U^{the}nofficial Guide® to
Chicago

5th Edition

Other *Unofficial Guides*

the Unofficial Guide® to Chicago

5th Edition

Joe Surkiewicz
and
Bob Sehlinger

Wiley Publishing, Inc.

Please note that prices fluctuate in the course of time, and travel information changes under the impact of many factors that influence the travel industry. We therefore suggest that you write or call ahead for confirmation when making your travel plans. Every effort has been made to ensure the accuracy of information throughout this book, and the contents of this publication are believed correct at the time of printing. Nevertheless, the publishers cannot accept responsibility for errors or omissions or for changes in details given in this guide or for the consequences of any reliance on the information provided by the same. Assessments of attractions and so forth are based upon the author's own experience, and therefore, descriptions given in this guide necessarily contain an element of subjective opinion, which may not reflect the publisher's opinion or dictate a reader's own experience on another occasion. Readers are invited to write the publisher with ideas, comments, and suggestions for future editions.

Published by:

Wiley Publishing, Inc.

909 Third Ave.

New York, NY 10022

Produced by Menasha Ridge Press
Cover design by Michael J. Freeland
Interior design by Michele Laseau

For information on our other products and services or to obtain technical support please contact our Customer Care Department within the U.S. at 800-762-2974, outside the U.S. at 317-572-3993 or fax 317-572-4002

Wiley also publishes its books in a variety of electronic formats. Some content that appears in print may not be available in electronic formats.

ISBN 0-7645-6754-3

ISSN 1083-1452

Manufactured in the United States of America

5 4 3 2 1

Contents

Part Two   Planning Your Visit to Chicago   51

Part Three   Hotels   61

List of Maps

About the Authors

Joe Surkiewicz has co-authored five titles in the *Unofficial Guide* series and written two guides to the best places to ride a mountain bike in the mid-Atlantic states. He lives in Baltimore with his best friend and counselor, Ann Lembo. When not traveling or bicycling, they enjoy evenings curled up on the sofa with their black-and-white feline companions, Molly and Trixie, to watch black-and-white movies starring 1930s film divas Barbara Stanwyck, Norma Shearer, and Jean Harlow.

Bob Sehlinger is the creator and Executive Publisher of the *Unofficial Guide* travel series.

Acknowledgments

Frequent *Outside* magazine contributor Debra Shore took a Sunday to show us around some of Chicago's ethnic enclaves—and then wrote our wit- and insight-infused section on neighborhoods. Her son, Ben Smith, chipped in with a kid's-eye view of what's really cool in Chicago.

Laurie Levy, who wrote our shopping section, contributes to the *Chicago Tribune, Mademoiselle, McCall's, Travel & Leisure,* and the *Christian Science Monitor.* Her handbook on child safety for parents and teachers, *The Safe and Sound Child,* is published by Good Year Books; she's also an award-winning short story writer and novelist.

Chicago Sun-Times staff writer and columnist Dave Hoekstra penned our chapter on entertainment and nightlife. He won a 1987 Chicago Newspaper Guild Stick-O-Type Award for Column Writing for outstanding commentary on Chicago nightlife. He's also a contributing writer for *Playboy* and has been a contributing editor for *Chicago* magazine.

Mike Steere, a frequent contributor to *Outside* magazine, gave us invaluable insights into Chicago's outdoors scene that only a native could know, such as pointing out the least-crowded stretches of the Lakeshore Trail and the best spots to windsurf on Lake Michigan. Robert Feder at the *Chicago Sun-Times* tuned us in to the latest on the Chicago TV talk show scene, while the folks at Performance Bike Shop on North Halsted Street loaned us a mountain bike (*and* a helmet) for a blustery cruise along the lakefront.

The dynamic duo of Laura Levy Shatkin and Alice Van Housen wrote our dining chapter. Shatkin is head instructor and owner of Ovens of Evanston Cooking School (a collaboration with Chicago's Whole Foods Markets). From 1997 to 1999, she wrote "The Curious Cook" food column for the Pioneer Press. In 1997, she joined the *Chicago Reader* to develop both a restaurant finder website (featuring 1,400 listings) and their first printed restaurant section. She's now the chief restaurant critic at the *Chicago Reader*, and has also written for the *Chicago Tribune, Chicago Magazine, Today's Chicago Woman, Crain's Chicago Business, New City,* and the *Evanston Review,* in addition to making television appearances on the NBC Morning Show, CLTV, Continental's Cafe, and WGN Evening News. Alice Van Housen is a food, travel, and lifestyle writer based in Chicago. She contributes to numerous periodicals, websites, and travel guides, including the *Chicago Sun-Times,* Los Angeles Times Syndicate, Food.com, *Wine & Spirits* magazine, and *Frommer's Chicago 2001.* She is also a contributing restaurant critic for the website Chicago.Citysearch.com.

Hotel inspectors Grace Walton and Dawn Charlton endured sore feet and hasty, high-cholesterol lunches as they zipped around the Windy City.

Finally, many thanks to Brian Taylor, Tim Krasnansky, Laura Poole, Annie Long, Steve Jones, Chris Mohney, Allison Jones, Holly Cross, and Ann Cassar, the pros who managed to transform all this effort into a book.

Introduction

The Most "American" of American Cities

When you think of great American cities, it's no wonder that Chicago is not the first to spring to mind. Chicago, it seems, has an image problem. You could say it's the Rodney Dangerfield of American cities.

The *Second* City? The *Windy* City?

Chicago gets no respect.

Funny thing, though—the people who live in Chicago get along very well without the external validation that fires and sustains New Yorkers. Chicago is big, brash, independent, and, most important, self-confident. With a magnificent lakefront park for a front yard, stunning architecture, a rich and colorful history, world-class cuisine and shopping, and a thriving arts and culture scene, Chicagoans don't require constant reassurance. They're just happy to be there.

Yet many of Chicago's charms remain a secret to outsiders; even worse, over the years some folks have nurtured decidedly unflattering notions about the town. Maybe it was the devastating fire of 1871 that leveled the center city, or the reeking, mile-square stockyards—a notorious Chicago landmark for more than a century. It could be the city's sinister reputation for gangsters, tough guys, and hardball politicians. Or perhaps it's the plight of the hapless Chicago Cubs, the National League club that hasn't won a World Series since 1908.

But out-of-towners who write Chicago off as a layover at O'Hare are missing a lot. Brassy and blowsy, Chicago is a place where people speak their minds and aren't reluctant to talk to strangers—especially about sports and politics. With a score of major museums, an impressive collection of public sculpture, thriving regional theaters, a frenetic nightlife scene, and hundreds of first-rate restaurants, Chicago is a city where people come to have a good time. Chicago is a blues and jazz town without compare, but it also boasts one of the finest symphony orchestras in

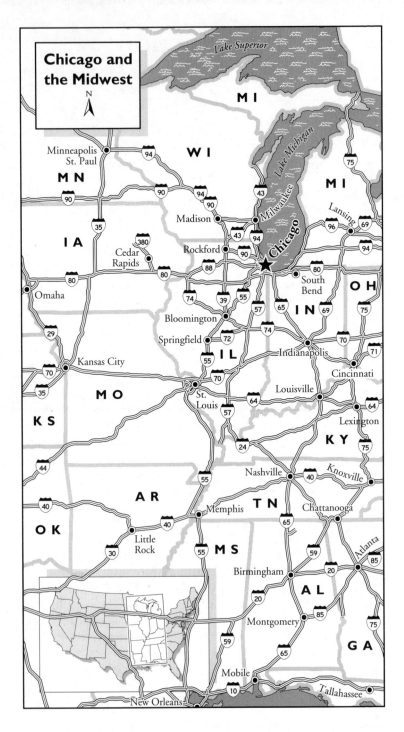

Chicago and
the Midwest

N

the world. Additionally, it's a city with a no-holds-barred literary tradition, from the muckraking of Upton Sinclair to the machine-gun dialogue of Pulitzer Prize–winning playwright David Mamet.

Chicagoans know their town as a city of strength, bold visions, and decisive action. In a remarkably short time, Chicago sprang from flat prairies and swampland and grew into an international trade center whose financial markets and commercial enterprises influence economies all over the world. There are miles of public beaches, the country's tallest building (third-tallest in the world), a river that runs backward, "Da Bears," the world's largest indoor aquarium, Oprah Winfrey, Michael Jordan . . . and the ever-popular deep-dish pizza. Yet for all that, Chicago has never been regarded as particularly cosmopolitan or "international" in the manner of, say, European capitals or waterfront American cities such as San Francisco or New Orleans. Chicago derives its identity from within, from its energy and from its diversity. Chicago is the melting pot. Chicago is a metaphor for America.

About This Guide

How Come "Unofficial"?

Most "official" guides to Chicago tout the well-known sights, promote the local restaurants and hotels indiscriminately, and leave out a lot of good stuff. This guide is different.

Instead of pandering to the tourist industry, we'll tell you if a well-known restaurant's mediocre food is not worth the wait. We'll complain loudly about overpriced hotel rooms that aren't convenient to the Loop or the airport, and we'll guide you away from the crowds and congestion for a break now and then.

Chicago's crush of world-class traffic jams and staggering size can bewilder first-time visitors. We sent in a team of evaluators who toured downtown and its outlying neighborhoods and popular attractions, ate in the area's best restaurants, performed critical evaluations of its hotels, and visited Chicago's best nightclubs. If a museum is boring, or a major attraction is overrated, we say so—and, in the process, hopefully make your visit more fun, efficient, and economical.

Creating a Guidebook

We got into the guidebook business because we were unhappy with the way travel guides make the reader work to find any usable information. Wouldn't it be nice, we thought, if we were to make guides that are easy to use?

Most guidebooks are compilations of lists. This is true regardless of whether the information is presented in list form or artfully distributed through pages of prose. There is insufficient detail in a list, and prose can present tedious helpings of nonessential or marginally useful information. Not enough wheat, so to speak, for nourishment in one instance, and too much chaff in the other. Either way, these types of guides provide little more than departure points from which readers initiate their own quests.

Many guides are readable and well researched, but they tend to be difficult to use. To select a hotel, for example, a reader must study several pages of descriptions with only the boldface hotel names breaking up large blocks of text. Because each description essentially deals with the same variables, it is difficult to recall what was said concerning a particular hotel. Readers generally must work through all the write-ups before beginning to narrow their choices. The presentation of restaurants, clubs, and attractions is similar except that even more reading is usually required. To use such a guide is to undertake an exhaustive research process that requires examining nearly as many options and possibilities as starting from scratch. Recommendations, if any, lack depth and conviction. These guides compound rather than solve problems by failing to narrow the average traveler's choices down to a thoughtfully considered, well-distilled, and manageable few.

How *Unofficial Guides* Are Different

Readers care about the author's opinion. The author, after all, is supposed to know what he is talking about. This, coupled with the fact that the traveler wants quick answers (as opposed to endless alternatives), dictates that authors should be explicit, prescriptive, and, above all, direct. The *Unofficial Guide* tries to do just that. It spells out alternatives and recommends specific courses of action. It simplifies complicated destinations and attractions and helps the traveler feel in control in even the most unfamiliar environments. The objective of the *Unofficial Guide* is not to have the most information or all of the information; it aims to have the most accessible, useful information, unbiased by affiliation with any organization or industry.

An *Unofficial Guide* is a critical reference work; it focuses on a travel destination that appears to be especially complex. Our authors and research team are completely independent from the attractions, restaurants, and hotels we describe. *The Unofficial Guide to Chicago* is designed for individuals and families traveling for the fun of it, as well as for business travelers and conventioneers, especially those visiting the Windy City for the first time. The guide is directed at value-conscious, consumer-oriented adults who seek a cost-effective, though not Spartan, travel style.

Special Features

The *Unofficial Guide* incorporates the following special features:

- Friendly introductions to Chicago's vast array of fascinating ethnic neighborhoods.
- "Best of" listings giving our well-qualified opinions on bagels to baguettes, four-star hotels to the best night views of Chicago.
- Listings keyed to your interests, so you can pick and choose.
- Advice to help sightseers avoid crowds; advice to business travelers on avoiding traffic and excess expense.
- A zone system and maps that make it easy to find places you want to go and avoid places you don't.
- A hotel chart that helps narrow your choices fast, according to your needs.
- Shorter listings that include only those restaurants, clubs, and hotels we think are worth considering.
- A detailed index to help you find things quickly.

What you won't get in an *Unofficial Guide:*

- Long, useless lists where everything looks the same.
- Insufficient information that gets you where you want to go at the worst possible time.
- Information without advice on how to use it.

How This Guide Was Researched and Written

Though a lot of guidebooks have been written about Chicago, very few have been evaluative. Some guides practically regurgitate hotel and tourist office promotional material. In preparing this book, nothing was taken for granted. Each museum, monument, art gallery, hotel, restaurant, shop, and attraction was evaluated and rated by a team of trained observers according to formal criteria. Interviews were conducted to determine what tourists of all ages enjoyed most—*and least*—during their Chicago visit.

While our observers are independent and impartial, they do not claim to have special expertise. Like you, they visited Chicago as tourists or business travelers, noting their satisfaction or dissatisfaction.

The primary difference between the average tourist and the trained evaluator is the evaluator's skills in organization, preparation, and observation. The trained evaluator is responsible for much more than simply observing and cataloging. While the average tourist is gazing in awe from the observation deck at the Sears Tower, for instance, the professional is rating the attraction in terms of pace, how quickly crowds move, the location of rest rooms, and how well children can see over the railing in front of the big plate glass windows. The evaluator also checks out nearby attractions, alternatives if the line at a main attraction is too long, and where to find the best local lunch options. Observer teams used detailed checklists to analyze hotel rooms, restaurants, nightclubs, and attractions. Finally, evaluator ratings and observations were integrated with tourist reactions and the opinions of patrons for a comprehensive quality profile of each feature and service.

In compiling this guide, we recognize that tourists' ages, backgrounds, and interests will strongly influence their taste in Chicago's wide array of activities and attractions. Our sole objective is to provide the reader with sufficient description, critical evaluation, and pertinent data to make knowledgeable decisions according to individual tastes.

Letters, Comments, and Questions from Readers

We expect to learn from our mistakes, as well as from the input of our readers, and to improve with each book and edition. Many of those who use the *Unofficial Guides* write to us to ask questions, make comments, or share their own discoveries and lessons learned in Chicago. We appreciate all such input, both positive and critical, and encourage our readers to continue writing. Readers' comments and observations will frequently be incorporated in revised editions of the *Unofficial Guide* and will contribute immeasurably to its improvement.

How to Write the Authors

Bob Sehlinger, Joe Surkiewicz
The Unofficial Guide to Chicago
P.O. Box 43673
Birmingham, AL 35243

When you write, be sure to put your return address on your letter as well as on the envelope—sometimes envelopes and letters get separated. And remember, our work takes us out of the office for long periods of time, so forgive us if our response is delayed.

Reader Survey

At the back of the guide you will find a short questionnaire that you can use to express opinions concerning your Chicago visit. Clip the questionnaire along the dotted line and mail it to the above address.

How Information is Organized: By Subject and by Geographic Zones

To give you fast access to information about the best of Chicago, we've organized material in several formats.

Hotels   Because most people visiting Chicago stay in one hotel for the duration of their trip, we have summarized our coverage of hotels in charts, maps, ratings, and rankings that allow you to quickly focus your decision-making process. We do not go on page after page describing lobbies and rooms which, in the final analysis, sound much the same. Instead, we concentrate on the variables that differentiate one hotel from another: location, size, room quality, services, amenities, and cost.

Restaurants   Because you will probably eat a dozen or more restaurant meals during your stay, and because not even you can predict what you might be in the mood for on Saturday night, we provide detailed profiles of the best restaurants in and around Chicago.

Entertainment and Night Life   Visitors frequently try several different clubs during their stay. Because clubs and nightspots, like restaurants, are usually selected spontaneously after arriving in Chicago, we believe detailed descriptions are warranted. The best nightspots and lounges are profiled by category under Chicago's Night Life in the same section.

Geographic Zones   Once you've decided where you're going, getting there becomes the issue. To help you do that, we have divided the Chicago area into geographic zones and created maps of each zone.

Zone 1.	North Side
Zone 2.	North Central/O'Hare
Zone 3.	Near North
Zone 4.	The Loop
Zone 5.	South Loop
Zone 6.	South Central/Midway
Zone 7.	South Side
Zone 8.	Southern Suburbs
Zone 9.	Western Suburbs
Zone 10.	Northwest Suburbs
Zone 11.	Northern Suburbs

All profiles of hotels, restaurants, and nightspots include zone numbers. For example, if you are staying at a hotel on Chicago's Magnificent Mile and want to sample the latest in the new Southwestern cuisine, scanning the restaurant profiles for those in Zone 3 (Near North) will provide you with the best choices.

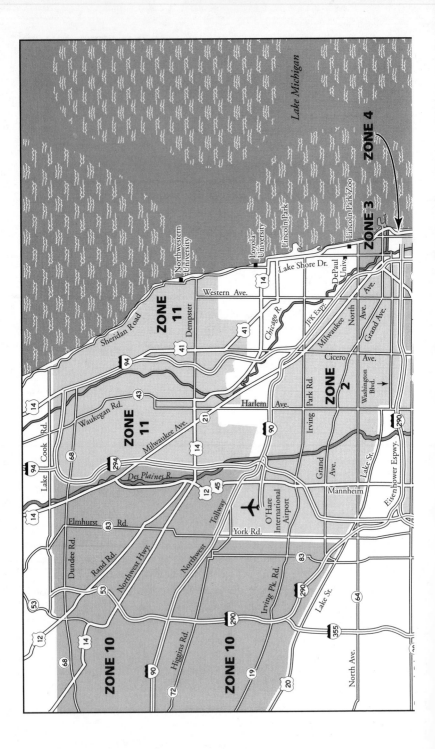

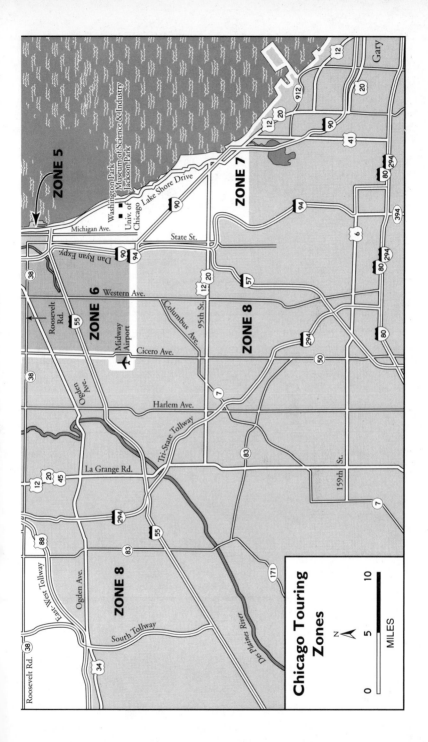

Chicago Touring Zones

N

0 5 10
MILES

ZONE 5
ZONE 6
ZONE 7
ZONE 8
ZONE 8

Washington Park
Museum of Science & Industry
Univ. of Chicago
Jackson Park

Michigan Ave.
Lake Shore Drive
State St.
Dan Ryan Expy.
Western Ave.
Roosevelt Rd.
Midway Airport
Columbus Ave.
95th St.
Cicero Ave.
Ogden Ave.
Harlem Ave.
Tri-State Tollway
La Grange Rd.
159th St.
Des Plaines River
South Tollway
East-West Tollway
Ogden Ave.
Roosevelt Rd.

Gary

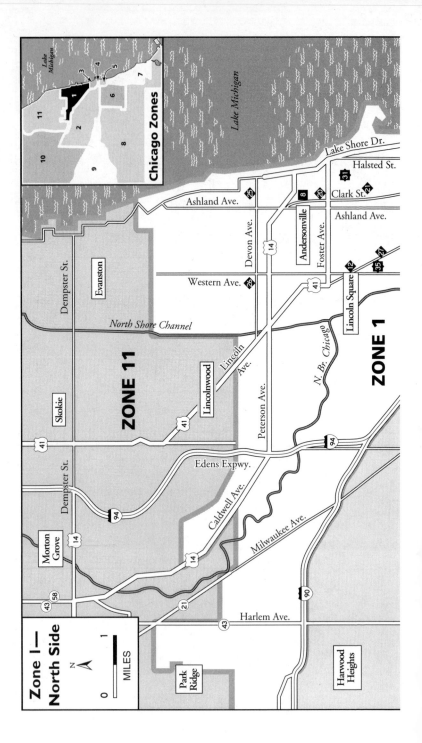

Zone 1—
North Side

Chicago Zones

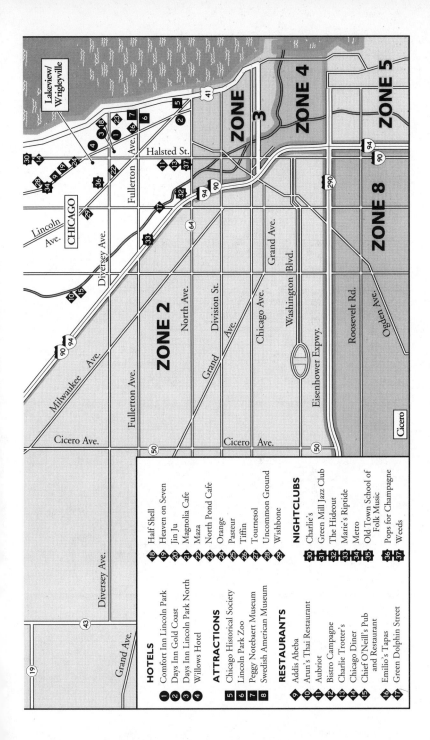

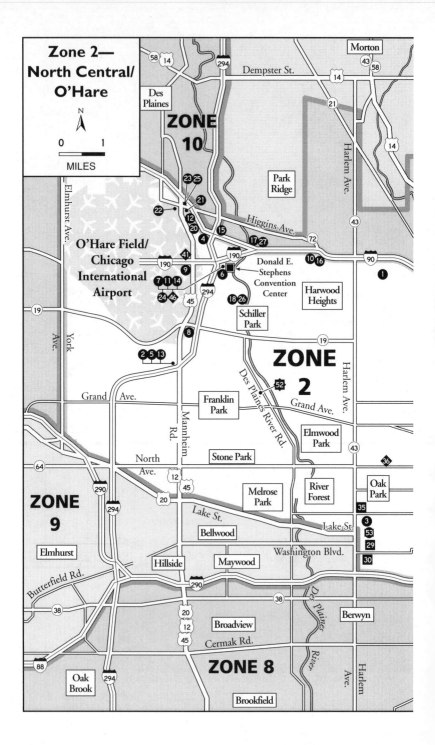

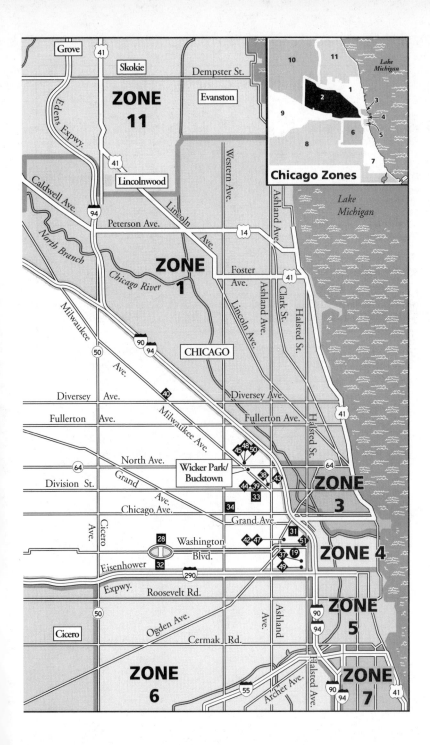

Grove
41
Skokie
Dempster St.
Evanston
ZONE 11
Edens Expwy.
41
Lincolnwood
Caldwell Ave.
94
Peterson Ave.
North Branch
Lincoln Ave.
Western Ave.
14
ZONE 1
Chicago River
Foster Ave.
Ashland Ave.
41
Milwaukee Ave.
90 94
50
CHICAGO
Lincoln Ave.
Ashland Ave.
Clark St.
Halsted St.
Lake Michigan
Diversey Ave.
Diversey Ave.
40
Fullerton Ave.
Milwaukee Ave.
Fullerton Ave.
41
45 48 50
64
North Ave.
Wicker Park/ Bucktown
38 43
Halsted St.
ZONE 3
64
Division St.
Grand
44 39 33
Ave.
Chicago Ave.
34
Cicero Ave.
Grand Ave.
31
42 47
51
28
Washington
17 19
ZONE 4
32
Blvd.
49
Eisenhower
290
Expwy.
Roosevelt Rd.
ZONE 5
50
Ogden Ave.
Ashland Ave.
90 94
Cicero
Cermak Rd.
ZONE 6
55
Archer Ave.
Halsted Ave.
90 94
ZONE 7
41

Chicago Zones
10   11
Lake Michigan
1
2
3
9
4
6
5
8
7

13

Zone 2—North Central/O'Hare

HOTELS

1. Best Western O'Hare
2. Candlewood Suites O'Hare
3. The Carleton at Oak Park
4. Comfort Inn O'Hare
5. Days Inn O'Hare South
6. DoubleTree O'Hare-Rosemont
7. Embassy Suites O'Hare
8. Four Points Sheraton O'Hare
9. Hilton O'Hare
10. Holiday Inn Chicago O'Hare
11. Holiday Inn O'Hare International
12. Holiday Inn Select
13. Howard Johnson Express O'Hare
14. Hyatt Regency O'Hare
15. Hyatt Rosemont
16. Marriott O'Hare
17. Marriott Suites O'Hare
18. Motel 6 O'Hare East
19. Quality Inn Downtown
20. Radisson O'Hare
21. Ramada Plaza Hotel O'Hare
22. Residence Inn by Marriott
23. Sheraton Gateway Suites O'Hare
24. Sofitel Chicago
25. Travelodge Chicago O'Hare
26. Twelve Oaks Suites
27. Westin Hotel O'Hare

ATTRACTIONS

28. Garfield Park Conservatory
29. Hemingway Museum
30. Hemingway's Birthplace
31. Museum of Holography
32. Peace Museum
33. Polish Museum of America
34. Ukrainian National Museum
35. Wright Home and Studio

RESTAURANTS

36. Amarind's
37. Artopolis
38. Bongo Room
39. Fortunato
40. Ixcapuzalco
41. Lou Mitchell's Restaurant
42. Marché
43. Mas
44. Mirai Sushi
45. Mod
46. Morton's
47. one sixtyblue
48. Piece
49. Santorini
50. Spring
51. Wishbone

NIGHTCLUB

52. Hala Kahiki

TOURING INFO

53. Oak Park Visitor Center

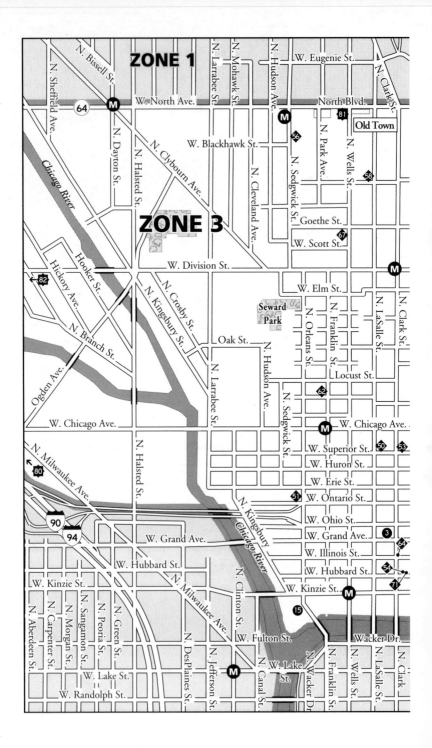

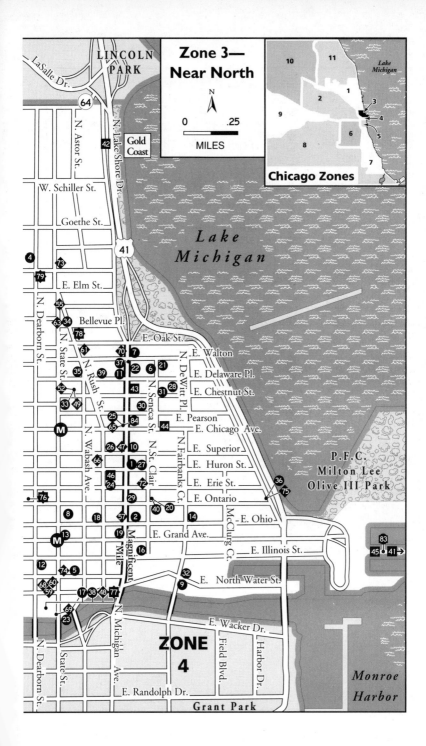

Zone 3—
Near North

N

0   .25
MILES

Chicago Zones

Lake Michigan

LINCOLN PARK

LaSalle Dr.

64

N. Astor St.

42

N. Lake Shore Dr.

Gold Coast

W. Schiller St.

Goethe St.

41

Lake
Michigan

E. Elm St.

N. Dearborn St.

N. State St.

Bellevue Pl.

E. Oak St.

E. Walton

N. DeWitt Pl.

E. Delaware Pl.

N. Rush St.

E. Chestnut St.

N. Seneca St.

E. Pearson

E. Chicago Ave.

N. St. Clair

N. Fairbanks Ct.

E. Superior

E. Huron St.

N. Wabash Ave.

E. Erie St.

E. Ontario

E. Ohio

McClurg Ct.

P.F.C.
Milton Lee
Olive III Park

Magnificent Mile

E. Grand Ave.

E. Illinois St.

E. North Water St.

E. Wacker Dr.

ZONE 4

N. Dearborn St.

State St.

N. Michigan Ave.

Field Blvd.

Harbor Dr.

Monroe
Harbor

E. Randolph Dr.

Grant Park

17

Zone 3—Near North

HOTELS

1 The Allerton Crowne Plaza
2 Best Western Inn Chicago
3 Best Western River North
4 Claridge Hotel
5 Courtyard by Marriott Downtown
6 DoubleTree Guest Suites
7 The Drake
8 Embassy Suites Chicago
9 Embassy Suites Downtown/ Lakefront
10 Fitzpatrick Hotel
11 Four Seasons Hotel
12 Hampton Inn & Suites Downtown
13 Hilton Garden Inn
14 Holiday Inn Chicago City Center
15 Holiday Inn Mart Plaza
16 Hotel InterContinental Chicago
17 House of Blues Hotel
18 Lenox Suites
19 Marriott Chicago Downtown
20 Marriott Fairfield Inn & Suites
21 Marriott Residence Inn Downtown
22 Millennium Knickerbocker Hotel
23 Omni Ambassador East
24 Omni Chicago Hotel
25 Park Hyatt Chicago
26 The Peninsula
27 Radisson Hotel & Suites Chicago
28 The Raphael Chicago
29 Red Roof Inn Downtown
30 Ritz-Carlton Chicago
31 The Seneca
32 Sheraton Chicago Hotel & Towers
33 Sofitel Water Tower
34 Sutton Place Hotel
35 Talbott Hotel
36 The W Lakeshore
37 Westin Hotel Chicago
38 Westin River North Chicago
39 Whitehall Hotel
40 Wyndham Chicago

ATTRACTIONS

41 Chicago Children's Museum
42 International Museum of Surgical Science
43 John Hancock Center Observatory
44 Museum of Contemporary Art
45 Navy Pier
46 Terra Museum of American Art

RESTAURANTS

47 Avenues
48 Bin 36
49 Cafe des Architectes
50 Cafe Iberico
51 Chilpancingo
52 Cru Cafe and Wine Bar
53 Erawan
54 Frontera Grill
55 Gibson's
56 Heat
57 Heaven on Seven
58 Kamehachi of Tokyo
59 Keefer's
60 Kevin's
61 Le Colonial
62 mk
63 Morton's
64 Naha
65 Nomi
66 Rosebud Cafe
67 Salpicon
68 Shaw's Crab House
69 Smith & Wollensky
70 Spiaggia
71 Topolabampo
72 Tru
73 Twelve 12
74 Vong's Thai Kitchen
75 Wave

NIGHTCLUBS

76 Excalibur
77 House of Blues
78 Jillyland
79 The Lodge
80 The Matchbox
81 Old Town Ale House
82 SLOW DOWN— Life's Too Short!

TOURING INFO

83 Illinois Market Place Visitor Information Center
84 Water Tower Welcome Center

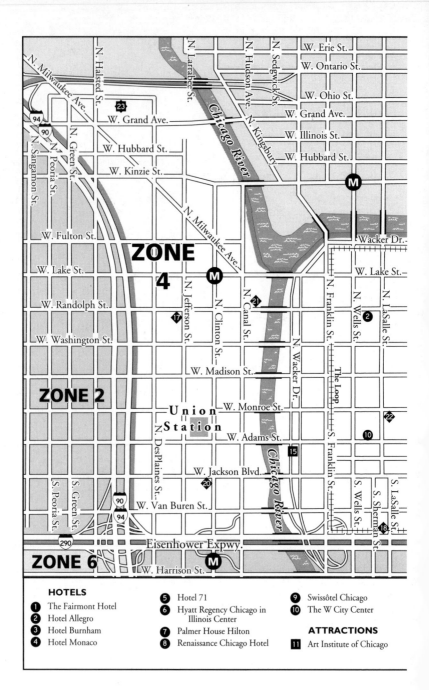

HOTELS

1. The Fairmont Hotel
2. Hotel Allegro
3. Hotel Burnham
4. Hotel Monaco
5. Hotel 71
6. Hyatt Regency Chicago in Illinois Center
7. Palmer House Hilton
8. Renaissance Chicago Hotel
9. Swissôtel Chicago
10. The W City Center

ATTRACTIONS

11. Art Institute of Chicago

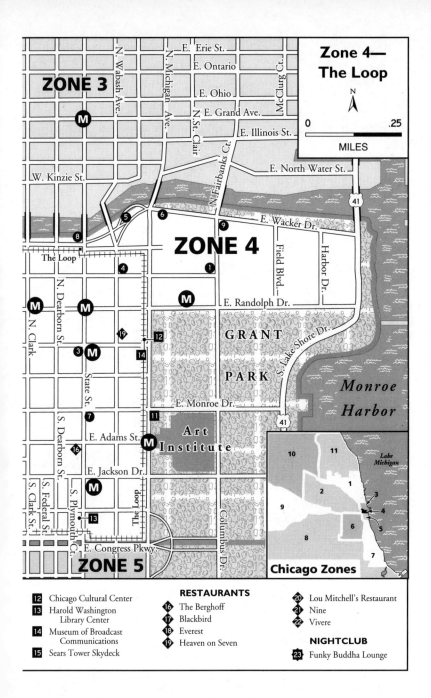

Zone 4—The Loop

N

0 .25

MILES

ZONE 3

ZONE 4

The Loop

GRANT

PARK

Art Institute

ZONE 5

N. Wabash Ave.
N. Michigan Ave.
N. St. Clair
McClurg Ct.

E. Erie St.
E. Ontario
E. Ohio
E. Grand Ave.
E. Illinois St.

W. Kinzie St.

N. Fairbanks Ct.

E. North Water St.

E. Wacker Dr.

Field Blvd.
Harbor Dr.

E. Randolph Dr.

S. Lake Shore Dr.

Monroe Harbor

E. Monroe Dr.

N. Dearborn St.
N. Clark
State St.
S. Dearborn St.
S. Clark St.
S. Federal St.
S. Plymouth Ct.
Columbus Dr.

E. Adams St.
E. Jackson Dr.

E. Congress Pkwy.

Chicago Zones

Lake Michigan

10 11
2   1
9   3
6   4
8   5
7

12 Chicago Cultural Center
13 Harold Washington Library Center
14 Museum of Broadcast Communications
15 Sears Tower Skydeck

RESTAURANTS
16 The Berghoff
17 Blackbird
18 Everest
19 Heaven on Seven

20 Lou Mitchell's Restaurant
21 Nine
22 Vivere

NIGHTCLUB
23 Funky Buddha Lounge

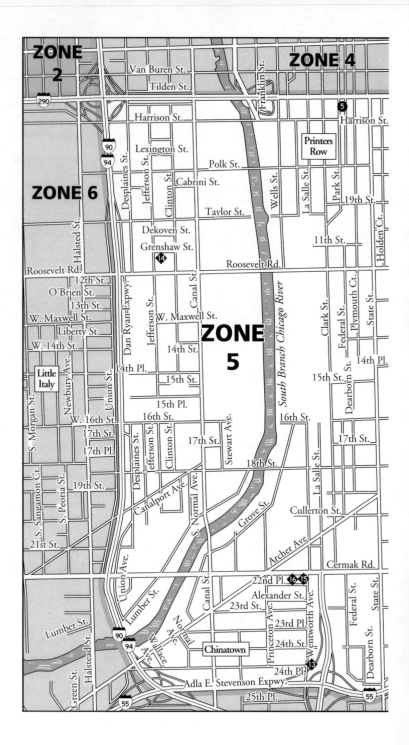

N

0 .25
MILES

Chicago Zones

Congress Pkwy.

Balbo Dr.

18th St.

19th St.

Grant Park

11th Pl.

13th St.

14th St.

McFetridge Dr.

Northerly Island Park

Northerly Island

Lake Michigan

Burnham Park

12th St. Beach

Merrill C. Meigs Field

Waldron Dr.

18th Dr.

Burnham Park Yacht Harbor

Cullerton St.

21st St.

23rd St.

24th St.

24th Pl.

25th St.

McCormick Place

Burnham Park

ZONE 6

Michigan Ave.
Indiana Ave.
16th St.
18th St.
Prairie Ave.
Cottage Grove Ave.
Martin Luther King Jr. Dr.
Wabash Ave.
Lake Shore Dr.
Columbus Dr.

HOTELS

1 Best Western Grant Park Hotel
2 Congress Plaza Hotel
3 Essex Inn
4 Hilton Chicago
5 Hyatt on Printer's Row Chicago
6 Hyatt Regency McCormick Place
7 Travelodge Downtown

ATTRACTIONS

8 Adler Planetarium and Astronomy Museum
9 Field Museum of Natural History
10 John G. Shedd Aquarium
11 National Vietnam Veterans Art Museums
12 Spertus Museum of Judaica

RESTAURANTS

13 House of Fortune
14 Manny's Coffee Shop & Deli
15 Penang
16 Three Happiness

NIGHTCLUB

17 Buddy Guy's Legends

23

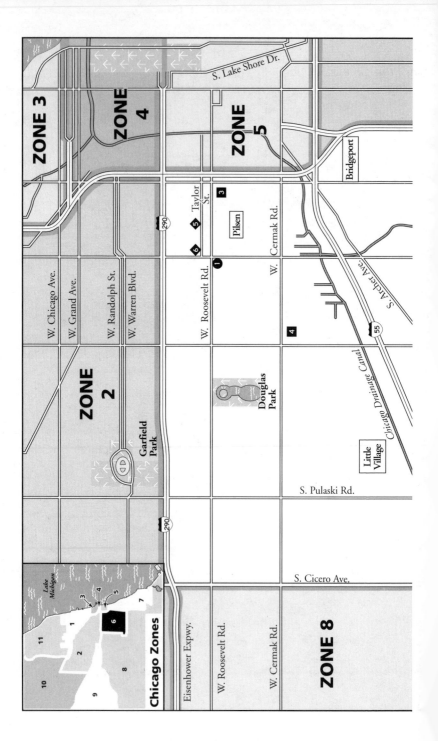

ZONE 3

ZONE 4

ZONE 5

Bridgeport

S. Lake Shore Dr.

5 Taylor St.

3

6

Pilsen

1

W. Cermak Rd.

W. Chicago Ave.

W. Grand Ave.

W. Randolph St.

W. Warren Blvd.

290

W. Roosevelt Rd.

4

S. Archer Ave.

55

ZONE 2

Garfield Park

Douglas Park

Chicago Drainage Canal

Little Village

S. Pulaski Rd.

290

S. Cicero Ave.

Lake Michigan

3 4 5
1   7
11   6
2
8
10
9

Chicago Zones

Eisenhower Expwy.

W. Roosevelt Rd.

W. Cermak Rd.

ZONE 8

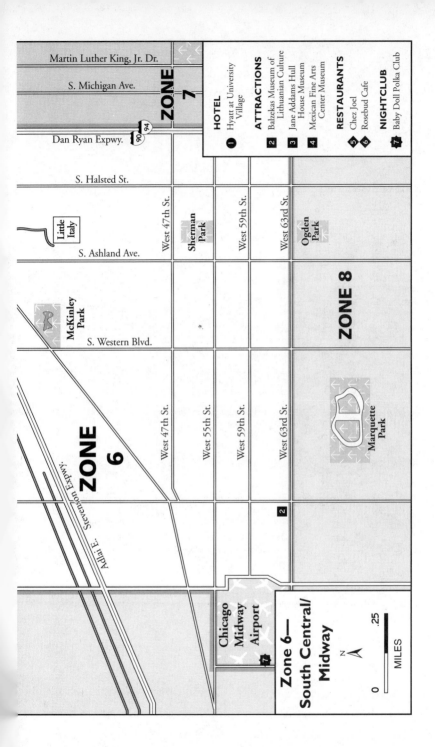

Martin Luther King, Jr. Dr.

S. Michigan Ave.

ZONE 7

Dan Ryan Expwy. 90 94

S. Halsted St.

Little Italy

West 47th St.

Sherman Park

West 59th St.

West 63rd St.

Ogden Park

S. Ashland Ave.

McKinley Park

S. Western Blvd.

ZONE 8

ZONE 6

Stevenson Expwy.

Adlai E.

West 47th St.

West 55th St.

West 59th St.

West 63rd St.

Marquette Park

2

Chicago Midway Airport

7

HOTEL
1 Hyatt at University Village

ATTRACTIONS
2 Balzekas Museum of Lithuanian Culture
3 Jane Addams Hull House Museum
4 Mexican Fine Arts Center Museum

RESTAURANTS
5 Chez Joel
6 Rosebud Cafe

NIGHTCLUB
7 Baby Doll Polka Club

**Zone 6—
South Central/
Midway**

N

0   .25
MILES

25

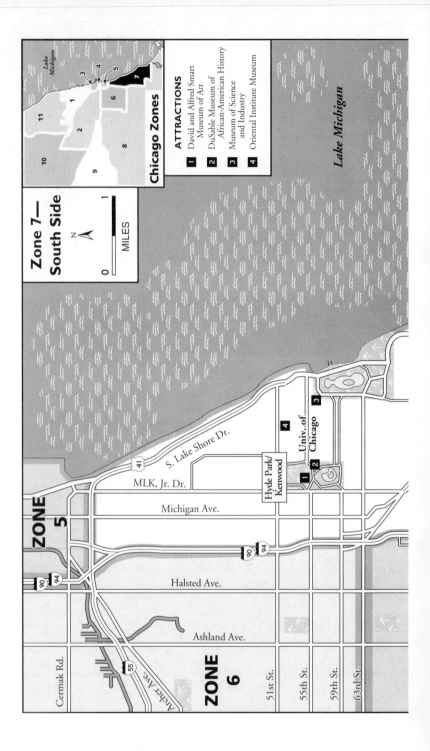

Zone 7—
South Side

N

MILES
0   1

ATTRACTIONS
1 David and Alfred Smart Museum of Art
2 DuSable Museum of African-American History
3 Museum of Science and Industry
4 Oriental Institute Museum

Chicago Zones

Lake Michigan

Lake Michigan

S. Lake Shore Dr.

MLK, Jr. Dr.

Michigan Ave.

Halsted Ave.

Ashland Ave.

Cermak Rd.

ZONE 5

ZONE 6

51st St.

55th St.

59th St.

63rd St.

Archer Ave.

Hyde Park/ Kenwood

Univ..of Chicago

41

90 94

90 94

55

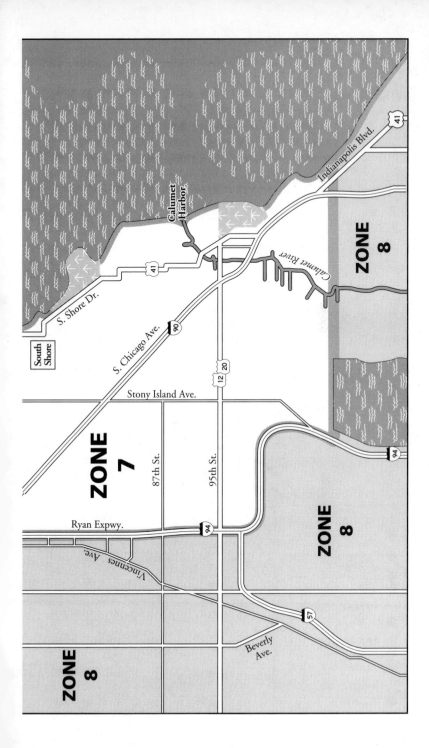

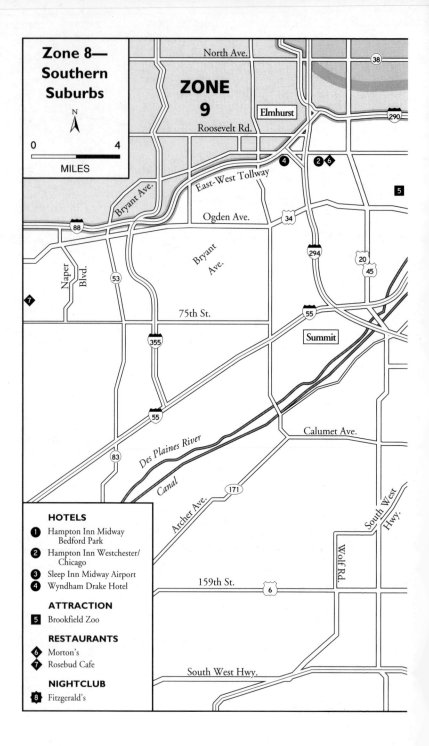

Zone 8—
Southern
Suburbs

N

0 ——— 4
MILES

North Ave.

ZONE 9

Elmhurst

Roosevelt Rd.

East-West Tollway

Ogden Ave.

Bryant Ave.

Naper Blvd.

75th St.

Summit

Des Plaines River

Canal

Calumet Ave.

Archer Ave.

South West Hwy.

Wolf Rd.

159th St.

South West Hwy.

HOTELS

1 Hampton Inn Midway
  Bedford Park
2 Hampton Inn Westchester/
  Chicago
3 Sleep Inn Midway Airport
4 Wyndham Drake Hotel

ATTRACTION

5 Brookfield Zoo

RESTAURANTS

6 Morton's
7 Rosebud Cafe

NIGHTCLUB

8 Fitzgerald's

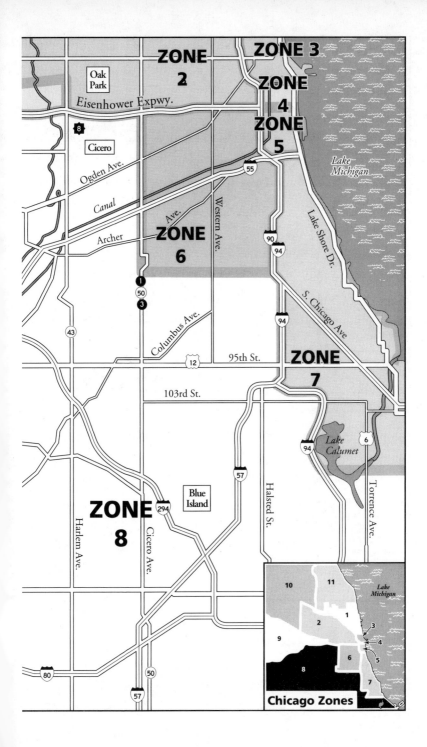

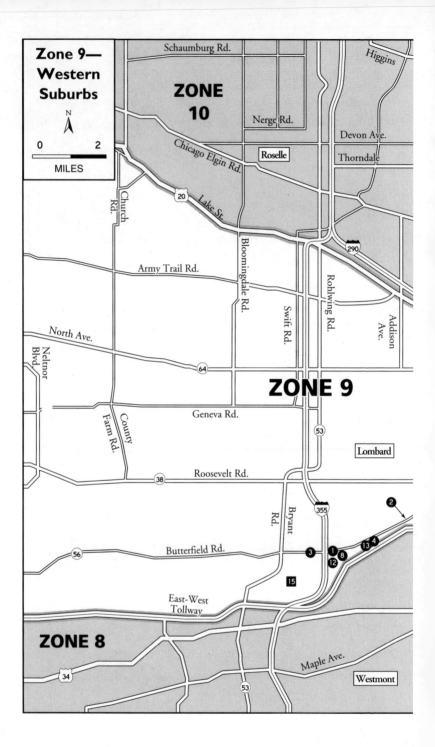

Zone 9—
Western
Suburbs

N

0   2
MILES

Schaumburg Rd.

Higgins

ZONE 10

Nerge Rd.

Devon Ave.

Chicago Elgin Rd.

Roselle

Thorndale

20 Lake St.

290

Church Rd.

Army Trail Rd.

Bloomingdale Rd.

Swift Rd.

Rohlwing Rd.

Addison Ave.

North Ave.

Nelnor Blvd.

64

ZONE 9

County Farm Rd.

Geneva Rd.

53

Lombard

38

Roosevelt Rd.

355

2

56

Butterfield Rd.

Bryant Rd.

3

1
8
12

13 4

15

East-West
Tollway

ZONE 8

Maple Ave.

34

53

Westmont

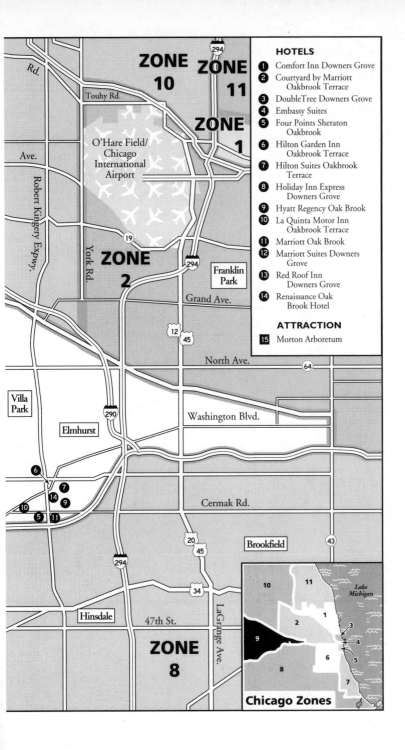

HOTELS

1. Comfort Inn Downers Grove
2. Courtyard by Marriott Oakbrook Terrace
3. DoubleTree Downers Grove
4. Embassy Suites
5. Four Points Sheraton Oakbrook
6. Hilton Garden Inn Oakbrook Terrace
7. Hilton Suites Oakbrook Terrace
8. Holiday Inn Express Downers Grove
9. Hyatt Regency Oak Brook
10. La Quinta Motor Inn Oakbrook Terrace
11. Marriott Oak Brook
12. Marriott Suites Downers Grove
13. Red Roof Inn Downers Grove
14. Renaissance Oak Brook Hotel

ATTRACTION

15. Morton Arboretum

Chicago Zones

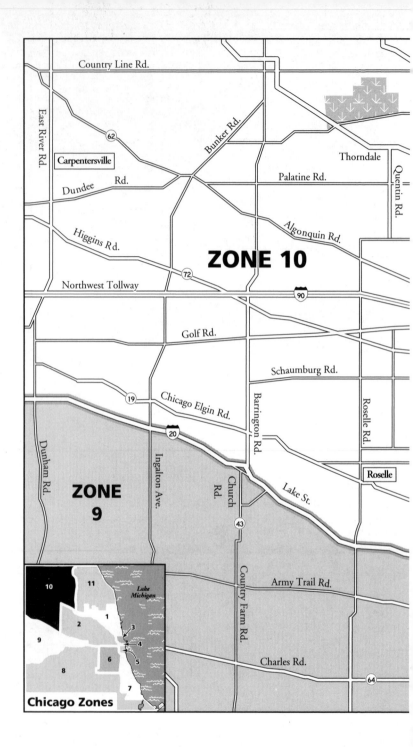

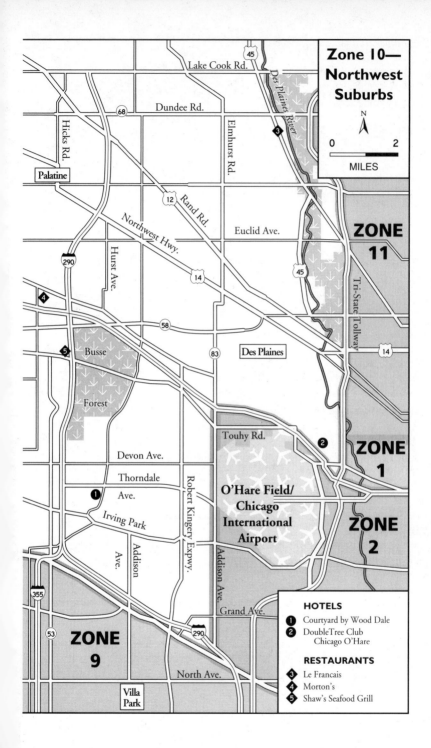

Zone 10—
Northwest
Suburbs

N

0   2
MILES

Lake Cook Rd.
Dundee Rd.
Palatine
Hicks Rd.
Elmhurst Rd.
Des Plaines River
ZONE 11
Rand Rd.
Northwest Hwy.
Euclid Ave.
Hurst Ave.
Busse
Forest
Des Plaines
Tri-State Tollway
Touhy Rd.
ZONE 1
Devon Ave.
Thorndale
Ave.
Irving Park
Ave.
Robert Kingery Expwy.
Addison
Addison Ave.
O'Hare Field/
Chicago
International
Airport
ZONE 2
ZONE 9
Grand Ave.
North Ave.
Villa
Park

HOTELS
❶ Courtyard by Wood Dale
❷ DoubleTree Club
   Chicago O'Hare

RESTAURANTS
◆ Le Francais
◆ Morton's
◆ Shaw's Seafood Grill

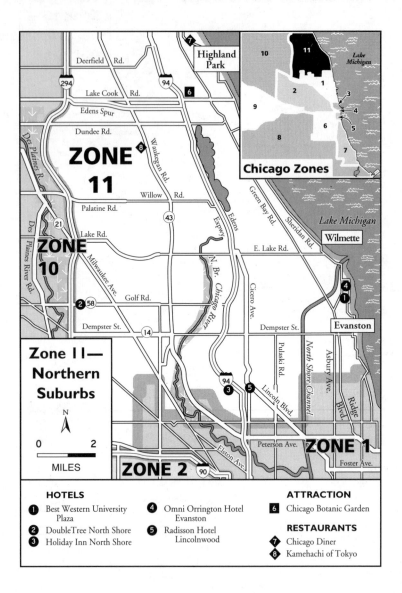

Zone 11—
Northern
Suburbs

N

0   2
MILES

HOTELS

1 Best Western University Plaza

2 DoubleTree North Shore

3 Holiday Inn North Shore

4 Omni Orrington Hotel Evanston

5 Radisson Hotel Lincolnwood

ATTRACTION

6 Chicago Botanic Garden

RESTAURANTS

7 Chicago Diner

8 Kamehachi of Tokyo

Understanding the City

A Brief History of Chicago

New York has always leaned toward Europe, and Los Angeles toward the Pacific Rim. But Chicago stands on its own: a freshwater port, a mid-continental city of big shoulders (from Carl Sandburg's famous 1916 poem "Chicago": "Stormy, husky, brawling/City of the Big Shoulders."). The town was founded on a swamp, and it later rebuilt itself from the ashes of a tremendous fire into the nation's third-largest city. With a lakefront skyline recognized around the world, it's a town that owes its verve to generations of strong backs. Chicago is a true American city.

It's also a cauldron of bubbling contrasts: Shimmering skyscrapers on Michigan Avenue and the squalor of Cabrini Green; a growing city beset by post-industrial urban decay; a town whose long-suppressed black minority points with pride to Chicagoan Carol Moseley-Braun, the first black woman U.S. senator. Chicago is Al Capone and Michael Jordan, Jane Addams and Hugh Hefner, perennial losers the Chicago Cubs and Nobel Prize winner Saul Bellow.

Chicago is a city of legends, of a few precious visionaries and quite a few scoundrels. Built on swampland at the edge of a prairie, the city has endured cycles of booms and busts. As the nation grew westward, Chicago found itself in a unique geographical position to supply the raw materials that fed the expansion. The city was incorporated on March 4, 1837.

Beginnings

Twelve thousand years ago, Lake Chicago was a larger version of Lake Michigan that covered much of what is now the Midwest. As this great glacial lake receded, it left behind a vast prairie and a shoreline swamp that linked North America's two great waterways: the Mississippi (via the Des Plaines and Illinois Rivers) and the Great Lakes.

The area's first residents were Native Americans who called it Checagou or Checaguar, which probably meant something like "wild onion" or "swamp gas"—no doubt a reference to the pungent smell of decaying marsh vegetation that permeated the swamp. Either way, the name implied great strength. The Potawatomi tribe, able to traverse the swamp in shallow-bottomed canoes during spring rains, was the first to take advantage of Chicago's bridge between the two waterways. It was about eight miles from the Des Plaines River to Lake Michigan; traders in those days dealt in furs and skins.

First Settlers

In 1673, two French explorers were the first Europeans to set eyes on what is now Chicago: Louis Jolliet, who was searching for gold, and Father Jacques Marquette, who was searching for souls. When their Native American allies showed them the portage trail linking the Mississippi Valley and the Great Lakes, Jolliet saw Chicago's potential immediately. He predicted to Marquette, "Here some day will be found one of the world's great cities."

In the late 18th century, the flat prairies stretching west were as empty and primeval as when the last glacier had retreated thousands of years before. Chicago's first nonnative resident, Jean Baptist Point du Sable, arrived in 1779 and erected a rough-hewn log house on the north bank of the Chicago River. A tall, French-speaking son of a Quebec merchant and a black slave, du Sable established a trading post at what is now Michigan Avenue. As the local Native Americans noted, "The first white man to live here was a black man."

After du Sable pulled up stakes and moved to Missouri in 1800 (leaving a handful of other traders at the mouth of the river), Chicago's first boom began. But first the frontier outpost had to endure a massacre. The Indians had been run out in 1795, ceding huge tracts of Midwestern land—including "six miles square at the mouth of the Chickago River." The swamp turned into a speculator's dream almost overnight.

Soldiers of the fledgling United States Republic arrived from Detroit in 1803 and erected Fort Dearborn near what is now the corner of Lower Wacker Drive and Michigan Avenue. After evacuating the fort during the War of 1812 against the British, settlers and soldiers fleeing the fort were ambushed by Indians in league with the enemy; 52 men, women, and children were slain in the Fort Dearborn Massacre.

Boom ...

Illinois became a state in 1818—a time when Chicago was still a struggling backwater far north of southern population centers—and in 1829 the state legislature appointed a commission to plot a canal route between Lake Michigan and the Mississippi River. Chicago was poised for a population explosion.

The pace of westward development from bustling Eastern Seaboard cities was accelerating in the early 19th century, and pioneers surged into the Midwest. Fort Dearborn was rapidly rebuilt, and the Erie Canal opened in 1825, creating a new water route between Chicago and the East. Pioneer wagons rolled in daily, and Chicago's population swelled from around 50 in 1830 to over 4,000 in 1837. As waves of Irish and German immigrants arrived, the town's population increased by another 100,000 in the following 30 years.

Speculators swooped in, and lots that sold for $100 in 1830 changed hands for as much as $100,000 in 1837 during a real estate frenzy fueled by visions of wealth to be made from the planned canal. Fort Dearborn closed in 1836, symbolizing the end of Chicago's frontier era, and the town started taking on the trappings of civilization. The first newspaper, the *Chicago Democrat,* was launched in 1833; the first brewery was opened in 1836; and the first policeman was hired in 1839—and no doubt had his hands full in a town overflowing with saloons.

...and Bust

The boom went bust, however, in the Panic of 1837, one of the nation's first economic depressions. Work on the canal ground to a halt, and many local investors went broke. Slowly, a recovery set in, work on the canal resumed, and Chicago spawned its first ethnic neighborhood.

Originally called Hardscrabble, it was an enclave of Irish laborers digging the waterway. By the time it was annexed in 1863, the South Side neighborhood was known as Bridgeport, later famous as the wellspring for generations of Irish-American politicians—including Mayor Richard J. Daley (aka Hizzoner) and his son, current mayor Richard M. Daley.

A Transportation Hub

Although the waterway was a boon to commerce when it opened in 1848, it was quickly overshadowed by a new form of transportation—railroads. Soon, locomotives were hauling freight along the tracks of the Galena and Chicago Union line, and the newly opened Chicago Board of Trade brokered commodities in what was to become the world's greatest rail hub. German and Scandinavian immigrants swelled the city's population, and horse-drawn street railways stimulated growth of the suburbs.

Before growth could proceed much farther, however, the swamp-bound city first had to elevate itself; streets were a quagmire most of the year. In the years prior to the Civil War, street grades were raised as many as a dozen feet, and first floors became basements. It was an impressive technological feat—the first of many to come.

By 1856, Chicago was the hub of ten railroad trunk lines. Lumber from nearby forests, iron ore from Minnesota, and livestock and produce from the fertile Midwest were raw materials shipped to the city and manufactured into the products that fueled the nation's rapid growth. Passenger rail service from New York began in 1857, cutting travel time between the cities from three weeks to two days. The population soared to 28,000 in 1850 and to 110,000 in 1860. Economically, Chicago was the national middleman between the East and West, a role it has never ceased to play.

Innovative Marketing and a Presidential Nomination

Just as the city mastered transportation and manufacturing, it spawned a generation of marketing geniuses. Mail-order giants Montgomery Ward & Co. and Sears, Roebuck & Co. were founded in Chicago. Other legendary names of Chicago merchandising include Marshall Field, Potter Palmer, Samuel Carson, and John Pirie.

By 1860 Chicago was the ninth-largest city in the United States and hosted the nominating convention of the fledgling Republican Party. A jerry-built convention hall with a capacity of 10,000 was thrown up at Lake and Market Streets on the fringe of today's Loop, where the Republicans nominated Abraham Lincoln on the third ballot. The city would host another 23 major-party nominating conventions, including the bruising 1968 Democratic Convention. In 1996, the Democrats returned after an absence of nearly 30 years.

One of Chicago's most famous—and odorous—landmarks opened in 1865: the Union Stockyards. The yards were Chicago's largest employer for half a century. By 1863, the city had earned the moniker "Porkopolis" by processing enough hogs to stretch snout-to-tail all the way to New York. Gustavus Swift of meatpacking fame boasted, "We use everything but the squeal." The darker sides of the yard—abysmal sanitation problems and horrific working and living conditions for its laborers—were brought to light in 1906 in Upton Sinclair's *The Jungle*.

Industrial Might

More growth: In the years following the Civil War, Chicago ranked as the world's largest grain handler and the biggest North American lumber market. The North Side's huge McCormick plant churned out reapers and other farm equipment that were shipped around the globe. George Pullman built his first sleeping car in 1864, the nation's first steel rails came out of the North Side in 1865, and the number of sea vessels docked at Chicago in 1869 exceeded the combined number calling on New York and five other major United States ports.

While knee-deep mud was a thing of the past, the city was still steeped in quagmires of different sorts. Cholera and typhoid struck regularly as

Chicago fouled its Lake Michigan drinking water via the dangerously polluted Chicago River. Corruption at City Hall became rampant, and the city was notorious for its gambling, saloons, and 400 brothels. Hundreds of thousands of poor Chicagoans were jammed into modest pine cottages on unpaved streets without sewers. Some observers warned of dire consequences unless the city cleaned up its act.

The Great Chicago Fire of 1871

They were right. Chicago in 1871 was a densely packed city of 300,000 whose homes were built almost entirely of wood. A lengthy drought had turned the town tinder-dry, setting the stage for the most indelibly mythic event in the city's history: the Great Fire of 1871.

Legend has it that Mrs. Maureen O'Leary's cow kicked over a lantern and started the conflagration, probably a myth created by a journalist of the era. But the fire spread rapidly from the O'Leary barn in the West Side and burned its way north and east through the commercial center and residential North Side. More than 17,000 buildings were destroyed, 100,000 people were left homeless, and 250 were killed. The city lay in ashes.

So they built it again—this time with fireproof brick. Architects, sensing unlimited opportunity, flocked to Chicago. In five years, the city's commercial core was restored with buildings erected to meet stringent fire codes, and a tradition of architectural leadership was established. In 1889, the city annexed a ring of suburbs and was crowned America's Second City in the census of 1890.

Chicago was emerging from an era of cutthroat Social Darwinism into an age of social reform. Jane Addams's Hull House became a model for the nation's settlement house movement. Addams and her upper-class cohorts provided fresh, clean milk for babies, taught immigrants English, and set up day-care centers for the children of working mothers.

The Columbian Exposition of 1893 was a fabulously successful world's fair that left indelible cultural marks on the city, including the Art Institute of Chicago and the Field Museum. The era ushered in the skyscraper, a distinctly urban form created in Chicago that has reshaped the look of skylines around the world. The University of Chicago, one of the world's great research institutions, was founded in 1892 with funds from the Rockefellers.

In 1900, another technological feat: The flow of the Chicago River was reversed, much to the relief of a population in desperate need of safe drinking water from Lake Michigan—and to the consternation of populations downstream.

In 1909, architect Daniel H. Burnham left his mark on the city by pursuing a plan to preserve Chicago's pristine lakefront through creation of a series of parks and the acquisition of a green belt of forest lands on the city's periphery. "Make no little plans," Burnham urged, and the city heeded his words. Today, with the exception of massive McCormick Place, the lakefront is an uncluttered recreational mecca.

Labor Troubles

Yet around the turn of the 19th century, Chicago seethed with labor unrest and the threat of class warfare. Nascent labor movements argued for better working and living conditions for the city's laborers. Seven policemen were killed in the 1886 Haymarket Riot and four anarchists were hanged; the Pullman Strike of 1894 was crushed by U. S. Army troops after wages were sharply cut by the sleeping-car magnate.

The lowest rung in Chicago's pecking order was reserved for blacks, who started to arrive from the South in substantial numbers, reaching 110,000 by 1920. Segregation formed a "black belt" ghetto with buildings in poor repair—often without indoor toilets—and substantially higher rents than white housing. A six-day riot in July 1919 left 23 blacks and 15 whites dead; the governor had to send in troops to quell the uprising. Yet the underlying causes of the unrest weren't addressed.

Carl Sandburg celebrated the city and its tradition of hard work in verse ("Hog Butcher for the World / Tool Maker, Stacker of Wheat / Player with Railroads and the Nation's Freight Handler; / Stormy, husky, brawling / City of Big Shoulders"). Other pre-Depression literary lights from Chicago include Theodore Dreiser and Ben Hecht; later came James T. Farrell, Nelson Algren, Richard Wright, and Saul Bellow.

The Roaring Twenties

Following World War I, the focus of power shifted from industrialists to politicians; crooked pols and gangsters plundered the city. The smoke-filled room was invented in Chicago at the 1920 Republican National Convention when Warren G. Harding's nomination was sewn up in Suite 804–805 at the Blackstone Hotel.

A baby-faced crook from New York named Alphonse Capone hit town in 1920, right after Prohibition became law. It wasn't a coincidence. Chicago was soon awash in bootleg hooch—much of it illegally imported by Capone and his mob. The short, pot-bellied gangster nicknamed Scarface still holds the world record for the highest gross income ever accumulated by a private citizen in a year—$105 million in 1927, when he was 28 years old.

Alas, Capone didn't pay his taxes and was put away by a group of Feds, known as the Untouchables, led by Eliot Ness. The gangster, probably Chicago's best-known historical figure, served eight hard years in Alcatraz and died of syphilis in his bed in 1947.

Another Depression . . . and Another Fair

In the 1930s, the Great Depression hit Chicago hard. Out-of-work men and women marched down State Street. Businessmen went bust. Nearly 1,400 families were evicted from their homes in the first half of 1931 alone. Hardest hit were Chicago's blacks, whose population then totaled about 250,000.

Yet in 1933 the city hosted another world's fair: the Century of Progress exposition, which occupied 47 acres of lakefront south of the Loop. The show attracted about 39 million visitors and actually made money. The star of the show was fan dancer Sally Rand, who went on stage nude with large props—not only fans but feather boas and large balloons. Like Little Egypt at the Columbian Exposition 40 years before, she drew mobs of men to her shows and further embellished the city's notorious reputation.

The Second World War

World War II and an unparalleled surge in defense spending lifted Chicago—and the rest of the country—out of the Depression. The $1.3 billion spent to build war plants in the city was unmatched anywhere else in the country.

In 1942, a team at the University of Chicago under the direction of physicist Enrico Fermi built the world's first nuclear reactor under the stands of Stagg Field. The feat provided critical technology for the development of nuclear power and allowed the nation to embark on the ambitious Manhattan Project, which led to the manufacture of the atomic bomb. Today the portentous site is marked by a brooding sculpture by Henry Moore.

A New Era

The city reached its peak population of 3.6 million in 1950, a year that marked the beginning of a long slide as Chicago's population drained off into surrounding suburbs. Following eras of settlement, growth, booms, busts, depression, and war, Chicago moved into one last period: the 21-year rule of Mayor Richard J. Daley, "da Boss." He was a powermonger who left yet another indelible mark on the city.

Elected in 1955, Daley bulldozed entire neighborhoods, built segregated walls of high-rise public housing, and constructed an elaborate system of freeway exchanges in the heart of the city. Critics noted with dismay that the maze of highways cut the hearts out of flourishing neighborhoods and provided handy corridors for suburban flight.

Daley was also a kingmaker for presidents; he delivered the winning—though slim—margin to John F. Kennedy in 1960. In 1968, at the peak of the Vietnam conflict, Daley unleashed his police on anti-war protesters at the Democratic Convention; some called it a "police riot." Hizzoner pugnaciously scowled at news cameras and growled, "Duh policeman isn't dere to create disorder, duh policeman is dere to preserve disorder." The whole world was watching.

Post-Industrial Chicago

Daley passed away in 1976, computer operators now outnumber steel mill workers, and post-industrial Chicago shuffles along. The Gold Coast and the Magnificent Mile are glitzier than ever, and Chicago's work force—what's left of it, anyway—is learning to survive in a service economy. More and more people have fled for greener horizons beyond the city limits, trading deteriorating schools and racial strife for safer neighborhoods.

Yet Chicago hangs on. In the 1970s and 1980s a forest of new skyscrapers shot up on the city's skyline, including the Sears Tower, the world's third-tallest building. Since Daley's death, the city has seen its first woman mayor (Jane Byrne) and its first black mayor (Harold Washington, a beloved figure who died in office in 1987). The city entered the 1990s with Mayor Richard "Richie" Daley, son of Hizzoner, solidly in office with his roots still embedded in the South Side. Although Chicago has been leaking population for decades, nearly three million people still live here.

"A Real City"

So what is Chicago today? It is 228 square miles stretching 30 miles along Lake Michigan's shore. It is 550 parks, 8 forest preserves, 29 beaches, 200 good restaurants, 2,000 lousy restaurants, and dozens of stands selling the best hot dogs in the world. Chicago is a city where football is a serious business and politics is a game. It's heaven for symphony lovers and nirvana for jazz buffs.

Come to Chicago and within half an hour someone will tell you it's "a city of neighborhoods." Sprinkled with curiosities, the city's ethnic neighborhoods offer visitors a flavor of the Old World and a chance for discovery.

And the Loop? Walk downtown along busy Michigan Avenue late on a Friday afternoon, watch the lights wink on in the skyscrapers overhead, feel the city's vitality, and you'll agree with what Rudyard Kipling wrote a century ago: "I have struck a city—a real city—and they call it Chicago."

Skyscrapers and the Prairie School: Chicago Architecture

Though no one seriously argues Chicago's status as the Second City— even the most avid boosters concede New York's status as America's leading city in population, culture, and finance—the Windy City lays claim to one superlative title that remains undisputed: the world capital of modern architecture.

And it's not just that the skyscraper was born here. A visit to Chicago is a crash course in the various streams of architecture that have helped shape the direction of twentieth-century building design. Even folks with an otherwise casual interest in architecture are bedazzled by the architectural heritage displayed here. Chicago is the world's largest outdoor museum of modern architecture.

A Bovine Beginning

A substantial amount of the credit for Chicago's status in the world of architecture can be laid at the feet of a cow—if it's true that Mrs. O'Leary's cow kicked over a lantern, starting an inferno of mythic proportions. The Great Chicago Fire of 1871 destroyed four square miles of the central city, and architects from around the world flocked to Chicago—not unlike Sir Christopher Wren, who rushed to London after a great fire leveled much of that city in the late 17th century.

Several other factors figured in Chicago's rise to preeminence in building design in the decades after the fire. The rapidly rising value of real estate in the central business district motivated developers to increase building heights as much as they could. Advances in elevator technology freed designers from vertical constraints; easily rentable space no longer needed to be an easy climb from street level.

But most important was the development of the iron and steel skeletal frame, which relieved the walls of the burden of carrying a building's weight. For the first time, a structure's exterior walls didn't need to grow thicker as the building grew taller. New technology also allowed for larger windows.

The Chicago School

As new technology took hold, many architects felt a building's external form should be equally innovative. The result was a style of architecture with a straightforward expression of structure. A masonry grid covered the steel structure beneath, while projecting bay windows created a lively rhythm on the facade. Any ornamentation was usually subordinated to the overall design and often restricted to the top and bottom thirds of the building, creating a kind of classical column effect. Collectively, the style came to be known as the Chicago School of Architecture.

Early skyscrapers that flaunt the technological innovations that made Chicago famous include the 15-story **Reliance Building** (32 North State Street; Burnham and Root; 1890) and the 12-story **Carson Pirie Scott & Company** department store (1 South State Street; Adler and Sullivan;

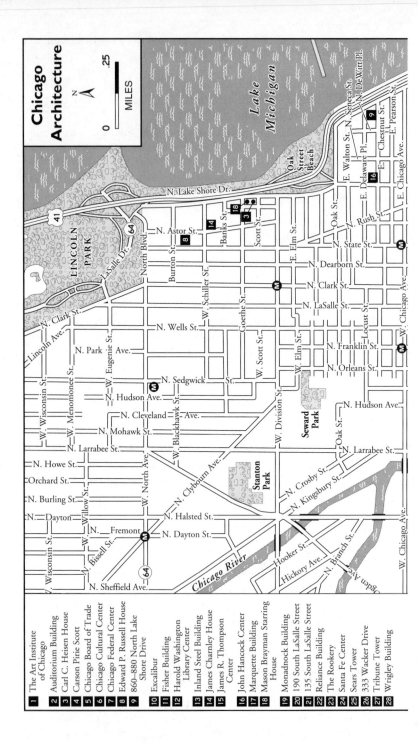

Chicago Architecture

N

0 .25
MILES

Lake Michigan

LINCOLN PARK

N. Lake Shore Dr.

Oak Street Beach

N. Astor St.

Banks St.

Scott St.

Burton St.

W. Schiller St.

Goethe St.

W. Scott St.

E. Walton St.

N. Seneca St.

N. DeWitt Pl.

E. Delaware Pl.

Chestnut St.

E. Pearson St.

E. Chicago Ave.

N. State St.

N. Dearborn St.

N. Clark St.

N. LaSalle St.

N. Rush St.

E. Elm St.

Oak St.

North Blvd.

LaSalle Dr.

N. Clark St.

Lincoln Ave.

N. Park Ave.

N. Wells St.

N. Eugenie St.

N. Sedgwick St.

N. Hudson Ave.

N. Cleveland Ave.

N. Mohawk St.

N. Larrabee St.

N. Franklin St.

N. Orleans St.

N. Hudson Ave.

N. Elm St.

W. Division St.

Seward Park

N. Wisconsin St.

W. Menomonee St.

W. Blackhawk St.

N. Howe St.

Orchard St.

N. Burling St.

N. Dayton

N. Fremont

W. Willow St.

W. Bissell St.

N. North Ave.

N. Clybourn Ave.

Stanton Park

N. Larrabee St.

N. Crosby St.

N. Kingsbury St.

Oak St.

N. Halsted St.

N. Dayton St.

Hooker St.

Hickory Ave.

N. Branch St.

W. Chicago Ave.

N. Sheffield Ave.

Chicago River

Ogden Ave.

1 The Art Institute of Chicago
2 Auditorium Building
3 Carl C. Heisen House
4 Carson Pirie Scott
5 Chicago Board of Trade
6 Chicago Cultural Center
7 Chicago Federal Center
8 Edward P. Russell House
9 860–880 North Lake Shore Drive
10 Excalibur
11 Fisher Building
12 Harold Washington Library Center
13 Inland Steel Building
14 James Charnley House
15 James R. Thompson Center
16 John Hancock Center
17 Marquette Building
18 Mason Brayman Starring House
19 Monadnock Building
20 190 South LaSalle Street
21 135 South LaSalle Street
22 Reliance Building
23 The Rookery
24 Santa Fe Center
25 Sears Tower
26 333 Wacker Drive
27 Tribune Tower
28 Wrigley Building

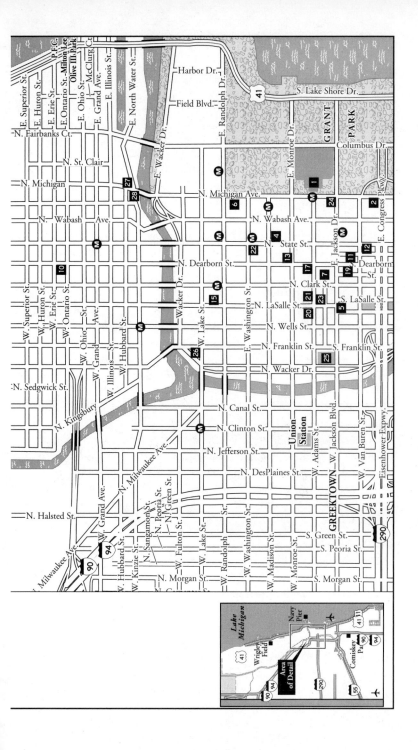

1899). These show-off buildings, held up by thin tendons of steel, are close in spirit to the modernist architecture that was to follow.

Classical Designs by the Lake

Daniel Burnham, who developed Chicago's urban plan and designed some of its most innovative buildings, also organized the 1893 World's Columbian Exposition. Yet the formal Beaux Arts style used in the major structures that remain were designed by East Coast architects. As a result, cultural institutions such as the **Art Institute** (Michigan Avenue at Adams Street; Shepley, Rutan & Coolidge; 1892) and the **Chicago Cultural Center** (78 East Washington Street; Shepley, Rutan & Coolidge; 1897) have their underlying structures disguised in white, neoclassical historical garb.

The Prairie School

Yet not all of Chicago's architectural innovations pushed upward or aped the classical designs of the past. In the early 1900s, Frank Lloyd Wright and his contemporaries were developing a modern style that's now called the Prairie School. The break from historically inspired Victorian house designs is highlighted by low, ground-hugging forms, hovering roofs with deep eaves, and bands of casement windows. Interiors feature open, flowing floor plans, centrally located hearths, natural woodwork, and uniform wall treatments.

Truly shocking in their day, Wright's designs now dot Chicago and its suburbs. The flowing horizontal planes sharply contrast with the upward thrust of skyscrapers in the Loop and convey a feeling of peace and calm. The largest groups of Prairie School houses are found in Oak Park, where Forest Avenue and nearby streets are lined with houses designed by Wright and his disciples.

1920s Prosperity and Art Deco

The prosperity of the 1920s resulted in a building boom; the construction of the Michigan Avenue Bridge encouraged developers to look for sites north of the Chicago River. It was the "heroic age" for the city's skyline, and designers borrowed heavily from European sources. The **Wrigley Building** (400 and 410 North Michigan Avenue; Graham, Anderson, Probst & White; 1922) is a dazzling white, terra cotta–clad lollipop of a building that's strikingly well lighted from the opposite shore of the river; the clock tower remains one of Chicago's most distinctive landmarks.

The **Tribune Tower** (435 North Michigan Avenue; Hood & Howells; 1925) is a neo-Gothic tower (considered "retro" when built) that soars upward like a medieval cathedral. At **333 North Michigan Avenue** stands Chicago's first Art Deco skyscraper, designed by Holabird & Root in 1928. More of the Art Deco impulse is displayed south of the river at the **Chicago Board of Trade Building** (141 West Jackson Boulevard; Holabird & Root; 1930), which anchors LaSalle Street's financial canyon and is topped with a 30-foot aluminum statue of Ceres, the Roman goddess of grain.

The International Style

When the Depression hit, most construction ground to a halt and didn't resume until after World War II. But after the postwar economic recovery arrived, German-born Ludwig Mies van der Rohe (who fled Nazi persecution before the war and later taught architecture at the Illinois Institute of Technology) found Chicago a receptive canvas for his daring designs.

Mies's motto was "Less is more," and the result was the sleek and unadorned International Style (often called the Second Chicago School). He was concerned with structural expression and the use of new technology as much as his predecessors in the 1890s, and Chicago boasts some of his most famous designs: the **Federal Center Complex** (Dearborn Street between Jackson Boulevard and Adams Street; 1964–75), the **Illinois Institute of Technology** (State Street between 31st and 35th Streets; 1940–58), and his last major design, the **IBM Building** (330 North Wabash; 1971).

Mies's signature style is the high-rise with an open colonnaded space around a solid shaft; the glass-and-steel skin is carefully detailed to represent the steel structure within. The designs are macho, strong, and sinewy, with great care given to proportion, play of light, and simplicity. Detractors sniff and call them "glass boxes."

Postmodernism

Inevitably, rebellion began, and the result was postmodernism, a catchall term describing anything outside the realm of mainstream modernist design. Often, the postmodernists overturned modernist beliefs while echoing the Chicago aesthetic of the past in new, often graceful designs. Macho and cold is out; whimsy and colorful are in. The starkness of Mies-inspired architecture gave way to purely decorative elements in designs that are still unmistakably modern.

Arguably the most graceful of the new buildings in Chicago, **333 North Wacker Drive** (Kohn Pedersen Fox/Perkins and Will; 1983) features a curved facade of glass that reflects the Chicago River in both shape and color. Another stunner is **150 North Michigan Avenue** (A. Epstein & Sons; 1984), whose sloping glass roof slices diagonally through the top ten floors.

Tipping its hat to the past is the **Harold Washington Library Center** (400 South State Street; Hammond, Beeby & Babka; 1991), which references numerous city landmarks. A red-granite base and brick walls pay tribute to the Rookery and Manadnock buildings (two Burnham and Root gems), while the facade and pediments along the roof recall the Art Institute. Even more retro is the **NBC Tower** (455 North Cityfront Plaza; Skidmore, Owings & Merrill; 1989), a 38-story Art Deco tower that successfully mines the architectural past.

One of Chicago's most controversial buildings is the **State of Illinois Center** (100 West Randolph Street; C. F. Murphy/Jahn Associates and Lester B. Knight & Associates; 1983). It's a 17-story, glass-and-steel interpretation of the traditional government office building created by the bad boy of Chicago architecture, Helmut Jahn. Inside, 13 floors of balconied offices encircle a 332-foot central rotunda that's topped with a sloping glass skylight 160 feet in diameter. You've got to see it to believe it. The controversy? Some people loathe it—and state employees often endure blistering heat in the summer and freezing cold in the winter.

Scraping the Sky

Another hard-to-ignore element in recent downtown Chicago designs is height: Chicago claims several of the world's ten tallest buildings, including the 1,454-foot **Sears Tower** (233 South Wacker Drive; Skidmore, Owings & Merrill; 1974). The world's third-tallest building is a set of nine square tubes bundled together to give strength to the whole; seven tubes drop away as the building ascends, and only two go the distance.

Yet the 1,127-foot **John Hancock Center** (875 North Michigan; Skidmore, Owings & Merrill; 1969) usually gets higher marks from critics for its tapered form that's crisscrossed by diagonal wind-bracing; locals say the view from the top is better, too. The Hancock Center is the world's 14th-tallest building, but the world's 13th-tallest is also in Chicago: the 80-story, 1,136-foot **AON Centre** (200 East Randolph Street; E. D. Stone/Perkins and Will; 1974). New white-granite cladding on the AON Centre replaced a Carrara marble skin that couldn't stand up to Chicago's wind and temperature extremes.

An Outdoor Museum

Most of Chicago's landmark buildings—and we've only described a few—are located in and around the Loop, making a comfortable walking tour the best way to explore this outdoor museum of modern architecture. If you've got the time and the interest, we strongly recommend taking one of the Chicago Architecture Foundation's two-hour walking tours of the Loop (info at (312) 922-3432 or **www.architecture.org**). It's by far the best way to gain a greater appreciation of one of the world's great architectural mosaics.

1. *Untitled* ("The Picasso"), Pablo Picasso (1967)
2. *Chicago*, Joan Miro (1981)
3. *Monument with Standing Beast*, Jean Dubuffet (1984)
4. *Freeform*, Richard Hunt (1993)
5. *Flight of Daedalus and Icarus*, 120 North LaSalle Street, Roger Brown (1990)
6. *Dawn Shadows*, Louise Nevelson (1983)
7. *Loomings and Knights and Squires*, Frank Stella
8. *Batcolumn*, Claes Oldenburg (1977)
9. *The Universe*, Alexander Calder (1974)
10. *Gem of the Lakes*, Raymond Kaskey (1990)
11. *San Marco II*, Ludovico de Luigi (1986)
12. *The Town-Ho's Story*, Frank Stella (1993)
13. *Ruins III*, Nita K. Sutherland (1978)
14. *Flamingo*, Alexander Calder (1974)
15. *Lines in Four Directions*, Sol Lewitt (1985)
16. *The Four Seasons*, Marc Chagall (1974)
17. *Untitled Sounding Sculpture*, Harry Bertoia (1975)
18. *Alexander Hamilton*, Bela Lyon Pratt (1918)
19. *Large Interior Form*, Henry Moore (1983)
20. *Celebration of the 200th Anniversary of the Founding of the Republic*, Isamu Noguchi (1976)
21. *The Fountain of the Great Lakes*, Lorado Taft (1913)

Sculpture in the Loop

Chicago, the world leader in modern architecture, also boasts one of the finest collections of public art in the United States. Major pieces by such 20th-century greats as Picasso, Chagall, Calder, Miró, Moore, Oldenburg, Nevelson, and Noguchi are scattered throughout the Loop.

It's a cornucopia of postmodern masterpieces—although some might take a little getting used to. After Picasso's untitled abstract sculpture in the Civic Center plaza was unveiled by Mayor Richard J. Daley in 1967, one Chicago alderman introduced a motion in the city council that it be removed and replaced by a monument to Cubs baseball hero Ernie Banks. Nothing came of the motion, and now the sculpture is a beloved city landmark. Here's an informal tour of some of the Loop's best:

1. *Untitled Picasso Sculpture* (1967, Pablo Picasso); Richard J. Daley Plaza (West Washington Street between North Dearborn and North Clark Streets); Cor-Ten steel.

2. *Flamingo* (1974, Alexander Calder); Federal Center (219 South Dearborn Street between West Adams Street and West Jackson Boulevard); painted steel.

3. *Miró's Chicago* (1967, Joan Miró; installed 1981); Chicago Temple (69 West Washington Street at North Clark Street); bronze, concrete, tile.

4. *The Four Seasons* (1975, Marc Chagall); First National Plaza (West Monroe Street between South Clark and South Dearborn Streets); hand-chipped stone, glass fragments, brick.

5. *Monument with Standing Beast* (1985, Jean Dubuffet); State of Illinois Center (100 West Randolph Street at North Clark Street); fiberglass.

6. *Ceres* (1930, John Storrs); Chicago Board of Trade (141 West Jackson Boulevard at South LaSalle Street); aluminum.

7. *Being Born* (1983, Virginio Ferarri); State Street Mall (at East Washington Street in front of Marshall Field's); stainless steel.

8. *Batcolumn* (1977, Claes Oldenburg); Social Security Administration Building Plaza (600 West Madison Street at North Clinton Street); painted steel.

9. *Dawn Shadows* (1983, Louise Nevelson); Madison Plaza (200 West Madison Street at North Wells Street); steel.

10. *Universe* (1974, Alexander Calder); Lobby, Sears Tower (233 South Wacker Drive); painted aluminum.

Part Two

Planning Your Visit to Chicago

When to Go: Seasons of the Windy City

Four Distinct Seasons

Chicago is a town that boasts four distinct seasons. Arrive on a blustery winter day—when pedestrians battle fierce winds off Lake Michigan that rake North Michigan Avenue—and you may assume Chicago is called "the Windy City" because of the weather. (It's not. The moniker was earned by long-winded nineteenth-century Chicago pols.) In January and February, Chicago's climate is often distinguished by a bone-chilling combination of subfreezing temperatures and howling winds. And the white stuff? The average winter snowfall is 40 inches.

CHICAGO'S AVERAGE TEMPERATURES AND PRECIPITATION		
Month	Average Daily Temperature (Minimum/Maximum in Fahrenheit)	Average Monthly Precipitation
January	18°/34°	1.6"
February	20°/36°	1.3"
March	29°/45°	2.6"
April	40°/58°	3.7"
May	49°/70°	3.2"
June	59°/81°	4.1"
July	65°/86°	3.6"
August	65°/85°	3.5"
September	56°/76°	3.4"
October	45°/65°	2.3"
November	32°/49°	2.1"
December	22°/36°	2.1"

A CALENDAR OF FESTIVALS AND EVENTS

January

Chicago Park District Holiday Flower Show   Garfield Park Conservatory and Lincoln Park Conservatory. Through the first week of January. Free. (312) 746-5100 (Garfield Park), (312) 742-7737 (Lincoln Park).

Chicago Boat, Sports, and RV Show   McCormick Place. Hands-on displays of sporting goods, boats, motor homes, and recreational vehicles. Admission fee. (312) 946-6200; **www.discoverboating.com.**

February

Chinese New Year Parade   Chinatown. A parade, firecrackers, and a paper dragon dance through the streets of Chinatown. Free. (312) 225-6198.

Chicago Park District Spring Flower Show   Garfield Park Conservatory and Lincoln Park Conservatory. Thousands of spring flowers on display from mid-February to mid-May. Free. (312) 746-5100 (Garfield Park), (312) 742-7737 (Lincoln Park).

Chicago Auto Show   McCormick Place. The largest commercial auto show in the world, featuring new models, classics, and race cars. Admission: $10. (630) 495-2282.

National African-American History Month   Various locations. A month-long, city-wide celebration of black Americans' lives, times, and art. Free. (312) 747-2536 (South Shore Cultural Center).

The summer months of June, July, and August, on the other hand, are noted for high temperatures and high humidity that frequently approach triple digits. Though the combination can make for miserably hot and sticky summer afternoons, breezes off Lake Michigan are often a mitigating factor that can make a stroll through Lincoln Park (or an afternoon at the Taste of Chicago festival) bearable.

Temperature-wise, spring and fall are the most moderate times of the year; many people say autumn is their favorite Chicago season. Evening temperatures in October and November may dip into the 40s, but the days are usually warm. Starting in mid-October, the fall foliage creates a riot of color that tempts thousands of folks to jump in their cars for day trips north of the city along scenic Sheridan Road.

One common cliché applies in Chicago: If you don't like the weather, just wait a while . . . it may change. In any season, the city's lakefront setting and location in a major west-to-east weather path make atmospheric

March

South Side Irish St. Patrick's Day Parade   Western Avenue from 103rd to 114th Streets the weekend before St. Patty's Day. Free. (773) 445-6764.

St. Patrick's Day Parade   Dearborn Street from Wacker Drive to Van Buren Street. Forty pounds of vegetable dye turns the Chicago River green, and everyone is Irish for the day. The parade starts at noon and features floats, marching bands, and hundreds of thousands of spectators. Free. (312) 744-3370.

Chicago Park District Spring Flower Show   Navy Pier, 600 E. Grand Avenue. An eyeful of spring. Free. (312) 746-5100 (Garfield Park), (312) 321-0077.

April

Cinco de Mayo Festival   McCormick Place. A two-day festival celebrating Mexican independence featuring food, drink, and more. Free. (312) 751-5560.

Chicago Latino Film Festival   Various locations. (312) 409-1757.

May

Art Chicago   Navy Pier. Art, both past and present, offered for sale by prestigious art galleries. Admission: $12. (312) 587-3300.

Polish Constitution Day Parade   Dearborn Street from Wacker Drive to Van Buren Street. Free. (773) 889-7125.

conditions highly changeable (and, as you'll discover during your stay, difficult to predict). Plan accordingly on all-day outings by bringing along appropriate rain gear and/or extra clothing.

For visitors in town enjoying Chicago's museums, galleries, shopping, restaurants, and other attractions, any season is okay. The city goes full-blast all year. In fact, while winter may be the least desirable time of year to hit town, it's the cultural season; theater, music, and special programs at museums are running at full steam.

Avoiding Crowds

In general, the summer months (mid-June through mid-August, when school is out) are the busiest times at most tourist attractions. Popular tourist sites are busier on weekends than weekdays, and Saturdays are busier than Sundays. Many major Chicago attractions offer free admission one day a week; it's usually the most crowded day.

A CALENDAR OF FESTIVALS AND EVENTS *(continued)*

May *(continued)*

Wright Plus   Oak Park. The only chance to tour the interiors of ten homes designed by Frank Lloyd Wright and his contemporaries. Admission: $85; tickets go on sale on March 1, and the event usually sells out by mid-April. The all-day tour is held on the third Saturday in May. (708) 848-1976.

June

Chicago Blues Festival   Petrillo Music Shell, Grant Park. Fabulous music, food, and dozens of artists from Chicago and beyond. Free. (312) 744-3315.

57th Street Art Fair   57th Street and South Kimbark Avenue. Oldest juried art fair in the Midwest. Free. (773) 493-3247.

Chicago Gospel Festival   Petrillo Music Shell, Grant Park. Free. (312) 744-3370.

Celebrate on State Street Festival   State Street from Wacker Drive to Van Buren Street. Free. (312) 782-9160.

Gay and Lesbian Pride Parade   Starts at Halsted Street and Belmont Avenue. Free. (773) 348-8243.

Midsummer Festival in Andersonville   Neighborhood festival on Clark Street from Foster to Catalpa avenues. Free. (773) 728-2995.

Chicago Country Music Festival   Petrillo Music Shell, Grant Park. Free. (312) 744-3370.

On weekdays during the school year, places such as the Art Institute of Chicago, the Field Museum, and the Lincoln Park Zoo are besieged by yellow school buses. If you'd rather tour when things are a little quieter, come back in the afternoon: The kids are whisked back to class by 1:30 p.m. because the buses are needed at the end of the school day.

Driving during Chicago's rush hour—for that matter, driving in Chicago at any time for out-of-town visitors—should be avoided. Massive tie-ups are routine on the main arteries leading in and out of the city, as well as on the major highways that connect the suburbs. If you must drive, stay off the road before 9 a.m. and after 4 p.m. so you'll miss the worst rush hour traffic. Generally, getting around by car on weekends and holidays is a breeze, although you may run into an occasional backup on the Eisenhower or Kennedy Expressways, the two major highways that lead in and out of downtown Chicago.

Taste of Chicago Grant Park. In the week preceding Independence Day more than 100 restaurants serve Chicago-style and ethnic cuisine at this alfresco food festival; musical entertainment. (312) 744-3370.

Ravinia Festival Highland Park from late June to late August. A 12-week season of the Chicago Symphony Orchestra, dance, jazz, ballet, folk, and comedy in a picnic setting. Admission: $10 lawn; pavilion tickets vary from about $20 to about $75. For information, call (847) 266-5000; for travel information, call (847) 266-5100.

Taste of River North Superior Street, between LaSalle and Wells Streets. Two days of food tastings from up to 40 restaurants located in this trendy Chicago neighborhood. Free. (312) 645-1047.

July

Chicago Country Music Festival Petrillo Music Shell, Grant Park. Free. (312) 744-3315.

Concerts in the Parks Various locations. More than 80 concerts performed in 64 Chicago parks in July and August. Free. (312) 747-0816.

Independence Day Concert and Fireworks Petrillo Music Shell, Grant Park. A classical concert kicks off Chicago's traditional Fourth of July celebration. Free. (312) 744-3370.

Sheffield Garden Walk and Festival Corner of Sheffield Avenue and Webster Street at St. Vincent's Church. Self-guided walking tour of private gardens, garage sales, food, and entertainment. Admission fee. (773) 929-9255.

Likewise, if you're driving to Chicago or planning to get from the airport to downtown by car or cab, avoid arriving during rush hour (especially on Friday afternoons). The drive from O'Hare to the Loop can take up to four hours as all those high-rise office buildings disgorge legions of office workers focused on getting home for the weekend. Don't get in their way.

Warning: Population Explosion

Be forewarned that Chicago is home to some of the largest conventions and trade shows in the world. If you attempt to visit the Windy City while one of these monsters is in progress, you will find hotel rooms scarce and expensive, restaurants crowded, and empty cabs impossible to find. This population explosion is often compounded between Thanksgiving and the third week in December when shoppers and conventioneers converge

A CALENDAR OF FESTIVALS AND EVENTS *(continued)*

July *(continued)*

Taste of Ireland Festival   Irish American Heritage Center, 4626 North Knox Avenue. Two days of continuous entertainment, 40 Irish bands, food, Irish step dancing, and museum and art gallery tours. Admission: $10. (773) 282-7035.

Newberry Library Annual Book Fair   60 West Walton Place. Free. (312) 255-3700.

Venetian Night   Chicago's lakefront, from Navy Pier to the planetarium. The Grant Park Symphony and a parade of animated floats and illuminated yachts. Free. (312) 744-3315.

August

Black Harvest Film Festival   Film Center of the Art Institute, Columbus Drive and Jackson Boulevard. Admission fee. (312) 846-2600.

Concerts in the Parks   Various locations. More than 80 concerts performed in 64 Chicago parks in July and August. Free. (312) 747-0816.

Bud Billiken Parade   King Drive to Washington Park. The South Side black community's fun-filled event for kids and grownups. Free. (312) 225-2400, ext. 142.

Chicago Air and Water Show   North Avenue Beach. The largest free air and water show and one of the largest spectator events in the United

on Chicago simultaneously. To help you avoid the crowds, consult our calendar of those conventions and trade shows large enough to affect your visit (see Part Four: Visiting Chicago on Business).

How to Get More Information on Chicago before Your Visit

For additional information on entertainment, sight-seeing, maps, shopping, dining, and lodging in the Chicago area, call or write:

Chicago Office of Tourism
Chicago Cultural Center
78 East Washington Street
Chicago, Illinois 60602
(877) CHICAGO, (312) 744-2964 (TDD)
(877) 244-2246
www.877chicago.com

States attracts two million people each year; powerboat racing and a dazzling aerial display in the sky over Lake Michigan. Free. (312) 744-3315.

Ginza Holiday Midwest Buddhist Temple, 435 West Menomonee Street. A celebration of Japanese culture featuring food, dance, mime, martial arts, music, origami, painting, and sculpture. Admission: $3.50. (312) 943-7801.

National Antique Show & Sale Stephens Convention Center (near O'Hare). A large semi-annual show of antiques and collector's items. Admission: $8. (847) 692-2220.

Gold Coast Art Fair Between Ontario, Huron, Franklin, and State Streets. For three days 400 artists display and sell high-quality paintings, photographs, and hand-crafted fine art. Free. (847) 432-3606.

Oz Festival Lincoln Park. Family-oriented fun featuring arts and crafts, entertainment for children, and food. Admission fee. (312) 409-5466.

New East Side ArtWorks Festival Michigan Avenue and Lake Street. Free. (773) 404-0763.

Chicago Jazz Festival Petrillo Music Shell, Grant Park. A jazz marathon over Labor Day weekend; the world's largest free jazz festival featuring the greats from traditional and swing to bebop, blues, and avant garde. Free. (312) 744-3370.

In addition, three visitor information centers are centrally located: in the Historic Water Tower on the Magnificent Mile (on North Michigan Avenue across from the Water Tower Place shopping mall); in the Chicago Cultural Center (downtown on South Michigan at Washington Street); and in the Explore Chicago kiosk inside the Sears on State store (2 North State Street, in the Loop). All are open daily, offer help planning an itinerary, make suggestions about things to do, and feature plenty of free information and maps.

Getting to Chicago

Folks planning a trip to the Windy City have several options when it comes to getting there: plane, train, or automobile. Your distance from Chicago—and your tolerance for such hassles as traffic congestion and interminable waits in holding patterns—will probably determine which mode of transportation you ultimately choose.

A CALENDAR OF FESTIVALS AND EVENTS *(continued)*

September

Berghoff Oktoberfest Adams Street between State and Dearborn Streets. Street party with beer tents, bands, and dancing. (312) 427-3170.

"Viva Chicago" Latin Music Festival Petrillo Music Shell, Grant Park. Free. (312) 744-3315.

October

Chicago International Film Festival Screenings at various theaters throughout the city. Exciting new international films, directors, and stars. Admission: $10. (312) 425-9400.

Columbus Day Parade Dearborn Street from Wacker Drive to Congress Parkway. Free. (312) 828-0010.

Historic Pullman District's Annual House Tour Historic Pullman Center, 614 East 113th Street. Annual fall tour of homes and historic buildings; refreshments available. Admission fee. (773) 785-8181.

Edgar Allan Poe Reading Clarke House Museum. Listen to an actor read Poe stories in a candlelit setting. Admission: $25. (312) 326-1480.

November/December

Annual Polish Film Festival in North America Various movie theaters. Admission: about $9, depending on program. (773) 486-9612.

Historic Pullman District's Candlelight Tour Historic Pullman Center, 614 East 113th Street. Candlelight tour of Historic Pullman Center and

Flying

If you're coming to Chicago from the east, west, Gulf coast, Europe, Asia, South America, or any other place that's more than a 12-hour drive away, you'll probably arrive the way most folks do: by plane into O'Hare International Airport, the world's busiest—and often, most frustrating—airfield.

Yet many domestic flyers can avoid the hassles of O'Hare by flying into Midway, an airport with architecture right out of the 1950s that's conveniently located about ten miles southwest of the Loop. Midway is a one-level airport that's considerably less congested than O'Hare, located on a subway line, and only about 20 minutes from downtown (longer during rush hour). Our advice: If you can, fly into Midway. (See Part Five: Arriving and Getting Oriented for maps of O'Hare and Midway.)

five homes, with dinner; $50 per person; reservations only. (773) 785-8181.

Chrysanthemum Show   Lincoln Park Conservatory and Garfield Park Conservatory. Mum's the word. (312) 746-5100 (Garfield Park), (312) 742-7737 (Lincoln Park).

Veteran's Day Parade   Dearborn Street from Wacker Drive to Van Buren Street. Free. (312) 744-7582.

Magnificent Mile Festival of Lights   North Michigan Avenue from the Chicago River to Oak Street. The kickoff of Chicago's traditional holiday shopping season features stage shows, a parade, fireworks, and 300,000 lights on Michigan Avenue and Oak Street. Free. (312) 642-3570.

Christmas around the World   Museum of Science and Industry. A grand ethnic festival, plus entertainment. Admission: $9. (773) 684-1414; **www.msichicago.org.**

Candlelight Tours of Prairie Avenue Houses   Near McCormick Place. Authentic period Christmas decorations; docents talk about the history of Christmas traditions in Chicago. Admission: $15. (312) 326-1480.

Chicago Park District Holiday Flower Show   Garfield Park Conservatory and Lincoln Park Conservatory. Free. (312) 746-5100 (Garfield Park), (312) 742-7737 (Lincoln Park).

Taking the Train

Just as O'Hare is a major air hub between the east and west coasts of the United States, Chicago's Union Station is the major rail station between the two coasts. Though long-distance travel by train can be tedious, people who live in the Midwest can travel by rail into Chicago without fear of getting stuck in a holding pattern over O'Hare or trapped in a traffic snarl on the Eisenhower Expressway.

The cities closest to Chicago with Amtrak passenger train service are Milwaukee (1.5 hours one-way) and Indianapolis (4.5 hours). Other cities offering daily rail service to Union Station include St. Louis (5 hours), Detroit (5 hours), Cincinnati (7 hours; three days a week), Cleveland (6 hours), Kansas City (8.5 hours), Toronto (12 hours), Omaha (9 hours), and Minneapolis (8 hours). For schedules and reservations, call Amtrak at (800) 872-7245; **www.amtrak.com.**

Driving

If you live close to Chicago and driving is an option, think again. Why? Chicago traffic congestion never lets up. Backups, accidents, and delays occur perpetually throughout the metropolitan area. And parking? Not a chance. Convenient, affordable, and/or secure places to leave your car are rare luxuries. Instead of enduring traffic and parking crises, try using Chicago's extensive public transportation systems and abundance of taxis to get around town, and airport vans to get to and from downtown hotels. For more information about travel in Chicago without a car, see "Public Transportation" in Part Six: Getting around Chicago.

But what if, in spite of our advice, you drive to Chicago? Here's the short list of things to do (and avoid) when driving around town: Make sure your hotel offers on-site or nearby off-street parking, don't arrive during rush hour, and be flexible about using public transportation throughout your stay. Often, it's less expensive and a lot less hassle to leave the car parked and to take a bus, the El, or a cab. For more information on getting around Chicago by car, see Part Six: Getting around Chicago.

Part Three

Hotels

Deciding Where to Stay

Though Chicago sprawls for miles north and south along Lake Michigan, and threatens on the west side to realize some suburban manifest destiny by creeping all the way to the Iowa border, the city is as focused and anchored as Manhattan. Chicago is defined by its city center. Downtown Chicago is not simply the heart of the city, it is the heart of the Midwest. As American as Valley Forge and as foreign as Warsaw, downtown Chicago is a magnet. If you visit Chicago, downtown is where you want to be.

The Chicago hotel scene reflects the dynamism and power of the city's bustling core. By and large, Chicago hotels are big, huge even, soaring 20, 30, and more stories above the lake. Although there are hotels near Midway and O'Hare Airports and in smaller towns that have expanded to surround the great city, the majority of Chicago's nearly 77,000 rooms are situated in a narrow strip bordered by Lake Michigan on the east, Clark Street on the west, North Avenue on the north, and Roosevelt Road on the south. All told, the area is about three miles north to south and less than a mile wide.

Though some of the finest hotels in the world are in Chicago, finding comfortable lodging for less than $100 a night is easier here than in New York. Chicago is not cheap, but the quality standards for hotels are generally high. Also in Chicago, unlike in Boston, Atlanta, or Washington, D.C., the option of booking a less expensive hotel in the suburbs and commuting to downtown is impractical. The commute is long, the suburban hotels few, and the savings insignificant to nonexistent.

Finally, Chicago is the busiest convention city in the United States. If your visit to Chicago coincides with one or more major conventions or trade shows, hotel rooms will be both scarce and expensive. If on the other hand, you are able to schedule your visit to avoid big meetings, you will have a good selection of hotels at suprisingly competitive prices. If you happen to be attending one of the big conventions, book early and use some of the tips listed below to get a discounted room rate. To assist in timing your visit, we have included a convention and trade show calendar in Part Four: Visiting Chicago on Business.

Some Considerations

1. When choosing your Chicago lodging, make sure your hotel is situated in a location convenient to your recreation or business needs, and that it is in a safe and comfortable area. Please note that although it is not practical to walk to McCormick Place (the major convention venue) from any of the downtown hotels, larger conventions and trade shows provide shuttle service.

2. Find out how old the hotel is and when the guest rooms were last renovated. Request that the hotel send you its promotional brochure. Ask if brochure photos of guest rooms are accurate and current.

3. If you plan to take a car, inquire about the parking situation. Some hotels offer no parking at all, some charge dearly for parking , and a few offer free parking.

4. If you are not a city dweller, or perhaps are a light sleeper, try to book a hotel on a more quiet side street. Ask for a room off the street and high up.

5. The Chicago skyline is quite beautiful, as is the lake. If you are on a romantic holiday, ask for a room on a higher floor with a good view.

6. If shopping is high on your agenda, try to book a hotel near Michigan Avenue between Oak Street and East Wacker Drive.

7. When you plan your budget, remember that Chicago's combined room and sales tax is a whopping 14.9%.

Getting a Good Deal on a Room

Special Weekend Rates

Although well-located Chicago hotels are tough for the budget conscious, it's not impossible to get a good deal, at least relatively speaking. For starters, most downtown hotels that cater to business, government, and convention travelers offer special weekend discount rates that range from 15–40% below normal weekday rates. You can find out about weekend specials by calling individual hotels or your travel agent.

Getting Corporate Rates

Many hotels offer discounted corporate rates (5–20% off rack). Usually you do not need to work for a large company or have a special relationship with the hotel to obtain these rates. Simply call the hotel of your choice and ask for their corporate rates. Many hotels will guarantee you the discounted rate on the phone when you make your reservation. Others may make the rate conditional on your providing some sort of bona fides, for instance a fax on your company's letterhead requesting the rate, or a company credit card or business card on check-in. Generally, the screening is not rigorous.

Half-Price Programs

The larger discounts on rooms (35–60%), in Chicago or anywhere else, are available through half-price hotel programs, often called travel clubs. Program operators contract with an individual hotel to provide rooms at deep discounts, usually 50% off rack rate, on a "space available" basis. Space available in practice generally means that you can reserve a room at the discounted rate whenever the hotel expects to be at less than 80% occupancy. A little calendar sleuthing to help you avoid city-wide conventions and special events will increase your chances of choosing a time when the discounts are available.

Most half-price programs charge an annual membership fee or directory subscription charge of $25 to $125. Once enrolled, you are mailed a membership card and a directory listing participating hotels. Examining the directory, you will notice immediately that there are many restrictions and exceptions. Some hotels, for instance, "black out" certain dates or times of year. Others may only offer the discount on certain days of the week, or require you to stay a certain number of nights. Still others may offer a much smaller discount than 50% off rack rate.

Programs specialize in domestic travel, international travel, or both. More established operators offer members between 1,000 and 4,000 hotels to choose from in the United States. All of the programs have a heavy concentration of hotels in California and Florida, and most have a very limited selection of participating properties in New York City or Boston. Offerings in other cities and regions of the United States vary considerably. The programs with the largest selections of Chicago hotels are **Encore, Travel America at Half Price** (Entertainment Publications), **International Travel Card,** and **Quest.** Each of these programs lists between 4 and 50 hotels in the greater Chicago area.

Preferred Traveler	(800) 638-0930
Entertainment Publications	(800) 285-5525
International Travel Card	(800) 342-0558
Quest	(800) 638-9819

One problem with half-price programs is that not all hotels offer a full 50% discount. Another slippery problem is the base rate against which the discount is applied. Some hotels figure the discount on an exaggerated rack rate that nobody would ever have to pay. A few participating hotels may deduct the discount from a supposed "superior" or "upgraded" room rate, even though the room you get is the hotel's standard accommodation. Though hard to pin down, the majority of participating properties base discounts on the published rate in the *Hotel & Travel Index* (a quarterly reference work used by travel agents) and work within the spirit of their agreement with the program operator. As a rule, if you travel several times a year, your room rate savings will easily compensate for program membership fees.

A noteworthy addendum: Deeply discounted rooms through half-price programs are not commissionable to travel agents. In practical terms, this means that you must ordinarily make your own inquiry calls and reservations. If you travel frequently, however, and run a lot of business through your travel agent, he or she will probably do your legwork, lack of commission notwithstanding.

Preferred Rates

If you cannot book the hotel of your choice through a half-price program, you and your travel agent may have to search for a lesser discount, often called a preferred rate. A preferred rate could be a discount made available to travel agents to stimulate their booking activity, or a discount initiated to attract a certain class of traveler. Most preferred rates are promoted through travel industry publications and are often accessible only through an agent.

We recommend sounding out your travel agent about possible deals. Be aware, however, that the rates shown on travel agents' computerized reservations systems are not always the lowest rates obtainable. Focus on a couple of hotels that fill your needs in terms of location and quality of accommodations, and then have your travel agent call the hotel for the latest rates and specials. Hotel reps almost always respond to travel agents because travel agents represent a source of additional business. As discussed earlier, there are certain specials that hotel reps will disclose only to travel agents. Travel agents also come in handy when the hotel you want is supposedly booked. A personal appeal from your agent to the hotel's director of sales and marketing will get you a room more than half of the time.

Wholesalers, Consolidators, and Reservation Services

If you do not want to join a program or buy a discount directory, you can take advantage of the services of a wholesaler or consolidator. Wholesalers and consolidators buy rooms, or options on rooms (room blocks), from hotels at a low, negotiated rate. They then resell the rooms at a profit through travel agents, tour packagers, or directly to the public. Most wholesalers and consolidators have a provision for returning unsold rooms to participating hotels, but are not inclined to do so. The wholesaler's or consolidator's relationship with any hotel is predicated on volume. If they return rooms unsold, the hotel may not make as many rooms available to them the next time around. Thus wholesalers and consolidators often offer rooms at bargain rates, anywhere from 15–50% off rack, occasionally sacrificing their profit margins in the process, to avoid returning the rooms to the hotel unsold.

When wholesalers and consolidators deal directly with the public, they frequently represent themselves as "reservation services." When you call, you can ask for a rate quote for a particular hotel, or alternatively ask for their best available deal in the area where you prefer to stay. If there is a maximum amount you are willing to pay, say so. Chances are the service will find something that will work for you, even if they have to shave a dollar or two off their own profit. Sometimes you will have to pay for your room with a credit card when you make your reservation. Other times you will pay as usual, when you check out. Two such services are **Hotel Reservations Network** (phone (800) 964-6835) and **Hot Rooms** (phone (773) 468-7666).

Alternative Lodging

B&Bs   **Bed & Breakfast Chicago** at (800) 375-7084 or (773) 248-0005 is a reservation service for guest houses and furnished apartments primarily in the downtown area. Rates usually range from $95–$295 for guest houses and $125–$325 for furnished apartments. For more information, visit **www.chicago-bed-breakfast.com.**

Condos   If you want to rent a condo for a week in Chicago, you are out of luck. Local law stipulates a minimum rental period of 30 days. If you are planning an extended stay and are interested in a condo, your best bet is to shop realtors in the area of town where you prefer to stay. If they don't handle rentals, they can refer you to someone who does.

How to Evaluate a Travel Package

Hundreds of Chicago package vacations are offered to the public each year. Packages should be a win/win proposition for both the buyer and the seller. The buyer only has to make one phone call and deal with a single salesperson to set up the whole vacation: transportation, rental car, lodging, meals, attraction admissions, and even golf and tennis. The seller, likewise, only has to deal with the buyer once, eliminating the need for separate sales, confirmations, and billing. In addition to streamlining sales, processing, and administration, some packagers also buy airfares in bulk on contract like a broker playing the commodities market. Buying a large number of airfares in advance allows the packager to buy them at a significant savings from posted fares. The same practice is also applied to hotel rooms. Because selling vacation packages is an efficient way of doing business, and because the packager can often buy individual package components (airfare, lodging, etc.) in bulk at discount, savings in operating expenses realized by the seller are sometimes passed on to the buyer, so that, in addition to convenience, the package is also an exceptional value. In any event, that is the way it is supposed to work.

All too often, in practice, the seller cashes in on discounts and passes none on to the buyer. In some instances, packages are loaded additionally with extras that cost the packager next to nothing, but inflate the retail price sky-high. As you may expect, the savings to be passed along to customers remain somewhere in Fantasyland.

When considering a package, choose one that includes features you are sure to use. Whether you use all the features or not, you will most certainly pay for them. Second, if cost is of greater concern than convenience, make a few phone calls and see what the package would cost if you booked its individual components (airfare, rental car, lodging, etc.) on your own. If the package price is less than the à la carte cost, the package is a good deal. If the costs are about the same, the package is probably worth buying just for the convenience.

If your package includes a choice of rental car or airport transfers (transportation to and from the airport), take the transfers unless you are visiting Chicago for the weekend. During the weekend, with the exception of some sections of Michigan Avenue, it is relatively easy to get around. During the week, forget it. Also, if you take the car, be sure to ask if the package includes free parking at your hotel.

Helping Your Travel Agent Help You

When you call your travel agent, ask if he or she has been to Chicago. If the answer is no, be prepared to give your travel agent some direction. Do not accept any recommendations at face value. Check out the location and rates of any suggested hotel and make certain that the hotel is suited to your itinerary.

Because some travel agents are unfamiliar with Chicago, your agent may try to plug you into a tour operator's or wholesaler's preset package. This essentially allows the travel agent to set up your whole trip with a single phone call and still collect an 8–10% commission. The problem with this scenario is that most agents will place 90% of their Chicago business with only one or two wholesalers or tour operators. In other words, it's the line of least resistance for them, and not much choice for you.

Travel agents will often use wholesalers who run packages in conjunction with airlines, like Delta's Dream Vacations or American's Fly-Away Vacations. Because of the wholesaler's exclusive relationship with the carrier, these trips are very easy for travel agents to book. However, they will probably be more expensive than a package offered by a high-volume wholesaler who works with a number of airlines in a primary Chicago market.

To help your travel agent get you the best possible deal, do the following:

1. Determine where you want to stay in Chicago, and if possible choose a specific hotel. This can be accomplished by reviewing the hotel information provided in this guide, and by writing or calling hotels that interest you.

2. Check out the hotel deals and package vacations advertised in the Sunday travel sections of the *Chicago Tribune* and *Chicago Sun-Times* newspapers. Often you will be able to find deals that beat the socks off anything offered in your local paper. See if you can find specials that fit your plans and include a hotel you like.

3. Call the hotels, wholesalers, or tour operators whose ads you have collected. Ask any questions you have concerning their packages, but do not book your trip with them directly.

4. Tell your travel agent about the deals you find and ask if he or she can get you something better. The deals in the paper will serve as a benchmark against which to compare alternatives proposed by your travel agent.

5. Choose from the options that you and your travel agent uncover. No matter which option you select, have your travel agent book it. Even if you go with one of the packages in the newspaper, it will probably be commissionable (at no additional cost to you) and will provide the agent some return on the time invested on your behalf. Also, as a travel professional, your agent should be able to verify the quality and integrity of the deal.

If You Make Your Own Reservation

As you poke around trying to find a good deal, there are several things you should know. First, always call the specific hotel as opposed to the hotel chain's national toll-free number. Quite often, the reservationists at the national toll-free number are unaware of local specials. Always ask about specials before you inquire about corporate rates. Do not be reluctant to bargain. If you are buying a hotel's weekend package, for example, and want to extend your stay into the following week, you can often obtain at least the corporate rate for the extra days. Do your bargaining, however, before you check in, preferably when you make reservations.

Chicago Lodging for Business Travelers

The primary considerations for business travelers are affordability and proximity to the site or area where you will transact your business. Identify the zone(s) where your business will take you, and then use either the zone maps in the Introduction or the zone lists later in this chapter to find hotels located in that area. Once you have developed a short list of possible hotels that are conveniently located, fit your budget, and offer the standard of accommodation you require, you (or your travel agent) can make use of the cost-saving suggestions discussed earlier to obtain the lowest rate.

Lodging Convenient to McCormick Place

If you are attending a meeting or trade show at McCormick Place, the most convenient lodging is downtown Chicago, though none of the hotels, practically speaking, are within walking distance. From most downtown hotels, McCormick Place is a 5–14-minute cab or 10–30-minute shuttle ride away. Parking is available at the convention center, but it is expensive and not all that convenient. We recommend that you leave your car at home and use shuttles and cabs. The Hyatt Regency McCormick Place has 800 rooms and is connected to McCormick's Grand Concourse.

Commuting to McCormick Place from the suburbs or the airports during rush hour is something to be avoided if possible. If you want a room downtown, book early . . . very early. If you screw up and need a room at the last minute, try a wholesaler or reservation service, or one of the strategies listed below.

Convention Rates:
How They Work and How to Do Better

If you are attending a major convention or trade show, it is probable that the meeting's sponsoring organization has negotiated "convention rates" with a number of hotels. Under this arrangement, hotels reserve a certain number of rooms at an agreed-on price for conventioneers. Sometimes, as in the case of a small meeting, only one hotel is involved. In the event of a large "city-wide" convention at McCormick Place, however, almost all downtown and airport hotels will participate in the room block.

Because the convention sponsor brings a lot of business to the city and reserves a large number of rooms, it usually can negotiate a volume discount on the room rates, a rate that should be substantially below rack rate. The bottom line, however, is that some conventions and trade shows have more bargaining clout and negotiating skill than others. Hence, your convention sponsor may or may not be able to obtain the lowest possible rate.

Once a convention or trade show sponsor has completed negotiations with participating hotels, it will send its attendees a housing list that includes all the hotels serving the convention, along with the special convention rate for each. When you receive the housing list, you can compare the convention rates with the rates obtainable using the strategies covered in the previous section. If the negotiated convention rate doesn't sound like a good deal, you can try to reserve a room using a half-price club, a consolidator, or a tour operator. Remember, however, that many of the deep discounts are available only when the hotel expects to be at less than 80% occupancy, a condition that rarely prevails when a big convention is in town.

CHAIN HOTEL TOLL-FREE NUMBERS

Best Western	(800) 528-1234 U.S. & Canada
	(800) 528-2222 TDD
Comfort Inn	(800) 228-5150 U.S.
Courtyard by Marriott	(800) 321-2211 U.S.
Days Inn	(800) 325-2525 U.S.
DoubleTree	(800) 528-0444 U.S.
DoubleTree Guest Suites	(800) 424-2900 U.S.
Econo Lodge	(800) 424-4777 U.S.
Embassy Suites	(800) 362-2779 U.S. & Canada
Fairfield Inn by Marriott	(800) 228-2800 U.S.
Hampton Inn	(800) 426-7866 U.S. & Canada
Hilton	(800) 445-8667 U.S.
	(800) 368-1133 TDD
Holiday Inn	(800) 465-4329 U.S. & Canada
Howard Johnson	(800) 654-2000 U.S. & Canada
	(800) 654-8442 TDD
Hyatt	(800) 233-1234 U.S. & Canada
Loews	(800) 223-0888 U.S. & Canada
Marriott	(800) 228-9290 U.S. & Canada
	(800) 228-7014 TDD
Quality Inn	(800) 228-5151 U.S. & Canada
Radisson	(800) 333-3333 U.S. & Canada
Ramada Inn	(800) 228-3838 U.S.
	(800) 228-3232 TDD
Residence Inn by Marriott	(800) 331-3131 U.S.
Ritz-Carlton	(800) 241-3333 U.S.
Sheraton	(800) 325-3535 U.S. & Canada
Renaissance Hotel	(800) 468-3571 U.S. & Canada
Wyndham	(800) 822-4200 U.S.

Strategies for Beating Convention Rates

There are several tactics for getting around convention rates:

1. Reserve early. Most big conventions and trade shows announce meeting sites one to three years in advance. Get your reservation booked as far in advance as possible using a half-price club. If you book well ahead of the time the convention sponsor sends out the housing list, chances are the hotel will accept your reservation.

2. Compare your convention's housing list with the list of hotels presented in this guide. You may be able to find a suitable hotel that is not on the housing list.

3. Use a local reservations agency or consolidator. This is also a good strategy to employ if, for some reason, you need to make reservations at the last minute. Local reservations agencies and consolidators almost always control some rooms, even in the midst of a huge convention or trade show.

Hotels and Motels: Rated and Ranked

What's in a Room?

Except for cleanliness, state of repair, and decor, most travelers do not pay much attention to hotel rooms. There is, of course, a discernible standard of quality and luxury that differentiates Motel 6 from Holiday Inn, Holiday Inn from Marriott, and so on. In general, however, hotel guests fail to appreciate the fact that some rooms are better engineered than others.

Contrary to what you might suppose, designing a hotel room is (or should be) much more complex than picking a bedspread to match the carpet and drapes. Making the room usable to its occupants is an art, a planning discipline that combines both form and function.

Decor and taste are important, certainly. No one wants to spend several days in a room whose decor is dated, garish, or even ugly. But beyond the decor, several variables determine how "livable" a hotel room is. In Chicago, for example, we have seen some beautifully appointed rooms that are simply not well designed for human habitation. The next time you stay in a hotel, pay attention to the details and design elements of your room. Even more than decor, these will make you feel comfortable and at home.

It takes the *Unofficial Guide* researchers quite a while to inspect a hotel room. Here are a few of the things we check:

Room Size While some smaller rooms are cozy and well designed, a large and uncluttered room is generally preferable, especially for a stay of more than three days.

Temperature Control, Ventilation, and Odor   The guest should be able to control the temperature of the room. The best system, because it's so quiet, is central heating and air conditioning, controlled by the room's own thermostat. The next best system is a room module heater and air conditioner, preferably controlled by an automatic thermostat, but usually by manually operated button controls. The worst system is central heating and air without any sort of room thermostat or guest control.

The vast majority of hotel rooms have windows or balcony doors that have been permanently sealed. Though there are some legitimate safety and liability issues involved, we prefer windows and balcony doors that can be opened to admit fresh air. Hotel rooms should be odor free, smoke free, and not stuffy or damp.

Room Security   Better rooms have locks that require a plastic card instead of the traditional lock and key. Card and slot systems allow the hotel, essentially, to change the combination or entry code of the lock with each new guest. A burglar who has somehow acquired a conventional room key can afford to wait until the situation is right before using the key to gain access. Not so with a card and slot system. Though larger hotels and hotel chains with lock-and-key systems usually rotate their locks once each year, they remain vulnerable to hotel thieves much of the time. Many smaller or independent properties rarely rotate their locks.

In addition to the entry lock system, the door should have a deadbolt, and preferably a chain that can be locked from the inside. A chain by itself is not sufficient. Doors should also have a peephole. Windows and balcony doors, if any, should have secure locks.

Safety   Every room should have a fire or smoke alarm, clear fire instructions, and preferably a sprinkler system. Bathtubs should have a nonskid surface, and shower stalls should have doors that either open outward or slide side to side. Bathroom electrical outlets should be high on the wall and not too close to the sink. Balconies should have sturdy, high rails.

Noise   Most travelers have been kept awake by the television, partying, or amorous activities of people in the next room, or by traffic on the street outside. Better hotels are designed with noise control in mind. Wall and ceiling construction are substantial, effectively screening routine noise. Carpets and drapes, in addition to being decorative, also absorb and muffle sounds. Mattresses mounted on stable platforms or sturdy bed frames do not squeak, even when challenged by the most acrobatic lovers. Televisions enclosed in cabinets, and with volume governors, rarely disturb guests in adjacent rooms.

In better hotels, the air conditioning and heating system is well maintained and operates without noise or vibration. Likewise, plumbing is quiet and positioned away from the sleeping area. Doors to the hall, and to adjoining rooms, are thick and well fitted to better block out noise.

If you are easily disturbed by noise, ask for a room on a higher floor, off main thoroughfares, and away from elevators and ice and vending machines.

Darkness Control   Ever been in a hotel room where the curtains would not quite meet in the middle? Thick, lined curtains that close completely in the center and extend beyond the edges of the window or door frame are required. In a well-planned room, the curtains, shades, or blinds should almost totally block light at any time of day.

Lighting   Poor lighting is an extremely common problem in American hotel rooms. The lighting is usually adequate for dressing, relaxing, or watching television, but not for reading or working. Lighting needs to be bright over tables and desks, and beside couches or easy chairs. Since so many people read in bed, there should be a separate light for each person. A room with two queen beds should have individual lights for four people. Better bedside reading lights illuminate a small area, so if one person wants to sleep and another to read, the sleeper will not be bothered by the light. The worst situation by far is a single lamp on a table between beds. In each bed, only the person next to the lamp will have sufficient light to read. This deficiency is often compounded by weak light bulbs.

In addition, closet areas should be well lit, and there should be a switch near the door that turns on room lights when you enter. A seldom seen but desirable feature is a bedside console that allows a guest to control all or most lights in the room from bed.

Furnishings   At bare minimum, the bed(s) must be firm. Pillows should be made with nonallergenic fillers and, in addition to the sheets and spread, a blanket should be provided. Bedclothes should be laundered with fabric softener and changed daily. Better hotels usually provide extra blankets and pillows in the room or on request, and sometimes use a second topsheet between the blanket and spread.

There should be a dresser large enough to hold clothes for two people during a five-day stay. A small table with two chairs, or a desk with a chair, should be provided. The room should be equipped with a luggage rack and a three-quarter- to full-length mirror.

The television should be color and cable-connected; ideally, it should have a volume governor and remote control. It should be mounted on a swivel base, and preferably enclosed in a cabinet. Local channels should be posted on the set and a local TV program guide should be supplied. The telephone should be touchtone, conveniently situated for bedside use, and should have on or near it easy-to-understand dialing instructions and a rate card. Local white and yellow pages should be provided. Better hotels install phones in the bathroom and equip room phones with long cords.

Well-designed hotel rooms usually have a plush armchair or a sleeper sofa for lounging and reading. Better headboards are padded for comfortable reading in bed, and there should be a nightstand or table on each side of the bed(s). Nice extras in any hotel room include a small refrigerator, a digital alarm clock, and a coffeemaker.

Bathroom   Two sinks are better than one, and you cannot have too much counter space. A sink outside the bath is a convenience when one person bathes as another dresses. Sinks should have drains with stoppers.

Better bathrooms have both a tub and shower with a nonslip bottom. Tub and shower controls should be easy to operate. Adjustable shower heads are preferred. The bath needs to be well lit and should have an exhaust fan and a guest-controlled bathroom heater. Towels and washcloths should be large, soft, and fluffy, and generously supplied. There should be an electrical outlet for each sink, conveniently and safely placed.

Complimentary shampoo, conditioner, and lotion are a plus, as are robes and bathmats. Better hotels supply bathrooms with tissues and extra toilet paper. Luxurious baths feature a phone, a hair dryer, sometimes a small television, or even a Jacuzzi.

Vending   Complimentary ice and a drink machine should be located on each floor. Welcome additions include a snack machine and a sundries (combs, toothpaste, etc.) machine. The latter are seldom found in large hotels that have restaurants and shops.

Hotel Ratings

Zone   The Zone column identifies the Chicago zone where you will find a particular property.

Overall Quality   To distinguish properties according to relative quality, tastefulness, state of repair, cleanliness, and size of standard rooms, we have grouped the hotels and motels into classifications denoted by stars. Star ratings in this guide apply to Chicago-area properties only and do not necessarily correspond to stars awarded by Mobil, AAA, or other travel critics. Because stars carry little weight when awarded in the absence of common standards of comparison, we have linked our ratings to expected levels of quality established by specific American hotel corporations.

★★★★★	Superior	Tasteful and luxurious by any standard
★★★★	Extremely Nice	What you would expect at a Hyatt Regency or Marriott
★★★	Nice	Holiday Inn or comparable quality
★★	Adequate	Clean, comfortable, and functional without frills (like a Motel 6)
★	Budget	Spartan, not aesthetically pleasing, but clean

Star ratings describe the property's standard accommodations. For most hotels, a "standard accommodation" is a room with either one king bed or two queen beds. In an all-suite property, the standard accommodation is either a one- or two-room suite. In addition to standard accommodations, many hotels offer luxury rooms and special suites not rated here. Star ratings are assigned without regard to whether a property has restaurant(s), recreational facilities, entertainment, or other extras.

Room Quality In addition to stars (which delineate broad categories), we also employ a numerical rating system. Our rating scale is 0 to 100, with 100 as the best possible rating, and zero (0) as the worst. Numerical ratings are presented to show the difference we perceive between one property and another. Rooms at the Omni Ambassador East, Marriott Chicago Downtown, and the Millennium Knickerbocker Hotel are all rated as three and a half stars (★★★½). In the supplemental numerical ratings, the Omni is rated an 82, the Marriott an 80, and the Knickerbocker a 77. This means that within the three-and-a-half-star category, the Marriott is a bit nicer than the Knickerbocker, and the Omni has an edge over both.

Cost Cost estimates are based on the hotel's published rack rates for standard rooms. Each "$" represents $60. Thus, a cost symbol of "$$$" means a room (or suite) at that hotel will cost about $180 a night.

How the Hotels Compare

Below is a hit parade of the nicest rooms in town. We've focused strictly on room quality and excluded any consideration of location, services, recreation, or amenities. In some instances, a one- or two-room suite can be had for the same price or less than that of a hotel room.

If you use subsequent editions of this guide, you will notice that many of the ratings and rankings have changed. In addition to the inclusion of new properties, these changes also consider guest room renovations or improved maintenance and housekeeping. A failure to properly maintain guest rooms or a lapse in housekeeping standards can negatively affect the ratings.

Finally, before you begin to shop for a hotel, take a hard look at this letter we received from a couple in Hot Springs, Arkansas:

We cancelled our room reservations to follow the advice in your book [and reserved a hotel room highly ranked by the Unofficial Guide*]. We wanted inexpensive, but clean and cheerful. We got inexpensive, but [also] dirty, grim, and depressing. I really felt disappointed in your advice and the room. It was the pits. That was the one real piece of information I needed from your book! The room spoiled the holiday for me aside from our touring.*

Needless to say, this letter was as unsettling to us as the bad room was to our reader. Our integrity as travel journalists, after all, is based on the quality of the information we provide our readers. Even with the best of intentions and the most conscientious research, however, we cannot inspect every room in every hotel. What we do, in statistical terms, is take a sample: We check out several rooms selected at random in each hotel and base our ratings and rankings on those rooms. The inspections are conducted anonymously and without the knowledge of the management.

Although unusual, it is certainly possible that the rooms we randomly inspect are not representative of the majority of rooms at a particular hotel. Another possibility is that the rooms we inspect in a given hotel are representative but that by bad luck a reader is assigned a room that is inferior. When we rechecked the hotel our reader disliked, we discovered that our rating was correctly representative but that he and his wife had unfortunately been assigned to one of a small number of threadbare rooms scheduled for renovation.

The key to avoiding disappointment is to snoop around in advance. We recommend that you look on the web, ask for a photo of a hotel's standard guest room before you book, or at least get a copy of the hotel's promotional brochure. Alas, some hotel chains use the same guest room photo in their promotional literature for all their properties; a specific guest room may not resemble the brochure photo. Find out how old the property is and when your guest room was last renovated. If you arrive and are assigned an inferior room, demand to be moved.

	HOW THE HOTELS COMPARE			
Hotel	**Zone**	**Overall Quality**	**Room Quality**	**Cost ($=$60)**
Omni Chicago Hotel	3	★★★★★	96	$$$$$
The Peninsula	3	★★★★½	96	$$$$$$$
The W City Center	4	★★★★½	95	$$$$$−
Four Seasons Hotel	3	★★★★½	95	$$$$$$$$$−
Sofitel Water Tower	3	★★★★½	93	$$$$+
The Fairmont Hotel	4	★★★★½	93	$$$$$−
The W Lakeshore	3	★★★★½	92	$$$$$−
House of Blues Hotel	3	★★★★½	92	$$$$$
Ritz-Carlton Chicago	3	★★★★½	92	$$$$$$$
DoubleTree O'Hare-Rosemont	2	★★★★½	91	$$$−
The Drake	3	★★★★½	91	$$$$$+
Westin River North Chicago	3	★★★★½	90	$$$$
Hotel Burnham	4	★★★★½	90	$$$$$
Hotel Monaco	4	★★★★½	90	$$$$$
Sofitel Chicago	2	★★★★½	87	$$$$
Swissôtel Chicago	4	★★★★	90	$$$$$$+

HOW THE HOTELS COMPARE (continued)

Hotel	Zone	Overall Quality	Room Quality	Cost ($=$60)
Hyatt Regency Chicago in Illinois Center	4	★★★★	89	$$$–
Westin Hotel O'Hare	2	★★★★	89	$$$+
Hilton Chicago	5	★★★★	89	$$$+
Renaissance Chicago Hotel	4	★★★★	89	$$$$$$$
DoubleTree Guest Suites	3	★★★★	88	$$$
Wyndham Chicago	3	★★★★	88	$$$
Hotel Allegro	4	★★★★	88	$$$+
Hotel InterContinental Chicago	3	★★★★	88	$$$$
Hotel 71	4	★★★★	88	$$$$+
Park Hyatt Chicago	3	★★★★	88	$$$$$$$$$
Hyatt Regency McCormick Place	5	★★★★	87	$$+
Hyatt on Printer's Row Chicago	5	★★★★	87	$$+
Sheraton Gateway Suites O'Hare	2	★★★★	87	$$+
Hilton Garden Inn	3	★★★★	87	$$$$–
Fitzpatrick Hotel	3	★★★★	87	$$$$
Candlewood Suites O'Hare	2	★★★★	86	$$+
Marriott Suites Downers Grove	9	★★★★	86	$$$–
Renaissance Oak Brook Hotel	9	★★★★	86	$$–
Palmer House Hilton	4	★★★★	86	$$$
Hyatt Regency O'Hare	2	★★★★	86	$$$+
Embassy Suites Downtown/ Lakefront	3	★★★★	86	$$$$–
Sutton Place Hotel	3	★★★★	86	$$$$$$–
DoubleTree Downers Grove	9	★★★★	85	$$–
Hilton Suites Oakbrook Terrace	9	★★★★	85	$$$–
Residence Inn by Marriott	2	★★★★	85	$$–
Marriott Oak Brook	9	★★★★	85	$$$
Hyatt Rosemont	2	★★★★	84	$$+
Radisson O'Hare	2	★★★★	84	$$+
Embassy Suites Chicago	3	★★★★	84	$$$$–
Sheraton Chicago Hotel & Towers	3	★★★★	84	$$$$$$–
DoubleTree North Shore	11	★★★★	83	$$$+
Whitehall Hotel	3	★★★★	83	$$$$$–
Marriott Suites O'Hare	2	★★★½	85	$$$$–
Holiday Inn Select	2	★★★½	82	$$+

HOW THE HOTELS COMPARE (continued)

Hotel	Zone	Overall Quality	Room Quality	Cost ($=$60)
Embassy Suites O'Hare	2	★★★½	82	$$+
Omni Ambassador East	3	★★★½	82	$$$$+
Marriott Chicago Downtown	3	★★★½	82	$$$$$$$–
Omni Orrington Hotel Evanston	11	★★★½	81	$$$+
Marriott Residence Inn Downtown	3	★★★½	81	$$$$+
Westin Hotel Chicago	3	★★★½	81	$$$$$–
Embassy Suites	9	★★★½	80	$$–
Twelve Oaks Suites	2	★★★½	80	$$
Claridge Hotel	3	★★★½	80	$$$
Hilton O'Hare	2	★★★½	80	$$$$–
The Allerton Crowne Plaza	3	★★★½	80	$$$$+
Hyatt Regency Oak Brook	9	★★★½	79	$$–
Courtyard by Wood Dale	10	★★★½	79	$$–
Hyatt at University Village	6	★★★½	79	$$
Best Western University Plaza	11	★★★½	79	$$+
Hilton Garden Inn Oakbrook Terrace	9	★★★½	79	$$$–
Marriott O'Hare	2	★★★½	78	$$$
Wyndham Drake Hotel	8	★★★½	78	$$$$–
Courtyard by Marriott Downtown	3	★★★½	78	$$$$
The Carleton at Oak Park	2	★★★½	77	$$+
Holiday Inn Chicago O'Hare	2	★★★½	77	$$+
Four Points Sheraton Oakbrook	9	★★★½	77	$$$–
Millennium Knickerbocker Hotel	3	★★★½	77	$$$$–
Holiday Inn Mart Plaza	3	★★★½	76	$$+
Courtyard by Marriott Oakbrook Terrace	9	★★★½	75	$$+
Radisson Hotel Lincolnwood	11	★★★½	75	$$+
Holiday Inn Chicago City Center	3	★★★½	75	$$$$+
Hampton Inn & Suites Downtown	3	★★★	76	$$$–
Holiday Inn O'Hare International	2	★★★	74	$$$–
Marriott Fairfield Inn & Suites	3	★★★	74	$$$–
Radisson Hotel & Suites Chicago	3	★★★	73	$$$+
Talbott Hotel	3	★★★	73	$$$$$$+

HOW THE HOTELS COMPARE *(continued)*

Hotel	Zone	Overall Quality	Room Quality	Cost ($=$60)
Holiday Inn North Shore	11	★★★	72	$$–
Willows Hotel	1	★★★	70	$$+
Best Western Grant Park Hotel	5	★★★	69	$$$–
Four Points Sheraton O'Hare	2	★★★	68	$$$+
Hampton Inn Westchester/ Chicago	8	★★★	68	$$
DoubleTree Club Chicago O'Hare	10	★★★	66	$$
Comfort Inn Downers Grove	9	★★★	65	$$–
La Quinta Motor Inn Oakbrook Terrace	9	★★★	65	$$–
Hampton Inn Midway Bedford Park	8	★★★	65	$$+
Days Inn Lincoln Park North	1	★★★	65	$$+
The Raphael Chicago	3	★★★	65	$$$
Comfort Inn O'Hare	2	★★½	64	$$+
The Seneca	3	★★½	64	$$$+
Best Western River North	3	★★½	63	$$+
Lenox Suites	3	★★½	63	$$+
Congress Plaza Hotel	5	★★½	63	$$$–
Howard Johnson Express O'Hare	2	★★½	62	$
Ramada Plaza Hotel O'Hare	2	★★½	62	$+
Quality Inn Downtown	2	★★½	62	$$+
Sleep Inn Midway Airport	8	★★½	61	$$–
Travelodge Downtown	5	★★½	61	$$–
Best Western Inn Chicago	3	★★½	61	$$$–
Essex Inn	5	★★½	61	$$$–
Best Western O'Hare	2	★★½	60	$$+
Holiday Inn Express Downers Grove	9	★★½	59	$$–
Days Inn O'Hare South	2	★★½	58	$+
Travelodge Chicago O'Hare	2	★★½	57	$+
Red Roof Inn Downtown	3	★★	57	$$+
Red Roof Inn Downers Grove	9	★★	55	$
Comfort Inn Lincoln Park	1	★★	55	$$+
Days Inn Gold Coast	1	★★	54	$$+
Motel 6 O'Hare East	2	★★	52	$

CHICAGO HOTELS BY ZONE

Hotel	Overall Quality	Room Quality	Cost ($=$60)
Zone 1: North Side			
Willows Hotel	★★★	70	$$+
Days Inn Lincoln Park North	★★★	65	$$+
Comfort Inn Lincoln Park	★★	55	$$+
Days Inn Gold Coast	★★	54	$$+
Zone 2: North Central/O'Hare			
DoubleTree O'Hare-Rosemont	★★★★½	91	$$$−
Sofitel Chicago	★★★★½	87	$$$$
Westin Hotel O'Hare	★★★★	89	$$$+
Sheraton Gateway Suites O'Hare	★★★★	87	$$+
Candlewood Suites O'Hare	★★★★	86	$$+
Hyatt Regency O'Hare	★★★★	86	$$$+
Residence Inn by Marriott	★★★★	85	$$−
Hyatt Rosemont	★★★★	84	$$+
Radisson O'Hare	★★★★	84	$$+
Marriott Suites O'Hare	★★★½	85	$$$$−
Holiday Inn Select	★★★½	82	$$+
Embassy Suites O'Hare	★★★½	82	$$+
Twelve Oaks Suites	★★★½	80	$$
Hilton O'Hare	★★★½	80	$$$$−
Marriott O'Hare	★★★½	78	$$$
The Carleton at Oak Park	★★★½	77	$$+
Holiday Inn Chicago O'Hare	★★★½	77	$$+
Holiday Inn O'Hare International	★★★	74	$$$−
Four Points Sheraton O'Hare	★★★	68	$$$+
Comfort Inn O'Hare	★★½	64	$$+
Howard Johnson Express O'Hare	★★½	62	$
Ramada Plaza Hotel O'Hare	★★½	62	$+
Quality Inn Downtown	★★½	62	$$+
Best Western O'Hare	★★½	60	$$+
Days Inn O'Hare South	★★½	58	$+
Travelodge Chicago O'Hare	★★½	57	$+
Motel 6 O'Hare East	★★	52	$
Zone 3: Near North			
Omni Chicago Hotel	★★★★★	96	$$$$$
The Peninsula	★★★★½	96	$$$$$$$

CHICAGO HOTELS BY ZONE *(continued)*			
Hotel	Overall Quality	Room Quality	Cost ($=$60)
Zone 3: Near North (continued)			
Four Seasons Hotel	★★★★½	95	$$$$$$$$$–
Sofitel Water Tower	★★★★½	93	$$$$+
The W Lakeshore	★★★★½	92	$$$$$$–
House of Blues Hotel	★★★★½	92	$$$$$$
Ritz-Carlton Chicago	★★★★½	92	$$$$$$$$
The Drake	★★★★½	91	$$$$$+
Westin River North Chicago	★★★★½	90	$$$$
DoubleTree Guest Suites	★★★★	88	$$$
Wyndham Chicago	★★★★	88	$$$
Hotel InterContinental Chicago	★★★★	88	$$$$
Park Hyatt Chicago	★★★★	88	$$$$$$$$$
Hilton Garden Inn	★★★★	87	$$$$–
Fitzpatrick Hotel	★★★★	87	$$$$
Embassy Suites Downtown/Lakefront	★★★★	86	$$$$–
Sutton Place Hotel	★★★★	86	$$$$$$–
Embassy Suites Chicago	★★★★	84	$$$$–
Sheraton Chicago Hotel & Towers	★★★★	84	$$$$$$–
Whitehall Hotel	★★★★	83	$$$$$–
Omni Ambassador East	★★★½	82	$$$$+
Marriott Chicago Downtown	★★★½	82	$$$$$$$–
Marriott Residence Inn Downtown	★★★½	81	$$$$+
Westin Hotel Chicago	★★★½	81	$$$$$–
Claridge Hotel	★★★½	80	$$$
The Allerton Crowne Plaza	★★★½	80	$$$$+
Courtyard by Marriott Downtown	★★★½	78	$$$$
Millennium Knickerbocker Hotel	★★★½	77	$$$$–
Holiday Inn Mart Plaza	★★★½	76	$$+
Holiday Inn Chicago City Center	★★★½	75	$$$$+
Hampton Inn & Suites Downtown	★★★	76	$$$–
Marriott Fairfield Inn & Suites	★★★	74	$$$–
Radisson Hotel & Suites Chicago	★★★	73	$$$+
Talbott Hotel	★★★	73	$$$$$$+
The Raphael Chicago	★★★	65	$$$
The Seneca	★★½	64	$$$+
Best Western River North	★★½	63	$$+
Lenox Suites	★★½	63	$$+
Best Western Inn Chicago	★★½	61	$$$–
Red Roof Inn Downtown	★★	57	$$+

CHICAGO HOTELS BY ZONE *(continued)*	Overall Quality	Room Quality	Cost ($=$60)
Hotel			
Zone 4: The Loop			
The W City Center	★★★★½	95	$$$$$–
The Fairmont Hotel	★★★★½	93	$$$$$–
Hotel Burnham	★★★★½	90	$$$$$
Hotel Monaco	★★★★½	90	$$$$$
Swissôtel Chicago	★★★★	90	$$$$$$+
Hyatt Regency Chicago in Illinois Center	★★★★	89	$$$–
Renaissance Chicago Hotel	★★★★	89	$$$$$$$
Hotel Allegro	★★★★	88	$$$+
Hotel 71	★★★★	88	$$$$+
Palmer House Hilton	★★★★	86	$$$
Zone 5: South Loop			
Hilton Chicago	★★★★	89	$$$+
Hyatt on Printer's Row Chicago	★★★★	87	$$+
Hyatt Regency McCormick Place	★★★★	87	$$+
Best Western Grant Park Hotel	★★★	69	$$$–
Congress Plaza Hotel	★★½	63	$$$–
Travelodge Downtown	★★½	61	$$–
Essex Inn	★★½	61	$$$–
Zone 6: South Central/Midway			
Hyatt at University Village	★★★½	79	$$
Zone 8: Southern Suburbs			
Wyndham Drake Hotel	★★★½	78	$$$$–
Hampton Inn Westchester/Chicago	★★★	68	$$
Hampton Inn Midway Bedford Park	★★★	65	$$+
Sleep Inn Midway Airport	★★½	61	$$–
Zone 9: Western Suburbs			
Renaissance Oak Brook Hotel	★★★★	86	$$–
Marriott Suites Downers Grove	★★★★	86	$$$–
DoubleTree Downers Grove	★★★★	85	$$–
Hilton Suites Oakbrook Terrace	★★★★	85	$$$–
Marriott Oak Brook	★★★★	85	$$$
Embassy Suites	★★★½	80	$$–
Hyatt Regency Oak Brook	★★★½	79	$$–
Hilton Garden Inn Oakbrook Terrace	★★★½	79	$$$–

Hotel	Overall Quality	Room Quality	Cost ($=$60)
CHICAGO HOTELS BY ZONE (*continued*)			
Zone 9: Western Suburbs (continued)			
Four Points Sheraton Oakbrook	★★★½	77	$$$–
Courtyard by Marriott Oakbrook Terrace	★★★½	75	$$+
Comfort Inn Downers Grove	★★★	65	$$–
La Quinta Motor Inn Oakbrook Terrace	★★★	65	$$–
Holiday Inn Express Downers Grove	★★½	59	$$–
Red Roof Inn Downers Grove	★★	55	$
Zone 10: Northwest Suburbs			
Courtyard by Wood Dale	★★★½	79	$$–
DoubleTree Club Chicago O'Hare	★★★	66	$$
Zone 11: Northern Suburbs			
DoubleTree North Shore	★★★★	83	$$$+
Omni Orrington Hotel Evanston	★★★½	81	$$$+
Best Western University Plaza	★★★½	79	$$+
Radisson Hotel Lincolnwood	★★★½	75	$$+
Holiday Inn North Shore	★★★	72	$$–

Top 30 Hotel Deals in Chicago

Having listed the nicest rooms in town, let's reorder the list to rank the best combinations of quality and value in a room. As before, the rankings are made without consideration of location or the availability of restaurant(s), recreational facilities, entertainment, and/or amenities. Remember that a ★★★ room at $75 may rank closely with a ★★★★ room at $150, but that does not mean the rooms will be of comparable quality. Regardless of whether it's a good deal or not, a ★★★ room is still a ★★★ room. These are the best room buys for the money, regardless of location or star classification, based on averaged rack rates.

THE TOP 30 BEST DEALS IN CHICAGO

Hotel	Overall Quality	Room Quality	Cost ($=$60)
1. DoubleTree Downers Grove	★★★★	85	$$–
2. Hyatt Regency Oak Brook	★★★½	79	$$–
3. DoubleTree O'Hare-Rosemont	★★★★½	91	$$$–
4. Courtyard by Wood Dale	★★★½	79	$$–
5. Hyatt Rosemont	★★★★	84	$$+
6. Howard Johnson Express O'Hare	★★½	62	$
7. Four Points Sheraton O'Hare	★★★	68	$$$+
8. Embassy Suites	★★★½	80	$$–
9. Candlewood Suites O'Hare	★★★★	86	$$+
10. Hyatt Regency McCormick Place	★★★★	87	$$+
11. Hyatt on Printer's Row Chicago	★★★★	87	$$+
12. Sheraton Gateway Suites O'Hare	★★★★	87	$$+
13. Twelve Oaks Suites	★★★½	80	$$
14. Hyatt at University Village	★★★½	79	$$
15. Radisson O'Hare	★★★★	84	$$+
16. Hilton Suites Oakbrook Terrace	★★★★	85	$$$–
17. Hyatt Regency Chicago in Illinois Center	★★★★	89	$$$–
18. Ramada Plaza Hotel O'Hare	★★½	62	$+
19. Days Inn O'Hare South	★★½	58	$+
20. Holiday Inn Select	★★★½	82	$$+
21. Holiday Inn Mart Plaza	★★★½	76	$$+
22. Courtyard by Marriott Oakbrook Terrace	★★★½	75	$$+
23. Marriott Suites Downers Grove	★★★★	86	$$$–
24. Residence Inn by Marriott	★★★★	85	$$–
25. Renaissance Oak Brook Hotel	★★★★	86	$$–
26. Best Western University Plaza	★★★½	79	$$+
27. Holiday Inn North Shore	★★★	72	$$–
28. Travelodge Chicago O'Hare	★★½	57	$+
29. The Carleton at Oak Park	★★★½	77	$$+
30. Holiday Inn Chicago O'Hare	★★★½	77	$$+

Hotel	Quality Ratings	Zone	Street Address & Website
The Allerton Crowne Plaza	★★★½ 80	3	701 North Michigan Avenue Chicago, 60611 www.crowneplaza.com
Best Western Grant Park Hotel	★★★ 69	5	1100 South Michigan Avenue Chicago, 60605 www.bestwestern.com
Best Western Inn Chicago	★★½ 61	3	162 East Ohio Street Chicago, 60611 www.bestwestern.com
Best Western O'Hare	★★½ 60	2	10300 West Higgins Road Rosemont, 60018 www.bestwestern.com
Best Western River North	★★½ 63	3	125 West Ohio Street Chicago, 60610 www.bestwestern.com
Best Western University Plaza	★★★½ 79	11	1501 Sherman Avenue Evanston, 60201 www.bestwestern.com
Candlewood Suites O'Hare	★★★★ 86	2	4021 North Mannheim Road Schiller Park, 60176 www.candlewoodsuites.com
The Carleton of Oak Park	★★★½ 77	2	1110 Pleasant Street Oak Park, 60302 www.carletonhotel.com
Claridge Hotel	★★★½ 80	3	1244 North Dearborn Parkway Chicago, 60610 www.claridgehotel.com
Comfort Inn Downers Grove	★★★ 65	9	3010 Finley Road Downers Grove, 60515 www.comfortinn.com
Comfort Inn Lincoln Park	★★ 55	1	601 West Diversey Parkway Chicago, 60614 www.comfortinn.com
Comfort Inn O'Hare	★★½ 64	2	2175 East Touhy Avenue Des Plaines, 60018 www.comfortinn.com
Congress Plaza Hotel	★★½ 63	5	520 South Michigan Avenue Chicago, 60605 www.congresshotel.com
Courtyard by Marriott Downtown	★★★½ 78	3	30 East Hubbard Street Chicago, 60611 www.courtyard.com
Courtyard by Marriott Oakbrook Terrace	★★★½ 75	9	6 Transam Plaza Drive Oakbrook Terrace, 60181 www.courtyard.com

Local Phone	Fax	Toll Free Reservations	Rack Rate	No. of Rooms	On-site Dining	Pool
(312) 440-1500	(312) 440-1819	(800) 227-6963	$$$$+	443	✔	
(312) 922-2900	(312) 922-8812	(800) GRANT-PK	$$$–	172	✔	✔
(312) 787-3100	(312) 573-3136	(800) 557-BEST	$$$–	357	✔	
(847) 296-4471	(847) 296-4958	(800) 528-1234	$$+	143	✔	✔
(312) 467-0800	(312) 467-1665	(800) 727-0800	$$+	148	✔	✔
(847) 491-6400	(847) 328-3090	(800) EVANSTON	$$+	159	✔	✔
(847) 671-4663	(847) 671-4653	(888) CANDLEWOOD	$$+	160		
(708) 848-5000	(708) 848-0537	(888) CARLETON	$$+	110	✔	
(312) 787-4980	(312) 787-4069	(800) 245-1258	$$$	170	✔	
(630) 515-1500	(630) 515-1595	(800) 228-5150	$$–	115		✔
(773) 348-2810	(773) 348-1912	(800) 228-5150	$$+	75		
(847) 635-1300	(847) 635-7572	(800) 228-5150	$$+	148	✔	
(312) 427-3800	(312) 427-3972	(800) 635-1666	$$$–	842	✔	
(312) 329-2500	(312) 329-0293	(800) 321-2211	$$$$	336	✔	✔
(630) 691-1500	(630) 691-1518	(800) 321-2211	$$+	147		✔

Hotel	Quality Ratings	Zone	Street Address & Website
Courtyard by Wood Dale	★★★½ 79	10	900 North Wood Dale Road Chicago, 60191 www.courtyard.com
Days Inn Gold Coast	★★ 54	1	1816 North Clark Street Chicago, 60614 www.daysinn.com
Days Inn Lincoln Park North	★★★ 65	1	644 West Diversey Chicago, 60614 www.daysinn.com
Days Inn O'Hare South	★★½ 58	2	3801 North Mannheim Road Schiller Park, 60176 www.daysinn.com
DoubleTree Club Chicago O'Hare	★★★ 66	10	1450 East Touhy Avenue Des Plaines, 60018 www.doubletree.com
DoubleTree Downers Grove	★★★★ 85	9	2111 Butterfield Road Downers Grove, 60515 www.doubletree.com
DoubleTree Guest Suites	★★★★ 88	3	198 East Delaware Place Chicago, 60611 www.doubletree.com
DoubleTree North Shore	★★★★ 83	11	9599 Skokie Boulevard Chicago, 60077 www.doubletree.com
DoubleTree O'Hare-Rosemont	★★★★½ 91	2	5460 North River Road Chicago, 60018 www.doubletree.com
The Drake	★★★★½ 91	3	140 East Walton Place Chicago, 60611 www.thedrakehotel.com
Embassy Suites	★★★½ 80	9	707 East Butterfield Road Lombard, 60148 www.embassysuites.com
Embassy Suites Chicago	★★★★ 84	3	600 North State Street Chicago, 60610 www.embassysuites.com
Embassy Suites Downtown/ Lakefront	★★★★ 86	3	511 North Columbus Drive Chicago, 60611 www.embassysuites.com
Embassy Suites O'Hare	★★★½ 82	2	5500 North River Road Rosemont, 60018 www.embassysuites.com
Essex Inn	★★½ 61	5	800 South Michigan Avenue Chicago, 60605
The Fairmont Hotel	★★★★½ 93	4	200 North Columbus Drive Chicago, 60601 www.fairmont.com

Local Phone	Fax	Toll Free Reservations	Rack Rate	No. of Rooms	On-site Dining	Pool
(630) 766-7775	(630) 766-7552	(800) 321-2211	$$−	149	✔	✔
(312) 664-3040	(312) 664-0348	(800) DAYS-INN	$$+	275	✔	
(773) 525-7010	(773) 525-6998	(800) 325-2525	$$+	128	✔	✔
(847) 678-0670	(847) 678-0690	(800) 329-7466	$+	144	✔	
(847) 296-8866	(847) 296-8268	(888) 444-CLUB	$$	245	✔	✔
(630) 971-2000	(630) 971-1021	(800) 222-TREE	$$−	250	✔	✔
(312) 664-1100	(312) 664-9881	(800) 222-TREE	$$$	345	✔	✔
(847) 679-7000	(847) 679-9841	(800) 222-TREE	$$$+	367	✔	✔
(847) 292-9100	(847) 292-9295	(800) 222-TREE	$$$−	369	✔	✔
(312) 787-2200	(312) 787-2549	(800) 55-DRAKE	$$$$$+	535	✔	
(630) 969-7500	(630) 969-8776	(800) EMBASSY	$$−	228	✔	✔
(312) 943-3800	(312) 943-5979	(800) EMBASSY	$$$$−	358	✔	✔
(312) 836-5900	(312) 836-5901	(800) EMBASSY	$$$$−	455	✔	✔
(847) 678-4000	(847) 928-7678	(888) EMBASSY	$$+	294	✔	✔
(312) 939-2800	(312) 922-6153	(800) 621-6909	$$$−	255	✔	✔
(312) 565-8000	(312) 856-1032	(800) 526-2008	$$$$ $$−	692	✔	

Hotel	Quality Ratings	Zone	Street Address & Website
Fitzpatrick Hotel	★★★★ 87	3	166 East Superior Street Chicago, 60611 www.fitzpatrickhotels.com
Four Points Sheraton Oakbrook	★★★½ 77	9	17 West 22nd Street Oakbrook Terrace, 60181 www.sheraton.com
Four Points Sheraton O'Hare	★★★ 68	2	10249 West Irving Park Road Schiller Park, 60176 www.sheraton.com
Four Seasons Hotel	★★★★½ 95	3	120 East Delaware Place Chicago, 60611 www.fourseasons.com
Hampton Inn Midway Bedford Park	★★★ 65	8	6540 South Cicero Avenue Bedford Park, 60638 www.hamptoninn.com
Hampton Inn & Suites Downtown	★★★ 76	3	33 West Illinois Street Chicago, 60610 www.hamptoninn.com
Hampton Inn Westchester/ Chicago	★★★ 68	8	2222 Enterprise Drive Westchester, 60154 www.hamptoninn.com
Hilton Chicago	★★★★ 89	5	720 South Michigan Avenue Chicago, 60605 www.hilton.com
Hilton Garden Inn	★★★★ 87	3	10 East Grand Avenue Chicago, 60611 www.hilton.com
Hilton Garden Inn Oakbrook Terrace	★★★½ 79	9	1000 Drury Lane Oakbrook Terrace, 60181 www.hilton.com
Hilton O'Hare	★★★½ 80	2	O'Hare International Airport Chicago, 60666 www.hilton.com
Hilton Suites Oakbrook Terrace	★★★★ 85	9	10 Drury Lane Oakbrook Terrace, 60181 www.hilton.com
Holiday Inn Chicago City Center	★★★½ 75	3	300 East Ohio Street Chicago, 60611 www.sixcontinentshotels.com
Holiday Inn Chicago O'Hare	★★★½ 77	2	8201 West Higgins Road Chicago, 60621 www.sixcontinentshotels.com
Holiday Inn Express Downers Grove	★★½ 59	8	3031 Finley Road Downers Grove, 60515 www.sixcontinentshotels.com

Local Phone	Fax	Toll Free Reservations	Rack Rate	No. of Rooms	On-site Dining	Pool
(312) 787-6000	(312) 787-6133		$$$$	119	✔	✔
(630) 833-3600	(630) 833-7037	(800) 325-3535	$$$–	233	✔	✔
(847) 671-6000	(847) 671-0371	(800) 323-1239	$$$+	296	✔	✔
(312) 280-8800	(312) 280-1748	(800) 332-3442	$$$$$ $$$$–	343	✔	✔
(708) 496-1900	(708) 496-1997	(800) HAMPTON	$$+	104		
(312) 832-0330	(312) 832-0333	(800) HAMPTON	$$$–	230	✔	✔
(708) 409-1000	(708) 409-105	(800) HAMPTON	$$	112		
(312) 922-4400	(312) 922-5240	(800) HILTONS	$$$+	1,544	✔	✔
(312) 595-0000	(312) 595-0955	(800) HILTONS	$$$$–	357	✔	✔
(630) 941-1177	(630) 941-1188	(800) HILTONS	$$$–	128	✔	✔
(773) 686-8000	(773) 601-1728	(800) HILTONS	$$$$–	858	✔	✔
(630) 941-0100	(630) 941-0299	(800) HILTONS	$$$–	212	✔	✔
(312) 787-6100	(312) 787-6238	(800) HOLIDAY	$$$$+	500	✔	✔
(773) 693-2323	(773) 693-3771	(800) HOLIDAY	$$+	120	✔	✔
(630) 810-9500	(630) 810-0059	(800) HOLIDAY	$$–	123		

Hotel	Quality Ratings	Zone	Street Address & Website
Holiday Inn Mart Plaza	★★★½ 76	3	350 North Orleans Street Chicago, 60654 www.sixcontinentshotels.com
Holiday Inn North Shore	★★★ 72	11	5300 West Touhy Avenue Skokie, 60077 www.sixcontinentshotels.com
Holiday Inn O'Hare International	★★★ 74	2	5440 North River Road Rosemont, 60018 www.sixcontinentshotels.com
Holiday Inn Select	★★★½ 82	2	10233 West Higgins Rosemont, 60018 www.sixcontinentshotels.com
Hotel Allegro	★★★★ 88	4	171 West Randolph Street Chicago, 60601 www.allegrochicago.com
Hotel Burnham	★★★★½ 90	4	1 West Washington Street Chicago, 60602 www.burnhamhotel.com
Hotel Inter-Continental Chicago	★★★★ 88	3	505 North Michigan Avenue Chicago, 60611 www.intercontinental.com
Hotel Monaco	★★★★½ 90	4	225 North Wabash Avenue Chicago, 60601 www.monaco-chicago.com
Hotel 71	★★★★ 88	4	71 East Wacker Drive Chicago, 60601 www.hotel71.com
House of Blues Hotel	★★★★½ 92	3	333 North Dearborn Chicago, 60610 www.loweshotels.com
Howard Johnson Express O'Hare	★★½ 62	2	4101 North Mannheim Road Schiller Park, 60176 www.hojo.com
Hyatt on Printer's Row Chicago	★★★★ 87	5	500 South Dearborn Street Chicago, 60605 www.hyatt.com
Hyatt Regency Chicago in Illinois Center	★★★★ 89	4	151 East Wacker Drive Chicago, 60601 www.hyatt.com
Hyatt Regency McCormick Place	★★★★½ 87	5	2233 Martin Luther King Drive Chicago, 60616 www.hyatt.com
Hyatt Regency O'Hare	★★★★ 86	2	9300 West Bryn Mawr Avenue Chicago, 60018 www.hyatt.com

Local Phone	Fax	Toll Free Reservations	Rack Rate	No. of Rooms	On-site Dining	Pool
(312) 836-5000	(312) 222-9508	(800) HOLIDAY	$$+	524	✔	✔
(847) 679-8900	(847) 679-7447	(800) HOLIDAY	$$–	248	✔	✔
(847) 671-6350	(847) 671-5406	(800) 642-7344	$$$–	507	✔	✔
(847) 954-8600	(847) 954-8800	(800) HOLIDAY	$$+	378	✔	
(312) 236-0123	(312) 236-0917	(800) 643-1500	$$$+	483	✔	
(312) 782-1111	(312) 782-0899	(877) 294-9712	$$$$$	122	✔	
(312) 944-4100	(312) 944-3050	(800) 628-2112	$$$$	844	✔	✔
(312) 960-8500	(312) 960-1883	(800) 397-7661	$$$$$	192	✔	
(312) 346-7100	(312) 346-1721		$$$$+	420	✔	
(312) 245-0333	(312) 923-2444	(800) 235-LOEWS	$$$$$$	367	✔	
(847) 678-4470	(847) 678-3837	(800) 446-4656	$	67		
(312) 986-1234	(312) 939-2468	(800) 233-1234	$$+–	161	✔	
(312) 565-1234	(312) 565-2966	(800) 233-1234	$$$–	1200	✔	
(312) 567-1234	(312) 528-4000	(800) 233-1234	$$+	800	✔	✔
(847) 696-1234	(847) 698-0139	(800) 233-1234	$$$+	1100	✔	✔

Hotel	Quality Ratings	Zone	Street Address & Website
Hyatt Regency Oak Brook	★★★½ 79	9	1909 Spring Road Oak Brook, 60523 www.hyatt.com
Hyatt Rosemont	★★★★ 84	2	6350 North River Road Rosemont, 60018 www.hyatt.com
Hyatt at University Village	★★★½ 79	6	625 South Ashland Avenue Chicago, 60607 www.hyatt.com
La Quinta Motor Inn Oakbrook Terrace	★★★ 65	9	1S666 Midwest Road Oakbrook Terrace, 60181 www.lq.com
Lenox Suites	★★½ 63	3	616 North Rush Street Chicago, 60611 www.lenoxsuites.com
Marriott Chicago Downtown	★★★½ 82	3	540 North Michigan Avenue Chicago, 60611 www.marriott.com
Marriott Fairfield Inn & Suites	★★★ 74	3	216 East Ontario Street Chicago, 60611 www.fairfieldinn.com
Marriott Oak Brook	★★★★ 85	9	1401 West 22nd Street Oak Brook, 60523 www.marriott.com
Marriott O'Hare	★★★½ 78	2	8535 West Higgins Road Chicago, 60631 www.marriott.com
Marriott Residence Inn Downtown	★★★½ 81	3	201 East Walton Street Chicago, 60611 www.marriott.com
Marriott Suites Downers Grove	★★★★ 86	9	1500 Opus Place, Business Corridor Downers Grove, 60559 www.marriott.com
Marriott Suites O'Hare	★★★½ 85	2	6155 North River Road Chicago, 60018 www.marriott.com
Millennium Knickerbocker Hotel	★★★½ 77	3	163 East Walton Place Chicago, 60611 www.millenniumhotels.com
Motel 6 O'Hare East	★★ 52	2	9408 West Lawrence Avenue Schiller Park, 60176 motel6.com
Omni Ambassador East	★★★½ 82	3	1301 North State Parkway Chicago, 60610 www.omnihotels.com

Local Phone	Fax	Toll Free Reservations	Rack Rate	No. of Rooms	On-site Dining	Pool
(630) 573-1234	(630) 573-1133	(800) 233-1234	$$−	425	✔	✔
(847) 518-1234	(847) 518-0855	(800) 233-1234	$$+	206	✔	
(312) 243-7200	(312) 529-6095	(800) 233-1234	$$	114	✔	
(630) 495-4600	(630) 495-2558	(800) 531-5900	$$−	150		✔
(312) 337-1000	(312) 337-7217	(800) 44-LENOX	$$+	325	✔	
(312) 836-0100	(312) 836-6139	(800) 228-9290	$$$$ $$−	1173	✔	✔
(312) 787-3777	(312) 787-8714	(800) 228-2800	$$$−	185	✔	
(630) 573-8555	(630) 573-1026	(800) 228-9290	$$$	347	✔	✔
(773) 693-4444	(773) 693-3164	(800) 228-9290	$$$	681	✔	✔
(312) 943-9800	(312) 943-8579	(800) 331-3131	$$$$+	221	✔	
(630) 852-1500	(630) 852-6527	(800) 228-9290	$$$−	254	✔	✔
(847) 696-4400	(847) 696-2122	(800) 228-9290	$$$$−	256	✔	✔
(312) 751-8100	(312) 751-9205	(800) 621-8140	$$$$−	305	✔	
(847) 671-4282	(773) 601-1728	(800) 4MOTEL6	$	143		
(312) 787-7200	(312) 573-5816	(800) 843-6664	$$$$+	285	✔	

Hotel	Quality Ratings	Zone	Street Address & Website
Omni Chicago Hotel	★★★★★ 96	3	676 North Michigan Avenue Chicago, 60611 www.omnihotels.com
Omni Orrington Hotel Evanston	★★★½ 81	11	1710 Orrington Avenue Evanston, 60201 www.omnihotels.com
Palmer House Hilton	★★★★ 86	4	17 East Monroe Street Chicago, 60603 www.hilton.com
Park Hyatt Chicago	★★★★ 88	3	800 North Michigan Avenue Chicago, 60611 www.hyatt.com
The Peninsula	★★★★½ 95	3	108 East Superior Street Chicago, 60611 www.peninsula.com
Quality Inn Downtown	★★½ 62	2	1 South Halsted Street Chicago, 60661 www.qualityinn.com
Radisson Hotel Lincolnwood	★★★½ 75	11	4500 West Touhy Avenue Lincolnwood, 60712 www.radisson.com
Radisson Hotel & Suites Chicago	★★★ 73	3	160 East Huron Street Chicago, 60611 www.radisson.com
Radisson O'Hare	★★★★ 84	2	6810 North Mannheim Road Rosemont, 60018 www.radisson.com
Ramada Plaza Hotel O'Hare	★★½ 62	2	6600 North Mannheim Road Rosemont, 60018 www.ramada.com
The Raphael Chicago	★★★ 65	3	201 East Delaware Place Chicago, 60611 www.raphaelchicago.com
Red Roof Inn Downers Grove	★★ 55	9	1113 Butterfield Road Downers Grove, 60515 www.redroof.com
Red Roof Inn Downtown	★★ 57	3	162 East Ontario Street Chicago, 60611 www.redroof.com
Renaissance Chicago Hotel	★★★★ 89	4	1 West Wacker Drive Chicago, 60601 www.renaissancehotels.com
Renaissance Oak Brook Hotel	★★★★ 86	9	2100 Spring Road Oak Brook, 60523 www.renaissancehotels.com

Local Phone	Fax	Toll Free Reservations	Rack Rate	No. of Rooms	On-site Dining	Pool
(312) 944-6664	(312) 266-3015	(800) 843-6664	$$$$$	347	✔	✔
(847) 866-8700	(847) 866-8724	(800) THE-OMNI	$$$+	280	✔	
(312) 726-7500	(312) 917-1707	(800) HILTONS	$$$	1544	✔	✔
(312) 335-1234	(312) 239-4000	(800) 233-1234	$$$$$ $$$$	213	✔	✔
(312) 337-2888	(312) 751 2888		$$$$$ $$	339	✔	✔
(312) 829-5000	(312) 829-8151	(800) 228-5151	$$+	406	✔	
(847) 677-1234	(847) 677-0234	(800) 333-3333	$$+	293	✔	✔
(312) 787-2900	(312) 787-5158	(800) 333-3333	$$$+	350	✔	✔
(847) 297-1234	(847) 297-5287	(800) 333-3333	$$+	475	✔	✔
(847) 827-5131	(847) 827-5659	(800) 2-RAMADA	$+	723	✔	✔
(312) 943-5000	(312) 943-9483	(800) 983-7870	$$$	172	✔	
(630) 963-4205	(630) 963-4425	(800) RED-ROOF	$	135		
(312) 787-3580	(312) 787-1299	(800) RED-ROOF	$$+	195		
(312) 372-7200	(312) 372-0093	(800) 228-9290	$$$$$ $$	553	✔	✔
(630) 573-2800	(630) 573-7134	(800) 228-9290	$$−	170	✔	✔

Hotel	Quality Ratings	Zone	Street Address & Website
Residence Inn by Marriott	★★★★ 85	2	7101 Chestnut Street Rosemont, 60018 www.marriott.com
Ritz-Carlton Chicago	★★★★½ 92	3	160 East Pearson Street Chicago, 60611 www.fourseasons.com
The Seneca	★★½ 64	3	200 East Chestnut Street Chicago, 60611 www.senecahotel.com
Sheraton Chicago Hotel & Towers	★★★★ 84	3	301 East North Water Street Chicago, 60611 www.sheraton.com
Sheraton Gateway Suites O'Hare	★★★★ 87	2	6501 North Mannheim Road Rosemont, 60018 www.sheraton.com
Sleep Inn Midway Airport	★★½ 61	8	6650 South Cicero Avenue Bedford Park, 60638 www.sleepinn.com
Sofitel Chicago	★★★★½ 87	2	5550 North River Road Rosemont, 60018 www.accorhotels.com
Sofitel Water Tower	★★★★½ 93	3	20 East Chestnut Street Chicago, 60611 www.accorhotels.com
Sutton Place Hotel	★★★★ 86	3	21 East Bellevue Place Chicago, 60611 www.suttonplace.com
Swissôtel Chicago	★★★★ 90	4	323 East Wacker Drive Chicago, 60601 www.swissotel.com
Talbott Hotel	★★★ 73	3	20 East Delaware Place Chicago, 60611 www.talbotthotel.com
Travelodge Chicago O'Hare	★★½ 57	2	3003 Mannheim Road Des Plaines, 60018 www.travelodge.com
Travelodge Downtown	★★½ 61	5	65 East Harrison Street Chicago, 60605 www.travelodge.com
Twelve Oaks Suites	★★★½ 80	2	9450 West Lawrence Avenue Schiller Park, 60176 www.12oaksohare.com
The W City Center	★★★★½ 95	4	172 West Adams Street Chicago, 60603 www.whotels.com
The W Lakeshore	★★★★½ 92	3	644 North Lakeshore Drive Chicago, 60611 www.whotels.com

Local Phone	Fax	Toll Free Reservations	Rack Rate	No. of Rooms	On-site Dining	Pool
(847) 375-9000	(847) 375-9010	(800) 228-9290	$$–	192		✔
(312) 266-1000	(312) 266-1194	(800) 621-6906	$$$$$ $$$	430	✔	✔
(312) 787-8900	(312) 988-4438	(800) 800-6261	$$$+	130	✔	
(312) 464-1000	(312) 464-9140	(800) 233-4100	$$$$ $$–	1200	✔	✔
(847) 699-6300	(847) 699-0391	(800) 325-3535	$$+	325	✔	✔
(708) 594-0001	(708) 594-0058	(800) SLEEP-INN	$$–	120		
(847) 678-4488	(847) 678-4244	(800) 763-4835	$$$$	300	✔	✔
(312) 324-4000	(312) 324-4025	(800) 763-4835	$$$$+–	415	✔	
(312) 266-2100	(312) 266-2103	(800) 606-8188	$$$$ $$–	246	✔	
(312) 565-0565	(312) 565-0540	(800) 637-9477	$$$$ $$+	630	✔	✔
(312) 944-4970	(312) 944-7241	(800) TALBOTT	$$$$ $$+	146	✔	
(847) 296-5541	(847) 803-1984	(800) 578-7878	$+	94		✔
(312) 427-8000	(312) 427-8261	(800) 578-7878	$$–	250	✔	
(847) 725-2200	(847) 725-2221	(866) 212-OAKS	$$	170		✔
(312) 332-1200	(312) 917-5771	(877) W-HOTELS	$$$$$–	376	✔	
(312) 943-9200	(312) 255-4411	(877) W-HOTELS	$$$$ $$–	556	✔	✔

Hotel	Quality Ratings	Zone	Street Address & Website
Westin Hotel Chicago	★★★½ 81	3	909 North Michigan Avenue Chicago, 60611 www.westin.com
Westin Hotel O'Hare	★★★★ 89	2	6100 River Road Rosemont, 60018 www.westin.com
Westin River North Chicago	★★★★½ 90	3	320 North Dearborn Street Chicago, 60610 www.westin.com
Whitehall Hotel	★★★★ 83	3	105 East Delaware Place Chicago, 60611 www.slh.com
Willows Hotel	★★★ 70	1	555 West Surf Street Chicago, 60657 www.cityinns.com
Wyndham Chicago	★★★★ 88	3	633 St. Clair Street Chicago, 60611 www.wyndham.com
Wyndham Drake Hotel	★★★½ 78	8	2301 York Road Oak Brook, 60521 www.wyndham.com

Local Phone	Fax	Toll Free Reservations	Rack Rate	No. of Rooms	On-site Dining	Pool
(312) 943-7200	(312) 397-5580	(800) WESTIN-1	$$$$$–	750	✔	
(847) 698-6000	(847) 698-3993	(800) 228-3000	$$$+	525	✔	✔
(312) 744-1900	(312) 527-2650	(800) WESTIN-1	$$$$	424	✔	
(312) 944-6300	(312) 944-8552	(800) 948-4255	$$$$$–	221	✔	
(773) 528-8400	(773) 528-8483	(800) 787-3108	$$+	55		
(312) 573-0300	(312) 346-0974	(800) WYNDHAM	$$$	417	✔	✔
(630) 574-5700	(630) 574-0830	(800) 996-3426	$$$$–	160	✔	✔

Part Four

Visiting Chicago on Business

Convention Central, U.S.A.

Chicago, the gateway to the Midwest and the third-largest city in the United States, attracts more than six million overnight pleasure visitors a year. Tourists from all over the world come to enjoy the city's fabled attractions, ogle the legendary skyline, and enjoy the summer season's free lakefront festivals. The numbers? The Shedd Aquarium and the Museum of Science and Industry, Chicago's most popular fee-charging attractions, drew 2 million and 1.8 million visitors, respectively, in 1998, and the Taste of Chicago attracts 3.7 million outdoor fun-seekers each summer.

Yet not everyone visiting the Windy City comes with a tourist agenda. Chicago bills itself as the Convention Capital of the World, hosting more top trade shows than any other city in the country. The town's central geographical location, 7,000 restaurants, and 67,000 hotel rooms make it a natural destination for nearly five million trade show and convention visitors annually.

The Windy City also boasts an unparalleled location to house all those exhibitions: **McCormick Place Convention Center**, the largest convention hall in North America. Located on the shores of Lake Michigan a mile or so south of downtown, McCormick Place is a sprawling, 27-acre venue with 2.2 million square feet of exhibit space, a 4,000-seat theater, and ceilings up to 50 feet high.

In May 1993, ground was broken on a $987 million expansion of McCormick Place. Now completed, the project included the construction of the 840,000-square-foot South Building (near the intersection of the Stevenson Expressway and Lake Shore Drive), a glass-enclosed Grand Concourse linking the three buildings that make up the convention center, a five-acre landscaped park, and renovations to existing facilities.

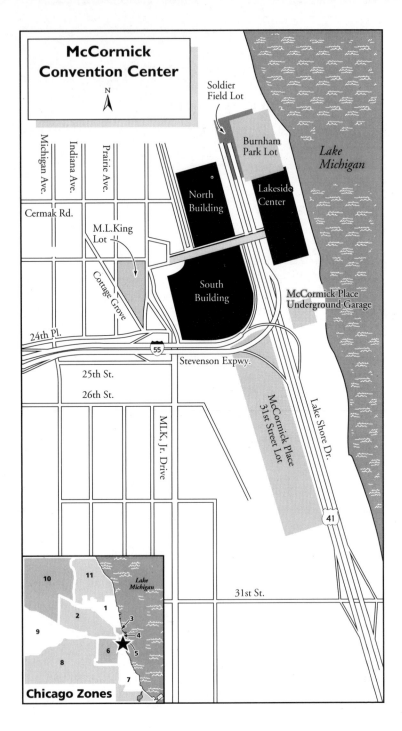

McCormick Convention Center

N

Soldier Field Lot

Burnham Park Lot

Lake Michigan

Michigan Ave.

Indiana Ave.

Prairie Ave.

North Building

Lakeside Center

Cermak Rd.

M.L.King Lot

Cottage Grove

South Building

McCormick Place Underground Garage

24th Pl.

55

Stevenson Expwy.

25th St.

26th St.

MLK. Jr. Drive

McCormick Place 31st Street Lot

Lake Shore Dr.

41

31st St.

10

11

Lake Michigan

1

2

3

4

9

6

5

8

7

Chicago Zones

Other Business Visitors

In addition to conventioneers and trade show attendees bound for McCormick Place or another convention hall, other people come to conduct business at the city's wide array of manufacturing and financial firms (many of which are located in Chicago's suburbs). In addition to Chicago's four major financial exchanges (Chicago Mercantile Exchange, Chicago Stock Exchange, Chicago Board of Trade, and Chicago Board Options Exchange), the Windy City is also home to many blue-chip public companies, including Sears, Amoco, Motorola, Allstate, Sara Lee, and Caterpillar.

The city's large number of higher learning institutions (including the University of Chicago, Northwestern University, the University of Illinois at Chicago, DePaul University, the Illinois Institute of Technology, and Loyola University) attract a lot of visiting academics, college administrators, and students and their families.

How the *Unofficial Guide* Can Help

In many ways, the problems facing business visitors and conventioneers on their first trip to Chicago don't differ much from the problems of tourists intent on seeing Chicago's best-known attractions. Business visitors need to locate a convenient hotel, want to avoid the worst of the city's traffic, face the same problems of navigating a huge city, must figure out the public transportation system, and want to pinpoint Chicago's best restaurants. This book can help.

For the most part, though, business visitors aren't nearly as flexible about the timing of their visit as people who pick Chicago as a vacation destination. While we advise that the best times for visiting the city are spring and fall, the necessities of business may dictate that you pull into the Windy City in hot and humid August—or even worse, January, a month when cold temperatures and stiff winds off Lake Michigan often create double-digit minus-zero windchill readings.

Yet much of the advice and information presented in the *Unofficial Guide* is as valuable to business visitors as it is to tourists. As for our recommendations on seeing the city's many sights . . . who knows? Maybe you'll be able to squeeze a morning or an afternoon out of your busy schedule, grab this book, and spend a few hours exploring some of the attractions that draw more than six million tourists each year.

McCormick Place Convention Center

It's Big . . .

Chicago's McCormick Place (2301 South Lake Shore Drive; (312) 791-7000; fax (312) 791-6543; **www.mccormickplace.com**) stands today as the largest exhibition and meeting facility in North America. With 2.2 million square feet of exposition space (1.3 million on one level), 345,000 square feet of meeting room, banquet, and ballroom space, as well as four theaters (including the 4,300-seat **Arie Crown Theater**), McCormick Place is the 800-pound gorilla of Chicago convention venues.

The original McCormick Place was the brainchild of Col. Robert R. McCormick, a former owner of the *Chicago Tribune.* It opened in 1960 and enjoyed seven years of success before being destroyed by fire in 1967. A new, more comprehensive structure (Lakeside Center) replaced it in 1971 and, along with the North Building (added in 1986) and the South Building (completed in late 1996), comprises today's McCormick Place.

... and It Has Its Drawbacks

While McCormick Place is huge, its drawbacks are varied. The convention center's location on Lake Michigan destroys any vestiges of an open, uncluttered Chicago lakefront; a formidable tangle of ramps and viaducts connects the Stevenson Expressway (I-55) to Lake Shore Drive. For weary conventioneers looking for a respite from crowded exhibition halls, there is nothing—repeat, nothing—within walking distance of the huge complex that can provide distractions—with the possible exception of a stroll along the bike path that follows the shoreline of placid Lake Michigan.

As one spokesman for the giant hall once commented, McCormick Place is "totally business-oriented. There is no lounge area in the lobby. There aren't even any clocks in this place. The reason this place is popular with exhibitors is once a guy is here, he's stuck." Though we spotted a few clocks in Lakeside Center, the rest of the statement remains essentially true: The closest hotels and restaurants (with the exception of eating places inside the center) are a $5 cab ride away. Even the food court in the South Building offers relatively few dining options—and with $7 hamburgers and $3 fries, it's overpriced.

McCormick Place also garnered a notorious reputation over the years for scandals and union problems. Recently, however, the trade unions involved with moving in, assembling, and moving out trade shows have agreed to some modifications of work rules to allow exhibitors to work on their own equipment. How liberal are the new rules? You be the judge. For example, full-time employees of the exhibiting company with verifiable documentation may screw in their own light bulbs if neither tools nor ladders are needed. At the American Booksellers Association show in June 1995, a certain travel publisher had a display that could be erected without any tools whatsoever. Employees of the publisher who were familiar with the design of the display could easily set the whole

McCormick Convention Center:
Understanding the Numbering System

Rooms E450–451

Rooms E350–354

Lakeside Center

Halls D1 and D2

Hall E1

Hall F1

Grand Concourse

Rooms S501–505

Rooms S401–406

Rooms N426–427

North Building

South Building

Halls B1 and B2

Rooms N226–231

Rooms N126–140

Halls C1 and C2

L–3

L–2.5

L–1

Halls A1 and A2

Rooms Grand S100–106 Ballroom

The McCormick Place Numbering System makes it easy to find your Exhibit Hall.

All Exhibit Halls are named alphabetically:
A, B, C, D...

Lakeside Center has
Hall D—Level 3
Hall E—Level 2 and
Hall F—Level 1

The North Building has
Hall B—Level 3
Hall C—Level 1

The South Building has
Hall A—Level 3

Finding your Meeting Room is just as simple.

All meeting rooms begin with either N, S, or E.
The Letters stand for North Building, South Building, or Lakeside Center (formerly the East Building).

The first numeral in the meeting room is 1, 2, 3, 4, or 5. This number stands for the level number.

The last two digits of the room number specify the exact room.

Some rooms have divider walls which create smaller rooms. These have an "a, b, c, or d" after the room number.

E271b

thing up in 45 minutes. Union representatives halted erection of the display and insisted that the task be turned over to a union carpenter. The carpenter required two hours to set up the display, one of which was considered double overtime. Recently, however, rule changes allow exhibitors with booths 300 square feet or smaller to do simple booth assembly and decorating. In addition, overtime policies were relaxed, which should save exhibitors money.

The Layout

McCormick Place is, in fact, three separate convention venues (Lakeside Center, the North Building, and the South Building). The three buildings are connected by the Grand Concourse, which serves as a unified entrance to McCormick Place and a link between the three. The spectacular, 100-foot-high, 900-foot-long pedestrian walkway includes visitor lobbies, a business center, cafes, coffee shops, specialty shops, and fountains. The glass-enclosed, multilevel concourse also crosses Lake Shore Drive to provide a seamless connection with the Lakeside Center and allows the South and North Buildings' exhibit halls to be combined for a total of 1.3 million square feet of exhibition space on one level.

Finding Your Way

Exhibit halls are named by consecutive letters. The South Building contains exhibit hall A; the North Building houses exhibit halls B (level 3) and C (level 1); and the Lakeside Center contains exhibit halls D (level 3), E (level 2), and F (level 1). Sometimes halls may be divided, for example: D1 and D2.

All meeting room numbers begin with either E, N, or S, and stand for Lakeside Center, North Building, and South Building. The next numeral (1, 2, 3, or 4) indicates the level, and the last two digits specify the exact room. To avoid confusion, no room numbers are duplicated between the three buildings. Rooms 1–25 are located in the South Building, 26–49 are in the North Building, and 50–75 are found in the Lakeside Center. Some meeting rooms with divider walls can create several smaller meeting rooms; these will have an "a," "b," "c," or "d" suffix following the number. Thus, meeting room N126b is located on the first level of the North Building, room 26.

Parking at McCormick Place

Our advice to Chicago visitors is the same whether you're vacationing or attending a convention at McCormick Place: Don't drive. Not only is the traffic congestion of epic proportions, but finding a place to put your car is equally frustrating—and expensive. While McCormick Place has 6,000 adjacent parking spaces and an underground parking garage ($12 a day for private cars), save yourself the expense and bother of fighting the traffic and leave the car at home.

In fact, so many people fly into Chicago for conventions that McCormick Place officials claim parking is only a major problem (read: nearly impossible) during large public shows that attract local residents. Example: The world's largest car show, held at McCormick Place each February, draws 1.1 million auto buffs.

Exhibitor Move-In and Move-Out

Though it's expensive, we recommend shipping your display as opposed to hauling it yourself. McCormick Place is not really set up to accommodate smaller exhibitors who want to bring in their own displays. If you elect to move yourself in and out, the easiest way is to arrive at McCormick Place in a cab. If you have too much stuff to fit in a cab, you can try to fight your way into one of the tunnels servicing the loading docks. (Access to the 65 loading docks serving the South Building should be easier—they're above ground and accessible from Martin Luther King Jr. Drive.) Because move-in and set-up usually take place over two- to three-day periods, getting in is less of a problem than getting out (when everyone wants to leave at the same time). In any event, be prepared to drag your exhibit a long way. Try to pack everything into cases with wheels or bring along some sort of handcart or dolly.

Getting to and from McCormick Place

Large conventions provide bus shuttle service from major downtown hotels to McCormick Place. On weekends, the shuttle service operates pretty smoothly. On weekdays, however, when the buses must contend with Chicago traffic, schedules break down and meeting attendees must wait a long time. To compound the problem, neither police nor convention authorities seem able to control the taxi cabs that constantly block the buses from getting to their convention center loading zones. The predictable result of this transportation anarchy is gridlock. If you depend on shuttle buses or cabs, prepare for long queues. Give yourself an hour to get to McCormick Place in the morning and two hours to get back to your hotel at night. If you want to take a cab to an outside restaurant for lunch, go before noon or after 1:30 p.m.

A preferable option to shuttle buses and cabs is to take the commuter train, accessible from the Grand Concourse. Each train can accommodate several thousand conventioneers at once. At most shows, we recommend using the shuttle buses in the morning to go to the convention center and returning in the evening by train. To commute to downtown hotels from McCormick Place, take the northbound train three stops to the Randolph Station at the end of the line. You will emerge from the station in the Loop area, a reasonably safe part of Chicago just south of the Chicago River. From here you can take a cab or walk to most downtown hotels in about 15 minutes. On weekdays, the trains run frequently enough that you don't really need to consult a schedule. On weekends, however, the trains run up to 45 minutes apart.

Getting to and from the Airport

Airport Express offers van service to and from McCormick Place and O'Hare and Midway Airports. The vans depart from the main entrance at the new Grand Concourse. The fare to O'Hare is $17 one-way; the ride to Midway is $12. For reservations and more information, call (800) 654-7871.

Cab fare to O'Hare is about $30, and $23 to Midway; actual fares vary depending on traffic conditions and don't include a tip. However, the cost will be the same regardless of the number of passengers.

Lakeside Center

Located east of South Lake Shore Drive on the shores of Lake Michigan, the Lakeside Center (formerly the East Building) underwent a $34 million renovation and reopened in late 1997. Upgrades include new carpeting, walls, ceilings, and lighting. The renovated building also features a new business center, cafe/bar, and gift shop.

Lakeside Center is able to operate independently of the rest of McCormick Place, separating smaller and midsized events from the huge shows taking place in the North and South Buildings across Lake Shore Drive. The building contains more than a half-million square feet of exhibit area and a 2,100-space underground parking garage.

Level 2, the lobby and mezzanine level, features the 283,000-square-foot Hall E1, the building's second-largest major exhibit area (which has its own loading docks). Also located on this level is the Arie Crown Theater, a site for major entertainment productions, corporate meetings, and convention keynote addresses; it's the largest theater in Chicago. Upgrades to the theater include reupholstered seats, improved acoustics, a new sound system, and theatrical lighting.

The 75,000-square-foot lobby on Level 2 accommodates registration and includes private show management offices and a press facility. The **McCormick Place Business Center** offers a wide array of services, including faxing, photocopying, equipment rentals, shipping, secretarial services, office supplies, foreign currency exchange on show management request, and more; the phone number is (312) 791-6400 and the fax number is (312) 791-6501. There's also an additional 10,000 square feet of meeting rooms on this level.

Level 3 contains a 45,000-square-foot Grand Ballroom and Lobby that's divisible into two 22,500-square-foot rooms. Hall D, with a north-south divider wall, can be divided into two 150,000-square-foot exhibition spaces for midsized shows. Two meeting rooms add another 58,000 square feet of space. The Grand Concourse connects Lakeside Center with the North and South Buildings across Lake Shore Drive. Loading docks are located at the north end of the building.

Level 1 offers Hall F1, a 60,000-square-foot room for extra exhibits, meetings, or registration; restaurants; two meeting rooms totaling nearly 5,000 square feet; and a coffee shop. Also located on this level are the McCormick Place administrative offices and an office of the **Chicago Convention and Tourism Bureau.** Level 4, the small upper level, contains three meeting rooms totaling 35,000 square feet.

The North Building

Completed in the mid-1980s and then expanded, the North Building boasts 188,000 square feet of new exhibit space, additional escalators, a business center, and a gift shop. Level 1, the lower level, contains Hall C1, a 148,500-square-foot exhibition space that can be used independently or in conjunction with the larger upper level hall; and Hall C2, a 61,000-square-foot extension area that can be used for additional exhibit space or crate storage. The lower-level lobby has dedicated taxi and areas for bus loading/unloading, 15 meeting rooms, and direct access to 4,000 outside parking spaces.

Level 3, the upper level, contains Hall B1, a 369,000-square-foot exhibition hall with an adjoining 127,000 square feet of space (Hall B2) that can be used for exhibits or crate storage; both halls can be combined with exhibition space in the South Building for a total of 1.3 million square feet of space on one level. A suspended roof design provides virtually column-free exhibition space and allows for clear ceiling heights of up to 40 feet. Loading docks are located at the north end of the building. The Grand Concourse connects the North Building with the South Building and the Lakeside Center.

Level 2, the mezzanine level, provides easy access to both the upper- and lower-level exhibition halls, as well as eight meeting rooms, two restaurants, and service areas. Over 50,000 square feet of lobby space is available for registration. Level 4 has two meeting rooms totaling 14,555 square feet.

The South Building

Completed in December 1997 at a cost of $675 million, the South Building provides an additional 840,000 square feet of exhibition space and 45 meeting rooms totaling another 170,000 square feet. It also boasts the 22,000-square-foot Vista Room and the 33,000-square-foot Grand Ballroom. Behind the scenes, the new building has 170,000 square feet of indoor crate storage and full in-floor utilities.

The South Building has 65 concealed truck docks and a special ramp for oversized exhibits. The weather-protected west entrance faces five-acre McCormick Square, featuring lighted 75-foot pylons, fountains, and landscaping.

Level 3 contains Hall A1 and Hall A2, which when combined total 840,000 square feet. Loading docks are located on the east and south ends of the building. Across the Grand Concourse is Level 3 of the North Building and another half-million square feet of exhibition space.

Level 1 features the main entrance and lobby, the Grand Ballroom, and six meeting rooms; Level 2.5 contains a food court, a restaurant, a business center, a first-aid station, access to Metra commuter trains, and retail stores; Level 4 has five meeting rooms totaling about 24,000 square feet and the two-story, 22,000-square-foot Vista Room; Level 5 contains five meeting rooms with nearly 19,000 square feet of space.

Lunch Alternatives for Convention and Trade Show Attendees
Eating at McCormick Place is a real hassle. There are too few food service vendors for the size of the facility, and even fewer table areas where you can sit and eat your hard-won victuals. Almost without exception, you must wait in one queue to obtain your food and in another to pay for it. We waited 35 minutes to get a turkey croissant sandwich and a lemonade, and then stood in line an additional 15 minutes to pay. How much? About $6 for two of us.

If you are an exhibitor, a small cooler should be an integral part of your booth. Ice frozen in a gallon milk jug lasts for days to keep drinks cold. Both exhibitors and nonexhibitors should eat breakfast before going to the show. After breakfast, but before you catch your shuttle, stop at one of the many downtown delis and pick up a sandwich, chips, fruit, and some drinks for lunch as well as for snacking throughout the day. If you want to leave campus for lunch, get in the cab queue before 11:30 a.m. or after 1:30 p.m. Getting back to McCormick Place by cab after lunch will not be a problem. For a rundown on the best restaurants for a quiet business lunch, see Part Nine: Dining and Restaurants.

Convention Overload
Business visitors have a huge impact on Chicago when, say, 70,000 exhibitors and trade show attendees come into town and snatch up literally every hotel room within a 100-mile radius of the Loop. Finding a place to sleep can be nearly impossible when most of the practicing radiologists in the United States converge on Chicago for their national convention.

The good news: The large trade shows register no discernible effect on the availability of cabs and restaurant tables, or on traffic congestion; it seems that only hotel rooms and rental cars become scarce when a big convention hits town. Consult our Convention and Trade Show Calendar when planning your trip to Chicago.

Navy Pier

In the summer of 1995, Navy Pier, a Chicago landmark jutting out nearly a mile into Lake Michigan, was reopened after a nearly $200 million facelift. (The pier first opened in 1916.) Today, it's a year-round tourist attraction and convention center for exhibitions, meetings, and special events. **Festival Hall,** located near the east end of the pier, contains 170,000 square feet of exhibit space and 65,000 square feet of meeting rooms designed for small- and medium-sized shows. The hall is surrounded by dining spots, cruise boats, a 150-foot Ferris wheel, a shopping mall, and a drop-dead view of Chicago's skyline.

Unlike visitors to McCormick Place, conventioneers and trade show attendees at Festival Hall have access to 13,000 hotel rooms located within a few blocks, enclosed parking for 1,900 cars (which still isn't enough; we recommend either walking, public transportation, or cabs to reach Festival Hall), and on-the-pier restaurants and catering providing choices ranging from fast food to elegant dining with skyline and waterfront views. Plus, Chicago's best hotels, shopping, and restaurants are only a few blocks away. Navy Pier is literally within walking distance of the Magnificent Mile and the Loop. For more information on Navy Pier, see its profile in Part Eight: Attractions in Chicago.

Navy Pier Convention Facilities

Festival Hall features more than 170,000 square feet of exhibit space divisible into two areas of 113,000 square feet (Hall A) and 56,000 square feet (Hall B). Taking maximum advantage of the pier's lakefront setting, the halls boast ceiling heights of up to 60 feet (30 feet minimum) and a full range of electrical and telecommunication amenities for exhibitors' needs.

The main halls are located on the second level; small exhibitors can carry or roll show material from the public parking area on the first level. Loading docks are located on the second (main hall) level at the west end of Festival Hall. The ramp to the loading docks is reached from the drive along the north side of Navy Pier.

Meeting rooms divisible into as many as 36 separate areas total more than 48,000 square feet and are located on a mezzanine overlooking the exhibition floor and on the exhibition level. The 18,000-square-foot Grand Ballroom, featuring an 80-foot domed ceiling and panoramic water views, continues to serve banquet, performance, and special exhibit functions as it has since the pier first opened in 1916.

CONVENTION AND TRADE SHOW CALENDAR

Estimated Dates	Convention Event	Location	Attendance
2003			
Mar. 3–5	National Manufacturing Week	McCormick	45,000
Mar. 16–18	GLOBALSHOP	McCormick	20,000
Mar. 30–Apr. 2	American College of Cardiology	McCormick	35,000
April 14–17	Converting Machinery & Materials	McCormick	35,000
April 15–17	COMDEX Chicago	McCormick	40,000
May 4–6	Supermarket Convention & Expo	McCormick	35,000
May 4–6	Int'l. Fancy Food & Confection	McCormick	20,000
May 17–20	Nat'l Restaurant Hotel-Motel	McCormick	77,000
May 31–Jun. 2	Amer. Soc. of Clinical Oncology	McCormick	30,000
June 16–18	NeoCon World's Trade Fair	Merchandise Mart	60,000
June 9–11	Nat'l. Cable & Telecommunications	McCormick	27,000
June 23–27	Society of Plastics Industry	McCormick	83,000
July 26–30	Chicago Gift & Home Market	Merchandise Mart	21,000
July 11–15	Maj. League Baseball—All Star Wk.	McCormick	50,000
July 12–16	IFT Annual Meeting & Food Expo	McCormick	25,000
Aug. 10–12	International Hardware Week	McCormick	55,000
Sept. 5–12	National Safety Council	McCormick	20,000
Sept. 16–18	The Motivation Show	McCormick	36,000
Sept. 16–18	Frontline Solutions	McCormick	20,000
Sept. 28–Oct.	IGRAPH/CONVERTING EXPO	McCormick	50,000

Donald E. Stephens Convention Center

Located northwest of downtown Chicago and five minutes from O'Hare International Airport, the **Donald E. Stephens** (formerly Rosemont) **Convention Center** (9301 West Bryn Mawr, Rosemont; (847) 692-2220, fax (847) 696-9700) is an exhibition venue offering convenience for fly-in exhibitors and trade show attendees—but not much else. Unfortunately, the location on the far fringe of Chicago's suburbs is strictly nowheresville in terms of easy access to the attractions, restaurants, nightlife, and ethnic diversity that make the Windy City a world-class travel destination.

Stephens is, however, a clean, modern facility offering 840,000 square feet of flexible convention space that can accommodate a con-

Estimated Dates	Convention Event	Location	Attendance
2003 *(continued)*			
Oct. 12–14	Nat'l. Assoc./Convenience Stores	McCormick	30,000
Oct. 19–23	American College of Surgeons	McCormick	30,000
Oct. 30–Nov. 2	Worldwide Food Expo	McCormick	30,000
Nov. 5–8	Nat'l Assoc. Educ./Young Children	McCormick	32,000
Nov. 16–20	SME—Fabtech International	McCormick	30,000
Nov. 30–Dec. 5	RSNA—Annual Meeting	McCormick	55,000
2004			
Jan. 24–28	Chicago Gift & Home Market	Merchandise Mart	24,000
Feb. 13–15	IOTOS 2004	Navy Pier	20,000
Feb. 20–22	Chicago Dental Society	McCormick	31,000
Feb. 23–26	National Manufacturing Week	McCormick	45,000
Mar. 8–12	PITTCON 2004	McCormick	30,000
Mar. 20–22	International Housewares Show	McCormick	58,000
Mar. 28–April 1	IMAX International	McCormick	40,000
April 2–4	Kitchen & Bath Industry Show	McCormick	40,000
April 14–16	COMDEX Spring eMobility	McCormick	40,000
May 2–4	Supermarket Convention & Expo	McCormick	35,000
May 2–4	Int'l. Fancy Food & Confection	McCormick	20,000
May 22–25	Nat'l Restaurant Hotel-Motel	McCormick	76,000

tinuous 250,000-square-foot space containing up to 1,150 booths. A 5,000-space parking garage and more than 3,000 nearby hotel rooms (in the Sofitel Chicago and Hyatt Regency O'Hare) are connected by a 7,000-linear-foot, enclosed pedestrian Skybridge Network. Heated in the winter and air conditioned in the summer, it's very nice when the weather is nasty outside and you want to get to your car or one of the nearby hotels.

Stephens handles a wide variety of both public and trade shows, ranging from the Chicago Midwest Bicycle Show (trade) to public ski shows. The center's six halls feature ceiling heights ranging from 16 to 26 feet and five drive-in freight doors. The conference center offers an additional 52,000 square feet of floor space in 34 meeting rooms located on two levels.

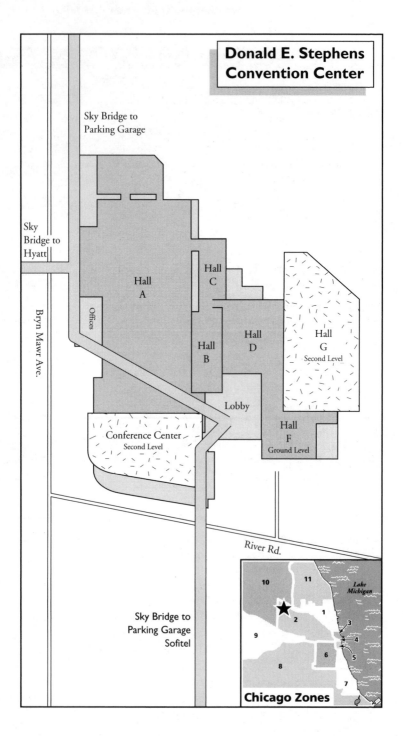

Donald E. Stephens Convention Center

Sky Bridge to Parking Garage

Sky Bridge to Hyatt

Bryn Mawr Ave.

Offices

Hall A

Hall C

Hall B

Hall D

Hall G
Second Level

Hall F
Ground Level

Lobby

Conference Center
Second Level

Sky Bridge to Parking Garage Sofitel

River Rd.

Chicago Zones

Lake Michigan

Other hotels close to Stephens include the **Westin Hotel O'Hare** (525 rooms), **Ramada Plaza Hotel O'Hare** (723 rooms), **Holiday Inn O'Hare International** (507 rooms), and **Sheraton Gateway Suites O'Hare** (325 suites). For places to eat that rise above standard hotel dining rooms, see Part Nine: Dining and Restaurants.

Getting to downtown Chicago from Stephens takes about 20 minutes by car (except during rush hours) and about 45 minutes by train. To drive, take I-90 (the Kennedy Expressway) east. You can board the CTA O'Hare Line train to downtown at either O'Hare or River Road in Rosemont (which has parking).

Part Five

Arriving and Getting Oriented

Coming into the City

By Car

The major route into Chicago from both the south and the north is Interstate 90/94 (better known locally as the Dan Ryan Expressway south of the Loop and the Kennedy Expressway to the north). The busy highway runs roughly north to south through Chicago (paralleling Lake Michigan) and features both express lanes (without exits) and local lanes (with exits); it's a setup guaranteed to exasperate first-time visitors.

South of the city, I-90/94 links with I-80, a major east-west route that connects Chicago to South Bend, Toledo, Cleveland, and New York City to the east, and Davenport, Des Moines, Omaha, and other points to the west. It also joins I-57, which continues south through Illinois to Kankakee and Champaign.

North of the Loop, I-90/94 changes names to become the Kennedy Expressway; it veers northwest toward O'Hare International Airport before splitting. I-90 (now called the Northwest Tollway) continues northwest past the airport to Madison, Wisconsin, where it meets I-94.

The Stevenson Expressway (I-55) enters Chicago near McCormick Place from the southwest; this interstate begins in New Orleans and goes north through Memphis and St. Louis before crossing I-80 and passing Midway Airport to its terminus in the city at Lake Shore Drive. From the west, the Eisenhower Expressway (I-290) comes into the Loop from I-88 (the East-West Tollway) and DeKalb.

West of the city limits, two highways run north and south through Chicago's suburbs to link the major roads coming into Chicago from the south, west, and north; the highways serve as de facto "beltways" in otherwise beltway-less Chicago. I-294 (the Tri-State Tollway) starts at I-80 south of the city and crosses I-55 (the Stevenson Expressway),

I-290 (the Eisenhower Expressway), and I-90 (the Kennedy Expressway) near O'Hare. North of Chicago it merges with I-94 en route to Milwaukee.

A few miles west of I-294, US 355 (the North-South Tollway) connects I-55 and I-88 (the East-West Tollway) to I-290 west of O'Hare; I-290 goes north to I-90, the Northwest Tollway that links Madison and Chicago.

US 41, the Edens Expressway, links I-90/94 in Chicago's North Side (north of the Chicago River) with the northern suburbs of Skokie, Highland Park, and Lake Forest before merging with I-94 south of the Wisconsin state line. Farther south in the city, US 41 becomes Lake Shore Drive, which follows Lake Michigan south past downtown and into Indiana.

By Plane

O'Hare International Airport is famous (or, as some cynics snort, infamous) as the busiest airport in the world. More than 72 million people a year fly in and out of the airport located 17 miles northwest of downtown Chicago. That means there are usually enough travelers on hand to turn the huge facility into a refugee camp when lousy weather snarls air traffic and strands travelers by the thousands.

Yet O'Hare isn't the only game in town. Midway Airport, located eight miles southwest of downtown, handles about one-tenth of the passenger traffic of its big brother to the north, making it a more hassle-free point of arrival and departure for many visitors to the Windy City.

O'Hare International Airport

Opened in 1955 and named for Congressional Medal of Honor winner Edward O'Hare (a navy pilot killed in the Battle of Midway), this sprawling airport includes four terminals connected by passenger walkways, moving sidewalks, and a "people mover" (an automated transit system that covers 2.7 miles of airport property).

Statistics on O'Hare are impressive. For decades, it has been the commercial aviation capital of the world, providing service to all 50 states and many foreign countries. The mammoth airport handles more passengers and aircraft than any other field in the world; about 195,000 travelers pass through O'Hare each day and an average of 100 aircraft arrive or depart each hour. The complex covers nearly 7,700 acres, and the airport serves nearly 60 commercial, commuter, and cargo airlines on a regular basis.

The airport is also connected to Chicago's subway system and is close to I-90 (the Kennedy Expressway), which goes downtown to the Loop. Although O'Hare is renowned for its headache-inducing holding patterns in the air, on the ground this modern airport boasts a new international

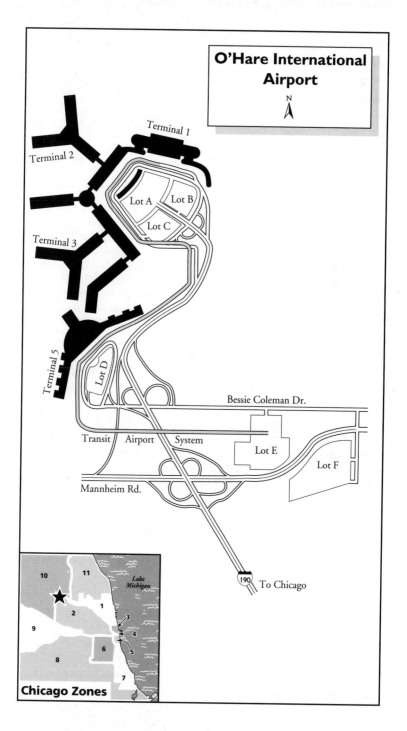

O'Hare International Airport

N

Terminal 1

Terminal 2

Terminal 3

Terminal 5

Lot A

Lot B

Lot C

Lot D

Bessie Coleman Dr.

Transit   Airport   System

Lot E

Lot F

Mannheim Rd.

190 To Chicago

10

11

Lake Michigan

1

2

3

4

5

9

6

8

7

Chicago Zones

terminal, is easy to get around, and is still growing. More than $700 million in improvements (including new runways) are planned over the next few years.

The Layout   The "core" of O'Hare contains terminals 1, 2, and 3, where most domestic flights come and go. Terminal 2 lies in the center of the horseshoe-shaped arrangement and faces the **Hilton O'Hare,** a parking garage, and parking lots. Terminal 5 (there's no terminal 4), which handles international flights, is located south of the core and is reached via the Airport Transit System (or "people mover").

In the three main terminals, the second-floor departure level features fast-food eateries, bars, shops, newsstands, and a "restaurant rotunda" between terminals 2 and 3. From the gate, arriving passengers follow signs to the baggage claim area on the lower level.

The People Mover   If you need to get from, say, terminal 1 to terminal 3, or your destination is the long-term parking area, take the "people mover." Escalators and elevators in front of the ticket counters take you over the roadway where departing passengers are dropped off. The people mover is free, and a train comes every few minutes.

Hint: If you've got some time to kill before your flight, explore this transportation system. It's fun to ride, and you'll be treated to some terrific views of the airfield. In addition, the international terminal has a food court with cheaper prices than the restaurants in the other terminals. And it's usually less crowded.

Getting Downtown

Cabs and Shuttles   Visitors who fly into Chicago have to make a choice when it comes to getting downtown. If your final destination is a major hotel near the Loop or the Magnificent Mile (which is where most of them are), **Airport Express** is the cheapest and easiest way to go—unless you're not schlepping luggage (take the train) or in a group (take a cab). Just inquire at the Airport Express desk in the baggage claim areas of either airport and ask if the van goes to your hotel. It's also a good idea to ask if your hotel is one of the first or last stops the van makes.

The service operates vans to major downtown hotels from 6 a.m. to 11:30 p.m. daily that leave about every 5–10 minutes. Ticket counters are located in the baggage claim areas of all four terminals. One-way fares are $20 for adults and $8.50 for children under age 12 with an adult. Round-trip fares for adults are $36. Figure on a 45-minute ride to your hotel during non–rush hour traffic. To make reservations for a pickup from your downtown hotel, for a guaranteed seat call (800) 654-7871 the day before you leave; last-minute reservations can be made up to an hour before departure on a space-available basis.

If your hotel isn't served by Airport Express, taxis, buses, hotel vans, and rental car pickups are located outside the lower-level baggage areas. Cab fares to downtown run about $35–$40 one-way for the normal travel time of 30 minutes; share-the-ride cabs cost $20 per person for a taxi shared between two to four passengers headed downtown. Allow at least an hour and a half during rush hour and expect to pay a higher fare for the longer cab ride.

Public Transportation If you're traveling light, the Chicago Transit Authority (CTA) Blue Line train terminal is located in front of and beneath terminal 2 (follow signs that read "Trains to Downtown"); it's about a 40-minute trip to the Loop that costs $1.50 one-way. Trains leave about every 10 minutes weekdays and about every 15 minutes early evenings and weekends. Unfortunately, there's no place to store luggage on the rapid-transit trains (although one piece of luggage is usually manageable, as many airline employees attest). For more information, call the CTA at (312) 836-7000.

Driving If you're renting a car and driving, getting to the Loop is pretty easy. Follow signs out of the airport to I-90 east, which puts you on the Kennedy Expressway; it's a straight, 18-mile ride to downtown that takes about a half hour (longer during rush hour—and Friday afternoons are the worst). As you approach the city, Chicago's distinctive skyline, anchored by the John Hancock Center on the left and the Sears Tower on the right, comes into view—if it's not raining.

If you're headed for the Loop, move into the right lane as you approach the tunnel (just before the city center) and get ready to exit as you come out of the tunnel. Take the Ohio Street exit to get to the north downtown area. The last of four exits to downtown is the Congress Parkway (where I-290 west, the Eisenhower Expressway, meets the Kennedy Expressway) to South Loop; miss it and you're on your way to Indiana. Taking the Congress Parkway exit scoots you *through* the U.S. post office building to the south edge of the Loop; South Michigan Avenue and South Lake Shore Drive lie straight ahead. For more information on getting around Chicago, see Part Six.

Visitor Services Twenty-six multilingual information specialists are on hand to provide information and translation assistance to travelers. Five airport information booths are located throughout the airport: on the lower levels of terminals 1, 2, and 3, and on both the lower and upper levels of terminal 5. The booths are open daily from 8:15 a.m. to 8 p.m. For more information, call the main airport number at (773) 686-2200.

The **U.S. Postal Service** operates an office in terminal 2 on the upper level. Hours are 7 a.m.–7 p.m. weekdays. Teletext phones for the hearing impaired are located next to the airport information booths in the three domestic terminals (lower level) and outside the customs area in the international terminal. More teletext phones are located in phone banks throughout the airport; (773) 601-8333.

Foreign currency exchanges are located in terminals 1, 3, and 5. Hours are 8 a.m.– 8 p.m. daily.

A duty-free shop, located in terminal 5 in the center court on the upper level, offers a wide range of merchandise free of export duties and taxes. Hours vary; the shop frequently stays open later than normal to serve international flights. Satellite shops are also located in terminal 1 near gate C18 and in terminal 3 across from gate K11; hours vary according to flight times.

ATMs are located on the upper levels of terminals 1, 2, and 3 near the concourse entrances (airside) and on the upper and lower terminals of terminal 5.

Kids on the Fly is an exhibit for youngsters operated by the Chicago Children's Museum. Centrally located in terminal 2 (near the security checkpoint), the 2,205-square-foot interactive playground lets children ages 1–12 burn off excess energy as they explore a kid-sized air traffic control tower, a ceiling-high model of the Sears Tower, a cargo plane, and a fantasy helicopter. It's free and open to all visitors during regular flight hours and to ticketed passengers after 10 p.m.

Parking   O'Hare provides more than 10,000 spaces in short- and long-term parking lots and a garage (call (773) 686-7530 for info). Short-term parking in the first level of the parking garage is $3 for the first hour, $21 for the next four hours (and another $21 for the next four hours after that), and finally $50 for 9–24 hours. Parking on levels 2–6 of the parking garage and in outside lots B and C costs $3 for an hour or less, with a maximum fee of $23 for 24 hours. Rates in short-term lot D (next to the international terminal) are $3 for an hour or less, and $30 for 13–24 hours. Long-term parking in lots E (served by the "people mover") and G costs $2 for an hour or less, with a $13 maximum fee per day.

Midway Airport

Located in a bungalow community eight miles southwest of downtown Chicago, this airport is everything O'Hare isn't: small, convenient, and uncongested. Our advice: If you can get a direct flight into Midway, take it. Why fight the hassles of the world's busiest airport?

The new terminal at Midway has six concourses. From your gate follow signs to the baggage area to pick up your bags. Passenger pick-up and drop-off, taxis, buses, car rental, and the CTA Orange Line train station are right outside the door. Free shuttles to the long-term economy parking lot arrive every 15 minutes.

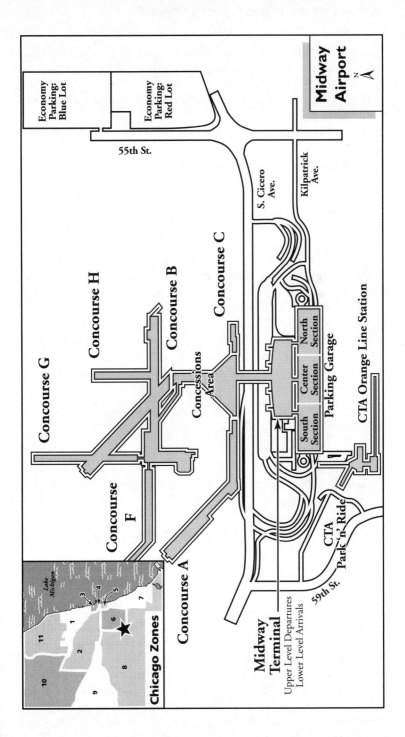

Cab fares from Midway to downtown run about $30, and the ride takes 20 minutes (in non–rush hour traffic; allow more time and figure on a higher fare during heavy traffic and/or bad weather). Share-the-ride cabs let you split the ride with up to three other passengers going downtown; the cost is $10 per person.

Airport Express offers van service to and from downtown hotels; the fare is $15 one-way for adults and $8.50 for children under age 12 with an adult. The trip takes about 30 minutes, and vans depart every 15 to 20 minutes. Round-trip fare for adults is $23. For a return reservation, call (800) 654-7871 a day in advance. Last-minute reservations can be made up to an hour before departure on a space-available basis.

CTA's Orange Line connects Midway to downtown, and trains offer plenty of room for luggage. The fare is $1.50 one-way, and the ride lasts 35 minutes. Trains run every day from 5 a.m. to 11 p.m. weekdays and Saturdays, and 7:30 a.m. to 11 p.m. Sundays and holidays. Trains run every six to eight minutes in rush hours and every ten minutes the rest of the time. Weekday *morning* rush hour bus service to downtown is via the #99M Midway Express bus (do *not* take this bus in the evening). Pick it up at the airport's center entrance. The #62 Archer bus provides 24-hour service to downtown. Bus fares are $1.50.

If you're renting a car and driving downtown, take South Cicero Avenue north a few miles to I-55 (the Stevenson Expressway) east. The highway ends at Lake Shore Drive and the McCormick Place complex; take Lake Shore Drive north to get downtown or places farther north.

As you bear left onto Lake Shore Drive, you're treated to a great view of the Chicago skyline and Lake Michigan. After passing the Field Museum on the right, turn left onto Balbo Avenue to reach Michigan Avenue, the Loop, and I-290 (the Eisenhower Expressway). Or continue straight along the lake across the Chicago River to reach the Magnificent Mile, Navy Pier, and other points north. From Midway, the ten-mile drive to downtown takes about 20 minutes (longer during rush hour).

By Train

Chicago's **Union Station,** located across the Chicago River a couple of blocks west of the Loop, is a hub for Amtrak rail service and Metra commuter service. Unfortunately, the train station's location makes it pretty inconvenient—it's not particularly close to anything (say, major hotels, tourist attractions, or subway stations)—and its layout is confusing.

Amtrak trains arrive on the concourse level of the station. After picking up your baggage, head for the taxi stand near the north concourse (Adams Street exit). Alas, Chicago's fabled "El" is several blocks to the east—too far to walk if you're carrying luggage. The only public transportation option is the #151 bus—also not a good idea if you're lugging a suitcase or two—which you can catch outside on Canal Street. The bus goes through the Loop and up North Michigan Avenue. To sum up: If you're not being picked up by someone in a car, a cab is your best option for getting out of Union Station.

Getting Oriented

The operative word for Chicago, currently the nation's third-largest city, is "big."

Located a third of the way between the East and West Coasts of the United States, the Windy City covers 227 square miles and stretches 33 miles along the southwestern coastline of Lake Michigan (the second-largest of the five Great Lakes, after Lake Superior). With a population of just under three million—in a metropolitan area of over six million—Chicago is not only the largest city in Illinois, it's the de facto economic and cultural capital of the Midwest. (But not the state capital; the state house is 200 miles away in Springfield.)

A Geography Lesson

Chicago is located in the northeast corner of Illinois, a large Midwestern state bordered by (starting clockwise southeast of the city) Indiana, Kentucky, Missouri, Iowa, and Wisconsin; Michigan is to the east and north across the eponymous lake. Most of the land that surrounds the city is flat—just like most of the Midwest—a fact, theorists say, that may explain the city's passion for tall buildings and the dizzying, easily recognized skyline.

To the southeast, just past the city line on the southern tip of Lake Michigan, lies the gritty industrial town of Gary, Indiana. North along the lake the city merges with the comfortable suburban enclave of Evanston (home of Northwestern University); farther north, but still within commuting range of Chicago, are Highland Park and Waukegan. The Wisconsin state line lies about 40 miles north of the Loop, the heart of downtown Chicago.

The closest major city is Milwaukee, a blue-collar town on Lake Michigan 90 miles to the north. Other big Midwestern cities arrayed around Chicago are Detroit (290 miles to the east), Indianapolis (180 miles to the southeast), St. Louis (300 miles to the southwest), Des Moines (360 miles to the west), and Minneapolis/St. Paul (410 miles to the northwest).

Chicago's Layout

River and Lake

The other major geographic feature of Chicago is the narrow Chicago River, which meets Lake Michigan downtown along the carefully preserved lakefront (which is lined with parks and a wildly popular bike and jogging trail, not factories and wharves). The direction of the river was reversed around 1900 and today flows away from Lake Michigan downstate to the Illinois River; it's a major shipping route to the Gulf of Mexico. Boat tours on the Chicago River provide some of the best views of the city's fabled architecture.

The Loop and Grant Park

Tucked south and east of a bend in the river is the Loop, Chicago's downtown core of skyscrapers, government buildings, financial and trading institutions, office buildings, hotels, and retail establishments. The name comes from the elevated train (the "El") that circles the downtown business district.

A couple of blocks east of the Loop and hugging Lake Michigan is Grant Park, a barrier of green where millions of Chicagoans and visitors flock each summer to enjoy a variety of outdoor events and music festivals. Grant Park also provides a campus-like setting for some of the city's largest museums, colorful Buckingham Fountain, and many softball fields. The view of the Chicago skyline from the park is spectacular.

Lake Shore Drive

Running north and south through Grant Park and along Lake Michigan is Lake Shore Drive. Although the multilane road's high speeds and congestion usually result in a white-knuckled driving experience for first-time visitors, a cruise along the venerable highway provides spectacular vistas of the Chicago skyline, yacht basins, parks full of trees and greenery, beaches, and ocean-like Lake Michigan stretching east to the horizon. (The views at night are even more mind-boggling.) It's also a major north-south corridor through the city, which is longer than it is wide.

In late 1996, Lake Shore Drive was relocated to the west of the Field Museum and Soldier Field. In 1997, the old lanes to the east were demolished and transformed into ten acres of new parkland, creating a traffic-free museum campus for the Field Museum, the Adler Planetarium, and the Shedd Aquarium. With its paths, bikeways, a pedestrian concourse under Lake Shore Drive serving as a gateway to the Museum Campus, and extensive landscaping, this new lakefront park provides Chicagoans and visitors with another place to stroll, bike, run, and relax as they take in the views. For drivers, an extensive system of new directional signs was installed.

Near North

North of the Chicago River are two areas popular with out-of-town visitors: the Magnificent Mile (a glitzy strip of North Michigan Avenue full of the city's toniest shops and galleries) and River North (Chicago's premier night club and restaurant district). Renovated and reopened in 1995 and jutting out into Lake Michigan is Navy Pier, featuring amusement rides, a shopping mall, clubs and restaurants, and a convention center. Farther north are the Gold Coast, an enclave of exclusive homes (and a great walking destination), and Lincoln Park, often called Chicago's "Central Park." It's surrounded by a residential neighborhood full of high-rises offering spectacular lake views and is home to the most visited zoo in the United States.

South and West of the Loop

South of the Loop along the lake is McCormick Place, North America's largest convention venue. Farther south is where visitors will find the huge Museum of Industry and Science, and Hyde Park, home of the beautiful University of Chicago campus (and more museums).

Some sections of the city west of downtown encompass the most economically distressed neighborhoods—and for out-of-town visitors, the most unsafe. Yet not-to-be-missed attractions west of the Loop include Hull House (where Nobel Prize winner Jane Addams gave turn-of-the-century Chicago immigrants a leg up on the American dream), ethnic restaurants in Greektown and Little Italy, huge Garfield Park Conservatory, and, just beyond the city line, Oak Park (hometown of famed architect Frank Lloyd Wright and equally famous Nobel-laureate novelist Ernest Hemingway).

Scattered throughout the city to the north, west, and south of downtown are a wide array of urban neighborhoods featuring shops, museums, and dining that reflect the ethnic diversity of the Windy City; see "Exploring Chicago's Neighborhoods" in Part Seven: Sight-Seeing Tips and Tours, for descriptions and locations. Beyond the city limits are more attractions worth the drive: Brookfield Zoo, Chicago Botanic Garden, and the Morton Arboretum are all less than an hour from downtown Chicago (allow more time in rush-hour traffic).

The Major Highways

The major interstate routes to Chicago's Loop are I-90/94 (better known to Chicagoans as the Dan Ryan Expressway south of downtown and the Kennedy Expressway to the north and west), I-290 (the Eisenhower Expressway), and I-55 (the Stevenson Expressway, which ends about a mile south of downtown at McCormick Place).

West of the city, I-294 (the Tri-State Tollway) parallels Lake Michigan through Chicago's suburbs as it heads north and links I-80 (a major transcontinental route south of the city) to I-90 (which goes to Milwaukee). I-294 also skirts O'Hare International Airport, where it intersects with I-90 (which links Chicago and Madison, Wisconsin).

A Word about Driving: Don't

With four major interstates converging downtown at or near the Loop, entering the city makes for a very interesting driving experience, especially if it's your first visit to Chicago . . . and it's rush hour.

Our advice: If you're staying in a downtown hotel, don't drive. Why? The congestion in America's third-largest city is unrelenting: morning and evening rush-hour traffic reports endlessly list backups, accidents, and delays occurring throughout the metropolitan area. And parking? Forget it. Chicago is notorious for its lack of convenient and/or affordable places to park.

Whether you're in town for business or pleasure, spare yourself the frustration of battling traffic, lanes that change direction depending on the time of day, and a tangle of highways. Instead, ride Chicago's extensive public transportation systems, take airport vans to and from downtown hotels, and take advantage of an abundance of taxis to get around town. (For more information on how to negotiate Chicago without a car, see "Public Transportation" in Part Six: Getting around Chicago.)

Finding Your Way around Chicago

Chicago's sheer size can be overwhelming, but here's some good news for visitors: The city is a relentlessly "right-angle" town, a characteristic that's invaluable in finding your way around. Except for the rare diagonal street, Chicago is laid out numerically on a grid, with State and Madison Streets (in the Loop) intersecting at the zero point.

It works like this: North Side Chicago is north of Madison Street and South Side is south of it. The West Side, logically enough, is west of State Street. And the East Side? It hardly exists; most of what could be termed "East Side" is Lake Michigan, since State Street is only a few blocks west of the lakefront.

Street numbers run in increments of 100 per block, with eight blocks to the mile. (Folks who like mental arithmetic can have fun figuring distances using street addresses.) Generally speaking, North Side streets and north-south streets on the South Side have names (Michigan Avenue, Erie Street), while east-west streets on the South Side usually are numbered (for example, the popular Museum of Science and Industry is at 57th Street and Lake Shore Drive).

After you've tried it a few times, navigating Chicago's grid gets to be fun (at least on weekends, when traffic is light). Locating, say, the Balzekas Museum of Lithuanian Culture is a snap. The address, 6500 South Pulaski Road, tells you the museum is at the corner of South Pulaski and 65th Street. It also helps that many (but not all) major avenues traverse the entire city from north to south. Like old friends, names such as Western, Cermak, Halsted, and Clark crop up over and over as you explore the city.

One last note that will help you stay oriented when exploring Chicago: Keep in mind that if the street numbers are going up, you're headed away from downtown; if they're going down, you're moving toward the center of the city.

Where to Find Tourist Information in Chicago

If you're short on maps or need more information on sight-seeing, hotels, shopping, or other activities in and around Chicago, there are several places to stop and pick up maps and brochures:

- In downtown Chicago, the **Visitor Information Center** located in the Randolph Lobby of the Chicago Cultural Center dispenses literature and advice to tourists. Just off the lobby, the Visitor Information Center provides orientation with videos and displays. Open Monday–Friday, 10 a.m.–6 p.m.; Saturday, 10 a.m.–5 p.m.; and Sunday, 11 a.m.–5 p.m. Closed on major holidays. 78 East Washington Street (at Michigan Avenue), Chicago, 60602; phone (312) 744-2400.

- On the Magnificent Mile north of the Loop, the **Water Tower Welcome Center** at Chicago and Michigan Avenues (you can't miss it; the tower is one of two structures that survived the Great Fire of 1871) provides tourist information, maps, hotel reservations, and advice. In addition, the Welcome Center stocks plentiful information on tourist attractions throughout Illinois. The Center is open daily, 7:30 a.m.–7 p.m; closed Thanksgiving and Christmas.

- In the Loop, the **Explore Chicago** kiosk inside the Sears on State store (2 North State Street) is open Monday–Saturday, 10 a.m.–6 p.m.; and Sunday, noon–5 p.m.

- In suburban Oak Park, visitors interested in touring the former residences of hometown heroes Frank Lloyd Wright and Ernest Hemingway should make their first stop at the **Oak Park Visitors Bureau,** 158 Forest Avenue, phone (888) OAK-PARK or (708) 848-1500. Visitors can park for free in the adjacent parking garage on weekends and can purchase tickets and pick up free maps in the visitor center. Open daily, 10 a.m.–5 p.m.

Things the Natives Already Know

Chicago Customs and Protocol

Chicagoans have earned a well-deserved reputation for friendliness and often display a degree of forwardness that can put off foreigners and visitors from more formal parts of our country. Sometimes Chicago natives come off as brash or blunt, since many value getting directly to the point. And that's mostly good news for tourists, who can count on plenty of help finding a destination when, say, riding a crowded rush hour bus. The moral is, don't hesitate to ask the natives for assistance.

Eating in Restaurants   By and large, casual is the byword when dining in the Windy City. Only the most chi-chi Chicago eateries require men to wear a jacket or prohibit ladies from wearing shorts or tank tops. Even swank places such as the Ritz-Carlton have dropped any requirement that men wear a tie at dinner.

Although people tend to get more dressed up for dinner downtown, you'll still find plenty of casual restaurants (the ones at North Pier, for example). Just about all ethnic restaurants beyond downtown have relaxed (read: nonexistent) dress codes. If in doubt, call ahead—or dress "chic casual": nice looking, but no T-shirts or running shoes.

Tipping   Is the tip you normally leave at home appropriate in Chicago? The answer is yes. Just bear in mind that a tip is a reward for good service. Here are some guidelines:

Porters and Skycaps   A dollar a bag.

Cab Drivers   A lot depends on service and courtesy. If the fare is less than $8, give the driver the change and a dollar. Example: If the fare is $4.50 give the cabbie 50 cents and a buck. If the fare is more than $8, give the driver the change and $2. If you ask the cabbie to take you only a block or two, the fare will be small, but your tip should be large ($3 to $5) to make up for his or her wait in line and to partially compensate him or her for missing a better-paying fare. Add an extra dollar to your tip if the driver handles a lot of luggage.

Parking Valets $2 is correct if the valet is courteous and demonstrates some hustle. A dollar will do if the service is just okay. Pay only when you check your car out, not when you leave it.

Bellmen and Doormen   When a bellman greets you at your car with a rolling luggage cart and handles all of your bags, $5 is about right. The more luggage you carry yourself, of course, the less you should tip. Add another $1 or $2 if the bellman opens your room. For calling a taxi, tip the doorman 50 cents to a dollar.

Waiters   Whether in a coffee shop, an upscale eatery, or ordering room service from the hotel kitchen, the standard gratuity ranges from 15–20% of the tab, before sales tax. At a buffet or brunch where you serve yourself, leave a dollar or two for the person who brings your drinks. Some restaurants, however, are adopting the European custom of automatically adding a 15% gratuity to the bill, so check before leaving a cash tip.

Cocktail Waiters/Bartenders   Here you tip by the round. For two people, a dollar a round; for more than two people, $2 a round. For a large group, use your judgment. Is everyone drinking beer, or is the order long and complicated? Tip accordingly.

Hotel Maids   On checking out, leave a dollar or two per day for each day of your stay, provided the service was good.

How to Look and Sound Like a Native   Good news: Chicagoans, by and large, are unpretentious, down-to-earth realists who, for example, take perverse pride in their city government's legendary corruptness. This town shuns phoniness, so visitors who want to blend in only need to be themselves. Yet, if it's important to you not to look like A Visitor on Holiday in the Windy City, we offer the following advice:

1. Don't crash diet. Except for razor-thin fashion victims haunting the over-priced boutiques along the Magnificent Mile, Chicagoans disdain the frou-frou svelteness that's the norm in New York or Los Angeles. Being overweight in Chicago isn't a social faux pas—this is, after all, a town renowned for its pizza, Italian beef and sausage sandwiches, and many other kinds of artery-clogging, waistband-expanding "hand food."

2. Be obsessive, if not maniacal, about the Cubbies, White Sox, Bears, Bulls, and Blackhawks.

3. Talk through your nose. Master the flat phonetics of the Midwest: give the letter "a" a harsh sound and throw in a few "dem's" and "dose's" when conversing with natives.

4. Occasionally, for no apparent reason, erupt in your best attempt at a Chicago accent, "Yah, but the city works."

5. Never, under any circumstances, put ketchup on a Chicago-style hot dog.

Publications for Visitors

Chicago has two major daily newspapers, the *Chicago Tribune* and the *Chicago Sun-Times*. Both are morning papers that cover local, national, and international news, and have Friday editions with up-to-the-minute information on entertainment for the weekend. Grab a Friday edition of both papers at a hometown newsstand before coming to Chicago for the weekend.

An even better source for entertainment and arts listings is the weekly *Reader,* a free tabloid that starts showing up on downtown newsstands (as well as a wide variety of clubs, bars, bookstores, coffee cafes, and shops) on Thursday afternoons. *New City*, another alt-weekly published on Thursdays, irreverently examines Chicago news, art, and entertainment.

Chicago is a monthly magazine that's strong on lists (top 20 restaurants, etc.) and provides a calendar of events, dining information, and feature articles. *Windy City Sports* is a free monthly guide to fitness and outdoor recreation that highlights seasonal sports such as skiing, bicycling, running, inline skating, and sailboarding. Pick up a copy at bike shops and outdoors outfitters.

Chicago Scene highlights Chicago's beautiful people and visiting celebs as they scarf canapés at the town's top fund-raising social events; the free monthly also contains articles on dining and fashion. Pick up a copy at swank shops, hair salons, and cafes up and down the Gold Coast. At the other end of the social spectrum, *StreetWise* is published twice monthly and is sold by homeless and formerly homeless men and women for a dollar (look for identifying vendor badges). The tabloid paper includes features, a calendar of events, local sports, poetry, and film reviews.

Chicago on the Air

Aside from the usual babble of format rock, talk, easy listening, and country music stations, Chicago is home to a few radio stations that really stand out for high-quality broadcasting. Tune in to what hip Chicagoans listen to, as listed below:

CHICAGO'S HIGH-QUALITY RADIO STATIONS		
Format	**Frequency**	**Station**
Jazz	95.5 FM	WNUA
NPR, News, Jazz	91.5 FM	WBEZ
Classical	98.7 FM	WFMT
Progressive Rock	93.1 FM	WXRT
Classical	97.1 FM	WNIB12

Access for the Disabled

Like most large U.S. cities, Chicago tries to make itself accessible to folks with physical handicaps. Most museums and restaurants, for example, feature wheelchair access. At the **Art Institute of Chicago,** wheelchair access is through the Columbus Drive (east) entrance, and a limited number of wheelchairs and strollers are available for free at both main entrances. Most public areas associated with the **Chicago Historical Society** are accessible to the disabled, and a limited number of wheelchairs are also available. Parking for disabled visitors is provided in the parking lot adjacent to the building.

The **Field Museum** has wheelchairs available on the ground level near the West Entrance and first-floor North Door, and the **Adler Planetarium** has wheelchair-accessible rest rooms on the first floor (down the vending machine hallway). Elevators are available for folks in wheelchairs, with strollers, or with other special needs.

Chicago Botanic Garden has wheelchairs available at the Information Desks in the Gateway and Education Centers. Accessible parking is located in parking lots #1, #2, and #3. The Orientation Center is equipped with assistive listening devices, closed caption monitors, and raised letters. **Brookfield Zoo** provides assistive listening devices in the

Administration Building near South Gate and in the Discovery Center near the North Gate. A telecommunication device for the deaf (TDD & TTY) is also available in the Administration Building.

Services for Disabled People

The **City of Chicago Department on Disability** offers information and reference: (312) 744-6673 and (312) 744-4964 (TDD only).

Handicapped visitors can arrange door-to-door transportation from the airport or train station to their hotel, as well as transportation anywhere in the city in special vans; the rate is $1.50 each time you board. Call the Chicago Transportation Authority Special Services Division at (312) 432-7025 (432-7116, TTY) for more information.

The **Chicago Transit Authority** operates 112 routes with lift-equipped buses; look for the blue wheelchair symbol displayed in the first bus/last bus chart on the Chicago Transit map. For routes, fares, schedules, and a copy of the latest Chicago Transit map, call (312) 836-7000 from 5 a.m. to 1 a.m. The TDD number is (888) 282-8891. Some (but not all) train stations are handicapped accessible. Here's the list; call (312) 836-7000 for hours of operation:

- **Blue Line** (O'Hare-Congress-Douglas): O'Hare, Rosemont, Cumberland, Harlem/Higgins, Jefferson Park, Logan Square, Western, Clark/Lake (Lake transfer), Jackson, UIC-Halsted/Morgan, Polk, 18th, Cicero/Cermak, Medical Center (Damen entrance), Kedzie-Homan, and Forest Park.

- **Red Line** (Howard-Dan Ryan): Loyola, Granville, Addison, Chicago, Lake, Washington, Jackson, Roosevelt, and Sox/35th, 79th, 95th/Dan Ryan.

- **Orange Line** (Midway): All stations between Midway Airport and Roosevelt; also Clark/Lake and Washington/Wells.

- **Brown Line** (Ravenswood): Kimball, Western, Clark/Lake, Washington/Wells, and Merchandise Mart.

- **Purple Line** (Evanston): Linden, Davis, Merchandise Mart, Clark/Lake, Library/Van Buren, and Washington/Wells.

- **Yellow Line** (Skokie).

- **Green Line** (Lake Street/Jackson Park): Ashland/63rd, Halsted, East 63rd–Cottage Grove, 51st, 47th, 43rd, 35-Bronzeville-ITT, King Drive, Roosevelt, Clark/Lake, Clinton, Ashland/Lake, California, Kedzie, Conservatory-Central Park Drive, Pulaski, Cicero, Laramie, Harlem/Lake (Marion entrance), and Central.

Time Zone

Chicago is located in the Central Time Zone, which puts Windy City clocks one hour behind New York, two hours ahead of the West Coast, an hour ahead of the Rocky Mountains, and six hours behind Greenwich Mean Time.

Phones

The Chicago area is served by five area codes: (312) in the Loop and downtown, (773) for the rest of the city, (630) for the far western suburbs, (708) for the near western and southern suburbs, and (847) for the northern suburbs. Calls from pay phones are 50 cents. To dial out of Chicago to the suburbs, dial 1, then the appropriate area code followed by the phone number you want to reach. While the initial call to the suburbs costs the same as an intra-city call, keep some change handy. On longer calls you may have to plug in more coins or get disconnected. If you're calling into the city from the suburbs, dial 1, then (312) or (773), followed by the number.

Liquor, Taxes, and Smoking

In Chicago the legal drinking age is 21, and no store may sell alcoholic beverages before noon on Sundays. The local sales tax is 8%, and the combined sales and hotel room tax is 14.9%. City laws require all restaurants to offer nonsmoking sections. In addition, smoking is prohibited in theaters, public buildings, and on public transportation.

How to Avoid Crime and Keep Safe in Public Places

Crime in Chicago

For most folks, Chicago and crime are synonymous. It's mostly left over from the Prohibition era, when bootlegger Al Capone and arch-gangster John Dillinger earned Chicago worldwide notoriety. Go almost anyplace in the world and mention Chicago and the response will likely be a pantomimed machine gun and a "rat-a-tat-tat" flourish.

The truth is, Chicago wasn't all that dangerous for John Q. Public in the 1920s. History shows that only 75 hoodlums went down in gang warfare in 1926—about 10% of today's annual murder count. Sadly, although metropolitan Chicago has about the same population as it did in the Roaring Twenties, the average person today is much more likely to become a crime statistic.

Places to Avoid

Like virtually all large U.S. cities, Chicago has its ghettoes, including (until recently) the nation's most infamous: the Cabrini Green projects, a series of high-rises that once stood as a monument to the failure of mid-twentieth-century urban planning. Located in Chicago's West Side, the housing project was an island of chronically unemployed and underemployed tenants, a segregated slum that was regularly regarded as one of America's worst neighborhoods.

While Cabrini Green is now undergoing mixed-use gentrification, much of the South Side and Near West Side contain areas that most visitors should avoid; exceptions include Chinatown, Hyde Park, and Pullman. On the North Side, glitzy neighborhoods are often next door to areas of high crime, so don't wander too far afield. Often in Chicago, relative safety is a question of day or night; the lakefront, public parks, Loop, and River North are active during the day, but except around restaurants and clubs, are deserted at night. Take a cab or drive directly to nighttime destinations in these areas.

Safe areas at virtually any time of the day or night include the Magnificent Mile and Oak, Rush, and Division Streets in the Gold Coast community. Just stay within well-lighted areas, and keep your eyes peeled for shady- looking characters who may have sinister designs on your purse or billfold. Pickpockets, by the way, are especially active in downtown shopping crowds during the holiday season and on subway trains to and from O'Hare.

Though we recommend that visitors stay away from unsafe public housing projects and other economically deprived areas, keep in mind that crime can happen anywhere. And Chicago, unfortunately, is an innovator when it comes to new ways of victimizing people; this is where carjacking and "smash and grab"—breaking a car window and snatching a purse off the seat—first gained national notoriety. Here are some security procedures that can help you avoid becoming a crime victim.

Crime Prevention Planning

Random violence and street crime are facts of life in any large city. You've got to be cautious and alert and plan ahead. Police are rarely able to actually foil a crime in progress. When you are out and about you must assume that you must use caution because you are on your own; if you run into trouble, it's unlikely that police or anyone else will be able to come to your rescue. You must give some advance thought to the ugly scenarios that might occur, and consider both preventive measures that will keep you out of harm's way and an escape plan just in case.

Not being a victim of street crime sort of parallels the survival of the fittest theory. Just as a lion stalks the weakest member of the antelope herd, muggers and thieves target the easiest victims. Simply put, no matter where you are or what you are doing, you want potential felons to think of you as a bad risk.

On the Street   You seldom represent an appealing target if you are with other people and act alert. Felons gravitate toward the preoccupied, the kind found plodding along staring at the sidewalk, with both arms encumbered by briefcases or packages. Visible jewelry (on either men or women) attracts the wrong kind of attention. Men, keep your billfolds in your front trouser or coat pocket. Women, keep your purses tucked tightly under your arm; if you're wearing a jacket, put it on over your shoulder bag strap.

Carry Two Wallets   If you're really concerned about mugging, this can give you a little peace of mind. Carry one inexpensive wallet, kept in your hip pocket, containing about $20 in cash and some expired credit cards. This is the one you hand over if you're accosted. Your real credit cards and the bulk of whatever cash you have should be in either a money clip or a second wallet hidden elsewhere on your person. Women can carry a fake wallet in their purses, and keep the real one in a pocket or money belt.

If You're Approached   Police will tell you that a felon has the least amount of control over his intended victim during the first few moments of his approach. A good strategy, therefore, is to short-circuit the crime as quickly as possible. If a felon starts by demanding your money, for instance, quickly take out your billfold (preferably your fake one), and hurl it in one direction while you run shouting for help in the opposite direction. Most likely, the felon would rather collect your billfold than pursue you. If you hand over your wallet and just stand there, the felon will likely ask for your watch and jewelry next. If you're a woman, the longer you hang around, the greater your vulnerability to personal injury or rape.

Secondary Crime Scenes   Under no circumstances, police warn, should you ever allow yourself to be taken to another location—a "secondary crime scene" in police jargon. This move, they explain, provides the felon more privacy and consequently more control. A felon can rob you on the street very quickly and efficiently. If he tries to remove you to another location, whether by car or on foot, it certainly indicates that he has more in mind than robbery. Even if the felon has a gun or knife, your chances are infinitely better running away. If the felon grabs your purse, let him have it. If he grabs your jacket, slip out of it. Hanging onto your money or jacket is not worth getting mugged, raped, or murdered.

Don't Believe Anything a Criminal Says   This holds true even if he's telling you something you desperately want to believe, for example, "I won't hurt you if you come with me." No matter how logical or benign he may sound, assume the worst. Always, *always,* break off contact as quickly as possible, even if that means running.

In Public Transportation   When riding a bus, try to take a seat as close to the driver as you can; avoid riding in the back if possible. In fact, many

Chicagoans who depend on public transportation don't ride buses at night (they take a cab). Likewise, on the subway or elevated train, sit near the driver's or attendant's compartment. These people have a phone and can summon help in the event of trouble.

In Cabs   When hailing a cab, you are somewhat vulnerable. Particularly after dusk, call a reliable cab company and stay inside while it dispatches a cab to your door. When your cab arrives, check the driver's certificate, which must, by law, be posted on the dashboard. Address the cabbie by his last name (for example, Mr. Jones) or mention his cab number. This alerts the cab driver that you are going to remember him and/or his cab. Not only will this contribute to your safety, it will keep your cabbie from trying to run up the fare.

If you are comfortable reading maps, familiarize yourself with the most direct route to your destination ahead of time. If you can say, "Pipers Alley movie theater on North Wells via State Street, please," the driver is less likely to take a longer route so he can charge you for extra mileage.

If you need to catch a cab at the train station or at one of the airports, always use the taxi queue. Taxis in the official queue are properly licensed and regulated. Never accept an offer for a cab or limo made by a stranger in the terminal or baggage claim area. At best, you will be significantly overcharged for the ride. At worst, you may be abducted.

Personal Attitude

Although some areas of every city are more dangerous than others, never assume that any area is completely safe. You can be the victim of a crime pretty much anywhere. If you go to a restaurant or night spot, use valet parking or park in a well-lighted lot. Women leaving a restaurant or club alone should never be reluctant to ask to be escorted to their car.

Never let your pride or sense of righteousness and indignation imperil your survival. This is especially difficult for many men, particularly for men in the presence of women. It makes no difference whether you are approached by an aggressive drunk, an imbalanced street person, or an actual felon, the rule is the same: forget your pride and break off contact as quickly as possible. Who cares whether the drunk insulted you, if everyone ends up safely back at the hotel? When you wake up in the hospital with a concussion and your jaw wired shut, it's too late to decide that the drunk's filthy remark wasn't really all that important.

Self-Defense

In a situation where it is impossible to run, you'll need to be prepared to defend yourself. Most police officers insist that a gun or knife is not much use to the average person. More often than not, they say, the weapon will be turned against the victim. Additionally, concealed firearms and knives are illegal in most jurisdictions. The best self-defense device for the average person is Mace. Not only is it legal in most states, it is nonlethal and easy to use.

When you shop for Mace, look for two things: it should be able to fire about eight feet, and it should have a protector cap so it won't go off by mistake in your purse or pocket. Carefully read the directions that come with your device, paying particular attention to how it should be carried and stored, and how long the active ingredients will remain potent. Wearing a rubber glove, test-fire your Mace, making sure that you fire downwind.

When you are out about town, make sure your Mace is someplace easily accessible, say, attached to your keychain. If you are a woman and you keep your Mace on a keychain, avoid the habit of dropping your keys (and your Mace) into the bowels of your purse when you leave your hotel room or your car. *Mace will not do you any good if you have to dig around in your purse for it.* Keep your keys and your Mace in your hand until you have safely reached your destination.

More Things to Avoid

When you do go out, walk with a minimum of two people whenever possible. If you have to walk alone, stay in well-lighted areas that have plenty of people around. And don't walk down alleys. Be careful about whom you ask for directions. (When in doubt, shopkeepers are a good bet.) Don't count your money in public, and carry as little cash as possible. At public phones, if you must say your calling card number to make a long-distance call, don't say it loud enough for strangers around you to hear. Avoid public parks and beaches after dark.

Carjackings

With the surge in carjackings, drivers also need to take special precautions. Keep alert when driving in traffic, and keep your doors locked, with the windows rolled up and the air conditioning on. Leave enough space in front of your car so that you're not blocked in and can make a U-turn if someone approaches your car and starts beating on your windshield. Store your purse or briefcase under your knees or seat when you are driving, rather than on the seat beside you.

Part Six

Getting around Chicago

Driving Your Car: A Really Bad Idea

Four major interstates and rush-hour traffic jams of mythic proportions are some of the unfortunate realities faced by drivers who venture into downtown Chicago on weekdays. Throw in a dearth of on-street parking, astronomical rates at most parking garages, and the in-your-face driving style of most Chicago drivers, and you've got a recipe for driver meltdown.

Yet as the traffic congestion attests, lots of people continue to brave the streets of the Windy City by car every day—and that includes some out-of-town visitors. What if you're one of them?

Time of Day

First-time Chicago drivers who are staying downtown should map out their routes in advance, avoid arriving or departing during rush hour (weekdays 7–9:30 a.m. and 4–7 p.m.), and then plan on leaving the car parked in their hotel garage during most of their stay. Exceptions to the don't-drive rule are weekday evenings and on weekends and holidays.

Parking

Chicago's lack of on-street parking is legendary. If you decide to try your luck at finding a space, however, bring lots of quarters—most meters demand two for 15 minutes, with a two-hour limit (which isn't much time for sight-seeing or attending a business meeting). The fine for parking at an expired meter, by the way, is $30. Be careful and read signs that may restrict parking—Chicago traffic cops are notoriously efficient at handing out tickets and towing illegally parked cars.

While the chances of finding an on-street spot in the Loop on weekdays are virtually nil, you'll have better luck east of the Loop on Congress Parkway between Lake Shore Drive and South Michigan Avenue (behind the Art Institute, facing the lake). Just be prepared to do a lot of circling before snagging a space.

A better idea: Head south of the Loop for one of the many outside commercial parking lots located along State and Wabash Streets south of Congress Parkway. After about 9:30 a.m. you can park the car for about $6 a day. On weekends, finding on-street parking in and around the Loop is usually easy.

Another option that's popular with savvy Chicago drivers is Field Harbor Parking Garage (165 North Field Boulevard at East Randolph Street), an underground parking garage located between the Loop and Lake Michigan, just south of the Chicago River. Parking is cheap ($6 for up to an hour, $7 for up to 10 hours, and $10 for up to 12 hours) and the location is particularly convenient for festivals in Grant Park. Call (312) 938-8989 for directions.

Parking near the Magnificent Mile is another headache-inducing experience; street parking is virtually impossible near this shopping mecca—and that includes evenings and weekends. Most major area hotels have under- or above-ground parking garages; be sure to check when making a reservation.

Farther from downtown, it is generally easier to find a parking spot, although exceptions abound. For example, in popular and hip Old Town, forget about finding street parking on a Friday or Saturday night; even the parking garages fill up. In addition, many neighborhoods have resident-only permit parking that prohibits nonresidents from grabbing scarce parking spaces in the evenings. A final note: When you do find a space, don't leave valuables in your car or trunk.

Insider Tips for Drivers

Many native Chicagoans who own cars routinely use public transportation or taxis to get downtown. They say the hassle and expense of parking just aren't worth it. It's especially true during the holidays, when out-of-towners and suburbanites converge on the city to shop—and parking the car for a long evening of shopping and enjoying the lights can cost $12–$15.

Yet because Chicago is relatively easy to navigate and traffic levels drop off significantly after rush hour and on weekends, sometimes driving makes sense—at least, if you've already got a car. For example, if you're going out to dinner, call ahead and see if the restaurant offers valet parking (as more and more Chicago eateries do) or is close to a commercial parking lot. In addition, some out-of-the-way museums provide convenient parking; the Museum of Science and Industry in Hyde Park is the best example.

Subterranean Chicago

Adventurous drivers can explore subterranean Lower Wacker Drive and Lower Michigan Avenue. (Actually, they're at lake level; Chicago's downtown streets were elevated before the Civil War.) They're generally less congested than their surface counterparts, but are a bit scary for drivers making the descent for the first time. Drawbacks include lots of truck traffic, poor signage, and underground murkiness; pluses include quick access to the Eisenhower Expressway and views of locations used in popular films such as *The Untouchables* and *Code of Silence.*

Public Transportation

The CTA

While Chicagoans may grouse about bus, subway, and train service, out-of-towners are usually impressed by the extensive public transportation system operated by the **Chicago Transit Authority** (CTA). So are we.

True, much of the system's infrastructure is aging, but many CTA routes run 24 hours a day, crisscrossing the city and providing service to a number of bordering suburbs. And consider the alternative: battling Chicago's epic traffic jams in a car.

For the most part CTA service is clean and dependable, even though it's an uneven mix of the sleek and seedy as some routes get upgraded while others are bypassed. Most routes take visitors to the places they want to be—or at least within a few blocks. (A notable exception is the lack of train service to McCormick Place.) *Warning:* After evening rush hour, for safety's sake don't use public transportation. Either drive or take a cab.

The El

For visitors, the most important and easiest-to-master segment of CTA service is rapid transit—what is usually called "the subway" in other cities. But in Chicago, it's called "the El" (for "elevated"), although large parts of the train system run underground or down the middle of expressways. Never mind: The entire train system is known as the El.

Chicago currently boasts seven train routes that run north, northeast, east, southeast, and south from downtown. The Brown (Ravenswood), Purple (Evanston), and Orange (Midway) lines are elevated, while the Red (Howard-Dan Ryan), Blue (O'Hare-Congress-Douglas), and Yellow (Skokie) line trains run underground or on the surface. The Green Line is an elevated line linking Jackson Park (south), the Loop, and Lake Street (east).

Downtown, the El defines the Loop as it circles Chicago's core financial and retail district; it's obvious that this part of the system is more than 100 years old as the trains rattle, shake, and roar overhead. The aging, peeling structures that hold the trains up don't inspire much confidence in most first-time visitors. Just think of the rickety system as a Chicago landmark and a bit of 19th-century charm.

Fares

Cash fares for the train are $1.50 ($0.75 for children ages 7–11). Don't worry about exact fare; attendants are on hand (except at stations on the Orange Line on the Southwest Side, where token vending machines accept $1, $5, and $10 bills). Attendants, however, won't change a $20 bill. Transfers cost $0.30 ($0.15 for children), must be purchased when you pay your fare, and allow two more rides within two hours—but not on the route you started on. They also allow transfers to a bus route (and vice versa).

If you plan to use the El or buses a lot during your stay in Chicago, consider purchasing a one-, two-, three-, or five-day visitor pass that allows unlimited rides. The passes range in price from $5 (one day) to $18 (five days) and are sold at both airports, Amtrak at Union Station, visitor information centers, Hot Tix, and most museums and major attractions.

Another option: In mid-1997, the CTA introduced a new electronic fare card system that allows you to purchase $1.50 to $100 worth of rides on the system's trains and buses, with a bonus of $1 worth for every $10 purchased. You can buy the fare cards at Transit Card machines installed in the stations as well as from the locations mentioned above.

Train Line Names

The seven El lines currently in operation are color coded, such as the Red Line. Watch out, though—some signs at stations and on the trains themselves have were never changed to show the color names. So it's good to know that the Red Line is also called the Howard-Dan Ryan line (the names identify the two ends of the line).

Trains run every 3 to 12 minutes during rush hours; every 6 to 15 minutes midday, early evening, and weekends; and every 6 to 20 minutes in the later evening. From 1:30 to 4:30 a.m. only four lines operate: the Red Line (every 15 minutes), the Purple Line (every 30 to 45 minutes), and the Blue and Green Lines (every 30 to 60 minutes). Late at night, you should take a cab.

Riding the El

In the Loop, finding the stations is easy: just look up. Then climb the rickety stairs up to the platform, pay the fare, and enjoy the weather as you await the next train—the elevated stations are partially covered, but not enclosed. To determine the direction of the train you want, use the maps displayed and the signs posted overhead and on columns.

Taking the Plunge in the Loop

Figuring out which lines are elevated and which lines are underground—and how they all interconnect—is a headache-inducing experience in the Loop, where all the El lines converge. Here's some help: On the elevated lines circling the Loop, as you face north, the Orange Line to Midway runs counterclockwise and the Brown Line to Ravenswood runs clockwise; at the Clark/Lake, State/Lake, Adams/Wabash, and LaSalle/Van Buren stations riders can transfer to other lines (at no extra charge), including the underground Blue Line to O'Hare and the Red Line to the North Side.

Our advice: To get familiar with the system, take the plunge and board the elevated Brown (Ravenswood) El in the Loop. The views as you circle the downtown area are spectacular. Next, the train passes the Merchandise Mart and continues northwest.

If it's a nice day, continue north to, say, the Diversey station; get off the train and reboard the next one south. The drop-dead view of the approaching Chicago skyline that unfolds as you return downtown should not be missed. At $1.50, the ride is one of the best tourist bargains in town. If you haven't had your fill of aerial views of Chicago, board the Orange Line and take the elevated train to Midway Airport and back (a half-hour ride one-way).

To reach the platform at underground stations, riders descend a set of narrow stairs to the (often) seedy stations; the first time feels much like a descent to Hades as you sink below sidewalk level into a grungy, dilapidated station. After paying the fare, descend to the next level and the platform, which is usually narrow, littered, not climate-controlled, and very noisy when a train comes through. The trains themselves, however, are usually clean and litter- and graffiti-free (but not carpeted).

Buses

Chicago's bus system is massive and complicated—and better left to commuters. Buses are also slower than trains, especially in Chicago's dense traffic. Yet a few bus lines that follow relatively unconvoluted routes are invaluable to visitors staying downtown—particularly those visitors lodging in a hotel along the subway-less Magnificent Mile. We don't recommend that visitors on vacation use the bus system exclusively when in town, but we do think judicious use of buses can save tourists, business travelers, and conventioneers a lot of shoe leather, not to mention cab fares or parking fees.

Examples: Though it's not a long walk to the below-ground Red Line train station at State and Chicago Streets from hotels on North Michigan Avenue, it's often more convenient to grab one of the many buses going up and down the Magnificent Mile. That's especially true when it is cold, raining, windy, snowing, or any combination of the above.

Buses #145, #146, and #151 (among others) provide easy, quick access south to the Loop and attractions such as the Field Museum along Lake Michigan. The #36 bus that goes north along State and Clark Streets provides easy access to Lincoln Park and Old Town. The #6 express bus, which can be boarded at State and Lake Streets in the Loop, quickly traverses the South Side to the Museum of Science and Industry (which doesn't have a convenient El station). The #56 bus heads out Milwaukee Avenue through Chicago's extensive Polish neighborhoods; think of it as an ethnic field trip. Buses #29, #56, #65, and #66 stop at Navy Pier, Chicago's most popular attraction.

Which Bus?

To get exact, efficient directions for the bus and El routes, check with your hotel concierge or call 836-7000 from anywhere in the Chicago area between 5 a.m. and 1 a.m. every day. CTA personnel who answer the phones are polite and helpful; just tell them where you are and where you want to go and they'll give you exact directions on routes and transfers (if any). Make sure you've got pencil and paper handy to write down the directions. If you have more lead time, you can also get extensive route maps and directions from the CTA's website, **www.transitchicago.com.**

More Information on Buses

Bus fares are $1.50 ($0.75 for children ages 7–11); a transfer is $0.30. Unlike the El, you need either exact change or a token to ride the bus; dollar bills are okay, but the drivers don't make change. If you need a transfer, purchase it when you board. (You can use the transfer to enter the El system or board a bus on a different route twice within two hours.) In our experience, Chicago bus drivers are friendly and will answer any questions you have about reaching your intended destination.

Two warnings, though, about riding Chicago's buses: First, rush-hour crowds, especially along hectic Michigan Avenue, are mind-boggling, and often you'll have to wait for a bus to come along that's not packed full. Second, after the evening rush hour, for safety's sake either drive or take a cab.

Taxis

In Chicago, taxis are plentiful and constitute one of the primary modes of transportation in this spread-out city. Along major thoroughfares it's easy to hail a cab, with the possible exception of rush hours and when the weather has just turned nasty (and you most need one). Stands in front of major hotels are another place to find a taxi.

Chicago's taxi fare system is straightforward and similar to New York City's. The fare is based on both distance and time—which means a $3.50 fare at non–rush hour can double when traffic is slow and heavy. The base charge is $1.50 and a three-mile jaunt downtown from, say, a hotel along the Magnificent Mile or from McCormick Place typically will run about $5 (non–rush hour). If you need to summon a cab, ask your hotel doorman or call a major cab company that offers 24-hour service.

CHICAGO'S MAJOR CAB AND LIMOUSINE COMPANIES

American United Cab	(773) 248-7600
Checker Cab	(312) 243-2537
Chicago Limousines	(800) 543-5466
Crown Cars & Limousines	(800) 876-7725
RightChoice Limousine Service	(312) 654-LIMO
Yellow Cab	(312) TAXI-CAB

Walking

While Chicago is a huge city stretching about 30 miles north and south along Lake Michigan and 15 miles to the west, the major areas of interest to visitors are concentrated in a few fairly compact areas: the Loop, the Magnificent Mile along North Michigan Avenue (also called Streeterville), Grant Park (a campus-like setting that's home to some of the city's best museums), and the Near North Side (with a wide range of shopping, dining, and night life options). Plus, there isn't a hill for miles around. Given good weather and a relaxed schedule, walking is the primary mode of discovering the city.

Great places to take a walk or a stroll include the Loop; Grant Park (great views of the skyline, the lake, and many museums), anywhere along the bike and jogging path that follows the Lake Michigan shoreline; the Gold Coast (where Chicago's richest citizens have lived since the 1890s); the Magnificent Mile (nearly peerless window shopping); and, just west of the city line, Oak Park (with 25 homes, churches, and fountains designed by Frank Lloyd Wright). Chicago's varied ethnic neighborhoods such as Andersonville (a charming mix of Swedish and Middle Eastern) are also great walking destinations.

Pedways

In addition, downtown is honeycombed with an underground system of pedestrian walkways that makes the Windy City a lot easier to negotiate for walkers when the weather is, well, windy. The "pedways" link train stations and major buildings (such as the State of Illinois Center, Marshall Field's, the Chicago Cultural Center, and the Prudential Building). Visitors seeking a mole's-eye view of the city will even find an occasional shop or cafe as they explore the still-growing underground walkway. Hours are 6:30 a.m. to 6 p.m., Monday through Friday.

Part Seven

Sight-Seeing Tips and Tours

Touring Chicago

Visitors to Chicago have a wealth of sight-seeing options to choose from. Consider: Not only does Chicago offer a wide selection of world-class museums—the city itself is a museum. The Loop and the lakefront encompass the world's largest collection of outdoor modern architecture. Turn any corner in the Loop and you're confronted with yet another structural, aesthetic, or technical innovation in building design.

There's more. Tourists, professionals, and residents clog Chicago's downtown streets year round to savor its stunning skyline, lakefront, art, history, shopping, cultural attractions, and festivals. Inevitably, out-of-towners rub shoulders with the city's outspoken (and often humorous) natives, most of whom are remarkably friendly to visitors. Here are tips to help first-time visitors discover this sprawling, dynamic city.

Taking an Orientation Tour

Visitors to Chicago can't help but notice the regular procession of open-air tour buses—"motorized trolleys" is probably a more accurate term—that prowl Michigan Avenue, the Loop, and the museums and attractions along the lakeshore. **The Chicago Trolley Co.** offers regularly scheduled shuttle buses that drop off and pick up paying customers along a route that includes the town's most popular attractions. Between stops, passengers listen to a tour guide talk about the city's cataclysmic fire of 1871, machine gun–toting gangsters, and spectacular architecture.

The guides also suggest good places to eat and drop tidbits of interesting—and often funny—Chicago trivia. Examples you're likely to hear include why Chicago was branded "The Windy City" by New York newspapers (because of blowhard politicians bragging about the city) and the best places to go for an Oprah sighting (her studio and the Crate & Barrel on Michigan Avenue).

Our advice: If this is your first visit to Chicago, take one of the tours early in your trip. Here's why: Seen from the air, Chicago is surprisingly contained. The city's towers rise up from the lakeside with a stunning vertical thrust, but then give way to the prairie flatness that characterizes the Midwest. Yet once on the ground, visitors discover that the city is too vast to get a quick handle on—and that includes its downtown. Although it's possible to embark on a walking tour that includes River North, the Magnificent Mile, the Loop, Grant Park, and Chicago's major museums, you'll murder your feet—and your enthusiasm for touring—in the process.

Think of the narrated Chicago shuttle-bus tours as an educational system that not only gets you to the most well-known attractions but also provides a timely education on the city's history and scope. (There's a downside to the narrator's spiel, too: a confusing litany of the skyscraper architects' names and a few too many references to the Roaring Twenties gangsters.)

The money you pay for your ticket allows unlimited reboarding privileges for that day, so you can get off at any scheduled stop to tour, eat, shop, or explore, and reboard a later bus. You can also determine which sights may warrant another day of exploration. Tour buses run about every 20 minutes or so, and boarding locations include the city's most popular downtown attractions. You can board at any stop along the route and pay the driver.

Chicago Trolley features San Francisco–style "trolleys" and a tour guide; the complete tour lasts about an hour and 20 minutes. Heated in the winter and open air in the summer, the trolleys operate rain or shine from 9:30 a.m. to 5 p.m. daily (hours are longer in the summer).

The tour buses make 16 stops: Sears Tower, Marshall Field's, the Chicago Art Institute, Field Museum, Adler Planetarium, the Museum of Science and Industry, Navy Pier, the Historic Water Tower, Michigan Avenue, Wacker Drive, the Hard Rock Cafe and other stops in River North, and House of Blues. Hint: If you didn't drive to Chicago and don't have a car, make this your chance to visit the popular Museum of Science and Industry; it's way off the beaten track and isn't near a train line. Getting off now can save on cab fare or navigating Chicago's bus system.

Chicago Trolley tickets are $20 for adults, $17 for seniors, and $10 for children ages 3–11. Youngsters can use their ticket to ride the trolley for free the next day; a two-day ticket for adults is $25 (Sunday–Thursday only) and family package for 2 adults and 2 children under 12 runs $54. Adults who only wish to tour without reboarding privileges can purchase a "city tour" ticket for $17 ($8 for children). For more information, call (773) 648-5000.

Architecture and Boat Tours

It's often said that in Chicago, architecture is a spectator sport. While an introductory bus tour of downtown Chicago gives first-time visitors a sense of the city's layout and a quick glimpse of Chicago architecture, things look different from the Chicago River. During the warmer months, riverboats glide down the Chicago River for a dockside view of downtown architecture and historical sites. And the Loop takes on a whole new perspective after embarking on an eye-opening walking tour with a docent pointing out and explaining the modern architectural trends on display in Chicago's downtown.

Boat Tours

Once scorned as a sewage canal, today the Chicago River offers visitors stunning views of the city's best buildings, including the Sears Tower, the Civic Opera Building on Wacker Drive, the IBM Building (Mies van der Rohe's last major Chicago structure), and the 1989 NBC Tower.

On downtown boat tours, tour guides weave history and technology as they tell the story of the Great Chicago Fire of 1871 and the role of the structural iron frame in rebuilding the city. The result was the skyscraper and a truly modern style unencumbered by any allegiance to the past.

Choosing a Boat Tour   Visitors can choose from several boat-touring companies that sail on 90-minute narrated cruises that either take them up the Chicago River or venture on Lake Michigan for a view of the city's fabled skyline. All the modern, motorized ships are enclosed and air conditioned, and they offer beverage services while en route; the cruises are offered spring through fall. Tours offered by the **Chicago Architecture Foundation** provide more focus on Chicago's spectacular buildings and the city's role as a leader in modern urban architecture; these trips are guaranteed to please culture vultures (see more details below). Boat tours leaving North Pier—just north of the Chicago River on the lake—offer lake and river tours with an emphasis on architecture or the town's colorful history. **Mercury Tours** and **Wendella Sightseeing Boats,** which board near the Michigan Avenue Bridge over the Chicago River, also offer a variety of tours on the lake and river and will appeal to general tourists who don't need to hear another word about Frank Lloyd Wright. Still can't make up your mind? Simply pick a cruise that best fits your schedule.

Chicago Architecture Foundation Tours

The Chicago Architecture Foundation offers 57 different tours by foot, bus, and boat. Each tour is led by a volunteer from an army of about 400 docents (tour guides). The tour leaders are witty, incredibly informed, and contagiously enthusiastic about Chicago architecture. These tours are far more detailed and enjoyable than any we could give you in these pages. Our advice: Go on at least one Foundation tour during your visit. Better yet, take a walking tour of the Loop *and* an architectural boat tour. You won't regret it.

By Boat *Chicago's First Lady* and *Chicago's Little Lady* push off from the southwest corner of Michigan Avenue and Wacker Drive for the CAF **Architecture River Cruise.** The yachts, which offer outside seating on the upper deck and air-conditioned interior seating, depart 3–6 times daily, June–November, for 90-minute tours; daily in May and November (3 times daily on weekends); tickets are $21on weekdays, $23 on weekends and holidays. In addition to a unique river perspective on Chicago architecture, you'll see the riverside railway that delivers newsprint to the *Sun-Times* and get a boater's-eye perspective of the city's bridges. For more information call (312) 922-TOUR, or visit **www.architecture.org.** For reservations, call (312) 922-3432.

By Foot Two-hour walking tours of the Loop and bus excursions to Chicago's neighborhoods start at the Foundation's headquarters and gift shop, 224 South Michigan Avenue (across from the Chicago Art Institute). The two-hour Loop walking tours excellently complement the boat tour, allowing you to see the buildings from street level, as well as letting you ogle some lobbies that are every bit as spectacular as the buildings' exteriors. Tours cost $10 per person and are offered daily on a varying schedule throughout the year. For more information, call (312) 922-TOUR, or visit **www.architecture.org.** For reservations, call (312) 922-3432.

More CAF Tours In addition to Loop walking tours and boat cruises, CAF offers the three-hour **Chicago Architecture Highlights by Bus** tour (March–November, every Saturday at 9:30 a.m.; $25 per person) and **Frank Lloyd Wright by Bus** tours (May–October, first Saturday of the month at 9:30 a.m.; $25). For more information, call (312) 922-TOUR, or visit **www.architecture.org.** For reservations, call (312) 922-3432.

Historical and Architectural Lake and River Cruises from North Pier

Boat tours depart from North Pier daily May through September for cruises on the Chicago River and Lake Michigan. On the historical cruise, visitors pass the spot where du Sable first established a trading post among the local native Americans and where Fort Dearborn stood to protect the community. The tour also passes through the heart of the city, where the fire of 1871 reduced buildings to ash at a rate of 65 acres an hour.

On Lake Michigan the boat passes Buckingham Fountain, where the Columbian Exposition of 1893 left its legacy of the Field Museum, Shedd Aquarium, Adler Planetarium, and Museum of Science and

Industry. But the highlight of the cruise is a view of the magnificent skyline of Chicago, a profile recognized around the world.

Architectural cruises take visitors downtown for up-close views of Chicago's most famous buildings, including the Tribune Tower, the Merchandise Mart, Lake Point Tower, and, of course, the Sears Tower, the third-tallest office building in the world. Visitors also see the spot near the Kinzie Street Bridge where the Chicago River flooded an old railroad freight tunnel in April 1992, shutting down the Loop and causing hundreds of millions of dollars in damage.

The 90-minute cruises leave North Pier daily on the hour, 9 a.m.–4 p.m., May–September, and on a reduced schedule in October. Prices are $23 for adults, $21 for seniors, and $14 for children and students ages 7–18. For more information and reservations (recommended), call (312) 527-1977.

Other Boat Cruises

Mercury Tours offers architectural, historical, and maritime sights tours May through September from the lower level and southwest corner of the Michigan Avenue Bridge over the Chicago River (at Wacker Drive). Cruises range from one to two hours in length, each with continuous commentary. Tours depart throughout the day from morning to late evening; prices range from $14 to $17 for adults and $7.50 for children. Tickets go on sale an hour before the cruise (no reservations necessary). For more information, call (312) 332-1353.

Wendella Sightseeing Boats offers cruises on the Chicago River and along the lakefront mid-April through mid-October. Lake-only tours lasting an hour are $13 for adults and $6.50 for children ages 11 and under, and the 90-minute lake and river tours cost $15 for adults and $7.50 for children. Two-hour river and lake tours in the evening feature a color light show at Buckingham Fountain; prices are $17 for adults and $8.50 for children. Tours leave throughout the day and evening from the base of the Wrigley Building at the northwest corner of the Michigan Avenue Bridge over the Chicago River. For more information, call (312) 337-1446.

Specialized Tours

American Sightseeing offers several general-interest tours (as opposed to CAF bus tours, which focus on architecture) around the city and special tours on architecture highlights and specific areas (such as the two-hour North Side Tour; $17 for adults and $9 for children ages 5–11). The Grand Tour takes visitors to most of Chicago's parks and most scenic locations, as well as the Loop, the Magnificent Mile, Wrigley Field, Lincoln Park Conservatory, the Adler Planetarium, the University of

Chicago campus, and the Museum of Science and Industry. The cost of the four-hour tour is $28 for adults and $14 for children.

American Sightseeing bus tours start at the Palmer House in the Loop (17 East Monroe Street). Unlike the hard benches on the "trolley" tours, the buses feature comfortable reclining seats, overhead lights, and air conditioning. For schedules, hotel pickup, and more information, call (312) 251-3100 or (800) 621-4153.

Gangsters and Ghosts

Would-be ghostbusters can explore Chicago's spooky sights on **Supernatural Tours.** The narrated bus tours highlight the city's heritage of ghost stories and folklore, weird tales, murder sites, cemeteries, gangsters, pubs, and restaurants. Tours are scheduled on select weekends from 7 p.m. to midnight; the cost is $33 per person, and reservations are required. The trips depart from the Goose Island Brewery Restaurant in River North; for more information and scheduled departures, call (708) 499-0300.

Though some may consider it inappropriate to emphasize Chicago's gangster past, the folks at **Untouchable Tours** say baloney. Two guys in pinstripe suits and fedoras escort visitors on a two-hour bus tour of Chicago's notorious yesteryear, including the site of Al Capone's former headquarters, the Biograph Theater on Lincoln Avenue (where Dillinger was shot), and the site of the St. Valentine's Day Massacre on Clark Street. The popular tour, led by actor-guides, is both historically correct and a crowd pleaser, especially for youngsters.

Tours are scheduled Monday through Saturday at 10 a.m., as well as Friday evenings at 7:30 p.m., Saturdays at 5 p.m., and Sundays at 11 a.m. and 2 p.m. There is also a 1 p.m. option on Thursdays, Fridays, and Saturdays. Tours depart from 610 North Clark Street, in front of the Rock 'n' Roll McDonald's in River North. The cost is $22 for adults and $16 for children and reservations are strongly recommended; call (773) 881-1195.

Airplanes and a Yacht

For a bird's-eye view of the city, head toward Meigs Field (south of Grant Park on Lake Michigan) and book a flight on **Chicago By Air.** Thirty-minute aero tours of Chicago in a single-engine Cessna 172 are $225 for two. A 45-minute champagne tour is $250 per couple. For reservations, call (708) 524-1172 between 6 a.m. and 10 p.m. daily.

While not strictly speaking a guided tour, Lake Michigan cruises on the *Odyssey* feature fine dining, live music, dancing, and breathtaking views of Chicago's skyline. Our local experts report cruising on the sleek and elegant yacht is a great way to see the city, and the operation is first-rate. Best bet: a sunset dinner cruise. Three-hour dinner cruises start at $80 per person (not including tax and gratuity) and two-hour lunch cruises start at $35. Odyssey departs from Navy Pier throughout the year. For more information and reservations, call (888) 741-0282.

Carriage Rides

An easy and fun way to see downtown Chicago is by horse and buggy. **The Noble Horse** at the southwest corner of Michigan Avenue and Chicago Street provides horse-drawn carriage rides weekdays from 10 a.m. to 4 p.m. and 7 p.m. to midnight; weekends from 10 a.m. to 1 a.m. The cost is $30 per half hour for up to four adults and $35 per half hour for five or six adults. Reservations aren't necessary; call (312) 266-7878 for more information.

The **Antique Coach & Carriage Company** offers rides daily from the southeast corner of Michigan Avenue and Huron Street. Hours are 6:30 p.m. to 1 a.m. Monday through Thursday; 6:30 p.m. to 2 a.m. Fridays; 1 p.m. to 2 a.m. Saturdays; and 1 p.m. to 1 a.m. Sundays. The cost is $35 per half-hour. For more information, call (773) 735-9400.

Touring on Your Own: Our Favorite Itineraries

If your time is limited and you want to experience the best of Chicago in a day or two, here are some suggested itineraries. The schedules assume you're staying at a downtown hotel, have already eaten breakfast, and are ready to go by around 9 a.m.

Day One

1. Tour downtown on one of the open-air shuttle bus services with unlimited reboarding privileges for the day. If the weather's clear, get off at the **Sears Tower** and check out the view. Then catch the next shuttle.

2. Pick one: Explore the **Shedd Aquarium** or the **Adler Planetarium** (they're close together). Then back on the bus.

3. Next stop is **Navy Pier** and lunch at the **Navy Pier Beer Garden** or **Charlie's Ale House** (featuring 38 different types of beer).

4. Next, climb aboard for a scenic, 30-minute skyline cruise on **Lake Michigan** that leaves Navy Pier every half hour in warm weather.

5. After the boat ride, take the shuttle bus to the **Historic Water Tower** on North Michigan Avenue. Explore the shops along **North Michigan Avenue** (one of the world's great shopping streets) and stop at the **Terra Museum of American Art** or the new **Museum of Contemporary Art.**

6. Dinner at a restaurant in **River North.** Afterward, listen to the real thing at **Blue Chicago** (937 North State Street), a blues bar with a roster of the city's finest musicians.

7. Finish the evening with a visit to the **John Hancock Center Observatory** for a knockout view of the city and beyond.

Day Two

1. Sleep in—but not too late. You don't want to miss the 10 a.m. Chicago Architecture Foundation walking tour of **the Loop.**

2. For lunch, sample the Wienerschnitzel or other German fare at the **Berghoff Restaurant** (17 West Adams Street), a Chicago institution. Then jump on the Ravenswood El for a ride around the Loop; take it north past the Merchandise Mart and catch the next train back for some terrific views of the city.

3. Explore the **Art Institute of Chicago.** Try to catch the free tour that begins daily at 2 p.m. near the Grand Staircase.

4. Reward the kids with a trip to the **Chicago Children's Museum** at Navy Pier. Or explore the other attractions—including a knockout view of the skyline—from this recently renovated Chicago landmark.

5. Dinner in a restaurant at Navy Pier. Two of the best are **Riva** and **Widow Newton's Tavern.**

6. An evening of improvisational comedy at **The Second City** (1616 North Wells Street).

If You've Got More Time ...

If you're spending more than two days in town or if this is not your first visit, consider some of these options for an in-depth Chicago experience.

1. Explore one of Chicago's many neighborhoods beyond the Loop. Suggestions: **Hyde Park** has the **University of Chicago** and several museums; shop and eat lunch in **Chinatown; Andersonville** features an eclectic mix of Swedish and Middle Eastern shops, and inexpensive ethnic restaurants.

2. **Oak Park,** just west of the city line, boasts two famous native sons: architect Frank Lloyd Wright and Nobel-winning novelist Ernest Hemingway. Spend a morning or afternoon learning more about them.

3. Two Chicago museums are so large that each requires a full day: the **Field Museum** and the **Museum of Science and Industry**.

4. Stretch your legs along the **Gold Coast,** where Chicago's wealthiest residents have made their homes for 100 years; it's just north of the Magnificent Mile. Or rent a bike and ride the path along **Lake Michigan.**

5. Go to a play. Chicago boasts well more than 100 active theater companies.

6. Kick back and enjoy a summer festival in **Grant Park.**

7. Spend a few hours browsing the art galleries in **River North.**

8. Check out **Marshall Field's** on State Street.

9. Attend a concert by the **Chicago Symphony Orchestra,** consistently rated one of the best orchestras in the world.

10. Root for the **Cubs** at **Wrigley Field,** the **White Sox** at **Comiskey Park,** or the **Bulls** or **Blackhawks** at **United Center.**

Exploring Chicago's Neighborhoods

Chicago is a big city—the country's third largest, America's Third Coast. You will hear again and again that it is a city of neighborhoods and, in truth, it is. The city's enviable vitality, rich architectural history, and cultural diversity are all found in the wide variety of ethnic enclaves—some mixed and some not—called neighborhoods.

What follows is not a comprehensive guide to Chicago's many neighborhoods, since the city officially claims 77 community areas, but our suggestions for dipping in and sampling the remarkably diverse array of architecture, cuisine, history, and culture that defines Chicago.

Taking an extended ride on the Ravenswood El, for instance, permits you to survey the spectacle of Chicago's neighborhoods—and back porches and rooftop graffiti—without getting your feet wet. (For route and fare information on CTA and Metra, call (312) 836-7000.) But apart from a bike ride along the lakefront, Chicago is a city best explored on foot. You can use the El, the bus system, or a car to get there, but in almost every case, we'd recommend stepping out for a stroll to get the feel and flavor of these neighborhoods.

Our sampling tour of Chicago neighborhoods starts in the north and generally flows south along the lake with several excursions to the northwest and southwest.

Andersonville (Zone 1)

You may register shock at the notion of "Swede-town" in Chicago, but amble north along Clark Street from Foster and you'll see Swedish flags flying, find the **Swedish American Museum** (5211 North Clark Street), and be tempted to savor excellent coffee cakes and pastries at the **Swedish Bakery** (5348 North Clark) or Swedish pancakes and limpa bread at **Svea Restaurant** (5236 North Clark). The cinnamon rolls from **Ann Sather's Restaurant** (5207 North Clark) are known to be addictive. At least you can buy a boxed dozen to take home.

Yet Andersonville, like most Chicago neighborhoods, is a mixing and melting pot. The well-kept red brick two-flats on the streets fanning east from Clark have become a new mecca for gays and lesbians, and the Clark Street strip features a number of feminist stores and shops, such as **Women & Children First Bookstore** (5233 North Clark), with its wide selection of books by women. Along Clark, you'll also find several thrift shops patronized by veteran deal-finders and **Reza's,** a Persian/Mediterranean restaurant (5255 North Clark).

To get there: Take the CTA Red Line (Howard) to the Berwyn station and then walk west on Foster about four blocks or transfer to the #92 Foster bus at the station.

By car from the Loop, drive north on Lake Shore Drive to the Foster exit and head west to Clark Street. There's metered parking along Clark or free parking on the side streets.

Devon Avenue (Zone 1)

On a Friday night along Devon Avenue you're likely to see Orthodox Jews in dark suits and black hats heading home from synagogue on the same sidewalks as Indians in bright, flowing saris. Mixed among the kosher butchers and Pakistani groceries on the stretch from Western (2400 West Devon Avenue) to the north branch of the Chicago River (3200 West Devon Avenue) is a newer sprinkling of Thai and Korean shops and restaurants. Truly, this is where the melting pot flows from *challah* to *naan* to *satay.*

You can visit **Rosenblum's World of Judaica** (2906 West Devon) for a treatise on Jewish life or **Taj Sari Palace** (2553 West Devon) for saris of all colors and styles. **Gitel's Kosher Pastry Shop** (2745 West Devon) and **Tel-Aviv Kosher Bakery** (2944 West Devon) sell the traditional Sabbath challah. For decent kosher restaurants, try **Mi Tsu Yun** (3010 West Devon) or **Jerusalem Kosher Restaurant** (3014 West Devon). **Viceroy of India** (2518 West Devon) comes highly rated for its curries and breads, and **Udupi Palace** (2543 West Devon) serves up South Indian vegetarian meals. Newer on the block is **Tiffin, the Indian Kitchen** (2536 West Devon).

Keep in mind that many stores close early on Friday night and remain closed on Saturday for the Jewish Sabbath.

To get there Take the CTA Red Line (Howard) north to Loyola, then transfer to a westbound #155 Devon Avenue bus.

By car from the Loop, drive north on Lake Shore Drive. At its northern end, take Ridge (west) to Devon and turn left (west); or take the Kennedy Expressway (I-90/94) north, then merge onto the Edens Expressway (I-94), exit at Petersen heading east and turn north (left) on Kedzie to Devon.

Uptown (Zone I)

One of Chicago's newer melting pots, Uptown, stretches north from Irving Park Road to Foster and west from the lakefront to Ashland. Though it has a decidedly seedy appearance in certain places where the once-magnificent homes have been neglected and allowed to deteriorate, other parts of Uptown bubble with vitality. Pockets of elegance remain in the huge homes that line Hutchinson Street and Castlewood Terrace. The community near Broadway and Argyle, often called New Chinatown, is in fact a brimming mix of Vietnamese, Laotian, Chinese, Cambodian, and Thai immigrants. You'll find Asian groceries, bakeries, and gift shops, barbecued ducks hanging in shop windows, and a profusion of restaurants. Try **Ha Mien** (4920 North Sheridan Road) for excellent Vietnamese fare or **Furama** (4936 North Broadway) for dim sum.

The **Green Mill Cocktail Lounge** (4802 North Broadway) offers jazz and Sunday night poetry slams of national renown each week.

Stray from the Broadway/Argyle axis and you'll quickly see the grubbier parts of Uptown; don't try it alone or on foot after dark.

To get there The CTA Red Line (Howard) stops at Argyle Street, where there's a $100,000 pagoda over the station.

By car from the Loop, drive north along Lake Shore Drive, exit at Lawrence (4800 North), head west to Broadway, then north to Argyle.

Lincoln Square (Zone I)

Illinois is Lincoln land, as the city's five outdoor "Abe" statues and numerous place names attest. Here, in the area known as Lincoln Square, his statue stands where Lincoln, Lawrence, and Western Avenues converge. The centerpiece of Lincoln Square is the small shopping area—virtually a pedestrian mall—along the 4700 block of Lincoln Avenue. Stores featuring Tirolean clothes and **Meyer's Delicatessen,** where the first language is often German, give the place a decided European feel. Stop in at **Merz Apothecary** (4716 North Lincoln Avenue) for imported soaps or any homeopathic remedies you might need. The light, airy space of **Cafe Selmarie,** just off the square, is a favorite place for locals to relax with coffee and pastries to threaten any waistline. Check out the wonderful Louis Sullivan facade of the **Kelmscott Building** (4611 North Lincoln Avenue) and the periodicals section—and modern design—of the **Conrad Sulzer Library** (4455 North Lincoln). **Fine Wine Brokers** (4621 North Lincoln) bills itself as a European-style wine merchant. The large wall mural at 4662 North Lincoln depicts scenes from the German countryside.

Lincoln Square's German residents are nestled against new Greektown west of the mall along Lawrence Avenue between Talman and Maplewood. **St. Demetrios Orthodox Church,** a 1928 basilica-style structure at 2727 West Winona serves the Greek community. **St. Matthias,** an 1887 German church, is at 2310 West Ainslie.

To get there Take the CTA Brown Line (Ravenswood) to the Western Avenue stop (Monday–Saturday until mid-evening; on Sunday, take the Red Line to Belmont and transfer to the Brown Line there) or the #11 bus, which connects the Loop with Lincoln Square, though the ride takes several months . . .

By car, take Lake Shore Drive north, exit at Lawrence Avenue (4800 North) and head west to Western Avenue (2400 West). There's metered parking on Lincoln Avenue or a lot at Leland next to the El station.

Lakeview/Wrigleyville (Zone 1)

Elderly Jews ensconced in lakefront condos, yuppies renovating graystones, gays and lesbians congregating at bars and bookstores—you name it, Lakeview's got vitality, history, espresso galore. Even the ivy-walled home of the ever-hapless, ardently supported Chicago Cubs—**Wrigley Field**—is a real neighborhood ballpark where fans stream in from the Addison El stop and those in the know watch from the roofs of nearby three-flats. (Don't be afraid to try for day-of-game tickets at the window.)

The remaining mansions along Hawthorne Place (a one-way street heading east between Broadway and Sheridan) give a sense of stately lakeside grandeur. The facing rows of townhouses on Alta Vista Terrace (1054 West between Byron and Grace Streets north of Wrigley Field) are mirror images.

Locals flock to **Ann Sather's Restaurant** (929 West Belmont Avenue, a branch of the one in Andersonville), drawn by the irresistible lure of addictive cinnamon rolls and well-prepared, moderately priced food. You'll find thrift shops, hip shops, bookstores, and espresso on nearly every corner, including the pungent smell of beans roasting at the **Coffee & Tea Exchange** (3311 North Broadway), one of the city's finest purveyors of coffee and equipment. **Unabridged Books** (3251 North Broadway) is one of the staunch independents holding out against the invasion of Borders and Barnes & Noble. You'll find the city's largest cluster of gay bars along Halsted and Broadway between Belmont and Addison and an eclectic variety of stores selling things antique to antic along the commercial strips of Belmont, Diversey, Broadway, Halsted, and Clark. (P.S., Lakeview is fine for solo strolling in the day, but at night it's best to go with a buddy.)

To get there From the Loop, take the CTA Red Line (Howard) or Brown Line (Ravenswood) to Belmont or the #151 bus along Michigan Avenue north to Belmont and then walk west. The #22 Clark Street bus, a quicker option, also puts you in the heart of Lakeview.

By car, drive north on Lake Shore Drive to the Belmont exit and head west on Belmont. Wrigley Field is located at Addison and Clark, about five blocks north of Belmont. (There's a CTA Red Line stop at Addison right near the ballpark.)

Milwaukee Avenue (Zone 2)

The locus of Chicago's Polish community, once situated at Milwaukee and Division, has angled north to the neighborhood called Avondale, although Milwaukee Avenue, especially between Central Park and Pulaski, remains the primary Polish corridor. On weekend afternoons, this section teems with shoppers and diners, all gossiping—in Polish—and debating the latest shifts in Eastern European alliances.

Your best bet is to stroll along the avenue, taking in the sights and sounds, stepping into **Andy's Deli** (3055 North Milwaukee Avenue) to gape at the 25 varieties of sausage lining the back wall and choose among packaged pierogi, gulasz, and Polish comic books. At the Polish department store, **Syrena** (3004 North Milwaukee), you can snap up that missing tuxedo for your children in white or black.

For a sit-down meal from which you'll struggle to rise, consider the buffet at **Red Apple** (3123 North Milwaukee) or the Polish specials at **Home Bakery & Restaurant** (2931 North Milwaukee).

St. Hyacinth's Roman Catholic Church (3636 West Wolfram) looms over the tidy bungalows and two-flats wedged on the side streets angling off Milwaukee. The church, built in ornate Renaissance Revival style, draws up to 1,000 people at a time for Polish-language masses.

To get there   The CTA #56 Milwaukee Avenue bus takes the s-l-o-w, scenic route through some of Chicago's oldest—and now graying—immigrant communities. Board at Randolph and Michigan (southbound) or along Madison (westbound) in the Loop. For a quicker ride, take the CTA Blue Line (O'Hare) to Logan Square and transfer to a northbound #56 Milwaukee Avenue bus.

By car from the Loop, take the Kennedy Expressway (I-90/94) north to the Kimball (Belmont) or Addison exits and head west (left) to Milwaukee Avenue.

Wicker Park and Bucktown (Zone 2)

If you want to see the hip, new Chicago where Generation X-ers congregate to hear pop artists such as Liz Phair and bands such as Urge Overkill and Smashing Pumpkins—if you want to hang out where slacker attitude prevails—then head for Wicker Park and Bucktown. Adjoining neighborhoods stretching from Division on the south to Fullerton on the north, between the Kennedy Expressway and Western Avenue, these formerly Polish, currently Puerto Rican communities have seen significant incursions by artists and yuppies of all stripes. Near Wicker Park itself, a small triangle at Schiller and Damen, are the late 1800s stone mansions of beer barons lining Pierce, Hoyne, Oakley, and Damen. Chicago author Nelson Algren once lived along here, which is why Evergreen Avenue is also Nelson Algren Avenue. Note the gingerbread house at 2137 West Pierce.

The cradle of the flourishing arts scene is the **Coyote Building** at 1600 North Milwaukee Avenue and its across-the-street landmark counterpart, the **Flatiron Building** (1579 North Milwaukee). Each year in September, the galleries and studios hold a celebratory open house called Around the Coyote. In one corner you'll find **Bella Bello** (1600 North Milwaukee), a charming store filled with flowers, linens, cards, and nifty perfume bottles. Nearby is **Pentimento** (1629 North Milwaukee) featuring clothes by local designers. Damen Avenue has become a mecca for small bistros, such as chef-owned **Le Bouchon** (1958 North Damen Avenue). Neighborhood stalwart **The Northside** (1635 North Damen) has an outdoor patio and a lively crowd.

Steep yourself in the late-night music scene at **The Double Door** (1572 North Milwaukee) or the supreme funk parlor known as **Red Dog** (1958 West North).

To get there   From the Loop, take the CTA Blue Line (O'Hare) to the Damen Avenue stop, which places you right at the confluence of Damen, North, and Milwaukee avenues in the heart of Bucktown. The #56 Milwaukee Avenue bus also takes you through Wicker Park and Bucktown.

By car from the Loop, drive north on the Kennedy Expressway (I-90/94) to the Division Street or North Avenue exits and head west.

Gold Coast and Old Town (Zone 3)

Behind the high-rises stretching north of Michigan Avenue along Lake Shore Drive are some of the most elegant townhouses and stately mansions in Chicago. It costs a fortune to live here—apropos the name, Gold Coast—but strolling along Astor Street or its neighbors from Division to North Avenue costs not a cent. Along the way, imagine urbane life in the former **Patterson-McCormick Mansion** (20 East Burton), which has since been divided into condominiums, or count the chimneys at the official residence of Chicago's Catholic archbishop (1555 North State Parkway). Consider treating yourself to lunch at the **Pump Room** in the Ambassador East Hotel (1301 North State Parkway), where you may see children in their dressed-up best dining with grandmother in her mink.

Old Town, which stretches west along North Avenue, was once a Bohemian center for folkies and artists. Now the rehabbed townhomes and coach houses have made it quieter (and costlier), with upscale boutiques and trendy shops along Wells. Many children of the city's blue-blood families enroll at the private Latin School (59 West North Avenue). Conversely, you'll find a young, beery crowd at some of the bars along Division. For picnic provisions, you'll want to browse among the many imported specialties at the **Treasure Island** grocery store (1639 North Wells Avenue), within walking distance of Lincoln Park.

To get there: Street parking is at such a premium on the Gold Coast, you might consider walking north from Michigan Avenue or taking the #151 bus and getting off anywhere between Oak Street and North Avenue. Walk west one block. For Old Town, there's a large parking garage next to the Piper's Alley theaters on North Avenue, or the #22 or #36 buses heading north (board downtown along Dearborn) put you in the heart of Old Town.

Chinatown (Zone 5)

Chicago's traditional Chinatown is a crowded, bustling area along the Wentworth Avenue corridor, its formal entrance marked by the ornate Oriental arch at Wentworth and Cermak. Walk south along Wentworth and note the temple-like **On Leong Building** (2216 South Wentworth), cornerstone of the commercial district where immigrant bachelors in years past rented space in apartments on the second floor. (Plans call for the building to be converted into a youth center.) Wentworth offers a lively, teeming mix of restaurants, shops, groceries, and even a wholesale noodle company. The Chinatown branch of the public library (2353 South Wentworth) circulates more books and cassettes (many in Chinese) than any other in the city. Newer shopping areas have spilled out across Cermak and Archer Avenues, and newer Chinese and Asian neighborhoods have evolved on the far north side near Argyle Street, but for the sights and smells most of us expect in Chinatown, this is where you'll find them.

To get there From the Loop, take the CTA southbound Red Line (Dan Ryan) from State Street to the Cermak/Chinatown stop. The #24 Wentworth bus heads south from Clark and Randolph in the Loop, and the #62 Archer Avenue bus travels south along State Street (exit at Cermak and Archer and walk one block east).

By car from the Loop, drive south on Michigan Avenue to 22nd Street (Cermak Road), turn right and drive five blocks to a public parking lot at Wentworth and Cermak; or drive south on the Dan Ryan Expressway and take the 22nd Street/Canalport turnoff, which leads to Chinatown.

Taylor Street (Zone 6)

Once the heart of Italian Chicago, this neighborhood was severely altered by the construction of the **University of Illinois** campus in the early 1960s, which displaced thousands of residents. Still, the Taylor Street area has undergone a renaissance with new townhouses being built and coffeehouses and fern bars offering proximity to the Loop with the lure of the university. Combine a tour of the area with a visit to the **Jane Addams Hull House** (800 South Halsted Street; see profile in Part Eight: Attractions in Chicago).

For a taste of Taylor, try **Al's No. 1 Italian Beef** (1079 West Taylor Street)—so famous that tour buses stop here—followed by an Italian ice at **Mario's Lemonade Stand** on Taylor between Aberdeen and Carpenter. (Open only in summer; you'll have to wait in line or wind your way through cars parked three abreast.) For Italian provisions, don't miss **Conte di Savoia** (1438 West Taylor) or the **Ferrara Original, Inc. Bakery** (2210 West Taylor). A real neighborhood joint is **Tufano's Restaurant**, also known as the **Vernon Park Tap** (1073 West Vernon Park Place).

On Polk Street between Laflin and Loomis, you can see some turn-of-the-19th-century buildings, including two wooden replicas of the style prevalent before the Great Fire of 1871. Bishop Street between Taylor and Polk, and Ada Street between Flournoy and Columbus Park also give a great feel to the neighborhood. **St. Basil Greek Orthodox Church** at Ashland and Polk bears witness to the neighborhood's transformation from a Jewish community to Greek to Italian—the church was once a synagogue and a Hebrew inscription is still visible on the exterior.

The new "Little Italy" is now along Harlem Avenue on the far western edge of the city between North Avenue and Irving Park.

To get there Take any CTA Blue Line train heading west to the UIC/Halsted stop or the Racine stop. During the week you can take the #37 bus southbound on Wells through the Loop.

By car from the Loop, drive west on the Eisenhower Expressway (290) to the Ashland exit and head south to Taylor Street.

Pilsen/Little Village (Zone 6)

Call these Chicago's barrios—home to the largest population of Mexican Americans in the Midwest—where the signs are Spanish and the smells are enticing. Pilsen lies principally along 18th Street between Canal and Damen. Little Village, considered somewhat more prosperous and stable, opens with its own pink stucco gateway arch at 26th Street and Albany and stretches in boisterous fashion west along 26th to Kostner.

Once the province of Bohemians and Poles, Pilsen is now the port of entry for thousands of Mexicans. It has a thriving artists' colony and is home to the **Mexican Fine Arts Center Museum** (1852 West 19th Street). The museum, which opened in 1987 in the converted Harrison Park Boat Craft Shop, strives to showcase the wealth and breadth of Mexican art in its exhibitions. You may want to survey some of the 20 handpainted murals depicting various cultural, religious, and political themes scattered throughout Pilsen (at 1305 West 18th Street, 18th and Racine, 18th and Wood, and lining the concrete wall along the tracks at 16th and Allport). When you visit, note the elaborate cornices and roofs of some of the 19th-century storefronts and two-flats along 18th west of Halsted. The Providence of God Church (717 West 18th Street) is the focal point for many celebrations, including a powerful Via Crucis (Way of the Cross) procession on Good Friday.

If the profusion of taquerías, bakeries, and taverns whets your appetite, try **Panaderia Nuevo Leon** (1634 West 18th Street) for sweets, **Carnitas Uruapan** (1725 West 18th) for barbecued pork and spicy salsa, or **Chicago's Original Bishop's Famous Chili** (1958 West 18th at Damen) for a simple bowl of hearty chili con carne served with locally brewed Filbert's root beer.

Little Village has its own colorful wall murals, such as the "Broken Wall Mural" in the back of Los Comales Restaurant next to McDonald's (26th Street and Kedzie). You'll find others at 26th and Homan, 25th and St. Louis, and 25th and Pulaski. Here, too, the neighborhood pulses along the commercial strip of 26th. Consider taking home a piñata selected from the many styles found at **La Justicia Grocery** (Millard and 26th). Watch the cooks grill Mexico City–style fast food at **Chon y Chano** (3901 West 26th), or try the dependable Mexican fare at **La Lo's** (3515 West 26th).

To get there   For Pilsen: Board the westbound CTA Blue Line (54th and Cermak) at Dearborn in the Loop and get off at the 18th Street stop right in the heart of Pilsen. By car, drive south on the Dan Ryan Expressway (I-90/94), exit at 18th Street, and head west.

For Little Village   By public transport, board the #60 Blue Island/ 26th Street bus westbound on Adams in the Loop.

By car from Pilsen, continue west along 18th to Western, go south (left) to 26th Street, and proceed west past the Cook County Courthouse and the turrets marking the perimeter of the Cook County Jail to the arch at Albany.

Bridgeport (Zone 6)

Bridgeport is the historic political centerpiece of Chicago for, despite a brief interregnum from 1979 to 1989, this working-class neighborhood has supplied the city with its mayors, including the present mayor, Richard M. Daley. In a city where politics are played at Super Bowl level, the political shrines are as you would expect: Mom's house, the neighborhood pub, and the ward organization office (or, in an earlier era, what might have irreverently been called the Machine Shop).

First stop on the pilgrimage, then, is Mom's house—home of "Sis" Daley, the late Richard J. Daley's widow and the current mayor's mom—

at 3536 South Lowe, a modest red brick bungalow distinguished only by the flagpole and police officer stationed in an unmarked squad car out front. At the end of the block—big surprise—is a police station whose handy placement was arranged by the late, great mayor. A few blocks to the west and south, you'll find the other two shrines right across the street from each other at 37th Street and Halsted: the 11th Ward Democratic Organization headquarters and **Schaller's Pump,** where the mediocre food is far surpassed by the atmosphere.

Stroll north along Halsted to sample the changing flavor of Bridgeport. You'll see Chinese, Mexican, Italian, and Lithuanian establishments all within a few blocks. Above all, don't miss **Healthy Food Restaurant** (3236 South Halsted Street), where slim waitresses in flowing skirts dish out ample portions of hearty Lithuanian food to the music of Tchaikovsky.

To get there   Take the CTA Red Line (Dan Ryan) to the 35th Street stop at Comiskey Park (from there it's a long hike to Halsted or to transfer to a #35 bus westbound), or board a #44 bus southbound on State Street in the Loop (weekdays only).

By car, drive south on Lake Shore Drive to the 31st Street exit and then west to Halsted; or drive south on the Dan Ryan Expressway to the 35th Street exit and then west to Halsted.

Hyde Park/Kenwood (Zone 7)

This is the place for big homes, big ideas, and a great cluster of cultural institutions. Drive along Ellis, Greenwood, and Woodlawn between 47th and East Hyde Park Boulevard (5100 South) and you'll marvel at the number of grand mansions on large lots. Years ago, they were homes of titans of industry; today more than likely they harbor Nobel laureates on the faculty of the nearby **University of Chicago,** which anchors Hyde Park with its cerebral gray presence between 57th Street and the Midway Plaisance, a wide, grassy boulevard created for the 1893 Columbian Exposition. Descend the stairs to the **Seminary Co-op Bookstore** (5757 South University) and you can't help but feel like a scholar yourself—or survey the eternal student scene at **Hutchinson Commons** in the Reynolds Club at 57th Street and University from behind one of the nouveau 'zines free for the taking.

Hyde Park, too, is one of the city's more integrated communities. The late Mayor Harold Washington used to live here, and the 5th Ward is considered one of the city's most liberal. **K.A.M. Isaiah Israel** (1100 East Hyde Park Boulevard) is the Midwest's oldest Jewish congregation. There are bustling commercial strips along 53rd and 57th Streets and in Harper Court at 52nd and South Harper. You'll certainly shed the tourist label if you tip back a brew at **Woodlawn Tap** (1172 East 55th Street) or eat at

Valois (1518 East 53rd Street), a cafeteria hang-out for cops, cabbies, and students of urban life where the motto is See Your Food.

To get there Be prepared for a lot of walking (not recommended after dark), or plan to tour the avenues by car. By public transportation, you can take the #6 Jeffrey express bus (30 cent surcharge) southbound from State Street to 57th and walk to the University of Chicago or the slower #1 Indiana/Hyde Park bus east on Jackson from Union Station, then south on Michigan to East Hyde Park Boulevard for a tour of Kenwood.

Metra electric trains also serve Hyde Park. Board underground at Randolph and Michigan or at Van Buren and Michigan and exit at either the 53rd and Lake Park stop, the combined 55th/56th/57th Street stop, or the University of Chicago stop at 59th Street and Harper. (The fare is $2.05 one-way.)

By car from the Loop, drive south on Lake Shore Drive to the 57th Street exit. Pass in front of the Museum of Science and Industry and follow signs for the University of Chicago. Or take the 47th Street exit, drive west, and then turn south on Woodlawn or Greenwood for a look at the mansions.

The Chicago Architecture Foundation offers two-hour walking tours of Kenwood in May, June, September, and October. Call (312) 922-3432.

South Shore (Zone 7)

Located between 67th and 79th and reaching from Lake Michigan on the east to Stony Island Avenue on the west, South Shore has been home to Chicagoans for more than 100 years. Today, many of the affluent African Americans who remain in Chicago dwell in some of the large, elegant homes lining South Euclid, Constance, and Bennett Streets between East 67th and East 71st at Jeffrey. Though the commercial strip along East 71st has suffered, the **South Shore Bank** (71st and Jeffrey) has become a national leader in innovative financing for community development projects.

The **South Shore Country Club** at the intersection of 71st Street and South Shore remains a gem. Once the site of elite South Side society gatherings, the stucco, Spanish-style structure and club fell on hard times until the Chicago Park District purchased the site 20 years ago. Now restored and open to the public, the club has a golf course, stables for the Chicago Police Department horses, and up-close lakefront views. In the winter you'll see a few solitary cross-country skiers; in the summer, there's picnicking and lakeside play.

The massive **Church of St. Philip Neri** (2132 East 72nd Street), one of Chicago's largest, has an exquisite sequence of mosaics depicting the Stations of the Cross. What was once the largest Greek Orthodox church in North America has become an Islamic mosque, the **Masjid Honorable Elijah Muhammad** (7351 South Stony Island Avenue).

For local cuisine, you may want to try **Army & Lou's** for soul food (422 East 75th Street) or **Alexander's Steak House and Cocktail Lounge** (3010 East 79th Street), where they've been dishing out prime rib and jazz at night for more than 50 years. **Salaam Restaurant & Bakery** (700 West 79th) is a showcase community investment by the Nation of Islam.

To get there   The CTA #6 Jeffrey express bus southbound on State Street will take you to 71st Street and Jeffrey (30 cent surcharge). A quicker option is the Metra electric train from Randolph and Michigan—the station is underground—which stops at Bryn Mawr (71st Street and Jeffrey; the fare is $2.05 one-way).

By car from the Loop, drive south along Lake Shore Drive through Jackson Park to South Shore.

Other Neighborhoods of Interest

Rogers Park (Zone 1)   The city's northernmost conglomeration of cultures and styles, Rogers Park mixes well-preserved lakeside condos with '60s hippie holdovers and ethnic groups ranging from Russian to Jamaican to Pakistani. Visit the **Heartland Cafe** (7000 North Glenwood) for vegetarian food–*cum*–radical politics. Sip espresso at **No Exit Cafe** (6970 North Glenwood) or at **Ennui** (6981 North Sheridan Road).

Rogers Park sprawls pretty far, and it's probably best not to wander alone or travel on foot after dark.

To get there   The CTA Red Line (Howard) stops at Morse, right near the Heartland Cafe, and at Loyola.

By car from the Loop, drive north to the end of Lake Shore Drive and continue north along Sheridan Road. Once you've curved around the buildings of Loyola University, you can turn right on any of the streets off Sheridan Road to view the older condos or continue up Sheridan to the city's border with Evanston.

Lincoln Park/DePaul (Zone 1)   This section, sandwiched between Old Town and Lakeview, may have the largest concentration of young urban white professionals in the city—or at least the most visible. Students at **DePaul University,** the large Catholic institution renowned for its Blue Demons basketball team, probably can't afford to live here after graduation unless they double up in one of the two- or three-flats along Bissell or Sheffield whose back porches face the El tracks.

Still, it's fun to roam the pleasant, tree-lined streets and gawk at the gentrified townhomes. The big ones line Fullerton Parkway as you head west from the lake, but a walk along any of the side streets, such as Hudson, Cleveland, Belden, or Fremont, will provide ample viewing pleasure.

Oz Park at Webster and Orchard is a favorite playground for kids and adults. The shops, galleries, boutiques, and restaurants clustered along Halsted, Armitage, and Clark are fun for browsing and spending.

Should you want to test the widely held theory that the best food in Chicago is to be found under the El tracks, stop by **Demon Dogs** at Fullerton Avenue near Sheffield for a hot dog and fries—you'll feel like a native.

To get there   The CTA Brown Line (Ravenswood) stops at Armitage or Fullerton and the Red Line (Howard) also goes to Fullerton (the stop closest to DePaul). The #151 bus travels through Lincoln Park; the #22 or #36 buses (board north along Dearborn) put you closer to the shopping district.

By car, drive north on Lake Shore Drive to the Fullerton exit and then head west. Or take the North Avenue exit to Stockton and drive through Lincoln Park.

Ukrainian Village (Zone 2)   A small pocket south of Wicker Park, Ukrainian Village has plenty of sustenance for body and soul. Note the gingerbread cutouts and stained glass on many of the tidy homes in this neighborhood, which stretches west along Chicago Avenue between Ashland and Western and north to Division. Stop in at the **Ukrainian National Museum** (721 North Oakley Boulevard, Thursday through Sunday 11 a.m.–4 p.m.) or the **Ukrainian Books and Gift Shop** (2315 West Chicago Avenue) for an Easter egg coloring kit, embroidered suits, or a wooden candelabra. Towering over the intersection of Oakley and Rice Streets you'll see the 13 copper-clad domes of **St. Nicholas Ukrainian Catholic Church,** modeled after the Basilica of St. Sophia in Kiev. But the real jewel is the much smaller Russian Orthodox **Holy Trinity Cathedral** (1121 North Leavitt at Haddon Street), designed by Louis Sullivan in 1901 and bearing his characteristic stenciling and ornamentation. **Ann's Bakery** (2158 West Chicago) is a social center as well as a source for great sweet rolls and plum cake.

To get there   By public transportation, take the CTA Blue Line (O'Hare) northbound to Chicago Avenue (not open on weekends), transfer to a westbound #66 bus, and travel to Damen or Ashland. Or you can get the #66 bus westbound right near Water Tower Place at Chicago and Michigan.

By car from the Loop, drive north on Michigan Avenue to Chicago Avenue. Turn left (west) and continue to Ukrainian Village.

Humboldt Park/Logan Square (Zone 2)   Originally settled by Polish and Russian Jews, then by Scandinavians, Ukrainians, and Eastern Europeans, Humboldt Park and Logan Square are now home to large numbers of Hispanic residents. A tour here opens a window onto an earlier era of residential gentility as the grand boulevards of Humboldt, Palmer, Kedzie, and Logan—one of the city's widest—are the site of many elegant graystones. In addition, Logan Square has Chicago's most unusual intersection—a traffic circle with a massive marble column commemorating the centennial of Illinois statehood. Much of the area off the boulevards has deteriorated; be careful here.

To get there   The CTA Blue Line (O'Hare) stops at Logan Square.

By car, drive west along North Avenue to Humboldt Boulevard and then north to Palmer Square.

Pullman (Zone 7)   Once a company town built by George Pullman to house workers at his Pullman Palace Car Works, Pullman is now a historic district with more than 80% of the original 1,800 buildings still standing. Start your tour at the **Historic Pullman Foundation,** housed in the Florence Hotel (named for Pullman's daughter) at 11111 South Forrestville Avenue. The neighborhood harbors architecturally unique mansions—the executives' houses—and far more modest two-story attached row houses in muted Queen Anne style.

To get there   Pullman is on the far southwest side of Chicago, almost at the city's southern boundary. Via public transport, take the Metra Electric train ($2.75 one-way) from the station under Randolph and Michigan to the Pullman stop at 111th and Cottage Grove (it's one block to the Florence Hotel) or to the Kensington stop at 115th, which has more frequent service.

By car, drive south on the Dan Ryan Expressway (I-90/94) and continue south on the Calumet Expressway (I-94) and exit at 111th Street. Head west a few blocks to South Forrestville.

Final Note

As rich as Chicago is in architecture, history, culture, and ethnic diversity, it *is* a major American city—which is to say, it is grappling with grave problems of unemployment, decaying infrastructure, crime, and besieged public schools. One recent study found that Chicago had four of the five poorest neighborhoods in the country—all located in the sprawling public housing projects that comprise today's ghettos. Many areas of the city's West Side still have not recovered from the fires and looting that followed the assassination of Dr. Martin Luther King Jr. in 1968. You need only drive west along 47th Street after touring the mansions of Kenwood to see the once stately buildings on Drexel Boulevard, now boarded up and barren. Or glance across the Dan Ryan Expressway from the gleaming new Comiskey Park to the forlorn hulks of Stateway Gardens and the Robert Taylor Homes (the largest public housing unit in the world) and in such juxtapositions of wealth and poverty you will recognize the challenges facing Chicago.

Chicago for Children

Question: After taking the kids on the requisite trip to the top of the Sears Tower, what else can a parent do to entertain kids on a Chicago vacation?

Answer: A lot. Chicago offers plenty of fun-filled places to visit and things to do that will satisfy the most curious—and fidgety—kids. Their folks will have fun, too.

The *Unofficial Guide* rating system for attractions includes an "appeal to different age groups" category indicating a range of appeal from one star (★), don't bother, to five stars (★★★★★), not to be missed. To get you started, we have provided a list of attractions in and around Chicago most likely to appeal to children.

More Things to Do with Children

Chicago has more for kids to enjoy than museums, zoos, and tall buildings. Some ideas: Swimming in Lake Michigan at **Oak Street Beach** and **North Avenue Beach,** roller skating at **United Skates of America** (Rainbow Entertainment Center, 4836 North Clark Street, phone (773) 271-6200), browsing at **NikeTown** (a high-tech shoe store at 669 North Michigan Avenue, phone (312) 642-6363) and **FAO Schwarz** (a giant toy store at 840 North Michigan Avenue, phone (312) 587-5000), and spotting the stones pirated from famous and ancient monuments worldwide (including the Parthenon, Notre Dame, and the Pyramids) embedded at street level in the **Tribune Tower** (435 North Michigan Avenue). Teens age 13 and older can relieve stress at the **Chicago Paintball Factory** (1001 West Van Buren Street—west of the Loop; phone (312) 563-1777); rates start at $18 an hour per person.

Pro Sports and a Really Big Amusement Park

Depending on the season and ticket availability, take the gang to a **Bears, Blackhawks, Bulls, Cubs,** or **White Sox** game. In the summer, don't forget **Buckingham Fountain** in Grant Park: Computer-controlled water displays send 14,000 gallons of water a minute through 133 jets. Colorful displays can be seen nightly from dusk to 11 p.m.

Farther afield (if you've got a car), take a drive to **Six Flags Great America,** a monster amusement park north of Chicago with more than 100 rides (including 8 roller coasters), shops, stage shows, and special theme sections representing different eras in American history. The park is open from May through October with varying hours; admission is $39.99 for adults, $29.99 for children and seniors. With prices like these, plan on spending the day. More advice: Avoid weekends (the place gets packed) and go early in the day. For more information and directions, call (847) 249-INFO.

Other neat activities kids will enjoy: bicycling or Rollerblading on the bike path along Lake Michigan, taking the **Untouchables Tour** and exploring the old haunts of Chicago's gangsters (phone (773) 881-1195), and watching airplanes take off and land at the **Meigs Airfield** observation deck (15th Street and Lakefront Drive, phone (312) 922-5454; it's free).

Helpful Hints for Visitors

How to Get into Museums for Half Price

Save over $30 when you visit Chicago's most popular museums and attractions with a **CityPass,** a book of tickets that cuts the price of admission in half. Participating attractions are the Art Institute of Chicago, Field Museum, Museum of Science and Industry, Adler Planetarium and Astronomy Museum, Shedd Aquarium, and Hancock Observatory.

The passes cost $39 for adults and $29 for children ages 3–11. Ticket books are sold at the participating attractions and are good for nine days, beginning with the the first day you use them. Don't remove the individual tickets from the booklet; just present the CityPass at each attraction. The clerk at the site removes the ticket, and you walk on in (usually without waiting in line to buy a ticket). These prices are valid April 2003– May 2004; for more information, visit **www.citypass.com.**

When the Admission Is Free

Many Chicago museums that usually charge admission open their doors for free one day a week. If you'd like to save a few bucks during your visit, use our list when planning your touring itinerary.

In addition, a few worthy attractions around town are free to the public all the time. Here's the list:

- Chicago Botanic Garden ($8.75 parking)
- Chicago Cultural Center
- Garfield Park Conservatory (donation requested during flower shows)
- Harold Washington Library Center
- Jane Addams Hull House Museum
- Lincoln Park Conservatory
- Lincoln Park Zoo
- Mexican Fine Arts Center Museum
- Museum of Broadcast Communications

- Oriental Institute Museum

- Polish Museum of America ($3 donation requested)

- Smart Museum of Art

- Smith Museum of Stained Glass

- Terra Museum of American Art

OTHER FREE ADMISSION DAYS

Monday

Balzekas Museum of Lithuanian Culture
Chicago Historical Society
Field Museum (January–February, September 23–December 24)
Museum of Science and Industry (August–February and first Monday in June)

Tuesday

Art Institute of Chicago
Brookfield Zoo (October–March; $4 parking)
Field Museum (January–February, September 23–December 24)
International Museum of Surgical Science
Museum of Contemporary Art
Museum of Science and Industry (August–February and first Tuesday in June)

Thursday

Brookfield Zoo (October through March; $6.75 parking)
Chicago Children's Museum (evenings)

Friday

Spertus Museum

Sunday

DuSable Museum of African-American History

Scenic Car Drives

Though we recommend that visitors to Chicago forego driving and rely on airport vans, taxis, and public transportation when in town, not everyone will heed our advice. In addition, rental cars are plentiful in Chicago, and traffic gets downright manageable on weekends. If you've got access to a set of wheels and feel the urge to roam, here are a few ideas.

Around Town

The best views of the city are revealed anywhere along **Lake Shore Drive.** (For safety's sake, don't get too distracted by the scenery as you navigate this busy highway.) For an urban exploration beyond the lakefront, tour

Chicago's boulevards and greenways, a series of wide streets laid out in the 19th century that link seven parks along what once was the city's western border.

Heading North

For a quick and scenic escape from the city, head north on Lake Shore Drive until it becomes Sheridan Road. This pleasant drive meanders along the lakeshore and passes through affluent neighborhoods full of gorgeous homes and mansions. In Evanston it skirts the beautiful campus of Northwestern University and, in Wilmette, the breathtaking Baha'i House of Worship.

Farther north along Sheridan Road in Glencoe is the **Chicago Botanic Garden**—worth a stop in any season—and, in Highland Park, the **Ravinia Festival,** where evening summertime performances range from Joan Baez to the Chicago Symphony Orchestra. Note: A drive along Sheridan Road is especially popular with Chicagoans in the fall when the leaves change; to avoid the worst of the traffic, go early in the day.

Great Views

Nobody comes to the Midwest for the views, right? Wrong—at least, in Chicago. Here's a list of ten great spots that offer breathtaking vistas of skyline, Lake Michigan, and the city stretching toward the horizon.

1. The observation decks atop the **Sears Tower** and the **John Hancock Center** offer stupendous vistas from vantage points over 1,000 feet high. Go on a clear day; better yet, go at night. Our preference is the Hancock Center, which is closer to the lake and usually not very crowded.

2. **Lake Shore Drive** offers dramatic views of the Chicago skyline and the lake all along its length. We especially like the vantage point looking north where the Stevenson Expressway joins Lake Shore Drive (at McCormick Place).

3. **Grant Park** is a great place to walk and look up at Chicago's downtown. Note: Unless there is a summer festival going on, consider the park unsafe at night.

4. The view of downtown from the **Shedd Aquarium** is a knockout, especially at dusk as the lights begin to wink on.

5. The **Michigan Avenue Bridge** over the Chicago River offers a heart-stopping view of downtown buildings, especially at night: the Wrigley Building and Tribune Tower are both illuminated.

6. Starting around Thanksgiving, the **Festival of Lights** along North Michigan Avenue features more than 300,000 white lights for the holidays.

7. The **Ravenswood El** features surprises around every corner as it encircles the Loop. Don't get off; take it north, then grab the next train toward downtown for more views of the city.

8. **Montrose Harbor** offers a spectacular view of the Chicago skyline, especially at night. You'll need a car: It's located near the northern end of Lincoln Park on a finger of land jutting out into Lake Michigan; get there from Lake Shore Drive.

9. As a lot of Chicago runners and bicyclists know, a stunning sunrise is a frequent reward on an early morning jaunt on the **Lakefront Trail** along Lake Michigan.

10. Or try this not-to-be-forgotten scene from anywhere on the lakefront (if the heavens cooperate on your trip): moonrise over **Lake Michigan.**

Getting into "Oprah"

Wanna be on national TV? Or would you just like to be in the audience at a taping of your favorite talk show? You've come to the right place—Chicago is home to three of America's most popular TV talk shows.

Numero uno, of course, is Oprah, a figure so well known that no more identification is needed. For audience reservations to **The Oprah Winfrey Show,** call (312) 591-9222 at least one month prior to your visit. There's no charge, and reservations are accepted for up to four people (who must be age 18 or older). Harpo Studios (that's Oprah spelled backward), where the shows are taped twice daily (early and late morning) on Tuesdays, Wednesdays, and Thursdays, is located at 1058 West Washington Street, a couple of blocks west of the Loop. The show goes on vacation from late June to late August and again from mid-December through mid-January.

To get into **The Jenny Jones Show,** call (312) 836-9485 at least six weeks before your trip to Chicago. Shows are taped on Tuesdays and Thursdays at the NBC Tower, 454 North Columbus Drive, and it's free. Reservations are accepted for up to four people.

For **The Jerry Springer Show,** call (312) 321-5365 at least one month in advance. Tickets are free, parties are limited to six people, and shows are usually taped at 10 a.m. and 1 p.m. on Mondays, Tuesdays, and Wednesdays, and on Tuesday evenings at 6 and 8 p.m. No shows are taped in July. The studios are in the NBC Tower, 454 North Columbus Drive, north of the Loop.

Part Eight

Attractions in Chicago

The Loop . . . and Beyond

Chicago is a sports town, a shopping town, a culinary grab bag of cuisines, a jumble of intriguing ethnic neighborhoods, a glimmering jewel by the lake that takes your breath away at night.

But that's not all. The nation's third-largest city offers visitors a potpourri of attractions that show off its fascinating (and often notorious) past. Visitors can also explore majestic art galleries crammed with world-class collections of paintings and sculpture, gigantic museums dedicated to natural history and technology, the world's largest indoor aquarium, the country's oldest planetarium, a polyglot of ethnic museums . . . and lots more.

The following zone descriptions provide you with a comprehensive guide to Chicago's top attractions, along with listing a few we think you should avoid. We give you enough information so that you can choose the places you want to see, based on your own interests. Each attraction includes a zone number so you can plan your visit logically without spending a lot of valuable time crisscrossing the city.

Attractions by Type and Zone

Because of the wide range of attractions in and around Chicago—from an unparalleled collection of French Impressionist paintings in the Art Institute to America's tallest building—we provide the following charts to help you prioritize your touring at a glance. Here, you'll find attractions organized by type and zone, complete with authors' ratings from one star (skip it) to five stars (not to be missed). Some attractions (usually art galleries without permanent collections) aren't rated because exhibits change. Individual attraction profiles follow the charts, organized alphabetically by attraction name.

CHICAGO ATTRACTIONS BY TYPE

Attraction	Zone	Author's Rating
Gardens, Parks, and Zoos		
Brookfield Zoo	8	★★★½
Chicago Botanic Garden	11	★★★★
Garfield Park Conservatory	2	★★★
Lincoln Park Zoo	1	★★★
Morton Arboretum	9	★★★½
Museums		
Art Institute of Chicago	4	★★★★
Balzekas Museum of Lithuanian Culture	6	★★
Chicago Children's Museum	3	★
Chicago Historical Society	1	★★½
David and Alfred Smart Museum of Art	7	★★★
DuSable Museum of African-American History	7	★★★½
Field Museum of Natural History	5	★★★★★
Hemingway Museum	2	★★
International Museum of Surgical Science	3	★★½
Jane Addams Hull House Museum	6	★★½
Mexican Fine Arts Center Museum	6	★★★½
Museum of Broadcast Communications	4	★★½
Museum of Contemporary Art	3	★★★★½
Museum of Holography	2	★★½
Museum of Science and Industry	7	★★★★★
National Vietnam Veterans Art Museums	5	★★★
Oriental Institute Museum	7	★★★★
Peace Museum	2	N/A
Peggy Notebaert Museum	1	★★★
Polish Museum of America	2	★★½
Spertus Museum of Judaica	5	★★★
Swedish American Museum	1	★★½
Terra Museum of American Art	3	★★★★
Ukrainian National Museum	2	★
Skyscrapers		
John Hancock Center Observatory	3	★★★★★
Sears Tower Skydeck	4	★★★★★
Tourist Landmarks		
Adler Planetarium and Astronomy Museum	5	★★½
Chicago Cultural Center	4	★★★½
Harold Washington Library Center	4	★★★
Hemingway's Birthplace	2	★½

CHICAGO ATTRACTIONS BY TYPE (continued)

Attraction	Zone	Author's Rating
Tourist Landmarks (continued)		
John G. Shedd Aquarium	5	★★★★★
Navy Pier	3	★★★★
Wright Home and Studio	2	★★★★

CHICAGO ATTRACTIONS BY ZONE

Attraction	Description	Author's Rating
Zone 1—The North Side		
Chicago Historical Society	Chicago, U.S. history	★★½
Lincoln Park Zoo	Urban animal park	★★★
Peggy Notebaert Museum	Nature museum	★★★
Swedish American Museum	Swedish immigrant story	★★½
Zone 2—North Central/O'Hare		
Garfield Park Conservatory	Botanical gardens	★★★
Hemingway Museum	Writer's memorabilia	★★
Hemingway's Birthplace	Victorian house	★½
Museum of Holography	3D photo gallery	★★½
Peace Museum	Exhibits on nonviolence	N/A
Polish Museum of America	Ethnic art and history	★★½
Ukrainian National Museum	Folk art	★
Wright Home and Studio	Famous architect's house	★★★★
Zone 3—Near North		
Chicago Children's Museum	High-tech playground	★
International Museum of Surgical Science	History of surgery	★★½
John Hancock Center Observatory	94th-floor view	★★★★★
Museum of Contemporary Art	Avant-garde art	★★★★½
Navy Pier	All-purpose tourist mecca	★★★★
Terra Museum of American Art	American art	★★★★
Zone 4—The Loop		
Art Institute of Chicago	Highbrow art palace	★★★★
Chicago Cultural Center	Art, architecture, tourist info	★★★½
Harold Washington Library Center	Largest library in U.S., art	★★★

CHICAGO ATTRACTIONS BY ZONE *(continued)*

Attraction	Description	Author's Rating
Zone 4—The Loop *(continued)*		
Museum of Broadcast Communications	TV and radio memorabilia	★★½
Sears Tower Skydeck	View from America's tallest building	★★★★★
Zone 5—South Loop		
Adler Planetarium and Astronomy Museum	Star show and space exhibits	★★½
Field Museum of Natural History	Nine acres of natural history	★★★★★
John G. Shedd Aquarium	Largest indoor fish emporium	★★★★★
National Vietnam Veterans Art Museums	Emotionally powerful art	★★★
Spertus Museum of Judaica	Jewish culture and history	★★★
Zone 6—South Central/Midway		
Balzekas Museum of Lithuanian Culture	Lithuanian culture and history	★★
Jane Addams Hull House Museum	Birthplace of social work	★★½
Mexican Fine Arts Center Museum	Mexican art and culture	★★★½
Zone 7—South Side		
David and Alfred Smart Museum of Art	Highbrow art gallery	★★★
DuSable Museum of African-American History	African American art and culture	★★★½
Museum of Science and Industry	Technology, hands-on exhibits	★★★★★
Oriental Institute Museum	Near East archaeology	★★★★
Zone 8—Southern Suburbs		
Brookfield Zoo	campus-like animal park	★★★½
Zone 9—Western Suburbs		
Morton Arboretum	1,500 acres of trees, shrubs	★★★½
Zone 11—Northern Suburbs		
Chicago Botanic Garden	formal, elegant gardens	★★★★

Attraction Profiles

Adler Planetarium and Astronomy Museum

Type of Attraction Narrative Sky Shows in a domed theater, a slide presentation, and exhibits on astronomy and space exploration. A self-guided tour.

Location Zone 5—South Loop; 1300 South Lake Shore Drive, Chicago, 60605

Admission $13 adults, $12 seniors, $11 children ages 4–17; $6 for all on Tuesday; admission includes one sky show exhibit

Hours Daily, 9 a.m.–6 p.m.; closed Thanksgiving and Christmas.

Phone (312) 922-STAR

When to Go Any time.

Special Comments The comfortable, high-backed seats in the theater almost guarantee you won't get a stiff neck from watching the show on the domed ceiling.

Appeal by Age Group

Pre-school ★	Teens ★★★	Over 30 ★★½
Grade school ★★★★	Young Adults ★★½	Seniors ★★½

Authors' Rating Some fascinating stuff on display, but the low-key planetarium show is geared to younger viewers and hard-core space cadets. ★★½

How Much Time to Allow 40 minutes for the show and at least half an hour to view the exhibits.

Description and Comments The Adler Planetarium was the first in the country when it opened in 1930. The 12-sided pink granite building that houses the Sky Theater was funded by a Sears, Roebuck & Company executive who had the Zeiss projector imported from Germany. In addition to the narrated Sky Shows (which change throughout the year), visitors can explore a wide range of exhibits on topics that include telescopes, the planets, man-made satellites, the moon, optics, and navigation. It's a modern, informative place that will delight youngsters and adults who read Carl Sagan. Good news for astronomy buffs: In early 1997 the Adler embarked on a $40 million expansion and renovation program that added 60,000 square feet of new space.

Touring Tips Enter the planetarium through the glass building that faces the planetarium, not the granite steps. On Friday nights (when the planetarium is open until 9 p.m.) visitors can tour the Doane Observatory and see its 20-inch telescope. Visit the planetarium late in a day of hard sight-seeing; relaxing in a comfortable, high-backed chair for 40 minutes is nirvana, even if you don't give a hoot about the cosmos. The view of the city skyline on the promontory leading to the building is spectacular, especially at sunset when the skyscrapers begin to light up.

Other Things to Do Nearby The John G. Shedd Aquarium and the Field Museum of Natural History are both within easy walking distance on the traffic-free Museum Campus. The half-mile promontory is a great place to watch planes taking off from Meigs Field; it's also a popular make-out spot for Chicago couples. Bad news if you're hungry: Getting something to eat beyond a hot dog requires flagging a cab or grabbing a bus downtown.

Art Institute of Chicago

Type of Attraction Internationally acclaimed collections of paintings and sculptures housed in a complex of neoclassical buildings erected for the World's Columbian Exposition of 1893. Guided and self-guided tours.

Location Zone 4—The Loop; 111 South Michigan Avenue, Chicago, 60603

Admission $10 adults, $6 children, students, and seniors; free admission on Tuesday; checkroom $1

Hours Monday, Wednesday, Thursday, and Friday, 10:30 a.m.–4:30 p.m.; Tuesday, 10:30 a.m.–8 p.m.; Saturday, 10 a.m –5 p.m.; Sunday and holidays, 10 a.m.–5 p.m.; closed Christmas and Thanksgiving Days.

Phone (312) 443-3600

When to Go During the school year, the museum is often besieged by groups of schoolchildren on field trips in the mornings; afternoons are usually less crowded. Because admission is free on Tuesdays, the museum is almost always packed.

Special Comments The first floor is the only level that connects the three buildings that comprise the Art Institute. It also provides access to Michigan Avenue (west) and Columbus Drive (east), food, rest rooms, and water fountains. Handicapped access is at the Columbus Drive entrance.

Appeal by Age Group

Pre-school ★	Teens ★★★	Over 30 ★★★★★
Grade school ★★½	Young Adults ★★★★	Seniors ★★★★★

Authors' Rating The best of a handful of attractions that elevate Chicago to world-class status. Not to be missed. ★★★★★

How Much Time to Allow At least two hours for a brief run-through, all day for art lovers. Better yet, try to visit the Art Institute more than once—the place is huge.

Description and Comments The massive, classical/Renaissance–style home of the Art Institute of Chicago was completed in 1892, just in time for the 1893 World's Columbian Exposition. Located on the edge of Grant Park near the Loop, the museum is easily identified by the two bronze lions standing guard on Michigan Avenue.

It's a world-class museum especially renowned for its Impressionist collection, which includes five of the paintings in Monet's haystack series, Caillebotte's *Paris, a Rainy Day,* and, perhaps the museum's best-known painting, Seurat's pointillist masterpiece *Sunday Afternoon on the Island of La Grande Jatte.* The large museum shop features calendars, books, cards, gifts (mugs, scarves, posters, CDs), and a huge collection of art books (some at reduced prices).

Touring Tips The second-floor gallery of European art is arranged chronologically from late medieval to post-Impressionist, with paintings and sculptures arranged in skylight-brightened rooms; prints and drawings are hung in corridor galleries. By taking a free tour, you'll get an overview of the place and see how various works are related.

For example, our guide linked different eras by explaining the evolution of paint— from egg and pigment used in the late Middle Ages to the stuff Jackson Pollock splattered on canvas with a stick. Fascinating. Tours start daily at 2 p.m. in Gallery 150, on the first floor near the Grand Staircase and the main entrance.

Other Things to Do Nearby The Loop is a block west; Grant Park and Lake Michigan are behind the Art Institute. Walking tours of downtown Chicago start across the street at the Chicago Architecture Foundation; no visit to the Windy City is complete until you've taken at least one. For lunch, Michigan Avenue has several fast-food places nearby, or try the Euro-deli next to the Chicago Architecture Foundation shop.

Balzekas Museum of Lithuanian Culture

Type of Attraction An eclectic collection of exhibits on Lithuanian history and culture. A self-guided tour.

Location Zone 6—South Central/Midway; 6500 South Pulaski Road, Chicago, 60629

Admission $4 adults, $3 seniors and students, $1 children; free on Monday.

Hours Daily, 10 a.m.–4 p.m.; closed Thanksgiving, Christmas, and New Year's Day.

Phone (773) 582-6500

When to Go Any time.

Special Comments Call in advance for information on special exhibits and programs. All exhibits are located on the ground floor.

Appeal by Age Group

Pre-school ★½	Teens ★★	Over 30 ★★
Grade school ★★	Young Adults ★★	Seniors ★★½

Authors' Rating Although there's some interesting stuff here, it's a small museum that lacks coherence. ★★

How Much Time to Allow 30 minutes to an hour.

Description and Comments Inside this small museum you'll find items ranging from a suit of armor to press clippings from World War II—and everything in between: old photos of immigrants, folk art (including dolls, toys, leather items, wooden household utensils), photos of rural Lithuania, genealogical information, a playroom for children (with a poster depicting the ancient kings of Lithuania), glass cases full of old prayer books, swords, rare books, jewelry, native costumes, coins, stamps. . . . There's a lot on display here, but it's all in a jumble.

Touring Tips Visitors can watch a short video about Lithuania that primes them for a tour of the museum.

Other Things to Do Nearby Not much. If you're flying in or out of Midway, it's only a few blocks away. Oak Park, the hometown of Frank Lloyd Wright and Ernest Hemingway, is about five miles to the north, just off the Eisenhower Expressway (I-290).

Brookfield Zoo

Type of Attraction A zoo featuring 2,500 animals and more than 400 species spread throughout 215 acres of naturalistic habitat. A self-guided tour.

Location Zone 8—Southern Suburbs; First Avenue and 31st Street, Brookfield (14 miles west of the Loop). By car, take I-55 (Stevenson Expressway), I-290 (Eisenhower Expressway), or I-294 (Tri-State Tollway) and watch for signs. By train, take the Burlington/Metra Northern Line to the Zoo Stop at the Hollywood Station. For information on reaching the zoo by bus, call (312) 836-7000 (city) or (800) 972-7000 (suburbs).

Admission $7 adults, $3.50 seniors and children ages 3–11; free admission October–March on Tuesday and Thursday. Parking is $6.75.

Hours Memorial Day–Labor Day: daily, 9:30 a.m.–6 p.m.; rest of year: 10 a.m.–5 p.m.

Phone (708) 485-0263

When to Go On weekdays in the spring and fall, come after 1:30 p.m. to avoid large school groups.

Special Comments Telecommunications devices for the deaf (TDD) are available in the administration building.

Appeal by Age Group

Pre-school ★★★★★	Teens ★★★★	Over 30 ★★★½
Grade school ★★★★★	Young Adults ★★★★	Seniors ★★★½

Authors' Rating Widely separated buildings, well-landscaped grounds, and a campus-like setting make for a pleasant (not spectacular) zoo. ★★★½

How Much Time to Allow Two hours to half a day.

Description and Comments Attractions at this lush, wooded park include bottlenosed dolphins, walruses, re-creations of steamy rainforests featuring exotic animals, and an "African waterhole" populated by giraffes, zebras, and topi antelope. More traditional sights include lions, tigers, snow leopards, reptiles, and elephants. The Australia House features a variety of unusual animals from Down Under.

Although the zoo is spread out, visitors don't necessarily have to hoof it from exhibit to exhibit. Motor Safari, an open-air tram that operates from late spring to early fall, lets you get off and reboard four times along its route; the trams run every 5 to 15 minutes. The fee is $2.50 for adults and $1.50 for seniors and children ages 3–11. In the winter, the deal gets better: The Snowball Express is a free, heated mini-bus that circulates throughout the zoo; flag it down any time and hop aboard.

Touring Tips The most popular exhibits at Brookfield Zoo are the dolphin show at the 2,000-seat Seven Seas Panorama ($2.50 for adults, $2 for children; for show times, check at zoo kiosks or the Seven Seas ticket booth; it's free anytime to watch the sea mammals underwater through plate glass windows), Tropic World (a huge indoor rainforest containing gorillas, monkeys, free-flying tropical birds, waterfalls, rocky streams, and big trees), Habitat Africa, "The Swamp" (a replica of a Southern cypress swamp), and summertime elephant demos.

First-time visitors can catch a free slide presentation at the Discovery Center that runs every 15 minutes (longer intervals in the winter). Finally, when planning a visit to the zoo, keep in mind that the most pleasant weather occurs in the spring and fall, animals are most active in the mornings and late afternoons, and the zoo is least crowded on rainy, chilly days.

Other Things to Do Nearby Oak Park, hometown of Ernest Hemingway and Frank Lloyd Wright, is a few miles east of the Brookfield Zoo on the Eisenhower Expressway. Take I-290 east to Harlem Avenue (Route 43 north), then turn right on Lake Avenue to Forest Avenue and the visitor center. In addition to snack bars in the zoo, there's fast-food on the road linking the zoo and the Eisenhower Expressway.

Chicago Botanic Garden

Type of Attraction 18 formal gardens featuring collections showcasing plants of the Midwest (including plants being tested for their performance in the Chicago area) and native and endangered flora of Illinois. Guided and self-guided tours.

Location Zone 11—Northern Suburbs; 1000 Lake-Cook Road, Glencoe, 60022. From Chicago, take Sheridan Road north along Lake Michigan, or I-94 (the Edens Expressway) to Lake-Cook Road. The gardens are about 15 miles north of the Loop.

Admission Free. Parking is $8.75, $5.75 for seniors on Tuesday.

Hours Daily, 8 a.m.–sunset; closed Christmas.

Phone (847) 835-5440

When to Go June through August to see the most flowering plants in bloom. Yet staffers say the gardens are gorgeous year-round—and especially after a heavy snowfall. Avoid summer afternoons on weekends, when crowds are at their heaviest; come in the morning and leave by 1 p.m. to miss the worst crowds.

Special Comments Prohibited activities include bicycling (except on designated bike routes), inline skating, or other sports activities such as Frisbee throwing, skiing, fishing, or skating; collecting plants and flowers; climbing on trees and shrubs; standing or walking in garden beds; and feeding wildlife. No pets are allowed except guide and hearing dogs.

Appeal by Age Group

Pre-school ★★★	Teens ★★★	Over 30 ★★★★
Grade school ★★★	Young Adults ★★★½	Seniors ★★★★½

Authors' Rating A stunning collection of beautifully designed gardens, pathways, ponds and pools, and outdoor sculpture. ★★★★

How Much Time to Allow Half a day.

Description and Comments This living museum is a 300-acre park of gently rolling terrain and water that contains 23 garden areas brimming with plants. Other collections include an herbarium of 5,000 dried plants, rare books, and an art collection of plant-related prints, drawings, sculpture, and decorative objects.

Among the most popular areas are the Japanese, English Walled, Naturalistic, Prairie, and Rose gardens. Linking the formal gardens are paths that wander past lakes, ponds, and greens that are meticulously groomed and provide impressive views. The Orientation Center near the parking lots features an audiovisual presentation, exhibit panels, computers, and a wall map to help visitors plan their visit. Food is available in the Gateway Center, and a picnic area is located between parking lots 1 and 2.

Touring Tips Narrated tram tours lasting 45 minutes are offered from April through October; the tours depart every 30 minutes from 10 a.m. to 3:30 p.m. Tickets are $5 for adults, $4 for seniors, and $3 for children ages 3–15.

If you're short on time and want to see the garden's highlights, cross the footbridge from the Gateway Center and turn left at the Heritage Garden. Then visit the Rose, English Walled, Waterfall, and Japanese gardens.

Combine a visit with a workout: The North Branch Bicycle Trail starts at Caldwell and Devon Avenues in Chicago and continues north 20 miles along the North Branch of the Chicago River to the Chicago Botanic Garden. Bring a lunch and eat it at the picnic area between parking lots 1 and 2.

Other Things to Do Nearby Ravinia, the summer home of the Chicago Symphony Orchestra, is on Sheridan Road; it's only a few minutes away. Sheridan Road follows Lake Michigan and is one of the best scenic drives around Chicago. Take a left onto Lake-Cook Road; it becomes Sheridan Road at the third traffic light.

Chicago Children's Museum

Type of Attraction A high-tech playground and engaging interactive exhibits for children up to age 12. A self-guided tour.

Location Zone 3—Near North; Navy Pier, 700 East Grand Avenue, Chicago, 60611 (just north of the Chicago River on the lakefront)

Admission $6.50 adults, $5.50 seniors; free for infants under age 1; free Thursday evenings, 5–8 p.m.

Hours Sunday–Tuesday, 10 a.m.–5 p.m.; Wednesday–Saturday, 10 a.m.–8 p.m.

Phone (312) 527-1000

When to Go During the summer, on weekends, and on school holidays, arrive when the museum opens at 10 a.m. During the school year, come in the afternoon to avoid school groups that arrive in the morning.

Special Comments This isn't a baby-sitting service. While all activities are supervised by the museum staff, all children must be accompanied by someone age 16 or older.

Appeal by Age Group

Pre-school ★★★★★	Teens ★	Over 30 ★
Grade school ★★★★★	Young Adults ★	Seniors ★

Authors' Rating Nirvana for youngsters through age 12. ★

How Much Time to Allow Half a day.

Description and Comments This $14.5-million, 60,000-square-foot "museum"— it's really a high-tech playground for ankle biters and children through the fifth grade— provides an active play and learning environment spread across three levels of Navy Pier. A dozen exhibits provide a range of age-appropriate activities that captivates toddlers as well as older children. One of the most popular is Waterways, where kids don raincoats (provided) and pump, squirt, and manipulate water (they can shoot a stream of water 50 feet into the air). In The Inventing Lab, children can build and launch gliders from a 50-foot tower. In Treehouse Trails and PlayMaze, toddlers can explore an indoor "nature park" (featuring a hiking trail, pond, waterfall, trees, log cabin, and animal homes) and play in a working bakery, service station, construction site, and the Play it Safe exhibit which teaches safety at home and in the the environment.

Touring Tips Start a visit with the Climbing Schooner, a three-story replica of a sailing ship that lets kids burn off energy by climbing the rigging up 35 feet to the crow's nest—and then sliding down a ladder. Then explore the rest of the museum.

Other Things to Do Nearby Make a day of it by exploring Navy Pier. Take a scenic cruise on Lake Michigan, relax in the IMAX theater, ride the Ferris wheel and carousel, eat lunch in the food court, or simply take a stroll to enjoy the Chicago skyline and Lake Michigan stretching out to the horizon.

Chicago Cultural Center

Type of Attraction A huge neoclassical structure containing the Museum of Broadcast Communications, eclectic art, and a free visitor information center; a downtown refuge for weary tourists. A self-guided tour.

Location Zone 4—The Loop; 78 East Washington Street, Chicago, 60602

Admission Free

Hours Monday–Wednesday, 10 a.m.–7 p.m.; Thursday, 10 a.m.–9 p.m.; Friday, 10 a.m.–6 p.m.; Saturday, 10 a.m.–5 p.m.; Sunday, 11 a.m.–5 p.m.

Phone (312) 346-3278

When to Go Any time.

Special Comments Free building tours are offered on Tuesday and Wednesday at 1:30 p.m. and Saturday at 2 p.m.

Appeal by Age Group

Pre-school ★½	Teens ★★½	Over 30 ★★★½
Grade school ★★	Young Adults ★★½	Seniors ★★★★

Authors' Rating An impressive building with a little bit of everything. ★★★½

How Much Time to Allow One hour for a quick run-through. Because of its convenient location and free admission, plan to stop here throughout your visit.

Description and Comments The nation's first free municipal cultural center served as Chicago's central library for nearly 100 years. Today it dispenses culture the way it once loaned books. Highlights of the building are spectacular stained-glass domes located in the north and south wings, which originally served as skylights. They were later enclosed in copper and backlighted to fully reveal and protect their beauty; the 38-foot dome in Preston Hall is thought to be the world's largest Tiffany dome, with a value estimated at $38 million. Preston Bradley Hall was renovated in the 1970s into a performance hall and hosts free weekly classical music concerts; the G.A.R. Rotunda and Memorial Hall will intrigue Civil War buffs.

First-time visitors to Chicago should take advantage of the Visitor Information Center in the main lobby and the Welcome Center, which provides orientation to the city and downtown. The coffee bar can inject a caffeine boost and give respite to weary feet; a number of nearby corridors serve as art galleries showcasing established and emerging artists.

The Grand Staircase features multicolored mosaics set in the balustrades, while the fourth floor of the Cultural Center boasts nearly 13,000 square feet of art exhibition space. The Museum of Broadcast Communications is located on the Washington Street side of the building (see profile).

Touring Tips Plan to stop at this prime example of 19th-century beaux arts architecture early in your visit; the Visitor Information Center in the lobby dispenses free information and touring advice. Then head up the Grand Staircase to view the Tiffany stained-glass dome on the third floor. From there, walk to the fourth-floor exhibition hall to see what's on display. Then take a peek into the beautiful Preston Bradley Hall.

Other Things to Do Nearby The Art Institute of Chicago is two blocks south on Michigan Avenue; the Loop is a block to the west. Directly across from the Art Institute on South Michigan Avenue is the Chicago Architecture Foundation, the starting point of not-to-be-missed daily walking tours of the Loop. For a great view, walk three blocks north to the Michigan Avenue Bridge and look up.

Chicago Historical Society

Type of Attraction A spacious museum highlighting Chicago history, from early frontier days to the present. A self-guided tour.

Location Zone 1—The North Side; Clark Street at North Avenue, Chicago, 60614
Admission $5 adults, $3 seniors and students ages 13–22, $1 children ages 6–13; $8 additional charge for Norman Rockwell exhibit; $3 additional charge for George Washington exhibit; general admission free on Monday
Hours Monday–Saturday, 9:30 a.m–4:30 p.m.; Sunday, 11 a.m.–5 p.m.
Phone (312) 642-4600
When to Go On weekdays during the school year, plan your visit in the afternoon after the school field trips are over.
Special Comments Parking for disabled visitors is provided in the adjacent lot. There's also a new parking garage at the corner of Clark and LaSalle that charges $5.50.

Appeal by Age Group

Pre-school ★	Teens ★★½	Over 30 ★★★
Grade school ★★½	Young Adults ★★★	Seniors ★★★

Authors' Rating There's a lot of neat stuff here, but it's also a bit austere ... and a little boring. ★★½

How Much Time to Allow Two hours.

Description and Comments The original entrance, which faces east, features a columned portico and a broad stairway stretching down to the broad lawn facing Lincoln Park and Lake Michigan. Today, the entrance is in the annex facing Clark Street, where large expanses of gridded glass welcome visitors to this large museum that showcases Chicago's history. The clean and modern interior features high ceilings and plenty of elbow room for visitors perusing the many exhibits.

Inside you'll find galleries hung with paintings, glass cases filled with artifacts (in the grand tradtion of Victorian collecting) and a seemingly endless procession of static displays explaining the city's past. Livelier exhibitions feature a real steam locomotive, an interactive gallery for hands-on fun, and eight miniature scenes depicting Chicago's rapid growth in the 19th century.

Touring Tips On the first floor, the Illinois Pioneer Life Gallery offers a fascinating glimpse of the state's early days, including a display of farm implements familiar to early settlers; test your ingenuity by guessing how they were used (answers are provided). The second floor's best exhibit is Chicago History, with a steam locomotive you can climb aboard. The American History Wing is less interesting, but Civil War buffs won't want to miss "A House Divided: America in the Age of Lincoln." Neither exhibit, however, focuses on Chicago. Hungry? The Big Shoulders Cafe on the first floor gets rave reviews from local diners.

Other Things to Do Nearby The Lincoln Park Zoo is within easy walking distance. Head west on North Avenue to find a selection of restaurants and fast-food restaurants. Or take the pedestrian bridge over Lake Shore Drive for views of Lake Michigan.

David and Alfred Smart Museum of Art

Type of Attraction A collection of art objects spanning five millennia, including works by Albrecht Dürer, August Rodin, Frank Lloyd Wright, Walker Evans, and Mark Rothko. A self-guided tour.
Location Zone 7—South Side; 5550 South Greenwood Avenue (on the University of Chicago campus), Chicago, 60637

Admission Free

Hours Tuesday, Wednesday, and Friday, 10 a.m.–4 p.m.; Thursday (spring and fall only), 10 a.m.–9 p.m., Friday and Saturday, noon–6 p.m.; closed Monday and holidays.

Phone (312) 702-0200

When to Go Any time.

Special Comments All the galleries are on one level and are wheelchair accessible. Free parking is available in the lot on the corner of 55th Street and Greenwood Avenue on weekends.

Appeal by Age Group

Pre-school ★	Teens ★★½	Over 30 ★★★
Grade school ★★	Young Adults ★★★	Seniors ★★★

Authors' Rating A sparkling white series of rooms featuring an eclectic array of art; you're sure to find something you like. ★★★

How Much Time to Allow One to two hours.

Description and Comments The art on display ranges from the ancient Greek to outrageous modern works culled from a permanent collection of more than 7,000 objects. In addition, the museum schedules eight special exhibitions each year. The feel of the place, like the campus around it, is serious, cerebral, and highbrow.

Touring Tips Don't miss the furniture on display designed by Frank Lloyd Wright, "Dining Table and Six Chairs," a prime example of the Chicago architect's spare, modern style. (And you thought the Wizard of Oak Park only designed houses you can't afford.) The Smart, a museum named for the founders of *Esquire* magazine, is a compact and easy gallery to explore. The bookstore features art books, posters, cards, children's books, and jewelry. A cafe offers sandwiches, salads, pastas, and other goodies.

Other Things to Do Nearby The Oriental Institute Museum and the DuSable Museum are close. If the weather is nice, stroll the beautiful University of Chicago campus; look for the Henry Moore sculpture (placed on the site of the first self-sustaining nuclear reaction on December 2, 1942) across from the Enrico Fermi Institute. The massive Museum of Science and Industry is on 57th Street. Join the locals for lunch at Valois, located at 1518 East 53rd Street.

DuSable Museum of African-American History

Type of Attraction A collection of artifacts, paintings, and photos that trace the black experience in the United States. A self-guided tour.

Location Zone 7—South Side; 740 East 56th Place (57th Street and Cottage Avenue near the eastern edge of the University of Chicago), Chicago, 60637

Admission $3 adults, $2 students, $1 children ages 6–13; free on Sunday.

Hours Weekdays, 10 a.m.–5 p.m.; wekends, noon–5 p.m.; closed Thanksgiving, Christmas, and New Year's Day.

Phone (773) 947-0600

When to Go Any time.

Special Comments The large main-floor gallery hosts temporary exhibits; check the *Chicago Reader* or call before visiting to find out what's on display.

Appeal by Age Group

Pre-school ★½	Teens ★★★	Over 30 ★★★★
Grade school ★★½	Young Adults ★★½	Seniors ★★★★

Authors' Rating Fascinating stuff, including, on our visit, an eye-opening show on the everyday lives of slaves in the antebellum South. ★★★½

How Much Time to Allow One to two hours.

Description and Comments This museum, which once served as a park administration building and a police lockup, is named after Jean Baptist Pointe du Sable, a Haitian of mixed African and European descent who was Chicago's first permanent settler in the late 18th century. Exhibits include paintings by African Americans, displays that vividly portray the lives of blacks in pre–Civil War days, and a room dedicated to black hero Joe Louis.

Touring Tips Paintings are located on the lower level, while temporary exhibits are displayed upstairs along with two small permanent exhibits on segregation (look for the sign, "For White Passengers") and on boxing champ Joe Louis. Avoid weekday mornings, when large school groups schedule visits; Thursdays, when admission is free, are also crowded. The gift shop features jewelry, fabrics, and arts and crafts created by African Americans.

Other Things to Do Nearby Outside the DuSable Museum, the beautiful lawns of Washington Park beckon in nice weather. The nearby University of Chicago campus is a great place to stroll; places to visit include the Oriental Institute Museum and the Smart Museum of Art. The immense Museum of Science and Industry is on 57th Street. Valois, a cafeteria where locals hang out, is located at 1518 East 53rd Street. Don't venture too far from the campus, though; it's only a marginally safe neighborhood.

Ernest Hemingway Museum

Type of Attraction A small collection of exhibits featuring rare photos of the Nobel laureate, his childhood diary, letters, early writing, and other memorabilia focusing on the writer's Oak Park years. A self-guided tour.

Location Zone 2—North Central/O'Hare; in the Oak Park Arts Center, 200 North Oak Park Avenue, Oak Park, 60302

Admission $7 adults, $5 seniors and students, free for children under age 5 with an adult; fee covers admission to both museum and birthplace

Hours Thursday, Friday, and Sunday, 1–5 p.m.; Saturday, 10 a.m.– 5 p.m.; closed Monday–Wednesday

Phone (708) 848-2222

When to Go Any time.

Special Comments Hemingway's Birthplace is about a block and a half away on the other side of Oak Park Avenue.

Appeal by Age Group

Pre-school ★	Teens ★½	Over 30 ★★
Grade school ★	Young Adults ★★	Seniors ★★

Authors' Rating A *very* narrow slice of the great writer's life that will be best appreciated by hard-core fans. ★★

How Much Time to Allow 30 minutes.

Description and Comments A handful of display cases in the basement of a former church house this small collection of Hemingway memorabilia. Artifacts on view range from photos, diaries, and family items to a violin and typewriter once owned by the writer, whom many critics consider the greatest U.S. author. A six-minute video recalls Hemingway's upper-middle-class high school years . . . but doesn't mention that he left town for good at age 20 and, unlike most famous writers from Chicago, wrote very little about his hometown.

Touring Tips There's one gem to be found in this smallish collection: the "Dear John" letter Hemingway received from Agnes Von Kurowsky, the nurse who tended his wounds in Italy after he was injured while serving as a volunteer ambulance driver during World War I. "For the rest of his life Hemingway was marked by his scars from battle and by an abiding distrust of women," the exhibit notes. Hem got his revenge, though; check out the ending of *A Farewell to Arms*—the beautiful nurse who tended the wounded hero croaks in the last chapter. What you *won't* find is any reference to his alleged remark that Oak Park is a town of "broad lawns and narrow minds."

Other Things to Do Nearby The Frank Lloyd Wright Home and Studio is only a few blocks away. Unity Temple, a National Historic Landmark designed by Wright in 1905, is located at 875 Lake Street; it's considered a masterpiece and is open weekdays 10 a.m. to 5 p.m. for self-guided tours ($4 for adults and $3 for seniors and children under age 18), and on weekends for guided tours at 1, 2, and 3 p.m. Guided tours are $6 for adults and $4 for seniors and children under age 18. Downtown Oak Park has a selection of dining and fast-food options. Brookfield Zoo is a few miles west off the Eisenhower Expressway (take Route 171 south).

Field Museum of Natural History

Type of Attraction One of the largest public museums in the United States, with more than nine acres of exhibits. A self-guided tour.

Location Zone 5—South Loop; East Roosevelt Road at Lake Shore Drive (in Grant Park)

Admission $8 adults; $4 seniors, children ages 3–11, and students; special exhibits: additional $6 adults, $3 children; January, February, and September 23–December 24: free general admission on Monday and Tuesday

Hours Daily, 9 a.m.–5 p.m.; closed Christmas and New Year's Day.

Phone (312) 922-9410

When to Go Any time.

Special Comments If someone in your party needs to make a pit stop while touring the special exhibits, go to the Dinosaur Hall exit and speak to a Visitor Services Representative (in a red jacket).

Appeal by Age Group

Pre-school ★★★★★	Teens ★★★★★	Over 30 ★★★★★
Grade school ★★★★★	Young Adults ★★★★★	Seniors ★★★★★

Authors' Rating This world-renowned institution draws on more than 20 million artifacts and specimens to fill its exhibits. If you can't find something you like here, it's time to get out of Chicago. ★★★★★

How Much Time to Allow Two hours for a brief run through; all day for a more leisurely exploration—but even then, you won't see it all.

Descriptions and Comments Founded in 1893 to create a permanent home for the natural history collections gathered in Chicago for the World's Columbian Exposition, the Field Museum today is one of the great institutions of its kind in the world, focusing on public learning and scientific study of the world's environments and cultures. For visitors, it's a chance to explore a mind-boggling assortment of the world's wonders.

While much of the museum reflects the Victorian mania for specimen collecting—aisle after aisle of wood-and-glass display cases and dioramas are filled with items from around the world—much of what you find here includes newer, more dynamic exhibits. Many emphasize hands-on fun and thematic exhibits, such as "Africa," "Inside Ancient Egypt," "Into the Wild," "Gems," "Traveling the Pacific," and "Life over Time," a high-tech journey that takes visitors through 3.8 billion years of the history of life.

"Life over Time" picks up where the dinosaur show leaves off. Fossils, dioramas, a nine-foot-tall walk-in hut built of mammoth bones, and videos in the 7,000-square-foot exhibit explore climatic change and mammal evolution during the Ice Age.

Touring Tips Folks with youngsters in tow or with a strong interest in dinosaurs should make their way to the second level to explore "Life over Time." It's a kid-oriented exhibit that's heavy on education, hands-on science stuff, and TV monitors showing "newscasts" by suit-clad anchors "reporting" on the beginning of life a billion years ago. It all ends up in a huge hall filled with dinosaur fossils and reconstructed skeletons. It's pure bliss for the Barney crowd.

After exploring the world of dinosaurs and mammoths (including Sue, the largest, most complete fossil of *T. rex* yet discovered) check your map and pick something of interest. Here's some help: Tots will enjoy the play area on the second floor, while older folks can check out exhibits of gems and jades also on the second floor. The popular Egyptian tomb (complete with mummies) is on the first floor, as are exhibits on Native Americans, Africa, birds, reptiles, a re-creation of a wilderness, and a "nature" walk. The ground floor features places to grab a bite to eat and exhibits on bushmen, sea mammals, prehistoric people, and ancient Egypt.

Other Things to Do Nearby The Shedd Aquarium and Adler Planetarium are both within easy walking distance on the new, traffic-free Museum Campus. Fast food is available inside the museum, but anything else requires taking a cab or bus downtown.

Frank Lloyd Wright Home and Studio

Type of Attraction The Oak Park home of famed architect Frank Lloyd Wright and the birthplace of the Prairie School of architecture. Guided and self-guided tours.

Location Zone 2—North Central/O'Hare; 951 Chicago Avenue, Oak Park, 60302. If you drive, park in the garage next to the Oak Park Visitor Center at 158 Forest Avenue. The center is open daily from 10 a.m. to 5 p.m. and centrally located, within easy walking distance to all the Wright and Hemingway attractions in town; purchase your tickets and pick up a map and more information inside. The visitor center is closed Thanksgiving, Christmas, and New Year's Day. Parking in the garage is free on weekends.

Admission $9 adults, $7 seniors and children under age 18; Forest Avenue walking tours (self-guided by audio cassette): $9 plus deposit; guided Forest Avenue walking tours: $9 adults, $7 seniors and children.

Hours 45-minute guided home and studio tours begin at 11 a.m., 1 p.m., and 3 p.m. Monday–Friday and about every 20 minutes 11 a.m.–3:30 p.m. on weekends; closed Thanksgiving, Christmas, and New Year's Day. Self-guided audio cassette tours of the exteriors of 13 Wright-designed houses along nearby Forest Avenue are available 10 a.m.–3:30 p.m. daily. Guided walking tours of the neighborhood are at 10:30 a.m., 11 a.m., noon, 1 p.m., 2 p.m., 3 p.m., and 4 p.m. weekends, March–October. Tours begin at noon, 1 p.m., and 2 p.m. November–February.

Phone (708) 848-1976

When to Go Any time. For the walking tours, bring an umbrella if it looks like rain.

Special Comments The house tour involves climbing and descending a flight of stairs.

Appeal by Age Group

Pre-school ★	Teens ★★	Over 30 ★★★★
Grade school ★½	Young Adults ★★★	Seniors ★★★★

Authors' Rating A fascinating glimpse into the life of America's greatest architect. ★★★★

How Much Time to Allow One hour.

Description and Comments Between 1889 and 1909, this house with prominent gables, window bays, and dark, shingled surfaces served as home, studio, and architectural laboratory for young Chicago architect Frank Lloyd Wright. Today it offers a permanent visual record of the beginnings of his continuous exploration of the relationship of light, form, and space. This is where Wright established the principles that guided his life work and launched a revolution that changed the architectural landscape of the 20th century. Yet this house Wright built with $5,000 borrowed from his employer doesn't reflect his Prairie School of design, the first distinctly American style of architecture featuring low, earth-hugging dwellings. That would come later.

Touring Tips What's fascinating about the tour—and what you should watch out for—are glimpses of early examples of elements that would become hallmarks of a Wright-designed home: large rooms that flow together, unity of design, minimal form, functionality, and the fusion of art and design elements. The tour guides do a good job of pointing them out.

The studio, which ends the tour and was added to the house by Wright in 1898, is a stunner, with walls supported by chains and a two-story octagonal drafting room. Here, working with 15 apprentices, Wright completed about 150 commissions and refined his Prairie School principles.

Other Things to Do Nearby The Ernest Hemingway Museum and the Hemingway Birthplace are only a few blocks away; both destinations are pleasant walks when the weather is nice. Unity Temple, a National Historic Landmark designed by Wright in 1905, is located at 875 Lake Street; it's considered a masterpiece and is open weekdays 10 a.m. to 5 p.m. for self-guided tours ($4 for adults and $3 for seniors and children under age 18; (708) 383-8873 for more information), and on weekends for guided tours at 1, 2, and 3 p.m. Guided tours are $6 for adults and $4 for seniors and children under age 18. Downtown Oak Park offers several places to grab something to eat.

Garfield Park Conservatory

Type of Attraction Four-and-a-half acres of grounds and 5,000 species and varieties of plants, most of them housed under the glass of a landmark 1907 structure. Self-guided tours.

Location Zone 2—North Central/O'Hare; 300 North Central Park Avenue, Chicago, 60624

Admission Free; $2 suggested donation for flower shows

Hours Daily, 9 a.m.–5 p.m.; 10 a.m.–5 p.m. during major flower shows

Phone (312) 746-5100

When to Go Any time.

Special Comments Garfield Park is located in a high-crime area. But stick close to the Conservatory and you'll be okay; the free parking lot is only a few steps away from the entrance.

Appeal by Age Group

Pre-school ★★½	Teens ★★½	Over 30 ★★½
Grade school ★★½	Young Adults ★★½	Seniors ★★★

Authors' Rating Some really big plants (many dating from 1907) and plenty of interior space promote a feeling of serenity. ★★★

How Much Time to Allow One hour (or longer if you've got a green thumb).

Description and Comments Four times larger than the conservatory in Lincoln Park, the Garfield Park Conservatory offers a world-class collection of botanical gardens for visitors to enjoy. The Palm House displays a variety of graceful palms, while the Cactus House encloses one of the nation's finest cactus displays (including giant saguaro) arranged in a typical Southwestern desert motif. A quiet visit here is soothing after a hectic morning of shopping on the Magnificent Mile or sight-seeing in the Loop.

Touring Tips Horticulture hounds and home gardeners can quiz the trained personnel that staff the conservatory about house plants and gardening in general. If you can't make it in person, call in your questions at (312) 746-5100. The conservatory hosts major flower shows throughout the year; see "A Calendar of Festivals and Events" in Part Two: Planning Your Visit to Chicago. Monet's Garden Cafe serves lunch daily from 10 a.m. to 5 p.m.; picnic lunches are available on weekends.

Other Things to Do Nearby The Peace Museum (see profile) is located in the Garfield Park Gold Dome, two blocks south of the conservatory. Garfield Park is one of the areas of green linked by the city's network of boulevards.

Harold Washington Library Center

Type of Attraction The world's second-largest public library (after the British Library in London). Guided and self-guided tours.

Location Zone 4—The Loop; 400 South State Street, Chicago, 60605

Admission Free

Hours Monday–Thursday, 9 a.m.–7 p.m.; Friday and Saturday, 9 a.m.–5 p.m.; Sunday, 1–5 p.m.

Phone (312) 747-4999

When to Go Any time.

Special Comments The library isn't very visitor-friendly: From the enclosed lobby on the first floor, take the escalators to the third floor, which serves as the main entrance to the library proper. From there, elevators and escalators provide access to the other seven levels. Conversely, to leave the building, you must return to the third floor and take the escalators down to the exit level (elevators are available for handicapped folks). What a pain.

Appeal by Age Group

Pre-school ★	Teens ★★	Over 30 ★★½
Grade school ★★	Young Adults ★★½	Seniors ★★½

Authors' Rating Though a trip to the library isn't on most travel itineraries, consider making an exception in Chicago. It's definitely worth a stop. ★★★

How Much Time to Allow One hour; consider joining a free public tour beginning at noon or 2 p.m., Monday through Saturday. The guided tour lasts an hour and starts in the third-floor Orientation Theater.

Description and Comments This neoclassical building with elements of beaux arts, classical, and modern ornamentation opened in 1991 and cost $144 million. Named after the late Chicago mayor (a notorious bookworm), the 750,000-square-foot Harold Washington Library Center serves as the Loop's southern gateway.

Inside are housed more than two million volumes; an electronic directory system that displays floor layouts, book locations, and upcoming events; a computerized reference system; more than 70 miles of shelving; a permanent collection of art spread over ten floors; and lots of nooks for curling up with a book.

Touring Tips Several not-to-be-missed attractions include the ninth-floor, glass-enclosed Winter Garden; the Harold Washington Collection (an exhibit located next to the Winter Garden); and the Jazz, Blues, Gospel Hall of Fame (eighth floor).

Folks with the time and interest should visit the eighth-floor Listening/Viewing Center, where patrons can watch videos and listen to music from the collection's 100,000 78 rpm records, LPs, and compact discs. Selections are particularly plentiful in popular music, jazz, and blues. Hours are Monday–Thursday, noon–6 p.m.; Friday and Saturday, noon–4 p.m.; closed Sunday. You don't have to be a Chicago resident to take advantage of the free service, although all patrons are limited to one session per day; there is a one-hour time limit if other people are waiting. Since the Center relies on a large array of electronics, it's often closed for maintenance; call (312) 747-4850 before going.

In addition, the library presents a wide range of special events throughout the year, including films, dance programs, lectures, storytelling sessions for children, concerts, special programs for children, art exhibits, and more. See the *Chicago Reader* (a free "alternative" paper) to find out what's happening during your visit.

Other Things to Do Nearby The Loop is a block to the north; hang a right to head toward Grant Park and the Art Institute of Chicago. Turn left at the elevated tracks to reach the Chicago Board of Trade and the Sears Tower. Eating and shopping establishments abound throughout the heart of downtown.

Hellenic Museum

Type of Attraction A small museum highlighting the history and contributions of Greek immigrants to American life and culture. A self-guided tour.

Location Zone 4—The Loop; National Bank of Greece Building, 168 North Michigan Avenue, Fourth Floor, Chicago, 60601

Admission $4

Hours Monday–Friday, 10 a.m.–4 p.m.; other times by appointment.

Phone (312) 726-1234

When to Go Any time.

Special Comments Long-term plans are to relocate the museum to larger quarters in Greektown, west of the Loop on Halsted Street.

Author's Rating Interesting, if narrow, slice of American immigrant history and culture. Worth a peek. ★★

How Much Time to Allow 30 minutes to an hour.

Description and Comments Greece may be one of the major sources of Western culture—and Greek immigrants' contributions to American life are the focus of this one-room museum located on North Michigan Avenue. The museum features temporary shows, such as a recent exhibit on Greek American soldiers who fought for their country from the Spanish-American War to the Gulf War.

Touring Tips The small bookstore has a wide array of books on Greek history and culture.

Other Things to Do Nearby The Art Institute of Chicago and the Loop are close, as is the Spertus Museum. Grant Park is a block east and the Chicago Cultural Center offers art and touring information, as well as a coffee shop.

Hemingway's Birthplace

Type of Attraction The partially restored Victorian house where Ernest Hemingway was born in 1899. A guided tour.

Location Zone 2—North Central/O'Hare; 339 North Oak Park Avenue, Oak Park, 60302

Admission $7 adults, $5 seniors and students, free for children under age 5 with an adult; fee covers admission to both museum and birthplace

Hours Thursday, Friday, and Sunday, 1–5 p.m.; Saturday, 10 a.m.–5 p.m.; closed Monday–Wednesday

Phone (708) 848-2222

When to Go Any time.

Special Comments One short but rather steep flight of stairs leads to the second floor.

Appeal by Age Group

Pre-school ★	Teens ★½	Over 30 ★½
Grade school ★	Young Adults ★½	Seniors ★★

Authors' Rating Strictly for die-hard Hemingway fans. ★½

How Much Time to Allow 45 minutes.

Description and Comments Open since the fall of 1993, this fine Victorian house has a long way to go before it becomes fully restored—and even then, it will only interest folks seeking a glimpse of upper-middle-class life in turn-of-the-19th-century Oak Park. Hemingway lived here for five years as a child, and only a few of the items on display are original. Upstairs, visitors can look into (but can't enter) the lavishly restored room where the writer was born.

Touring Tips Look for the embalmed muskrats (at least, that's what the docent and I guessed they are) that Hemingway and his doctor father stuffed when the great writer was a boy. Unfortunately, visitors are subjected to a much-too-long video (15 minutes, actually) that tells them more than they'll ever want to know about the Nobel Prize winner's grandparents. Unless you've got an abiding interest in Hemingway's genealogy, plead a tight schedule and try to skip the film.

Other Things to Do Nearby The Ernest Hemingway Museum is down the street; the Frank Lloyd Wright Home and Studio is only a few blocks away. Unity Temple, a National Historic Landmark designed by Wright in 1905, is located at 875 Lake Street; it's considered a masterpiece and is open weekdays 10 a.m. to 5 p.m. for self-guided tours ($4 for adults and $3 for seniors and children under age 18), and on weekends for guided tours at 1, 2, and 3 p.m. Guided tours are $6 for adults and $4 for seniors and children under age 18. Downtown Oak Park offers several dining and fast-food options. Brookfield Zoo is a few miles west, off I-290.

International Museum of Surgical Science

Type of Attraction Exhibits from around the world trace the history of surgery and related sciences. A self-guided tour.

Location Zone 3—Near North; 1524 North Lake Shore Drive, Chicago, 60610

Admission $6 adults, $3 seniors and students; free on Tuesday with a suggested donation of the regular admission

Hours Tuesday–Sunday, 10 a.m.–4 p.m.; closed Monday

Phone (312) 642-6502

When to Go Any time.

Special Comments Though the truly squeamish should avoid this place like the plague, there's actually very little on display that's overtly gory or upsetting. The museum is located on the #151 bus route, and limited parking is available in a small lot behind the building; additional parking is located in Lincoln Park and at North Avenue Beach. It's a short, pleasant stroll away from North Michigan Avenue.

Appeal by Age Group

Pre-school ★	Teens ★★	Over 30 ★★½
Grade school ★½	Young Adults ★★½	Seniors ★★½

Authors' Rating A must-see for folks in the medical field; otherwise, it's a nice fill-in spot when exploring the Gold Coast on foot. ★★½

How Much Time to Allow One hour for most folks; half a day for those with a keen interest in medical science.

Description and Comments The mysteries, breakthroughs, failures, and historic milestones of surgical science are on display in this unusual museum housed in an elegant mansion facing Lake Michigan. Implements on display range from the truly horrifying (2,000-year-old skulls with holes bored into them and tin-and-wood enema syringes from the 1800s) to the quaint (such as an X-ray shoe fitter from the early 1950s). The first floor features a re-creation of a 19th-century pharmacy and an early-20th-century dentist's office.

Touring Tips Start on the first floor and explore displays of antique medical instruments, then work your way up to the fourth floor. The second floor's Hall of Immortals features 12 eight-foot statues representing great medical figures in history, while the third floor includes an exhibit of antique microscopes and early X-ray equipment. Look for Napoleon's original death mask and more ancient medical instruments on the fourth floor.

Other Things to Do Nearby Explore Chicago's opulent Gold Coast neighborhood on foot. It's only a few blocks south to the Magnificent Mile, which features expensive shops, malls, department stores, and a knock-your-socks-off view from the 94th-floor observatory in the John Hancock Center (when it's not raining).

Jane Addams Hull House Museum

Type of Attraction The restored 1856 country home that became the nucleus of the world-famous settlement house complex founded by Jane Addams (a Nobel Peace Prize winner) at the end of the 19th century. A self-guided tour.

Location Zone 6—South Central/Midway; 800 South Halsted Street, on the campus of the University of Illinois at Chicago

Admission Free

Hours Monday–Friday, 10 a.m.–4 p.m.; Sunday, noon–5 p.m.; closed Saturday.

Phone (312) 413-5353

When to Go Any time.

Special Comments Park across the street in the University of Illinois parking lot.

Appeal by Age Group

Pre-school ★	Teens ★★½	Over 30 ★★½
Grade school ★★	Young Adults ★★½	Seniors ★★★

Authors' Rating An oasis of dignity, this restored museum is all that remains of a once-vibrant ethnic melting pot once served by the Nobel Peace Prize winner. ★★½

How Much Time to Allow One hour.

Description and Comments This square, brick, 19th-century house in the shadow of the University of Illinois at Chicago is where Jane Addams and Ellen Gates Starr began the settlement work that helped give immigrants a better shot at the American dream.

The lush Victorian interior includes Addams's desk, an old Oliver typewriter, photos of the staff, and several rooms of rich furnishings.

Touring Tips Start your tour upstairs in the Residents' Dining Hall with the 15-minute slide show on the settlement house movement. The tour ends in the restored mansion.

Other Things to Do Nearby Sample some pasta in Little Italy, southwest of the University of Illinois campus. Greektown and more great ethnic dining is north on Halsted, just past the Eisenhower Expressway. The Loop is a few blocks to the northeast.

John Hancock Center Observatory

Type of Attraction A 39-second elevator ride leading to a spectacular, 94th-floor view of Chicago. A self-guided tour.

Location Zone 3—Near North; 875 North Michigan Avenue, Chicago, IL 60611

Admission $9.50 adults, $7.50 seniors, $6 children ages 5–12, free for children under age 4. Individual sky tours, $3 with admission.

Hours Daily, 9 a.m.–11 p.m. (no tickets sold after 10:45 p.m.)

Phone (888) 875-VIEW or (312) 751-3681

When to Go Any time.

Special Comments This is an excellent alternative to the Sears Tower Skydeck, where the lines can be very long. In fact, most Chicagoans say the view is better. If the top of the building is hidden in clouds, come back another day.

Appeal by Age Group

Pre-school ★★★★★	Teens ★★★★★	Over 30 ★★★★★
Grade school ★★★★★	Young Adults ★★★★★	Seniors ★★★★★

Authors' Rating A stunning view, especially at sunset or at night. ★★★★★

How Much Time to Allow 30 minutes.

Description and Comments This distinctive building with the X-shaped exterior crossbracing is the 14th-highest building in the world. Although the 94th-floor observatory is nine floors lower than the Sears Tower Skydeck, some folks say the view is better here, perhaps due to its proximity to Lake Michigan.

Touring Tips The ideal way to enjoy the vista (you're 1,030 feet above Michigan Avenue) is to arrive just before sunset. As the sun sinks lower in the west, slowly the city lights blink on—and a whole new view appears.

Other Things to Do Nearby The 95th and 96th floors of the John Hancock Center house the highest restaurant and lounge in the city. (You can relax with a drink for about the same cost as visiting the observatory, but there's no guarantee you'll get a seat with a view.) Or return to street level and shop till you drop along chi-chi North Michigan Avenue; the Water Tower Place shopping mall is next door.

John G. Shedd Aquarium

Type of Attraction The world's largest indoor aquarium; the Oceanarium, the world's largest indoor marine mammal facility, re-creates a Pacific Northwest coastline. A self-guided tour.

Location Zone 5—South Loop; 1200 South Lake Shore Drive

Admission Aquarium and Oceanarium: $15 for adults, $11 for seniors and children ages 3–11. Aquarium is free on Mondays and Tuesdays, September through February.

Hours Monday–Friday, 9 a.m.–5 p.m. (until 6 p.m. in summer); Saturday and Sunday, 9 a.m.–6 p.m.; closed Christmas and New Year's Day.

Phone (312) 939-2438

When to Go Before noon during the summer and on major holidays. A time-ticket system is in effect for visitors to the extremely popular Oceanarium and tickets are often sold out by 3 p.m.; if you get a ticket, waits of two to three hours are not uncommon on busy days. (If you're waiting, tour the aquarium or other attractions.) Try to time your visit to coincide with the aquarium's coral reef feedings—a diver enters the circular 90,000-gallon exhibit and hand-feeds an assortment of tropical fishes; kids love it. Feeding times are 10:30 a.m., noon, 1:30 p.m., 3 p.m., and 4:30 p.m. daily.

Special Comments Three continuous nature slide shows lasting about 30 minutes are featured in the Phelps Auditorium. The seats are comfortable, and it's a great place to chill out when crowds are heavy.

Appeal by Age Group

Pre-school ★★★★★	Teens ★★★★★	Over 30 ★★★★★
Grade school ★★★★★	Young Adults ★★★★★	Seniors ★★★★★

Authors' Rating Whales breaching the surface with Lake Michigan in the background is an unforgettable sight. ★★★★★

How Much Time to Allow Two hours.

Description and Comments Not only does the Shedd Aquarium house more than 6,000 aquatic animals, the building itself is an architectural marvel, featuring majestic doorways, colorful mosaics, and wave and shell patterns on the walls. For most folks, however, the highlight of a visit is the Oceanarium, which treats visitors to a wide array of sea mammals—both from the surface and underwater through glass windows. The huge exhibit, which features a Lake Michigan backdrop, is quite spiffy.

In the aquarium, cool and dark rooms are lined with tanks filled with a wide assortment of creatures, including a huge alligator snapping turtle, electric eels, piranhas, and an especially creepy-looking green moray eel (which, we're sad to report, is actually blue; its skin appears green because it's coated with thick yellow mucus—yuck). The The Amazon Rising exhibit features 250 species in a re-creation of the Amazon River Basin.

Touring Tips Purchase a ticket that includes admission to the Oceanarium; from the foyer, head left around the circular Coral Reef Exhibit to the entrance. After touring both levels of the sea mammal emporium, return to the aquarium for a leisurely stroll past the many tanks; don't forget about the feedings in the coral reef (see above for times).

Other Things to Do Nearby The Adler Planetarium and the Field Museum of Natural History are both within walking distance on the traffic-free Museum Campus. If it's late in the afternoon and the sun's about to set, stick around; the Chicago skyline is about to do its nighttime thing. It's a view you won't soon forget.

Lincoln Park Zoo

Type of Attraction The most visited zoo in the nation, featuring more than 1,600 animals, birds, and reptiles. A self-guided tour.

Location Zone 1—The North Side; 2200 North Cannon Drive (Lincoln Park, off Lake Shore Drive at Fullerton Avenue north of the Magnificent Mile), Chicago, 60614

Admission Free; parking $9

Hours Daily, 8 a.m.–6 p.m. (until 7 p.m. in summer for Satruday, Sunday, and holidays)' buildings open at 10 a.m.

Phone (312) 742-2000

When to Go Any time, except weekday mornings from mid-April to mid-June, when as many as 100 school buses converge on the zoo; by 1:30 p.m., the hordes of youngsters are gone. Weekend afternoons during the summer also attract big crowds.

Special Comments Don't rule out a visit on a rainy or cold day: a lot of the animals are housed indoors. Interestingly enough, neighbors residing in nearby high-rises report they can hear wolves howling on warm summer nights.

Appeal by Age Group

Pre-school ★★★★	Teens ★★★★½	Over 30 ★★★
Grade school ★★★★★	Young Adults ★★★½	Seniors ★★★★

Authors' Rating Alas, this stately, old-fashioned zoo isn't in the same league as newer animal parks springing up around the nation. But it's still a refreshing oasis in the heart of bustling Chicago. ★★★

How Much Time to Allow Two hours.

Description and Comments Beautifully landscaped grounds, Lake Michigan, nearby high-rises, and the Chicago skyline in the distance are the hallmarks of this venerable but smallish park. Plus, the stately old buildings that house many of the zoo's inhabitants lend a Victorian elegance. Adults and especially children won't want to miss the Farm-in-the-Zoo (a farm featuring chickens, horses, and cows) and a children's zoo where the kids can enjoy a collection of small animals at eye level.

Touring Tips If you're pressed for time, the most popular exhibits at the zoo are the polar bear, elephants, and (hold your nose) the Primate House, where great apes cavort behind thick panes of glass. Before or after your visit, stop by the Lincoln Park Conservatory, three acres of Victorian greenhouses built in 1891 that provide a lush rainforest setting for flora and fauna from around the world. Seasonally, the Christmas poinsettias and Easter lilies draw huge crowds.

The conservatory is just outside the zoo's northwest entrance (near the elephants), and it's free. The restored Cafe Brauer serves salads and sandwiches; the Penguin Palace Ice Cream Shoppe dishes up ice cream during the summer.

Other Things to Do Nearby The Chicago Historical Society (and its acclaimed cafe) is an easy stroll from the zoo. A walk west for a block or two leads to a number of fast-food restaurants. Or take the pedestrian bridge across Lake Shore Drive and watch the waves crash against the Lake Michigan shoreline.

Mexican Fine Arts Center Museum

Type of Attraction The only Mexican museum in the Midwest features permanent and temporary exhibits by local, national, and international artists. A self-guided tour.

Location Zone 6—South Central/Midway; 1852 West 19th Street, Chicago, IL 60608

Admission Free

Hours Tuesday–Sunday, 10 a.m.–5 p.m.; closed Monday and major holidays.

Phone (312) 738-1503

Website mfacmchicago.org

When to Go Any time.

Special Comments All the exhibition space is on one level.

Appeal by Age Group

Pre-school ★	Teens ★★★	Over 30 ★★★½
Grade school ★	Young Adults ★★★½	Seniors ★★★½

Authors' Rating The galleries are attractive and well lighted; the Day of the Dead exhibit shown during our visit was an entertaining collection of colorful, funny, and bizarre folk art. ★★★½

How Much Time to Allow One hour.

Description and Comments When approaching Harrison Park in the Pilsen neighborhood, there is no doubt as to which building is the Mexican Fine Arts Museum (there's an Aztec design in the brickwork along the top of the structure). There are five different areas inside the museum: the permanent collection, the interactive room, the temporary art exhibits, the museum store, and the performing arts theater. The permanent collection offers a walk-through tour of Mexican history. Starting in Ancient Mexico, you then visit colonial Mexico, the Mexican Revolution, and the Mexican experience in the United States. Each exhibit displays artifacts, social structures, and significant developments along with the people that brought them about. An abundance of information accompanies each display (written in both English and Spanish). At the end, a large screen display runs a short movie about the Mexican experience. After leaving the permanent collection, the interactive room offers touchscreen computers which provide a look into other Mexican traditions as well as the opportunity to hear indigenous music. Most computers are set up for standing interaction, but there are a few terminals on a small desk for children. The temporary collection displays artwork from local, national, and international artists in a spacious gallery. Call ahead for a schedule of upcoming exhibits and performances, or visit the museum's website.

Touring Tips The large gift shop offers an extensive selection of Mexican items such as handicrafts, posters, toys, and books. Free guided tours are offered every Sunday at noon (English) and 1 p.m. (Spanish). In addition to changing exhibits by Hispanic artists, the Mexican Fine Arts Center Museum presents an ongoing series of readings, performances, and lectures. To see what's going on during your visit, pick up a free copy of the *Chicago Reader*.

Other Things to Do Nearby Pilsen, located along 18th Street between Canal and Damen streets, is a thriving Hispanic neighborhood with signs in Spanish and lots of spicy smells (good ethnic eateries, too). The Jane Addams Hull House Museum is about two miles northeast of the museum on Halsted Street (at the University of Illinois at Chicago). On weekends and holidays, the Blue Line does not stop at the museum; however, the city has provided a free trolley service to the museum that runs every 20 minutes on these off-days. More information on the other locations the free trolley visits can be found by visiting **www.877chicago.com** or by calling (877) CHICAGO.

Morton Arboretum

Type of Attraction A 1,700-acre, landscaped outdoor "museum" featuring more than 3,000 kinds of trees, shrubs, and vines from around the world. Guided and self-guided tours.

Location Zone 9—Western Suburbs; Route 53 (just off I-88) in Lisle (25 miles west of the Loop)

Admission $7 per car; $3 per car on Wednesdays only.

Hours April–October: daily, 7 a.m.–7 p.m.; November–March: daily, 7 a.m.–5 p.m. On major holidays, the grounds are open but the buildings are closed.

Phone (630) 719-2400 and (630) 968-0074

When to Go Spring and fall are the most beautiful seasons to visit, although the arboretum is worth a look year round. May and October weekends are the busiest; come in the morning to avoid the heaviest crowds.

Special Comments If throngs are packing the arboretum during your visit, head for the trails in Maple Woods at the east side of the park; most visitors don't venture far from the visitor center.

Appeal by Age Group

Pre-school ★★½	Teens ★★★	Over 30 ★★★½
Grade school ★★★	Young Adults ★★★½	Seniors ★★★★

Authors' Rating You don't have to be a tree hugger to appreciate this unusual and beautiful park. ★★★½

How Much Time to Allow One hour for a scenic drive; half a day to explore by foot.

Description and Comments In 1922, Joy Morton, the man who started the Morton Salt Company, founded this arboretum, a large park honeycombed with 25 miles of trails and 12 miles of one-way roads for car touring. Terrains here include native woodlands, wetlands, and prairie. The visitor center provides information on tours, trails, and places of special interest, such as the Plant Clinic, and houses a free library with books and magazines on trees, gardening, landscaping, nature, and other plant-related subjects.

The park, approximately four miles long and a mile wide, is divided into two segments bisected by Route 53; the visitor center is located on the east side. By car or on foot, visitors can explore a wide range of woodlands ranging from Northern Illinois and Western North American forests to collections of trees from Japan, China, the Balkans, and Northeast Asia. Interspersed between the woods are gently rolling hills and lakes.

Touring Tips Driving the 12 miles of roadway takes about 45 minutes without stopping. Good places to park the car and stretch your legs include Lake Marmo on the west side (park in lot P24) and the Maple Woods on the east side (lot P14). Foot trails range from pavement to wood chips, mowed paths, and gravel.

One-hour, open-air tram tours of the grounds are offered spring through fall from the visitor center. In May and October, the busiest months, tours start at 10:45 a.m., noon, 1:15 p.m., and 2:30 p.m. on weekends, and at noon, 1:15 p.m., and 2:30 p.m. weekdays. In June, July, and August, tours are offered at noon and 1:15 p.m. on weekends and Wednesdays. Tickets are $2 per person.

Other Things to Do Nearby Argonne National Laboratory, one of the nation's largest centers of energy research, is about five miles south of the Morton Arboretum. Saturday tours are available and advanced reservations are required; call (630) 252-5562. If you're heading back to Chicago on I-88 to I-290 (the Eisenhower Expressway), both the Brookfield Zoo and Oak Park are convenient stopping-off points.

Museum of Broadcast Communications

Type of Attraction A look at American culture through broadcasting memorabilia, hands-on exhibits, and public archives of more than 60,000 radio and television programs and commercials. A self-guided tour.

Location Zone 4—The Loop; In the Chicago Cultural Center, 78 East Washington Street, Chicago, 60602 (Washington Street entrance)

Admission Free

Hours Monday–Saturday, 10 a.m.–4:30 p.m.; Sunday, noon–5 p.m.; closed on state and national holidays.

Phone (312) 629-6000

When to Go Any time.

Special Comments Hour-long group tours are offered Monday through Friday at 10:30 a.m. and 2:30 p.m. The charge is $2.50 per person, and tours must be scheduled in advance; call (312) 629-6014.

Appeal by Age Group

Pre-school ★★½	Teens ★★★	Over 30 ★★★
Grade school ★★★★½	Young Adults ★★★	Seniors ★★★★½

Authors' Rating A small, attractive museum heavy on nostalgia. ★★½

How Much Time to Allow 30 minutes to an hour.

Description and Comments Chicago hosts a number of national talk shows, so it's only natural it should be home to this small, modern museum dedicated to TV and radio. Among the attractions are a TV exhibit gallery with changing video presentations, a news center that lets visitors play news anchor, two mini-theaters presenting award-winning TV commercials, and the Radio Hall of Fame (with a comprehensive collection of vintage radio sets).

Touring Tips In the A. C. Nielsen Jr. Research Center, visitors can see and hear TV and radio programs from the past. The museum's public archives contain 6,000 TV shows, 49,000 radio shows, and 8,000 commercials accessible for screening in 26 study suites (fee charged).

Other Things to Do Nearby Explore the rest of the Chicago Cultural Center or stroll down Michigan Avenue to the Art Institute of Chicago. The Loop, featuring plenty of skyscraper gazing, places to eat and shop, and unlimited people-watching, is a block west. Sign up for a Chicago Architecture Foundation walking tour of the Loop in their shop across from the Art Institute.

Museum of Contemporary Art

Type of Attraction An art museum dedicated to the avant garde in all media. A self-guided tour.

Location Zone 3—Near North; 220 East Chicago Avenue, Chicago, IL 60611

Admission $10 adults; $6 students and seniors; free for children age 12 and under; free on Tuesday

Hours Wednesday–Sunday, 10 a.m.–5 p.m.; Tuesday, 10 a.m.–8 p.m.; closed on Monday, Thanksgiving, Christmas, and New Year's Day.

Phone (312) 280-2660

When to Go Any time.

Special Comments Paid parking is available in the museum's parking garage; the MCA has wheelchair-accessible entrances, elevators, and rest rooms

Appeal by Age Group

Pre-school ★★½	Teens ★★★	Over 30 ★★★★½
Grade school ★★★	Young Adults ★★★½	Seniors ★★★★

Authors' Rating Chicago's spanking-new venue for modern art is bright, cheerful, and filled with paintings and sculpture, as well as some other difficult-to-categorize art-work. A not-to-be-missed destination for anyone who enjoys art that's both beautiful and challenging. ★★★★½

How Much Time to Allow One to two hours. Dyed-in-the-wool culture vultures should figure on at least half a day.

Description and Comments This five-story art museum opened in 1996 and provides a major world-class showcase for the MCA's permanent collection of late-20th-century art. Bright and airy on the inside, the new building doesn't overwhelm visitors like, say, the huge Art Institute. Most of the art is displayed on the fourth floor, with two smaller galleries on the second floor dedicated to special and traveling exhibitions. With lots of seating, carpeting, and sunlight streaming in through large windows, the MCA is an easy place to visit.

The permanent exhibit shows off paintings, sculpture, prints, and a wide variety of art utilizing a mind-boggling range of materials: acrylics, video, sound, neon, an inflatable raft, flashing lights. . . . Kids, perhaps unsaddled with preconceptions of what defines "art," seem to especially enjoy the MCA's eclectic offerings. Artists represented include Andy Warhol, Roy Lichtenstein, Robert Rauschenberg, Alexander Calder, Marcel Duchamp, Franz Kline, Rene Magritte, and Willem de Kooning.

Touring Tips From either the ground-floor entrance or the second-floor entrance at the top of the stairs facing Michigan Avenue, take the elevator to the fourth floor. Free 45-minute tours depart from the second floor at 6 p.m. on Tuesdays, 1 p.m. on Wednesdays, and 11 a.m., noon, 1 p.m., and 2 p.m. on Saturdays and Sundays. The bilevel book and gift shop features a wide selection of art books and kids' stuff, such as games, stuffed animals, T-shirts, and toys. The high-ceilinged cafe, which overlooks the outdoor sculpture garden and Lake Michigan, is comfortable and offers a European-style menu with prices in the $5–$8 range. Rest rooms are located on the ground floor near the entrance.

Other Things to Do Nearby The MCA is only a block off the Magnificent Mile, Chicago's shopping mecca; the Water Tower Place shopping mall (and its huge food court) is only a stone's throw away. The John Hancock Observatory, the Terra Museum of American Art, and a wide array of restaurants are all within easy walking distance. Children will enjoy Nike Town at 669 North Michigan Avenue, which features an actual basketball court on the second floor and a 22-foot-long aquarium.

Museum of Holography

Type of Attraction A small gallery exhibiting holograms, laser-produced photographic images that are three-dimensional and often feature movement, color change, and image layering. A self-guided tour.

Location Zone 2—North Central/O'Hare; 1134 West Washington Boulevard, Chicago, 60607

Admission $4 adults, $3 children 6–12; under age 6 free

Hours Wednesday–Sunday, 12:30–4:30 p.m.; closed Monday and Tuesday

Phone (312) 226-1007

When to Go Any time.

Special Comments Located just west of the Loop in an otherwise drab neighborhood of warehouses; one flight of stairs. Images are at adult eye level, so small fry will need a lift to get the full effect.

Appeal by Age Group

Pre-school ★½	Teens ★★½	Over 30 ★★½
Grade school ★★	Young Adults ★★½	Seniors ★★½

Authors' Rating Not high art, but fascinating—sometimes startling—images. ★★½

How Much Time to Allow 30 minutes to an hour.

Description and Comments It would probably take a physics degree to really understand how holograms are created, but the results are fascinating just the same. The museum, the only one of its kind in the United States, features stunning 3D images, such as a microscope that leaps off the surface; when you look into the "eye piece" you're rewarded with the sight of a bug frozen in amber!

Other holograms produce a motion-picture effect as you move your head from left to right in front of the image. Though the museum is small—it's essentially two small galleries and a gift shop—the stuff on display is unusual, to say the least.

Touring Tips The gift shop offers a wide array of holograms for sale, ranging from bookmarks and cards to framed images. Prices range from a few bucks to several hundred dollars for large, framed holograms. Most, however, are four-inch by six-inch images that start at $60 (including the frame). Note: Before purchasing a hologram, keep in mind that to get the full effect at home, it needs to be illuminated by an unfrosted incandescent bulb mounted at a 45° angle to the image.

Other Things to Do Nearby Nothing within walking distance. But the Loop is only a few blocks to the east.

Museum of Science and Industry

Type of Attraction 14 acres of museum space housing more than 2,000 wide-ranging exhibits (many of them hands-on), an Omnimax Theater, the Henry Crown Space Center, and a replica of a coal mine. A self-guided tour.

Location Zone 7—South Side; 57th Street and Lake Shore Drive, Chicago, 60637

Admission Museum: $9 adults, $7.50 seniors, $5 children ages 3–11; combination tickets for museum and Omnimax Theater: $15 adults, $12.50 seniors, $9.25 children.

Hours Memorial Day–Labor Day and on holidays: daily, 9:30 a.m.–5:30 p.m.; weekends and rest of year, 9:30 a.m.–4 p.m.; closed Christmas Day.

Phone (773) 684-1414 or (800) GO TO MSI

When to Go Monday through Wednesday are the least crowded days, while Thursday, when admission is free, attracts the most visitors. Weekends are usually packed, but Sundays are generally less crowded than Saturdays.

Special Comments Expect to get lost (well, disoriented) while exploring this immense—and often bewildering—museum. The public address system, by the way, is reserved for summoning the parents of lost children.

Appeal by Age Group

Pre-school ★★★★★	Teens ★★★★★	Over 30 ★★★★★
Grade school ★★★★★	Young Adults ★★★★★	Seniors ★★★★★

Authors' Rating Can there be too much of a good thing? Probably not, but this huge place comes close. Anyway, you'll find one full-sized wonder after another, plus plenty of hands-on fun that makes other museums seem boring by comparison. ★★★★★

How Much Time to Allow Even a full day isn't enough time to explore the museum in depth. First-time visitors should figure on spending at least half a day and plan to come back.

Description and Comments It might be easier to catalog what you *won't* find in this mega-museum, which once held the distinction of being the second-most-visited museum in the world (after the National Air and Space Museum in Washington, D.C.) before it started charging admission in 1991. Even with its rather steep admission price, the place still attracts nearly two million visitors a year.

Full-size exhibits include a real Boeing 727 jetliner, a Coast Guard helicopter, World War II German fighter planes—all suspended from the ceiling; the Apollo 8 command module that circled the moon in 1968; a mock-up of a human heart you can walk through; exhibits on basic science and, of all things, plumbing; and re-creations of 19th-century living rooms. Visitors can also thrill to a film in the domed Omnimax Theater, which boasts a five-story, 76-foot-diameter screen and a 72-speaker, 20,000-watt sound system. It's like nothing at your local mall.

Touring Tips Unless you've got all day and feet of steel, do some homework. Grab a map at the entrance and make a short list of must-see attractions. Just make sure you walk past the information booth to the Rotunda and the eye-popping view of that 727 docked at the balcony overlooking the main floor.

To get to the Henry Crown Space Center and the Omnimax Theater, walk through the Food for Life exhibit near the main entrance and descend to the ground floor near the U.S. Navy exhibit. The space exhibit features lunar modules, moon rocks, and a mock-up of a space shuttle. Nearby is U-505, a German submarine captured on June 4, 1944; on busy days the wait to tour the interior can last an hour.

At "Navy: Technology at Sea," kids can man the helm of a war ship. Other exhibits include Petroleum Planet, antique cars, bicycles, historic locomotives, computers, an energy lab, dolls, architecture. . . . The list goes on and on and on.

Other Things to Do Nearby The University of Chicago campus is full of beautiful buildings and interesting museums that offer a nice contrast to the hectic—and sometimes confusing—Museum of Science and Industry. It's a short walk from the museum. For a bite to eat, join the locals at Valois (1518 East 53rd Street), a cafeteria frequented by cops, cab drivers, and students.

National Vietnam Veterans Art Museum

Type of Attraction An art museum featuring more than 500 works of art (paintings, sculpture, and photographs) created by combat veterans from all nations that fought in the Vietnam War. A self-guided tour.

Location Zone 5—South Loop; 1801 South Indiana Avenue, Chicago, 60616 (in the Prairie Avenue Historic District)

Admission $5 adults, $4 seniors and students under age 16.

Hours Tuesday–Friday, 11 a.m.–6 p.m.; Saturday, 10 a.m.–5 p.m.; Sunday, noon–5 p.m.; closed Monday and major holidays.

Phone (312) 326-0270

When to go Any time.

Special Comments The museum is off the beaten tourist path; if you don't have a car, consider public transportation. From Michigan Avenue, take the bus south to 18th Street, then walk a block east (toward Lake Michigan) to the museum.

Appeal by Age Group

Pre-school ★		Teens ★½		Over 30 ★★★
Grade school ★		Young Adults ★★		Seniors ★★★

Authors' Rating Spartan and grim—and a potentially wrenching experience for anyone who served in Vietnam, lost a friend or relative in the war, or is old enough to remember the conflict. ★★★

How Much Time to Allow One to two hours.

Description and Comments Opened in a renovated industrial space in August 1996, this museum—the only one of its kind—is filled with disturbing images of a conflict many Americans would rather forget. But the 95 artists who created the 500 works on display can't forget; they all pulled combat duty in Vietnam, and their work is visceral and gut-wrenching. Images of death and dying are a recurrent theme, as are shredded American flags, bombs with dollar bills as fins, a painting of LBJ with an American flag shirt and tie, a GI strung to a post by barbed wire (titled *Waiting for Kissinger*), and a wide array of weapons and artillery displayed as works of art (including a Viet Cong 122mm rocket launcher sitting in front of a painting titled *Rocket Attack*). The bare concrete floors and exposed piping and air ducts add to the no-nonsense, serious tenor of the gallery.

Touring Tips Be warned: A visit to this museum is no stroll in the park—it's relentlessly grim and powerful. A good way to start a tour is in the small multimedia theater on the first floor, which continuously shows slide images of the war through the eyes of the soldiers. Many of the images reappear later in the art on display.

Other Things to Do Nearby Next door are the Glessner House Museums, two historic houses that provide visitors a glimpse into Chicago's prairie heritage and later Victorian splendor. Docent-guided tours are offered Wednesday through Sunday, noon to 4 p.m.; the cost is $7 for adults and $6 for students and seniors. For more information, call (312) 326-1480.

Navy Pier

Type of Attraction A renovated landmark on Lake Michigan with over 50 acres of parks, gardens, shops, restaurants, a 150-foot Ferris wheel, an IMAX theater, a convention center, a children's museum, and other attractions. A self-guided tour.

Location Zone 3—Near North; 700 East Grand Avenue, Chicago, 60611 (just north of the Chicago River on the lakefront)

Admission Free; some attractions such as the Chicago Children's Museum, the Ferris wheel, cruise boats, the Wave Swinger (a 40-foot-high thrill ride), Time Escape (a multisensory ride through Chicago history), and the IMAX theater have separate admission charges.

Hours Memorial Day–Labor Day: Sunday–Thursday, 10 a.m.–10 p.m.; Friday and Saturday, 10 a.m.–midnight. Fall: Monday–Thursday, 10 a.m.–9 p.m.; Friday and Saturday, 10 a.m. to 11 p.m.; Sunday, 10 a.m.–7 p.m. Spring: Monday–Thursday, 10 a.m.–8 p.m.; Friday and Saturday, 10 a.m.–10 p.m.; Sunday, 10 a.m.–7 p.m. Restaurants are open later throughout the year.

Phone (312) 595-PIER, (800) 595-PIER (outside the 312 area code), and (312) 595-5100 (administrative offices)

When to Go Attracting five million visitors a year, Navy Pier has catapulted past the Lincoln Park Zoo to become Chicago's number-one attraction—and during warm weather, the place is jammed. Try to arrive before 11 a.m., especially if you're driving and on weekends.

Special Comments Although the 700-space parking garage helps, finding a place to put the family car remains a problem at this very popular attraction. Arrive early—or, better yet, take public transportation (the Nos. 29, 56, 65, 66, 120, and 121 buses stop at the entrance) or a cab.

Appeal by Age Group

Pre-school ★★★★★	Teens ★★★★★	Over 30 ★★★★
Grade school ★★★★★	Young Adults ★★★★	Seniors ★★★★

Authors' Rating The view of Chicago's skyline alone makes this a must-see destination. The ultimate is dinner at a window table at Riva or an evening dinner cruise on the *Odyssey*. ★★★★

How Much Time to Allow Depending on the weather, anywhere from an hour to half a day—or longer if a festival or concert is taking place during your visit.

Description and Comments A former U.S. Navy training facility and a campus of the University of Illinois, Navy Pier reopened in 1995 after a $196 million facelift as Chicago's premier visitor attraction. There's something for everyone: a children's museum; a shopping mall and food court; a huge Ferris wheel and a carousel; a six-story-high, 80-foot-wide IMAX theater screen; scenic and dinner cruises on Lake Michigan; a convention center; a beer garden; a concert venue; ice skating in the winter … the list goes on.

Here's the scoop on Navy Pier's most popular attractions: The Ferris wheel is open year-round (weather permitting) and costs $4 for adults and $3.50 for children and seniors; it's a 7½-minute ride. Long waits in line aren't a problem because it rotates nonstop at a slow speed that lets visitors load and unload almost continuously. The IMAX theater is located near the entrance of the Family Pavilion shopping mall; tickets for the shows are $10 for adults, $8 for seniors, and $7 for children.

Crystal Gardens (a one-acre indoor tropical garden with fountains and public seating), Festival Hall, Skyline Stage, and the Grand Ballroom feature performances of jazz, blues, rock, theater, and dance, as well as special events such as consumer trade shows, art festivals, miniature golf, and ethnic festivals; most charge admission. The Chicago Shakespeare Theater opened in October 1999. For tickets, call (312) 595-5600. For more information on the popular Chicago Children's Museum, see its attraction profile. Cruise boats depart from Navy Pier's south dock, as does the Shoreline Shuttle, a sightseeing boat that departs every 30 minutes for the Shedd Aquarium.

Touring Tips Unless your visit to Navy Pier is midweek during the winter, avoid the hassles and expense of parking (more than $5 an hour) by arriving via bus or cab. And try to pick a nice day: the Ferris wheel shuts down in the rain, and the view of Chicago's magnificent skyline is what separates this shopping, restaurant, and festival venue from all the others. If you're taking the kids to the Chicago Children's Museum, either arrive when it opens in the morning (when school is out) or in the afternoon during the school year (to avoid school groups that often arrive in the mornings). Before leaving home, call Navy Pier for a schedule of special events taking place during your visit.

Other Things to Do Nearby North Pier Festival Market is about two blocks west, offering more shopping and another food court. Kids will enjoy the Battle Tech Center and Virtuality Center game rooms on the third level. You can also stroll the Lakefront Trail or, better yet, rent a bike or inline skates at Bike Chicago (in Navy Pier).

Oriental Institute Museum

Type of Attraction A showcase for the history, art, and archaeology of the ancient Near East. A self-guided tour.

Location Zone 7—South Side; 1155 East 58th Street (on the campus of the University of Chicago), Chicago, 60637

Admission Free; suggested donation $5 adults, $2 children under 12

Hours Tuesday, Thursday, Friday, and Saturday, 10 a.m.–4 p.m.; Wednesday, 10 a.m.–8:30 p.m.; Sunday, noon–4 p.m.; closed Monday, Independence Day, Thanksgiving, Christmas, and New Year's Day.

Phone (773) 702-9520

When to Go Any time.

Special Comments The Oriental Institute Museum features several exhibits in its Egyptian Gallery, such as artifacts from the Nile Valley and the ancient Near East, as well as a reconstruction of part of the palace of an Assyrian king dominated by a 40-ton winged bull. Other goodies on display include a 17-foot-tall statue of King Tut and a jar and fragment of the Dead Sea Scrolls. The remaining four galleries will reopen over the next few years.

Appeal by Age Group

Pre-school ★★	Teens ★★★★	Over 30 ★★★★
Grade school ★★★	Young Adults ★★★★	Seniors ★★★★

Authors' Rating An often-overlooked gem that shouldn't be missed. ★★★★

How Much Time to Allow One to two hours.

Description and Comments Most of the artifacts displayed in this stunning collection are treasures recovered from expeditions to Iraq (Mesopotamia), Iran (Persia), Turkey, Syria, and Palestine. The University of Chicago's Oriental Institute has conducted research and archaeological digs in the Near East since 1919, and since 1931 has displayed much of its collection in this impressive building. Items date from 9000 B.C. to the tenth century A.D. and include papyrus scrolls, mummies, everyday items from the ancient past, and gigantic stone edifices.

Touring Tips Not-to-be-missed artifacts on display include a cast of the Rosetta Stone (195 B.C.), which provided the key for unlocking the meaning of Egyptian hieroglyphics; huge, wall-sized Assyrian reliefs; a striding lion from ancient Babylon that once decorated a gateway; a colossal, ten-ton bull's head from Persepolis (a Persian city destroyed by Alexander the Great in 331 B.C.), and a 13-foot-high statue of King Tut.

The museum is a real find for archaeology buffs and anyone interested in ancient history. It's safe to say the ongoing renovation will make it even better.

Other Things to Do Nearby The DuSable Museum, the Smart Museum of Art, and the rest of the University of Chicago campus are all close—and well worth exploring. The huge Museum of Science and Industry is on 57th Street. For lunch, try Valois, a cafeteria hangout for local gendarmes and residents located at 1518 East 53rd Street.

Peace Museum

Type of Attraction A museum promoting peace and nonviolence through the arts. A self-guided tour.

Location Zone 3—Near North; 100 North Central Park Avenue (two blocks south of the Garfield Park Conservatory), Chicago, 60624

Admission Suggested donation of $4 for adults, $3 for children, students, and seniors

Hours Tuesday–Friday, 1 p.m.–5 p.m., Saturday by appointment; closed December 24, 25, 31, January 1

Phone (773) 638-6450

When to Go Any time.

Special Comments Take the elevator directly across from the building entrance to the fourth floor and turn right. Because the Peace Museum doesn't have a permanent collection, it's not possible to rate the museum; exhibits change about four times a year.

How Much Time to Allow 30 minutes to an hour.

Description and Comments This essentially one-room exhibit space may be the only museum in the world dedicated to world peace. On our visit, the exhibit was "A Piece of the Peace: Poetry for the Walls," which examined the role of language in making and breaking peace. Some of the original manuscripts on display were by Joan Baez, Bono, and Phil Ochs.

Touring Tips To find out what's on display during your visit, pick up a copy of the *Chicago Reader*.

Other Things to Do Nearby The Merchandise Mart and the Loop are a few blocks south on LaSalle Street.

The Peggy Notebaert Nature Museum of the Chicago Academy of Sciences

Type of Attraction An interactive museum dedicated to nature, from microcosms to wilderness walks, and a children's play gallery with puppets and a beaver lodge.

Location Zone 1—The North Side; 2430 North Cannon Drive in Lincoln Park, Chicago, 60614. On the northwest corner of Fullerton Parkway and Cannon Drive.

Admission $7 adults, $5 seniors and students, $4 children ages 3–12; free for children under age 3. Some exhibits may require an additional charge.

Hours Monday–Friday, 9 a.m.–4:30 p.m.; Saturday and Sunday, 10 a.m.–5 p.m.

Phone (773) 755-5100; 24-hour information line (773) 871-2668 Recorded message including information on bus routes.

When to Go Any time.

Special Comments The museum runs special public programs for adult and child education alike. For information on group programs and an online workshop, check out

www.chias.org. If traveling by car, park on the east side of Cannon Drive only; move your car by 4 p.m. Wheelchair and stroller accessible. Bike lockup is available.

Appeal by Age Group

Pre-school ★★★★★	Teens ★★	Over 30 ★★
Grade school ★★★★★	Young Adults ★★	Seniors ★★

Authors' Rating Educational for the young and refreshing for adults. ★★★

How Much Time to Allow A good two hours for adults, teenagers, and young adults. For families or groups with children, allow at least three hours.

Description and Comments A mellow, kid-centric museum to visit with a beautiful array of photographs and fun, interesting exhibits—including a live haven of butterflies, a wilderness walk, city science environmental center, an active water lab and children's gallery. A pleasant visit that is full of interesting scientific information. There is a small, comfortable cafeteria that sells slightly pricey but healthy sandwiches and snacks. In the summer, a patio provides a pleasant dining area overlooking the river.

Touring Tips Visit the butterfly haven first and enjoy the spectacular beauty of these graceful and docile creatures in their natural environment. Please be sure to respect the do's and don'ts video at the entrance. There is a nature museum shop for souvenir hunters.

Other Things to Do Nearby Head South on Cannon Drive to Chicago's Lincoln Park Zoo or East to Lake Michigan for a bike ride, stroll, or Rollerblade. During the summer months, call the museum for trolley tour information.

Polish Museum of America

Type of Attraction One of the largest and oldest ethnic museums in the United States, featuring Polish and Polish American paintings, sculptures, drawings, and lithographs. A self-guided tour.

Location Zone 2—North Central/O'Hare; 984 North Milwaukee Avenue, Chicago, 60622

Admission Free; $3 donation per adult requested.

Hours Daily, 11 a.m.–4 p.m.; closed Thursday

Phone (773) 384-3352

When to Go Any time.

Special Comments The museum is located on the second and third floors; visitors must climb two flights of stairs.

Appeal by Age Group

Pre-school ★½	Teens ★★½	Over 30 ★★½
Grade school ★★	Young Adults ★★½	Seniors ★★★

Authors' Rating An eclectic collection of high-quality art, colorful crafts, and historical items ranging from 17th-century armor to modern paintings. ★★½

How Much Time to Allow One hour.

Description and Comments Located in the heart of Chicago's first Polish neighborhood, the Polish Museum emphasizes the art and history of an ethnic group that maintains a strong national identity; famous Poles include Paderewski, Pulaski, Kosciuszko, Copernicus, Madame Curie, and Chopin. Interesting items on display include a one-horse open sleigh carved from a single log in 1703 that a Polish king gave to his daughter, Princess Maria, who married Louis XV of France.

Other stuff on display here—much of it colorful and reflecting a high degree of craftsmanship—include Polish folk costumes, exquisite hand-decorated Easter eggs, wood sculpture, prints, and paintings. It's not a very large place, but there's a lot to see.

Touring Tips The third floor contains an attractive, well-lighted art gallery featuring modern graphic art, paintings, and busts. Check out the stairwell and you'll find a Picasso lithograph and a Chagall etching.

Other Things to Do Nearby Walk a few blocks north on Milwaukee Avenue to explore the old Polish neighborhood, which still has a few shops and restaurants with signs written in Polish; there's an El station at Ashland and Milwaukee Avenues.

Sears Tower Skydeck

Type of Attraction Spectacular views into four states from the world's third-tallest building. A self-guided tour.

Location Zone 4—The Loop; 233 South Wacker Drive (enter at Jackson Boulevard)

Admission $9.50 adults, $6.75 children ages 5–12, $7.75 seniors, free for children under 3

Hours May–September: daily, 10 a.m.–10 p.m.; October–April: daily, 10 a.m.–8 p.m.

Phone (312) 875-9696

When to Go Early or late on weekends and holidays March through November; waits in line for the elevator ride to the top can exceed two hours on busy afternoons. On hot days, go after 6:30 p.m. to avoid the heat and to see the city in sunset or at night. Skip it in inclement weather or when clouds obscure the top of the building.

Special Comments Don't enter the main lobby of the building facing South Wacker Drive; go to the Skydeck entrance on Jackson Boulevard. If the line is long, consider this alternative: the John Hancock Center on North Michigan Avenue. Though not quite as high (it's only the 14th-highest building in the world), some people say the view is better ... and long waits are rare.

Appeal by Age Group

Pre-school ★★★★★	Teens ★★★★★	Over 30 ★★★★★
Grade school ★★★★★	Young Adults ★★★★★	Seniors ★★★★★

Authors' Rating Incredible. Part of the fun is looking down on all those other sky-scrapers. ★★★★★

How Much Time to Allow At least 30 minutes once you reach the viewing deck; signs posted at various points in the waiting area in the basement tell you how long you'll stand in line before boarding an elevator.

Description and Comments The distinctive, 110-story Sears Tower (easily identi-fied by its black aluminum skin, towering height, and twin antenna towers) reaches 1,454 feet; the Skydeck on the 103rd floor is 1,353 feet above the ground. It's a 70-sec-ond elevator ride to the broad, wide-windowed viewing area, where you're treated to a magnificent 360° view of Chicago, Lake Michigan, and the distant horizon.

Touring Tips Enter the building at the Skydeck entrance on Jackson Boulevard; take the elevator *down* to purchase a ticket. Try to visit the tower on a clear day; or go at night when the crowds are thinner and a carpet of sparkling lights spreads into the distance.

Other Things to Do Nearby   The Chicago Mercantile Exchange is around the corner on Wacker Drive; go downstairs for something to eat from a wide array of eateries. To view more unrestrained capitalism in action, head south toward the Sears Tower, then east on Jackson Boulevard to the Chicago Board of Trade.

Spertus Museum of Judaica

Type of Attraction   3,500 years of Jewish history on display, from ceremonial treasures to the Zell Holocaust Memorial. A self-guided tour.

Location   Zone 5—South Loop; 618 South Michigan Avenue, Chicago, 60605

Admission $5 adults; $3 seniors, children, students; $10 for families; free on Friday.

Hours   Sunday–Wednesday, 10 a.m.–5 p.m.; Thursday, 10 a.m.–7 p.m.; Friday, 10 a.m.–3 p.m.; closed Saturday.

Phone   (312) 322-1747

When to Go   Any time.

Special Comments   The permanent collection is located on one floor.

Appeal by Age Group

Pre-school ★★	Teens ★★½	Over 30 ★★★
Grade school ★★½	Young Adults ★★★	Seniors ★★★½

Authors' Rating   Small, tasteful, and full of beautiful objects artfully displayed in a modern setting. ★★★

How Much Time to Allow   One hour.

Description and Comments   The theme of this museum is the survival of the Jewish people as embodied in their art, including Torahs, Torah arks, ceremonial coats, parchment manuscripts, Hanukkah lamps, and tableware, just to name a few of the beautiful items on display. On a more somber note, the Zell Holocaust Memorial recalls the horrors of the concentration camps with heaps of clothing, piles of buttons, and video monitors slowly scrolling through the names of victims.

The Artifact Center, a level down from the museum, is a place where children through age 12 can play archaeologist by digging on a model tel, a mound built up over time by layers of successive human settlement. Other hands-on activities are available in the Marketplace, a group of market stalls where kids can examine objects from ancient Israel. All activities are supervised, so parents can leave the kids for an hour or so and view the permanent exhibits and special shows in the museum. Hours are 1–4:30 p.m., Sunday–Thursday; closed Friday and Saturday.

Touring Tips   Check at the admission desk to find out what's on display in the second-floor, temporary-exhibit galleries.

Other Things to Do Nearby   The Loop, the Art Institute of Chicago, and the Chicago Architecture Foundation are all close.

Swedish American Museum Center

Type of Attraction   An attractive store-front museum highlighting Swedish culture and the Swedish immigrant experience. A self-guided tour.

Location   Zone 1—The North Side; 5211 North Clark Street, Chicago, 60640

Admission $4 adults, $3 seniors and children; $10 family rate

Hours Tuesday–Friday, 10 a.m.–4 p.m.; Saturday and Sunday, 10 a.m.– 3 p.m. Closed Monday.

Phone (773) 728-8111

When to Go Any time.

Special Comments All the exhibits are located on the ground floor.

Appeal by Age Group

Pre-school ★	Teens ★★½	Over 30 ★★½
Grade school ★★	Young Adults ★★½	Seniors ★★★½

Authors' Rating Small, but attractive and interesting—and located in a great ethnic neighborhood. ★★½

How Much Time to Allow 30 minutes to an hour.

Description and Comments Swedes were a major immigrant group in 19th-century Chicago, and this museum provides insight into Swedish history and culture and the life of early immigrants. Items on display include jewelry from Lapland, old family Bibles, 19th-century hand tools, and a re-creation of a typical Swedish American home from the early 20th century.

The gallery also exhibits fascinating black-and-white photos, including old pictures of the departed laid out in their coffins before burial: "Death was present everywhere, in a different way than it is today, and the local photographer would often be asked to immortalize deceased persons, both old and young." How things change.

Touring Tips The well-stocked and attractive museum shop features a wide range of items such as Swedish videos (including several films directed by Ingmar Bergman), books, road maps of Scandinavia, audio crash courses in Swedish, and traditional handicrafts from the Old Country. The Children's Museum of Immigration tells the story of immigration for youngsters ages 3–12.

Other Things To Do Nearby Explore Andersonville, the last ethnic stronghold of Swedes in Chicago. It's a fascinating neighborhood—an unusual mix of Swedish and Middle Eastern—full of interesting shops and inexpensive ethnic restaurants. (See "Exploring Chicago's Neighborhoods" in Part Seven: Sight-Seeing Tips and Tours.)

Terra Museum of American Art

Type of Attraction A gallery on the Magnificent Mile (North Michigan Avenue) featuring 19th- and 20th-century American art. A self-guided tour.

Location Zone 3—Near North; 664 North Michigan Avenue, Chicago, 60611

Admission Free; $5 suggested donation

Hours Tuesday, 10 a.m.–8 p.m.; Wednesday–Saturday, 10 a.m.–6 p.m.; Sunday, noon–5p.m.; closed Monday

Phone (312) 664-3939

When to Go Any time.

Special Comments The five-floor museum is wheelchair accessible.

Appeal by Age Group

Pre-school ★	Teens ★★½	Over 30 ★★★★
Grade school ★★	Young Adults ★★★	Seniors ★★★★

Authors' Rating Elegant, quiet, modern; an oasis of quiet and beauty on bustling North Michigan Avenue. ★★★★

How Much Time to Allow One to two hours.

Description and Comments The Terra Museum's permanent collection of 19th- and 20th-century art relies heavily on Impressionists. But you'll also find paintings by Homer, Whistler, and other American masters, as well as changing exhibitions of American art. The museum is elegant, wide, and comfortable—a pleasant surprise for folks visiting this highly commercial area for the first time.

Touring Tips Take the (huge) elevator to the fourth floor to begin the tour. After walking up to the fifth-floor gallery, work your way down to the first-floor lobby. Free public tours are offered at noon weekdays and at 2 p.m. on weekends.

Other Things to Do Nearby The Historic Water Tower is three blocks north on Michigan Avenue, and the Magnificent Mile is primo shopping territory. Kids will enjoy Nike Town, a high-tech shoe store at 669 North Michigan Avenue. For more art, try the Museum of Contemporary Art on East Chicago Street (a block east of the Water Tower).

Ukrainian National Museum

Type of Attraction A collection of Ukrainian folk art, embroidery, wood carvings, ceramics, beadwork, and painted Easter eggs. A self-guided tour.

Location Zone 2—North Central/O'Hare; 721 North Oakley Boulevard, Chicago, 60612

Admission $3

Hours Thursday–Sunday, 11 a.m.–4 p.m.; Monday–Wednesday, by appointment only

Phone (312) 421-8020

When to Go Any time.

Special Comments Visitors must climb a set of stairs to reach the entrance.

Appeal by Age Group

Pre-school ★	Teens ★½	Over 30 ★½
Grade school ★½	Young Adults ★½	Seniors ★★

Authors' Rating Though some beautiful objects are on display here, this museum is too small and out of the way to recommend a special trip. ★

How Much Time to Allow 30 minutes to an hour.

Description and Comments The Ukraine, a nation of 52 million people that was once part of the former Soviet Union and an independent state since 1991, is the second-largest country in Europe. Crammed into this tiny but bright museum is a wide variety of folk art, including linens, colorful costumes, exquisitely detailed painted Easter eggs, musical instruments, wood models of native Ukrainian houses, swords, and paintings.

Touring Tips Make this a stop on an ethnic exploration of Chicago; see our description of the Ukrainian Village in "Exploring Chicago's Neighborhoods" in Part Seven: Sight-Seeing Tips and Tours.

Other Things to Do Nearby Next door is Sts. Volodymyr and Olha Ukrainian Catholic Church, topped by three gold domes and decorated by rich mosaics over the door. On nearby Chicago Avenue are several Ukrainian eateries and bakeries.

Part Nine

Dining and Restaurants

Dining in Chicago

In a year wrought with financial instability, the Chicago restaurant scene remained steadfast and strong. While customers are leaning more towards reasonable and familiar fare, a good showing of high-end eateries to emerged nevertheless, reinforcing Chicago's status as one of the most dynamic and exciting restaurant towns in the U.S. We've attracted Chef talent from across the globe in addition to spawning off fine talent from larger local kitchens into quaint solo ventures. New restaurants have sprouted up fairly equally across our neighborhoods, with a heavier concentration in the River North area, just north of the Loop. Other significant changes of late include a. growth in upscale hotel restaurants, the landing of national high-end chain branches, spin-offs and duplicates of local favorites, and a growing number of dressed up ethnic eateries.

Upscale Hotels and Restaurants

Several of the finest new restaurants to emerge in the past year have been housed in upscale hotels. Seafood-oriented **Avenues** (108 East Superior Street; (312) 573-6754) opened inside the new lux Peninsula hotel, directly across the street from its major competitor **NoMi** (800 North Michigan Avenue; (312) 239-4030), both nestled on the seventh floors of their respective hotels. Also in the Peninsula, though on the fourth floor, the elegant Chinese dining room **Shanghai Terrace** (phone (312) 573-6754) opened. Swanky **Cafe des Architectes** (20 East Chestnut Street; (312) 324-4000) is the first of two restaurants to open inside the first Chicago branch of Parisian Hotel Sofitel (**Cigale** opened in fall 2002). The W Hotels came in full force this year, opening two chic restaurants—Mediterranean-inspired **Wave** (644 North Lake Shore Drive; (312) 255-4460) in the W Chicago Lakeshore and the global eclectic **We** (172 West Adams Street; (312) 917-5608) on the street level of the W Chicago City Center. As part of the multi-million dollar renovation of the Hotel Intercontinental, the Mediterranean **Zest** (525 North Michigan Avenue; (312) 321-8766) now graces Michigan Avenue with floor to ceiling windows from the hotel lobby.

Chains Keep Coming

While local independently owned restaurants dominate Chicago's restaurant industry, this year we've also welcomed several branches of well-known chain restaurants. California-style **Napa Valley Grille** (626 North State Street; (312) 587-1166) popped into the River North area, as did **Roy's** (720 North State Street; (312) 787-7599), Roy Yamaguchi's chi-chi Hawaiian eatery. **Sushi Samba** also plans to move into the former River North Hudson Club space, while Brazilian churascurria (steakhouse) **Fogo de Chão** (661 North LaSalle Street; (312) 932-9330) joined the ranks of massive, theme-oriented restaurants on touristy LaSalle Street.

Spin-Offs and Siblings

Several local dining establishments expanded their families by opening suburban branches of urban originals or vice-versa. Suburban **Weber Grill,** with locations in Lombard and Wheeling, opened at 10 East Grand Avenue (phone (312) 595-0000) and Wheeling-based **Bob Chinn's Crabhouse** opened an 800-seat branch in the old traffic courthouse at 315 North LaSalle Street (phone (312) 822-0100). Contemporary American **mk** (868 North Franklin Street; (312) 482-9179) duped itself with suburban **mk North** (305 Happ Road, Northfield; (847) 716-6500), while popular Nuevo Latino Wicker Park **Mas** (1670 West Division Street; (773) 276-8700) branched into Lakeview with **Otro Mas** (3651 North Southport Avenue; (773) 348-3200).

Ethnic Diversity Gets a Makeover

Global Dining

While many millennial newcomers stayed true to American cuisine, some with a global twist or two **(Cloud 9, One North, Magnolia Cafe, 1212),** several others brought higher-end versions of various global ethnic fare, something supported and embraced in our melting pot community. **Erawan Royal Thai Cuisine** (729 North Clark Street; (312) 642-6888) turned Thai street food into a royal affair, while Andersonville's **Jin Ju** (5203 North Clark Street; (773) 334-6377) finally brought delectable Korean fare into the mainstream. The Market District gained the upscale Cuban **Marysol** (812–816 West Randolph Street; (312) 563-1763) and clubby Japanese **Starfish** (804 West Randolph Street;

(312) 997-2433). The ever-expanding restaurant strip of Milwaukee Avenue in Wicker Park became home to Mexican **Mi Sueno Su Realidad** (1250 North Milwaukee Avenue; (773) 782-1500). A fabulous art deco hotel lobby in Rogers Park landed Persian **Cafe Suron** (1146 West Pratt Avenue; (773) 465-6500), and the north side's Vietnamese Argyle Street saw one of its first higher-end dining rooms with **Hai Yen** (1055 West Argyle Street; (773) 561-4077).

Asian Infusion

Asian newcomers usually top the list, and this year is no exception. We welcomed refined **Kevin** (9 West Hubbard Street; (312) 595-0055) to River North, and Zen-like **Spring** (2039 West North Avenue; (773) 395-7100) by former Trio Chef Shawn McClain. More casual contenders include Wrigleyville's **Shabu-Ya** (3475 North Clark Street; (773) 388-9203) where shabu-shabu–style cook-your-own fare is featured; sushi restaurant **Bob San** (1805 West Division Street; (773) 235-8888), Thai eatery **Roong** (1633 North Milwaukee Avenue; (773) 252-3488), and Japanese **Rise** (3401 North Southport Avenue; (773) 525-3535).

Never-Ending French Bistros

A short few blocks west and north of the popular Lincoln Park neighborhood is Lincoln Square, an area rich with cultural diversity. While several restaurants have thrived there for years, they're now giving way to a wave of new French eateries. High-end Lincoln Parker **Aubriot** (1962 North Halsted Street; (773) 281-4211) turned a vacant storefront into its well-appointed sibling **Tournesol** (4343 North Lincoln Avenue; (773) 477-8820), a more casual French bistro. Just down the block, the former home to Villa Kula teahouse morphed into French **Bistro Campagne** (4518 North Lincoln Avenue; (773) 271-6100), the sibling to Evanston's rustic Italian **Campagnola** (815 Chicago Avenue, Evanston; (847) 475-6100). Also opening in fall 2002 at the former Grecian Taverna (4535 North Lincoln Avenue) will be another new, as-yet-unnamed French bistro by chef-owner Charlie Socher of **Cafe Matou** (1846 North Milwaukee Avenue; (773) 384-8911).

Noteworthy Neighborhoods

West Loop–Randolph Street Market District

Just west of the Chicago River, Randolph Street has developed into one of the fastest-growing restaurant rows, offering several fine contemporary American establishments and multiple upscale ethnic spots. **Nine** (440 West Randolph Street; (312) 575-9900) marks the easternmost edge of the strip, and the culinary concentration moves west out Randolph Street with chef-owned and -operated gem **Blackbird** (619 West Randolph Street; (312) 715-0708).

Moving further west over the expressway, the market district restaurant row includes bustling French bistro **Marché** (833 West Randolph Street; (312) 226-8399), trendy Italian **Vivo** (838 West Randolph Street; (312) 733-3379), swanky Cuban newcomer **Marysol** (812–16 West Randolph Street; (312) 562-1763), and sushi house **Starfish** (804 West Randolph Street; (312) 997-2433). Further west are the casual noodle house **Hi Ricky** (941 West Randolph Street; (312) 491-9100) and a new Mexican contender, **The Executives** (1300 West Randolph Street; (312) 666-1220). Anchoring the far-western boundary of the strip are the acclaimed **one sixtyblue** (160 North Loomis Street; (312) 850-0303) and the stylish wine bar **The Tasting Room at Randolph Wine Cellar** (1415 West Randolph Street; (312) 942-1212).

Central and South Loop

New gentrification in the South Loop represents new opportunities for restaurants. Longstanding favorites like **Printer's Row** (550 South Dearborn Street; (312) 461-0780) and **Prairie** (500 South Dearborn Street; (312) 565-6655) still thrive, but a few newcomers have ventured even further south, notably the classic American **Chicago Firehouse Restaurant** (1401 South Michigan Avenue; (312) 786-1401) and the rustic Italian **Gioco** (1312 South Wabash Avenue; (312) 939-3870).

The heart of the Loop has taken major culinary strides, with several capable and convenient eateries near or adjacent to downtown hotels, theaters, and the CSO Symphony Center. The regional American **Atwood Cafe** (1 West Washington Street; (312) 368-1900) opened in 2000 inside the Hotel Burnham; **312 Chicago** (136 North LaSalle Street; (312) 696-2420) offers American-Italian fare adjacent to the Hotel Allegro; and **Mossant Bistro** (225 North Wabash Street; (312) 236-9300) is housed inside the fabulous Hotel Monaco. Several longstanding Loop favorites still draw out-of-towners **(Trattoria #10, Everest Room, The Berghoff)**, while recent transitions warrant visits to **Rhapsody** (65 East Adams Street; (312) 786-9911), now under the culinary direction of Roemy Jung; and **The Grillroom Chophouse and Wine Bar** (33 West Monroe Street; (312) 960-0000).

Wicker Park

The sizzling, artsy-chic Wicker Park neighborhood surrounding the bustling intersection of Damen, North, and Milwaukee Avenues continues its heart-stopping rate of restaurant expansion. There's the family-run **Soju** (1745 West North Avenue; (773) 782-9000), serving traditional Korean fare in a sleek setting; exotic **Souk** (1552 North Milwaukee

Avenue; (773) 227-9110), where Egyptian food mingles with Syrian and Lebanese fare and after-dinner hookahs; and groovy **MOD** (1520 North Damen Avenue; (773) 252-1500) serving contemporary American fare in a trippy 1960s setting.

Soul Kitchen (1576 North Milwaukee; (773) 342-9742), featuring upscale soul food in a funky setting, and innovative American **Cafe Absinthe** (1954 West North Avenue; (773) 278-4488) remain local favorites. Other Wicker Park destinations worth a visit include **Phlair** (1935 North Damen Avenue; (773) 772-3719), a good spot for simple pasta at reasonable prices; and Japanese newcomer **Kudos** (1635 North Milwaukee Avenue; (773) 252-2233), just east of the cozy and competent **Cafe Matou** (1846 North Milwaukee Avenue; (773) 384-8911). Contemporary American **Feast** (1616 North Damen Avenue; (773) 772-7100) remained in the area but moved down the block, and **Spring** (2039 West North Avenue; (773) 395-7100) now inhabits a former Roman bathhouse.

Everyone's keeping an eye on the west-bound strip of Division Street, an inevitable outgrowth of restaurant-saturated Wicker Park. In little more than a year, we've seen the arrival of new sushi restaurants **Mirai Sushi** (2020 West Division Street; (773) 862-8500) as well as **Bob San** (1805 West Division Street; (773) 235-8888); the seasonal Italian of **Fortunato** (2005 West Division Street; (773) 645-7200); and **Settimana,** a new neighborhood Italian (2056 West Division Street; (773) 394-1629)—and there's more on the way.

And Now for the New New ...

As this book goes to press, we are anxiously awaiting the opening of several newcomers, including Indian-inspired Asian **Monsoon** (2813 North Broadway Avenue; (773) 665-9463), contemporary Mexican **Platiyo** (3313 North Clark Street; (773) 477-6700), Cajun **Nola's 32nd Ward Seafood House** (1856 West North Avenue; (773) 395-4300), and the contemporary American **Lovitt** (1466 North Ashland Avenue; (773) 252-1466). On the next page is a rundown of those establishments either too new to review or which have undergone recent, substantial changes.

Restaurants: Rated and Ranked

Our Favorite Chicago Restaurants: Explaining the Ratings

We have developed detailed profiles for what we consider the best restaurants in town. Each profile features an easy-to-scan heading that allows you to check out the restaurant's name, cuisine, star rating, cost, quality rating, and value rating very quickly.

NEW AND CHANGING RESTAURANTS

RESTAURANT	ADDRESS/PHONE	CUISINE
Bob Chinn's Chicago Crabhouse	315 North LaSalle Street; (312) 822-0100	Seafood
Buona Terra	2535 North California Avenue; (773) 289-3800	Italian
Butterfield 8	718 North Wells Street; (312) 327-0940	American
Cafe Suron	1146 West Pratt Avenue; (773) 465-6500	Middle Eastern/ Persian
Calliope Cafe	2826 North Lincoln Avenue; (773) 528-8055	American/ Sandwiches
Cloud 9	1944 North Oakley; (773) 486-3900	Global/Eclectic
Como	695 North Milwaukee Avenue; (312) 733-7400	Italian
Dioneses	510 North Western Avenue; (312) 243-7330	Mexican
Fogo de Chao	661 North LaSalle Street; (312) 932-9330	Latin/Brazilian
Frankie J's	4437 North Broadway Avenue; (773) 769-2959	American
Garrett Ripley's	712 North Clark Street; (312) 642-2900	Irish
Giocco	1312 South Wabash Street/(312) 939-3870	Italian
Grand Lux Cafe	600 North Michigan Avenue; (312) 276-2500	Global/Eclectic
Green Room	130 South Green Street; (312) 666-9813	Global/Eclectic
La Mora	2132 West Roscoe Avenue; (773) 404-4555	Italian
Marysol	812-16 West Randolph Street; (312) 563-1763	Latin/Cuban
Merlo Ristorante	2638 North. Lincoln Avenue; (773) 529-0747	Italian
Mi Sueno Su Realidad	1250 North Milwaukee Avenue; (773) 782-1500	Mexican

Overall Rating The overall rating encompasses the entire dining experience, including style, service, and ambience in addition to the taste, presentation, and quality of the food. Five stars is the highest rating possible and connotes the best of everything. Four-star restaurants are exceptional, and three-star restaurants are well above average. Two-star restaurants are good. One star is used to connote an average restaurant that demonstrates an unusual capability in some area of specialization—for example, an otherwise unmemorable place that has great barbecued chicken.

Cost To the right of the star rating is an expense description which provides a comparative sense of how much a complete meal will cost. A

RESTAURANT	ADDRESS/PHONE	CUISINE
Monsoon	2813 North Broadway Avenue; (773) 665-9463	Eclectic/ Indian
Napa Valley Grille	630 North State Street; (312) 587-1166	New American
Nola's 32nd Ward Seafood House	1856 West North Avenue; (773) 395-4300	Cajun
One North Kitchen and Bar	1 North Wacker Drive; (312) 750-9700	New American
Prego	2901 North Ashland Avenue; (773) 472-9190	Italian
RL	115 East Chicago Avenue; (312) 475-1100	American
Roy's	720 North State Street; (312) 787-7599	Hawaiian/ American
Rushmore	1023 West Lake Street; (312) 421-8845	New American
Shanghai Terrace	180 East Superior Street; (312) 573-6744	Chinese
Swank	710 North Wells Street; (312) 274-9500	Global/Eclectic
Think Cafe	2235 North Western Avenue; (773) 394-0537	Global/Eclectic
Trio (chef change)	1625 Hinman Avenue; (847) 733-8746	New American
Vong's Thai Kitchen	6 West Hubbard Street; (312) 644-8664	Thai
We	172 West Adams Street; (312) 332-1200	Global/Eclectic
Weber Grill	539 North State Street; (312) 467-9696	American/Steak
West Town Tavern	1329 West Chicago Avenue; (312) 666-6175	New American
Xippo	3759 North Damen Avenue; (773) 529-9135	New American
Zest	525 North Michigan Avenue; (312) 944-4100	Mediterranean

complete meal for our purposes consists of an entree with vegetable or side dish, and choice of soup or salad. Appetizers, desserts, drinks, and tips are excluded.

Inexpensive $16 and less per person   **Moderate** $17–$29 per person

Expensive $30–$40 per person   **Very Expensive** Over $40 per person

Quality Rating   The food quality rating is rated on a scale of one to five stars, with five stars being the best rating attainable. It is based expressly on the taste, freshness of ingredients, preparation, presentation, and creativity of food served. There is no consideration of price. If you are a person who wants the best food available and cost is not an issue, you need look no further than the quality ratings.

Value Rating   If, on the other hand, you are looking for both quality and value, then you should check the value rating. The value ratings, expressed as stars, are defined as follows:

★★★★★	Exceptional value, a real bargain
★★★★	Good value
★★★	Fair value, you get exactly what you pay for
★★	Somewhat overpriced
★	Significantly overpriced

Location   Just below the restaurant address and phone number is a designation for geographic zone. This zone description will give you a general idea of where the restaurant described is located. For ease of use, we divide Chicago into 11 geographic zones.

Zone 1.	North Side	Zone 7.	South Side
Zone 2.	North Central/O'Hare	Zone 8.	Southern Suburbs
Zone 3.	Near North	Zone 9.	Western Suburbs
Zone 4.	The Loop	Zone 10.	Northwest Suburbs
Zone 5.	South Loop	Zone 11.	Northern Suburbs
Zone 6.	South Central/Midway		

If you are in the Loop area and intend to walk or take a cab to dinner, you may want to choose a restaurant from among those located in Zone 4. If you have a car, you might include restaurants from contiguous zones in your consideration. (See pages **x-ref** for detailed zone maps.)

Our Pick of the Best Chicago Restaurants

Because restaurants are opening and closing all the time in Chicago, we have tried to confine our list to establishments—or chefs—with a proven track record over a fairly long period of time. Newer or changed establishments that demonstrate staying power and consistency will be profiled in subsequent editions.

The list is highly selective. Noninclusion of a particular place does not necessarily indicate that the restaurant is not good, only that it currently does not rank among the best or most consistent in its genre. Detailed profiles of each restaurant follow in alphabetical order at the end of this chapter. Also, we've listed the types of payment accepted at each restaurant using the following codes:

AMEX	American Express	CB	Carte Blanche
D	Discover	DC	Diners Club
JCB	Japan Credit Bank	MC	MasterCard
V	Visa		

THE BEST CHICAGO RESTAURANTS

Name	Overall Rating	Price Rating	Quality Rating	Value Rating	Zone
American					
Naha	★★★★	Exp	★★★★	★★★	3
Keefer's	★★★½	Exp	★★★★	★★	3
Uncommon Ground	★★½	Inexp	★★★★	★★★★★	1
Bongo Room	★★½	Inexp	★★★★	★★★★	2
Lou Mitchell's Restaurant	★★	Inexp	★★★★	★★★★	2, 4
Asian					
Vong's Thai Kitchen	★★★½	Mod	★★★★½	★★★★	3
Kevin	★★★½	Exp	★★★★	★★	3
Penang	★★★	Inexp	★★★★	★★★★	5
Breakfast					
Orange	★★	Inexp	★★★	★★★★	1
Brew Pub					
Piece	★★	Inexp	★★★	★★★★	2
Cajun					
Wishbone	★★½	Inexp	★★★★	★★★★★	1, 2
Heaven on Seven	★★½	Mod	★★★★	★★★	1, 3, 4
Chinese					
House of Fortune	★★★	Mod	★★★★	★★	5
Three Happiness	★★½	Inexp	★★★★	★★★★★	5
Deli					
Manny's Coffee Shop & Deli	★★	Inexp	★★★★	★★★	5
Ethiopian					
Addis Abeba	★★	Inexp	★★★½	★★★★★	1
French					
Everest	★★★★★	Exp/ Very Exp	★★★★★	★★★	4
Le Francais	★★★★★	Exp/ Very Exp	★★★★★	★★★	10
Chez Joel	★★★½	Mod	★★★★½	★★★	6
Le Colonial	★★★½	Mod	★★★★½	★★★	3
Marché	★★★	Mod	★★★★½	★★★	2
Tournesol	★★★	Mod	★★★★	★★★	1
Bistro Campagne	★★★	Inexp	★★★½	★★★★	1

THE BEST CHICAGO RESTAURANTS (continued)

Name	Overall Rating	Price Rating	Quality Rating	Value Rating	Zone
German					
The Berghoff	★★	Mod	★★★½	★★★	4
Greek					
Santorini	★★★	Exp	★★★★	★★★	2
Artopolis	★★½	Inexp	★★★★	★★★★	2
Indian					
Tiffin	★★★	Mod	★★★★	★★★★	1
Irish					
Chief O'Neill's Pub and Restaurant	★★	Mod	★★	★★★	1
Italian					
Spiaggia	★★★★★	Exp/ Very Exp	★★★★★	★★★	3
Vivere	★★★★	Exp	★★★★½	★★★	4
Fortunato	★★★½	Mod	★★★★	★★★	2
Rosebud Cafe	★★★	Mod	★★★★	★★★	3, 6, 8
Japanese					
Heat	★★★★	Exp	★★★★	★★	3
Mirai Sushi	★★★½	Mod	★★★★½	★★★	2
Kamehachi of Tokyo	★★★	Inexp	★★★★	★★★★	3, 11
Korean					
Jin Ju	★★★	Inexp	★★★	★★★½	1
Malaysian					
Penang	★★★	Inexp	★★★★	★★★★	5
Mediterranean					
Naha	★★★★	Exp	★★★★	★★★	3
Wave	★★★	Mod	★★★	★★★	3
Mexican					
Topolabampo	★★★★½	Exp	★★★★★	★★★	3
Frontera Grill	★★★★	Mod	★★★★½	★★★	3
Ixcapuzalco	★★★½	Mod	★★★★½	★★★★	2
Salpicon	★★★	Mod	★★★★½	★★★	3
Chilpancingo	★★★	Mod	★★★★	★★★	3
Middle Eastern					
Maza	★★★	Mod	★★★★½	★★★★	1

THE BEST CHICAGO RESTAURANTS *(continued)*					
Name	**Overall Rating**	**Price Rating**	**Quality Rating**	**Value Rating**	**Zone**
New American					
Charlie Trotter's	★★★★★	Very Exp	★★★★★	★★★	1
Tru	★★★★★	Very Exp	★★★★★	★★★	3
Spring	★★★★½	Mod	★★★★	★★	2
Blackbird	★★★★	Exp	★★★★½	★★★	4
mk	★★★★	Exp	★★★★½	★★★	3
Nomi	★★★★	Exp	★★★★½	★★★	3
North Pond Cafe	★★★★	Exp	★★★★½	★★★	1
one sixtyblue	★★★★	Exp	★★★★½	★★★	2
Bin 36	★★★	Exp	★★★★½	★★★	3
Mod	★★★	Mod	★★★★½	★★	2
Green Dolphin Street	★★★	Mod	★★★★	★★	1
Twelve 12	★★★	Exp	★★★	★★	3
Magnolia Cafe	★★½	Mod	★★★	★★	1
New French					
Avenues	★★★★½	Very Exp	★★★★	★★	3
Aubriot	★★★★	Exp	★★★½	★★★	1
Kevin	★★★½	Exp	★★★★	★★	3
Cafe des Architectes	★★★½	Exp	★★★★	1½	3
Nuevo Latino					
Mas	★★★½	Mod	★★★★½	★★★	2
Chilpancingo	★★★	Mod	★★★★	★★★	3
Pizzeria					
Piece	★★	Inexp	★★★	★★★★	2
Seafood					
Spring	★★★★½	Mod	★★★★	★★	2
Avenues	★★★★½	Very Exp	★★★★	★★	3
Shaw's Crab House	★★★½	Exp	★★★★½	★★	3, 10
Santorini	★★★	Exp	★★★★	★★★	2
Wave	★★★	Mod	★★★	★★★	3
Half Shell	★★	Mod	★★★★	★★★★	1
Southern					
Wishbone	★★½	Inexp	★★★★	★★★★★	1, 2
Spanish/Tapas					
Cafe Iberico	★★★	Mod	★★★★	★★★★	3
Emilio's Tapas	★★★	Mod	★★★★	★★★★	1

THE BEST CHICAGO RESTAURANTS *(continued)*

Name	Overall Rating	Price Rating	Quality Rating	Value Rating	Zone
Steak					
Gibson's	★★★½	Exp	★★★★½	★★★	3
Morton's	★★★½	Exp	★★★★½	★★	2, 3, 8, 10
Nine	★★★½	Exp	★★★★½	★★	4
Smith & Wollensky	★★★½	Exp	★★★★½	★★	3
Keefer's	★★★½	Exp	★★★★	★★	3
Sushi					
Heat	★★★★	Exp	★★★★	★★	3
Mirai Sushi	★★★½	Mod	★★★★½	★★★	2
Thai					
Arun's Thai Restaurant	★★★★½	Very Exp	★★★★★	★★	1
Vong's Thai Kitchen	★★★½	Mod	★★★★½	★★★★	3
Amarind's	★★★	Inexp	★★★	★★★★★	2
Erawan	★★★	Very Exp	★★★	★	3
Vegetarian					
Chicago Diner	★★	Inexp	★★★½	★★★★	1, 11
Vietnamese					
Pasteur	★★★½	Inexp	★★★★½	★★★★	1
Le Colonial	★★★½	Mod	★★★★½	★★★	3
Wine Bars					
Bin 36	★★★	Exp	★★★★½	★★★	3
Cru Cafe and Wine Bar	★★½	Mod	★★★★	★★★	3

CHICAGO RESTAURANTS BY ZONE

Name	Cuisine	Overall Rating	Price Rating	Quality Rating	Value Rating
Zone 1—The North Side					
Charlie Trotter's	New American	★★★★★	Very Exp	★★★★★	★★★
Arun's Thai Restaurant	Thai	★★★★½	Very Exp	★★★★★	★★
North Pond Cafe	New American	★★★★	Exp	★★★★½	★★★
Aubriot	New French	★★★★	Exp	★★★½	★★★
Pasteur	Vietnamese	★★★½	Inexp	★★★★½	★★★★
Maza	Middle Eastern	★★★	Mod	★★★★½	★★★★

CHICAGO RESTAURANTS BY ZONE (continued)

Name	Cuisine	Overall Rating	Price Rating	Quality Rating	Value Rating
Zone 1—The North Side (continued)					
Emilio's Tapas	Spanish/Tapas	★★★	Mod	★★★★	★★★★
Tiffin	Indian	★★★	Mod	★★★★	★★★★
Tournesol	French	★★★	Mod	★★★★	★★★
Green Dolphin Street	New American	★★★	Mod	★★★★	★★
Bistro Campagne	French	★★★	Inexp	★★★½	★★★★
Jin Ju	Korean	★★★	Inexp	★★★	★★★½
Uncommon Ground	American	★★½	Inexp	★★★★	★★★★★
Wishbone	Cajun/Southern	★★½	Inexp	★★★★	★★★★★
Heaven on Seven	Cajun	★★½	Mod	★★★★	★★★
Magnolia Cafe	New American	★★½	Mod	★★★	★★
Half Shell	Seafood	★★	Mod	★★★★	★★★★
Addis Abeba	Ethiopian	★★	Inexp	★★★½	★★★★★
Chicago Diner	Vegetarian	★★	Inexp	★★★½	★★★★
Orange	Breakfast	★★	Inexp	★★★	★★★★
Chief O'Neill's Pub and Restaurant	Irish	★★	Mod	★★	★★★
Zone 2—North Central/O'Hare					
Spring	Seafood/New American	★★★★½	Mod	★★★★	★★
one sixtyblue	New American	★★★★	Exp	★★★★½	★★★
Ixcapuzalco	Mexican	★★★½	Mod	★★★★½	★★★★
Mas	Nuevo Latino	★★★½	Mod	★★★★½	★★★
Mirai Sushi	Japanese/Sushi	★★★½	Mod	★★★★½	★★★
Morton's	Steak	★★★½	Exp	★★★★½	★★
Fortunato	Italian	★★★½	Mod	★★★★	★★★
Marché	French	★★★	Mod	★★★★½	★★★
Mod	New American	★★★	Mod	★★★★½	★★
Santorini	Greek/Seafood	★★★	Exp	★★★★	★★★
Amarind's	Thai	★★★	Inexp	★★★	★★★★★
Wishbone	Cajun/Southern	★★½	Inexp	★★★★	★★★★★
Artopolis	Greek	★★½	Inexp	★★★★	★★★★
Bongo Room	American	★★½	Inexp	★★★★	★★★★
Lou Mitchell's Restaurant	American	★★	Inexp	★★★★	★★★★
Piece	Pizzeria/Brew Pub	★★	Inexp	★★★	★★★★

CHICAGO RESTAURANTS BY ZONE (continued)

Name	Cuisine	Overall Rating	Price Rating	Quality Rating	Value Rating
Zone 3—Near North					
Spiaggia	Italian	★★★★★	Exp/ Very Exp	★★★★★	★★★
Tru	New American	★★★★★	Very Exp	★★★★★	★★★
Topolabampo	Mexican	★★★★½	Exp	★★★★★	★★★
Avenues	Seafood/ New French	★★★★½	Very Exp	★★★★	★★
Frontera Grill	Mexican	★★★★	Mod	★★★★½	★★★
mk	New American	★★★★	Exp	★★★★½	★★★
Nomi	New American	★★★★	Exp	★★★★½	★★★
Naha	Mediterranean/ American	★★★★	Exp	★★★★	★★★
Heat	Japanese/Sushi	★★★★	Exp	★★★★	★★
Vong's Thai Kitchen	Asian/Thai	★★★½	Mod	★★★★½	★★★★
Gibson's	Steak	★★★½	Exp	★★★★½	★★★
Le Colonial	Vietnamese/ French	★★★½	Mod	★★★★½	★★★
Morton's	Steak	★★★½	Exp	★★★★½	★★
Shaw's Crab House	Seafood	★★★½	Exp	★★★★½	★★
Smith & Wollensky	Steak	★★★½	Exp	★★★★½	★★
Keefer's	Steak/American	★★★½	Exp	★★★★	★★
Kevin	New French/ Asian	★★★½	Exp	★★★★	★★
Cafe des Architectes	New French	★★★½	Exp	★★★★	★½
Bin 36	New American/ Wine Bar	★★★	Exp	★★★★½	★★★
Salpicon	Mexican	★★★	Mod	★★★★½	★★★
Kamehachi of Tokyo	Japanese	★★★	Inexp	★★★★	★★★★
Cafe Iberico	Spanish/Tapas	★★★	Mod	★★★★	★★★★
Chilpancingo	Nuevo Latino/ Mexican	★★★	Mod	★★★★	★★★
Rosebud Cafe	Italian	★★★	Mod	★★★★	★★★
Wave	Mediterranean/ Seafood	★★★	Mod	★★★	★★★
Twelve 12	New American	★★★	Exp	★★★	★★
Erawan	Thai	★★★	Very Exp	★★★	★

CHICAGO RESTAURANTS BY ZONE (continued)

Name	Cuisine	Overall Rating	Price Rating	Quality Rating	Value Rating
Zone 3—Near North (continued)					
Cru Cafe and Wine Bar	Wine Bar	★★½	Mod	★★★★	★★★
Heaven on Seven	Cajun	★★½	Mod	★★★★	★★★
Zone 4—The Loop					
Everest	French	★★★★★	Exp/ Very Exp	★★★★★	★★★
Blackbird	New American	★★★★	Exp	★★★★½	★★★
Vivere	Italian	★★★★	Exp	★★★★½	★★★
Nine	Steak	★★★½	Exp	★★★★½	★★
Heaven on Seven	Cajun	★★½	Mod	★★★★	★★★
Lou Mitchell's Restaurant	American	★★	Inexp	★★★★	★★★★
The Berghoff	German	★★	Mod	★★★½	★★★
Zone 5—South Loop					
Penang	Asian/Malaysian	★★★	Inexp	★★★★	★★★★
House of Fortune	Chinese	★★★	Mod	★★★★	★★
Three Happiness	Chinese	★★½	Inexp	★★★★	★★★★★
Manny's Coffee Shop & Deli	Deli	★★	Inexp	★★★★	★★★
Zone 6—South Central/Midway					
Chez Joel	French	★★★½	Mod	★★★★½	★★★
Rosebud Cafe	Italian	★★★	Mod	★★★★	★★★
Zone 8—Southern Suburbs					
Morton's	Steak	★★★½	Exp	★★★★½	★★
Rosebud Cafe	Italian	★★★	Mod	★★★★	★★★
Zone 10—Northwest Suburbs					
Le Francais	French	★★★★★	Exp/ Very Exp	★★★★★	★★★
Morton's	Steak	★★★½	Exp	★★★★½	★★
Shaw's Seafood Grill	Seafood	★★★½	Exp	★★★★½	★★
Zone 11—Northern Suburbs					
Kamehachi of Tokyo	Japanese	★★★	Inexp	★★★★	★★★★
Chicago Diner	Vegetarian	★★	Inexp	★★★½	★★★★

More Recommendations

Best Ribs

Hecky's BBQ   Zone 11   1902 Green Bay Road, Evanston (847) 492-1182

Leon's Bar-B-Q   Zone 7   8259 South Cottage Grove Avenue (773) 488-4556; 1158 West 59th Street (773) 778-7828; 1640 East 79th Street (773) 731-1454

Merle's Ribs   Zone 11   727 Benson Avenue, Evanston (847) 475-7766

Miller's Pub   Zone 4   134 South Wabash Avenue (312) 645-5377

Robinson's #1   Zone 1   Ribs 655 West Armitage Avenue (312) 337-1399

Smoke Daddy   Zone 2   1804 West Division Street (773) 772-6656

Twin Anchors   Zone 1   1655 North Sedgwick Street (312) 266-1616

Weber Grill   Zone 4   539 North State Street (312) 467-9696

Best Beer Lists

Bistro Campagne   Zone 1   4518 North Lincoln Avenue (773) 271-6100

Chief O'Neill's   Zone 2   3471 North Elston Avenue (773) 583-3066

Clark Street Ale House   Zone 1   743 North Clark Street (312) 642-9253

Goose Island Brewing Company   Zone 1   1800 North Clybourn Avenue (312) 915-0071; 3535 North Clark Street (773) 832-9040

Green Door Tavern   Zone 4   678 North Orleans Street (312) 664-5496

Hopleaf   Zone 1   5148 North Clark Street (773) 334-9851

Red Lion Pub   Zone 1   2446 North Lincoln Avenue (773) 348-2695

Resi's Bierstube   Zone 2   2034 West Irving Park Road (773) 472-1749

Rock Bottom Brewery   Zone 4   1 West Grand Avenue (312) 755-9339

Village Tap   Zone 1   2055 West Roscoe Street (773) 883-0817

Best Brunch

Ann Sather's   Zone 1   929 West Belmont Avenue (773) 348-2378; 5207 North Clark Street (773) 271-6677

Bongo Room   Zone 2   1470 North Milwaukee Avenue (773) 489-0690

Brett's   Zone 1   2011 West Roscoe Street (773) 248-0999

Cafe Selmarie   Zone 1   4729 North Lincoln Avenue (773) 989-5595

Deleece   Zone 1   4004 North Southport Avenue (773) 325-1710

Feast   Zone 2   1835 West North Avenue (773) 235-6361

Frontera Grill (Saturday only)   Zone 4   445 North Clark Street (312) 661-1434

Hilary's Urban Eatery   Zone 2   1599 West Division Street (773) 235-4327

House of Blues   Zone 4   329 North Dearborn Street (312) 527-2583

Jane's   Zone 2   1655 West Cortland Avenue (773) 862-5263

Munch   Zone 2   1800 West Grand Avenue (312) 226-4914

North Pond   Zone 1   2610 North Cannon Drive (773) 477-5845

Orange   Zone 1   3231 North Clark Street (773) 549-4400

Phoenix   Zone 6   2131 South Archer Avenue (312) 328-0848

Park Avenue Cafe   Zone 3   DoubleTree Guest Suites Hotel, 199 East Walton Place (312) 944-4414

Ritz-Carlton Dining Room   Zone 3   Ritz-Carlton Hotel, 160 East Pearson Street (312) 573-5223

Salpicón   Zone 3   1252 North Wells Street (312) 988-7811
Soul Kitchen   Zone 2   1576 North Milwaukee Avenue (773) 342-9742

Best Late-Night Eateries

Bar Louie   American   Zone 1: 3545 North Clark Street (773) 296-2500;
800 North Lincoln Avenue (312) 337-9800; Zone 2: 1704 North Damen
Avenue (773) 645-7500; Zone 4: 123 North Halsted Street (312) 207-0500;
1800 North Lincoln Avenue (312) 337-9800; 226 West Chicago Avenue (312)
337-3313; Zone 5: 47 West Polk Street (312) 347-0000

Beat Kitchen   Global/Eclectic   Zone 1   2100 West Belmont Avenue
(773) 281-4444

Eau   French   Zone 1   1962 North Halsted Street (773) 281-4211

Gibson's Steak House   Steakhouse/American   Zone 3   1028 North Rush
Street (312) 266-8999

Lucille's Tavern and Tapas   Global/Eclectic   Zone 1   2470 North Lincoln
Avenue (773) 929-0660

Mike Ditka's   American   Zone 3   Tremont Hotel, 100 East Chestnut Street
(312) 587-8989

Nola's 32nd Ward Seafood House   Cajun   Zone 2   1856 West North
Avenue (773) 395-4300

Pepper Lounge   Global/Eclectic   Zone 1   3441 North Sheffield Avenue
(773) 665-7377

Tavern on Rush   Italian/American   Zone 3   1031 North Rush Street
(312) 664-9600

Three Happiness   Chinese   Zone 6   2130 South Wentworth Avenue
(312) 791-1228

Twisted Spoke   Burgers/American   Zone 2   501 North Ogden Avenue
(312) 666-1500

Best Outdoor Dining

Bistro Campagne   French   Zone1   4518 North Lincoln Avenue
(773) 271-6100

Cafe Ba-Ba-Reeba   Tapas/Spanish   Zone 1   2024 North Halsted Street
(773) 935-5000

Carmichael's Chicago Steakhouse   Steakhouse   Zone 2   1052 West
Monroe Boulevard (312) 433-0025

Don Juan on Halsted   Mexican   Zone1   1729 North Halsted (312) 981-4000

Jackson Harbor Grill   Seafood   Zone 7   6401 South Lake Shore Drive
(773) 288-4442

John Barleycorn Memorial Pub   American/Pub Grub   Zone1   658 West
Belden Avenue (773) 348-8899

Keefer's   Steakhouse   Zone 4   20 West Kinzie Street (312) 467-9525

Le Colonial   Vietnamese   Zone 3   937 North Rush Street (312) 255-0088

North Pond   New American   Zone1   2610 North Cannon Drive
(773) 477-5845

Pasteur   Vietnamese   Zone 1   5525 North Broadway (773) 878-1061

Pegasus   Greek   Zone 4   130 South Halsted Street (312) 226-3377

Puck's at the MCA   Global/Eclectic   Zone 3   220 East Chicago Avenue (312) 397-4034

Thyme   French   Zone 2   464 North Halsted Street (312) 226-4300

Topo Gigio   Italian   Zone 1   1516 North Wells Street (312) 266-9355

Best Bistros

Bistrot Margot   Zone 1   1437 North Wells Street (312) 587-3660

Bistro Ultra   Zone 2   2239 North Clybourn Avenue (773) 529-3300

Brasserie Jo   Zone 4   59 West Hubbard Street (312) 595-0800

Chez Joel   Zone 6   1119 West Taylor Street (312) 226-6479

Cyrano's Bistrot & Wine Bar   Zone 4   546 North Wells Street (312) 467-0546

Kiki's Bistro   Zone 3   900 North Franklin Street (312) 335-5454

La Sardine   Zone 2   111 North Carpenter Street (312) 421-2800

Le Bouchon   Zone 2   1958 North Damen Avenue (773) 862-6600

Mon Ami Gabi   Zone 1   2300 North Lincoln Park West (773) 348-8886

Tournesol   Zone 1   4343 North Lincoln Avenue (773) 477-8820

Best Soul Food

Army & Lou's   Zone 7   422 East 75th Street (773) 483-3100

BJ's Market and Bakery   Zone 7   8734 South Stony Island Avenue (773) 374-4700

Creole   Zone 4   226 West Kinzie Street (312) 222-0300

Gladys' Luncheonette   Zone 7   4527 South Indiana Avenue (773) 548-4566

Heaven on Seven   Zone 1: 3478 North Clark Street (773) 477-7818; Zone 3: 600 North Michigan Avenue (312) 280-7774; Zone 4: Garland Building, 111 North Wabash Avenue, 7th Floor (312) 263-6444

Soul Kitchen   Zone 2   1576 North Milwaukee Avenue (773) 342-9742

Wishbone   Zone 1: 3300 North Lincoln Avenue (773) 549-2663; Zone 4: 1001 West Washington Boulevard (312) 850-2662

Best Places with Music

Bite   Alternative Rock   Zone 2   1039 North Western Avenue (773) 395-2483

Brother Jimmy's BBQ   Blues   Zone 1   3660 North Clark Street (773) 755-4444

Chief O'Neill's   Irish   Zone 2   3471 North Elston Avenue (773) 583-3066

El Nandu   Argentine Guitar   Zone 2   2731 West Fullerton Parkway (773) 278-0900

Fado Irish Pub   Irish   Zone 4   100 West Grand Avenue (312) 836-0066

Green Dolphin Street   Jazz   Zone 1   2200 North Ashland Avenue (773) 395-0066

House of Blues   Blues, Rock   Zone 4   329 North Dearborn Street (312) 527-2583

Joe's Be-Bop Cafe and Jazz Emporium   (Jazz) Navy Pier, 600 East Grand Avenue (312) 595-5299 Zone 4

Pete Miller's Steak House   Jazz   Zone 11   1557 Sherman Avenue, Evanston (847) 328-0399

Reservation Blues Blues Zone 2 1566 North Milwaukee Avenue
(773) 645-5200

Smoke Daddy Blues, Jazz Zone 2 1804 West Division Street
(773) 772-6656

Best Delis

The Bagel Zone 1 3107 North Broadway (773) 477-0300

Cold Comfort Zone 2 2211 West North Avenue (773) 772-4552

5 Boroughs Zone 4 738 North Wells Street (312) 915-0188

Manny's Coffee Shop and Deli Zone 6 1141 South Jefferson Street
(312) 930-2855

New York City Bagel Deli Zone 1 1001 West North Avenue
(312) 274-1278

Best Pizza

Bricks Zone 1 1909 North Lincoln Avenue (312) 255-0851

California Pizza Kitchen Zone 3: Water Tower Place, 845 North Michigan
Avenue, 7th Floor (312) 787-7300; Zone 4: 52 East Ohio Street
(312) 787-6075

Edwardo's Zone 3: 1212 North Dearborn Street (312) 337-4490; Zone 5:
521 South Dearborn Street (312) 939-3366 Zone 5

Gino's East Zone 4 633 North Wells Street (312) 943-1124

Lou Malnati's Zone 4 439 North Wells Street (312) 828-9800

O Famé Zone 1 750 West Webster Avenue (773) 929-5111

Pizzeria Due Zone 4 619 North Wabash Avenue (312) 943-2400

Pizzeria Uno Zone 4 29 East Ohio Street (312) 321-1000

Elegant Prix-Fixe Menus

Ambria Zone 1 2300 North Lincoln Park West (773) 472-5959

Arun's Zone 2 4156 North Kedzie Avenue (773) 539-1909

Avenues Zone 3 180 East Superior Street (312) 573-6754

Campagnola Zone 11 815 Chicago Avenue, Evanston (847) 475-6100

Carlos Zone 11 429 Temple Avenue, Highwood (847) 432-0770

Charlie Trotter's Zone 1 816 West Armitage Avenue (773) 248-6228

Erawan Royal Thai Cuisine Zone 4 729 North Clark Street (312) 642-6888

Everest Zone 4 440 South LaSalle Street, 40th Floor (312) 663-8920

La Petite Folie Zone 6 1504 East 55th Street (773) 493-1394

Le Francais Zone 11 269 South Milwaukee Avenue, Wheeling (847) 541-7470

Les Nomades Zone 3 222 East Ontario Street (312) 649-9010

mk Zone 4 868 North Franklin Street (312) 482-9179

NoMi Zone 4 800 North Michigan Avenue (312) 239-4030

Ritz-Carlton Dining Room Zone 3 Ritz-Carlton Hotel, 160 East Pearson
Street (312) 573-5223

Seasons Four Zone 3 Seasons Hotel 120 East Delaware Place
(312) 649-2349

Spiaggia Zone 3 980 North Michigan Avenue (312) 280-2750

Tallgrass Zone 9 1006 South State Street, Lockport (815) 838-5566

Topolobampo Zone 4 445 North Clark Street (312) 661-1434
Tru Zone 3 676 North St. Clair Street (312) 202-0001
Twelve Zone 3 12 1212 North State Parkway (312) 951-1212
Zealous Zone 4 419 West Superior Street (312) 475-9112

Trendy Scene Places

Bin Zone 4 36 339 North Dearborn Street (312) 755-9463
Blackbird Zone 4 619 West Randolph Street (312) 715-0708
Butterfield 8 Zone 4 718 North Wells Street (312) 327-0940
Cafe Absinthe Zone 2 1954 West North Avenue (773) 278-4488
Gibson's Steak House Zone 3 1028 North Rush Street (312) 266-8999
Gioco Zone 5 1312 South Wabash Avenue (312) 939-3870
Le Passage Zone 3 937 North Rush Street (312) 255-0022
Marché Zone 4 833 West Randolph Street (312) 226-8399
Mas Zone 2 1670 West Division Street (773) 276-8700
Mirai Sushi Zone 2 2020 West Division Street (773) 862-8500
MOD Zone 2 1520 North Damen Avenue (773) 252-1500
Nine Zone 4 440 West Randolph Street (312) 575-9900
one sixtyblue Zone 4 160 North Loomis Street (312) 850-0303
Red Light Zone 4 820 West Randolph Street (312) 733-8880
Roy's Zone 4 720 North State Street (312) 787-7599
Tavern on Rush Zone 3 1031 North Rush Street (312) 664-9600
Wave Zone 3 644 North Lake Shore Drive (312) 255-4460

Best Fast Food

Byron's Hot Dogs Zone 2: 1017 West Irving Park Road (773) 281-7474; 1701
  West Lawrence Avenue (773) 271-0900; Zone 4: 680 North Halsted Street
  (312) 738-0968
Mr. Beef Zone 4 666 North Orleans Street (312) 337-8500
Muskie's Zone 1 2878 North Lincoln Avenue (773) 883-1633
Muskie's Hamburgers Zone 1 963 West Belmont Avenue (773) 477-1880
The Wiener's Circle Zone 1 2622 North Clark Street (773) 477-7444

Restaurant Profiles

ADDIS ABEBA ★★

ETHIOPIAN | INEXPENSIVE | QUALITY ★★★½ | VALUE ★★★★★ | ZONE 1

3521 North Clark Street; (773) 929-9383

Reservations Recommended on weekends **When to go** Dinner **Entree range**
$6–$15 **Payment** V, MC, AMEX, D **Service rating** ★★ **Friendliness rating** ★★★
Parking Public lots, street **Bar** Full service **Wine selection** Limited, $20–$22.50; 11
by the glass, $5–$7 **Dress** Casual **Disabled access** Wheelchair accessible **Customers** Grad students, hippies, and casual diners

Dinner Monday–Thursday, 5–10 p.m.; Friday and Saturday, 5–11 p.m.; Sunday, 4–10 p.m.

Setting & atmosphere The low-budget decor is enlivened by touches of exotic fabrics, artifacts, and food service in the traditional mesob (hand-woven basket). There's a small raised area with stools and tables designed for the authentic Ethiopian dining experience (intriguing if somewhat uncomfortable).

House specialties Sambusa (seasoned lentils with onions and jalapeño stuffed in a crusty roll); katenya (spinach and cheese blended with spiced butter and cardamom, spread on injera, rolled, and served with spicy yogurt sauce); asa (fish cubes sautéed in herb butter with garlic, pepper, and lemon pepper); doro wot (chicken simmered in berbere red pepper sauce, spiced butter, and honey wine, seasoned with garlic, cloves, cinnamon, and cardamom); yebeg alitcha (succulent pieces of lamb, slow cooked in mild sauce with spiced butter, onions, garlic, and turmeric).

Other recommendations Shorba (plain yogurt and cucumber soup with fresh mint and honey); kitfo (Ethiopian steak tartar seasoned with spiced butter, cardamom, and powdered hot peppers); zilzil tibs (strips of tender beef marinated in red wine, red pepper sauce, garlic, cardamom, and other spices); Ethiopian-style shish kebab.

Summary & comments A longstanding neighborhood ethnic favorite, Addis Abeba is a refreshing change from contrived concepts and high prices. The house T-shirt bears the ubiquitous red circle/slash international symbol for "no"—this time surrounding a knife, fork, and spoon. Expect to eat with your hands, grabbing bits of food with the moist injera bread. It's decidedly downscale in price, ambience, and dress code, but the food is flavorful and intriguing. Service can be quite slow.

AMARIND'S ★★★

THAI | INEXPENSIVE | QUALITY ★★★ | VALUE ★★★★★ | ZONE 2

6822 North Avenue; (773) 889-9999

Reservations Accepted **When to go** Dinner or lunch, weekday or weekends **Entree range** $6.95–$11.95 **Payment** MC, V, D, AMEX, DC **Service rating** ★★★ **Friendliness rating** ★★ **Parking** Street **Bar** Beer and wine only **Wine selection** Limited selection from Italy, France, Chile and California, $22–$40 per bottle; by the glass, $5–$7 **Dress** Casual **Disabled access** Yes **Customers** All ages and types, from urban to suburban

Hours Tuesday–Thursday, 11:30 a.m.–9:30 p.m.; Friday and Saturday, 11:30 a.m.– 10 p.m.; Sunday, 3 p.m.–10 p.m.; closed Monday.

Setting & atmosphere The simple room has classic Thai artifacts, crisp white unadorned linen cloths, and fresh, natural wood paneling. The clean lines make it serene, relaxing and tasteful.

House specialties Chive dumplings with chili black soy sauce; shrimp and pork shumai; catfish in yellow curry; holy basil squid; pad see ewe; garlic prawns.

Other recommendations Miniature eggrolls; mooping (sliced marinated pork); crispy omelet with shrimp, tofu, peanuts; asparagus chicken with shiitake mushrooms, squash, and scallion.

Summary & comments There's nothing remarkable about this simple room or the far-west location, but the casual Thai cuisine is second to none. Dishes are priced like any number of neighborhood Thai eateries, but the vivid flavors and exquisite presentations make it a truly great value.

ARTOPOLIS   ★★½

GREEK | INEXPENSIVE | QUALITY ★★★★ | VALUE ★★★★ | ZONE 2

306 South Halsted Street; (312) 559-9000

Reservations Not accepted **When to go** Weekday lunch **Entree range** $4.95–$9.75 **Payment** V, MC, AMEX, DC **Service rating** ★★ **Friendliness rating** ★★★ **Parking** Pay lot, $3; street **Bar** Full service **Wine selection** Mostly Greek, Italian, and Californian, $4–$6 by the glass, $5–$35 per bottle **Dress** Casual **Disabled access** Yes **Customers** Urban workers

Hours Daily, 9 a.m.–midnight

Setting & atmosphere The French doors at this Greek cafe and bakery (located in the heart of Greektown) spill onto bustling Halsted Street. There's a small balcony perched over the cafe tables in the front, and a spacious, dark-oak, copper-trimmed, marble-topped bar in the center divides the back retail area from the dining room. Terra cotta tile floors are handsomely set off by the rich cherry tables and chairs arranged closely in the cafe seating area.

House specialties Mediterranean fest appetizer (a sampling of hummus, fava beans, baba ghanoush, tzatziki, and olives); smoky harvest sandwich with oven-roasted vegetables; smoked Provolone and herbs on homemade sourdough bread; artopitas (signature flaky calzone-like stuffed pockets with a variety of fillings, such as spinach and feta, ham and kasseri cheese, zucchini and Gouda, and portabella mushroom and Emmenthaler cheese).

Other recommendations Frutti de mare salad with rock shrimp, octopus, and calamari; kotosalata sandwich (mesclun greens topped with chicken salad, pine nuts, green apple, and pesto on walnut bread); roasted lamb with mint aïoli sauce; seasonal fresh fruit tart; all fresh breads.

Summary & comments This Greektown newcomer brings a French pastry chef's exquisite rustic breads and pastries together with innovative, casual Greek fare. The ambitious staff is eager to please, although lunch is self-service. Wood-fired pizzas and artopitas (cheese-, meat-, and vegetable-stuffed pastries) make a nice light lunch, while other specialties are heartier. During nice weather, French doors open for inviting sidewalk dining.

ARUN'S THAI RESTAURANT   ★★★★½

THAI | VERY EXPENSIVE | QUALITY ★★★★★ | VALUE ★★ | ZONE 1

4156 North Kedzie Avenue; (773) 539-1909

Reservations Recommended **When to go** Reservations can be difficult for weekend dinner, but it's the best time. **Entree range** $85 for a multi-course tasting menu **Payment** V, MC, AMEX, DC, D **Service rating** ★★★★ **Friendliness rating** ★★★½ **Parking** Valet, $7 **Bar** Full service with several Asian beers **Wine selection** Concise and reasonable list featuring American, French, and Austrian bottles, with several by the glass, $7–$12; by the bottle, $28–$100, with a few reserve bottles near $200 **Dress** Dressy **Disabled access** Yes **Customers** Mature patrons, some professionals

Hours Tuesday–Sunday, 5–10 p.m.

Setting & atmosphere The nondescript exterior is no indication of the exquisite interior at this upscale Thai restaurant. The tranquil, narrow room is clean and simple with several semi-private alcoves and a raised gallery seating area. The mustard-colored walls are trimmed in deep mahogany wood and adorned with Thai artifacts, paintings, and silk panels.

House specialties Crab spring rolls; spicy roast duck salad with fresh Thai basil, cilantro, and snap peas in a vinegar-fish sauce; Thai-style sweet and sour striped bass with shiitake mushrooms and crispy egg noodles; garlic prawn and sea scallops; Mussaman beef curry; lemongrass ice cream.

Other recommendations Chicken curry soup with soft and crispy egg noodles; steamed assorted mini-rice dumplings filled with chicken or pork; green curry chicken with Thai eggplant; spicy green papaya salad with skewers of grilled chicken and hot chile flakes; lychee sorbet.

Summary & comments The Chef's Design Menu leaves the ordering up to Chef Arun Sampanthavivat, a master of creative and innovative Thai cooking. Servers inquire about patrons' likes, dislikes, and spice tolerance; then, more than a dozen small tasting courses come streaming out. Acclaimed chef Arun has received accolades since he opened in 1985 for his exquisite balance of flavors, intricate and artistic garnishes, and ability to raise Thai food to new heights of elegance. Some find it pricey, but most revel in the luxury.

Honors & awards 1995–1999, nominated Best Chef in the Midwest by the James Beard Foundation; 1998 and 1999, awarded DiRoNA Award of Excellence; 1995, Ivy Award from *Restaurants & Institutions* magazine.

AUBRIOT   ★★★★

NEW FRENCH | EXPENSIVE | QUALITY ★★★½ | VALUE ★★★ | ZONE 1

1962 North Halsted Street; (773) 281-4211

Reservations Accepted **When to go** Weekend dinner **Entree range** $17–$29 **Payment** MC, V, D, AMEX, DC **Service rating** ★★★ **Friendliness rating** ★★ **Parking** Valet, $8 **Bar** Full **Wine selection** Mostly French with some Californian and Oregonian, $34–$96; by the glass, $7–$12 **Dress** Moderately upscale **Disabled Access** Yes **Customers** Professionals, older locals

Hours Tuesday–Thursday, 5:50 p.m.–9:30 p.m.; Friday and Saturday, 5 p.m.–10 p.m.; Sunday, 5 p.m.–8:30 p.m.

Setting & atmosphere The cheerful, slender room is simply adorned with etched-glass sunflowers bordered by natural wood paneling. The atrium-like sunroom has several coveted tables, surrounded by windows overlooking the bustling street.

House specialties Pan-seared foie gras with toasted brioche, lemon cream, and lime juice-sugar reduction; caramelized cauliflower ravioli with asparagus, capers, and beurre noisette; smoked duck breast and pear salad with haricot vert, tomatoes, and coriander vinaigrette; seared lamb loin with tomato, Parmesan, mache, and a curry-honey reduction; roasted veal tender with lentils, chanterelle mushrooms, and a corn broth; sautéed sea bass with parsnip puree, mascarpone, and egg ravioli in an almond vegetable foam.

Other recommendations Sautéed escargot with porcini mushrooms, baby carrots, chives, and mushroom foam; salad of shaved fennel, Parmesan, bacon, and lemon vinaigrette; sautéed sea scallops with beets, orange confit, pea shoots, and truffle butter; goat cheese ravioli with asparagus, oven-dried tomatoes, enoki mushrooms, and parsley sauce.

Summary & comments The highly skilled chef-owner at this quaint Lincoln Park charmer comes with an impressive resume and the uncanny ability to lighten up French food while maintaining incredibly concentrated flavors. The room is small, so reservation are usually a must—but the clean flavors and intriguing combinations make it worth a visit. A good approach for those with culinary curiosity is the six-course degustation, available with or without matched wine.

AVENUES ★★★★½

SEAFOOD/NEW FRENCH | VERY EXPENSIVE | QUALITY ★★★★ | VALUE ★★ | ZONE 3

108 East Superior Street; (312) 573-6754

Reservations Recommended **When to go** Friday or Saturday dinner **Entree range** $25–$40 **Payment** MC, V, D, AMEX, DC **Service rating** ★★★½ **Friendliness rating** ★★★ **Parking** Valet, $18 **Bar** Full, with extensive spirits and Asian beers, sake, and dessert wines **Wine selection** Global varieties; Alsace, Rhone, Austria, Napa Valley, $36–$75; half bottles, $16–$90; by the glass, $8–$19 **Dress** Upscale, dressy **Disabled access** Yes **Customers** Hotel guests, corporate executives

Hours Monday–Saturday, 6 p.m.–11 p.m.; closed Sunday.

Setting & atmosphere This luxe seventh-floor room in the Peninsula Hotel is understated yet elegant, with earth-toned fabric covering the walls, billowing slate satin curtains, and nicely spaced tables with comfy high-backed chairs. Views of Michigan Avenue and the Water Tower are worth the trip alone.

House specialties Pan-seared langoustine and foie gras; Alaskan king crab, osetra caviar, and watercress salad; grilled live scallops with baby carrots and hazelnut quinoa in a shellfish emulsion; whole roasted sea bass baked in coarse sea salt crust with candied garlic and parsley (for two); wild loup de mer with sunchoke puree, glazed shallots, baby arugula, and a beurre blanc; rabbit loin with morel mushrooms, candied tomatoes, and a sage jus; Guanaja bitter chocolate mellow with white peach sorbet and basil syrup.

Other recommendations Tournedos langoustine with crisp pancetta in a squid ink sauce; terrine of ahi tuna with carpaccio of live scallops in a lime crème fraîche; couscous crusted halibut with braised cipollini onions and sauce vierge; roasted sturgeon with sweetbreads, braised puy lentils, celeriac, and a red wine sauce; rhubarb beignet with buttermilk ice cream and marmalade.

Summary & comments No detail is missed at this high-end French seafood dining room. The luxurious room is inviting and comfortable, but Avenues is best experienced on a special occasion since it's not easy on the pocketbook. Dishes are artistically presented, using the freshest and most extravagant ingredients. The waitstaff is extremely professional—just short of intimidating.

THE BERGHOFF ★★

GERMAN | MODERATE | QUALITY ★★★½ | VALUE ★★★ | ZONE 4

17 West Adams Street; (312) 427-3170

Reservations Accepted **When to go** Weekday lunch **Entree range** $10–$18 **Payment** V, MC, AMEX **Service rating** ★★½ **Friendliness rating** ★★½ **Parking** Discounted garage, 55 East Monroe ($8 after 4 p.m.) **Bar** Full service, specialty beers **Wine selection** Limited American and German, $16.95–$21.95 **Dress** Casual **Disabled access** Wheelchair accessible **Customers** Loop workers and tourists

Lunch/Dinner Monday–Thursday, 11 a.m.–9 p.m.; Friday, 11 a.m.–9:30 p.m.; Saturday, 11:30 a.m.–10 p.m.; closed Sunday and holidays.

Setting & atmosphere A Chicago institution, this traditional German favorite is graced with beautiful quarter-sawn oak woodwork, stained glass, and a historic, archival photography collection highlighting the 1883 Columbian Exposition and images of Old Chicago. It's usually noisy and teeming with Loop action; lines can be long, but the pace is fast.

House specialties Bratwurst and knockwurst, with potato salad and sauerkraut; creamed herring; sauerbraten (marinated roast sirloin of beef with sweet and sour gravy and spaetzle); Wienerschnitzel (breaded veal cutlet with German fried potatoes); rahm schnitzel (breaded pork cutlet with sautéed mushrooms in a wine sauce).

Other recommendations Turkey meat loaf; hot corned beef sandwich with German potato salad; braised lamb shank with white wine, fresh herbs, tomatoes, pearl onions, carrots, potatoes, and beans; broiled fresh Lake Superior whitefish; grilled Cornish hen marinated with cinnamon and nutmeg with fried apples and spaetzle; creamed spinach.

Summary & comments These hallowed halls have seen a lot of schnitzel served since the restaurant opened in 1913 (prior to that, the Berghoff was a saloon, opened in 1898, with the distinction of having received Chicago's first post-Prohibition liquor license). Stick to the German classics, served by no-nonsense, professional waiters— many of whom have been around for decades. Try the house beers (light, dark, and red are occasional specialty brews, brewed by Augsburger in Wisconsin).

Honors & awards 1999 Chicago Visitors Choice Awards, 1999 James Beard Foundation Award for Excellence, 2002 America's Regional Classics Award from Zagat Survey.

BIN 36 ★★★

NEW AMERICAN/WINE BAR | EXPENSIVE | QUALITY ★★★★½ | VALUE ★★★ | ZONE 3

339 North Dearborn Street; (312) 755-9463

Reservations Accepted **When to go** Weekday lunch or dinner **Entree range** $11–$28 **Payment** V, MC, AMEX, DC, D **Service rating** ★★½ **Friendliness rating** ★★★ **Parking** Valet, $8 weekdays, $10 weekends **Bar** Full service **Wine selection** From all wine-producing nations; flights of four 2½-ounce pours, $2.20–$5.65; 49 by the glass, $5.25–$16.50. **Dress** Casual to chic **Disabled access** Yes **Customers** Suburbanites, well-dressed yuppies, show-goers

Breakfast Monday–Friday, 6:30–10 a.m.; Saturday and Sunday, 7 a.m.–noon

Lunch Monday–Friday, 11 a.m.–2 p.m.

Dinner Monday–Thursday, 5–10 p.m.; Friday and Saturday, 5–11 p.m.; Sunday, 5–9 p.m.

Setting & atmosphere This spacious room has a wall of 30-foot windows draped with rich velvet floor-to-ceiling curtains, a zinc-topped oval bar at center, and a dining room tucked under an overhanging mezzanine used for private parties. The minimalist decor features stark white walls, high ceilings, and lots of glass, lending the feeling of a Jetsons space station.

House specialties Farm-raised Atlantic salmon, with olive oil crushed purple potatoes, fava beans, and sweet 100 tomatoes; chile relleno with goat cheese and smoked gouda with grilled tomatillo and avocado salad, fritto mistro (fried calamari, artichoke, lemon, and sauce remoulade); housemade pâtés; steamed black mussels and crispy fries; smoked turkey breast and pancetta club sandwich.

Other recommendations Skillet-roasted lamb chops; five-spice ribs; rotisserie Amish chicken.

Summary & comments There are two dining areas in this ultra-swanky Marina City restaurant—the full service "Cellar" dining room and the "Tavern" tasting area—along with a small wine retail corner and breakfast coffee bar. Though the fare can be hit or miss, the cheese selection is top notch, as is the diverse selection of wine and tasting flights. There's also a raw bar for a late-night snack.

BISTRO CAMPAGNE ★★★

FRENCH | INEXPENSIVE | QUALITY ★★★½ | VALUE ★★★★ | ZONE 1

4518 North Lincoln Avenue; (773) 271-6100

Reservations Accepted **When to go** Weekend brunch, weekday dinner, in warm weather for outdoor dining **Entree range** $8–$15 **Payment** MC, V **Service rating** ★★★ **Friendliness rating** ★★★★ **Parking** Coin lot across the street; $1 per hour **Bar** Full with unique microbrews **Wine selection** Limited but well selected, mostly French, $24–$48; by the glass, $6–$10 **Dress** Casual **Disabled Access** Yes **Customers** Young to middle-aged locals, musicians from neighboring music school.

Lunch Wednesday–Friday, 11:30 a.m.–1:30 p.m.

Dinner Tuesday–Thursday, 5:30–10 p.m.; Friday and Saturday, 5:30–10:30 p.m.

Setting & atmosphere The slender room is homey and smart with simple white walls, dark oak trim and modern works of local art. The garden surrounding the outdoor patio is second to none, with an equal number of tables as the dining room holds.

House specialties Brandade de morue; onion soup, niçoise salad; croque monsieur; warm goat cheese and field greens salad with a Dijon vinaigrette; steak frites; roasted organic pork chop with peasant bread salad; sautéed spinach; profiteroles; crème brûlée.

Other recommendations Mussels steamed in Belgian ale; caramelized onion strudel; lamb loin chop with flageolets in a lamb jus; ratatouille stuffed ravioli with pistou sauce; pan-seared trout in brown butter with almonds and haricots verts; chocolate soufflé.

Summary & comments Casual and comfortable, this Lincoln Square French bistro draws a steady crowd for a limited but solid menu of classic bistro fare. The outdoor patio is one of the best in town, and the wine list is well selected. Even the beer offerings were compiled with utmost attention to detail. Don't let the low prices fool you— the expertly prepared organic ingredients used make this one of the best values in town.

BLACKBIRD ★★★★

NEW AMERICAN | EXPENSIVE | QUALITY ★★★★½ | VALUE ★★★ | ZONE 4

619 West Randolph Street; (312) 715-0708

Reservations Recommended **When to go** Weekend evenings **Entree range** $10–$29 **Payment** V, MC, AMEX, DC, D **Service rating** ★★★★ **Friendliness rating** ★★★★ **Parking** Valet, $7 **Bar** Full service **Wine selection** Mostly French and Californian, some German and Oregonian, $27–$200 per bottle, with a few up to $300 (or even $1,300!); ample by the glass options, $6–$14 **Dress** Stylish, chic **Disabled access** Yes **Customers** Hip urban dwellers, professionals by day

Lunch Monday–Friday, 11:30 a.m.–2 p.m.

Dinner Monday–Thursday, 5:30–10:30 p.m.; Friday and Saturday, 5:30–11:30 p.m.

Setting & atmosphere This minimalist, stark white West Loop hot spot exudes a New York attitude. A diverse and always well-dressed crowd flocks here weekdays through the weekend, making reservations necessary. An exposed kitchen at back is the main visual attraction in the otherwise sparsely decorated space. Tables are extremely close and the noise level often high.

House specialties The ever-changing seasonal menu might feature confit of duck salad with French green lentils in a red wine–shallot vinaigrette; sautéed Maine diver scallop "carpaccio" with blood orange, candied ginger, scallion, starburst radish, and mint; Koren's curried ragoût with grilled loin, chanterelles, autumn squash, roasted shallots, and tarragon; roasted breast of squab with homemade noodles, matsutake mushrooms, brussels sprout leaves, and aromatics; wild striped sea bass with lobster and heart of palm; roast quail with leeks and oyster mushrooms in an asparagus and barley broth; roast rack of lamb and braised shoulder with pine nuts and green olives.

Other recommendations Foie gras with rhubarb chutney, ginger, and aged balsamic vinegar; pan-roasted Alaskan halibut "agradolce" with roasted fingerlings, zucchini, sungold tomatoes, pine nuts, and extra virgin olive oil; pan-roasted walleyed pike with fennel, chioggia beets, red potatoes, saffron, and lemon fleur de sel; wood-grilled Columbia River sturgeon and Manilla clams with artichoke barigoule, chickpeas, and aïoli ; ragoût of rabbit with braised leg; wood-grilled sturgeon in a braised oxtail jus; rustic apple tart with homemade honey lavender ice cream.

Summary & comments Stylish patrons fill this hip eatery located on an offbeat stretch of west Randolph Street. Chef Paul Kahan consistently dazzles diners with his French-rooted, contemporary American fare, which takes full advantage of peak ingredients. The seasonal menu has its share of classic combinations along with just enough innovative dishes to keep it interesting. The wine list is one of the best in town, with hard-to-find selections in a range of prices.

Honors & awards 1999 *Food and Wine's* America's Ten Best New Chefs; three stars from the *Chicago Tribune;* Top Five Chicago Restaurants, 2000 *Gourmet* magazine.

BONGO ROOM   ★★½

AMERICAN | INEXPENSIVE | QUALITY ★★★★ | VALUE ★★★★ | ZONE 2

1470 North Milwaukee Avenue; (773) 489-0690

Reservations Required for large parties **When to go** Early, before the crowds **Entree range** $6–$12 **Payment** V, MC, AMEX, D **Service rating** ★★ **Friendliness rating** ★★★ **Parking** Street **Bar** Full service **Wine selection** None **Dress** Casual **Disabled access** Wheelchair accessible **Customers** Funky bedheads, mother-and-daughter duos, and morning-after dates

Breakfast/Lunch Monday–Friday, 8 a.m.–2:30 p.m.; Saturday and Sunday, 9:30 a.m.–2:30 p.m.

Setting & atmosphere Funky, colorful loft atmosphere with an open grill. Casual—and crowded, especially for weekend brunch.

House specialties Breakfast/brunch: Fluffy omelets with choice of ingredients; seasonal flapjacks (e.g., pumpkin, buttermilk-lemon, etc.); banana-pecan flapjacks; brioche French toast; breakfast burrito; chocolate tower French toast; eggs Benedict; roasted red pepper feta Benedict. Lunch: chicken-avocado club; chicken-pear club with Gorgonzola; spinach and roasted baby beet salad; broiled eggplant sandwich with Moroccan olive salad.

Other recommendations Breakfast/brunch: Oreo crumb flapjacks; strawberry cheesecake pancakes; vegetarian croissant sandwich; smoked salmon and asparagus Benedict. Lunch: Mediterranean sandwich with artichoke hearts, plum tomatoes, roasted red pepper, fresh mozzarella, and crushed garlic; roast pork sandwich with apple-radicchio slaw, sage pesto, and melted Brie.

Summary & comments If you can stand the wait, complete with jostling crowd vying for standing room only (and the occasional fashion tip from the mostly Bucktown crowd), it's well worth it for the yummy fare. This is the sort of breakfast/brunch/lunch fare you like to think you'd make yourself if you took the time and invested the creativity—but at the Bongo Room, they do all the work, and they wait on you, too.

CAFE DES ARCHITECTES   ★★★½

NEW FRENCH | EXPENSIVE | QUALITY ★★★★ | VALUE ★½ | ZONE 3

20 East Chestnut Street; (312) 324-4000

Reservations Accepted **When to go** Weekday lunch **Entree range** $15–$25 **Payment** MC, V, D, AMEX, DC **Service rating** ★★★ **Friendliness rating** ★★ **Parking** Pay lot $22; valet, $18 **Bar** Full bar **Wine selection** French and Californian, $32–$92; by the glass, $7–$15 **Dress** Business attire, upscale **Disabled Access** Yes **Customers** Fashion executives, other worker bees, and hotel guests

Hours Daily, 6 a.m.–11:30 p.m.

Setting & atmosphere The dramatically appointed room, situated inside the Sofitel Hotel Chicago Water Tower and designed by Pierre-Yves Rochon, is quite stunning. White walls are highlighted by bright purple high-backed banquettes and brilliant crimson carpeting, with six-foot-long satin light fixtures affixed to the 30-foot ceilings.

House specialties Lemon and tarragon–infused lobster BLT on ciabatta with tabouleh salad; calamari and shrimp tagliatelle Bolognese; seared diver scallops with cannellini bean puree, braised endives, and fava beans; Atlantic salmon tartare with avocado, caviar, and vine ripe tomatoes in lemon oil; chilled red pepper gazpacho; avocado and cucumber tian with basil olive oil; fish stew of mussels, clams, shrimp, and monkfish.

Other recommendations Vichyssoise with Peeky Toe crab salad and beet-infused oil; grilled marinated shrimp with beet couscous and white port and ginger sauce; Muscovy duck two ways with red endive, arugula, and herb salad in a walnut vinaigrette; grilled Colorado lamb chops with rosemary jus and red bell pepper polenta.

Summary & comments The first branch of this ultra luxurious hotel to hit Chicago is making a splash. The spectacular structure jets into the Gold Coast sky, with the cafe overlooking the street and a main dining room, Cigale, at back. You could just as easily be in Paris when you enter, and the brasserie fare could have come straight from the Place de Vosges. Lovely and sprightly dishes tantalize with innovative combinations of infused oils and grains. Service can be stern, but it makes the place feel more European.

CAFE IBERICO ★★★

SPANISH/TAPAS | MODERATE | QUALITY ★★★★ | VALUE ★★★★ | ZONE 3

739 North LaSalle Street; (312) 573-1510

Reservations For parties of six or more only, Sunday–Thursday, **When to go** Weekday evenings for no waits and quieter room **Entree range** Tapas, $4–$6; entrees, $8–$14 **Payment** V, MC, AMEX, DC, D **Service rating** ★★ **Friendliness rating** ★½ **Parking** Valet after 5 p.m., $9 **Bar** Full service **Wine selection** Sangria, $11.95 per pitcher; several sherries; Californian and Spanish wines, $3.50–$5 by the glass; $16–$100 per bottle **Dress** Casual to trendy **Disabled access** Yes **Customers** Loop workers, young lively diners

Hours Sunday, noon–11 p.m.; Monday–Thursday, 11 a.m.–11:30 p.m.; Friday, 11 a.m.–1:30 a.m.; Saturday, noon–1:30 a.m.

Setting & atmosphere The two rooms at this casual, fun tapas bar (plus the basement on busy Wednesday through Saturday, nights) get more character from the crowds than from the decor. There's only a few Spanish artifacts along with a tile border to add a splash of color to the otherwise underwhelming space. The food is the main attraction; always fresh, intriguing, and plentiful.

House specialties Roasted veal served cold with raspberry vinaigrette; Spanish cured ham with manchego cheese and tomato bread; grilled squid in olive oil, garlic, and lemon juice; grilled mushrooms; croquetas (chicken and ham puffs with an aïoli sauce); paella Iberico with seafood, chicken, pork, and saffron rice.

Other recommendations Spanish potato salad with tuna and peas; tortilla Espanola (vegetarian Spanish omelet); grilled salmon with green peppercorn sauce; grilled Spanish sausages; Galician white bean and rappini soup.

Summary & comments The atmosphere is lively and the food just right at this River North tapas bar. The menu has more than a dozen each of hot and cold tapas along with a few entrees, the paella Iberico being the best pick. Large parties are common and work best with the tasting menu, meant to be shared. Service can be slow at times and even forgetful, but pitchers of sangria help pass the time painlessly.

CHARLIE TROTTER'S ★★★★★

NEW AMERICAN | VERY EXPENSIVE | QUALITY ★★★★★ | VALUE ★★★ | ZONE 1

816 West Armitage Avenue; (773) 248-6228

Reservations Required weeks in advance **When to go** Any day you can get in; reserve several months in advance **Entree range** Grand and vegetable dégustation menus only; $125 **Payment** V, MC, AMEX, DC, D **Service rating** ★★★★½ **Friendliness rating** ★★★ **Parking** Valet, $10 **Bar** Wine only **Wine selection** Award-winning wine list with over 1,500 French, Italian, Californian, Australian, German, and South African bottles, $25–$19,000; 22 by the glass, $8–$60. **Dress** Jackets required, formal attire **Disabled access** Yes **Customers** Tourists, suburbanites, and food aficionados

Dinner Tuesday–Saturday, 6–11 p.m.

Setting & atmosphere This attractive Lincoln Park two-flat is easy to miss, tucked behind a billowing trellis of greenery. The three small dining rooms, with a subdued decor in rich tones of burgundy and green (each seating only 30), are quite formal yet intimate with white linens and exquisite stemware and silverware. There's even a kitchen table for four to six guests, allowing a behind-the-scenes view of the masterful kitchen.

House specialties The daily changing menu might include specialties like shellfish-infused heirloom tomato soup with curry-scented lobster, smoked tomato, and spicy yogurt; roasted rabbit loin with chanterelle mushrooms, roasted turnips, and foie gras tortellini in a red wine–mushroom sauce; lamb loin and rack with braised daikon, jasmine rice cake, miitake mushrooms, and hijiki-red wine sauce; or yogurt–white pepper sorbet with melon soup. Vegetable menu features items such as terrine of leek confit with radish, fromage frais, preserved Hon Shimenji mushrooms, and arugula sauce; braised faro with heirloom eggplant, trumpet royale mushrooms, and Vidalia onion–brown butter vinaigrette.

Other recommendations Ragoût of fire beans and dragon tongue beans with fingerling potatoes and garlic-infused mushroom sauce; monkfish liver with lemongrass and ginger root; poached breast of poussin (chicken) with zucchini and hen of the woods mushroom sauce.

Summary & comments Early planning is required for a table at the world-renowned Lincoln Park eatery where award-winning chef Charlie Trotter consistently turns out culinary masterpieces. Trotter's dégustation menus, grand and vegetable, are each like a symphony—one petite course lays the foundation for the next. All dishes involve impeccably fresh ingredients in innovative preparations and presentations. For a real splurge, the table in the kitchen is the way to go both for an exquisite menu, fine entertainment, and brushing shoulders with the man himself. Service is top notch and the wine list unparalleled, with selections from all wine-producing regions of the world at a range of prices. The selection of large-format wines (such as magnums) is remarkable.

Honors & awards *Wine Spectator* Best Restaurant in the U.S. Award, 2000; James Beard Outstanding Restaurant Award, 2000; *Wine Spectator* Grand Award; four stars from the *Chicago Tribune, Chicago Sun Times,* and *Chicago* magazine; Mobil five stars; AAA five diamonds; Avero Outstanding Service Award, 2002.

CHEZ JOEL ★★★½

FRENCH BISTRO | MODERATE | QUALITY ★★★★½ | VALUE ★★★ | ZONE 6

1119 West Taylor Street; (312) 226-6479

Reservations Recommended **When to go** Weeknight dinner **Entree range** $12.95–$23.95 **Payment** V, AMEX, DC, D **Service rating** ★★★ **Friendliness rating** ★★★★ **Parking** Valet, $6; street **Bar** Full service **Wine selection** 50+ French and American selections, $18–$57; limited reserve list to $130; 12 wines by the glass, $5.50–$6.75 **Dress** Casual **Disabled access** Wheelchair accessible **Customers** Savvy diners, dates, and Little Italy denizens

Lunch Monday–Friday, 11 a.m.–3 p.m.

Dinner Monday–Thursday, 5–10 p.m.; Friday and Saturday, 5–11 p.m.; closed Sunday

Setting & atmosphere Cozy, warm, and inviting bistro, with buttery yellow walls; a small, chic bar; and outdoor garden dining in warmer months.

House specialties Bouillabaisse Marseillaise, an assortment of shellfish and seafood in saffron broth with a touch of Pernod; coq au vin à la mode rustique, a half chicken in white wine with frites or mashed potatoes; steak frites, a ten-ounce grilled sirloin served with maître d'hôtel butter (garlic-parsley-Pernod) and pommes frites; sautéed duck breast and duck leg confit over wild mushrooms fricassee with potatoes galettes, crème de cassis, and port wine sauce.

Other recommendations Salade gourmande (arugula, Belgian endive, and chicory frisée in a honey-mustard dressing with pecans and dried mission figs); escargots Bourguignonne (snails with garlic butter, Pernod, and herbed crumbs); coquilles St. Jacques (sea scallops sautéed with saffron broth and tobiko over leeks); steak au poivre; night and day (chocolate sponge cake soaked in Meyer's rum with two layers of chocolate ganache and vanilla cream).

Summary & comments What started out as a little French steak joint in the heart of Little Italy quickly became known as one of Chicago's top bistros. Reservations are highly recommended; Chez Joel is small and usually packed. The steak frites are arguably the best in the town; we've had some really caring, enthusiastic service here, too, though it can vary. They pride themselves on not freezing any of their ingredients, and Moroccan chef-owner Joel Kazouini's daily specials are usually fabulous—often it's hard to know what to order.

Honors & awards: Three Stars from *Chicago Tribune* and *Chicago Sun Times;* four crosses ("Don't Miss") from Zagat Survey; *Chicago* magazine, Best New Restaurants, 2000.

CHICAGO DINER ★★

VEGETARIAN | INEXPENSIVE | QUALITY ★★★½ | VALUE ★★★★ | ZONES 1, 11

3411 North Halsted Street; (773) 935-6696;
581 Elm Place, Highland Park; (847) 433-1228

Reservations Accepted **When to go** Brunch; any time **Entree range** $7–$11 **Payment** All major credit cards **Service rating** ★★½ **Friendliness rating** ★★★ **Parking** Free lot weekends and weekday evenings after 6 p.m. **Bar** Beer and wine, limited liquor **Wine selection** Limited American organic wines, $19–$30; 6 by the glass,

$5–$6 **Dress** Casual **Disabled access** Patio only **Customers** Eclectic

Hours Halsted Street: Monday–Thursday, 11 a.m.–10 p.m.; Friday, 11 a.m.–11 p.m.; Saturday, 10 a.m.–11 p.m.; Sunday, 10 a.m.–10 p.m. Highland Park: Friday, 11 a.m.–3 p.m., 5–9 p.m.; Saturday, 11 a.m.–9 p.m.; Sunday, 10 a.m.–9 p.m.; closed Monday–Thursday

Setting & atmosphere Cool and cozy, this low-lit space features classic diner elements like wooden booths and tables, a small diner counter, and a refrigerator case full of desserts and beer. Eclectic art by local artists lines the walls.

House specialties Biscuits and gravy hash scrambler (scrambled eggs or tofu with seasoned tempeh-potato hash browns, served with biscuits and veggie gravy; dairy and nondairy pancakes and French toast; vegan caesar salad; tofu loaf with onions, celery, sunflower seeds, garlic, and creamy miso sauce; no meata fajita (sizzling seitan with citrus-tequila marinade and fajita fixin's); smoothies.

Other recommendations Pesto bruschetta; radical Reuben (seasoned, marinated seitan on rye with onions, zucchini, peppers, and sauerkraut with melted Swiss or soy cheese); grilled portobello sandwich; hummus platter; lentil loaf; breakfast burrito; blue corn cakes.

Summary & comments The local vegetarian standard-bearer since opening in 1983, this is a casual, comfy spot for good veggie fare, with funky servers and funny menu names such as "yes, doggy dog" and "our seitanic Caesar." The menu includes kiddie vegetarian fare like quesadillas, pasta marinara, and granola. This smoke-free restaurant is sensitive to allergies and dietary concerns; food fact sheet available.

CHIEF O'NEILL'S PUB AND RESTAURANT ★★

IRISH | MODERATE | QUALITY ★★ | VALUE ★★★ | ZONE 1

3471 North Elston Avenue; (773) 473-5263

Reservations Accepted **When to go** Weekdays during music jam sessions; Sunday, Irish brunch **Entree range** $8–$20 **Payment** MC, V, D, AMEX, DC **Service rating** ★★★ **Friendliness rating** ★★★★ **Parking** Street **Bar** Full, with an excellent array of imported and tap beers, $4–$6 **Wine selection** Limited with California and French, $20–$30 per bottle; by the glass, $6–$9 **Dress** Casual **Disabled Access** Yes **Customers** Locals, Irish Chicagoans, police, music fans

Hours Monday–Thursday, 4 p.m.–1 a.m.; Friday and Saturday, noon–3 a.m.; Sunday, 10:30 a.m.–1 a.m.

Setting & atmosphere It's all things Irish at this traditional pub, from the Celtic knots on the tin ceiling to the instruments mounted in glass cases around the room. Most of the staff have thick accents. The dark wood-trimmed space is mammoth, especially when the outdoor picnic tables are available.

House specialties Beer-battered Alaskan cod fish and chips; shepherd's pie; Irish fish pot (steamed seafood and fish in a tomato, fennel, and saffron broth); braised lamb shank; Irish breakfast.

Other recommendations Cheddar cheese and Guinness soup; braised mussels; house-cured salmon; corned beef and cabbage; grilled salmon in an artichoke ragoût with lemon butter.

Summary & comments Irish food and music fans are regulars at this huge but homey pub. Live music and jam sessions are staged most nights and pints of beer are the norm. The fare is the real Irish deal as is the Sunday breakfast with bangers and mash, shepherd's pie, curry chicken with apples, and eye-opening Bloody Marys. The mostly Irish staff adds to the ambience with cheerful greetings and friendly service.

CHILPANCINGO ★★★

NUEVO LATIN/MEXICAN | MODERATE | QUALITY ★★★★ | VALUE ★★★ | ZONE 3

358 West Ontario Street; (312) 266-9525

Reservations Recommended **When to go** Weekend dinner, Sunday, brunch **Entree range** $15–$25 **Payment** MC, V, D, AMEX, DC **Service rating** ★★★ **Friendliness rating** ★★★★ **Parking** Valet, $8 **Bar** Full bar with extensive tequila selection and margaritas **Wine selection** Chilean, Spanish, Argentine, and Californian, $24–$44; by the glass, $6–$8.50 **Dress** Casual chic **Disabled Access** Yes **Customers** Worker bees from downtown for lunch, business executive for dinner

Brunch Sunday, 10:30 a.m.–2:30 p.m.

Lunch Monday–Sunday, 10:30 a.m.–2:30 p.m.

Dinner Sunday, Monday–Thursday, 5 p.m.–10 p.m.; Friday and Saturday, 5 p.m.–11 p.m.

Setting & atmosphere The bigger-than-life space at this former warehouse opens with a gurgling fountain and semi-circular staircase into a colorful dining room. Mural-sized works of Mexican folk art hang over the upholstered booths.

House specialties Corn masa boats with chicken, plantain, and black beans; tosaditas with ceviche; homemade tortillas in a savory pumpkin-seed sauce filled with hardboiled egg; carne asada; roasted duck breast with chipotle chiles, fresh mushrooms, and zucchini; garlic-marinated jumbo sea scallops in sour cream sauce with fingerling potatoes.

Other recommendations Fresh corn tamales filled with queso fresco and roasted chilaca creme; Oaxacan sausage grilled and served in a salsa with organic greens; fava bean soup with marinated chile pasilla and queso anejo; grilled black tiger shrimp in green mole with roasted chayote and Mexican rice.

Summary & comments The experience is always lively and enjoyable at this high-end Nuevo Latino eatery. The colorfully decorated and enormous space has a handsome bar on one side where wonderfully strong margaritas are mixed with your choice of premium tequila. The refined Mexican fare is beautifully presented with sauces so divine that you can't resist coming back for more.

CRU CAFE AND WINE BAR ★★½

WINE BAR | MODERATE | QUALITY ★★★★ | VALUE ★★★ | ZONE 3

888 North Wabash Avenue; (312) 337-4078

Reservations Not accepted **When to go** A good after-work crowd, especially on Friday; also good late night **Entree range** $8–$15 **Payment** V, MC, AMEX, DC, D **Service rating** ★★★ **Friendliness rating** ★★ **Parking** Street **Bar** Full service with six beers on tap, an extensive wine list, and a good selection of single malts, tequila, bourbon, vodka, and cognac **Wine selection** Extensive wine list spanning the globe with American, French, Australian, Spanish, and Italian selections; by the glass, $6–$18; half bottles, $17–$70; bottles, $20–$100 **Dress** Casual chic **Disabled access** Yes **Customers** Mostly well-dressed urbanites

Hours Daily, 11:30 a.m.–2 a.m.; Sunday, brunch, 11:30 a.m.–4 p.m.

Setting & atmosphere The ambience is clubby chic with contemporary gray and black couches and chairs scattered about the L-shaped room. Stylish light fixtures illuminating the sleek space and shelves behind the bar are cleverly built into ornate picture frames. Even the menu has style—it's a leather-bound book full of wines from around the world with excellent descriptions.

House specialties Lobster club sandwich; salmon tartare appetizer with quail egg, asparagus, and cucumber; fresh oysters of the day; B.L.A.S.T (bacon, lettuce, avocado, shrimp, and tomato sandwich with lemon mayonnaise).

Other recommendations Interesting selection of global cheese flights—French Sainte Maure, English Coolea, and American artisanal cheeses (e.g. Wabash Cannonball).

Summary & comments This casual Gold Coast restaurant and wine bar offers an extensive selection of wines spanning the globe from Australia to Spain. The fare is light but creatively prepared, full of appetizers, salads, sandwiches, and interesting cheese flights. The comfortable room fills up in the evenings and often late at night.

EMILIO'S TAPAS ★★★

SPANISH/TAPAS | MODERATE | QUALITY ★★★★ | VALUE ★★★★ | ZONE 1

444 West Fullerton Parkway; (773) 327-5100

Reservations Recommended **When to go** Dinner **Entree range** $6–$22 (Tapas–entrees) **Payment** V, MC, AMEX, DC **Service rating** ★★ **Friendliness rating** ★★★ **Parking** Valet, $7 (dinner only) **Bar** Full; emphasis on sherries, ports, and brandies **Wine selection** Extensive Spanish, $20–$100; 12 by the glass, $6–$8 **Dress** Casual **Disabled access** Wheelchair accessible **Customers** Dates, families of all ages

Lunch/Dinner Friday and Saturday, 11:30 a.m.–midnight; Sunday, 11:30 a.m.–10 p.m.

Dinner Monday–Thursday, 5–10 p.m.

Setting & atmosphere Emilio's offers expansive dining rooms with Mediterranean splashes of color, tile, and artifacts, and a wonderful open-air room in warm weather. The restaurant is comfortable and easy on the nerves—though often busy.

House specialties Paella (two variations); sautéed wild mushrooms with Amontillado sherry sauce; grilled salmon with asparagus, potatoes, and mustard-seed sauce; marinated leg of lamb with garlic potatoes, onions, and red-wine sauce; grilled shrimp in garlic butter; baked goat cheese in tomato sauce with olives; grilled eggplant with tomatoes, caramelized onions, capers, goat cheese, and shrimp; dates wrapped in bacon with red pepper sauce.

Other recommendations Black bean soup with Serrano ham; cold potato salad with aïoli or with tuna, peas, carrots, and eggs; cold tuna cannelloni with asparagus, basil, and green olives; tostadas of shrimp, scallops, and monkfish; rolled mozzarella with sun-dried tomatoes, basil, and black olives; wood-roasted piquillo peppers filled with duck pâté; seafood stew of shrimp, mussels, clams, fish, and angel hair pasta in saffron broth; grilled beef brochette rolled in cracked black pepper with caramelized onions and horseradish cream.

Summary & comments The fare is consistently good here, with an extensive menu in addition to daily specials. The sangria isn't the best, but it suffices; service varies.

ERAWAN   ★★★

THAI | VERY EXPENSIVE | QUALITY ★★★ | VALUE ★ | ZONE 3

729 North Clark Street; (312) 642-6888

Reservations Accepted **When to go** Weekend dinner **Entree range** $20–$38 **Payment** MC, V, D, AMEX, DC **Service rating** ★★★ **Friendliness rating** ★★ **Parking** Valet, $8 **Bar** Full bar **Wine selection** German, Austrian, and Alsatian whites, $28–$105 per bottle; California reds, $32–$230 per bottle; half bottles $23–$90; mostly French reserve list, $110–$900 **Dress** Upscale **Disabled Access** Yes **Customers** Urban food lovers; after-work crowd

Hours Sunday–Thursday, 5–10 p.m.; Friday and Saturday, 5–10:30 p.m.

Setting & atmosphere The exquisitely detailed room at this Royal Thai eatery feels more like a sanctuary, with hand-carved wood-trim walls, chairs, and tables along with gold leaf wallpaper, and dozens of precious artifacts. The large space never seems crowded as tables are spaced generously.

House specialties Snow bird dumplings; venison satay; papaya salad with grilled honey pork; lamb Mussaman; roast duck curry with pineapple; ginger soy escolar in miso-soy ginger sauce with shiitake mushrooms and scallions.

Other recommendations Baby soft-shell crab, foie gras and chanterelle mushroom shumai; crab spring rolls; herbal ginseng soup; whole red snapper with chile-shallot sauce; Panang curry with coriander-kaffir lime leaf essence.

Summary & comments This high-end Thai restaurant features elegant versions of Thai classics, some infused with Western ingredients. Carved vegetable garnishes are stunning, though actual dishes aren't as consistently stellar. Rich dishes prevail, matched to an impressive selection of Austrian and German acidic white wines. The seven-course degustation is a good way to sample the variety of options.

EVEREST   ★★★★★

FINE FRENCH | EXPENSIVE/VERY EXPENSIVE | QUALITY ★★★★★ | VALUE ★★★ | ZONE 4

440 South LaSalle Street (One Financial Place, 40th Floor); (312) 663-8920

Reservations Required **When to go** Special occasions **Entree range** À la carte, $29–$39; pre-theater menu, $44; evening tasting menu, $79 **Payment** All major credit cards, plus JCB **Service rating** ★★★★★ **Friendliness rating** ★★★★ **Parking** Complimentary valet parking in building **Bar** Full service **Wine selection** Extensive award-winning list with 1,200 international wines, mostly French, Alsatian, and American; $39+ per bottle; 15–20 selections by the glass **Dress** Jacket and tie strongly recommended **Disabled access** Wheelchair accessible; call ahead for special accommodations **Customers** Upscale, professionals, couples

Dinner Tuesday–Thursday, 5:30–9 p.m.; Friday and Saturday, 5:30–10 p.m.; closed Sunday and Monday

Setting & atmosphere Everest offers a luxurious, softly lit setting for spectacular dining with a view to match; the twinkling city lights far below your posh perch add a wonderful, far-from-the-madding-crowd element to dining here. The decor blends traditional elegance with modern flash; the table appointments are stunning, with lots of great specialty serving gewgaws.

House specialties Foie gras terrine with apple and Alsace Tokay gelée; salmon soufflé attributed to Paul Haeberlin of L'Auberge de LIII (Chef Jean Joho's mentor); roasted Maine lobster in Alsace Gewurztraminer, butter, and ginger; fillet of halibut wrapped and roasted in potato; poached tenderloin of beef, pot au feu style, with horseradish cream.

Other recommendations Cream of Alsace cabbage soup with home-smoked sturgeon and caviar; cold bouillabaisse terrine of seafood and shellfish; mosaic of guinea hen and duck with petite salade; sautéed medallions of venison with wild huckleberry sauce; lemon soufflé parfait with tapioca almond milk; caramelized banana tart with maple cap mushroom ice cream; warm almond nougatine and roasted figs with cardamom ice milk.

Entertainment & amenities Spectacular view.

Summary & comments Everest rides high atop the Chicago Stock Exchange, continuing to enjoy a superlative reputation as one of Chicago's finest. In partnership with Lettuce Entertain You Enterprises, Chef Jean Joho's culinary vision is the true heart of this excellent restaurant as he weaves authentic Alsatian touches into his artful French fare. Joho's pedigree includes an early entry into the business at the age of 13, many subsequent years of European training, and a position as sous chef at a Michelin two-star restaurant at the age of 23. Service is carried out seamlessly by a tuxedoed service team.

Honors & awards Four stars from the *Chicago Tribune, Chicago Sun-Times, Chicago* magazine; Gault Millau honors; *Wine Spectator* Award of Excellence, 1992, 1997–1999; James Beard Award for Best Chef in Midwest, 1995; *Nation's Restaurant News'* Fine Dining Hall of Fame; Reba Mandari Culinary Award of Excellence, 1998; AAA five diamonds; *Gourmet* magazine America's Top Table winner–Top Food, 1999.

FORTUNATO ★★★½

REGIONAL ITALIAN | MODERATE | QUALITY ★★★★ | VALUE ★★★ | ZONE 2

2005 West Division Street; (773) 645-7200

Reservations Recommended **When to go** Friday or Saturday, dinner **Entree range** $15–$25 **Payment** MC, V, D, AMEX, DC **Service rating** ★★★½ **Friendliness rating** ★★★ **Parking** Valet, $8 **Bar** Full bar, specializing in herbal-infused liquors and spirits **Wine selection** Esoteric Italian, $24–$60 per bottle; by the glass, $6–$9 **Dress** Hip, casual **Disabled Access** Yes **Customers** Trendy locals, restaurant industry people

Brunch Sunday, 10 a.m.–2 p.m.

Dinner Sunday–Thursday, 5:30–10 p.m.; Friday and Saturday, 5:30–11 p.m.

Setting & atmosphere Subdued tones of gun metal and slate fill the chic space which is perched on the edge of this up-and-coming neighborhood. Gray granite and silver leaf back the stunning front bar and oversized black-and-white photos of magnolias cover the exposed brick walls.

House specialties Oven-roasted mussels in fennel cream; wood-grilled baby octopus with bean salad; baby artichoke salad with honey thyme vinaigrette; proscuitto and mortadella mezzaluna pasta; black-and-white tagliatelle with clams, mussels, and calamari in a spicy saffron tomato broth.

Other recommendations Polenta with Marsala prunes; braised duck with buckwheat honey; fritto misto; golden purslane and wheat berry salad; oven roasted quail with pancetta and braised celery; Bing cherry cornmeal almond cake with zabaglione.

Summary & comments Special attention to detail is apparent in not only the attractive decor but in each innovative dish at this Ukrainian Village Italian. The ultra-fresh and mostly organic ingredients are combined into flavorful dishes, which are executed precisely. The intriguing and unfamiliar Italian wine list takes the meal to a new height, highlighted by a waitstaff that's extremely wine savvy, not to mention young and well dressed.

FRONTERA GRILL ★★★★

REGIONAL MEXICAN | MODERATE | QUALITY ★★★★½ | VALUE ★★★ | ZONE 3

445 North Clark Street; (312) 661-1434

Reservations Accepted only for parties of 5–10 at Frontera Grill **When to go** Lunch; early weeknight dinner; Saturday, brunch **Entree range** $15–$24 **Payment** All major credit cards **Service rating** ★★★½ **Friendliness rating** ★★★ **Parking** Valet, $10; pay lots, street **Bar** Beer, tequilas, brandy, and margaritas **Wine selection** Extensive global, 120 selections, $30–$175; 10 by the glass, $6–$12 **Dress** Casual **Disabled access** Wheelchair accessible **Customers** Mixed

Lunch Tuesday–Friday, 11:30 a.m.–2:30 p.m.; Saturday, 10:30 a.m.–2:30 p.m.; closed Sunday and Monday

Dinner Tuesday, 5:30–10 p.m.; Wednesday and Thursday, 5–10 p.m.; Friday and Saturday, 5:30–11 p.m.; closed Sunday and Monday

Setting & atmosphere With vibrantly colored walls and scene-setting Mexican artwork, Frontera Grill is casual, even boisterous, while still managing to convey an almost reverent sense of commitment to authenticity and quality. This is not your neighborhood chips-and-salsa, refried beans Mexican joint—not by a long shot.

House specialties Menus evolve constantly. Some evergreen items include: daily tamale specials; ensalada de jicama (crunchy jicama salad with oranges, grapefruit, and pineapple, tossed with orange-lime vinaigrette); sopa de tortilla (rich tortilla soup with chile pasilla, avocado, and queso fresco); tostaditas de seviche (crisp little tortillas piled with lime-marinated marlin, manzanillo olives, tomato, serrano chile, and cilantro); pollo a la Mexicana con verdolagas (Amish country chicken with roasted tomatoes, poblano chiles, braised purslane, and mashed organic Yukon gold potatoes); carne asada (naturally raised Limousine rib eye, marinated in spicy red chiles and wood-grilled, served with black beans, fried plantains, sour cream, and guacamole); tacos al carbon (wood-grilled meat, poultry, fish, or vegetables sliced and served with roasted pepper rajas, two salsas, frijoles charros, guacamole, and housemade tortillas).

Other recommendations Examples of changing seasonal dishes include: vitaminas al vapor estile Los Jorges (a spicy, rustic Oaxacan seafood soup flavored with smoky chipotle chile and epazote, "chock-full" of fresh Louisiana shrimp, crab, fish, fingerling potatoes, fresh corn, and a poached egg); borrego a la brasas (grilled, red chile–marinated Jamison lamb steak with slow-simmered tomato-guajillo salsa, mashed Mexican red beans, braised lamb's quarters, greens, and grilled red onions); dorado en escabeche de hongos (garlicky grilled mahi mahi in classic escabeche, a rich broth of fruit vinegar, olive oil, and spices, simmered with woodland mushrooms, sweet local organic beets, and roasted fingerlings, topped with pickled red onions).

Summary & comments Serving a seductive menu of grilled dishes, moles and chile-thick braises, Frontera Grill ups the ante on casual Mexican cuisine. The fare here is informed by the world-renowned commitment and talents of chef-owner Rick Bayless; there's a lot to explore in the exciting universe of Mexican regional cooking, and Bayless is one of the world's foremost guides through this tastebud-tantalizing terrain. The adjacent, more formal Topolobampo takes things to an even higher plane. If you've had your fill of omelets and pancakes, try the Saturday-only brunch.

Honors & awards Three stars from *Chicago* magazine; *Restaurants & Institutions* Ivy Award, 1991; World's Third Best Casual Restaurant, *International Herald Tribune*, 1994.

GIBSON'S   ★★★½

STEAK | EXPENSIVE | QUALITY ★★★★½ | VALUE ★★★ | ZONE 3

1028 North Rush Street; (312) 266-8999

Reservations Recommended **When to go** Weekends for the scene **Entree range** $12.75–$107 for surf and turf **Payment** V, MC, AMEX, DC, D, CB **Service rating** ★★★½ **Friendliness rating** ★★ **Parking** Valet, $8 **Bar** Full service **Wine selection** American, Italian, New Zealand, $24–$375 per bottle; $6–$15 per glass **Dress** Trendy to dressy **Disabled access** Yes **Customers** Mature, showy locals; middle-aged singles

Dinner Daily, 3 p.m.–midnight

Setting & atmosphere The 1940s men's-club decor, with dark wood wainscoting and trim along with tile floors, continues to draw fans who pack the front bar most nights. There's usually a wait, but patrons don't seem to mind; mingling before dinner is part of the allure.

House specialties Caesar salad; bone-in sirloin; veal chop; New York sirloin; double baked potato; green beans with garlic butter.

Other recommendations Spicy lobster cocktail; baby back ribs; double-cut lamb chops; giant lobster tail; sautéed spinach with garlic; small fillet with peppercorns.

Entertainment & amenities Live piano nightly.

Summary & comments High-quality steaks are served in obscene quantities, usually in straightforward preparations, at this popular Gold Coast steak house. There's also a limited selection of fish and chicken offered along with classic sides, but fans rave most about the prime, dry-aged beef. It's a happening scene on most nights, with live piano and a bounty of singles with eyes wide open.

GREEN DOLPHIN STREET   ★★★

NEW AMERICAN | MODERATE | QUALITY ★★★★ | VALUE ★★ | ZONE 1

2200 North Ashland Avenue; (773) 395-0066

Reservations Accepted **When to go** Weekend evenings and late night **Entree range** $25–$30 **Payment** V, MC, AMEX, DC, D **Service rating** ★★★½ **Friendliness rating** ★★★ **Parking** Valet, $6 **Bar** Full bar with ample single malts, small batch bourbons, cognacs, and ports **Wine selection** French, Californian, Italian, German, South African, Argentinean, Australian, and Chilean, $28–$305 per bottle; over 20 by the glass, $6–$14 **Dress** Casual to chic **Disabled access** Yes **Customers** Jazz fans, local yuppies

Dinner Monday–Thursday, 5:30–10 p.m.; Friday and Saturday, 5:30–11 p.m.; jazz club, 8 p.m.–3 a.m.

Setting & atmosphere This former auto repair shop still feels industrial with its high ceilings and a wall of exposed brick, but it's softened up a bit with white linens and faux-finished walls. The large, square room, which spills into a jazz lounge, has banquettes surrounding the perimeter and several rows of tables down the center.

House specialties Caviar service with assorted caviar and traditional accompaniments; pan-roasted rabbit saddle and caramelized honey jus; beef tenderloin medallions with caramelized onion gratin and red wine vinaigrette; sautéed Alaskan halibut with tropical fruits, red onion, cilantro, and fresh jalapeños.

Other recommendations Seared foie gras with caramelized bananas, fall greens, and a quince reduction; potato-crusted day boat scallops with citrus melange, arugula, crème fraîche, and caviar; butternut squash soup with scallop strudel; an interesting variety of intermezzo sorbets, such as sage-infused cranberry with orange-sage melange; pheasant pot-au-feu with a fall vegetable and oxtail consommé.

Entertainment & amenities Nightly jazz.

Summary & comments The swanky room at this huge restaurant and jazz club draws a well-dressed crowd for its French-inspired American fare. It's somewhat overpriced, perhaps reflecting the no-cover policy (diners get in free), but the fare is intriguing and well-executed. Chefs come and go, resulting in a frequently changing and inconsistent menu, but the caviar and cheese selections along with the extensive and well-selected wine list (with ten half bottles available) are worth the visit.

HALF SHELL ★★

SEAFOOD | MODERATE | QUALITY ★★★★ | VALUE ★★★★ | ZONE 1

676 West Diversey Parkway; (773) 549-1773

Reservations Not accepted **When to go** Any time **Entree range** $7–$20 **Payment** Cash only **Service rating** ★½ **Friendliness rating** ★★★ **Parking** Street **Bar** Full service **Wine selection** 2 white, 2 red, $18+; 5 wines by the glass, $5.50 **Dress** Casual **Disabled access** No **Customers** Seafood lovers of all kinds

Lunch/Dinner Monday–Saturday, 11:30 a.m.–midnight; Sunday, noon–midnight

Setting & atmosphere Ancient diner tables, Christmas lights, and nautical kitsch.

House specialties Six cherrystone clams cooked on open fire; steamed jumbo shrimp; Half Shell mulligan stew; dressed smelts, deep fried; thirty-two pointer (generous combination platter of French fried shrimp, frog legs, smelts, perch, and clams); Dungeness crab; whole broiled red snapper; king crab legs.

Other recommendations Oysters and clams on the half shell; whole fried catfish; French fried eggplant in sauce; steamed mussels and sauce; French fried squid; deep-fried clam strips.

Summary & comments This popular neighborhood seafood place is a distinctive dive—a dark half-basement with down-to-earth ambience, fresh seafood, and a great jukebox.

HEAT   ★★★★

JAPANESE/SUSHI | EXPENSIVE | QUALITY ★★★★ | VALUE ★★ | ZONE 3

1507 North Sedwick Avenue; (312) 317-9818

Reservations Recommended **When to go** Thursday–Sunday, for dinner; weekdays for a prix fixe lunch. **Entree range** $14–$60 **Payment** MC, V, D, AMEX, DC **Service rating** ★★★ **Friendliness rating** ★★★ **Parking** Valet, $8 **Bar** Full bar with over 50 varieties of sake, $30–$250 per bottle. **Wine selection** Global selections from Alsace (France), New Zealand, Oregon, South Africa, and Australia; $50–$100 per bottle; $12–$22 by the glass **Dress** Stylish **Disabled Access** Yes **Customers** Food savvy, young, Asian

Lunch Monday, Wednesay–Saturday, 11:30 a.m.–2 p.m.

Dinner Monday–Saturday, 5–10 p.m.; closed Sunday

Setting & atmosphere Slate gray and earth tones dominate the subdued swanky room. There's a natural stone backsplash behind the sushi bar along with a 20-foot-long fish tank at knee level, from which live fish are pulled and cooked on the spot. The slender room only fits a dozen tables, making the quarters tight but comfortable.

House specialties Freshly killed spiny lobster, eel, fluke, sea raven, and grouper, served while still twitching; Kaiseki progressive seven-course prix fixe meal; ultra-fresh sushi and sashimi combinations.

Other recommendations Tiny sawa-gani (river crabs) deep fried with spicy honey sauce; mebaru itame (pan-fried rockfish with spinach dressing); yakimono (pan-fried white salmon with king crab and asparagus).

Summary & comments It doesn't get much fresher than the sushi and freshly killed fish served at this high-end Japanese eatery. There's barely a sign outside the door, so you're in the know if you find it. Service is quick and precise, and wine suggestions are helpful. Sit at the sushi bar to enjoy the chef's choice menu that'll keep coming until you tell them to stop.

HEAVEN ON SEVEN   ★★½

CAJUN/CREOLE | MODERATE | QUALITY ★★★★ | VALUE ★★★ | ZONES 1, 3, 4

Heaven on Seven on Clark, 3478 North Clark Street; (773) 477-7818;
Heaven on Seven on Rush, 600 North Michigan Avenue; (312) 280-7774;
Heaven on Seven on Wabash, 111 North Wabash Avenue; (312) 263-6443

Reservations Accepted **When to go** Any time **Entree range** $10–$25; brunch, $6–$10 **Payment** All major credit cards **Service rating** ★★½ **Friendliness rating** ★★★ **Parking** Valet: Rush, $9; Clark, $7, Friday and Saturday only; no valet at Wabash

Bar Full service **Wine selection** Limited, $20–$28; by the glass, $6–$8 **Dress** Casual **Disabled access** Wheelchair accessible **Customers** Professionals and Mag Mile shoppers

Hours Rush, Clark: Sunday–Thursday, 11 a.m.–10 p.m.; Friday and Saturday, 11 a.m.–11 p.m. Wabash: Monday–Friday, 8:30 a.m.–5 p.m.; Saturday and Sunday, 11 a.m.–2 p.m. Brunch: 11 a.m.–3 p.m.

Setting & atmosphere Fun, low-down Bayou kitsch; oceans of hot sauce (both as decoration and covering the tables), lively zydeco music.

House specialties New Orleans BBQ shrimp; gumbo; Cajun fried chicken; red beans and rice with andouille sausage; shrimp po' boy sandwich; jerked chicken wings with habañero mango sauce; avocado and Alabama rock shrimp cocktail; Mardi Gras jambalaya; etouffée of the day.

Other recommendations Grilled andouille sausage with sweet potato polenta; shrimp and Parmesan-Reggiano cheese grits; coconut-crusted Louisiana Gulf shrimp with red curry sauce, mango, and papaya paint; grilled beef tips with sweet corn, cheddar cheese, and tasso ham mashed potatoes, served with guajillo and chicory coffee BBQ sauce; chocolate peanut butter pie.

Summary & comments This N'awlins favorite is a real hot spot—literally—as the walls are adorned with rows upon rows of hot sauce, many with outrageous names, from the far reaches of the globe. It's fun and casual (though the real favorite is the original location on the seventh floor of the Garland Building in the Loop—hence the name—that serves a limited menu).

HOUSE OF FORTUNE ★★★

CHINESE | MODERATE | QUALITY ★★★★ | VALUE ★★ | ZONE 5

2407 South Wentworth Avenue; (312) 225-0880

Reservations Accepted **When to go** Sunday, evenings, weekday lunch **Entree range** $8–$24 **Payment** V, MC, AMEX, DC, D **Service rating** ★½ **Friendliness rating** ★ **Parking** Free lot **Bar** Full bar **Wine selection** American and Chinese, $4+ by the glass, $16–$32 per bottle **Dress** Casual to dressy **Disabled access** Yes **Customers** Locals and Loop workers by day

Hours Daily, 11:30 a.m.–10 p.m.

Setting & atmosphere Spacious Chinatown restaurant set at the far south end of the Wentworth strip. The stark white walls and bright lighting are only softened by a few scattered modern Oriental art pieces. Large round tables are abundant and frequently filled.

House specialties BBQ pork; lemon chicken; Mongolian beef; Peking duck (doesn't need to be ordered ahead); seaweed egg drop soup; spicy shrimp with ginger sauce.

Other recommendations Szechuan eggplant; stir-fried clams in black bean sauce; shredded pork in savory brown sauce; Singapore noodles (stir-fried glass noodles with BBQ pork and shrimp in a curry sauce).

Summary & comments For traditional Cantonese fare, this long-standing Chinatown restaurant is a safe bet. There aren't many surprises on the massive menu, but all the favorites are made to satisfaction. The Peking duck is one of the best in town—worth a trip alone. Service can be painfully slow at times.

IXCAPUZALCO ★★★½

REGIONAL MEXICAN | MODERATE | QUALITY ★★★★½ | VALUE ★★★★ | ZONE 2

2919 North Milwaukee Avenue; (773) 486-7340

Reservations Accepted; recommended on weekends **When to go** Mid-week for intimacy, weekends for bustle **Entree range** $15–$25 **Payment** All major credit cards **Service rating** ★★½ **Friendliness rating** ★★★ **Parking** Valet, $7; street **Bar** Full service; 65 sipping tequilas **Wine selection** Limited but well-chosen $22–$48; short reserve list, $37–$87; 11 by the glass, $5–$8 **Dress** Upscale casual **Disabled access** Yes **Customers** Foodies and Bahena followers, artsy and mature couples, parties

Brunch Sunday, 11:30 a.m.–2:30 p.m.

Lunch Daily, 11:30 a.m.–2:30 p.m.

Dinner Sunday, Monday, Wednesday, and Thursday, 5:30–9:30 p.m.; Friday and Saturday, 5:30–11 p.m.; closed Tuesday

Setting & atmosphere The open kitchen with bright red tiles and gleaming copper pots greets you upon entering this storefront restaurant. Heavy, carved-wood chairs and colorful Mexican paper cutouts accent the dining rooms; bright, somewhat bizarre Mexican artwork lines the walls.

House specialties Sopa Azteca (dark broth flavored with chile pasilla, garnished with chicken breast, avocado, cheese, and tortilla strips); tostaditas de seviche "Chichihuhuliti" (crisp tortillas piled with lime-marinated marlin, Manzanillo olives, tomato, Serrano chiles, and cilantro); Sopes surtidos (a sampler of corn masa boats with a variety of fillings, including chicken in red mole and sweet plantains with sour cream). The real stars are Bahena's sensational Oaxacan moles, which can be ordered with chicken, duck, or quail. Sunday: Negro (spicy and sweet, black from the charring of the chiles and seeds); Monday: Coloradito (light red, robust with sesame seeds and almonds); Tuesday: Amarillo (orange, thickened with masa and flavored with hoja santa leaves); Wednesday: Manchamanteles (literally "tablecloth stainer"; deep, rich red, with chorizo, pineapple, and sweet potato); Thursday: Verde (classic green, with tomatillos, cilantro, epazote, and pumpkin seeds); Friday: Chichilo (dark red and sharp, with a variety of chiles); Saturday: Rojo (smooth red mole with tomatoes, plantains, and chocolate).

Other recommendations A five-course chef's tasting menu is available for $45.

Summary & comments Chef-owner Geno Bahena was sous chef for many years at Rick Bayless's temples of fine Mexican cuisine, Frontera Grill and Topolobampo. Bahena draws on the ancient roots of Mexican cuisine in his seasonal, regional fare. The food is soulful and often scintillating, overriding occasional communication difficulties with the service staff and less-than-stellar dessert offerings. If you like the bustle of a busy kitchen/service area, sit in the front room; if not, opt for the larger, calmer back room.

Honors & awards *Chicago* magazine, Best New Restaurants, 2000.

JIN JU   ★★★

KOREAN | INEXPENSIVE | QUALITY ★★★ | VALUE ★★★½ | ZONE 1

5203 North Clark Street; (773) 334-6377

Reservations Accepted **When to go** Any day for dinner **Entree range** $12–$15
Payment MC, V, D, AMEX, DC **Service rating** ★★★ **Friendliness rating** ★★★
Parking Street only **Bar** Full bar **Wine selection**   Ordinary and limited French,
Australian, Californian, Chilean; bottles $24–$45; by the glass, $5–$7 **Dress** Casual
Disabled Access No **Customers** Young locals

Lunch Saturday and Sunday, 11:30 a.m.–3 p.m

Dinner Monday–Thursday, 5–11 p.m.; Friday and Saturday, 5 p.m.–midnight; Sunday,
5–10 p.m.

Setting & atmosphere The dining room at this Korean establishment feels more
like a sushi bar with clean lines, dark oak floors, and black spinning fans overhead. Original tin ceilings remain, but the overall feeling is contemporary—mimicking the style of
the food, which puts a new spin on traditional Korean fare.

House specialties Pajun (lightly fried scallion pancake served with a soy dipping sauce);
mandoo (Korean dumplings filled with beef, onions, scallions, and tofu); te gim (tempura-
style fried shrimp, squid and vegetables); crab and cucumber salad; chap chae (vermicelli
noodles with beef sirloin, spinach, roasted red peppers, shiitake mushrooms, and scallions); kim chee chigae (kim chee soup with pork, tofu, and green chiles); kalbi (beef short
ribs marinated in a sweet soy sauce then grilled and served with lettuce and bean paste).

Other recommendations Miyuk soup (mild seaweed soup with scallions in a mus-
sel broth); kim bap (seaweed roll filled with rice, bulgogi, and yellow pickled radish); dol
sut bi bim bap (rice bowl with beef, mushrooms, fried egg, and spicy red pepper paste
served in a hot stone pot); o junga bokum (sautéed squid with green chili peppers,
onions, and carrots in a spicy red pepper sauce).

Summary & comments It's the first of its kind to bring traditional Korean fare into
the mainstream. The hip room makes tasting this unusual cuisine more palatable,
although after an initial introduction, it's not all that intimidating. Flavorful dishes are
spiced just hot enough for the American palate, but many still have kick. It's a charming
addition to the Asian restaurant scene, situated conveniently in Andersonville.

KAMEHACHI OF TOKYO   ★★★

JAPANESE | INEXPENSIVE | QUALITY ★★★★ | VALUE ★★★★ | ZONES 3, 11

1400 North Wells Street; (312) 664-3663;
1320 Shermer Road, Northbrook; (847) 562-0064

Reservations Recommended on weekends **When to go** Weeknight dinner **Entree
range** $9–$16 **Payment** V, MC, AMEX, DC, D **Service rating** ★★½ **Friendliness
rating** ★★★ **Parking** Valet, $8; street **Bar** Full service **Wine selection** 16 bottles,
$15–$68; 12 by the glass, $5–$8 **Dress** Casual **Disabled access** Wheelchair accessible **Customers** North-side yuppies

Lunch Monday–Saturday, 11:30 a.m.–2 p.m.

Dinner Monday–Thursday, 5 p.m.–12:30 a.m.; Friday and Saturday, 5 p.m.–1:30 a.m.; Sunday, 4:30–11 p.m.

Setting & atmosphere The somewhat sterile, very bright first floor has tables and a sushi bar; the darker, intimate second floor has a clubby atmosphere with another, smaller sushi bar. Nice outdoor patio in warm weather.

House specialties Kamehachi roll (tuna, avocado and cucumber rolled in tobiko; dragon roll (freshwater eel, tempura crunchies, and cucumber, wrapped in an avocado shell); softshell crab, prepared kara age style (dusted in special flour, delicately deep fried, and served with dipping sauce); steak teriyaki (New York strip steak, broiled with teriyaki sauce); rainbow trout teriyaki (whole trout broiled until crispy with teriyaki sauce).

Other recommendations Sugaki (fresh chilled oysters with vinegar-soy sauce); agedashi tofu (deep-fried bean curd in seasoned soy sauce); shumai (selection of steamed dumplings with dipping sauce); cha soba (green tea noodles with dipping sauce, wasabi, and scallions); negi maki (thinly sliced beef rolled with green onions and broiled in teriyaki sauce); unagi kabayaki (marinated eel broiled in teriyaki sauce).

Summary & comments This popular, social Old Town Japanese/sushi restaurant is often packed, with a long waiting line. Making a reservation definitely greases the wheels, though you may have to wait if you want the second floor, and the tiny second floor bar is often standing room only. The fare is well executed, if perhaps not the most original.

KEEFER'S ★★★½

STEAKHOUSE/AMERICAN | EXPENSIVE | QUALITY ★★★★ | VALUE ★★ | ZONE 3

20 West Kinzie Street; (312) 467-9525

Reservations Recommended **When to go** Weekday lunch, Friday evening happy hour **Entree range** $17–$33 **Payment** MC, V, D, AMEX, DC **Service rating** ★★★★ **Friendliness rating** ★★★ **Parking** Valet, $9 **Bar** Full bar **Wine selection** Californian and French, $17–$139 per bottle; by the glass, $7–$13 **Dress** Business attire, moderately dressy **Disabled Access** Yes **Customers** Power media executives, business lunchers

Hours Monday–Friday, 11:30 a.m.–10:30 p.m.; Saturday, 4:30–11:30 p.m.; closed Sunday

Setting & atmosphere The enormous space is flashy and bustling with 25-foot curved glass windows overlooking the semicircular outdoor patio. Mirrors and deep tones of green along with a powerful sound system attract a power crowd.

House specialties Smoked salmon and potato cake; lobster bisque; clams casino; New York strip; roast rack of lamb; smoked grilled pork chop; Dover sole; orange chocolate crème brûlèe.

Other recommendations Jumbo lump crab cakes; asparagus wrapped with proscuitto; roasted veal chop; pommes frites; creamed spinach; homemade ice creams and sorbet; poached pear with caramel sauce.

Summary & comments This River North newcomer was packed the day it opened and continues to draw a serious crowd that's ready to indulge. The spacious and stylish room has vaulted, high ceilings and lots of glass and mirrors. Service is ultimately professional, tables are generously spaced, and the hosts are gentlemanly.

KEVIN ★★★½

NEW FRENCH/ASIAN | EXPENSIVE | QUALITY ★★★★ | VALUE ★★ | ZONE 3

9 West Hubbard Street; (312) 595-0055

Reservations Recommended **When to go** Weekend dinner or weekday lunch **Entree range** $23–$27 **Payment** MC, V, D, AMEX, **Service rating** ★★★ **Friendliness rating** ★★★ **Parking** Valet, $8 **Bar** Full **Wine selection** French and Californian, $34–$180; half bottles $25–$60; extensive by the glass selection, $7–$12 **Dress** Upscale, dressy **Disabled Access** Yes **Customers** Business workers at lunch, suburbanites and food lovers for dinner

Lunch Monday–Friday, 11:30 a.m.–2 p.m.

Dinner Monday–Thursday, 5:30–10 p.m.; Friday and Saturday, 5:30–11 p.m.

Setting & atmosphere The natural wood room is appointed with various stainless-steel details, like a curving wine-glass rack and brushed-steel bar. Tables can be close, but the room is charming.

House specialties Grilled asparagus salad with balsamic vinegar, goat cheese and strawberry coulis; seared ostrich with greens in a tart cherry vinaigrette; roasted squab on potato pancake in ginger plum sauce; soy-glazed king salmon in yuzu dressing with crisp sushi terrine; poached peaches with a cinnamon cream napoleon.

Other recommendations Arugula salad with capers, croutons and Manchego cheese; wild mushroom, goat cheese and pine nut pot sticker in truffle oil; crisp crab cake with saffron tomato dressing and garlic rouille.

Summary & comments This long awaited Asian-inspired New French dining room showcases the chef's lightness of hand with exquisite ingredients. The serene space is comfortable and the service cheerful. An extensive and well-selected wine list with ample half bottles and by-the-glass pours make it a wine-lover's dream.

LE COLONIAL ★★★½

VIETNAMESE/FRENCH | MODERATE | QUALITY ★★★★½ | VALUE ★★★ | ZONE 3

937 North Rush Street; (312) 255-0088

Reservations Recommended **When to go** Weekend evenings, during warm weather **Entree range** $14–$22 **Payment** V, MC, AMEX, DC **Service rating** ★★½ **Friendliness rating** ★★★ **Parking** Valet, $8 weekdays, $9 weekends (dinner only) **Bar** Full service **Wine selection** French and Californian, $28–$225 per bottle; 6–8 selections by the glass, $8–$10; champagne, $10–$12 per glass **Dress** Stylish to dressy **Disabled access** Yes **Customers** Older local crowd, well dressed

Lunch Daily, noon–2:30 p.m.

Dinner Monday–Friday, 5–11 p.m.; Saturday, 5 p.m.–midnight; Sunday, 5–10 p.m.

Setting & atmosphere Sultry, French colonial–style room with spinning ceiling fans, live palm plants, bamboo shutters, and sepia-toned vintage photos of Vietnam. There's an intimate upstairs lounge that's a real find, and balcony seating in warm weather.

House specialties Goi bo (spicy marinated beef salad); bo bia (soft salad rolls with julienne vegetables and a sweet apricot dipping sauce); ca chien Saigon (crisp Vietnamese whole red snapper); vit quay (ginger-marinated roast duck with a tamarind sauce); banh uot (grilled sesame beef rolls with lettuce, cucumber, and fresh herbs).

Other recommendations   Ca tim nuona (spicy basil-lime-grilled eggplant); com tho ga (ginger chicken with vegetables and rice in a clay pot); com chien (house fried rice with chicken and vegetables); bahn cuon (steamed Vietnamese ravioli with chicken and mushrooms).

Summary & comments   The appealing, film-set-like dining room at this Rush Street Vietnamese draws crowds regularly, as does the sultry upstairs lounge. The flavors are quite authentic, and the combinations of warm and cold, sweet and spicy, and soft and crunchy make the fare tasty and sensuous. The food here is approachable enough for a timid American palate—if not overly toned down.

LE FRANCAIS ★★★★★

FRENCH | EXPENSIVE/VERY EXPENSIVE | QUALITY ★★★★★ | VALUE ★★★ | ZONE 10

269 South Milwaukee Avenue, Wheeling; (847) 541-7470

Reservations Strongly recommended **When to go** Special occasions, big deals, and business lunches **Entree range** Prix-fixe dinner only, $95–$500; lunch, $9–$12 (multi-course appetizer portions) **Payment** V, MC, AMEX, DC, D **Service rating** ★★★★½ **Friendliness rating** ★★½ **Parking** Complimentary valet **Bar** Full service **Wine selection** 350 selections, predominantly French and Californian, $30–$3,500; 12 by the glass, $8–$15 **Dress** Jackets required **Disabled access** Wheelchair accessible **Customers** Older, moneyed crowd

Dinner Monday–Thursday, 5:30–9 p.m.; Friday and Saturday, 5:30–9:30 p.m.; closed Sunday

Setting & atmosphere   Subdued in the dining room, bustling in the view-through kitchen. The tastefully updated room is all done in neutrals, with banquettes lining the room and a suited, alert service team resembling a Secret Service contingent. The efficient, talented kitchen corps runs like clockwork beneath the gleaming copper pots dangling from the ceiling. A Picasso, a Chagall, and a Lalique collection greet patrons in the foyer.

House specialties   Salmon paillard with olive oil mashed potatoes and grainy mustard cream; Maine lobster ravioli with creamed spinach, lobster sauce and sturgeon caviar; roasted squab breast with quinoa, tomato tian, pea puree and tarragon; grilled flank steak with spicy greens, crispy won tons and peanut vinaigrette; seared yellowfin tuna with olive oil and pink peppercorns; roasted rack of lamb with taro-black truffle puree, artichokes, basil and asparagus; black trumpet crusted salmon with a strawberry-pineapple jam; porcini crusted foie gras, fresh morels, Minus vinegar; house-made peach, lychee, and mango sorbet; warm chocolate cake with hazelnut ice cream.

Other recommendations   Green and white asparagus salad with black truffles and black truffle vinaigrette; roasted half poussin with mushrooms, red wine sauce, and tarragon; braised beef short ribs with roasted vegetables and celery root puree; braised oxtail risotto with horseradish oil; coconut-mussel soup with lemongrass and Peeky Toe crab meat; mushroom-crusted lamb with curry kaffir lime sauce, porcini, and celery root puree; orange cream caramel with orange zest and fresh orange.

Summary & comments The new regime is firmly ensconced at this world-class French establishment. Chef and co-owner Don Yamaguchi (Carlos', Gordon) now mans the kitchen, bringing his more eclectic style to classic dishes. Much of the professional staff that served under Jean Banchet remains, as does the dining room's recent redesign, including lighter colors and a large picture window that looks into the kitchen. The menu is still opulent, but now it's set off by a lightness of hand and a bit more innovation. Even the foie gras feels fresh when it's paired with dried cherries, red onions, and a peanut cream sauce. Sommelier Frederic Fuschetto does a masterful job of pairing the wonderful wines with dishes. Petits fours and chocolates are a perfect finish if you don't have room for, say, crispy crêpes filled with lemon curd and raspberries. Service remains top-notch but now has more personality.

Honors & awards Four stars from *Chicago Tribune* and *Chicago Sun-Times; Bon Appetit* and *Chicago* magazine's Best New Restaurants, 2000; AAA five diamonds; Relais & Châteaux/Relais Gourmand.

LOU MITCHELL'S RESTAURANT ★★

AMERICAN | INEXPENSIVE | QUALITY ★★★★ | VALUE ★★★★ | ZONES 2, 4

Lou Mitchell's Express, O'Hare Airport, Terminal 5, 5600 North Manheim Road, Chicago; (773) 601-8989
Lou Mitchell's Restaurant, 565 West Jackson Boulevard; (312) 939-3111;

Reservations Accepted for parties of six or more, Monday–Friday only **When to go** Breakfast, lunch **Entree range** $6–$15 **Payment** Cash, checks **Service rating** ★★ **Friendliness rating** ★★½ **Parking** Public lots, street **Dress** Casual **Disabled access** No **Customers** Loop workers, die-hard fans

Breakfast/Lunch Monday–Saturday, 5:30 a.m.–3 p.m.; Sunday, 7 a.m.–3 p.m.

Setting & atmosphere Lou Mitchell's celebrates the technological breakthroughs of naugahyde, formica, and fake plants. This is lowbrow, high camp, retro diner authenticity at its finest, complete with Rat Pack background music.

House specialties Eggs and fluffy, in-the-skillet omelets made with double-yolk eggs (e.g., Greek sausage, tomato, green pepper, and onion, or Michigan sweet apples with old English cheddar cheese); Belgian malted waffles; grilled French toast; homemade pie. Extensive daily specials run the gamut from corned beef hash and hot turkey sandwiches to chicken pot pie, baked short ribs, and "creamed baked macaroni au gratin."

Other recommendations Pot roast sandwich with jardinière sauce; club sandwich; baked meat loaf; grilled patty melt; fresh banana pancakes; milkshakes.

Summary & comments Head back in time at this legendary diner-restaurant opened in 1923. Lou Mitchell's is notorious for its gruff anti-service, free Milk Duds for the ladies, and classic diner schtick. A commitment to freshness is evident in the fresh-squeezed juice, fresh breads, pastries, and marmalade.

MAGNOLIA CAFE ★★½

NEW AMERICAN | MODERATE | QUALITY ★★★ | VALUE ★★ | ZONE 1

1224 West Wilson Avenue; (773) 728-8787

Reservations Accepted **When to go** Weekends for dinner or Sunday brunch **Entree range** $15–$23 **Payment** MC, V **Service rating** ★★★ **Friendliness rating** ★★★★ **Parking** Street **Bar** Full bar **Wine selection** Mostly Californian, $27–$56 per bottle; by the glass, $6.25–$8.50 **Dress** Casual chic **Disabled Access** Yes **Customers** Young professionals

Hours Tuesday–Thursday, 5:30–10:30 p.m.; Friday and Saturday, 5:30–11:30 p.m.; Sunday, 10 a.m.–3 p.m.

Setting & atmosphere A lofted ceiling and dim lighting give a stylish twist to this edgy Sheridan Park neighborhood storefront. Exposed brick walls are hung with tasteful black-and-white photos of magnolias, and large windows face onto the sidewalk where tables are set up during nice weather.

House specialties Grilled calamari with pesto and spaghetti squash in a Champagne cream sauce; chipotle pork quesadillas with roasted pepper and caramelized onions; salad of sugar snap peas, shaved fennel, and oranges in a mustard vinaigrette; wild mushroom and blue cheese ravioli in brown butter; grilled Amish chicken and shiitake mushroom risotto.

Other recommendations Gulf shrimp and English pea risotto; heirloom tomato salad with arugula, goat cheese, and cucumbers; grilled beef tenderloin with Parmesan potato gratin in a red wine sauce; spicy Italian sausage with shrimp in penne pasta.

Summary & comments Surprisingly located in a far north, nondescript neighborhood, this New American incorporates global flavors in successful combinations. The quaint space and gracious servers make the experience enjoyable, as do the daily specials like pan-seared mahi mahi with morel and oyster mushrooms.

MANNY'S COFFEE SHOP & DELI ★★

DELI/CAFETERIA | INEXPENSIVE | QUALITY ★★★★ | VALUE ★★★ | ZONE 5

1141 South Jefferson Street; (312) 939-2855

Reservations Not accepted **When to go** Breakfast, lunch **Entree range** $6–$12 **Payment** Cash only **Service rating** ★★ **Friendliness rating** ★★★ **Parking** Street, small lot **Bar** None **Wine selection** None **Dress** Shirt and shoes required **Disabled access** Wheelchair accessible **Customers** Blue and white collar

Breakfast/Lunch Monday–Saturday, 5 a.m.–4 p.m.

Setting & atmosphere This beloved cafeteria-style deli, dishing it up since 1942, oozes authenticity with the fast-paced counter service, no-frills furnishings, water served in paper cones, and cashier station/candy counter selling sweet treats and el cheapo cigars. Down-to-earth, city of big shoulders patrons are here to tie on a serious feedbag.

House specialties Mile-high corned beef and pastrami sandwiches; Reubens; steamship round and beef brisket; meat loaf; beef stew; liver and onions; short ribs; knishes; borscht and matzo ball soup.

Other recommendations Corned beef omelets; lox breakfast; chopped liver. Daily specials run the gamut from chop suey and chopped liver to tongue with mushrooms and franks and beans.

Summary & comments This place is a Chicago institution, and deservedly so. To quote Manny's website, "At Manny's you don't diet. You don't snack. You don't nosh. You come to this landmark lunchroom to pile your tray high and eat like there's no tomorrow." Gruff, old-timey counter staff in paper hats sling heavenly, hearty fare; at the end of the line is a time-warp sweets section featuring stewed prunes, Jell-O, rice pudding, and German chocolate cake.

Honors & awards *USA Today* Top Ten Jewish Noshes, *Gourmet* magazine's Best Deli in Chicago.

MARCHÉ   ★★★

FRENCH BSTRO | MODERATE | QUALITY ★★★★½ | VALUE ★★★ | ZONE 2

833 West Randolph Street; (312) 226-8399

Reservations Highly recommended **When to go** Semi-noisy weeknight dinners, noisy weekend dinners, business lunch **Entree range** $12–$38; tasting menu: 4-course $50, 5-course $65 **Payment** V, MC, AMEX, DC, JCB **Service rating** ★★★ **Friendliness rating** ★★½ **Parking** Valet, $8; street **Bar** Full service **Wine selection** 200 bottles, mostly Californian, French, and German, $24–$339; 10 by the glass, $7–$12 **Dress** Casual chic **Disabled access** Wheelchair accessible **Customers** Hip urbanites of all ages

Lunch Monday–Friday, 11:30 a.m.–2 p.m.

Dinner Sunday–Wednesday, 5:30–10 p.m.; Thursday, 5:30–11 p.m.; Friday and Saturday, 5:30 p.m.–midnight

Setting & atmosphere Colorful—phantasmagoric even—with bright walls, outre furnishings, and wildly painted pillars dotting the large, noisy, open dining room with open kitchen. The design screams "scene"—and so do the patrons.

House specialties Giant shrimp with vanilla bean nage and red wine syrup; spit-roasted chicken with onion confit, herbs de Provence and pommes frites; escargots Bourguignonne; prime 16-ounce New York strip with green peppercorn cognac sauce and pommes frites; 10-ounce sliced sirloin with Paris mustard sauce and pommes frites; grilled 32-ounce bone-in prime rib steak with au gratin potatoes (for one or two).

Other recommendations Roasted beet salad with watercress, chèvre and horseradish vinaigrette; peppercorn-crusted ostrich with oven-roasted Roma tomatoes and charred red onion relish; wild salmon with fiddlehead ferns and mustard vinaigrette; braised lamp shank with whipped potatoes, carrots, parsnips, and lemon-thyme aïoli; double-cut pork chop with tropical fruit relish and mustard green pistou.

Summary & comments Cavernous Marché offers a chic circus atmosphere that appeals to a wide variety of clientele. Expect noise—the bar is an integral part of the dining room, and the scene is part of the appeal. The wild decor adds to a sense of revelry and abandon, enhanced by the scents and sounds of the open kitchen with rotisserie. The fare is hearty and satisfying, with some dishes a bit more creative than simple bistro standards. This is a great dinner date destination—if you like to be surrounded by lots of energy.

MAS ★★★½

NUEVO LATINO | MODERATE | QUALITY ★★★★½ | VALUE ★★★ | ZONE 2

1670 West Division Street; (773) 276-8700

Reservations Not accepted **When to go** Weekdays to avoid crowds **Entree range** $17–$27 **Payment** V, MC, AMEX, DC **Service rating** ★★★ **Friendliness rating** ★★★ **Parking** Valet, $7 **Bar** Full bar specializing in Latin cocktails—caipirinhas, batidas, pico sours, Mas margaritas, and high-end tequilas **Wine selection** Spanish, Argentinian, Chilean, and Californian, $22–$90 per bottle; over a dozen by the glass, $6–$12 **Dress** Casual to trendy **Disabled access** Yes **Customers** Local young hipsters

Dinner Monday–Thursday, 5:30–10:30 p.m.; Friday and Saturday, 5:30–11:30 p.m.; Sunday, 5:30–10 p.m.

Setting & atmosphere Tables are close and the room usually crowded at this popular Latin hangout—but nobody seems to mind. Even with a no-reservation policy, the bar is packed with locals, either waiting to eat or just sipping on one of several tasty Latin cocktails.

House specialties Caldo (black bean and bacon or white bean and chorizo soup); antojo de salmon (tequila-cured salmon gravlax served with arugula, tomato, bacon, and a chipotle-dill dressing); chupe de mariscos (lobster and shrimp bisque, sweet corn, serrano-chive oil); gazpacho (chilled, roasted tomato and cucumber soup, crouton, jonah crab meat); ceviche of the day; carbonada (chipotle-braised pork shoulder, roasted pumpkin, preserved peaches); pan-roasted salmon, lentil salsa, smoked tomato criolla; sautéed tilapia, boniato, saffron nage, oven-roasted tomato and caper salsa; churrasco atun (rare yellowfin tuna with chimichurri and yuca frites).

Other recommendations Arepas (spiced fried shrimp with beberete salsa and a beurre blanc); acorn and butternut squash, wild mushrooms, boniato, pumpkin seed oilpollito; ancho-roasted poussin, braised bacon, wild mushrooms, asparagus; lombo (chili-cured pork tenderloin, white beans, truffle-scented jus); dry-aged New York strip.

Summary & comments There's never a dull moment at this Nuevo Latin gem; the bar is packed with diners who'll wait over an hour to sample chef John Manion's version of upscale Latin fare. Unique flavor sensations rule in dishes like tuna and papaya tacos, and wild mushroom empanadas. The lights are always dim, the music loud, and the crowd well dressed for a party-like atmosphere, best enjoyed on weekends.

MAZA ★★★

MIDDLE EASTERN | MODERATE | QUALITY ★★★★½ | VALUE ★★★★ | ZONE 1

2748 North Lincoln Avenue; (773) 929-9600

Reservations Accepted **When to go** Weekday dinner to avoid crowds **Entree range** $10–$21 **Payment** V, MC, AMEX **Service rating** ★★★½ **Friendliness rating** ★★★★ **Parking** Valet on weekends only, $7 **Bar** Full service **Wine selection** Californian, Australian, French, and Italian; $20–$25 per bottle; several by the glass, $4–$7 **Dress** Casual **Disabled access** Yes **Customers** Local yuppies, suburbanites

Dinner Sunday–Thursday, 5–11 p.m.; Friday and Saturday, 5 p.m.–midnight.

Setting & atmosphere This stylish Lincoln Park storefront is fresh and cozy, with high ceilings, exposed ductwork, and colorful modern art covering the white walls. Graceful fabric drapes across the front windows, and ethnic music abounds. Tables are nicely spaced, and lights are dim for romance or quiet conversation.

House specialties Fool modamas (simmered fava beans in herbs and spices with lemon juice, garlic, and olive oil); labneh (creamy yogurt with mint and black olives); fattoush (salad with crisp pita chips in a sumac dressing); lamb or chicken brochettes; whole trout with fine herbs.

Other recommendations Tabouleh (cracked wheat with scallions, tomato, and parsley); seafood grill (scallops, shrimp, and salmon over rice pilaf); lamb sausage; lentil soup; mamoul bi tamr (couscous baked with dates and poached figs in an apricot sauce).

Summary & comments Former chef and manager of the venerable Uncle Tannous opened this upscale Middle Eastern in an attractive, lofty space in west Lincoln Park. Elegant floor-length curtains adorn the storefront windows, and artifacts are scattered throughout. The fare is decidedly more elegant—both in preparation and presentation—than most typical restaurants of this cuisine, which tend to pay little attention to details.

MIRAI SUSHI　　★★★½

JAPANESE/SUSHI | MODERATE | QUALITY ★★★★½ | VALUE ★★★ | ZONE 2

2020 West Division Street; (773) 862-8500

Reservations Recommended **When to go** Dinner (weeknights for less crowding) **Entree range** $6–$18 **Payment** All major credit cards **Service rating** ★★★ **Friendliness rating** ★★★ **Parking** Valet, $7; street **Bar** Full service, emphasis on sake **Wine selection** 54 global, $34–$106; 13 by the glass, $7–$12 **Dress** Casual **Disabled access** Wheelchair accessible first floor only **Customers** Hip urbanites of all ages

Dinner Sunday–Wednesday, 5:30–10 p.m.; Thursday–Saturday, 5:30–11 p.m.; upstairs lounge open 5:30 p.m.–1 a.m.

Setting & atmosphere This bustling, bilevel Wicker Parker place is a sushi scene, with a bright first floor restaurant and sushi bar and a dark, sensuous sake lounge upstairs with living room furniture, dining tables, and bar. Try the house cocktail, a "Red One," comprised of vodka, cranberry juice, fresh passion fruit, orange, and lime juices.

House specialties Daily sushi selection based on season and market (usually several varieties of tuna, salmon, shrimp, and roe); ise ebi (minced lobster served with fresh seaweed, quail egg, lotus, and sesame-lobster miso soy dressing); sakana carpaccio moriawase (tuna, salmon, and whitefish carpaccio with cilantro, capers, and sesame oil); sakana mushi (steamed flounder with shiitake mushrooms in a ginger-sake-scallion sauce).

Other recommendations Kamo (grilled duck sashimi over mixed greens, marinated seaweed, and baby lotus with orange-sesame-ginger dressing); ebi tempura (jumbo shrimp with sweet potato, pumpkin, shiitake mushroom, and ohba leaf with tempura sauce); udon (udon noodles, tempura vegetables, and shrimp, with negi, fish cake, and shiitake mushrooms); tuna tataki (seared tuna sashimi with scallions and red radish in ponzu sauce); filet mignon with taro potatoes, asparagus, baby carrots, and cauliflower.

Entertainment & amenities Live DJ Friday and Saturday.

Summary & comments Fresh fish and funky patrons are the allure at this fashionable sushi hot spot. The cut-above Japanese fare is creative and well executed, the sake menu extensive and informative, and the ambience decidedly Wicker Park artsy chic. Focus on the extensive nightly specials for the most intriguing dishes, both sushi and otherwise. Consider reserving a dining spot among the lounge furniture and low tables on the second floor.

Honors & awards *Chicago* magazine, Best New Restaurants, 2000; three stars from the *Chicago Tribune.*

---

mk ★★★★

NEW AMERICAN | EXPENSIVE | QUALITY ★★★★½ | VALUE ★★★ | ZONE 3

868 North Franklin Street; (312) 482-9179

Reservations Highly recommended **When to go** Stylish dinner **Entree range** $10–$34; 4-course dégustation menu, $54–$62 **Payment** V, MC, AMEX, DC **Service rating** ★★★½ **Friendliness rating** ★★★ **Parking** Valet, $8 **Bar** Full service **Wine selection** 550 well-chosen international bottles, $29–$700; 12 by the glass, $7–$18 **Dress** Upscale casual to business **Disabled access** Wheelchair accessible **Customers** Trendies and power money, nice age mix

Dinner Sunday–Thursday, 5:30–10 p.m.; Friday and Saturday, 5:30–11 p.m.

Setting & atmosphere Stylish and contemporary without being severe, mk's architectural dining room is spacious and airy, with a pleasantly sophisticated neutral color palette. Plush lounge furniture in the entry area is a great stop for a glass of bubbly before or after.

House specialties Belgian endive salad with French beans, apple, Roquefort cheese, and pecans; cumin-scented lobster soup with Maine lobster and cumin-spiced carrots; young arugula, shaved fennel, and Humboldt Fog goat cheese with lemon and olive oil; pan-roasted Alaskan halibut with trumpet royal mushrooms and white and green asparagus; Alaskan king crab with roasted pepper coulis, scallions, and poached garlic; prime New York sirloin grilled over hardwood charcoal with green peppercorn–cognac sauce and baby spinach.

Other recommendations Variations of lobster salad; naturally raised and roasted guinea hen with Tuscan bread salad; chilled tomato terrine with basil-scented tomato water, grilled rabbit, arugula, and parmesan; Niman ranch naturally raised pork loin with watercress, Granny Smith apple, and Stilton vinaigrette; thinly sliced calves' liver with stone ground mustard, burnt onions, applewood-smoked bacon, and aged balsamic vinegar; bittersweet chocolate ganache tart with cappuccino semifreddo; plum and brown butter custard tart with warm caramel and triple vanilla ice cream; housemade ice creams and cookies.

Summary & comments Mk is a mainstay of Chicago's foodie faithful, a restaurant of both style and substance. Chef-owner Michael Kornick has a talent for clean flavor combinations and plate presentations—gratifying without contrivance, handsome without preciousness. Kornick's background (opening chef of Marché, chef/partner in Red

Light, and a history that includes Gordon, the Quilted Giraffe, and the Four Seasons in Boston) shows in the dining room, too, where staff reaches a fine balance between personable and efficient. Mindy Segal's desserts are worth saving room for.

Honors & awards Three stars from *Chicago Sun-Times, Chicago Tribune,* and *Chicago* magazine; Best New Restaurants, *Esquire* and *Chicago* magazines; "Hottest Restaurants in the World," *Condé Nast Traveler; Bon Appetit's* "A List."

MOD   ★★★

NEW AMERICAN | MODERATE | QUALITY ★★★★½ | VALUE ★★ | ZONE 2

1520 North Damen Avenue; (773) 252-1500

Reservations Accepted **When to go** Weekday evenings **Entree range** $14–$26 **Payment** V, MC, AMEX, DC **Service rating** ★★½ **Friendliness rating** ★★★ **Parking** Free lot **Bar** Full service **Wine selection** Austrian, American, German, French, $20–$105 per bottle; $5–$9 by the glass **Dress** Trendy casual **Disabled access** Yes **Customers** Hip, urban locals

Dinner Sunday–Thursday, 5–10:30 p.m.; Friday and Saturday, 5–11 p.m.

Setting & atmosphere The ultra-modern, eccentric room features brightly colored acrylic room dividers, light fixtures, and egg-shaped chairs. Hanging lights over the entryway bar are encased in plastic wrap for an odd effect. Shoplifting mirrors hang in the corners for distorted views of neighboring tables.

House specialties Iron skillet–roasted black mussels in Meyer lemon butter; foie gras in rum-flambéed Maui pineapple; beet, frisée, and goat cheese salad in a citrus vinaigrette; oven-roasted red grouper, Merquez lamb sausage, manila clams, and fresh oregano; shellfish stew with cannelini bean puree, and provencal style vegetables; "Texas truck stop" (jumbo rib-eye chop with Stilton fondue, onions, and wild mushrooms).

Other recommendations Duck confit with honey-roasted nectarines in a rosemary broth; crispy fried green beans with two dipping sauces; grilled double-cut pork chop with mascarpone macaroni and cheese; MOD tropical split (brûléed bananas, passionfruit, and gianduja ice creams; coconut gelato, macadamia nut brittle, and passionfruit caramel.

Summary & comments Terry Alexander (Soul Kitchen) does it again with another stylized, hip eatery, this one serving ambitious, seasonal American fare. While the Peter Max–style room can be fun and lively, the food can be hit or miss—with more hits likely over time. Service falters at times but is savvy about the well-selected, albeit pricey wine list.

MORTON'S   ★★★½

STEAK | EXPENSIVE | QUALITY ★★★★½ | VALUE ★★ | ZONES 2, 3, 8, 10

9525 Bryn Mawr Avenue, Rosemont; (847) 678-5155
1050 North State Street; (312) 266-4820
1 Westbrook Corporate Center, Westchester; (708) 562-7000
1470 McConnor Parkway, Schaumburg; (847) 413-8771

Reservations Recommended **When to go** Any time **Entree range** $22–$35 **Payment** All major credit cards **Service rating** ★★★ **Friendliness rating** ★★★ **Parking**

On-site garage (validated) **Bar** Full service **Wine selection** 275 wines, primarily Californian, French and German, $28–$3,200; 15 by the glass, $6–$12 **Dress** Business casual **Disabled access** Yes, all locations **Customers** Business diners, couples

Dinner Monday–Saturday, 5:30–11 p.m.; Sunday, 5–10 p.m.

Setting & atmosphere Morton's is renowned for its clubby, masculine decor; this is quintessential Chicago steakhouse territory, complete with photo-lined walls and a discreet entrance reminiscent of a speakeasy. The main section of the dining room is smoking.

House specialties Jumbo lump crabmeat or shrimp cocktail; caesar salad; lobster bisque; double filet mignon, sauce béarnaise; 24-ounce porterhouse steak, also available as a 48-ounce double; whole baked Maine lobster; farm-raised salmon; hash browns; steamed asparagus with hollandaise.

Other recommendations Bluepoint oysters on the half shell; broiled sea scallops wrapped in bacon with apricot chutney; Sicilian veal chop; shrimp Alexander, sauce beurre blanc; domestic rib lamb chops; Godiva hot chocolate cake; soufflé for two (chocolate, Grand Marnier, lemon, or raspberry).

Entertainment & amenitie "See food" menu cart presentation by the servers, theatrically displaying enormous cuts of steaks, chops, live lobsters, and vegetables.

Summary & comments Founded by Chicago restaurateur Arnie Morton, this steak-lover's sanctuary is now a thriving national chain of near-legendary status. This is the original, a real bastion of old-guard, carnivorous dining delights; steady as she goes, Morton's delivers quality and consistency without a hint of high-falutin' fussiness.

Honors & awards *Restaurants & Institutions,* Top 400 Restaurant Concepts, 2000; Zagat Survey Certificate of Distinction, 1999.

NAHA ★★★★

MEDITERRANEAN/AMERICAN | EXPENSIVE | QUALITY ★★★★ | VALUE ★★★ | ZONE 3

500 North Clark Street; (312) 321-7561

Reservations Accepted **When to go** Weekday lunch, weekend dinner **Entree range** $25–$39 **Payment** MC, V, D, AMEX, DC **Service rating** ★★★½ **Friendliness rating** ★★★★ **Parking** Valet, $9 **Bar** Full bar **Wine selection** Mostly French; Rhone Valley, Burgundy, Provence, some New Zealand, Californian, and German, $35–$175 per bottle; by the glass, $7.50–$10 **Dress** Upscale casual **Disabled Access** Yes **Customers** Professional, older crowd, with locals people by day

Lunch Monday–Friday, 11:30 a.m.–2 p.m.

Dinner Monday–Thursday, 5:30–10 p.m.; Friday and Saturday, 5:30–10:30 p.m.

Setting & atmosphere The contemporary space features walls of windows on two sides, low backed chrome and leather chairs, and works of abstract modern art on the cool gray walls. The front bar area is spacious for waiting.

House specialties Mediterranean Greek salad with sautéed shrimp and a warm feta turnover; mustard seed–glazed hot-smoked Sockeye salmon with heirloom greens; Chesapeake Bay soft shell crabs with polenta; Moulard duck breast with Bing cherries and baby turnips; rib eye of veal with potato-parsley gnocchi.

Other recommendations Tartare of big eye tuna and wild King salmon in an aigrelette sauce; sea scallops with pears four ways; Delmonico rib-eye steak with gratin of macaroni and goat cheese.

Summary & comments The ever-changing seasonal menu never ceases to dazzle diners at this Mediterranean-inflected New American, former home to the venerable Gordon. Service is ultra-professional without intimidating. Wonderful harder-to-find bottles grace the wine list, and the beautifully presented fare tastes as good as it looks.

NINE ★★★½

STEAK | EXPENSIVE | QUALITY ★★★★½ | VALUE ★★ | ZONE 4

440 West Randolph Street; (312) 575-9900

Reservations Highly recommended **When to go** Early evening for quieter dining; later and weekends for scene **Entree range** $14–$34 **Payment** V, MC, AMEX, DC **Service rating** ★★★★ **Friendliness rating** ★★★½ **Parking** Valet, $9; street **Bar** Three full-service bars; emphasis on specialty martinis, champagne cocktails, and sake **Wine selection** Well-chosen, well-rounded list of 150+ selections; emphasis on France and California; large champagne selection and several magnums; 15–20 wines by the glass, $6.50–$25 **Dress** Officially "casual chic"; unofficially, the greatest fashion show in town **Disabled access** Wheelchair accessible **Customers** Celebs and beautiful people; all-ages diners and bar denizens

Lunch Monday–Friday, 11:30 a.m.–2 p.m.

Dinner Monday–Wednesday, 5:30–10 p.m.; Thursday, 5:30–11 p.m.; Friday and Saturday, 5:30 p.m.–midnight; closed Sunday

Setting & atmosphere Grand, sizzling, spectacular. Nine calls out the adjectives with its tastefully Vegas-tinged ambience, soaring silver-leaf domed ceiling, waterfall wall, mirrored pillars, light show, and plushy ultra-suede booths. Pose in the cushy lounge; imbibe at the main bar; indulge at the central champagne and caviar bar; dine in the vast dining room with ultra-social sightlines; hold a private party with state-of-the-art audiovisual capabilities; or climb the stairs to the ethereal Ghost Bar, one of the hippest hangouts in town.

House specialties American caviar parfaits (black tobiko, salmon, and whitefish) with crisp potato pancakes; cones of lobster with avocado and Asian tuna tartare; crispy Carolina rock shrimp with two dipping sauces; shellfish platters; Chilean sea bass wrapped in pancetta with celery root, black truffle mushrooms, and white truffle oil; 12-ounce filet mignon with béarnaise sauce; 16-ounce New York strip steak; 14-ounce veal porterhouse; roasted whole red snapper.

Other recommendations Cold or steamed Alaskan king crab legs; 24-ounce bone-in rib eye; seared rare ahi tuna with tropical fruit compote, cilantro oil and baby anchocress salad; carpaccio of sliced raw sirloin with endive, radicchio, arugula, Parmigiano, and balsamico; caviar-stuffed new potatoes; warm chocolate brownie with banana ice cream and hot fudge sauce.

Summary & comments When it opened in April 2000, Nine wowed Chicago with its luxury ambience and contemporary-decadent menu and bar offerings. This place is a great scene—with great steakhouse-and-beyond food—the perfect place for an evening of well-earned indulgence. The fashionable, often eye-popping crowd is a big part of the action here, but the food assures that Nine goes beyond the "now you're hot, now you're not" fate of many trendy restaurants. Make an evening of it—make a reservation for the champagne and caviar bar before dinner, and head up to the Ghost Bar afterward. Thanks to the Loop location, Nine also does a busy business lunch.

Honors & awards Three stars from *Chicago Tribune; Chicago* magazine readers' poll Best New Restaurant, 2000.

NOMI ★★★★

NEW AMERICAN | EXPENSIVE | QUALITY ★★★★½ | VALUE ★★★ | ZONE 3

800 North Michigan Avenue; (312) 239-4030

Reservations Recommended **When to go** Weekend evenings **Entree range** $24–$42 **Payment** V, MC, AMEX, DC, D **Service rating** ★★★½ **Friendliness rating** ★★★★ **Parking** Valet, $10 **Bar** Full service **Wine selection** American, French, Australian, New Zealand, Italian, and Spanish, $30–$245 per bottle; 12 wines by the glass, $8–$22 **Dress** Chic to dressy **Disabled access** Yes **Customers** Tourists, mature patrons

Breakfast Monday–Friday, 6:30–10:30 a.m.; Saturday and Sunday, 7–11 a.m.

Lunch Monday–Friday, 11:30 a.m.–2:30 p.m.; Saturday and Sunday, noon–3 p.m.

Dinner Monday–Saturday, 6–10:30 p.m.; Sunday, 6–10 p.m.

Setting & atmosphere The spectacular room, designed by Tony Chi and perched on the seventh floor of the new Park Hyatt hotel, has fabulous views of North Michigan Avenue (hence the name). The entryway alone is worth a visit; it's a temperature-controlled wine cellar that opens into a handsome adjoining lounge. The white linen–topped tables in the dining room are nicely spaced, stemware is elegant, and the exposed kitchen is finished in eye-catching iridescent aqua tile.

House specialties Chilled white bean soup with shaved black truffles; warm Maine lobster salad (haricots verts, domestic and wild asparagus, creamy chunks of avocado, and generous pieces of lobster in a Ligurian olive oil); Hudson Valley foie gras artfully arranged atop a scoop of heirloom tomato jam, surrounded by a fluffy bed of mâche tossed in a balsamic reduction; grilled Maine lobster tail with glazed fennel and lobster claw in lobster knuckle bisque; sautéed pampano with ragoût of fava beans, yellow teardrop tomatoes, cucumber, and an eight-year-old Trebbiano balsamic vinegar; roasted beef tenderloin with fingerling potatoes, glazed spanish peach, foie gras, and beef jus; roasted peaches with Tahitian vanilla ice cream and caramel sauce; raspberry tart.

Other recommendations Yellowfin tuna tartare with osetra caviar, blinis, and a crème fraîche aigrelette sauce; sautéed daurade with tomatoes, olives, and fried basil in a fennel-spice sauce; chilled cucumber soup with tomato-avocado ratatouille, lemon olive oil and osetra caviar; seared sea scallop with haricot vert, baby artichoke and rosemary goat cheese sauce; Maine lobster ragoût with fava beans, asparagus, and a classic armoricaine sauce (lobster and olive oil emulsion).

Summary & comments Chef Sandro Gamba, whose resume includes stints at Alain Ducasse's Louis XV in Monte Carlo and Lespinasse in Washington, D.C., executes straightforward fare, highlighting the intrinsic flavors of ingredients in a most artistic and refined manner. The wine list, created in consultation with former Charlie Trotter's sommelier Joseph Spellman, offers affordable gems along with slightly pricier options—but nothing too outrageously priced. It's an experience best reserved for a special occasion.

Honors & awards   Three stars from *Chicago Tribune;* best new chef, *Food & Wine,* 2001.

NORTH POND CAFE ★★★★

NEW AMERICAN | EXPENSIVE | QUALITY ★★★★½ | VALUE ★★★ | ZONE I

2610 North Cannon Drive; (773) 477-5845

Reservations Recommended **When to go** Weekday evenings, lunch during warm weather **Entree range** $24–$28; brunch, $28 **Payment** V, MC, AMEX, DC, D **Service rating** ★★★★ **Friendliness rating** ★★★★ **Parking** Street **Bar** Full service with a nice selection of local microbrews and spirits **Wine selection** Well-appointed list featuring ample American wines from California, Oregon, and Washington, along with a few French sparkling wines; by the bottle, $35–$70; by the glass, $7–$12 **Dress** Casual to upscale **Disabled access** Yes **Customers** Mix of suburban diners and young neighborhood patrons

Brunch Sunday, 11 a.m.–2 p.m.

Lunch Tuesday–Saturday, 11:30 a.m.–2 p.m.

Dinner Tuesday–Sunday, 5:30–10 p.m.

Setting & atmosphere This renovated warming house is perched on the edge of a serene pond in Lincoln Park, with windows covering three wood-trimmed walls. The Prairie-style room harmonizes nicely with the park; the ceiling frescoes depict wild prairie grass, and Arts and Crafts light fixtures illuminate the Frank Lloyd Wright–style tables and chairs. It's sophisticated but still lively and energetic, with a bustling exposed kitchen running the length of one wall.

House specialties Seasonally changing dishes include red, white and candy striped beets with baby arugula, gorgonzola dressing and bacon croustillant; seared skin-on cod with couscous, dry-cured sausage, pistachios, glazed beets and arugula; seared breast of duck with a wine-braised leg in potato crust with glazed carrots and bing cherry sauce. Brunch items worth a try include hazelnut pancakes with fresh seasonal berries; mushroom and goat cheese omelet with browned fingerling potatoes; sautéed sea scallops with lobster sauce, braised leeks, and roasted parsnip purée.

Other recommendations Roasted eggplant puree with warm tomato coulis, black olive tapenade and a wild herb salad; goat cheese and caramelized onion tart with sun gold tomatoes, basil cream and herb salad; sautéed wild striped bass with new potatoes, braised baby fennel, tomato basil fondu with olives; pan-browned quail with a sunny-side up egg, braised rainbow chard, corn cake, and a foie gras emulsion.

Summary & comments This charming Arts and Crafts–style room is inconveniently located in the heart of Lincoln Park, and parking can be tricky. The room has room to wait at the bar and a few dozen additional tables overlooking the pond. The American fare is skillfully executed, incorporating seasonal ingredients in intriguing combinations. The lunch menu is more casual, and the Sunday brunch is a great option.

The mostly American wine list is well selected and reasonable. Service has its missteps, but the food and ambience more than make up for it.

one sixtyblue ★★★★

NEW AMERICAN | EXPENSIVE | QUALITY ★★★★½ | VALUE ★★★ | ZONE 2

160 North Loomis Street; (312) 850-0303

Reservations Recommended **When to go** Dinner any time; special occasions and with favored visitors **Entree range** $19–$30; prix fixe: $28, 2-course; $32, 3-course **Payment** V, MC, AMEX, DC **Service rating** ★★★★ **Friendliness rating** ★★★ **Parking** Valet, $7 **Bar** Full service **Wine selection** Eclectic, international list organized by varietals; about 150 selections, from $32 up; 15 by the glass, $9–$13 **Dress** Chic casual to dressy **Disabled access** Complete **Customers** Savvy diners of all ages; international glitterati and smart money

Dinner Monday–Thursday, 5–10 p.m.; Friday and Saturday, 5–11 p.m.; closed Sunday

Setting & atmosphere Designed by Adam Tihany, one sixtyblue is a remarkably chic, high-concept restaurant. The color scheme of black, neutrals, and citrus hues manages to be crisp and clean without sterility; table dividers with light boxes provide the illusion of privacy, while allowing for discreet spying on fellow diners.

House specialties Homemade gnocchi with rock shrimp, asparagus, and lobster tarragon sauce; pan-seared sea scallops with sweet corn puree, baby corn and truffle vinaigrette; arparagus vichyssoise with jumbo lump crab and truffle honey; 160 blue duck à l'orange with truffle honey and blood orange; pan-roasted grouper with braised artichokes, kalamata olives, and Morroccan oil; pan-roasted chicken with morel mushrooms, pearl onions, asparagus, natural jus; honey-glazed salmon with tomato ginger relish, shaved fennel salad, mushrooms; trio of lamb with couscous, dried apricot, vegetable medley, and cumin lamb jus; filet mignon au poivre with whipped potato, caramelized endive, and roasted shallots; crunchy Napoleon with crème brûlée and butterscotch sauce; hot chocolate cake with candied orange and Grand Marnier sauce.

Other recommendations Poached jumbo shrimp with vegetable tartare in woodroasted piquillo pepper vinaigrette; pan-seared foie gras with rhubarb, lemon confit, and strawberry sauce; mixed green salad with tomato, croutons, and roasted hazlenut vinaigrette; roasted pineapple with coconut ice cream.

Summary & comments One sixtyblue enjoys an excellent reputation as one of Chicago's best—among many—contemporary American culinary destinations. The fare is innovative and attractive on the plate, served with polish and precision by a smartly clad service team. Michael Jordan, His Airness himself, is a partner in this gem of a restaurant, anchoring the west end of the Randolph Street restaurant row.

Honors & awards Named one of the Best New Restaurants of 1998, *Esquire;* three stars from *Chicago* magazine; three stars from the *Chicago Tribune.*

ORANGE ★★

GLOBAL/BREAKFAST | INEXPENSIVE | QUALITY ★★★ | VALUE ★★★★ | ZONE 1

3231 North Clark Street; (773) 549-4400

Reservations Not accepted **When to go** Weekend breakfast or brunch **Entree range** $4–$8 **Payment** MC, V, D, AMEX, DC **Service rating** ★★ **Friendliness rating** ★★★ **Parking** Street **Bar** Juice only **Wine selection** None **Dress** Casual **Disabled Access** Yes **Customers** Young local, hungover late-night club hoppers

Hours Tuesday–Sunday, 8 a.m.–3 p.m.

Setting & atmosphere A homey, cheerful storefront with orange crates as art, exposed brick walls, natural floors, and an eye-appealing fresh juice bar.

House specialties Frushi specialty (rice rolled with fresh fruit in fruit leather), do-it-yourself crêpes; green eggs and ham (scrambled eggs with basil pesto, roasted tomatoes, buffalo mozzarella, and diced pancetta); jelly doughnut pancakes with lingonberries.

Other recommendations French toast kabobs (coconut-infused French toast skewered and grilled with fresh strawberries and pineapple); succotash with honey-roasted shiitake mushrooms, black-eyed peas, haricot vert, parsnips, turnips, and applewood smoked bacon.

Summary & comments For a fresh lively early morning spot, this Lakeview gem is just the place. Fresh ingredients are the keys to clever and creative dishes and drinks. Even the coffee gets infused with orange zest. It's one of the most neighborly breakfast haunts in town.

PASTEUR ★★★½

VIETNAMESE | INEXPENSIVE | QUALITY ★★★★½ | VALUE ★★★★ | ZONE I

5525 North Broadway; (773) 878-1061

Reservations Accepted **When to go** Dinner any night **Entree range** $8–$27 **Payment** V, MC, AMEX, DC, D **Service rating** ★★★½ **Friendliness rating** ★★★½ **Parking** Free lot or street **Bar** Full service **Wine selection** Mostly French with Californian and Argentinian selections; 10 by the glass, $7–$8; bottles $28–$110 **Dress** Casual **Disabled access** Yes **Customers** Diverse crowd with mature suburbanites and young urbanites

Lunch Thursday–Sunday, noon–5 p.m.

Dinner Monday–Thursday, Sunday, 5–10 p.m.; Friday and Saturday, 5–11 p.m.

Setting & atmosphere The sultry room feels like French Saigon, with spinning overhead fans, large palm plants, and delicate Asian paintings in jewel tones. The front bar waiting area is also inviting, with deep crimson walls, straw bar seats, and a comfortable couch.

House specialties Cha gio (rice paper eggrolls with pork, woodear mushrooms, and cellophane noodles served with a tangy fish sauce for dipping); thit nuong rau song (lemongrass, sesame, and honey-marinated beef, grilled and served with rice paper and fresh vegetables for hand-rolling); chao tom (sugar cane stalks surrounded by ground shrimp with a peanut-plum dipping sauce); Asian bouillabaisse (shrimp, blue crab, cuttlefish, scallops, and vegetables in a shrimp broth); cochinchin (chicken and shrimp sautéed with wide rice noodles, bean sprouts, and scallions); Saigonese duck à l'orange.

Other recommendations Banh xeo (rice flour crêpe seasoned with turmeric and coconut milk, then filled with chicken, shrimp, mushrooms, and bean sprouts with a tangy fish sauce for dipping); bo tai chanh (grilled flank steak, chilled and served with a lime vinaigrette and fresh mint); canh chua tom (hot and sour tamarind soup with shrimp, okra, mushrooms, and pineapple); ca hap (whole bass steamed in a ginger soy sauce); cua rang muoi (whole sautéed Dungeness crab in a rich garlic sauce).

Summary & comments This reincarnation of one of Chicago's original Vietnamese restaurants is better than ever, with a pleasant decor to match. The fare manages to combine raw and cooked ingredients in sweet and savory combinations that dazzle even the most jaded taste buds. Service is always congenial and accommodating by a waitstaff elegantly dressed in authentic silk robes. It's off the beaten path for urban dwellers, but certainly worth the trip.

PENANG ★★★

ASIAN/MALAYSIAN | INEXPENSIVE | QUALITY ★★★★ | VALUE ★★★★ | ZONE 5

2201 South Wentworth Avenue; (312) 326-6888

Reservations Accepted **When to go** Any time **Entree range** $7–$20 **Payment** V, MC **Service rating** ★★½ **Friendliness rating** ★★½ **Parking** Validated **Bar** Full service **Wine selection** Limited, $25–$39; 3 by the glass, $6 **Dress** Casual **Disabled access** Wheelchair accessible **Customers** A melting pot of locals and tourists

Lunch/Dinner Daily, 11 a.m.–1 a.m.

Setting & atmosphere Casual, tiki-influenced atmosphere with large wood tables, open ductwork, and wood beam accents.

House specialties Roti telur (a traditional Indian pancake filled with egg, onion, and green chiles with curry chicken potato dipping sauce); Penang satay chicken/beef (marinated chicken or beef on skewers, charcoal grilled and served with peanut sauce); Penang udang mee (noodles in chef's special shrimp broth with shrimp, pork, and bean sprouts); seafood tom yum mee hoon (rice noodles in spicy-sour lemongrass broth with seafood and straw mushrooms); Penang char kway teow (stir-fried flat rice noodles with fresh shrimp, squid, bean sprouts, eggs, soy sauce, and chile paste); Buddhist yam pot (fried taro stuffed with shrimp, chicken, and Chinese mushroom); beef rending (beef, coconut milk, chiles, cinnamon, and clove spices cooked over low heat); mango udang (shrimp with fresh mango in Penang sauce); kari sayur, mixed vegetables in a clay pot with spicy curry broth); Penang ikan (BBQ fish wrapped in banana leaf).

Other recommendations Dragon roll (eel cucumber and avocado); rainbow roll (tuna, salmon, yellowtail, crabmeat, avocado, and tobiko); chile chicken (deep-fried sliced chicken with fresh chile curry leaves, onion, and delicate spices); volcano BBQ baby spare ribs; sizzling beef; kang kung belacan (sautéed water spinach with spicy Malaysian shrimp paste).

Summary & comments If you're looking for a different dining experience, the mostly Malaysian fare at this unique restaurant fills the bill. Though you can easily have an entree and soup here for under $15, half the fun is trying several dishes. The main menu is exhaustive, and by the time you start perusing the second sushi menu, you may be overwhelmed—try sitting back and letting your server make some selections for the table.

PIECE ★★

PIZZERIA/BREW PUB | INEXPENSIVE | QUALITY ★★★ | VALUE ★★★★ | ZONE 2

1927 West North Avenue; (773) 772-4422

Reservations Not accepted **When to go** Weekdays, late-night, quick lunch **Entree range** $8–$12 **Payment** MC, V, D, AMEX **Service rating** ★★ **Friendliness rating** ★★★★ **Parking** Valet, $6 **Bar** Full bar notable for 7 house-made award-winning brews, plus 10 regional microbrews **Wine selection** Limited Italian and American, $20–$36 per bottle; by the glass, $5–$8 **Dress** Casual **Disabled Access** Yes **Customers** Young, urban locals, actors, and athletes

Hours Daily, 11 a.m.–2 a.m.

Setting & atmosphere Formerly a truck garage, this lofted space still has an industrial feel with poured cement floors and high ceilings with a long glass skylight running the length. That's not to say there aren't any stylish details—a sunken lounge area up front sports blue and green comfy couches and floor-to-ceiling windows which open onto bustling North Avenue.

House specialties East coast (New haven, Connecticut)–style pizza pies topped with traditional ingredients, along with some more adventurous toppings like meatballs, clams, and broccoli raab. Choose your base: plain (tomato with Parmesan and garlic), white (olive oil with garlic), or red (tomato with mozzarella).

Other recommendations Wild mushroom quesadillas; salad of candied pecans, pears, and Gorgonzola.

Summary & comments It's a natural location for this pizzeria and microbrewery— right in the heart of the young and happening Wicker Park neighborhood. Not only does their original East Coast crust recipe come straight from the source, but a former Sierra Nevada brewmaster was installed to supervise the microbrewery attached to this 5,800-square-foot dining room. It all works like a well-oiled machine, and there's space for crowds—even on a major game night when the many TVs are all tuned in.

ROSEBUD CAFE ★★★

ITALIAN | MODERATE | QUALITY ★★★★ | VALUE ★★★ | ZONE 3, 6, 8

720 North Rush Street; (312) 266-6444
1500 West Taylor Street; (312) 942-1117
48 West Chicago Avenue, Naperville; (630) 548-9800

Reservations Recommended **When to go** Weeknight dinner **Entree range** $12– $30 **Payment** All major credit cards **Service rating** ★★½ **Friendliness rating** ★★½ **Parking** Valet. West Taylor: $5 lunch, $7 dinner; Rush: $9 lunch and dinner; Naperville: $4 dinner only. Limited street parking. **Bar** Full service **Wine selection** 48 Italian and American selections, $20–$250; 10 available by the glass, $6–$8 **Dress** Casual **Disabled access** Wheelchair accessible **Customers** Tourists, goombahs, and Little Italy habitués

Lunch Daily. West Taylor: 11 a.m.–3 p.m.; Rush, Naperville: 11 a.m.–3 p.m.

Dinner Daily. West Taylor: 3–11 p.m.; Rush: 5–11 p.m.; Naperville: weeknights, 4–10 p.m.; weekends, 4–11 p.m.

Setting & atmosphere The dated decor of carved wood, leaded and stained glass, mirrors, and celebrity photos is comforting in its familiarity; the crowd is a real slice.

House specialties Calamari fritti; sausage and peppers (broiled Italian sausage with sautéed sweet peppers); chicken Vesuvio (pan-roasted crispy chicken served in a garlic-wine sauce with roasted potatoes and sautéed peas); pappardelle (square semolina noodles in a rich marinara sauce); cavatelli with sautéed mushrooms, roasted peppers, and green beans in garlic and oil sauce.

Other recommendations Stuffed artichoke with garlic and Parmesan breading; panzanella (bread salad with mixed greens, tomatoes, olives, capers, onions, and basil); fish salad (shrimp, octopus, calamari, and scungilli in olive oil and lemon); zuppa di pesce; strip steak Italian style (with potato wedges and vinegar peppers in white wine sauce); veal saltimbocca or Marsala.

Summary & comments Rosebud epitomizes the hearty fare and back-slapping goodwill of Chicago's Little Italy. Though prices can run high, portions are notoriously oversized; everyone leaves with a doggie bag. Weekends are mobbed, and reservations can be virtually meaningless.

SALPICON ★★★

REGIONAL MEXICAN | MODERATE | QUALITY ★★★★½ | VALUE ★★★ | ZONE 3

1252 North Wells Street; (312) 988-7811

Reservations Recommended **When to go** Lively weekend dinner **Entree range** $17–$27 **Payment** V, MC, AMEX, DC, D **Service rating** ★★★ **Friendliness rating** ★★½ **Parking** Valet, $7 **Bar** Beer, wine, and tequila drinks only **Wine selection** French, American, Australian, Chilean, Austrian, and German, $25–$400 per bottle; several by the glass, $6–$17 **Dress** Chic to casual **Disabled access** Yes **Customers** Urban workers, mature locals

Brunch Sunday, 11 a.m.–2:30 p.m.

Dinner Sunday–Thursday, 5–10 p.m.; Friday and Saturday, 5–11 p.m.

Setting & atmosphere The lively two-room storefront space is splashed with color, from the brightly painted walls to the large Mexican canvases and artifacts. Tables are tightly spaced, making it feel inordinately crowded at times.

House specialties Crepa de huitlacoche (earthy corn mushrooms sautéed with onion and serrano chile, folded into a cilantro crêpe and topped with a roasted poblano cream sauce); enchiladitas Oaxaquenas (shredded chicken mini-enchilada with a Oaxacan black mole and queso fresco); costillitas de borrego en coloradito (rack of Australian baby lamb served with a red mole and papas con chorizo); pescado en salsa de cuatro chiles (grilled Chilean sea bass topped with sautéed portobello mushrooms, epazote, and chiles with a fresh mango sauce).

Other recommendations Tostaditas de tinga (crispy small tortillas with shredded pork and chorizo in a roasted tomato-chipotle sauce); camarones al carbon (grilled tiger shrimp served with an avocado-tomatillo sauce and a spicy roasted tomato and chipotle sauce garnished with refreshing mango slices); chiles dona queta (stuffed poblano chile with huitlacoche, corn, and zucchini in a roasted poblano crème sauce); chef's seven-course tasting menu ($55, subject to availability, check when reserving).

Summary & comments Formerly from Frontera Grill, chef Priscilla Satkoff prepares the Mexican cuisine of her homeland in an elegant, upscale manner. Dishes can be spicy, so it's best to inquire before ordering. The menu features clean, authentic flavors from the indigenous ingredients, like chipotle chiles, mangos, tomatillos, and her fabulous homemade mole. An on-site wine cellar houses over 800 bottles of wine for an outstanding selection, not to mention a killer premium tequila list.

Honors & awards Three stars from the *Chicago Tribune*.

SANTORINI   ★★★

GREEK/SEAFOOD | EXPENSIVE | QUALITY ★★★★ | VALUE ★★★ | ZONE 2

138 South Halsted Street; (312) 829-08820

Reservations Accepted **When to go** Before United Center events **Entree range** $11–$35 **Payment** V, MC, AMEX, DC, D **Service rating** ★★★½ **Friendliness rating** ★★★ **Parking** Free lot **Bar** Full service **Wine selection** Greek, French, Californian, Italian, $15–$220 per bottle; $5 per glass **Dress** Casual to dressy **Disabled access** Yes **Customers** Mixed crowd; professionals by day, families and suburbanites by evening

Hours Sunday–Thursday, 11 a.m.–midnight; Friday and Saturday, 11 a.m.–1 a.m.

Setting & atmosphere This upscale Greektown eatery has a wood-burning fireplace in the center of the dining room, with various Mediterranean artifacts and baskets scattered about. It's rustic, homey, and comfortable.

House specialties Roasted whole fish (red snapper or black sea bass), prepared simply with olive oil and lemon juice; Kamari beach calamari char-grilled with garlic, lemon juice, and olive oil; lemon sole; seafood platter (lobster, shrimp, oysters, and fish).

Other recommendations Char-grilled octopus; tzatziki; kolokithakis (fried zucchini with garlic sauce); Florida grouper.

Summary & comments This cozy yet bustling addition to Greektown specializes in seafood, with Mediterranean-style whole fish that's a standout. Service is professional and attentive, accommodating sports fans on their way to a game. Family-style multi-course dinners are offered for large parties.

SHAW'S CRAB HOUSE   ★★★½

SEAFOOD | EXPENSIVE | QUALITY ★★★★½ | VALUE ★★ | ZONES 3, 10

21 West Hubbard Street; (312) 527-2722
Shaw's Seafood Grill, 1900 East Higgins Road, Schaumburg; (847) 517-2722

Reservations Recommended **When to go** Any time **Entree range** $10–$50 **Payment** All major credit cards **Service rating** ★★★½ **Friendliness rating** ★★★½ **Parking** Valet, $9 **Bar** Full service **Wine selection** 175+ domestic selections, $19–$280; 20 by the glass, $6–$13 **Dress** Business casual, dressy **Disabled access** Wheelchair accessible **Customers** Professionals, tourists, and seafood lovers

Lunch Monday–Friday, 11:30 a.m.–2 p.m.

Dinner Monday–Thursday, 5:30–10 p.m.; Friday and Saturday, 5–11 p.m.; Sunday, 5–10 p.m.

Setting & atmosphere Upscale and clubby, with rich woods and all the accoutrements of fine dining.

House specialties Fresh oysters, generally seven regional selections plus a sampler plate; seasonal crab (e.g., chilled Florida stone crab claws, Alaskan "red" king crab legs, Alaskan Dungeness); Shaw's crab cakes; fresh Maine lobster, whole or stuffed.

Other recommendations Fried oysters caesar salad; grilled Block Island swordfish with Parmigiano Reggiano mashed potatoes and roasted artichoke sauce; grilled Florida red grouper with chanterelle and oyster mushrooms, Vidalia onion, and Cabernet Sauvignon sauce; grilled Gulf yellowfin tuna with tomato and Vidalia onion and green and black olive tapenade; sautéed Canadian walleye, blue crab, almond wild rice pilaf, and cipollini onion sauce; sautéed Virginia flounder Grenobloise (with capers, croutons, and lemon butter sauce).

Summary & comments Though the tariff is high, this is the price we pay for fresh seafood in the Midwest. The quality and selection are there for lovers of the bounties of the sea, and the clubby atmosphere is suitably toney. Service is polished and professional. The adjoining Blue Crab Lounge is more casual, with a great East Coast oyster bar feel and occasional live music.

SMITH & WOLLENSKY ★★★½

STEAK | EXPENSIVE | QUALITY ★★★★½ | VALUE ★★ | ZONE 3

318 North State Street; (312) 670-9900

Reservations Suggested **When to go** Deals and dates **Entree range** $16–$42 **Payment** All major credit cards **Service rating** ★★★ **Friendliness rating** ★★★ **Parking** Valet, $9 **Bar** Full service **Wine selection** 200+ selections, mostly Californian, French, Italian, and German, $19–$2,800; 20 by the glass, $6–$15 **Dress** Casual, business **Disabled access** Wheelchair accessible **Customers** Older power money, professionals, and upscale diners

Lunch/Dinner Daily, 11:30 a.m.–1a.m.

Setting & atmosphere Smith & Wollensky has one of the most beautiful, inviting buildings and locations in town, with a grand entrance and clubby steakhouse atmosphere of dark wood, marble, creamy walls, and globe light fixtures. The pomp is punctuated with a whimsical collection of American folk art, including a group of antique carved bears commemorating Chicago Bear greats. Great outdoor dining on the Chicago River in warm weather.

House specialties Smoked pastrami salmon; Wollensky's salad; split pea soup; Maryland crab cakes; filet au poivre; sirloin steak; crackling pork shank with firecracker applesauce; "angry" lobster.

Other recommendations Caesar salad; Maine lobster, steamed or broiled; veal chop; mustard-crusted tuna; lemon pepper chicken; creamed spinach; Cape Cod lobster and shrimp roll (lunch only).

Summary & comments This pedigreed New York import gives great steak and great steakhouse ambience, making it a great place to satisfy those carnivorous cravings. It has the feel of a classic, though it's only been around a few years. Prices for similar items are lower at the more casual Wollensky's Grill, located below the main restaurant.

SPIAGGIA ★★★★★

ITALIAN | EXPENSIVE/VERY EXPENSIVE | QUALITY ★★★★★ | VALUE ★★★ | ZONE 3

980 North Michigan Avenue; (312) 280-2750

Reservations Required Friday and Saturday nights, recommended at other times **When to go** Big deals, special occasions **Entree range** $14–$40 **Payment** All major credit cards **Service rating** ★★★★½ **Friendliness rating** ★★★½ **Parking** Lot in building, $7 (validated) **Bar** Full service; numerous grappas, brandies, and amari (digestivi) **Wine selection** 600–700 Italian varietals and prestige cuvee champagnes, $35–$2,000; 10 wines by the glass, $8–$20 **Dress** Jacket required for dinner, recommended for lunch; tie optional; no jeans or gym shoes **Disabled access** Wheelchair accessible **Customers** Mature couples, international business types, upscale special occasion celebrants

Lunch Tuesday–Saturday, 11:30 a.m.–2 p.m.

Dinner Monday–Thursday, Sunday, 5:30–9:30 p.m.; Friday and Saturday, 5:30–10:30 p.m.

Setting & atmosphere Spiaggia's ultra-sophisticated ambience is dramatically enhanced by looming 40-foot windows overlooking the fashionable intersection of Oak Street and Michigan Avenue. The multi-tiered, architectural dining room is done in subtle neutrals with spectacular light fixtures, black marble pillars, and topiary. Tables are sumptuously appointed.

House specialties Delicatezze di mare agli olii soprafini (a tasting of three seafood antipasti: peekytoe crabmeat alla Veneziana with tangerine-infused olive oil); yellowtail crudo with white truffle oil and celery hearts; and spaghettini with Petrossian osetra caviar and chives); insalata di astico alla Catalana (Sardinian-style lobster salad with arugula, tomatoes, onion, lobster caviar, and crispy focaccia); tortelloni di fagiano tartufato (pheasant-filled ravioli with Umbrian black truffles); taglio di manzo "Piemontese" con purea al tartufo nero e erbe (seared Piemontese Better Beef strip steak with black truffle potato purée and herb salad).

Other recommendations Corzetti alla ligure con granchio e fagiolini al pesto (traditional Ligurian pasta coins with pesto, king crab meat, green beans, and potatoes); halibut con funghi porcini (wood-roasted, bacon-wrapped halibut with porcini mushroom sauce and potato puree); torta al mascarpone in salsa di Illy caffe (chilled mascarpone cheese torte with espresso sauce).

Summary & comments Spiaggia has long been known as Chicago's finest Italian restaurant. Since the departure of chef Paul Bartolotta, opening chef Tony Mantuano recently returned to the Spiaggia kitchen, and the restaurant hasn't skipped a beat. Expect luxury ingredients, simply beautiful presentations, fine wines, and gracious service—in short, a superlative, fine Italian dining experience.

Honors & awards Four stars, *Chicago Tribune,* 1999; four stars, *Mobil Travel Guide,* 2000; Insegna del Ristorante Italiano del Mondo, 1997; Ivy Award, *Restaurants & Institutions,*

1993; DiRoNA Award, 1993, 1997, 1999, 2000; inducted into the *Nation's Restaurants News* Restaurant Hall of Fame, 1992.

SPRING ★★★★½

SEAFOOD/NEW AMERICAN | MODERATE | QUALITY ★★★★ | VALUE ★★ | ZONE 2

2039 West North Avenue; (773) 395-7100

Reservations Required **When to go** Weekday dinner to avoid long waits **Entree range** $15–$25 **Payment** AMEX, MC, V, D **Service rating** ★★★★ **Friendliness rating** ★★ **Parking** Valet, $8 **Bar** Full Bar **Wine selection** French, Californian, Italian and Austrian, $36–$250; half bottles $21–$85; by the glass, $8–$14 **Dress** Casual chic **Disabled Access** yes **Customers** Trendy young locals and suburbanites

Dinner Tuesday–Thursday, 5:30–10 p.m.; Friday and Saturday, 5:30–11 p.m.; Sunday, 5:30–9 p.m.; closed Monday

Setting & atmosphere Formerly a Roman bath house, the subterranean pool area is now the dining room with a Zen-garden at the entrance and minimalist decor. The feng shui space has tables zigzagging down the center, separated by high banquets for privacy. Pistachio-colored walls are illuminated by recessed lights, making the room glow.

House specialties Fresh Hawaiian hearts of palm and green papaya salad with Maine lobster, shrimp, fresh mint, and a ginger dressing; lobster spring rolls in a curry-passion fruit sauce; lemongrass and coconut soup with red Thai curry and cellophane noodles; skate wing with Indian spiced lentils and chickpeas; roasted black grouper with preserved lemon couscous and orange soy reduction; fresh figs with a Muscat sabayon and cinnamon basil ice cream.

Other recommendations Chilled golden tomato soup with Thai basil-infused olive oil; soft shell crab, lobster, and corn chowder; buckwheat soba noodles with wild mushrooms and mustard-soy broth; Atlantic striped bass with wild mushrooms, edamame, and sweet corn sauce; Alaskan halibut with spring vegetable risotto and white asparagus-truffle emulsion; Valrhona chocolate mint honeycomb with lavender ice cream and citrus confit.

Summary & comments It didn't take this elegant newcomer long to make a splash in the dining scene. It's already highly touted as one of the best new restaurants in town, and reservations can take months to secure. But the serene space—combined with the exquisitely prepared and executed dishes, fabulously broad wine list, and professional servers—make it no wonder. It's garnering just attention for the innovative Asian-inspired fare, which incorporates layers of ingredients in innovative combinations.

THREE HAPPINESS ★★½

CHINESE | INEXPENSIVE | QUALITY ★★★★ | VALUE ★★★★★ | ZONE 5

209 West Cermak Road; (312) 791-1228

Reservations Accepted **When to go** Busy for lunch, crowds on weekend evenings **Entree range** $8–$15 **Payment** V, MC, AMEX, DC, D **Service rating** ★★★ **Friendliness rating** ★★★★ **Parking** Pay lot, $1 **Bar** Full service **Wine selection** Limited, but sake and plum wine also served **Dress** Casual **Disabled access** Yes **Customers** Diverse crowd; university and Loop workers

Hours Daily, 9 a.m.–2 a.m.

Setting & atmosphere The simple, small room isn't fancy, but it's clean and efficient, and the friendly staff and owner help make it comfortable. Simple linoleum floors, a red Tsing Tao paper dragon hanging from the ceiling, and booths lining the perimeter of the room complete the decor. The family-style dining with revolving lazy Susans at most tables makes for lively conversation both at lunch and dinner.

House specialties Spare ribs with black bean and garlic sauce; Szechwan diced chicken; shrimp lobster style; pork chop Mandarin style; seaweed soup; Buddhist delight (vegetarian medley of stir-fried vegetables).

Other recommendations Pan-fried prawn in the shell; five-spice soy chicken; beef with ginger and scallion; various dim sum dishes served all day long, such as pan-fried taro root cake; rice in lotus leaf with pork and chicken; kow wong (chicken and bean sprouts in rice pancake).

Summary & comments As the oldest establishment in Chinatown, this small store-front maintains high-quality fare. Lunch is a real bargain—$3.95 for a meal soup-to-nuts—but dinner or à la carte ordering allows for sampling of more interesting dishes from the incredibly broad menu. Dim sum, the small dishes normally served for a unique brunch, is available all day, every day. It's a midweek delight for adventurous nibblers.

TIFFIN ★★★

INDIAN | MODERATE | QUALITY ★★★★ | VALUE ★★★★ | ZONE 1

2536 West Devon Avenue; (773) 338-2143

Reservations Accepted **When to go** Lunch for the buffet, dinner for a quieter meal **Entree range** $9–$16 **Payment** V, MC, AMEX, DC, D **Service rating** ★★★ **Friendliness rating** ★★★★ **Parking** None **Bar** Full service **Wine selection** Limited selection of Italian, French, and Chilean wines from $10–$20 per bottle; 2 by the glass, $4 **Dress** Casual **Disabled access** Yes **Customers** Local Indian crowd along with younger Americans and families

Lunch Daily, 11:30 a.m.–3:30 p.m.

Dinner Sunday–Thursday, 5:30–10 p.m.; Friday and Saturday, 5:30–10: 30 p.m.

Setting & atmosphere One of the nicer rooms on this crowded stretch of Devon Avenue, this Indian restaurant sports dark wood–trimmed walls, white linen table-cloths, a clean heated buffet for lunch, and congenial hosts and waiters. The ceiling is cheerfully covered with a fresco of the sky, and tables are comfortably spaced.

House specialties Masala dosai (thin pancake with potatoes and vege-tables in a spicy curry sauce); tandoori chicken and lamb; lamb seekh kabab; chicken tikka masala; puloa (yogurt dip); assorted biryanis (spiced long grain rice with vegetables, lamb, or chicken); a variety of clay-oven-baked traditional breads, such as naan, onion kulcha, paratha, and poori.

Other recommendations Fish peri peri; paneer tikka; tandoori shrimp; Bengal fish curry.

Summary & comments On this busy Indian stretch of Devon Avenue, restaurants are interspersed between retail grocers selling ethnic ingredients and spices. The cheerful, friendly establishment has garnered a fine reputation; the room is comfortable, the service is attentive, the food fresh and always hot. The lunch buffet is frequently refilled, and the breads are a taste sensation, each warm and fluffy. All tandoori dishes stand out, as does the lamb vindaloo and the fresh yogurt–based raita.

TOPOLOBAMPO ★★★★½

REGIONAL MEXICAN | EXPENSIVE | QUALITY ★★★★★ | VALUE ★★★ | ZONE 3

445 North Clark Street; (312) 661-1434

Reservations Accepted for parties up to 8 **When to go** Weeknight dinner **Entree range** $19–$29; chef's 5-course tasting menu, $70 **Payment** All major credit cards **Service rating** ★★★★ **Friendliness rating** ★★★½ **Parking** Valet, $10; public lots, street **Bar** Extensive premium tequila list, margaritas, brandies, and beer **Wine selection** Extensive global, 120 selections, $30–$175; 10 by the glass, $6–$12 **Dress** Casual **Disabled access** Wheelchair accessible **Customers** Upscale locals and travelers, professionals, and couples

Lunch Tuesday–Friday, 11:30 a.m.–2 p.m.; closed Saturday–Monday

Dinner Tuesday–Thursday, 5:30–9:30 p.m.; Friday and Saturday, 5:30–10:30 p.m.; closed Sunday and Monday.

Setting & atmosphere Jeweled blues and sun-drenched hues of oranges and golds; colorful, evocative Mexican folk and fine art. Though more formal than the more casual Frontera Grill adjacent, the Topolobampo dining room tempers its sophistication with a sense of fun.

House specialties The menu of Mexican celebratory dishes, game, and little-known regional specialties changes every two weeks, and no single dish is considered a house specialty. Sample items might include ensalada de chayote (tender, delicate chayote salad dressed with Spanish sparkling wine vinaigrette, housemade goat-milk queso fresco, Neuske bacon, watercress, and pickled red onions); langosta en crema de calabaza (super-sweet roasted Maine lobster in ancho-tinged pumpkin cream with mushroom and chard–stuffed delicata); cochinita adobada (Maple Creek Farm pork slow-roasted in banana leaves with guajillo chile marinade, served with rich pan juices, grilled acorn squash, and braised greens).

Other recommendations A few lunch items remain constant, including pollito en mole verde (roasted, marinated free-range baby chicken with classic green pumpkin seed mole, Mexican greens, and heirloom beans); Milanese de puerco (crunchy-coated pork tenderloin, pan-fried in olive oil, with a spicy salsa of tomatoes, habañeros, onions, and sour orange with baby lettuces and pickled red onions); chilaquiles verdes (tangy tomatillo sauce simmered with crispy tortillas, topped with grilled chicken, thick cream, and jicama); cuatro cositas (a sampler plate of chicken enchilada in roasted tomatillo sauce; griddle-baked quesadilla of Jack cheese, duck, and peppers; tostada of marinated cactus salad; and black beans); lime tart.

Summary & comments Considered by many the nation's forerunner of fine Mexican dining, Topolobampo opens up a whole new world of soulful flavors from the regions of Mexico. Owner Rick Bayless is a true culinary artist and a dedicated scholar of Mexican cuisine (author of several cookbooks, he is also the host of *Mexico—One*

Plate at a Time on PBS). The ever-changing menu creates a sense of unfolding seasonal pageantry that keeps loyalists returning frequently for another trip to Mexican culinary heaven. Make reservations well in advance. The adjacent sister restaurant, Frontera Grill, offers a less formal (and less expensive) variation on Bayless's trailblazing, regional Mexican theme.

Honors & awards Three and a half stars from *Chicago* magazine and the *Chicago Tribune; Wine Spectator* Award of Excellence since 1990; *Restaurants & Institutions* Ivy Award, 1999; *Food & Wine* magazine's Best New Chef of 1988; *Esquire* Best New Restaurant, 1991; Best American Chef: Midwest, James Beard Foundation, 1991; National Chef of the Year, James Beard Foundation, 1995; International Association of Culinary Professionals' Chef of the Year, 1995; Humanitarian of the Year, James Beard Foundation, 1998.

TOURNESOL ★★★

FRENCH | MODERATE | QUALITY ★★★★ | VALUE ★★★ | ZONE 1

4343 North Lincoln Avenue; (773) 477-8820

Reservations Accepted **When to go** Weekday dinner **Entree range** $8–$15 **Payment** MC,V **Service rating** ★★★ **Friendliness rating** ★★★★ **Parking** Street **Bar** Full bar **Wine selection** Wide range of Austrian, Italian, and French wines, $24–$60 per bottle; half bottles $19–$58; more than a dozen by the glass, $5.50–$12 **Dress** Casual **Disabled Access** Yes **Customers** Locals and French food-lovers

Dinner Tuesday–Thursday, 5:30–9:30 p.m.; Friday and Saturday, 5:30–11 p.m.; Sunday, 5–9 p.m.

Setting & atmosphere The smart room was a labor of love for the owners, who did it all themselves. Dark wood booths and trim flank large mirrors, which open up the medium-sized room. Earth-tone drapes grace the front windows, and works of local artists cover the open walls.

House specialties Escargot fricassee; salads Lyonnaise and niçoise; poached leeks with red wine vinaigrette; mussels marinière; steak frites; braised leg of rabbit.

Other recommendations French onion soup; pan-seared trout with haricots verts in a caper brown butter; steak au poivre; sautéed veal kidneys in shallot cream sauce.

Summary & comments A new entry in the French bistro scene in Lincoln Square, this quaint yet elegant room is pleasant and inviting. Classic dishes are expertly prepared but reasonable enough for dinner during the week. Masterful wine matches are a bonus, as is the accommodating staff.

TRU ★★★★★

NEW AMERICAN | VERY EXPENSIVE | QUALITY ★★★★★ | VALUE ★★★ | ZONE 3

676 North St. Clair Street; (312) 202-0001

Reservations Highly recommended **When to go** Dinner **Entree range** Prix fixe "collections" only, ranging from 3 courses ($75) to 8 courses ($125) **Payment** All major credit cards **Service rating** ★★★★½ **Friendliness rating** ★★★ **Parking** Valet, $10; nearby lots and garages **Bar** Full service **Wine selection** 950 wines, diverse with an emphasis on France and California, $32–$2,300; 16 wines and champagnes by the glass, $10–$44 **Dress** Jackets required for men; ties requested **Disabled access** Wheelchair accessible **Customers** Power money, Michigan Avenue denizens, creative professionals

Dinner Monday–Thursday, 5:30–10 p.m.; Friday and Saturday, 5–10 p.m.; closed Sunday

Setting & atmosphere The dining room is ultra-contemporary, stark, and simple with a few original artworks (Warhol, Mapplethorpe); the buzz of the patrons and the plushy blue velvet purse stools keep the space from feeling sterile. The restaurant's signature whimsy appears in touches like a "Zen garden" of handmade lollipops in sugar "sand." Don't miss the gravity-defying bathroom sinks.

House specialties With a constantly changing menu, regular items are few. Some mainstays include the caviar staircase, a sculptural glass spiral staircase dotted with various caviars and fixin's; a tasting of various exquisite soups in eye-popping Gianni Versace cappuccino cups; any of chef Rick Tramonto's various foie gras preparations; Gale Gand's roasted pineapple carpaccio with coconut-cilantro dressing and buttermilk–key lime sherbet; duet of soufflés flavored with truffle-stuffed chocolate and blood orange; and her housemade animal crackers and mignardises (petits fours).

Other recommendations Sample menu items might run along the lines of potato-crusted Scottish salmon with artichokes, fennel salad, and herb vinaigrette; assiette of milk-fed veal, roasted loin, butter-poached breast, and crispy sweetbreads; roasted duck breast with foie gras wontons and duck consommé; truffle-stuffed chocolate with passion fruit; peanut butter and banana bread pudding.

Summary & comments Stunning Tru represents another collaboration between Rich Melman's Lettuce Entertain You and established, high-end chef talent. The high-concept fare is renowned for its contemporary creativity with touches of humor leavening the sophistication (like a dish served perched on a "fishbowl" with live tropical fish). This is très chic—and très lengthy—dining, so plan to make an evening of it, especially if you want to experience the full spectrum of the larger collection menus (choices also include vegetarian and seafood). European-style team service; no smoking, and no cell phones in the dining room.

Honors & awards Four stars from *Chicago* magazine and *Chicago Tribune*; *Chicago* magazine, Best New Restaurants, 2000; *Wine Spectator* Award of Excellence; *Wine Spectator*, America's Best Restaurants (top 20); *Condé Nast Traveler* Top 50 Best Restaurants; AAA five diamonds; Mobil four stars.

TWELVE 12   ★★★

NEW AMERICAN | EXPENSIVE | QUALITY ★★★ | VALUE ★★ | ZONE 3

1212 North State Parkway; (312) 951-1212

Reservations Recommended **When to go** Weekends for dinner **Entree range** $16–$30 **Payment** MC, V, D, AMEX **Service rating** ★★ **Friendliness rating** ★★★ **Parking** Valet, $9 **Bar** Full **Wine selection** Primarily American, most from Napa Valley; $33–$180 per bottle; extensive list of half-bottles, $20–$120; by the glass, $6–$14 **Dress** Stylish **Disabled Access** Yes **Customers** Well-dressed Gold Coast locals, club hopper-types on special party nights.

Dinner Monday–Thursday, 5–10 p.m. (late-night menu offered until midnight); Friday and Saturday, 5–11 p.m. (late-night menu offered until 1:00 a.m.)

Setting & atmosphere The spacious, minimalist room on the Gold Coast is tasteful with simple black and white details, a raised dining area, and an attractive lounge with colorful couches up front. Tables are nicely spaced, and booths on the perimeter allow for privacy.

House specialties Roasted veal sweetbreads and fresh ricotta tart with caramelized onions and blackberry glaze; sautéed ivory salmon on Swiss chard ravioli with apple-wood smoked bacon sauce and frisée lettuce; heirloom tomato salad with tomato sorbet and chilled tomato broth; pan-seared walleyed pike with lemon-fennel nage, artichokes, and ramps; roasted veal rib chop with creamy mascarpone polenta, morel ragoût, and black peppercorn jus; warm nectarine compote with crème fraîche pound cake and vanilla ice cream.

Other recommendations Grilled foie gras with sweet onion rings, potato, and aged balsamic; chilled lobster salad with lemon crème fraîche, shaved fennel salad, and American sturgeon caviar; seasonal ceviches; sautéed cod with braised fennel and olive oil-poached tomatoes; grilled Amish chicken breast with barbecue glaze, warm potato salad, Swiss chard, and whole grain mustard sauce; baby spring vegetable tart with smoked goat cheese ravioli and mushroom glacé.

Summary & comments While this space has been home to several eateries, this one looks more permanent with a steady flow of regulars, locals, and visitors alike. Dishes are pleasantly artistic, combining flavors and ultra-fresh ingredients in memorable ways. Desserts are especially interesting, as is the domestic artisanal cheese plate.

UNCOMMON GROUND ★★½

AMERICAN | INEXPENSIVE | QUALITY ★★★★ | VALUE ★★★★★ | ZONE 1

1214 West Grace Street; (773) 929-3680

Reservations Accepted **When to go** Breakfast, coffee break, casual dinner **Entree range** $8–$14 **Payment** All major credit cards **Service rating** ★★★ **Friendliness rating** ★★★★★ **Parking** Street **Bar** Beer, wine, some liquor **Wine selection** 10 eclectic, mostly American choices; $17–$19 per bottle; $6–$8 by the glass **Dress** Casual **Disabled access** Wheelchair accessible **Customers** Savvy northsiders, families, and students

Hours Sunday–Thursday, 8 a.m.–11 p.m.; Friday and Saturday, 8 a.m.–midnight.

Setting & atmosphere The hip, family-owned TLC of owners Michael and Helen Cameron is palpable in this funky-charming coffee house and restaurant, with exposed brick walls, fireplace, displays of work by vicinity artists, and regular live acoustic music.

House specialties Uncommon Huevos (two black bean, corn, and chipotle cakes topped with eggs over easy, ancho chile sauce, Chihuahua cheese, and cilantro, served with crispy potatoes); Montana omelet (filled with bacon, potatoes, green onions, and cheddar cheese topped with sour cream); sundried tomato, fresh basil, and smoked mozzarella omelet; house granola (oats, honey, walnuts, almonds, and cinnamon, served with fruit and yogurt); baked artichoke, goat cheese, and pesto dip with toasted French bread; apple, walnut, and Amish blue cheese salad (also with grilled chicken); Helen's marinated and grilled breast of chicken topped with Swiss cheese, avocado, red onion, tomato, sprouts, and honey-mustard dressing on hearth-baked bread; pumpkin ravioli with sage-spice butter, Amish blue cheese, and toasted hazelnuts; Louisiana spiced grilled chicken salad with griddled veggies in balsamic vinaigrette.

Other recommendations Buttermilk pancakes; fresh scones; homemade vegetarian chili; rigatoni Diablo with spicy fire-roasted tomato sauce and goat cheese (available with grilled chicken); roast vegetable sandwich; fresh carrot cake with caramel sauce; deep dish apple cobbler. In addition to excellent coffee drinks, Uncommon Ground is also known far and wide for its great hot chocolate.

Entertainment & amenities Live acoustic music five nights a week, from local singer-songwriters to national touring artists on major record labels. For information about upcoming shows, visit **www.uncommonground.com.**

Summary & comments This is a great place for an inexpensive date, to sit back with your laptop over a coffee, to meet friends for breakfast, or just to hang in front of the fireplace on a chilly Chicago day. The fresh food is akin to going to a friend's house for a meal, and the colorful atmosphere is welcoming and decidedly low key.

Honors & awards Named "Chicago's Best Coffeehouse" by *New City* Reader's Poll.

VIVERE ★★★★

ITALIAN | EXPENSIVE | QUALITY ★★★★½ | VALUE ★★★ | ZONE 4

71 West Monroe Street; (312) 332-4040

Reservations Recommended **When to go** Any time **Entree range** $16–$30 **Payment** All major credit cards **Service rating** ★★★½ **Friendliness rating** ★★★ **Parking** Valet, $9 after 5 p.m. **Bar** Full service **Wine selection** Broad and deep, in both quality and value; 1,000+ selections, $20–$1,750; 18 by the glass, $6–$13 **Dress** Business casual **Disabled access** Wheelchair accessible **Customers** Loop business denizens and seekers of fine Italian fare

Lunch Monday–Friday, 11:30 a.m.–2:30 p.m.

Dinner Monday–Thursday, 5–10 p.m.; Friday and Saturday, 5–11 p.m.; closed Sunday

Setting & atmosphere The dramatic, fantasy decor by leading designer Jordan Mozer separates stylish, contemporary Vivere from its more staid, traditional surroundings in the Italian Village restaurant complex.

House specialties Gocce di pomodoro e melanzana (timbale of plum tomatoes, eggplant, sweet herbed oil, balsamic vinegar and mixed greens); involtini di capesante (diver scallops, Belgian endive, olive oil, butternut squash-amaretto sauce, chervil); salsa olivata e spinaci (ligurian olives, sun-dried tomatoes, oregano, capers, olive oil, and sautéed spinach; insalata di verdure grigliate con agnello (mixed grilled vegetable, grilled lamb, mixed greens, and herb dressing); barbabietole miste con arugula e formaggio di capra condito (assorted beets, goat cheese, and arugula with blackberry balsamic dressing); salto di riso capesante con salsa di porcini tartufati (seared diver scallop with crispy Italian rice cake and porcini-truffle butter sauce); tortine di funghi misti (garlic-infused mushrooms with onion-thyme cream sauce; agnolottini di fagiano (pheasant-filled pasta with butter, sage, and Parmesan cheese); daily risotto specials.

Other recommendations Cappellacci de zucca (butternut squash–filled pasta, cinnamon, nutmeg, parmesan, eggs, mostarda di cremona, caramelized pears; terrina d'astice e salmone (lobster and salmon terrine, sevruga caviar, mixed herb sauce and pine nuts); salame di fichi con Sambuca (dry-aged fig roll with Sambuca, walnuts, anise seeds, and pecorino shavings); gelato di Parmigiano e caviale (creamy Parmesan quenelles and tobiko caviar with cracked black pepper and port glaze); tortelli di branzino con salsa di mare (bass-filled squid ink pasta with calamari, shrimp, and mussels in spicy tomato sauce); rotollo di faraona (roasted guinea hen with foie gras, baby vegetables, and blackberry marmalade).

Summary & comments Don't let the Loop location fool you. Several years ago, the younger generation of the Capitanini family transformed the Italian Village's dated Florentine Room into this ambitious, contemporary Italian contender, worthy of a spot in Chicago's upper echelon of fine Italian dining. Chef Marcelo Gallegos manages to keep it fresh creatively while staying true to the roots of Italian culinary authenticity; it can be difficult to choose from his soulful seasonal menu. Noteworthy desserts and an award-winning wine list. Good spot for pre-theater dining.

Honors & awards DiRoNA Award since 1998; *Wine Spectator* Grand Award winner since 1990; Best New Restaurant, *Esquire*, 1990; three stars from the *Chicago Tribune*.

VONG'S THAI KITCHEN ★★★½

ASIAN/THAI FUSION | MODERATE | QUALITY ★★★★½ | VALUE ★★★★ | ZONE 3

6 West Hubbard Street; (312) 644-8664

Reservations Recommended **When to go** Lunch is less crowded and less expensive **Entree range** $14–$20 **Payment** V, MC, AMEX, DC, D **Service rating** ★★★ **Friendliness rating** ★★½ **Parking** Valet, $9 **Bar** Full service **Wine selection** Broad list with offerings from Australia, Austria, Germany, America, and France, $20–$75; 14 by the glass, $7–$11 **Dress** Dressy/business attire **Disabled access** Yes **Customers** Stylish and mature by evening, professional crowd by day

Lunch Monday–Friday, 11:30 a.m.–2 p.m.

Dinner Monday–Thursday, 5:30–9:30 p.m.; Friday, 5:30–10:30 p.m.; Saturday, 5–11 p.m.; Sunday, 5–9 p.m.

Setting & atmosphere Acclaimed designer David Rockwell is responsible for the elegant dining room at this New York transplant. The formerly sleek and stylish room has been overhauled, now sporting crimson walls, a more casual ambience, and a more approachable menu.

House specialties Black plate appetizer combination with items like crab spring rolls or warm duck roll with sweet and sour plum sauce; Asian pear and Roquefort salad with frisée, walnuts, and honey-balsamic vinaigrette; crab spring rolls with tamarind dipping sauce; chicken and scallion satay with cucumber salad; chili shrimp with spicy pepper sauce; sesame-glazed duck with baby bok choy, sesame sauce, and pineapple fried rice; salmon pad Thai with rice noodles, Thai basil, lime, and peanuts.

Other recommendations Thai mixed leaf salad with ginger vinaigrette; warm asparagus salad with avocado; portobello mushroom satay with balsamic glaze; panang curry shrimp with peanut coconut curry and kaffir lime leaf; roasted chicken and long beans with sticky rice; seared sea scallops and shrimp with spiced butternut squash. warm Valrhona chocolate cake with coconut sorbet and a peppered tuile (cookie).

Summary & comments River North is home to this casual Thai fusion eatery, once a higher end Thai restaurant that didn't make the Chicago cut. Lunch is a good time to visit for slightly more upscale versions of Thai classics like satay, pad Thai, and curry dishes. The desserts are worth the trip alone, especially the warm Valrhona chocolate cake topped with coconut sorbet.

WAVE   ★★★

MEDITERRANEAN/SEAFOOD | MODERATE | QUALITY ★★★ | VALUE ★★★ | ZONE 3

644 North Lake Shore Drive; (312) 255-4460

Reservations Accepted **When to go** Dinner on weekends to be part of the scene; weekdays for quiet **Entree range** $16–$30 **Payment** MC, V, D, AMEX, DC **Service rating** ★★½ **Friendliness rating** ★½ **Parking** Valet, $10 **Bar** Full Bar with extensive spirits and martinis **Wine selection** Californian, French, and Spanish, $29–$95 per bottle; $7–$12 by the glass **Dress** Casual chic with an emphasis on black attire **Disabled Access** Yes **Customers** Hip, trendy see-and-be-seen types; hotel guests

Hours Daily 6:30 a.m.–10 p.m.; Friday and Saturday, 6:30 a.m.–11p.m.; Sunday, 6:30 a.m.–9 p.m.

Setting & atmosphere The ultra-swanky lobby of the W Hotel Lakeshore spills into the dining room, where woven leather mats cover the floor, a continuous abstract video runs on one wall, and a community table draws single travelers and locals. Loud music and a well-dressed staff add to the clubby ambience.

House specialties Seared jumbo sea scallops with chilled gazpacho and rock shrimp ceviche; grilled baby octopus with poached Manila clams; cioppino-style bouillabaisse with seafood and fish in a tomato chili broth; oven roasted black tail grouper with braised celery, pancetta, and oranges.

Other recommendations Ahi tuna tartare in a kalamata olive vinaigrette topped with an over easy quail egg; panzanella peasant salad of tomato, red onion, feta cheese, and red wine vinegar–laced croutons; whole roasted seasonal fish.

Summary & comments The room and music are anything but understated at this trendy lakefront hotel restaurant. The fare is nicely executed, although the staff is young and at times uninformed. It's a place to be seen with a multi-ethnic crowd who heads up to the 33rd-floor Whiskey Sky bar to see even more. For a great late-night snack, small plates of mini-pannini, hummus, and olives are a good bet.

WISHBONE   ★★½

CAJUN/SOUTHERN | INEXPENSIVE | QUALITY ★★★★ | VALUE ★★★★★ | ZONES 1, 2

3300 North Lincoln Avenue; (773) 549-2663
1001 West Washington Boulevard; (312) 850-2663

Reservations Required at lunch for parties of 6 or more **When to go** Brunch, casual dinner **Entrée range** $8—$15 **Payment** V, MC, AMEX, DC, D **Service rating** ★★

Friendliness rating ★★★ **Parking** Valet, $6; street **Bar** Full service **Wine selection** Limited, $14–$25; 13 by the glass, $5–$8 **Dress** Casual **Disabled access** Wheelchair accessible **Customers** Come-as-you-are locals, families

Breakfast Monday–Friday, 7–11 a.m.; Saturday and Sunday, 8–11 am

Lunch Monday–Friday, 11 a.m.–3 p.m.; Saturday and Sunday, 11 a.m.–2:30 p.m.

Dinner Tuesday–Thursday, 5–10 p.m.; Friday and Saturday, 5–11 p.m.; Sunday, 5–9 p.m.

Setting & atmosphere This funky-casual, warehouse-style restaurant is a big, exposed brick room with lots of windows and whimsical chicken-and-egg art. There's a cafeteria-style counter for quick, inexpensive meals.

House specialties Menu specialties change daily. Possibilities include: shrimp sautéed with bacon, mushrooms, and scallions, served over cheese grits; baked bone-in ham with honey mustard sauce; blackened catfish (fresh farm-raised catfish fillet, blackened with Cajun spices); yardbird (charbroiled chicken with a sweet red pepper sauce); red eggs (two eggs over corn tortillas with black beans, cheese, chili ancho sauce, scallions, sour cream, and salsa); crunchy French toast (French toast dipped in corn flakes).

Other recommendations Louisiana chicken salad (enormous salad with blackened chicken breast and corn muffin); North Carolina crab cakes; hoppin' John or hoppin' Jack (vegetarian black-eyed peas or black beans on rice with cheddar cheese, scallions, and tomatoes); breakfast burrito; omelets; biscuits and gravy.

Summary & comments Now that the good ol' original Wishbone is closed, the other two locations take on the casual dining and tousled brunch crowd. The food is hearty and inexpensive, though hit or miss. There are numerous vegetarian options, as well as full-pint Bloody Marys. When it's busy, it's a big, mostly happy free-for-all, and the servers in their corn zeppelin disaster T-shirts (and the scrambling bussers, too) deserve combat pay.

Part Ten

Shopping in Chicago

Nothing Like It Back Home

Visitors who come here expecting second (or third) city are overjoyed. Time was, fashion was the resultant mélange of trends that blew in from the Coast (either one). No more. Said mélange floated down Boul Mich, blew west across the Loop, fanned north and south, and became Chicago Style. Suddenly, the world sat up and took notice.

The City of Big Shoulders still takes the best of the West, combines it with the best of the East, imports every possible plum from abroad, adds the dash that is all its own, and comes up with the formula that puts the chic in Chicago. As a clever copywriter for Marshall Field's said so succinctly long ago: "There's nothing like it back home."

The savviest locals will tell you style has nothing to do with how much you spend; it's how you spend it. Chic, elan, verve, and all those natty synonyms are rooted in curiosity and vitality, indigenous to Chicago. Style has nothing to do with what's In or Out, and everything to do with aesthetics (and fun). Great taste means it would be nice to own an original Cézanne, but you can still stir the senses with a stunning litho created by a local artist and purchased at a local gallery.

The question is, in a city this size, where should you look? There's always the obvious Michigan Avenue, but what about those neighborhood boutiques that are the natives' well-kept secrets? Sorry, natives, it's time to divulge the wheres and how-to-find-its.

The Where of It

Chicago shopping is centered downtown. First, bordered by the Chicago River on both the north and west is **the Loop,** a 35-block cornucopia of retail action circumscribed by elevated train tracks and home of the giant Marshall Field's and Carson Pirie Scott department stores. For years, the empty lot known as "Block 37" (which, in winter becomes a skating rink and in summer houses an art gallery) has been chronically reputed to become another big Loop department store; so far, it hasn't happened, but hope springs eternal. It should be mentioned, additionally, that the area is a busy theater district.

Moving north of the river is the so-called **Magnificent Mile** where grand malls and opulent boutiques flank both sides of Michigan Avenue. The **Near North Side**—our Zone 3, known for streets that fan east and west of the Magnificent Mile, including the "tree streets": Maple, Chestnut, Oak, etc.—is home to small pockets of eclectic shopping pleasures. Off the north end of Michigan Avenue, heading west, **Oak Street** is a shopping venue in its own right. Ritzy, upscale, exclusive, and generally expensive, Oak's single block is designer fashion headquarters. **River North,** on the west side of Near North, is the epicenter of Chicago's art, antique, and designer furniture scene.

Moving beyond Near North and River North and away from downtown are **Lincoln Park** and the ever-burgeoning **Bucktown** (and Wicker Park) area. The latter, west of downtown, is filled with shopping, gallery hopping and great dining, too, since some of the city's most interesting restaurants are nearby. Some galleries, moving even further west, have created an area known as the **New West Side.**

Lincoln Park's parallel streets of **Webster** and **Armitage** are such fun they warrant time of their own, though neither has shopping areas that are all that large. Because most of these shops are "Mom and Pop" operations, with the owners usually on site, they provide an antidote to any impersonality you might find on Boul Mich. In this same area, the north-south streets of **Halsted, Clark,** and **Southport** amble for miles, sometimes in a drab fashion, occasionally glowing with a shop or two and restaurants to rival top areas in the city. **Lincoln Avenue,** slanting northwest from Lincoln Park, is less likely to glow, but has some surprising charmers that refute that theory.

Cut east and head north along the lake into **Evanston.** When you're finished trooping the Northwestern campus, avail yourself of some of the town's good shopping. North of Evanston are affluent and shopping-rich communities such as **Wilmette, Winnetka, Glencoe, Northbrook, Highland Park,** and **Lake Forest.** To the north is **Milwaukee** (Wisconsin), but before you get there, stop at **Gurnee Mills** in Gurnee for your Ph.D. in outlet shopping.

To the west, suburban communities such as **Schaumburg, Oakbrook, Hinsdale, Geneva, St. Charles, Elgin,** and many others offer occasionally awesome browsing (both shopping centers and boutiques).

The How of It

Because people shop Chicago's Michigan Avenue as if it's one huge consolidated shopping center, that is the way we have presented it. Block by block, we describe the malls and the stores in and between them without attempting to organize what's available into specific categories of goods and services. As much an attraction as a repository of goods, Michigan Avenue is a browser's paradise. No shopping list or agenda is required. Simply set off to walk the Magnificent Mile and some article or item will thrust itself upon you and insist you buy it. The aggregation of merchandise is so vast that you generally don't need to concern yourself with its availability. If it can be sold in a store, you'll find it on Michigan Avenue.

In discussing the other downtown and Greater Chicago shopping venues, however, the territory is immense and the stores geographically dispersed. Off Michigan Avenue it's more important, and sometimes necessary, to define what you are shopping for. When we talk about shopping in the myriad stores of the Loop, Oak Street, Near North, River North, and beyond, we organize our discussion around specific genres of merchandise. Some Michigan Avenue stores not incorporated in malls are also included in these categories.

Michigan Avenue: The Magnificent Mile

From the Chicago River north along Michigan Avenue is America's largest concentration of upscale shopping, known collectively as the "Miracle" or "Magnificent" Mile. Leading department stores anchor a dazzling array of chain stores, boutiques, and malls. It is a place where department stores are grander and boutiques more specialized, and where even chain habitués of suburban malls are enticingly fashioned (Gap, take a bow). Many stars in this shopping galaxy are neatly integrated into malls tucked away inside huge buildings. Imagine ducking into a streetside shop that opens unexpectedly into canyons of retail concourses. To shopping junkies, the discovery of these merchandise cities is akin to passing through the looking glass. And the malls are fairly gorgeous: Chicago Place, Water Tower Place, and 900 North Michigan, for three.

It is no secret that Oprah loves Michigan Avenue (and Chicago shopping, in general). Another talk-show host, Jenny Jones, who once arrived from L.A. to set up in Chicago, confided that she was dazzled by the proximity of so many great stores. "Everything in L.A.," she lamented, "is a car ride away."

True. Add five B's (Bloomingdale's, Barneys, Burberry, Brooks Brothers, and Bulgari) to the likes of Field's, Lord & Taylor, Saks Fifth Avenue,

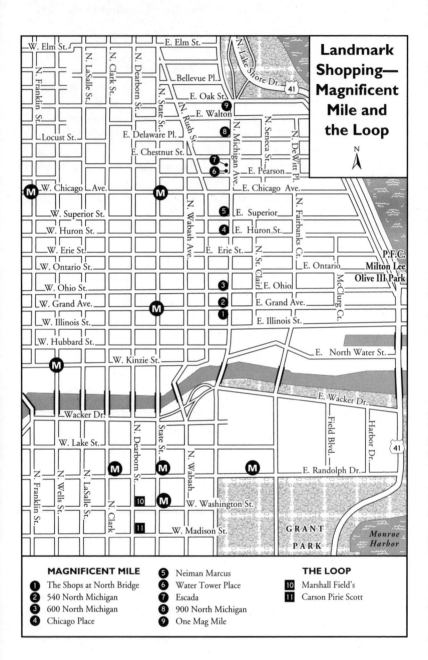

Landmark Shopping—Magnificent Mile and the Loop

N

MAGNIFICENT MILE

1. The Shops at North Bridge
2. 540 North Michigan
3. 600 North Michigan
4. Chicago Place
5. Neiman Marcus
6. Water Tower Place
7. Escada
8. 900 North Michigan
9. One Mag Mile

THE LOOP

10. Marshall Field's
11. Carson Pirie Scott

Neiman Marcus, Chanel, Ralph Lauren, and dozens more sometimes within a two-block area, and it's shopper's paradise.

Michigan Avenue's Grand Malls

Until September 2000, while there was some shopping on Michigan Avenue between the river and Ohio Street, most of the primo shops were concentrated in the nine blocks from Ontario north to Oak. This changed when the "mall" at 520 North Michigan known as North Bridge and housing the city's first **Nordstrom** (phone (312) 379-4300) opened (though suburban Nordstroms were already ensconced). The 271,000-square-foot, four-level fashion specialty store is strong on cosmetics, "style stations," men's bath and spa shop, fitting rooms to accommodate persons with disabilities, kid stuff on level three, a concierge desk, and two restaurants. For general information about **The Shops At North Bridge,** call the concierge desk at (312) 327-2300). The Shops include 35 other retailers, such as **Tommy Bahama** (sportswear), **Oilily** (vivid fashions for women and children), **A/X Armani** and **F. Carriere** (apparel), **Mephisto** (shoes, courtesy of Peter Hanig, whose store **Hanig's** is at 660 North Michigan), **Soco** (handbags), **C.D. Peacock** (another big-name Chicago area jeweler), **Benetton** (women and children), third-level joys for kids called **LEGO® Store** and **Lego Construction Zone** play area, and **Store of Science,** plus children's wear (well-priced and fashionable) at **The Children's Place, Jordan Marie** (clothing for babies, toddlers), and the girlhood rave **Sanrio's Hello Kitty. Sephora** (grooming aids and women's designer cosmetics by the ton) and the first **Hugo Boss** on Michigan Avenue are here, and on the fourth level are eight Chicago-style eateries, including **Cafe Salsa, Tuscany Cafe,** and **Fluky's, Cafe Typhoon,** and **Chen & Weinstein** (a deli).

540 North Michigan   This block houses a **Virgin Entertainment** (phone (312) 245-0488) emporium and **Kenneth Cole** (phone (312) 644-1163) for clothing, shoes, and accessories. Among the chains of note, there's a new **Gap** at 555 North Michigan (there are three Gap stores on Michigan Avenue, and they wrap up clothes for adults, kids, and babies). **Guess** at 605 North Michigan (phone (312) 440-9665) of course attracts the younger crowd.

600 North Michigan   This mall houses **Eddie Bauer** (phone (312) 951-5888), where you'll find outdoor goods and gear for men and women, with everything from parkas to stainless-steel lunch bottles. At **Levi's the Original Store,** (phone (312) 642-9613) women can buy "customized" Levi's (thanks to the store's unique Personal Pair jeans-that-fit service). Also in this mall are **Marshalls** (phone (312) 280-7506), **Linens & Things** (phone (312) 787-0462), **Cineplex Odeon** theaters (entrance at the corner of Rush and Ohio Streets, phone (312) 255-9340), **Ann Taylor** (phone (312) 587-8301), and **H₂O Plus** (phone (312) 397-1243).

Chicago Place   The eight-level shopping center at 700 North Michigan known as Chicago Place has one of the nation's prettiest **Saks Fifth Avenue** stores and some 45 specialty stores, including **Ann Taylor; Talbots** (phone (312) 944-6059), with clothes from petites to slightly larger sizes; outstanding furs at **Abby & Yanni** (phone (312) 988-7188); terrific togs at **Tall Girl Shops** (phone (312) 649-1303); a hugely expanded **Room & Board** home furnishings (phone (312) 266-0656), and its contemporary furniture sibling **Retrospect** (phone (312) 440-1270); and a refurbished **Williams-Sonoma** (phone (312) 787-8991). There are also decorative arts galleries, such as famed **Chiaroscuro** (phone (312) 988-9253), where the wares of 300 artists and artisans are shown (including jewelry, glass, furniture, and mixed media); and a terrific collection of fine art direct from their French headquarters (wonderful street scenes of Paris) at **Matignon Galleries,** level three, (phone (312) 255-0909). In that same international mode, **Russian Creations** (phone (312) 573-0792) may or may not be the only place in Chicago where you can find some brilliantly painted Russian nesting dolls (called matryoshka, a symbol of Russian folk art), $35 and up.

If you can't jet to County Cork, **Joy of Ireland** (phone (312) 664-7290) imports gifts and goodies to compensate. Another attraction is **Umbria Ceramics** (phone (312) 266-9600), where authentic Italian housewares and gifts are sublime. A recent traveler to Deruta, home of Umbrian ceramics, returned from her Italian trip and soon after dropped into this beautiful gallery to find the same up-to-the-minute pasta bowl she'd been sure no one else had in the United States.

700 also houses bath and body products at **The Body Shop** (phone (312) 482-8301), coffee blends at **Torrefazione Italia** on the first level (phone (312) 266-6400), a winning food court with at least nine sources for yummies (including McDonald's), a fine florist shop, **A New Leaf** (phone (312) 649-7008), sprawling fragrantly throughout the first and fourth levels, and a year-round Christmas store called **Christmas on the Avenue,** third level (phone (312) 751-0506).

Finally, give the last word to glossy **Saks Fifth Avenue** (phone (312) 944-6500): The retailer has been on the avenue since 1929, and this is one of their showcase stores; everything always sparkles here. Find traditional and cutting-edge designers, a children's department, and an expanded home section on the seventh floor. Across the street at 717 North Michigan Avenue, the **Saks Men's Store** also dispenses fine wares. There are also Saks stores at Oakbrook Shopping Center, Old Orchard, and a new beauty in Highland Park. The low-end (one hesitates to say "cut-rate" about anything Saks-ish) **Saks Off Fifth Avenue** stores are in Schaumburg and Gurnee Mills.

Neiman Marcus   Just down the avenue from 700 is a nonmalled titan, **Neiman Marcus,** at 737 North Michigan (phone (312) 642-5900). Suburbanites (who adore the NM at Northbrook Court in Northbrook) swear that NM is the only reason they trek into the city. Says one, firmly: "This is Michigan Avenue's best store. I can find evening wear there and designer jewelry I can't find anywhere else." You have been warned. (Note also great gift wrapping with ornamentation of packages a specialty, a **Zodiac** restaurant known for signature popovers, a superb designer shoe salon, unique home decor items in their gift galleries, and cosmetics, beauty, and bath items on the first floor).

Water Tower Place   At 835 North Michigan is the seven-level marble palace known as Water Tower Place, anchored by **Marshall Field's** and **Lord & Taylor.** Once past the beautiful entrance (the bubbling waterfall is soothing), you may think this is chainsville, but some of the retailers may surprise you. Take **The Goldsmith** (phone (312) 751-1986) on the mezzanine, where designer Sherry Bender is turning out some of the most entrancing custom jewelry in the city. Of the more than 100 specialty shops at WTP, some are exclusive to Chicago, some to the area. In apparel, there's everything from Tweety Bird sweatshirts at the **Warner Bros.' Studio Store** and kids' things at **Abercrombie (& Fitch) Kids, Baby Gap, Gymboree, Jacadi,** and **Limited Too,** to **Louis Vuitton** leathers on three, and clothing stores for women such as beauteous **Eileen Fisher** (phone (312) 943-9190) on level two, **J.Jill** (the only one in Chicago; (312) 712-9940) on level six, **BBSP, Elisabeth, Chico's,** and **August Max Woman.** A must-investigate specialty shop is **Chiasso** (phone (312) 280-1249), with things for the home , the kids (ladybug night lights), the hostess (the Anna corkscrew in a metal "dress"), and more. A new attraction is **Aura Science** (phone (312) 440-0517), filled with the spacious store's own beautifully packaged cosmetics and skin care products on level five.

One of the more interesting aspects of this fun shopping center is the vast food court called **foodlife,** where you can dig into (or take out) almost anything, from tacos to freshly baked pies. Ensconced here, lounging amid the fake greenery while forking good pasta, it may become easy to forget you're in the middle of a huge city. A noteworthy plus is that foodlife has a market, so you can run in and pick up a bottle of wine, beautiful breads, sauces, home-cooked meals (even macaroni and cheese, poached salmon, etc.). Tucked into a space behind the food court is a restaurant called **Mity Nice Grill;** calm and filled with delicious menu items, it's one of the mall's best-kept secrets, as is the market. Other new dining options are on the horizon, soon to be announced. And if you can't wait, run up to **Harry & David** on level three for some jams, fruits, and other goodies.

The children's paradise, **FAO Schwarz,** opened its luscious free-standing candy store, **FAO Schweetz,** on level two here, delighting families with a giant gumball machine, a lollipop forest, and over 250 bulk candy bins. FAO Schwarz, the stunning toy emporium, is not in this mall but across the street at 840 North Michigan, where adults have as much fun gawking at the stuffed animals, toys, and games as the diminutive shoppers.

Escada   On this block is **Escada** (840 North Michigan; (312) 915-0500), a smaller, luxe, four-floor mall that offers **Escada, Escada Sport, Escada Couture,** a full line of accessories (including leather goods), an enlarged shoe salon, and **Escada Beaute** fragrance. The shoes are particularly good here, and the store director can arrange for same-day delivery to homes, offices, and hotels; the director will also provide gratis gift wrap and car service if needed.

900 North Michigan   Close by is the formidable 900 North Michigan, which houses **Bloomingdale's** (phone (312) 440-4460), gorgeous **Gucci** (phone (312) 664-5504), silvery **Pavilion Christofle** (phone (312) 664-9700), and a city mall of elegant laid-back charm that makes it easy to shop. Bloomie's is full of surprises, offering a range of prices. Find shoes (divine ripoffs of styles attempted by only top designers, featured right along with shoes by the latter), superb housewares (bedding, kitchen, and tabletop items), and stop for a cappuccino at the cafe on six. They have everything; after you've found inexpensive jeans, you can go up a floor or two and find the priciest of import gowns. Cosmetics on the first floor offers extraordinary abundance.

A knockout boutique is on the fifth floor: the **Pavo Real Gallery of Animal Arts & Sculptures,** featuring artist Todd Warner's magical menagerie (including zebras, birds, and a sprawling frog). Also on five, **Galt Toys + Galt Baby** has items for kids who have a lot (but would always like a little more); tiny **Glove Me Tender** is the place to buy (natch) gloves, and they have hats, too. Among other clothing stores are the very major **Max Mara** (phone (312) 475-9500), at street level, **bebe, Yolanda Lorente** (phone (312) 867-0900), the designer whose exquisite gowns have long adorned local fashionables, **Club Monaco** (phone (312) 787-8757), and **Linda Campisano Millinery,** sixth level (phone (312) 337-1004), featuring custom-designed hats for women (and men). Here too is the **Mario Tricoci Hair Salon and Day Spa** (phone (312) 915-0960); and even more special, the fifth U.S. location of **Lalique** (phone (312) 867-1787), where you can pick up crystal, along with perfume, scarves, leather accessories, and porcelain. This store will be known for its commitment to Lalique's accessories collection (how about a crystal ring?). While on the first level, check the home accessories at **Rue Royale** (phone (312) 751-1700) and the divine shoes at **Stuart Weitzman** (phone (312) 943-5760), then waltz off to the sixth level to dine on Asian goodies at **Baisi Thai.**

You can't help but love 900 for its chic occasional pianist and its charm; the escalators are rather awkwardly spaced, but elevators make getting around easier

One Mag Mile   Across the street from the Drake Hotel is another marble palace, dubbed **"One Mag Mile"** by the developer, but it didn't stick (so don't expect a cabbie to know what you're talking about if you drop the name on him . . . the building is actually at 980 North Michigan). It's primarily residential, except for one of the best Italian cashmere houses, **Manrico Cashmere** (970 North Michigan; (312) 649-1114). After you've finished your sweater spending, go upstairs and have a glass of pinot grigio at **Spiaggia,** one of the city's best Italian restaurants. More shopping is in evidence across the street, where you'll find **Chanel, Georg Jensen,** and a mini cluster of other retailers housed at the Drake Hotel.

East of Michigan

East of Michigan Avenue (don't go too far, or you'll wind up in the lake) is a former shopping enclave, now dedicated exclusively to food. At 401 East Illinois is the massive food emporium **Fox & Obel** (see "Food and Wine"), and at 455 East Illinois, there's **Tavern on the Pier** and a **Starbucks.**

At **Navy Pier,** 600 East Grand Avenue on the Lake, you'll find one of the best places in the city to take the kids: the **Chicago Children's Museum,** with hands-on exhibits. Afterward, take them for a ride on the pier's Ferris wheel or to the Crystal Gardens for a snack. Call (312) 595-PIER for Pier info, and if you want to take a dinner cruise (ships depart from Navy Pier) you can choose between *Spirit of Chicago* cruises (phone (312) 836-7899), **Duck Cruises** (phone (800) 662-5285), or the more expensive **Odyssey** cruises (phone (800) 947-9367). Also at Navy Pier: the **Imax Theatre,** the terrific **Chicago Shakespeare Theatre,** and the **Smith Museum of Stained Glass Windows** (phone (312) 595-5024), where you'll find contemporary and vintage stained glass. Trinket shopping is available throughout the Pier premises.

The Landmark Department Stores of the Loop

South of the Chicago River and just west of Michigan Avenue is **the Loop,** circumscribed by elevated train tracks. As concerns shopping, this area falls into the "obvious" category. Nevertheless, even many locals don't realize just how interesting the Loop's treasure houses are. (And there are, usually, rumors of more to come.) The cliché for tourists, some say, is to avoid them; so, do the opposite. Even though these great stores can't obscure the fact that the Loop's glory comes and goes, visitors to the city, influenced by locals who shop only boutiques (whether they be Armani or thrift shops), may pass up a chance to investigate, and thus fail to bask in the light of these stars. So don't listen. Tell naysayers you know the stars aren't Out, they're very In. Go see.

Marshall Field's

Star One is **Marshall Field's** (111 North State Street; (312) 781-1000). The 7¼-ton clocks (at Randolph and Washington corners) that tower over this grandaddy of Chicago stores signal your arrival. Ongoing renovations include a fabulous new Beauty Department under the Tiffany Dome that arcs seven stories above the selling floor. The fragrance area features glass art, and there's a beautiful flower shop allowing you to pick a bouquet before trying cosmetics (from Armani to Yves Saint Laurent; a new line is Qiora). The Marketplace on the "lower level" (all basements should look like this) is where you can grab a sandwich. Of all the floors, chock-full of goods, their high-fashion "28 Shop" is a renovated stunner, as are their children's and accessories departments.

Marshall Field's is, arguably, the most beautiful department store in the country. It is also a source of firsts: first to establish a European buying office (in England in 1871); first to open a dining room in a department store; first to delight customers with lavish store window displays; and first United States store to start a bridal registry. Also notable is their Christmas season "Great Tree," towering 45 feet, which has delighted patrons for more than 82 yuletide seasons.

Architecturally, Field's is awesome. About that State Street Tiffany dome: it's the largest glass mosaic of its kind and the first ever built of iridescent glass. A 1992 addition—an 11-floor, 165-foot-high atrium—is another knockout.

Field's is probably the only store of its kind that burned down twice in its history (once, when it was Field & Leiter, during the great Chicago Fire of 1871, and again, in 1873). Leiter retired in 1881, and the store became Marshall Field & Co., reigning in this fashion almost a century until it became part of the Department Store Division of the Dayton Hudson Corporation in 1990, re-named Target Corporation. Field's owns 64 stores in Illinois, Wisconsin, Ohio, Indiana, Minnesota, Michigan, North Dakota, and South Dakota.

But, back to this one. Perhaps the best way to shop Field's is to pretend you're exploring a small village.

There's a huge store for men (the largest selection of shirts and ties in the Midwest). On two are **men's suits and coats,** with designer separates,

Armani, Donna Karan, Tommy Hilfiger, and Polo Shop. Women enjoy designer wares on three as well at **Select** (free personal shopping). Also on three is **Petites.** On four is the renovated **women's shoe department** (now 16,000 square feet).

Five is for **kid stuff,** as well as **intimate apparel,** the **beauty salon,** and Women's Way **larger-sized fashions.**

The highlight of six is the **home store,** with crystal galleries, antique silver, a shop for designer bed linens, and more than 500 china patterns on display (but thousands may be ordered). The hot new **gallery in crystal,** joining huge collections of Hoya, Orrefors, Baccarat, Waterford, Swarovski, and Lalique, is Steuben. Field's **Christofle** joins in offering flatware patterns, china, and crystal, and there are also departments here for **quilts** and corporate gifts. This is the only department store in the country that has Pickard china; they're known for doing embassy china.

The newly renovated seventh floor (State Street) is largely dedicated to **food.** A recent renovation has created and updated some fine attractions. The famed **Walnut Room** has a center fountain, and the plates here feature the Norman Rockwell painting of Field's famous Great Clock. (Both natives and tourists make a point to come to the Walnut Room at Christmas to gape at the Great Tree.) The **Frango Cafe** is a 140-seat cafe featuring soups, salads, sandwiches, ice cream delights, a children's menu, bakery, and dessert bar. An open atrium area houses the **7 on State Gourmet Food Stations,** seating 450 people and with goodies that range from soups to noodles. A new **Visitor Services Center** has been relocated to the seventh floor as well.

On the lower level of State the newly-remodeled **Marketplace Food Court** includes a deli, a bakery, and "Marketplace Lite" foods for calorie counters, and **Hinky Dink Kenna's** pub (on the pedway) connects you underground to other Loop addresses.

The eighth floor is earmarked for **furniture,** including separate galleries for Ralph Lauren Furniture, Thomas O'Brien for Hickory Chair, Kindel, and Barbara Barry for Baker. The 2,000-square-foot **Trend House** rooms are here, and what Field's people claim (who knows?) is the largest **Oriental carpet** collection of any U.S. department store.

Carson Pirie Scott

Heading south on State, shoppers find another Loop star, **Carson Pirie Scott** (1 South State Street; (312) 641-7000). When the great architect Louis H. Sullivan designed the building at State and Madison, he utilized the most modern construction technology available at the time, ensuring the store's place in the history of retailing. This flagship store was named a Chicago landmark in 1970 (and it's listed in the National Register of

Historic Places). Today, having passed its 142nd year, CPS deserves its status for its ever-innovative direction. The 1994 first-floor State renovation revitalized the original Sullivan floor plan and the columns; 1999 brought even more remodeling.

You can find the best here, from fashion to furniture. Beginning on the lower level are **men's career apparel, men's outerwear, luggage, optical, shoe repair, juniors,** and a **John's** popcorn and subs franchise.

On the main level are **cosmetics, handbags, accessories,** and the new **hosiery** shop has its own entrance. The first-floor Wabash side is home to **men's furnishings, fragrance,** a **Dockers'** shop, **Polo by Ralph Lauren, Nautica,** and **Roots** shops.

On level two, women find **better sportswear, bridge lines,** and **maternity** and **petite** departments, while men find a **Big & Tall** shop, **better sportswear, young men's,** and **men's shoes.** A busy **TicketMaster** ticket center is also on this floor, plus a small **post office, dry cleaner,** and **Wardrobe Consulting,** housed in the historic Rotunda. On level three is the newly remodeled **women's shoe** department—one of the country's largest at 30,000 square feet—and here too are **women's coats, furs,** and the **Salon at Carson Pirie Scott.** On level four for women are the remodeled **intimate apparel** and **Moderate** departments, while level five houses a collectors' **Sports Memorabilia Shop** (rare coins, signed footballs), plus **stationery** and a 40,000-square-foot **furniture** gallery with an interior design studio.

Level six features the **Home Store,** with a computerized gift registry (type in the giftees' names to see what they've registered for). Level seven is home to the **children's** departments and a magical **Trim-A-Home Shop** (open mid-September through early January).

Hungry? The **Cream City Cafe** on first floor Wabash is open at 7:30 a.m. Grab coffee, muffins, and other goodies; you'll also find postcards, Chicago-themed T-shirts, local crafts, and boxed candy in this section, as well as a great selection of team merchandise, for fans (Cubs and Sox jerseys, for instance).

The Corporate Gifts division enables one-stop shopping to enhance a corporate image; for company gifts and awards, call (800) 945-GIFT.

Carson's also has the ability to assist disabled customers. Full-time shoppers serve this clientele, but you must call in advance for an appointment (whether single or group).

There are 27 CPS stores and 4 furniture galleries in the Chicago area. In addition to the State Street store, there are other city stores at Harlem-Irving Plaza on the north side and at 120 South Riverside Plaza (near Union Station). They're also at suburban malls, including Chicago Ridge, Ford City, Stratford Square, Spring Hill, Lincoln Mall

(Matteson), Randhurst, North Riverside, Orland Square, Edens Plaza (take the Lake East exit on the Edens Expressway) and the new Woodfield store.

Where to Find . . .

If you choose not to shop in a Michigan Avenue mall or in one of the huge department stores in the Loop, there is a distinct possibility that you are looking for something specific. We have, therefore, chopped the remainder of the Chicago shopping iceberg into neat little categories to make it easy to find what you want.

Glaring Omissions

There are some rather glaring omissions here, so before someone says, "What about **Old Navy, Victoria's Secret,** or **Barnes & Noble**?" let us hasten to say they are very much alive and glowing. You may also have heard of **Enzo Angiolini Shoes** (701 North Michigan does carry the full line, though many stores carry a limited amount). Of course there are many more, but that's enough about chain stores. Seek and ye shall find them easily enough, as they're everywhere in Chicago.

Art and Fine Crafts

In the Loop   Be sure to take a thorough look-see at one of the city's most tasteful (and too-little-known) galleries: the **Illinois Artisans Shop** (100 West Randolph Street; (312) 814-5321), at Clark Street, otherwise known as the State of Illinois building, Suite 2–200. Everything here is handmade by Illinois artists. Into this category fall jewelry, glass, ceramics, handwoven wearable art, quilts, baskets, dolls, woodworking, ironwork, prints, paintings, sculpture, and photographs. Trust us on this. Hours are 9 a.m.–5 p.m., Monday–Friday.

At the south end of Michigan Avenue is the **Chicago Architecture Foundation Store** (224 South Michigan Avenue; (312) 922-3432), full of architecture and design books and quality Chicago memorabilia. At 618 South Michigan Avenue, the **Spertus Museum** (phone (312) 322-1747) of the Spertus Institute of Jewish Studies, the **Bariff Shop of Judaica** (phone (312) 322-1740) is a lovely place to buy anything from books and jewelry to a Passover plate or a menorah made in Israel.

Several fine galleries are going into what's sometimes known as **West Loop Gate,** west of the Loop. Notable among them is **Donald Young Gallery** (933 West Washington Boulevard; (312) 455-0100), where Young specializes in contemporary art, displaying such artists as Bruce Nauman, Sol LeWitt, and others in the gallery's 5,000 square feet of space. Nearby, at 835 West Washington Boulevard, other fine galleries have set up shop: **Jan Cicero** (phone (312) 733-9551), **Vedanta Gallery** (phone (312) 492-6692), and others mentioned later.

On North Michigan Avenue   There was a time when Michigan Avenue not only was the retail repository of the Midwest's best but also was dotted with a parcel of some of the city's best art galleries. Many have moved to the River North area, but among those remaining are the **Richard Gray Gallery,** one of Chicago's outstanding dealers in fine art (875 North Michigan Avenue, the John Hancock Building, level 25; (312) 642-8877), and **R. S. Johnson Fine Art** (Suite 234, 645 North Michigan; (312) 943-1661). **Stephen Solovy Fine Arts** (phone (312) 664-4860) joins only a few others still on the Avenue at 980 North Michigan.

When you say "art in Chicago," your number one thought should be the **Art Institute of Chicago,** the magnificent institution south of the Chicago River (Michigan Avenue at Adams—Zone 4) that consistently outpaces the finest museums in the world. Also extraordinary is the **Art Institute Museum Store** (phone (312) 443-3583), which was one of Chicago's best-kept secrets for too long; it provides a fascinating array of delectables. Find the Midwest's best art books, posters, T-shirts, and notecards—everything from a Monet-inspired paperweight to Impressionist-inspired scarves, unique designs of Baltic amber jewelry, Monet prints, even umbrellas, such as a scenic one called "Paris Street, Rainy Day" by "urban impressionist" Gustave Caillebotte ($36, and there's a collapsible size at $20, one of the most popular items ever carried in the store). And much more.

Another beauteous store, generously trimmed in oak, is a highlight of the **Museum of Contemporary Art** (220 East Chicago Avenue; (312) 280-2660). Called **Culturecounter,** the MCA Store & Bookstore (the store is on the first level, with the bookstore on the second floor), the two levels are connected by a sweeping two-story winding staircase under a skylight centering this light, bright, and airy backdrop for artful works, wares, books and toys. You'll find such items as rare and fine contemporary art books, compact discs (they shine in experimental music), wonderful animal masks, mobiles, interesting jewelry, candles, and (a particular strength) high design in home and tabletop gifts. **Puck's at the MCA** is the cafe for lunch. Dine al fresco in good weather on the granite terrace off the sculpture garden. It's just a few feet from the shops on Michigan Avenue, but it feels like a world away.

At the **Terra Museum of American Art** (666 North Michigan; (312) 664-3939), which concentrates on American art and exhibitions, a bright museum store features a wide variety of collectible art prints, books, paper goods, children's interactive games, and crafts; all are suffused with Americana. Exhibits here have ranged from the American

West to the photography of Robert Capa; all bear testimony to the great taste of founder Daniel J. Terra.

The **Chicago Cultural Center** (78 East Washington Street; (312) FINE-ART) has ongoing exhibits that are original, usually intriguing, new to the city, and feature both emergent and recognized artists. The exhibits are free of charge and a real attraction.

Near North **Joy Horwich** closed her gallery to become an art consultant running wonderful tours to art-filled places (from the Getty Museum in California to Bilbao, Spain, to Berlin and Prague, as well as to the Milwaukee Museum). She also takes individuals and families on personalized, offbeat, and conventional artistic and cultural jaunts in Chicago (such as trips to an auction house or to an artist's studio). Call (773) 327-3366 for information.

Just off Michigan Avenue is **The American Artisan** (44 East Superior Street; (312) 787-5780), an invaluable treasure trove if you're looking for crafts you don't see elsewhere. The tiny gallery is packed with unique finds, such as blown glass in gorgeous colors, ceramics, wood- and metalwork, contemporary pewter serving pieces, and more.

Two other finds must be mentioned just off Michigan Avenue. **The Hart Gallery** (64 East Walton; (312) 932-9646) has contemporary European drawings, paintings, and sculpture, with an emphasis on artists from Eastern Europe and Germany. Just east of Michigan Avenue is **Johnson Antiques** (172 East Walton Street; (312) 440-9466) a lovely shop with a green awning where Phyllis Johnson offers antique jewelry (Georgian to Art Deco) and silver (Georgian to the Arts and Crafts period).

Several galleries brighten Oak Street. One is **Aaron Galleries** (second floor, 50 East Oak), where you'll find 19th- and early-20th-century American paintings and master prints; there's also **Malcolm Franklin** (34 East Oak; (312) 337-0202).

Another Oak Street gem is **The Colletti Collection** (67 East Oak; (312) 664-6767), offering a primarily European collection of posters circa 1880–1940, fine art ceramics, stunning furniture, glass, and more. If you're in the market for a Mucha or Toulouse-Lautrec poster, this is the spot for you.

River North Van Gogh might have given his other ear to stroll the hugely expanded **Pearl Art & Craft Supply** (225 West Chicago Avenue; (312) 915-0200). The mostly discount store provides an incredibly wide supply of materials for artisans. Making jewelry? Beads overflow. Want a choice of brushes? Options abound. Staffers get a feel for what you want, whether you're a professional or a hobbyist. Hundreds of new handmade papers come from around the world.

To begin our discussion of the gallery district, we'll attempt a quick summation (then you can go and make up your own mind). Two antiques sources are **Jay Roberts Antiques Warehouse** (149 West Kinzie; (312) 222-0167) and **Spencer Jolly** (124 West Kinzie; (312) 595-0018), a specialist in early 17th- through 19th-century European antiques.

Robert Henry Adams Fine Art (715 North Franklin; (312) 642-8700) features American modern paintings, drawings, and sculpture, prior to 1950. The **Douglas Dawson Gallery** (222 West Huron; (312) 751-1961) is widely known for ancient and historic ethnic arts from Asia, Africa, and the Americas (textiles, ceramics, furniture, and sculpture); nearby is the **Zolla/Lieberman Gallery** (325 West Huron; (312) 944-1990), featuring contemporary painting, sculpture, and works on paper. You'll find **Aldo Castillo Gallery** (233 West Huron; (312) 337-2536) here, specializing in Latin American art.

When you hit Superior Street, the galleries come thicker and faster. It's fun to wander Superior and stop when the feeling (or the gallery) moves you. **Portia Gallery** (207 West; (312) 932-9500) is the place for fine contemporary art glass. In the **300 Building** are **Catherine Edelman** (phone (312) 266-2350) for contemporary photography and the **Judy A. Saslow Gallery** (phone (312) 943-0530) for a global mix of outsider, self-taught, folk, and ethnographic works, and contemporary artists.

Another notable is **Steven Daiter Gallery** (311 West; (312) 787-3350); photography is special here, especially vintage black-and-white photos. **Printworks** (phone (312) 664-9407), with contemporary prints, drawings, photographs, and artists' books, is also at 311 West, as is **Michael Fitzsimmons Decorative Arts** (phone (312) 787-0496), home of Arts & Crafts–era works in most media. **Perimeter Gallery** (210 West; (312) 266-9473), specializes in contemporary fine art (also ceramics, works on paper, and metalwork) by internationally recognized artists.

A word must be said about **Architech** (730 North Franklin; (312) 475-1290), where you'll see a wonderful array of architectural drawings. You may also want to drop into **Carol Ehlers Gallery, Ltd.** (750 North Orleans Street; (312) 642-8611); she specializes in 20th-century master and contemporary photography. And it's always fun to stop into **Tigerman Himmel Decorative Arts & Design** (212 West Chicago Avenue; (312) 337-8300) for antique and contemporary furniture, fine art, and Euro-Asian objects.

One of the best galleries in this area is **Roy Boyd** (739 North Wells Street; (312) 642-1606). Exhibits here tend not to disappoint, and they're likely to be contemporary. Nearby is **Carl Hammer Gallery** (740 North Wells; (312) 266-8512) with contemporary and selected masterworks, with an emphasis on self-taught artists. **Primitive Art Works** (706 North Wells; (312) 943-3770) features four floors of tribal and ethnic displays of authentic international textiles, rugs, jewelry, and artifacts.

You can hang the goods at **Vintage Posters International** (1551 North Wells; (312) 951-6681). Here, owner Susan Cutler not only displays fashion and Euro advertising posters, but also 20th-century furniture, lighting, accessories, some costume/vintage jewelry, and 20th-century objects of art.

West (and West Loop Gate) **Aron Packer Gallery** (phone (312) 226-8984) has moved to 118 North Peoria, where you'll find contemporary, outsider, and folk art in all media. Also at 118 is **Rhona Hoffman Gallery** (phone (312)455-1990). Featured here are contemporary works by Americans and Europeans, both established and less-well-known artists. **Moniquemeloche** (951 West Fulton Market; (312) 455-0299) is the place for contemporary work in all media by primarily emerging and mid-career artists. A final suggestion in this area is **Thomas McCormick** (835 West Washington; (312) 226-6800), for modern and contemporary American painting.

Lincoln Park/Clybourn Corridor/and Farther North **Fortunate Discoveries** (1022 West Armitage; (773) 404-0212) purveys ethnic art accessories such as Swat (Pakistan) windows; wonderful Kilim rugs from Turkey, Afghanistan, Persia, and Russia; and interesting, one-of-a-kind pillows and artifacts from around the world.

Art Effect (934 West Armitage Avenue; (312) 664-0997) is one of the first stores to feature wearable art, and that's still one of its strong points. National artists' works are displayed here, with attention paid to clothes, jewelry, and items for the home. There are several interesting stores and galleries to be found in Wicker Park/Bucktown. One of the most enticing is **Pagoda Red** (1714 North Damen; (773) 235-1188) an urban oasis with an oriental garden full of 18th- to 19th-century Chinese furniture and artifacts. **Pavilion Antiques** (2055 North Damen; (773) 645-0924) has French antiques, mostly furniture. Another fulsome boutique is **Cielo Vivo** (1528 North Milwaukee Avenue; (773) 276-8012). This is sort of a don't-follow-your-first-instinct-to-skip-this-place place; it's crammed with everything from Han dynasty figurines to amber necklaces from Morocco and Afghanistan. Here are some antique African American dolls, a Chinese wooden chair from the 19th century ($300), basketry, and some of the best textiles collected in the city.

A find to the north in an area blooming with galleries lately is the **Judith Racht Gallery** (3727 North Southport Avenue; (773) 261-3705) in the Music Box (theater) building. Known for her Michigan/Indiana Dunes country gallery, Racht features a mélange of contemporary art, outsider art, furniture, and even antique quilts.

Baby Furniture

Bellini (2001 North Halsted Street; (312) 6696) is a synonym for beautiful furniture for baby. From cribs to dressing tables to first beds for tots, they're here, along with rocking chairs, high chairs, strollers, clothing (up to toddler 4), and fun bedroom furnishings such as colorful crib linens and mobiles. Many of these pieces are imports; few are bargain priced, but all are unusual and will make baby sit up and take notice. They also do teen beds and bedding.

Cradles of Distinction (2100 North Southport; (773) 472-1001) is a unique store where you can pick up not only layettes and kids' designer clothing (jackets in animal prints, faux furs, funky playwear) but also custom-designed bedding, furniture, gifts, and accessories. Cradles has another smaller chic store at 838 North Rush Street (phone (312) 703-9912) and there's a third store in the suburbs (Winnetka).

For the best in ordering childproofing services and safety products for the home, the leader is **Safety Matters** (phone (773) 281-BABY, and **www.safetymatters.com** on the web.

Beauty Items

Michigan Avenue   This probably should be filed under grooming, rather than beauty, because it's strictly for men: **Truefitt & Hill** (sixth level, 900 North Michigan Avenue; (312) 337-2525) is the perfect man's getaway from everything; in these English club–ish surroundings, he can have a hot lather shave, haircut, pedicure, bootshine, and all manner of stress-reducing packages.

Near North   On Oak Street, lined with really beautiful stores, the jewelbox salon of international perfume/cosmetic creator **Marilyn Miglin** (112 East Oak Street; (312) 943-1120) is right up there at the top for any woman. For one thing, this immaculate salon sparkles divinely, and it smells so good. Marilyn's perfumes include Pheromone ("the world's most precious perfume"), Goddess, Nirvana, and Destiny, and more are available. Her salon is known for its exquisite goods and services including facials, nail services, massage, and, of course, makeup applications.

Face & Facial (104 East Oak Street; (312) 951-5151) features internationally known facialist Mila Bravi. There are manicurists here, too, who are among the best (and not the most expensive) in the city. Another trained esthetician with a soothing touch is **Kathleen Peara,** a bit to the north at 154 West Schiller, Studio 2D (phone (312) 337-6734) where indulging in an aromatherapy facial will have you purring.

Hair salons in Near North aren't likely to indulge you with bargain prices, but they do deliver the goods. **Charles Ifergan** (106 East Oak; (312) 642-4484) is a trendsetting hair designer who wins national awards for his styles for men and women. The **Anita Russum Salon** (10 East Delaware Place; (312) 944-8533) is an oasis of tranquility where hair colorist Anita Russum works her magic. Again, no bargain prices, but the artistry performed by Russum (plus the skill of staffers) will win your heart.

Spas are proliferating in Chicago, and followers of the **Elizabeth Arden Red Door Salon** (919 North Michigan Avenue; (312) 988-9191) will be pleased with the beautiful, large environs (the entrance is on the Walton Street side). Hair colorist Maurice Bonamigo (direct line: (312) 664-6353) is big here. Then there's **Urban Oasis** (12 West Maple; (312) 587-3500), specializing in stress-freeing massage, and **Kiva** (196 East Pearson; (312) 840-8120) is very popular, with its Am-I-in-Santa Fe? ambience. No, you're next door to the Ritz-Carlton hotel, enjoying an oasis for body/mind/spirit nurturing, with every type of treatment—from aromatherapy and massages at the spa to pedicures and scalp analysis at the salon, and snacking on such treats as low-fat brownies. An outstanding salon/spa is **Spa Emilia** (21 West Elm; (312) 951-7415), a serene environment where Grace, Elizabeth, and their staff offer manicures and pedicures people rave about. A pampering pedicure might include the Royal Gelee (with warm paraffin). Spa Emelia facials center on Helena Kuchynkova, trained in Prague and an esthetician for ten years. The fabulous **Janet Sartin Institute of Skin Care** (46 East Pearson Street; (312) 397-1550) is ready and waiting to attend to facials (the Golden Spoons Facial Treatment with Collagen is a winner), massages, and everything from crystal exfoliation and oxygen treatments for the face to manicures. All of the super Sartin products are here, too, in their shiny bright yellow boxes. Finally, one of the best spas is **Urbana Salon and Spa** (70 East Walton; (312) 932-0345), known for facials, massages, and other beauty pleasures.

Also at 70 East Walton, note the **Robert Lucas Studio** (phone (312) 642-6640); Lucas excels as a stylist and color expert and has high-profile clients who swear by his expertise. Also in the Goldcoast area is **Anna Kay** (100 East Walton, #300; (312) 944-8500), a favorite among fashionables for her skin care. One of the city's top makeup artists is definitely **Diane Ayala** at Mon Ami Coiffeur Chicago (65 East Oak; (312) 943-4555) and in Highland Park. Finally, a welcome addition is **Marlena's Factory Outlet Store** (127 West Huron; (312) 266-4600), where you can pick up fragrances, makeup, and skincare products, all at prices less than retail. Goods change every two weeks: totes and cosmetics bags (closeouts, perfect quality), gift baskets, assorted bed and bath accessories, etc. We found crystal powder shakers here you don't see coming and going. This place is a find.

Bikes and Skateboards

Many find their way to **Turin Bicycle Store** in Evanston (1027 Davis Street; (847-864-7660), but let's stay in the city. If we start at North Avenue and work our way north on Halsted, we'll encounter a bike shop, **Quick Release** (1623 North Halsted Street; (773) 871-3110). They sell mostly mountain bikes, 26"-wheel type; Ross and Canadian Peugeot brands are sold here, among others; full- service repair shop. Beloved to others: **Kozy's Cyclery** (3712 North Halsted, (773) 281-2263); 1451 West Webster at Clybourn, (773) 528-2700); and 601 South LaSalle Street in the South Loop, (312) 360-0020). Voted the number one bike shop in Chicago by *Windy City Sports,* Kozy's carries Cannondale, Specialized, Gary Fisher, Schwinn, and Trek. **Cycle Smithy** (2468½ North Clark Street; (773) 281-0444) is popular, too (a lot of Lincoln Park's yups hang out here to get air in their tires).

A state-of-the-art hangout for the skateboard aficionado, **Push** (50 East Chicago Avenue; (312) 573-9996) has at least 250 skateboards, caps, skate products, urban streetwear, and shoes ("The toe must be reinforced to do the trick," says co-owner Brad Court).

Boats, Yachts, and Sailing Craft

Chicago has a limited boating season, but there are numerous marine dealerships in the area, particularly in the far north suburbs, including Fox Lake and Grayslake. **Brunswick,** based in Lake Forest, makes Sea Rays, Bayliners, Boston Whalers, Maxums, and others. Most are powered by Mercury Marine engines, another Brunswick company. **Outboard Marine Corporation,** based in Waukegan, produces marine engines under the brand name Johnson and Evinrude. Chicago has powerboat retailers in the suburbs, though none in the city proper. Notes Dave Leli of *Boating Magazine,* "Chicagoland is an active area for purchasing and selling pleasure boats." Meryl Papanek, Vice President of Marketing for the National Marine Manufacturers' Association says that the best way to check on what boat best suits you is to check their website **discoverboating.com**, put out by the trade association for the recreational boat industry. Their "boating guy" responds to e-mail questions (though he won't recommend brand names), and there's a calendar of events. "Another database for where to take lessons and find out about ramp sites and marinas is **waterworks.org,** which can help people narrow their focus. Visit by state." Papanek reports that there are three boat shows in the area: the **Chicago Boat, RV, and Outdoors Show,** held in January, with all the boats under one roof at McCormick Place (Zone 5); the (all-sailboat) **Strictly Sailboat Show** at Navy Pier (Zone 3), usually in February; and the **Midwest Boat Show,** generally in February in Rosemont (Zone 10).

Books, Cards, and Stationery

In the Loop   The son of legendary bookseller Stuart Brent, whose store stood on Michigan Avenue for 50 years, is Adam Brent. **Brent's Books & Cards, Ltd.** in the Loop (309 West Washington; (312) 364-0126) is where Adam has won success with his dedication to personal service. His well-read staff has a reverence for books, and the store offers author appearances and a huge selection of titles (including a wide selection of children's books). He's out to "match and exceed discounts at the mega-bookstores," with 10% off some hardcovers and 30% off current *New York Times* best sellers. The table where Adam seats authors for signings has a lot of history: Saul Bellow, Tom Wolfe, Nelson Algren, Truman Capote, Gore Vidal, and hundreds of others sat at that table with Stuart Brent. **Distinctive Bookbinding** (231 South LaSalle Street; (312) 658-1319) is the place to find the distinctive paper goods made by the Italian firm Pineider.

On Michigan Avenue   At Water Tower Place, **Papyrus** (phone (312) 266-9945) sells stationery, cards, and gifts (they're also at 209 South LaSalle). When it comes to books, the national chain titans continue to battle the small independent booksellers around the city, but even among the giant discounters, there are favorites. One of the best is **Borders** (830 North Michigan Avenue; (312) 573-0564), which has won over many readers with a caring staff, a vast supply of tomes (some 200,000 titles), music, a coffee cafe (featuring live jazz on occasional Friday evenings), children's story hours, and exciting author appearances.

What are stationery and cards without pens? Find the latter at **Montblanc** (900 North Michigan Avenue), home of the Limited Edition "Writer's Series" pens (coveted collectibles). And while you're here, pick up a Montblanc sport watch; they're gorgeous.

Near North   Rush Street, which once housed cabarets, now is home to several unique shops. **Children in Paradise Bookstore** (909 North Rush; (312) 951-5437) is a kids-only first in Chicago, where both children and their parents can browse among the tomes in happy-making surroundings. They sell kids' software in a complete section called Children in Technology. Older readers (11–15 years of age) might be found upstairs in an art supplies and activities section, separating them from the tots. A carpeted reading pit with pillows is used for weekly story hours (mornings, twice weekly).

On Oak Street   Oak isn't all fashion. You can find custom stationery and gifts (such as antique magnifying glasses and leather journals) at **The Watermark** (109 East Oak; (312) 337-5353).

River North   **Write Impressions** (211 West Huron Street; (312) 943-3306) is a source of paper goods (invitations are good here). **Paper**

Source (232 West Chicago Avenue; (312) 337-0798) is where we've noticed handmade rag papers (in fact all manner of unusual and special papers and notebooks), specialty books, ribbons, and wax seals. There are also gifts, such as glass pens. In short, shopping here is fun.

Lincoln Park/Clark/Clybourn Corridor A bookstore that has scored high with much of literary Chicago is **Barbara's Bookstore** (1350 North Wells Street; (312) 642-5044). Barbara's has been based in Old Town since 1963. Readings and author signings are regularly scheduled; staffers know their stuff; and the store pays attention to local authors. (Barbara's has another store at Navy Pier, and kiosks for downtown readers are located at Sears Tower and Northwestern Memorial Hospital; two suburban stores are in Oak Park and Lincolnshire.) **Hyde Park 57th Street Books** (1301 East 57th Street; (773) 684-1300) is also exemplary.

Used Books In the Loop, **Rain Dog Books & Cafe** (408 South Michigan Avenue; (312) 922-1200) is a first-rate source of books in high quality condition, and they have a good selection. Buy your choice and dine in their cafe.

North, on Lincoln Avenue at 2850 is another good used bookstore, **Powell's** (phone (773) 248-1444), which can also be found at 828 South Wabash (phone (312) 341-0748) and at 1501 East 57th Street in the Hyde Park neighborhood (phone (773) 955-7780). South Wabash is the largest, but we like the Lincoln Park location because it's usually so quiet that it's almost ghostly. In Hyde Park, a huge favorite (particularly for antiquarian books) is **O'Gara & Wilson** (1448 East 57th; (773) 363-0993). A friend says she found a book here that was printed circa 1500. And, for sheer atmosphere, hurry to rambling **Bookman's Alley** (rear of 1712 Sherman Avenue, Evanston; (847) 869-6999).

Cameras

Photo-fans, check out **Helix Camera & Video,** where prices are fair and the selection is great (over 100 types of film). They have several locations: 2 Illinois Center, (312) 565-5901; 3 First National Plaza, (312) 444-9373; and the main store at 310 South Racine Avenue, (312) 421-6000. **Central Camera Company** (232 South Wabash; (312) 427-5580) is an old-timer and dependable. They carry a large, varied selection of cameras, lenses, flashes, and other equipment, plus darkroom items. Another top choice is **Calumet Photographic** (1111 North Cherry Street, off Division Street; (312) 440-4920), and don't forget the national biggies, **Wolf/Ritz Cameras** (they merged), and several smaller independents.

Canoes and Kayaks

West and north of Wicker Park (4000 north and 6400 west) is what may be the largest (certainly is the most unusual) dealer in the country for canoes and kayaks. **Chicagoland Canoe Base** (4019 Narragansett; (773) 777-1489) retails over 150 models of canoes and kayaks and builds canoes from 14½ feet long to 34 feet long. Owner Ralph Frese, in business over 50 years, says his full-fledged blacksmith shop comes in handy for designs and repairs on everything from fittings to boat trailers. He not only makes custom canoes for films (such as birchbark models for Universal Studios) but also sells accessories from clothing to paddles to camping gear to trailers. See Frese, too, for restoration of antique canoes.

Clothing and Shoes

In the Loop   Pick up flannel shirts at **Pendleton Woolen Mills Products Store** (119 South State; (312) 372-1699) in the Palmer House Hotel arcade. The store has been there for 77 years, offering goods from Pendleton woolen mills in Oregon. But here they go beyond woolens for men and women to cotton knit sweaters, sweatshirts, jewelry, umbrellas, tote bags, and more. In woolens there are scarves, blankets, men's sport coats and slacks, and coats aplenty in winter. (Note: If you're visiting the western suburbs, there's a Pendleton at 777 North York Road, Gateway Square Shopping Center, in Hinsdale; phone (630) 323-1314.)

LaSalle Street houses an enclave of men's stores and emporiums dedicated to business accessories (men shoppers involved in law and finance in this area outnumber the women). You'll find a men's store called **Leading Man Clothiers** (32 East Adams Boulevard; (312) 346-1733). And the suits you buy at **Syd Jerome Men's Wear** (2 North LaSalle Street; (312) 346-0333) will also make you someone's leading man.

Brooks Brothers (209 South LaSalle Street; (312) 263-0100) is the menswear powerhouse attended by both men and women. The BB many prefer is at 713 North Michigan Avenue (phone (312) 915-0060), and BB is also big in the suburbs (Northbrook Court, Old Orchard, Woodfield, and Oak Brook Center).

A popular men's retailer is **Men's Wearhouse,** with a Loop location at 25 East Washington Boulevard (phone (312) 263-2306). The action here is discounted, name-brand menswear, plus personal service. Other branches are Near North at 48 East Walton Place and at 2070 North Clybourn Avenue, as well as in the suburbs.

Another menswear supplier is **Jos. A. Bank Clothiers** (25 East Washington; (312) 782-4432), with several suburban stores. A final men's outfitter is **Duru's,** known for custom-tailoring shirts and suits (221 North LaSalle Street; (312) 782-4443).

On Michigan Avenue   For men, let's begin with an old-time custom tailor recognized for expertise with hand-tailored suits, "architects of fashion for Chicago's living legends" **Lawrence Pucci** (333 North

Michigan Avenue; (312) 332-3759). And, while you're cruising the Magnificent Mile, peruse the premises at **NikeTown** (669 North Michigan; (312) 642-6363). If you don't, people won't believe you've been to Chicago. It's the gathering place for sports enthusiasts—a veritable retail sports arena of Nike footwear, apparel, accessories, and equipment. There's a lot going on here (audio-video presentations, for example), and they're attracting active femmes as well as men, thanks to remodeling the third floor for women.

Speaking of shoes, **Hanig's** shoes for men and women get around: In addition to the large emporium at 660 North Michigan Avenue (phone (312) 642-5330), there's yet another branch at located 102 West Monroe (phone (312) 263-1365), plus **Hanig's Mephisto** at 520 North Michigan (phone (312) 494-9808), and other stores, even a **Hanig's Birkenstock Shop** at 847 West Armitage (phone (773) 929-5568).

The beauteous **Burberry** (633 North Michigan; (312) 787-2500) is where men and women seek the instantly recognizable camel-and-cream (with a touch of black) icon on plaid that enhances so many raincoats, scarves, and other fashion items, which are becoming less traditional and more modern. At 645 North Michigan is the local outpost of the great Italian design house of **Ermenegildo Zegna** (phone (312) 587-9660). The clothing is carried at several other stores, but the boutique housing this exclusive menswear is here.

Huge is the word for **The Gap** (679 North; (312) 335-1896). The sales staff are really friendly, and they have Gap shoes and Gap kids' clothes, too. One of the chic names for men to hit on the Avenue is **Saks Fifth Avenue Men's Store** (717 North Michigan; (312) 475-9195). Still another national classic is **Polo Ralph Lauren** (750 North Michigan; (312) 280-1655). This 37,000-square-foot Chicago flagship is said to be the largest Polo Ralph Lauren store anywhere. You'll find the designer's men's, women's, and children's clothing and accessories, plus home furnishings; there's even **RL,** the first Ralph Lauren restaurant. Within the Georgian facade is everything from linens to Polo Golf to a women's equestrian shop (fourth floor). Things for the home are presented in unique lifestyle environments.

Banana Republic (744 North Michigan and other locations) started as a repository for clothes you wished you could afford to buy to go camping; it's graduated to providing really nice sportswear and accessories, but you already knew that. What you may not know is that **Georgio Armani** left Oak Street and is now holding court (and charging *molto lire* for the Italian designer's divine duds) at 800 North Michigan Avenue (phone (312) 573-4220). The Park Hyatt Chicago Hotel is home to **Marlowe** (800 North Michigan Avenue; (312) 988-9398), a very luxe store focusing on ultra-chic Italian-made cashmere knitwear, handbags, and leathers. This is their first flagship store in the U.S.

If we had a separate category in this section for girls age seven and up, the following would be number one: **American Girl Place** (111 East Chicago Avenue, across from the Water Tower) is chock-full of the American Girl collection of books, dolls (one is Kit, a girl from the 1930s; the newest is Kaya, the Native American girl), doll clothes, and other delights, including the latest fashions for real live girls from A.G. Gear. There's a cafe here for lunch, tea, or dinner, and a theater, too (call (877) AG-PLACE for tickets).

Another titan, **Rochester Big & Tall** (840 North Michigan Avenue; (312) 337-8877) echoes its name with top fashions for larger men (notable clients include many basketball players from all teams). The emphasis is on the best of Italian designers, from Zanella dress trousers to cashmere coats from Movimento, as well as Donna Karan, Levi, Polo, Versace (dress and casual), Zegna (sportswear and clothing), and more.

At 875 North Michigan is the stunning nearly 100-story-high **John Hancock Building,** which houses the veddy chic men's clothiers **Paul Stuart** (phone (312) 640-2650), which came west from Manhattan; they carry women's clothing, too. While you're there, check out the Hancock's newsy restaurants, little shops (such as **Aveda's** Lifestyle store, phone (312) 664-0417), and, of course, the view from the 95th floor.

A word (or more) about **Bloomingdale's** belongs here: Lyman and Joseph Bloomingdale set up a little notions shop in New York, and by 1872 it had become an East Side bazaar. It took until the 1980s for the big B to hit Chicago at 900 North Michigan Avenue. Of the current 23 stores, Chicago has one of the most beautiful. There are stores in Old Orchard and Oakbrook Center, too. Another source for menswear and women's wear is at 900—**Mark Shale** (phone (312) 440-0720)—which has suburban stores, too. Don't leave 900 without stopping at **Max Studio** (phone (312) 944-4445) for hot styles that won't decimate your wallet.

Does anyone need a reminder that the north end of Michigan Avenue is Shoe Paradise? Note the before-mentioned **Gucci** and **Stuart Weitzman.** Also special is **Avventura** (men's) footwear, at Water Tower Place (phone (312) 337-3777). **Salvatore Ferragamo** has a sparkling store here (645 North Michigan; (312) 397-0464)—the company's first in the Midwest, housing women's and men's shoes, handbags, and other fine accessories from the Italian master.

Stop to see the cashmere sweaters at **Malo** (909 North Michigan; (312) 440-1060). Then peruse the **Chanel Boutique** (935 North Michigan Avenue; (312) 787-5500), a lush store filled with awesome, internationally known clothes, jewelry, and accessories.

A tiny-but-mighty shop with staying power is **Giovanni,** on the Avenue for more than 20 years, the last dozen at 140 East Walton (phone (312) 787-6500). The accent is on special occasion clothing—gowns for balls, mothers of the bride, and nontraditional brides, plus ready-to-wear (suits, separates, leathers, suedes) and accessories (handbags, scarves, hats, costume jewelry).

On Oak Street   World-class shopping begins on (no, not Rodeo Drive) Oak Street. Early ambience was strictly beads and wampum. Then the settlers descended. By 1850, Oak was a residential street—among the first to turn to ashes in the Chicago Fire of 1871. By the 1880s, chic mansions gave new meaning to the words "Gold Coast," and this probably set Oak on its lifelong mission to cross sophistication with cozy hospitality. Now, the low-rise, high-fashion city block rimmed by Rush Street and the northernmost end zone of Michigan Avenue has come into its own, evolving into the style center it is today.

In most major cities, visions of the world's most exotic bazaars suddenly crystallize into one prototypical street, teeming with treasures arrayed before the eyes of dazzled shoppers. Surrounded by urban canyons, that single special avenue stands apart, its unique charm inviting, delighting. Such is Oak, Chicago's blockbuster block of fabulous fashion. The Oak Street council carefully keeps the 38 Art Deco street lights new, the 33 trees replaced if winter has been particularly rough, and even its sidewalks colored a distinctive charcoal gray.

What's in store? The ultimate by the world's most prestigious designers, presented with hometown flair. You can go crazy spending money on Oak, as you waltz the long block from the Michigan Avenue end to the corner of Rush at 25 East Oak Street (where you'll find the newly expanded **Barneys New York** (phone (312) 587-1700). Designers love it here, including **Sansappelle** (34 East Oak; (312) 642-9642). Founded in 1976, this is a top manufacturer of late-day, evening, and special occasion fashions for women. But one of Oak's secrets is that you can actually save money at the street's only drugstore: **Bravco,** the beauty center at 43 East Oak (phone (312) 943-4305) where you can find anything from false eyelashes to toothpaste.

One of the newest Oak stars is **dunhill** (55 East Oak; (312) 943-9030). The clothing/leathers house is in gorgeous quarters with English Beefeater–red walls, sporting everything a man could wish, from ties to cashmere/nutria overcoats. The second floor houses areas for bespoke suitings, a barbershop, and of course the fabled Humidor, with leather couches, private lockers, plasma screen TV, and of course, cigars.

Oak's most uniquely homegrown high-fashion treasure is **Ultimo** (114 East Oak; (312) 787-1171), known internationally for the ultimate in designer clothing for women as well as their tomorrow-flavored accessories. Under the direction of founder Joan Weinstein, this store paved the way for the roster of international stars that now dot Oak—**Jil Sander** (48 East Oak; (312) 335-0006) for one.

International flavor is ever-present on Oak. Begin your Italian fling at **Prada** (30 East Oak; (312) 951-1113). **Luca Luca** (59 East Oak; (312) 664-1512) presents more Italian women's wear (the colors are lush); **Hermès of Paris** (110 East Oak; (312) 787-8175) sends us its exclusive scarves, ties, leather goods, and other goodies à la Française; and **The Wolford Boutique** (54 East Oak; (312) 642-8787) offers imported fun and fashionable hosiery and bodywear. Wolford is an international chain (originating in Austria); the hosiery, bodywear, and swimwear are pricey, but women like them because they fit, last, and are so incredibly luxe. Another favorite is **Kate Spade** (101 East Oak; (312) 654-8853), the company's largest freestanding boutique to date, packed with all the Spade bags and shoes, handpicked items to match, and a line of men's accessories (Jack Spade), designed by Kate's husband and business partner, Andy.

Among other Oak shops to peruse are the **(Max Azria) BCBG** (103 East Oak; (312) 787-7395) for young figures; **Nicole Miller** (63 East Oak; (312) 664-3532), with a full line of the New York designer's often whimsical prints and an extensive bridal collection; Marie Gray's exquisitely tailored fashions at **St. John Boutique** (51 East Oak; (312) 943-1941); maternity fashions at **A Pea in the Pod** (46 East Oak; (312) 944-3080), and men's fashions (many by the hand-tailoring genius Pal Zileri) at **Tessuti** (50 East Oak; (312) 266-4949). One of the most right-now bridal salons (specializing in couture gowns) in the country is **Ultimate Bride** (106 East Oak; (312) 337-6300); there's also **Fenaroli for Regalia** (56 East Oak; (312) 642-3300). And, juniors make a beeline for hot fashions and accessories at **Sugar Magnolia** (34 East Oak; (312) 944-0885). Newcomer **Marina Rinaldi** (113 East Oak; (312) 867-8700) will prove that "style is not a size," featuring sizes 10–22.

A bright outpost of style is **Chacok** (47 East Oak; (312) 943-9391), with fashions for women shipped from Paris by owner Barbara Travers. The boutique is the first in the United States, and the flavor is fresh, imaginative, and bursting with gorgeous color, whether the clothes are knits for winter or gauzy silks for summer. A recent collection featured Venice (Italy, not California) as a theme, and it was smashing. Another Euro gift to Oak Street is **Chasalla** (70 East Oak; (312) 640-1940), a German-based store opened by Marc Engel and Richard Settlemire with clothing, shoes, and accessories for men and women from Hugo Boss, D&G (Dolce & Gabbana), Roberto Cavalli, Cinque, Moschino, and others. Top service here from Marco Engel and his expert staff.

And still more international flavor: **Rikei** (50 East Oak; (312) 573-9655) is the only North American location to carry the unique collections of Lithuanian designer Ramune Piekautaite. The fabrics are lush, the designs feminine and stunning.

The last word goes to **George Greene** (49 East Oak; (312) 654-2490) for menswear that is truly exceptional. The designers here are the ones who count.

Because parking is such a nuisance, choose from two solutions: valet parking (attendant stationed mid-block approximately in front of 101 East Oak) or the 1 East Oak garage (corner of Oak and State Streets).

Near North   One of the newer and most important high fashion emporiums in town is **Ikram** (873 North Rush Street; (312) 587-1000)—very special because of owner Ikram's exquisite taste in everything from shoes to vintage jewelry. Located amid Rush Street's unique shops is **Diesel** (923 North Rush; (312) 255-0157), the third of 24 U.S. stores. Here are men's and women's clothes and accessories (including tons of five-pocket jeans, as one of the specialties here is denim).

More luxe is **Hana K** (100 East Walton Street, 4th level; (312) 280-8188), where outerwear for men and women reigns. Here are lightweight shearlings, gorgeous rainwear, (cashmere-, flannel-, or fur-lined), coats of cashmere and baby alpaca, and more.

At 46 East Walton Place is one of 90 exclusive, worldwide boutiques set up by Parisian designer **agnes b.** (phone (312) 642-7483). The look is spare, sleek, simple, luxe, and stunning, and they've added selected wardrobe items for men, too.

Back at 946 North Rush Street is an improbable boutique—**Tender Buttons,** by name (phone (312) 337-7033)—which no doubt has that missing button you'd love to re-sew on your favorite jacket. Here are men's blazer buttons and imports (including gold buttons from France). Button, button, who's got the button? They do.

High fashion by a Chicago designer who sells all over the country is now available in her own studio/salon. The designer's name is **Patricia Rhodes** (434 West Ontario; (312) 664-4200). Patricia is on the premises to customize the fit of every garment (her specialty is gorgeous evening gowns), and her staff is at your service.

A terrific store—because the owner Terri Vizzone is so adept—is **Only She** (8 East Delaware; (312) 335-1353). Fashion is the point here, but more specifically, wearable art culled from designers and artisans who know how to dazzle. An unqualified rave.

Material Possessions (54 East Chestnut Street; (312) 280-4885) is also a haven for wearable art (from wovens to jewelry). But you're more likely to find unusual items for your table (pottery, glasses, and serving pieces). See "Home Furnishings" for more info.

Realta (1 East Delaware Place; (312) 664-8902) is an elegant store housing sophisticated Italian suitings for men by Sartoni and Gianfranco Ferre, and such pleasures as nonwrinkle pure cotton dress shirts by Eton of Sweden. Find sportswear from Spain and Italy, and neckwear by such designers as Ferre, Christian LaCroix, and Brioni.

A source for gently used women's fashions is **Shabby Chic** (46 East Superior; (312) 649-0080. For those in the market for new clothes, a lot of stunning women think **Mary Walter** (650 North Dearborn Street, at Erie; (312) 266-1094) is their own best-kept secret, but of course they're not alone. In this attractive store, removed from hectic Avenue shoppers, you can browse among beautifully chosen suits, jackets, and other must-haves for work and leisure, such as hand-painted scarves and jewelry (a lot of one-of-a-kind pieces). There's also a full-time tailor here.

Wells Street At 678 North Wells Street are the French sportswear creations of Marithe + François Girbaud's **Girbaud Boutique** (phone (312) 787-2022). **Biba Bis** (732 North Wells; (312) 988-9560) has cutting-edge fashion design for women, including professionals (we've seen great suits here), and unique home accessories and gifts. Customers are aged 20–60; Oprah, Madonna, and Julia Roberts have come to call. They do custom non-trad bridal fashions, too.

At 1706 North Wells is **Handle with Care** (phone (312) 751-2929) famous for up-to-the-second women's fashions. **Fabrice** (1714 North Wells; (312) 280-0011) is a must-visit for faux and fab jewelry (the kind featured by Fabrice in Paris; it's resin-based and painted, the kind of piece you wear and people say, "Where did you get that?" Here too are accessories, home items, soaps, and other gifts. Another Wells fashion stop is **Etre** (1361 North Wells; (312) 266-8101), where upscale runway looks and design names are important; besides clothing they also have handbags and shoes. **Vagabonds Boutique** (1357 North Wells; (312) 787-8520) has upscale fashion designs, from suedes to career separates; gift items include beaded bracelets and bags. Chicago's premier hemp market of high-quality textiles, apparel, and sundries grown in harmony with the environment is **O'Fields** (1547 North Wells; (312) 867-0624), and a much-applauded pit stop for the hip is **Sofie** (1343 North Wells; (773) 255-1343), for the latest jeans, accessories, handbags, and shoes.

Lincoln Park/Clybourn Corridor 859 West Armitage Avenue houses one of the reasons area fashionables don't always have to dash to Michigan Avenue or the Loop. The name is **Celeste Turner** (phone (773) 549-3390), a contemporary clothing boutique that serves the best in brand names (particularly good in sportswear). If you're desperate for something new (if used), note **Cynthia's Consignments** (2218 Clybourn Avenue; (773) 248-7714).

The Kangaroo Connection (1113 West Webster; (773) 248-5499) carries goods and gear from Australia and animal souvenirs (cuddly toy koalas, kangaroos, wombats), as well as stationery, clothing, and jewelry. The owner is open "by appointment or by chance," and fills orders mainly from her website at **www.kangarooconnection.com.**

After 50 years in business, **Davis for Men** is at 824 West North Avenue (phone (312) 266-9599). There's also a store at 900 North Michigan (third level of Bloomingdale's) offering menswear for business, leisure, classic, and avant-garde tastes.

A fine place for lingerie is **Isabella** (1101 West Webster; (773) 281-2352), and another of Webster's outstanding shops is **Krivoy** (1145 West Webster; (773) 248-1466). It's not a big place, and with the walls lined with home furnishings, you may not focus at first on the fashion. Then it hits you: this is the place to find a hat (they're made by the owner). There are also clothes and bags, and everything here is as tasteful as it is desirable. Also on Webster, pull up to **Underthings** (804 West Webster; (773) 472-9291). Don't be embarrassed; this is another store dedicated to (and for) lingerie, and it's complete from robes to bras.

At 808 West Armitage Avenue you'll find clothes by the inventive Chicago designer **Cynthia Rowley** (phone (773) 528-6160). Handmade wearables by national artisans are at **Isis On Armitage** (823 West Armitage; (773) 665-7290); they show more glossy wearables at 900 North Michigan Avenue.

At 1115 West Armitage, **Jane Hamill** plies her trade, which is creating women's clothes that are both chic and affordable. With each season, her design talents grow; her accessories are always well chosen, too. Looking for unique goods by leading artists and craftsmen? **Art Effect** (651 West Armitage; (312) 664-0997) is chock full of wearable art and jewelry. **Shopgirl** (1206 West Webster; (773) 935-7467) is a sexy, sophisticated boutique. Find clothes by Trina Turk, Shoshanna, and accessories such as necklaces by mariechavez and some Chicago designers. A maternity store called **Swell** is tucked inside Shopgirl, with fashions by Olian and Japanese Weekend; there's a Winnetka Swell, too.

The next stop should be **Studio 910** (910 West Armitage) for upscale women's wear. So many desireables, so little time: designers from Tahari to White & Warren, and jewelry by many local and national designers. **Marilena's Boutique** (705 West Armitage; (312) 440-1606) showcases the designs of Marilena Serbanescu, who does lovely handknits and some couture gowns. To the west is **Su-zen** (2241 North Clybourn; (773) 477-9919), the place to pick up Chicago-area designer Hahn's dresses and separates.

Wicker Park/Bucktown   Damen Avenue is a booming source for boutiques, and some of the most popular have both affordables and "little-bit-moreables." Start with **Robin Richman** (2108 North Damen), rich with hot accessories, such as handmade felt rings and beaded coin purses, as well as vintage bags and shoes (collectibles come from the far corners of French and U.S. flea markets); they also have a good selection of ribbons and Richman's own handknit sweaters. At **Saffron** (2064 North Damen; (773) 486-7753), look for spicy, sari-inspired silks and separates created by the Indian-born owner, plus the creations of others who love color and fine fabrics. A great source for clothes, shoes, jewelry, and other accessories (including local talents) is on tap at **p. 45** (1643 North Damen; (773) 862-4523), and loads of chic types love **Tangerine** (1659 North Damen), home to clothes, hats, jewelry, and other accessories purveyed by a savvy mother/daughter team. Another special store is **Toshiro,** (1719 North Damen; (773) 772-9314) where international designers (Tufi Duek from Brasil is one, with his wonderful printed leathers) have created wonderful exclusives in leather and handwoven fabrics; there are some great accessories, too. A lot of women love the clothing and accessories at **Clothes Minded** (1649 North Damen; (773) 227-3402); so do women who wear larger sizes, who have finally found a fashion home at **Vive La Femme**—"style beyond size"—(2115 North Damen; (773) 772-7429). They not only have chic dresses and separates, but great accessories too, such as larger handbags for larger women. is **Belly Dance Maternity** (1647 North Damen; (773) 862-1133 is filled with the best high-end lines in maternity clothes, workout wear, skincare, lingerie, and accessories. In the area is the slightly edgy **Xcito** (1557 North Milwaukee Avenue; (773) 278-5619), with clothes and stunning accessories for men and women. In Wicker Park, a new store is **Sorbino** (1924 West North Avenue; (773) 235-5511), an Italian men's shop carrying the unique Sorbino men's line of jeans, plus shirts, sweaters, jackets, shoes, and more. Find **Smack** (1650 West Division; (773) 227-2008) for women's wear which smacks of L.A. culture (owner Lailani Orlanes just came back from California), thanks to clinging duds by Juicy Couture, Japanese designer Kosiuko's patchwork jeans, and more. Finally, if you continue to explore the area, you'll probably find several more stores that were still on the drawing board when we went to press.

On Halsted, Clark, and Lincoln   Young women love to shop on North Halsted Street, thanks to stores like **Banana Republic** (2104 North Halsted; (773) 832-1172); and, for shoes and bags, **Nine West** (2058 North Halsted; (773) 871-4154). **All Our Children** (2217 North Halsted; (773) 327-1868) is a lovely store that attracts grandparents looking for fashions for their little darlings (parents can come, too). There are clothes for newborns up to preteens.

Further north on Halsted is **1154 Lill** (2523 North Halsted; (773) 477-5455), where you can use their leathers and your imagination to fashion your own handbag ($72–$130), wallet ($24–$40) or a fabric creation.

Clark Street fashion stores mostly for women include trendsetting sportswear and edge-y accessories (handbags and jewelry, especially) at **Panache** (2252 Clark Street; (773) 477-4537); this is a neighborhood fave with a variety of prices and sizes. A sleek store nearby that fits its Italian name (it looks like a shop you might encounter in Milan) is **Palazzo,** (2262 Clark Street; (773) 665-4044). Designs here focus on custom contemporary wedding gowns (unruffly, nothing traditional). A **Limited Express,** women's fashions (phone (773) 871-2738), and a former **Structure,** men's sportswear, now re-named men's **Express** (phone (773) 868-4670) are on the corner of Clark and Belden. Across the street is **Nonpareil** (2300 Clark Street; (773) 477-2933), where you're likely to see incredibly eclectic goods: fashions as well as vases and table treasures, silk jackets, trinkets, expensive imported jewelry, and more. There's also a large **Urban Outfitters** (2352 North Clark; (773) 549-1711), where some things are real finds and others real junque, both in clothes and home design. Further north on Clark Street is **Public I** (2839 North Clark; (773) 868-1744), an intriguing source for both menswear and women's wear. Quality rules, so expect good, unusual stuff, and not always the most expensive: Parasuco jeans, menswear by Arkun and Theory, Lance Koresch's separates for her, and much more. **Tribeca** (2480 North Lincoln Avenue; (773) 528-5958) has sportswear for women by designers such as Parallel, Cambio pants, Three Dots, Follies, and Sharagano, among others.

A few blocks west is a superb new store called **Krista K** (3458 North Southport Avenue; (773) 248-1967). Owner Krista Meyers carries only the most chic women's wear, including maternity fashions by Liz Lange, and there are handbags and jewelry from baguettes by Susan Fitch to necklaces by Me & Ro.

Back to Clark Street: head north to **Hubba-Hubba** (3309 North Clark; (773) 477-1414), for vintage fashions, and since we've arrived at that subject, more may be found in the Belmont area and a bit further north. Shoppers at **Flashy Trash** (3524 North Halsted Street; (773) 327-6900) might like to skate over to **Land of the Lost** (614 West Belmont Avenue; (773) 529-4966) for more vintage fashions. **The Alley** (858 West Belmont; (773) 883-1800), is popular; one teen shopper told us, "They have really neat jewelry and those hard-to-find Chicago cop leather jackets." They also have a vast number of T-shirts emblazoned with the name of your favorite band. Other vintage sources are **Vintage Deluxe** (2127 West Belmont; (773) 529-7008) and **Kitschy Koo** (1614 West Belmont; (773) 404-4510). **Tragically Hip (**931 West Belmont; (773) 549-1500) carries mostly junior sizes. A huge golden retriever belonging to owner Kathleen Jamieson guards the premises, and you'll find cutting-edge fashions at ultra-reasonable prices, notes one young shopper. Two more vintage and thrift sources are at 812 West Belmont: **Hollywood Mirror** (phone (773) 404-4510) and (upstairs) **Ragstock.**

To finish our brief youngish wrapup, **Pink Frog** (857 West Belmont Avenue; (773) 525-2680) has relatively inexpensive items, and **Strange Cargo** (3448 North Clark Street; (773) 327-8090) is a thrift shop crossed with a vintage store (some 1970s shoes were here when we last looked). The trendy young women who like all of the above will also like shoes by **Alternatives** (1969 North Halsted; (312) 943-1591).

Now, as they say, for something completely different: At **Blake Women's Apparel** (2448 North Lincoln Avenue; (773) 477-3364), don't be fooled by the storefront aspect. It's only one of the best high fashion sources in the city. Here are very selective designer clothing and accessories—some outré designers, some Gaultier, some Euro notables. There are always a few accessories you must have.

Go back to Fullerton and continue west to 1880 West Fullerton Avenue, and you'll find **Chicago Tennis & Golf** (phone (773) 489-2999), where you can pick up great sportswear, including warmups, shoes, headbands, vests, hats—everything you need for tennis and golf. (This membership club also has services for restringing racquets and same-day regripping of golf clubs.)

Beyond Wicker Park Do costumes belong in the clothing category? Why not? **Fantasy Headquarters** (4065 North Milwaukee Avenue; (773) 777-0222 or (800) USA-WIGS), is the place to buy and rent costumes and wigs (both crazy and serious), makeup, and party props. Here's an entire area with "1,001 gags" (talking, singing skeletons for Halloween and whenever you need 'em), plus a magic section, and this is the largest costume (and wig) store in the Midwest. If you're in need of a Santa Claus suit, characters from Harry Potter to Easter bunnies, a cow mask, or a vegetable (tomato, carrot) mask, it's here.

In Glencoe, Winnetka, and Beyond When it comes to women's clothes, people from the city drive to **Shirise** (341 Park, Glencoe; (847) 835-2595) in Glencoe for snazzy shoes, and while they're in that suburb they never miss **Nicchia** (688 Vernon, Glencoe; (847) 835-2900) for gorgeous sportswear (great knits) for men and women. Then it's off to **Perlie** (897 Green Bay, Winnetka; (847) 441-8585) and **Jolie Femme** (899

Green Bay, Winnetka; (847) 501-4322) in Hubbard Woods (Winnetka) for top-flight, upscale women's wear. Many prefer the **Neiman Marcus** at Northbrook Court (phone (847) 564-0300)—in the suburb of Northbrook, bordering Highland Park and Deerfield—to the NM downtown; there's a huge parking lot, for one thing, and the sales force tends to be the shoppers' neighbors, dedicated to the fine art of Finding Something. Northbrook Court is perhaps more fun to shop than most malls, thanks to its size (not too excessive) and goods (upscale, but not desperately pricey). There's also a small, good shopping center in downtown Highland Park (1849 Green Bay Road) called **Renaissance Place** with, among other stores, a pretty **Saks Fifth Avenue, Ann Taylor, Eddie Bauer, Pottery Barn, Restoration Hardware,** and more. Among other Highland Park designers, **Sandra Joy, Inc.** is hot for (expensive, in the hundreds) one-of-a-kind antique framed handbags, frames of sterling silver, bakelite, and the like with fabrics such as beaded lace, silk, satin, and leathers; each is a collector's item. By appointment only; phone (847) 831-2318.

Clothing and Shoes Discount Outlets

In the Loop **Designer Resale of Chicago** (658 North Dearborn; (312) 587-3312) offers mostly high-end fashion (Chanel, Versace). **The Daisy Shop** (67 East Oak; (312) 943-8880) has both current and vintage gently used items. The way Chicagoans have embraced the Boston biz **Filene's Basement** (1 North State; (312) 553-1055), you'd think it was a native operation. Clothes here sometimes surprise you: rakeoff DKNY and Calvin Klein, shoes, wedding dresses. There are FB stores out north and west in the suburbs, as well as Designerland (Michigan Avenue).

On Michigan Avenue Above Borders Bookstore at 830 North Michigan is the first "discount" store to hit the Avenue, and the powers that be determined it couldn't open on the ground floor. Therefore, **Filene's Basement** (phone (312) 482-8918) opened on the third and fourth floors in a 50,000-square-foot shop that's a bit glossier than most FBs (as befits Michigan Avenue). They offer a variety of bargains.

Lincoln Park/Clybourn Corridor A top outlet store is **Fitigues Outlet** (1535 North Dayton; (312) 255-0095), with the Fitigues' distinctive look for women and children. Sportwear buys here are excellent, but a season later than you might find in their fashion stores (five in Illinois). Look for seasonal sales twice a year (February and July) for special values. If you're hunting for menswear, head west (5–10 minutes) to Elston Avenue, then just north to Fullerton (east of I-94). At 2593 North Elston Avenue is **Mark Shale Outlet** (phone (773) 772-9600). Shale does women's wear, too, on the tailored side. Here: 30–70% off, much of it private-label Shale merchandise; men can find Calvin Klein, Joseph

Abboud, and dozens more designers. Look for summer and winter blowouts (around the time of July 4th and New Year's) from 50–75% off already marked-down goods.

Lori's Discount Designer Shoes (824 West Armitage Avenue; (773) 281-5655) does exactly what it says: gives you discount prices on shoes sold elsewhere for more (can we put it more succinctly?) They're always up to the minute, with a vast stock; the emphasis is on variety, with a shoe for every style. We've seen great-looking bags in here . . . jewelry, hosiery, and socks, too. (There's also a Northfield store and one in Highland Park.)

On Halsted, Clark, and Lincoln   A New York based women's clothier is a favorite savings-stop here: **Fox's** (2150 North Halsted; (773) 281-0700), with kicky women's wear from 50–70% off. There are two consignment boutiques to visit: **Buy Popular Demand** (2629 North Halsted; (773) 868-0404), with clothes (some new) for women to buy and sell; and **Selections** (2152 North Clybourn Avenue; (773) 296-4014), with low, low prices.

Finally, it's reported that you can find a good selection and save 20–50% off department store regular prices at **DSW Shoe Warehouse** (phone (773) 975-7182), in Lincoln Park at the Pointe, where Clark and Halsted Streets meet at 3131 North Clark Street.

In the Suburbs   North (several blocks East off the Edens Expressway) in Lincolnwood is **Imperial Clothiers, Ltd.** (4560 West Touhy Avenue; (847) 676-2020), with good prices on menswear: suits, sport coats, tuxedos, trousers by Imperial wholesalers, and shirts, coats, ties, shoes, and sweaters by recognizable designers. Alterations on the premises.

A number of outlet malls are described in "Suburban Shopping Centers, Discount Malls, and Shops," later in this chapter.

Crystal, China, and Kitchen Items

On Michigan Avenue   "Major" is the word for **Crate & Barrel's** flagship store (646 North Michigan; (312) 787-5900); it's as luminous at night as an oceanliner. Contemporary home furnishings are provided at mostly moderate prices. You may run across Mexican glass, Danish teak, Italian pottery, you name it. The store also purveys furniture.

Lalique is a new crystal palace at 900 North Michigan (phone (312) 867-1787). Though you can find Lalique pieces all over town, this is the one place that gathers them all together. You can spend under $100 for a tabletop item or find a crystal dining table for $100,000—and everything in between.

Lincoln Park/Clybourn Corridor   If you're looking for houseware bargains, it may pay to drive north to browse at **Krasny & Company** (2829 North Clybourn Avenue, Damen and Diversey area; (773) 477-5504).

There's everything for the tabletop (miles of glassware and professional cookware, plus some spices and herbs). Heavy-duty commercial frypans and stainless-steel stock pots can be found here below retail. **Bed, Bath, & Beyond** (1800 North Clybourn; (312) 642-6596) is a huge warehouse loaded with exactly what it says. There are some great values here in bedding, towels, and accessories.

At 2525 North Elston Avenue is the **Edward Don Outlet** (phone (773) 489-7739), where they sell everything for your kitchen and dining room thanks to "at cost" prices. Not everything is great, but if your tastebuds are in bloom, there's gold in them thar aisles. Some china is swell, some glassware can be found at $0.50 per piece (especially if it's sale time). Commercial cookware is here, as well as a back room for closeouts.

Two finds are **Tabula Tua** (1015 West Armitage Avenue; (773) 525-3500) and **Faded Rose** (1017 West Armitage Avenue; (773) 281-8161). Tabula Tua (which means "your table") has the slogan "beautiful wares," and that's the truth. Half of the tablewares are imported, such as pottery from Provence, and half are American, such as a handpainted pear dish. There are tables, picture frames, and other home accessories; prices are mixed.

The big news in a convenient mall at 800 West North Avenue is the **Crate & Barrel Outlet** (phone (312) 787-4775). As one of Chicago's own housewares successes (see Michigan Avenue), C&B here offers goods more gently priced than at their other stores (such as one close by at 854 West North Avenue) making it worth a shopping stop. Usually, prices are 20–70% off discontinued and sample C&B merchandise.

Those searching for kitchenware, woks, electric rice cookers, bread makers, knives, and other implements used to cook Oriental foods will find the **J. Toguri Mercantile Company** (851 West Belmont Avenue; (773) 929-3500) a treasure. (Here, too, are nonperishable foods, as well as goods from kimonos to CDs of hard-to-find Japanese music.)

In Glencoe and Wilmette At 657 Vernon Avenue in Glencoe, **Madeleine At Home** (phone (847) 835-9100) is chock full of ultra-tasteful home accessories, tabletop items, serving pieces, and other gifts for the home. In Wilmette, **The Crystal Cave** (1141 Central; (847) 251-1160) features a master artisan who repairs crystal and designs crystal pieces (they've done award pieces for the Olympics). They also carry dozens of china and crystal patterns.

Florists

A truly unique Chicago florist is **A New Leaf** (1645 North Wells Street; (312) 642-1576), packed with fresh posies to adorn your hotel room or take to a lucky hostess. We've seen things here that nobody else seems to stock. (See "Home Furnishings" for news of their second store.)

In a city where many floral designers seem to create look-alike bouquets, the following attract attention: **Bukiety** (phone orders for corporate clients only: (312) 733-4580); and their Marshall Field's outlet called **Uroda** for portable botanic or floral related gifts (phone (312) 781-5077); **Alice's Garden** (900 North Michigan Avenue; (312) 649-2100); and **Italian Court Flowers** (phone orders, (312) 666-6950).

That Flower Shop (537 South Dearborn Street; (312) 341-0808) also shines. Owners Peter and Michelle Daut use fresh-cut Holland flowers to do natural designs (they're in demand a lot by celebrities). The shop also has dried flowers, candles, unusual French wire baskets, and an all-natural line of bath products called Blue Moon Botanicals.

Food and Wine

In the Loop   If you miss the Rue Cler in Paris, now is your moment. Just be in the Loop in the summer months, and shop at the City of Chicago **Farmer's Market,** usually held at Daley Plaza. The city sponsors these merry markets (overflowing with trucked-in fleurs, fruits, and vegetables) at some 24 locations during various times weekly. The Saturday market on Armitage (off Halsted) is one of our favorites. Call (312) 744-9187 for details on where and when.

Chocoholics should know about the fulfilling **Godiva Chocolatier** (10 South LaSalle Street; (312) 8551588). (There's another at 845 North Michigan.) And, if you're feeling a chocoholic's yearning for really terrific brownies, Lauren Mitchell will ship her **Aunt Maimee's Brownies** anywhere. For the original, nut, white chocolate chip, caramel, peanut butter, mocha, peppermint, and Bliss balls (powdered sugar–covered, not for shipping, as are her cookies), phone order at (773) 342-6218.

Michigan Avenue   To the east of the Avenue is **Fox & Obel** (401 East Illinois Street; (312) 379-0146), home of gourmet foods; the emphasis is on freshness, and chefs prepare an array of delectables (the breads and cheeses are among the best in town).

On South Michigan Avenue is **Caffee Baci** (332 South Michigan Avenue) an upscale but moderately priced place to grab a quick lunch while shopping. Still south of the bridge, find a new **Moonstruck Chocolate Co.** (320 North Michigan Avenue; (312) 696-1201) for good hot chocolate in winter. Great candy is at **Long Grove Confectionery** (35 West Wacker Drive; (312) 443-1440); this shop is an offshoot of the popular original in the village of Long Grove. The exotic truffle emporium **Vosges Haut-Chocolat** (phone (312) 644-9450) has joined the roster of **The Shops At North Bridge.** This shop creates some of the most delectable chocolates in the world (being allied in partnership with the Paris-based culinary center Le Cordon Bleu). Chocolates may contain flowers as well as rare spices, and they range from $1 apiece to $16 for a special gift package, on up. Yum.

Near North   The place to find fresh mozzarella is **L'Appetito** (30 East Huron Street; (312) 787-9881), along with many imported Italian goodies; there's a second L'Appetito on the ground floor of the John Hancock Building. The divine breads from **The Corner Bakery** (516 North Clark Street; (312) 644-8100) are much praised. There are more than a dozen Corner Bakeries in the city (including one at the Field Museum and one at the Chicago Cultural Center), as well as in the suburbs and around the nation. All have delish sandwiches, pizzas, and muffins.

In addition to Chicago's multiple **Starbucks** and **Seattle's Best** coffee bars, a cozy cafe (both coffee and food) with a hometown flavor is **The 3rd Coast** (1260 North Dearborn Street).

Lincoln Park/Clybourn Corridor   At 2121 Clybourn Avenue is **Market Square.** The "market" refers to a huge **Treasure Island** (phone (773) 880-8880); some consider this food store chain the city's best, and this one best of all; others like the TIs at 1639 North Wells and 75 West Elm. To the west, take Elston south till you reach North Avenue; you'll soon bump into **Stanley's** (1558 North Elston; (773) 276-8050), notable for good fruits and veggies. Some prefer the **Whole Foods** shopping mall (1000 West North Avenue; (312) 587-0648). Here you'll find everything from health aids to top-notch meats and poultry, and many rave about their huge salad bar (it's one of few places that has diced celery).

Near Whole Foods, look for **Sam's Wines & Liquors** (1720 North Marcey; (312) 664-4394). This is a place beloved by many Chicagoans, who know they can pick up the best wines for the best prices. Staffers here know how to advise you, so listen. You may come in for a California Cabernet Sauvignon and walk out with a Piemontese Barolo. You won't be sorry. Also check out **The House of Glunz** (1206 North Wells Street; (312) 642-3000), wine merchants with a very broad range thanks to their extensive cellar. If you are from certain (very few) states, you may order your selections by mail, and your wines will be shipped to you sans Illinois sales tax. **The Chopping Block,** which also houses a cooking school at 1324 West Webster (phone (773) 472-6700), attracts shoppers for its appealing cookware, not to mention its cooking classes. But equally enticing are the (highly selective) foodstuffs (i.e., a walnut mustard from France we haven't seen elsewhere that's out of this world).

At 609 West North Avenue, **Burhop's** (phone (312) 642-8600) delights Lincoln Parkers and Near North neighbors who crave the freshest fish and seafood, great crab cakes, party trays, and such pleasures as good soups and Key lime tarts. They're also at Plaza Del Lago, 1515 North Sheridan Road, in Wilmette.

In Evanston, Wilmette, and Glenview   For those with a sweet tooth: **Belgian Chocolatier Piron** (509 Main Street, Evanston; (847) 864-5504). And, the last word in English toffee is at **Cora Lee Candies** (1844 Waukegan Road, Glenview; (847) 724-2754). If you hate to cook, stop at **Foodstuffs** (2106 Central Avenue, Evanston; (847) 328-7704), or further north in Glencoe at 338 Park Avenue (phone (847) 835-5105). Both stores have huge delis, bake their own pastries, feature fish (Glencoe) and meats and fish (Evanston), and offer gift baskets and catering—both are outstanding. In Wilmette, the best take-out place is **A La Carte** (111 Green Bay Road; (847) 256-4102). All their homemade foods are marvelous, but special raves go to their soups, salads, and desserts. (You can also eat here, in the small lunchroom and, in summer, outdoors.) Back in Evanston, a further treat are the coffees roasted on the premises at **Casteel Coffee** (2924 Central Avenue; (847) 733-1187); many prefer these to the (let's keep it nameless) chain stores' flavors. Another Evanston attraction is the original **Spice House** (1941 Central; (847) 328-3711). This is the last word in everything from Back-of-the-Yards garlic pepper to Saigon cinnamon. People came from miles around for these extraordinary spices, until, happily, they opened a fragrant store in Chicago, too (1512 North Wells Street; (312) 274-0378).

Finally, full-service catering is yours from **Entertaining Company** (1640 West Walnut Street, Chicago; (312) 829-2800), but it's their luxe green baskets that ring bells. They have appetizer baskets, bread and dessert baskets, and more. They need 48 hours advance notice.

Formalwear

The best source for men is the ever-popular hometown favorite, **Gingiss Formalwear** (151 South Wabash Avenue, in the Loop; (312) 263-7071), to buy and to rent. There are three more far-flung Gingiss city stores (including an outlet store at 542 West Roosevelt Road, south of the Loop) and umpteen (21, actually) suburban outlets.

Furs

The **Chicago Fur Mart,** after a tremendous remodeling, is now in its permanent location at the Summerfield Hotel (166 East Superior; (312) 951-5000). On the edge of the Lincoln Park area is a satisfying new and "gently used" fur shop called **Chicago Fur Outlet** (777 West Diversey Parkway; (773) 348-3877), the "home of the furry godmother." They have furs for both men and women, as well as shearlings and leathers. Of course, if you're interested in higher-end furs, see **Maximilian At Bloomingdale's** (900 North Michigan Avenue; (312) 337-8882) or longtime Chicago favorite **S. Garber Furs,** also at 900 Michigan (phone (312) 6442-6600), where 50% of the fur coats here are private label. One of the city's best fur departments is **Marshall Field's Fur Salon** (opened in 1859, the original salon is perhaps the oldest fur business in Chicago and the first in a Chicago department store). This is a very large, pretty full-service fur salon on third-floor State Street, offering sales, remodeling, repair, cleaning, and storage. Mink (lately, the sheared variety) comprises the bulk of their sales, but they have everything from beaver to sable and chinchilla (tsk! Not too practical, except as trim). And if you can't find what you want, they'll make it for you. Many fur fanciers like **Andriana Furs** (535 North Michigan; (312) 943-8080). Others prefer **Abby & Yanni** (700 North Michigan Avenue, in Chicago Place). And, in the suburb of Elmhurst, an all-round favorite is **York Furrier** (107 North York Road, Elmhurst; (630) 832-2200), where they're as likely to do a full length sable as a denim jacket lined with mink.

Garden and Landscaping

At 1006 West Armitage Avenue is another "world" in itself: At **Urban Gardener** (phone (773) 477-2070), the backdrop is the home garden, and an eclectic variety of related items are spread throughout two floors. The two owners have a grasp of both architecture and landscaping, and they display architectural salvage (fragments for the garden, including old metal gates and coach lanterns). There are dried flowers, housewares with floral themes, books, baskets, floral soaps, and pillows.

Another house/garden force is **Jayson Home and Garden** (1885 & 1911 North Clybourn; (773) 525-3100), a warehouse holding varieties of indoor and outdoor furnishings. Much condensed but still there to the north is **Fertile Delta** (1560 West Diversey Parkway; (773) 929-9330).

Home Furnishings, Linens, and Bath Supplies

On Michigan Avenue   See "Crystal, China, and Kitchen Items" for more details on Crate & Barrel stores.

West of the Loop   This discounter advertises itself as "locationally challenged," as it's indeed off-the-beaten-path, but if you happen to be driving while looking for furniture bargains, trek to **EFW,** or European Furniture Warehouse (2145 West Grand; (312) 243-1955). They offer modern classics and contemporary furniture for all home needs.

On Oak Street   One of the city's top home furnishings emporiums is **Elements** (102 East Oak; (312) 642-6574). Tabletop accessories can be found here, along with everything from picture frames to men's and women's jewelry and wedding gifts. The owners have been on the avant scene for years and buy with wisdom; what you get will be a knockout.

Luxe bed, bath, and table linens come with love (and great taste) from Italy at **Pratesi Linens** (67 East Oak; (312) 943-8422). They're not inexpensive, but the quality is high. And, a newcomer is the fabled Italian linens emporium **Frette** (41 East Oak; (312) 649-3744), fresh from Milan with the company's signature linens, fragrances (scented candles and sachets), and an at-home clothing line lush with cashmeres. They're best known for their jacquard print bedding of 300–600-thread-count Egyptian cotton and linen. Pricey, but pop in and pop for a divine sachet.

Near North   For 15 years, a leading purveyor of Asian antique furniture and accessories has been stunning **Decoro** (224 East Ontario Street; (312) 943-4847). They also have a second and larger showroom west at 2000 West Carroll Avenue (phone (312) 850-9260), which is hard to find—but this treasure-house is so worth the trek. Find anything here from Japanese tansu (cabinetry) and tribal rugs to exquisitely embroidered pillows from Paris and Venice. Definitely a place to browse, **Cambium** (119 West Hubbard; (312) 832-9920) offers furniture, kitchen items, and some wonderful home and tabletop gifts.

The **Morson Collection** (100 East Walton Street; (312) 335-9417) is impressive, with its European contemporary furniture, area rugs, lighting, and accessories. At **Material Possessions** (54 East Chestnut Street; (312) 280-4885), eclectic spirit is combined with a sense of humor in showcasing a unique selection of original home furnishings, specializing in tabletop items. The display of custom-made dinnerware, glassware, and linens complements other areas of the store, where contemporary items are sold alongside antiques. This is a must-see for the discerning shopper. There's another MP in the suburbs (Winnetka).

A bit west of Michigan Avenue: If you're into "faded, classical slipcovered furniture," slip into **Shabby Chic** (46 East Superior Street; (312) 649-0080). On Walton is an enchanting boutique with a French accent: **La Maison Francaise** (66 East Walton; (312) 943-3988). The latter features a mélange of gifts, home accessories, antiques, even furniture.

River North   Along with most of the city's best galleries are some of its most cherished home decor emporiums. There are, in fact, so many of them, it's not easy to pick and choose. The problem is, of course, that what one person detests, another will adore. We'll try to give you a quick summary; then you can go and make up your own mind.

One more necessary disclaimer: Stores, like galleries, come and go; at this writing, everything's in place. Who knows about tomorrow? We've tried to include the enduring ones, but, just to be sure, call to check before you go shopping.

The scene here began with a few furniture and antiques galleries that first moved west from LaSalle to cluster around Superior and Huron Streets (wags named it SuHu, after New York's Soho, but it didn't take). Today, the area is larger, extending in spots to Clark Street on the east, and south of Grand Avenue as far as Illinois, Hubbard, and Kinzie, in some cases. The cut-off point is usually Chicago Avenue to the north, but then again, rules are made to be broken.

First contenders are **Champagne Furniture Gallery** (65 West Illinois Street; (312) 923-9800) and **The Golden Triangle Imports** (Clark at 72 West Hubbard Street; (312) 755-1266). Dazzling goods might include a teak/cane plantation chair from Thailand or Burmese wooden puppets. **Sawbridge Studios** (153 West Ohio Street; (312) 828-0055) is a gallery of custom-made designs by craftspeople from around the world. Furniture (from Shaker to traditional to Prairie) is predominant, and, considering the high cost for custom-made pieces, it's affordable. Many other craft items are also here, including pottery, glass, quilts, handpainted rugs, and a fine assortment of lamps. Sawbridge features one of the largest collections of handblown crystal by craftsman Simon Pearce of Vermont. There is also a suburban gallery in Winnetka.

The Antiques Centre at Kinzie Square (220 West Kinzie Street; (312) 464-1946) is an exciting enclave for shoppers to enjoy more than 500 selections in furniture, lighting, decorative objects, rugs, fine art, and estate jewelry. There are vendors who purvey everything from vintage Miriam Haskell pearl pins to antique rocking chairs to sterling flatware with inlaid mother-of-pearl handles. There's no musty attic feeling here, either; everything's bright and light.

Also on Kinzie is **Asian House** (159 West Kinzie; (312) 527-4848), boasting a complete line of Oriental furniture and accessories, such as cloisonné vases and animals, bronze statues, porcelain fishbowls, Korean furniture, antique Chinese furniture, coromandel screens, and more.

On Hubbard Street, furniture reigns at **Roche-Bobois** (222 West Hubbard; (312) 951-9080) and also at the **Kreiss Collection** showroom (415 North LaSalle Street; (312) 527-0907). The Kreiss family designs and manufactures its own elegant pieces; you can pick out the finishes, fabrics, and accessories right here.

Rita Bucheit (449 North Wells Street, use the Illinois Street entrance; (312) 527-4080) is the major Biedermeier expert and importer for the Midwest. She searches for furniture made by the Austrian master after 1840; at Christmastime, she has small silver pieces, small furniture items (such as accent chairs for additional seating), and ornaments. Also on Wells, the place to go if you're looking for exquisite floor tiles is **Ann**

Sacks Tile & Stone (501 Wells; (312) 923-0919), where you'll also see stone flooring that is gorgeous but not necessarily expensive.

Mig & Tig (corner of 549 North Wells Street at Ohio; (312) 644-8277) has a fine furniture mix: upholstered pieces, some wood, wrought iron from Mexico, and other imports. They are pieces that would fit in all settings, from contemporary to country. Nearby is **Arrelle Fine Linens** (445 North Wells Street; (312) 321-3696). This is where you'll find an Italian sheet as silky as gelato that might set you back $100 or more. At least go in and look at the table linens and gorgeous bed settings (maybe you can afford pillowcases).

Atn extraordinarily artful collection of furniture and furnishings—half the pieces are Italian, some are designed by the owner/architect—is at **Manifesto** (755 North Wells Street; (312) 664-0733). You'll see some Herman Miller pieces (reissues of top 1950s designers) if you peruse the two floors; we saw a dining room table, sofas, and benches (from their Austrian company), lounge chairs, vases, lighting, wine racks, and some accessories.

Luminaire (301 West Superior; (312) 664-9582) is a 16,000-square-foot showroom that began as a fine lighting emporium and graduated into retail home furnishings. Everything is top-flight here; find the very best international designers, from Philippe Stark to a Boffi kitchen center on the third level to the largest B & B Italia retailer in the world.

The **Spicuzza Collection** (415 North Franklin Street; (312) 661-0360) is the showroom for furniture designer and interior architect Martin Spicuzza. You'll find his woods beautiful and adornments (from luxe fabrics to drawer and door pulls) impressive.

Galleria M (313 West Superior; (312) 988-7791) is Chicago's version of the New York–based **Dialogica.** The hot furniture design collection, by the team of Monique and Sergio Savarese, was brought to the Midwest by owner M. J. Foreman-Daitch. Pieces here are quirkily contemporary (though they'd fit in anywhere) and mostly affordable and unforgettable. Tabletop accessories have been added, and Dialogica also has come out with a lower-priced line called the Saba Collection.

Lincoln Park/Clybourn Corridor   Right next door to Jayson Garden at 1915 North Clybourn is **Jayson Home** (1911 North Clybourn; (773) 525-3100), which has become one of the hottest retail stores in the Lincoln Park area. In vintage warehouses, you'll find treasures that interestingly combine old and new, domestic and imported. Unusual gifts include heirloom photo albums; opulent sofas, chairs, and ottomans; and Euro bath luxuries. For the garden, there are plants, fresh flowers, and outdoor furniture, among other goodies.

A charming source for antiques and reproduction pine furniture is **Pine & Design** (511 West North Avenue; (312) 640-0100), with an in-house cabinetry shop and a gift boutique of eclectic accessories. Farther west is one of the top storage and organization leaders in the housewares industry, **The Container Store** (908 West North; (312) 654-8450). They have everything for storage—every type of shelving from bookcases to entertainment centers, and storage containers for kitchens, bath-rooms, and every room in the house, including closets. They also have stores in Schaumburg, Northbrook, and Oak Brook.

An absolute standout is **Fortunate Discoveries** (1022 West Armitage Avenue; (773) 404-0212). The owner has a marvelous eye for interna-tional treasures, such as handwoven kilim ("flatly woven") rugs from the Middle East using various weaving techniques, or old windows from the Swat Valley (Pakistan). Here, too, are one-of-a-kind pillows and furnish-ings from Africa, Afghanistan, and Indonesia, including benches, armoires, side tables, and multiple accessories.

Another find on Armitage is **Findables, Inc.** (907 Armitage; (773) 348-0674), a treasure trove of items past, present, and future. You're as likely to find antique beads or a piece of antique crystal or silver as a new woolen throw from Italy or table linens from France. Here, too, are unique books, decorative dinnerware and home furnishings, and luxe bath items, including body lotions and scented soaps.

At 1925 North Clybourn Avenue is a store with a therapeutic aim: **Relax the Back** (phone (773) 348-2225). It's bent on relief of back pain, thanks to such things as the best-selling Backsaver Zero Gravity Recliners and ergonomic executive office chairs. Farther north and west is **Interior Design Concepts** (4200 West Diversey; (773) 202-9200), where Daryl Michaels' helpful showroom focuses on home safety concepts for the elderly and disabled, such as tubs with doors for people who can't lift their legs over the edge.

Popular florist **A New Leaf** has opened **A New Leaf Studio & Garden** (1818 North Wells Street; (312) 642-8553), where shoppers can find antique Mexican curio cabinets, antique armoires, tables, pottery, can-dles, and ceramics, plus dried flowers and potted plants.

On Halsted, Clark, and Lincoln   Halsted has so much to offer, not the least of which are galleries full of decorative furnishings. One of the best is **Gallimaufry** (3345 North Halsted Street; (773) 348-8090).

If you're bound for the western suburbs, look for **Home Bodies,** which has moved to 1263 Main Street, Suite 180, Lombard. This eclectic spe-cialty shop has thousands of items, from lamps to wind chimes. Back on North Halsted, a store that sets the style for sleepyheads is **Bedside Manor Ltd.** (2056 North Halsted; (773) 404-2020), with beds, beautiful linens, and fluffy down comforters. They also have stores in Winnetka, Hinsdale, and Lake Forest.

On Broadway is the **Broadway Antique Market** (6130 Broadway; (773) 868-0285). It's an unlikely setting, but a good place to shop (though there are actually more vintage items—1950s and 1960s—than antiques). Some furniture, some Russell Wright and Eva Zeisel pottery, some vintage clothes and posters—it's all here.

The store that bows to your budget is **Cost Plus World Market** (2844 North Broadway; (773) 477-9912). Some of the items here are truly junque, but in between are necessities that can save you a bundle. At the other end of the spectrum, an outstanding source for fine antique furnishings is **Ile de France Antiques** (2009 North Fremont; (773) 525-4890). Here are many international (but mostly 19th-century French) antiques, as well as Art Deco and Art Nouveau furniture. Mirrors, tables, chairs, and clocks are here, as well as art (paintings, prints). They also have other stores, and a warehouse for restoration of furniture and decoration (gilding, etc.) at 2222 North Elston (phone (773) 227-0704).

On Clark Street, you'll find a superb design emporium called **I.D.** (3341 Clark Street; (773) 755-IDID). Co-owned by Steven Burgert, Anthony Almaguer, and Joseph Almaguer, the contemporary lifestyle store is a source of Paola Lenti furniture, Hackman tabletop, titanium eyewear, and lighting. Our spies report nothing but raves when it comes to shopping here. Nearby, **Aiko's Art Materials Import** (3347 North Clark Street; (773) 404-5600) would properly be listed under paper goods (handmade Japanese paper in 500 different varieties) but for the fact that they also offer some interesting folk art pottery.

Last, but certainly not least to the budget-conscious urban tastemakers who frequent it is the 6,000-square-foot **CB 2** (3745 North Lincoln Avenue; (773) 244-1188), the cool design offspring of Crate & Barrel. The product mix is contemporary and full of priced-right furniture, hip accessories, home office gadgets, and storage objects.

In Bucktown and Wicker Park   At **Eclectic Junction** (1630 North Damen Avenue; (773) 342-7865), Erika Judd shows a permanent collection of furniture and one-of-a-kind pieces by other artisans. Her wares, she says, are "functional, affordable, traditional installations, as well as useables and wearables." The upholstered leather furniture casts **Embelezar** (1639 North Damen; (773) 645-9705) into the furniture category, but that doesn't do the place justice. A browse-through revealed picture frames, soaps, incredible drawer pulls, a ton of antiques and newly made imports, and finds by international artists.

Many shoppers for furnishings love the leather furniture and custom upholstery at **Stitch** (1723 North Damen Avenue; (773) 782-1570);

they have terrific leather handbags here, too. When it comes to antiques, put **Pagoda Red** (1714 North Damen Avenue; (773) 235-1188) on your list. It's notable for unusual furniture and artifacts from China, Tibet, and Southeast Asia. At **Kachi Bachi** (2041 North Damen; (773) 645-8640) are pillows, duvet covers, and window treatments; and a must-see is **Pavilion** (2055 North Damen Avenue; (773) 645-0924), where Deborah Colman and Neil Kraus specialize in all things French. The owners of **Orange Skin** 1429 North Milwaukee Avenue; (773) 394-4500) do plastic big-time: chairs, lava lamps, rubbery housewares, etc. They've also assembled hard-to-find Euro lines, from Tacchini to Alessi. Go to **Asian Essence** (2025 West North Avenue, just north of Milwaukee Avenue; (773) 782-9500) for unique Asian imports, and **Indochina Company** (1442 North Milwaukee; (773) 486-3058) offers antiques, art, and crafts from Laos, Cambodia, and remote villages of the Golden Triangle. **Virtu** (2034 North Damen; (773) 235-3790) is probably one of the most interesting shops, offering a potpourri of crafts from teapots to felt scarves. And consider looking into the 1950s–1970s goods on tap at **Modern Times** (1538 North Milwaukee Avenue; (773) 772-8871), a fount of 20th-century-modern furnishings, including the collectibles of Charles and Ray Eames. A final recommendation: The Chinese antiquities at **Wow and Zen** (2105 West Armitage; (773) 269-2600) are really wow. An early-19th-century Chinese wine basket is $135; Tibetan marriage boxes (like chests to hold wedding gifts) are $50–$90, and they usually fetch twice that. The hours here are very erratic, so phone first.

Off the Beaten Path   Discover **Vintage Pine** (904 West Blackhawk; (312) 943-9303), a 13,000-square-foot showroom overflowing with current custom, antique, and vintage looks in both furniture and accessories. It's two blocks south of North Avenue and two blocks west of Clybourn Avenue. The goods here range from shipments of English pine armoires, farm tables, chairs, and silver pieces to items sold by on-site galleries that deal in antiques and more contemporary home furnishings.

Off the Bolt (1333 North Kingsbury; (312) 587-0046) is owner Norene Fremont's dream come true: high-end, highest-quality textiles for interiors at mill-direct prices, immediately available. In one locale, you won't believe your eyes: silks, chenilles, mohairs, tapestries, and a wall of shimmering taffetas that seems as fluid as a waterfall.

A small shop called **POSH Tablewares** (3729 North Southport Avenue; (773) 529-7674) has such interesting items as the kind of vintage water carafes found in French bistros, as well as vintage hotel silver and commercial china (manufactured for hotels and country clubs, but unused). If you continue north, you'll arrive at **Architectural Artifacts** (4325 North Ravenswood; (773) 348-0622), an extraordinary outlet for furniture and decorative items from around the world. In this huge warehouse, find everything from garden furniture to old (but sometimes beautiful) fireplace mantels. Another sprawling warehouse stocked with retro and just plain old artifacts from long-ago buildings, **Salvage One** (1840 West Hubbard Street; (312) 733-0098) is reported to have some 250,000 items—some of them treasures, including stained-glass windows, odd cornices, bathtubs, garden ornaments, and hardware on sale.

West Loop　The unique **Morlen Sinoway Design Atelier** (1052 West Fulton Street; (312) 432-0100) shows Sinoway's own furniture designs, artisan lighting, flooring materials and objects of art. **Hollis** (949 West Fulton Street; (312) 266-5242) is a sparkling source of interior design. One of the newest entries in the West Loop area is **Gallery 1040** (1040 West Randolph Street; (312) 421-1040). Here, in a spacious former food products building, is a potpourri of 15 furniture lines (including the only Bassett Furniture Direct dealer and the only Kincaid Furniture Gallery in Chicago), plus oriental rugs, accent pieces, lighting, mattresses and box springs, and much more.

In Evanston　Of the many fun and attractive stores in this near-northern suburb, one of the best is **Perennials** (2022 Central Avenue; (847) 475-8327), where you'll find everything from English soaps, teas, and teapots to picture frames and other home accessories.

Jewelry

In the Loop　A big Loop attraction for those who must have baubles, bangles, and beads is a series of jewelers (both wholesale and retail) at the renovated **Jewelers' Center** at the Mallers Building (5 South Wabash Avenue; (312) 853-2057). It's worth a look just to see how beautifully one of the oldest buildings in the Loop has been redesigned, and there are reputed to be over 200 jewelers in the building to lure you. **Wabash Jewelers Mall** (street level at 21 North Wabash Avenue; (312) 263-1757) also entices with good values.

On Michigan Avenue　On the second level of Water Tower Place glows **The Goldsmith,** where Sherry Bender does every kind of commission, from updating a fun heirloom to creating a spectacular diamond necklace. The Midwest's only **Bulgari** is a gorgeous outpost of the Roman designer at 909 North Michigan. All of the contemporary classics are here, from Tubogas (hand-wrapped flexible band) designs to the double-stone ring called Doppio Buccellato. Here, too: Bulgari fragrances for men and women (some with green tea), scarves, handbags, and sunglasses. One of the most exclusive boutiques in the country is **Cartier** (630 North Michigan Avenue; (312) 266-7440), where you can pick up anything from a silver cup for baby to an engagement ring. In the former

Waterford/Wedgwood shop at 636 North Michigan, **Van Cleef & Arpels** brings its posh baubles to your wondering eyes (no competition with Cartier; they have the same owner). And you mustn't slight **Tiffany & Co.** (730 North Michigan Avenue; (312) 944-7500), where you can find a crystal vase, Tiffany stainless-steel flatware, pictures frames, and all manner of gems to take home in that unmistakable Tiffany blue box. New here is the Tiffany Mark, the original watch creation that replaces all former Tiffany watches, in stainless steel, 18K gold, and platinum.

Just west of Michigan Avenue is **Sidney Garber** (118 East Delaware Street; (312) 944-5225), a creative jeweler here since 1945 that deals in fine watches as well as diamonds and pearls. Also off Michigan Avenue, multi-talented goldsmith and jewelry designer Gia Hammond, owner of **Gisela** (64 East Walton), presents some of the world's most interesting designers in her exquisite gallery.

The Drake Hotel houses **Georg Jensen** (959 North Michigan; (312) 642-9160), a mélange of gorgeous jewelry and tabletop items. Note a Danish artist (all the designers featured here seem to be Danish) named Viviana Torun, who does super silversmithing.

West of the Avenue is **Geneva Seal** (1033 North Rush Street; (312) 377-0100), where fine jewelry and watches vie for prominence, many of them non-mainstream beauties like Chronoswiss, Dubey & Schaldenbrand, and Alain Silberstein.

On Oak Street   Jewelry here is in the capable hands of two longtime Chicago favorites, one being master designer **Lester Lampert** (57 East Oak; (312) 944-6888), offering three floors of custom-made contemporary and classic designs, estate jewelry, and a huge array of fine watches. The other, **Trabert & Hoeffer,** has operated since 1937, most of that time on Michigan Avenue, but currently at 111 East Oak (phone (312) 787-1654). Fine gemstones and custom designs are the rule here; you're not bombarded by lots of jewelry cases; they bring items to you, somewhat in the style of an extra-haute fashion house. But don't be intimidated. Gems are expensive, but the staff here can make buying them pleasant. The fluid style of **Judith Ripka** (129 East Oak; (312) 642-1056) incorporates interchangeable components (an earring can be a stud or evolve into a pendant drop on a French wire), and whether she's working in gold or platinum, people like Senator Hillary Clinton seem to crave her creative work. A relative newcomer is **Sabbia** (106 East Oak Street; (312) 440-0044), formerly Alex Sepkus New York. They find fabulous designers, including Sepkus himself, and showcase them; wearing these pieces is truly wearing art.

Off the Beaten Path   **Ancient Echoes** (1022A West Armitage; (773) 880-1003) is where the jewelry is as appealing as the mélange of home accessories (everything from furniture to amazing Christmas ornaments) and gifts. The owner Ivy Hofstadter, seems to know major artisans throughout the world, and she shows them here. Look for the jewelry of Judith Jack, Patricia Locke, and Ayala Bar. In the Lincoln Park area, a boutique not to be missed is that of **Ani Afshar** (2009 North Sheffield Street; (773) 477-6650). Nationally known as a jeweler who works exclusively with beads, Afshar's Logan Square loft originates this stunning beadwork, sold at such outposts as the Asia Society of New York and Harrods of London, as well as here. (For customizing, call her at (773) 645-8922). In Bucktown, find fun jewelry among the interesting accessories at **Robin Richman** (2108 North Damen; (773) 278-6150) and pieces made by artisans at **p. 45** (1643 North Damen; (773) 862-4523).

In Evanston Custom-designed jewelry is on tap at **Eve J. Alfille** (623 Grove Street; (847) 869-7920), where they love nature's images; and at **Peggie Robinson Designs** (1514 Sherman Avenue; (847) 475-2121), where one customer here has been wearing different versions of her hand-hammered silver hoops for 30 years.

Luggage

In the Loop **Emporium Luggage** (128 North LaSalle Street; (312) 372-2110) offers Tumi, Hartmann, Swiss Army, North Face, Timberland, and others. Their discount store is **Irv's Luggage** (820 West North Avenue; (312) 787-4787). Both stores also have messenger bags, backpacks, travel related merchandise, and accessories.

Deutsch Luggage Shop (39 West Van Buren, (312) 939-2935); and 40 West Lake, (312) 236-2935) is another family-owned business and a source for fine luggage, leather goods, business cases, and gifts. Among many national brand names are Tumi, Hartmann, Andiamo, and Swiss Army. (They also have a store at Oakbrook Center.) **Flite Luggage & Repair** (309 West Chicago Avenue; (312) 664-2142) is also a good source, and they do great zipper repair, too.

Michigan Avenue The Shops at North Bridge include a fine luggage store, **El Portal** (level two; (312) 644-4315). They carry their own exclusive El Portal brand, everything from duffles to uprights, and also Tumi, Hartmann, Swiss Army, Travelpro, Delsey, Zero Haliburton, and more. The merchandise is rather high-end but impressive at **Louis Vuitton** (Water Tower Place; (312) 944-2010).

Lincoln Park/Clybourn Corridor **Kaehler Travelworks** may be found in multiple locations, including Water Tower Place, but one of the best sources is 2070 North Clybourn Avenue (phone (773) 404-1930). The store specializes in luggage, leather goods, and gifts, and there are some terrific buys here.

Marine Specialty Items

Lincoln Park/Clybourn Corridor   An unusual store in this area is **West Marine** (627 West North Avenue; (312) 654-1818), the last word in supplies, books, and gifts for those who love the sea and ships. Find everything here for the boater but the boat, from personal flotation devices (a.k.a life jackets) to books on boat safety.

Musical Instruments and Recorded Music

In the Loop   If you are looking for music, you'll find plenty at the **Chicago Music Mart** at DePaul Center (333 South State Street, park at Crosstown Auto Park, 328 South Wabash Avenue; (312) 362-6700). Here are 20 stores that can supply everything from drums to karaoke tapes. **Chicago Band & Orchestra** (phone (312) 341-0102) sells instruments and manages the **Percussion Center** (drums). Tapes and pop sheet music are at Carl Fischer (phone (312) 427-6652); **Crow's Nest** offers CDs and tapes. **American Music World** (phone (312) 786-9600) is the place to buy pianos and keyboards, and so are **Karnes Music** (phone (312) 663-4111) and **Fandrich Pianos** (phone (312) 427-4200). There are even souvenirs of musical Chicago at **Accent Chicago** (phone (312) 922-0242). Among the outposts of the latter is one at O'Hare Airport, which specializes in nonjunky items that represent (and accent) Chicago products and arts. Look for free daily performances at the **Mart's Tunes at Noon,** with outdoor performances in the summer at the DePaul Center Plaza.

Our friends at **Carl Fischer of Chicago** at the Chicago Music Mart note that Carl Fischer has been a local musicians' mecca since 1909, purveying band, choral, handbell, piano, vocal, guitar and popular print music. They also sell guitars and all manner of novelty and gift items, from metronomes to colored guitar straps. They gave us some great tips. For one thing, at a super used bookstore called **Selected Works** (3510 North Broadway; (773) 975-0002), Keith Peterson sells used sheet music (some vintage); he's open noon–9 p.m. daily. Speaking of vintage, **Pedals, Pumpers & Rolls** restores and repairs old pianos and other automatic musical instruments (player pianos, nickelodeons, reproducing grands, music boxes, etc.), but they're far west of the city (relocated near the Joliet area). By appointment only; call (815) 634-2829.

On Michigan   Avenue Another recommendation is **Sherry-Brener** (226 South Michigan Avenue; (312) 427-5611), selling violins and other stringed instruments, bagpipes and pan pipes, mandolins, guitars handmade in Spain, used guitars, and more. They also teach violin lessons.

It's fun to look into the futuristic **Sony Gallery** (663 North Michigan; (312) 943-3334), even though it's a bit touristy. But how else can you check out state-of-the-art electronics? Of course there's much more here than music items; you'll admire the hot new digital cameras and gadgets galore (even their talking electronic dog that never needs to be fed!).

On Oak Street **Bang & Olufsen** (15 East Oak; (312) 787-6006) is prime territory for admirers of the great Danish music and video systems. Note gorgeous TVs (the Plasma 42" screen; the Beo Vision 5, the plasma version of the Avant TV) and audio items like the MP3 players (digital music). The Beo Com 2-line speaker phone is also stunning.

Near North Not far from Michigan Avenue in the area of North Bridge, **Bose** (55 East Grand Avenue; (312) 595-0152) is a great place to look for great sound, from the Wave Radio/CD in white and graphite gray to their great Quiet Comfort head set, to computer speakers and home theater technology. A block south of Grand Avenue at the edge of the Loop—and a must if you're feelin' groovy—is **Jazz Record Mart** (444 North Wabash Avenue; (312) 222-1467), which bills itself as the world's largest jazz and blues shop.

Oriental Rugs

Near North One of the best names to note is **Oscar Isberian** (122 West Kinzie Street; (312) 467-1212). There is also an Oscar Isberian at 1028 Chicago Avenue in the suburb of Evanston.

On Halsted, Clark, and Lincoln Check out **Peerless Rug Co.** (3033 North Lincoln; (773) 525-9034). Riches include Oriental rugs and unusual European tapestries, skillful reproductions of centuries-old designs. The motto here is "It's worth the trip," and if you're looking for carpets, indeed it is. For kilim rugs, **Fortunate Discoveries** (1022 West Armitage Avenue; (773) 404-0212) is the place to go.

Outdoor Gear

On Michigan Avenue **The North Face** (875 North in the John Hancock Building; (312) 337-7200) is newsworthy, with great skiwear and ski equipment, as well as climbing and other outdoor gear. There is also a suburban store at Oak Brook Center Mall.

On Halsted, Clark, and Lincoln What started as a discount army-navy surplus store has graduated to a sporting goods, camping, and travel emporium where you can pick up anything from a pea coat to mountain climbing gear. The name is **Uncle Dan's Army-Navy, Camping & Travel** (2440 North Lincoln Avenue; (773) 477-1918), and it's nothing fancy, but is very service-minded. They're also in the suburbs, including Highland Park.

Sports Cars and Vintage Automobiles

A day trip to the northern suburbs (Zone 11) takes you to two sources for vintage cars and other antique car collectibles, which may be why some international shoppers find Chicago a hub for these auto prizes.

Chicago Car Exchange is in Libertyville (take I-94 to Route 176 east) at 14085 West Rockland Road (phone (847- 680-1950). Philip J. Kuhn, III, his father, Philip Kuhn, Sr., and his brother Charlie run the family business, featuring antique and collectible cars: vintage sports cars, classic cars from the 1920s-through-1950s, and racy "muscle" cars with big engines from the 1960s. One hundred and fifty cars are gathered in an indoor showroom and sold worldwide. "New cars depreciate in value," says Phil Kuhn. "These cars are viewed as an investment to drive." There is an admission charge of $3.

Not far from there is the **Volo Antique Auto Museum** on 30 wooded acres (27582 Volo Village Road, near Routes 12 and 120; (815) 385-3644). Here are over 250 Hollywood pre-war muscle and collector cars. All cars are for sale (values range from $7,000–$750,000). Official collector classifications include antique, brass-era, classic, milestone, muscle, exotic, and sports cars, domestic and foreign, from the early 1900s through the 1980s. The museum is owned and operated by the second- and third-generation Grams family (Greg Grams and sons Jay and Brian, and Greg's brother Bill), and the museum is a guest exhibitor at the annual Chicago Auto Show every February. There are other sources for collector cars, but this is the largest. The **American Classics Gift and Book Shop** (museum food court) has auto-related gifts. There are also three separate but connected (not auto-related) antiques malls representing over 300 established antiques dealers. The museum and malls are open daily, 10 a.m.–5 p.m.

Tobacco

The reemergence of cigars has caused some minor interest in this category, but the following sources are the most interesting:

The **Up Down Tobacco Shop** (1550 North Wells Street; (312) 337-8025) is an old-timer (and one of the original few) dedicated to smokers who cherish the art of enjoying and buying fine cigars. Up Down goes the same ways, but perseveres mightily. They claim to have the largest selection of premium cigars in Chicago.

The **Blue Havana Smoke Gallery** (906 West Belmont Avenue; (773) 242-8262) features a walk-in humidor filled with 200 varieties of cigars, and various cigar guides and accessories.

On the upscale side, cigars are classic and impressive at the **dunhill** humidor (2nd floor at dunhill, 55 East Oak; (312) 943-9030).

Toys, Games, and Gifts for Children

The Loop   It's a chain store, but the stuff for kids is varied, and they have just about everything that's ever advertised, in case your little darling saw it on TV. It's none other than **Toys R Us** (10 South State; (312) 857-0667); they're also in several suburbs, often with their Kids R Us clothing for kids.

On Michigan Avenue   After **FAO Schwarz** (840 North Michigan; (312) 587-5000), the others often play follow the leader. Sugarplums here include everything from books and art supplies (we found an "art studio" for kids with 14 watercolors, 36 pastel crayons, 36 colored pencils, and 2 brushes in a portable wooden case,) to dolls, including limited edition Barbies, and a forest of stuffed animals). See **The Lego Store** at 520 North Michigan, too.

On Halsted, Clark, and Lincoln   Arguably the city's most charming store for children's toys, books, and games, **Saturday's Child** (2146 North Halsted Street; (773) 525-8697) has been a longtime favorite of children born every day of the week. **Toyscape** (2911 North Broadway; (773) 665-7400) is an adventurous toy store and bookstore . . . adventurous because you won't find TV-advertised stuff, but unique toys that even collectors covet.

The Red Balloon Company (2060 North Damen Avenue; (773) 489-9800) has imported furniture and accessories for kids, some antique and one-of-a-kind gifts.

In Evanston   **Rosie** (620 Grove Street; (847) 869-1721) is highly recommended for children's toys, books, and games. Everything at Rosie looks hand selected, and the service is savvy, too.

Western Goods, Boots, and Saddles

Out of the West (1000 West Armitage Avenue; (773) 404-9378) is a stunning western lifestyle emporium that's a cross between a luxe ranch and an old-fashioned general store. Savvy buying is obvious in the various categories of goods: Navajo rugs, silver jewelry, silver buckles and handmade belts, a wall of boots, racks of urban-focused sportswear, home decor, lamps, and tableware. The store deserves cheers for succeeding in establishing the ambience it seeks.

Way out West is **Alcala Western Wear** (1733 Chicago Avenue; (312) 226-0152), definitely the place to be if you're in the market for 10,000 pairs of boots (including exotic skins), some 3,000 hats, and heaven knows how many belts. There's lots of leathers and Native American jewelry, too. (It's a five-minute cab ride from the Loop.)

Suburban Shopping Centers, Discount Malls, and Shops

Some Chicago area malls are musts (mostly downtown), a few are recommended if you happen to be in the area, and some don't warrant a visit, even if you're visiting relatives in that suburb.

Most shoppers—whether they're from Lucca in Tuscany or Las Vegas, Nevada—know that a Gap store is a Gap store, Saks Fifth Avenue is SFA, Osco is Osco, and a rose is a rose. Sometimes, however, a mall store will surprise; those are the ones you want to hear about.

If you're driving past the beautiful Baha'i House of Worship on Sheridan Road into Wilmette, you may want to stop at the second-oldest shopping center in the United States, **Plaza Del Lago** (phone (847) 256-4467). The distinctive style of a romantic Spanish courtyard serves as a backdrop for 30 stores—everything from Crate & Barrel to a fine fish store called **Burhop's** (they not only sell fish and basic as well as gourmet foods, but they make wonderful soups and crabcakes, too). With so many places to shop here, you'll get hungry, so stop at **Convito Italiano** or **Betise** for lunch. Convito features Italian foods (their take-out counter and retail food and wine counters are always packed), and Betise has a French bistro flavor.

One of the newsiest, and the biggest shopping center on the north shore is Westfield Shoppingtown's **Old Orchard** (Skokie Boulevard and Old Orchard Road, Skokie). Westfield also owns **Hawthorn,** a large mall in far north Vernon Hills. One of the prettiest outdoor malls, OO was renovated at the time of **Nordstrom's** entrance. This is a beautiful store, as is **Marshall Field's. Saks Fifth Avenue** is another chic anchor, and so are **Lord & Taylor** and **Bloomingdale's.** There are also about 125 more stores, from **FAO Schwarz** to **The Disney Store,** as well as theaters and eateries. Another dining suggestion: two blocks up the road (south) is a terrific seafood restaurant, **Don's Fishmarket** (9335 Skokie Boulevard; (847) 677-3424).

An equally busy and beautiful shopping center is **Northbrook Court,** Northbrook (phone 847) 498-1770). In addition to **Neiman-Marcus, Lord & Taylor, Marshall Fields,** and dozens of other stores that range from the chains **(Gap, Keds, Ann Taylor,** etc.) to more unique stores that aren't found much on the North Shore **(Mark Shale)** and the only **Bice Restaurant** this side of Chicago.

Oakbrook Center (Zone 9) in Oak Brook is what they call premier shopping and what you'd call first-run in the performance lineup of shopping centers. **Saks** anchors here, along with **Nordstrom** (this was the first in the Midwest), **Neiman Marcus, Marshall Field's, Lord &**

Taylor, and **Sears.** Stores here also include **Tiffany & Co., Tommy Hilfiger,** the **Eddie Bauer** (prototype) home store, one of the best museum shops of the **Art Institute, FAO Schwarz, Crate & Barrel, Camille Et Famille** (gifts and artsy home accessories), **Mario Tricoci Hair Salon and Day Spa,** and some 146 others. The Williams-Sonoma store expanded to become **Williams-Sonoma Grande Cuisine** (lots of product demonstrations here).

Woodfield Shopping Center (Zone 10) in Schaumburg (about 40 minutes northwest of Chicago and not far from O'Hare) has been joined by a handful of other shopping centers in the area. Add the **Barrington Ice House** in Barrington, the folksy charm of **Long Grove Shopping Village,** and several small malls in Schaumburg to Woodfield, and you've got Greater Woodfield's four million square feet of retail (and what we last heard was nearly 500 stores). Whew.

Woodfield Shopping Center itself is one of the largest of its kind in the United States, so wear comfy shoes to walk its miles of indoor track. **Nordstrom, Lord & Taylor, Marshall Field's, Sears, J.C. Penney,** and some 230 more are here. Nifty stores vary from **Abercrombie & Fitch** (phone (847) 619-6271) to "learning" stores such as the **Discovery Channel Store** (phone (847) 619-7430), **Rand McNally** (phone (847) 995-8058), and **Imaginarium** (phone (847) 619-1915), where you can find great toys that are educational and fun. At **Build-A-Bear** (phone (847) 517-4155), kids can make their own teddy bears. Another fun place is **Mary Engelbreit** (phone (847) 303-9370), where you'll find products from a nifty designer who invents phrases such as "Let's put the fun back in dysfunctional" and puts 'em on coffee cups. Take the kids to the **Rainforest Cafe** (phone (847) 619-1900), a faux Disney-esque rainforest, to dine.

While out west, it's an excellent idea to investigate the stores in Geneva: **Cocoon** (home/bath accessories), **The Past Basket, Kris Kringle** (a year-round Christmas store), **Paper Merchant,** and **Graham's Chocolate,** all on Third Street; and **Lily of the Valley** (home, garden), **Les Tissus Colbert, One** (an art gallery), **Nature's Gallery,** and **Valley Golf,** all on State Street. And **Galyan's** (sporting goods) leads the lineup at the new **Geneva Commons.** While you're visiting Geneva, it's a great idea to stay at the beautiful **Herrington Inn** (phone (630) 208-7433). Also, in the western suburb of Elgin, several superb shopping sites are **State Street Market Shops** (701 North State Street), **The Painted Lady** (95 South Gilbert Street) gifts and furniture, **The Milk Pail** (north of I-90 on Route 25), and, nearby, **Port Edward** (20 West Algonquin Road, Algonquin) for nautical gifts and antiques.

While we're on the subject of day-tripping, the following destinations may add further incentive to get behind the wheel, shopping bags poised to be filled. All are an hour or two from the city (one-way), so allot enough time. In many cases, however, the savings can be sky-high.

Gurnee Mills Mall, the Midwest's largest value retail and manufacturer outlet mall at the intersection of I-94 and Grand Avenue (Illinois Route 132, Gurnee) is bigger than Soldier Field and attracts more visitors than Graceland. Among the 200 stores are the **Bass Pro Shops Outdoor World** (which is more of an environment than a store, fishing included), **Marshall's Megastore, T.J. Maxx, American Eagle Outfitters, Circuit City, Fuzzwig's Candy Factory, Auntie Ann's Pretzels, Off 5th Saks Fifth Avenue Outlet, J.C. Penney Outlet,** and so many more. For more information, call their tourism department at (800) 937-7467.

Take I-94 and Highway 50 to exit 344 in Kenosha, Wisconsin, and you're at the **Original Outlet Mall** (phone (262) 857-7961): 100 outlet stores include **Eddie Bauer, Carter's** (the kidswear is great), **Oneida, Casio, Hush Puppies Factory Direct, General Nutrition Center**, and **Reebok.**

Prime Outlets at Kenosha (I-94, exit 347 in Kenosha): More chic names are found here than at the other centers. Their big draws are seldom attached to the word "outlet": **Donna Karan, Ralph Lauren, Tommy Hilfiger,** and **J. Crew.** They're joined by other unexpected outlet names, such as **Nordic Trak, Geoffrey Beene, Liz Claiborne, Nike, Jones New York & Co.,** and **Sara Lee Bakery,** among others. Call the center at (414) 857-2101.

And more bargains are available from the **Prime Outlets at Huntley** at 11800 Factory Shop Boulevard, way out west in Huntley, Illinois (phone (847) 669-9100). Of the 50 outlet stores, find **The Gap, Izod, Reebok, Rockport, Casual Corner, Mikasa,** and **Carter's.**

Part Eleven

Exercise and Recreation

Handling Chicago's Weather

Most of the folks on our *Unofficial Guide* research team work out routinely. Some bike, some run, and some lift weights, while others play tennis or do aerobics. We discovered that Chicago is a city of extremes when it comes to climate. In the summer, humidity is intense and temperatures often climb above 90° by midafternoon, making outdoor exercise and recreation problematic unless you plan to lounge on a Lake Michigan beach or go for a swim. Winter, on the other hand, can be positively arctic in intensity, especially in January and February, when cold temperatures and icy blasts off the lake plunge windchill factors to well below zero.

The solution in the summer is to exercise early, before the sun and humidity make conditions outdoors too hot and muggy. In the winter, only hearty outdoor types such as cross-country skiers will want to brave the cold and wind; everyone else should plan to exercise indoors. The good news is that spring and fall are usually delightful for enjoying the outdoors.

Regardless of the season, however, keep in mind that Chicago's weather is highly variable. As the locals like to say, if you don't like the weather, just wait a while; it'll change.

Keep that in mind before setting out on an all-day outing, and take along appropriate rain gear and/or warm clothing.

Indoor Activites

Free Weights and Nautilus

Many of the major hotels in Chicago have either a spa or fitness room with weight-lifting equipment on site, or have reciprocity with a nearby health club that extends privileges to hotel guests. For an aerobic workout, most of the fitness rooms offer a Lifecycle, Stairmaster, or rowing machine.

Fitness Centers and Aerobics

Many Chicago fitness centers are coed and accept daily or short-term memberships. The **Chicago Fitness Center,** located at 3131 North Lincoln Avenue (at Belmont) offers a weight room with 50 pieces of equipment, including free weights, and Nautilus and Universal fixed-weight machines. Aerobic equipment includes Stairmasters, treadmills, and exercise bikes. The daily fee is $10; bring a lock. For more information, call (773) 549-8181.

World Gym and Fitness Center, located at 909 West Montrose (at Sheridan), offers free weights and Nautilus fixed-weight machines, Stairmasters, exercise bikes, Nordic Track, and steam and sauna rooms. The cost is $12 a day; for more information, call (773) 348-1212.

Exercising in Your Hotel

You work out regularly, but here you are stuck on a rainy day in a hotel without an excercise room. Worse, you're out of sorts from overeating, sitting in airplanes, and not being able to let off steam. Don't despair. Unless your hotel is designed like a sprawling dude ranch, you have stairs to play on. Put on your workout clothes and find a nice interior stairwell, which all hotels are required to have in case of fire. Devise a step workout consistent with your fitness level.

Bob's Plan (for a ten-story hotel): From your floor, descend to the very bottom of the stairwell. Walk up ten flights and down again to get warmed up. Then, taking the stairs two at a time, bound up two floors and return to the bottom quickly, but normally (i.e., one step at a time). Next, bound up three floors and return. Add a floor after each circuit until you get to the top floor. Then reverse the process, ascending one less floor on each round trip: nine, eight, seven, etc. You get the idea. Tell somebody where you'll be in case you fall down the stairs or something. Listen to your body and don't overdo it. If your hotel has 30 stories, don't feel compelled to make it to the top.

Joe's Plan (for a ten-story hotel): Sit in the stairwell on the fourth-floor landing with a sixpack of Bud and laugh at Bob every time he chugs past. Thank God that you are not a Type-A obsessive-compulsive.

If steps aren't your gig, you might consider buying a Reebok Slide exerciser. Self-contained, compact, and weighing less than 12 pounds, the slide can be spread out on your hotel room floor for a great workout. Take it with you wherever you travel.

Outdoor Activities

Walking

Though not as compact as, say, most European cities, Chicago is still a great town for getting around by foot. After all, the city is as flat as an Illinois corn field. If you mentally break the city up into discrete chunks—the Loop, River North, the Magnificent Mile, etc.—and you don't overextend yourself, walking is the best way to explore Chicago. Folks who are fit and enjoy using their own two feet should bring comfortable walking shoes and regularly give themselves a rest by occasionally taking a taxi, a bus, or the El.

Along the Lake

Serious walkers and people in search of great scenery and primo people-watching as they stretch their legs should head for Chicago's premier walking destination, the **Lakefront Trail** along Lake Michigan. The 20-mile paved path is flat, clean, well lighted—and usually crowded with people who have the same idea as you. You really haven't done Chicago unless you've experienced the Lakefront Trail.

Some safety notes: The stretch of path from McCormick Place south to Hyde Park is considered bandit turf; stay to the north in daylight hours and you'll be okay. Pedestrian tunnels under Lake Shore Drive make it possible to reach the trail without getting killed on the busy roadway.

City Walks

Other great destinations for a scenic stroll include the **Gold Coast** (a neighborhood of sumptuous mansions and townhouses located just above the Magnificent Mile), **Lincoln Park** (featuring 1,200 acres of greenery, three museums, and a zoo), and **Oak Park** (where strollers can explore a shady neighborhood full of homes designed by Frank Lloyd Wright).

In late 1996, the northbound lanes of Lake Shore Drive were relocated to the west of the Field Museum. New landscaping created a new, traffic-free **Museum Campus** comprising the Field Museum, the Shedd Aquarium, and the Adler Planetarium. Other pedestrian-friendly amenities planned for the ten-acre park include rows of elm trees; a large, sloping lawn in front of the Field Museum and to the west of the Shedd Aquarium; and a series of decorative plazas linked by walkways between the museums. A new pedestrian concourse underneath Lake Shore Drive at Roosevelt Road will serve as an entranceway to the Museum Campus.

The planetarium, by the way, sits on a former island in Lake Michigan that's now linked to the shore by a half-mile peninsula. The view of

Chicago's skyline, as you can imagine, is stupendous, and it's a great place to watch private planes landing and taking off at Meigs Field. It's one of Chicago's top make-out spots.

Another outstanding place to walk is the Gothic—and beautiful—campus of the **University of Chicago** in Hyde Park. Don't miss the unmistakable 12-ton abstract sculpture, *Nuclear Energy,* by Henry Moore; it's located on the spot where Enrico Fermi and other University of Chicago scientists achieved the first self-sustained nuclear chain reaction in 1942.

Farther afield, more great walking destinations include **Brookfield Zoo** (14 miles west of the city), the **Morton Arboretum** (25 miles west of the Loop; 1,500 acres of native woodlands and 25 miles of trails), and the **Chicago Botanic Garden** (300 acres of landscaped gardens and islands located 18 miles north of downtown Chicago).

Running

The Big Enchilada of Chicago running routes is the **Lakefront Trail** along Lake Michigan. And runners, without handlebars sticking out or the need to weave like in-line skaters, have it easier when it comes to penetrating the throngs that choke the path in nice weather. And this is where you'll routinely see the Windy City's most serious runners working out.

Folks looking for more elbow room can go a little north of downtown and run on the section of trail between Belmont Harbor and the northern neighborhood of Edgewater. While the same holds true for the six-mile stretch starting below McCormick Place, it's not nearly as safe.

Good news for runners who prefer training on a soft surface instead of asphalt: Chicago is surrounded by a network of forest preserves that are easy to reach by car. To run in a sylvan setting, head to **Palos Forest Preserve District** in southwest Cook County, about 20 miles from downtown. The nation's largest forest preserve (nearly 14,000 acres) features 80 miles of multipurpose trails, which are ten feet wide and covered with gravel or grass. For more information on Palos and other forest preserves, call (773) 261-8400.

Tennis

The Chicago Park District has close to 700 outdoor tennis courts, and some of them are convenient to visitors staying downtown. The nets go up in mid-April and usually stay up through October. Reservations aren't required for most courts; just put your racquet by the net and the players using the court will know you want to use it next. Other courts require phone reservations; see below.

Daley Bicentennial Plaza, located downtown at 337 East Randolph Street (between Columbus and Lake Shore drives), features 12 lighted courts. For reservations, call (312) 742-7529 after 10 a.m. the day before you plan to play. Hours are 7 a.m. to 10 p.m. weekdays and 8 a.m. to 5 p.m. weekends; the fee is $7 an hour.

Another 12 lighted courts are available in **Grant Park** at 900 South Columbus Drive; reservations aren't accepted, courts are free during the day, and there's a nominal charge after 5 p.m. **Lake Shore Park,** 808 North Lake Shore Drive (across from Northwestern University), has two lighted courts; no reservations are accepted, hours are 7 a.m. to 11 p.m. daily, and they can be used for free. **Waveland,** located in Lincoln Park, features 20 lighted courts. Reservations are required and fees are charged.

McFetridge Sports Center, located at 3843 North California Avenue in northwest Chicago, has six indoor tennis courts. Rates are $13 per person/per hour from 7 a.m.–4 p.m. daily; $20 in the evening from 4 p.m.–10 p.m.; and on weekends, $22 from 7 a.m.–7 p.m., reduced to $20 from 7 p.m.–10 pm. Call (312) 742-7586 for reservations.

Golf

The Chicago Park District boasts six public golf courses managed by Kemper Golf Management. The courses are open mid-April through November from dawn to dusk. Make reservations at least a week in advance on Kemper's helpful automated phone tee-time reservation system, which provides directions to and descriptions of all six courses. Have a credit card handy and keep in mind that no rain checks or refunds are issued; call (312) 245-0909.

The **Sydney R. Marovitz Golf Course** (usually called "Waveland," the course's former name) is the *crème de la crème* of Chicago's public courses. Located close to the ritzy Gold Coast and Lake Michigan, the course features great views, a location close to downtown, and a design modeled on Pebble Beach. Not a lot of trees, but the fairways are fairly long (3,290 yards) compared to other municipal courses.

It's the place to go to impress a client—and you won't be alone. The nine-hole course handles about 400 golfers a day; figure on three hours to play a round. Fees for adult nonresidents are $16 on weekdays, $18 on weekends, and $9 on weekdays, $10 on weekends for seniors and kids. The course is located at the lakefront in Lincoln Park; (312) 742-7930.

South Shore Golf Course, located at 7059 Lake Shore Drive, is a nine-holer that's fairly short (2,903 yards). But the holes are well designed and moderately challenging, and South Shore is considered an undiscovered gem. The setting on the lake means that every hole is a visual feast, whether it's waves of Lake Michigan crashing along the fairway or spectacular views of the city. It's also the only municipal course that rents driving carts ($14 per round). Fees for adult nonresidents are $12 on weekdays, $14 on weekends, and $9 on weekdays; $10 on weekends for seniors and kids.

Robert A. Black Golf Course, located at 2045 West Pratt Street (near the lakefront and the city's northern boundary), is a nine-hole, 3,200-yard course with no water hazards. But it does have 21 bunkers (sand traps), making it a challenging course. Adult nonresident fees are $14 weekdays, $15 weekends, and $9 on weekdays; $10 on weekends for seniors and kids. Call (312) 742-7931.

Chicago's only 18-hole municipal course is at **Jackson Park,** located near the southern terminus of Lake Shore Drive at 63rd Street and Stony Island Avenue. It's a moderately difficult, 5,538-yard course with a lot of trees, but not much sand or water. Fees for adult nonresidents are $19 weekdays, $20 weekends, and $11 on weekdays; $12 on weekends for seniors and kids. Call (312) 747-2763.

Marquette Park Golf Course, a nine-holer located at 6700 South Kedzie Avenue (at 67th Street near Midway Airport), offers wide fairways and water on seven holes. The 3,300-yard course is rated pretty easy. Adult nonresident fees are $13 weekdays, $14 weekends, and $9 on weekdays; $10 on weekends for seniors and kids. Call (312) 747-2761.

Located west of downtown near Oak Park, **Columbus Park Golf Course** (5700 West Jackson Boulevard) is recommended for novices. The 2,832-yard course offers wide, open fairways and large greens. Fees for adult nonresidents are $12 weekdays, $14 weekends, and $9 on weekdays; $10 on weekends for seniors and kids. Call (312) 746-5573.

Road Bicycling and In-Line Skating

With the exception of hardened urban cyclists and former bike messengers, recreational riders should stay off Chicago's mean streets. And that goes double for weaving in-line skaters.

So where's the best place to ride a skinny-tire bike or skate the black ice? That's easy—the **Lakefront Trail,** which hums with throngs of the Lycra-clad and sportif, is the Windy City's primo riding and Rollerblading destination. Any excursion on the paved path along Lake Michigan is an out-and-back endeavor, so try to figure out which way the wind blows before starting out. Then ride or skate out into a head wind, which becomes a helpful tail wind on the way back. If you want to avoid the worst of the crowds, try riding or 'blading north of downtown between Belmont Harbor and the neighborhood of Edgewater.

The six-mile stretch of trail south of McCormick Place is considered unsafe, in spite of beefed-up bike-mounted police patrols. "Gangs use two-way radios to spot riders on bikes with suspension forks, beat the shit out of them and steal their bikes," reports Chicago cyclist Ron Bercow, former manager of the Performance Bike Shop on North Halsted Street. Ride with a friend and go early, and you should be all right.

Renting Bikes and In-Line Skates

Bike Chicago rents bikes at three locations along the Lakefront Trail and offers free maps, group guided tours, and delivery to your hotel. For more information, check out **www.bikechicago.com;** you receive a 10% discount for reserving online. You can also call (800) 915-BIKE.

For rental of high-quality in-line skates, your best bet is **Windward Sports,** located at 3317 North Clark Street. Rates are $15 a day; the shop is only three blocks from the Lakefront Trail. For more information, call (773) 472-6868.

Road Rides

Local roadies who like to go the distance say the best road riding is out Sheridan Road and north to Kenosha, Wisconsin—a 115-mile round-trip ride, if you're up for it. A shorter option is to drive to Evanston, park at Northwestern University, and ride north on Sheridan Road to Fort Sheridan, about 30 miles round-trip. Although Sheridan Road is scenic and even has a couple of hills (!), it's not very bicycle-friendly—there's no bike lane, often not much shoulder, and traffic is heavy—so it's a route best left to experienced road cyclists.

Mountain Biking

Even though it's paved, the **Lakefront Trail** is Chicago's number one fat-tire route. But what if you want the feel of mud between your knobbies? While mountain biking has taken the Windy City by storm (just like everywhere else), we're sad to report that challenging single-track trails are scarce around Chicago.

The **Palos Forest Preserve District** in Cook County has restricted bicycles to designated single-track trails in the immensely popular 14,000-acre Palos Preserve. It's a ravine-sliced forest located 20 miles southwest of the city and the best place around for dedicated fat-tire fanatics to rock 'n' roll in the dirt. Call Palos at (708) 771-1330 for a free map showing the trails that are okay to ride.

For comprehensive, detailed info about all the single-track options in the immediate area and beyond, consult *Mountain Bike! Midwest* and *Mountain Bike! Wisconsin,* both published by Menasha Ridge Press.

For the Hard-Core

Local hammerheads report the most adventurous, varied, and accessible single-track action is found at **Kettle Moraine** in Wisconsin, about a 90-minute drive from Chicago. A system of trails originally cut for hikers (and now legal for mountain bikes) features some steep and narrow stuff that will thrill experienced mountain bikers, but might put off first-time riders. For more information, call (262) 594-6200.

To get there, take I-94 to Wisconsin Highway 50 to US 12. Park at the LaGrange General Store and pick up sandwiches and maps; then head down County Road H a mile to the main parking area. The parking fee is $10, and there's a $3 per person trail-use fee (must be 16 or older).

Easy Riding

Other off-road options close to Chicago are considerably tamer than the challenging trails in Palos. Forty miles west of Chicago, the **Fox River Trail** provides relative solitude and easy pedaling on a 37-mile stretch of asphalt and crushed limestone that follows the eponymous river between the *Wayne's World*–type suburbs of Aurora and Elgin. **Mill Race Cyclery,** located in the western suburb of Geneva at 11 East State Street, rents hybrid and mountain bikes for use on the trail. Rates are $6 an hour (two-hour minimum), and $25 a day on weekends. For more information, call the shop at (630) 232-2833.

The **Busse Woods Bicycle Trail** is an 11-mile scenic bike path weaving through the woods and meadows of the 3,700-acre Ned Brown Preserve, located in northwestern Cook County about 20 miles from the Loop.

The **North Branch Bicycle Trail** starts at Caldwell and Devon Avenues in Chicago and continues north 20 miles along the North Branch of the Chicago River to the Chicago Botanic Garden. Pack a lunch and picnic at the gardens; freshwater wells are located along the trail.

Swimming

The Lake Michigan shore is lined with 31 sand beaches for sunning and swimming. These public beaches are manned with lifeguards from June to mid-September daily from 9 a.m. to 9 p.m. and are free. Lockers are available at the major beaches.

Oak Street Beach, the closest to downtown and only a credit card's throw away from Bloomingdale's, is called the St. Tropez of the Midwest. It's also the most crowded of the lakefront beaches; the young and the beautiful, perfect-ten models, jet-setting flight attendants, all-American Frisbee-tossing frat brothers and sorority sisters, Eurotrash, ordinary folk, and voyeurs blanket the sand on steamy summer weekends. Pedestrians can get there safely via the underpass across from the Drake Hotel at Michigan Avenue and Oak Street.

North Avenue Beach is more family-oriented than hip Oak Street Beach and stretches north for a mile, from just above North Avenue to Fullerton Avenue. Farther north, **Montrose Avenue Beach** offers great views of the Chicago skyline.

Rule of thumb: The crowds at the popular beaches tend to thin out the farther north you go. Example: Unabashed bare-it-all types flock to **Pratt Boulevard Beach** for illegal skinny-dipping in the wee hours. Separated by a seldom-used park, a wide beach, no spotlights, no high-rises, no searchlights, and even a little hill to block joggers' views, the dark, sandy beach near Morse Avenue may be the perfect place to take it all off and dive into the surf.

A practical note: Lake Michigan water can be chilly, even in August.

Paddling

For folks in search of a touch of wilderness solitude, the best bet in lake-bound Chicago is by water. While powerboat traffic on Lake Michigan can make the lake a misery of chop, noise, and exhaust on summer afternoons, tranquility in a canoe or sea kayak can be found early in the morning or late at night. On the main branch of the Chicago River, canoeing may be the best way of enjoying the architectural delights of the city, while a canoe trek on the North Branch of the river reveals an astounding amount of wildlife for an urban stream.

Headquarters for paddling information and rentals in the Windy City is **Chicagoland Canoe Base,** located at 4019 North Narraganset Avenue (phone (773) 777-1489). Vic Hurtowy points clients toward some of the Midwest's best-kept paddling secrets, such as the Skokie Lagoons, a nearby urban jewel where boaters can sneak up on deer, coyote, fox, great blue heron, egrets, and other fish-eating birds.

Canoe rentals are $40 the first day and $20 each additional day, and include a car-top carrier, paddles, personal flotation devices, and plenty of advice. The shop also schedules more than 100 organized trips a year; they're free. Give Vic a call to find out what's on tap.

Windsurfing

The Windy City earns its epithet with nine-mile-an-hour average winds on Lake Michigan. Hey, it ain't Oregon's Columbia River Gorge, but Chicago boardsailors aren't complaining. **Montrose Beach** is rated Chicago's safest launch point, with the **South Side Rainbow Beach** next in popularity.

Never tried windsurfing? **Windward Sports** offers a two-day certification course that will teach you all you need to know for $120. Lessons are given at Wolf Lake, south of Chicago near the Indiana state line; it's a controlled environment that's safe and lets novices concentrate on learning skills. Board rentals, offered June through August by Windward Sports at Montrose Beach, are $35 a day. For more information, call the shop at (773) 472-6868.

To get a marine weather forecast before setting out, call the National Weather Service at (815) 834-0675. Keep in mind that Chicago's quick-change weather can leave novices stranded far from shore.

Ice Skating

Daley Bicentennial Plaza, located at 337 East Randolph, features an outdoor, 80-by-135-foot rink with stunning views of Lake Michigan and the Loop. The season on the prepared rink (which is equipped with chillers) starts in November and runs through mid-March. Hours are 10 a.m. to 10 p.m. daily. Admission is $3 for adults and $2 for children age 14 and under; figure-skate rentals are the same price as admission. For more information, call (312) 742-7648

At **Skate on State** (in the Loop at State and Randolph Streets) skating admission is $3 during a season that lasts from November through mid-March. During the week, two-hour sessions run 9 to 11:15 a.m., noon to 2 p.m., 2:30 to 4:30 p.m., and 5 to 7:15 p.m. On weekends, shorter sessions run 9 to 11 a.m., 11:30 a.m. to 1 p.m., 1:30 to 3 p.m., and 3:30 to 7:15 p.m. Skate rentals per session are $4 for adults and $3 for children. For more information, call (312) 744-3315.

Downhill Skiing

The closest ski resort to Chicago is **Wilmot Mountain,** about an hour's drive north of O'Hare, just over the Wisconsin state line. The resort features 25 runs with a 230-foot vertical, snowmaking, night skiing until 11 p.m., a pro shop, rentals, instruction, cafeteria, and bar. Weather permitting, Wilmot is open from December 1 through mid-March; call their local snow information line at (773) 736-0787. For directions and a list of local motels, call (262) 862-2301.

Cross-Country Skiing

When Mother Nature lays down a blanket of the white stuff, a lot of Chicagoans strap on skinny skis and head for the nearest park or forest preserve to enjoy a day of kicking and gliding.

Camp Sagawau, located about 20 miles southwest of the Loop in the Cook County Palos Forest Preserve District, features a system of groomed cross-country ski trails that traverse a scenic landscape of forest and prairie. The Sag Trail is gentle and ideal for novices, while rolling Ridge Run accommodates intermediate and advanced Nordic skiers.

The trails are open whenever there's enough snow on the ground to ski; ski rentals and lessons are also available. Camp Sagawau is on Route 83 east of Archer Avenue at 12545 West 111th Street in Lemont. For more information, a snow report, and directions, call (630) 257-2045.

Spectator Sports

A Sports-Crazy Town

Chicago is quite possibly the most sports-crazy town in the United States, a city famous for its teams that win frequently . . . and those that don't. Either way, Chicago sports fans are renowned for their tenacity, whether it's for the oft-winning Bears, Bulls, or Blackhawks, or those perennial losers, the Chicago Cubs.

The enthusiasm is fueled by a sports culture steeped in tradition and folklore. Consider this: In 1876, the same year General George Custer was shut out by Sitting Bull at Little Big Horn, the team that would evolve into today's Chicago Cubs won the National League championship in its first season of baseball. Since then, Chicagoans have shown an unwavering passion for pro sports. Other notable events and personalities from Chicago's sports past include the "Black Sox" betting scandal of 1919, Hall of Fame TV and radio sports announcer Harry Caray singing an off-key "Take Me Out to the Ballgame" during the seventh-inning stretch at Wrigley Field, the glorious Bears triumph of 1986, and Michael Jordan, the world's most famous athlete, leading the Chicago Bulls to consecutive NBA championships.

For visitors, the quintessential Chicago sporting experience is an afternoon baseball game at Wrigley Field, home of the Cubs. It's a place where fans feel like they've stepped back in time to the days before World War II. Spectators love the ivy-covered walls, the way errant breezes can turn pop-ups into home runs, and the opportunity for some first-rate people-watching as all sizes, shapes, and classes of Chicagoans root for the Cubs.

Chicago is also blessed with many colleges and universities, which provide a wide array of spectator sports. For current listings and goings-on of both pro and amateur events, check the sports sections of the *Chicago Tribune* and the *Chicago Sun-Times*.

Pro Teams

Baseball

Chicago is home to two professional baseball teams: The **Chicago Cubs** (National League), who play at venerable Wrigley Field on the North Side (1060 West Addison) and the **Chicago White Sox** (American League), who play at Comiskey Park on the South Side (333 West 35th Street). The season starts around the first week of April and continues through early October.

The Cubs, as most baseball fans know, are a testament to Chicago's unstoppable allegiance in the face of adversity; the team hasn't won a

World Series since 1908. No matter—like the New York Mets of yester-year, the Cubbies are affectionately embraced by Chicago fans and picture-perfect Wrigley Field draws more than two million fans each year for a taste of baseball history. Although lights were added to the stadium in 1988, most games are still played during the day; aficionados insist it's still the only way to see a game at the park.

For schedule information, call (773) 404-2827; tickets can be ordered by calling (312) 831-CUBS (in Illinois) or (800) 347-CUBS (outside Illinois). Get tickets as far in advance as possible, but you can try your luck at the ticket window or outside the gates before game time; some gracious souls occasionally sell or even give away extra tickets. Scalpers are another source.

Street parking is restricted during day games in the neighborhood around Wrigley Field; public transportation is the best way for visitors to reach the park. Take the Englewood/Howard El line to the Addison Street station.

While geography divides the fans of the North Side Cubs from the South Side White Sox, they're at least joined together by a long tradition of championship futility; the Sox last won the World Series in 1917. Today the White Sox play in Comiskey Park, which replaced the old stadium of the same name in 1991. The new facility features unobstructed views of the action and TV monitors in the walkways so fans don't miss a thing. *Warning:* The upper-deck seats should be avoided by folks who are prone to nose bleeds or scared of heights.

To find out when the White Sox are playing at home or for tickets, call (312) 674-1000. Forget about parking at Comiskey; on-street parking is virtually nonexistent and the official lots are a nightmare to get in and out of. Take the train: El service runs along the Dan Ryan Expressway two blocks to the east; get off at 35th Street. Large crowds flocking to and from the game virtually eliminate the chance of getting mugged on the short walk, but watch out for pickpockets working the throngs.

Football

Sports tradition in Chicago isn't restricted to baseball. The **Chicago Bears** can point to a football history that goes back to the 1930s. Yet like their baseball counterparts, "da Bears" suffer from an inability to win championships. Only in 1986 has the team won the Super Bowl—a game that made William "Refrigerator" Perry a household name.

Pro gridiron action takes place at Soldier Field, where a colonnade of paired 100-foot concrete Doric columns rise majestically behind fans brave enough to endure icy blasts off Lake Michigan. Glassed-in skyboxes added in 1981 to shelter corporate hotshots cost over $7,500 a game; the price is negotiable if rented for the season. Soldier Field is located at 425 East McFetridge Drive (at South Lake Shore Drive, just south of the Field Museum).

For tickets and information on Bears games, call (847) 615-2327 Monday through Friday from 9 a.m. to 4 p.m. Alas, subscription sales account for most tickets. Your best bet is to locate a subscriber trying to unload a ticket before the game. Parking is relatively plentiful and nearby. Public transportation: By bus, take the #146 State Street/North Michigan Avenue downtown, or the Red or Orange Line train to the Roosevelt Road station and walk east.

Basketball

The NBA **Chicago Bulls** always sell out. Currently, the team plays in the United Center, a $170 million arena that seats 21,500 and is adorned with 217 luxury skyboxes. For game times, call (312) 455-4000. To purchase tickets, call (312) 559-1212; the season starts in October and runs through April.

Tickets go on sale in September for the season and some games sell out in a few weeks. Scattered single tickets are sometimes available two weeks before a game, but day-of-game tickets are never available. The United Center is located at 1901 West Madison Street, west of the Loop; take the #20 Madison Street bus.

Hockey

Loud, gregarious fans like to watch the NHL **Chicago Blackhawks** mix it up on the ice as much as they like to mix it up in the stands. They're also fiercely devoted to the team, which has claimed three National Hockey League championship trophies—in 1934, 1938, and 1961.

The Blackhawks share quarters with the Chicago Bulls in the United Center, located at 1901 East Madison Street; take the #20 Madison Street bus. For schedules and game times, call (312) 455-4500; for tickets, call (312) 559-1212. The season runs October through April.

Soccer

For fast indoor soccer action, watch the **Chicago Power** play at the Rosemont Horizon near O'Hare. Order tickets by calling (312) 559-1212. To get there, take the Blue Line train to the River Road station. The season starts in November and ends in April.

College Sports

Chicago's only Division I conference (Big Ten) football/basketball representatives are the **Northwestern University Wildcats,** who play in nearby Evanston. Gridiron action takes place in Ryan Field, 1501 Central Avenue; call (847) 491-7503. Basketball is played at McGaw Hall/Welsch-Ryan Arena, 2705 Ashland Avenue; call (847) 491-7887.

Other college basketball teams include the **DePaul Blue Demons,** who play at DePaul University, 1011 West Belden (phone (312) 362-8000); the **Loyola Ramblers,** who provide on-the-court action at Loyola University, 6525 North Sheridan Road (phone (773) 508-2560); and the University of Illinois at **Chicago Flames,** who play ball at the University of Illinois Pavilion, 1150 West Harrison Street (phone (312) 413-5700).

Horse Racing

Out of the ashes of the old Arlington Park Race Track (which burned in 1985) has risen **Arlington International Race Course,** rated as an even bigger and better thoroughbred racing/entertainment venue. The horses run May through October; the track is located at Euclid and Wilkie Roads in Arlington Heights (about 25 miles northwest of the Loop). For more information, call (847) 255-4300.

Hawthorne Race Course in Cicero features harness-racing excitement and thoroughbred racing. The track is located at 3501 South Laramie Avenue, about five miles southwest of the Loop. For post times and more information, call (708) 780-3700. **Sportsman's Park,** next to Hawthorne in Cicero, is now a multipurpose facility, featuring thoroughbred racing from February through mid-May. Call (773) 242-1121 for more information. Other offerings include auto racing and concerts.

Off-Track Betting and Riverboat Casinos

Folks allergic to real horses and mud can still play the ponies at off-track betting locations downtown. There are two locations: **State Street OTB** at 177 North State Street (phone (312) 419-8787) and **Jackson OTB** at 223 West Jackson (phone (312) 427-2300).

Riverboat gambling is as close as an hour away from downtown Chicago. **Hollywood Casino Aurora** features slots, table games, dining, Las Vegas–style entertainment, and movie memorabilia. Hollywood's boats depart every 90 minutes from 8:30 a.m. to 9:30 p.m. (often later on weekends) daily for three-hour sessions on the Fox River. Admission is free. Patrons must be age 21 or older and a photo ID may be required. For more information and directions, call (800) 888-7777.

Empress River Casino offers more than 1,000 slots and more than 60 table games, plus Empress Off-Track Betting. Fourteen gaming sessions are offered daily; gaming and boarding begin 30 minutes prior to departure. Express bus service is only available from downtown hotels to the Hammond location; call (888) 436-7737 for more information.

Harrah's Northern Star and *Southern Star II* cruise the Des Plaines River with three levels of gaming, entertainment, and dining. **Harrah's Joliet Casino** operates daily from 8:30 a.m. to 6:30 p.m. Cruises are free. Reservations are suggested on Friday and Saturday. Call (800) HARRAHS for more information.

Part Twelve

Entertainment and Nightlife

Chicago after Dark

It's easier to navigate the neon passages of Chicago than those in New York or Los Angeles. The city's clearly defined neighborhoods create landscapes of welcome or warning. A majority of Chicagoans have lived here most of their lives. They are honest and sometimes homespun to a fault. They will always point you in the right direction.

Chicago is a hands-on city:

A true Chicagoan plays 16-inch softball—without a glove.

A true Chicago nightcrawler makes the rounds—without a doubt.

People go out at night to see reflections of themselves. When you see Chicago's nightlife, you will bear witness to a muscular city where people drink beer with one hand and munch a deep-dish pizza with the other.

For the maximum Chicago experience, check out neighborhood bars, diners, music clubs, and theater groups. Stay away from the chains like Hard Rock Cafe and the Cheesecake Factory. Do not go to a nightclub where people are waiting in line between fancy velvet ropes. Chicagoans identify with close-to-home culture more than any big city in America.

Chicago's wide and deep ethnic classes shape a unique sense of purity. New York and Los Angeles are about a "scene." Chicago is about a spirit. Urban blues, soul, alternative country, and house music began as determined underrcurents of Chicago culture—they are now part of America's music lexicon. The **Second City** improvisational troupe named itself because of the shadow cast by New York. Now Second City is world famous.

Architect Louis Sullivan's beautiful **Auditorium Theatre** tumbled into disrepair for more than 20 years, but in the mid-1960s, Chicagoans came together to save the historic palace. In the late 1990s, the city's downtown theater district was reborn with the renovation of classic movie palaces like the **Shubert Theatre,** the **Ford Center/Oriental Theatre,** and the **Cadillac Palace**—all within walking distance of each other. The historic **Goodman Theater** opened an extravagant two-theater space downtown. All of the city's major sports teams carry a storied legacy of coming back from one disaster or another. Chicagoans identify with this. They are a forgiving lot.

Live Entertainment

There's a feisty, eclectic ethic at the heart of Chicago's live entertainment scene, which can be divided into seven hands-on categories: live rock, jazz, country music, live blues, cabaret, theater, and classical music. The profiles of clubs that follow focus on live music, dance clubs, and the storied neighborhood taverns.

Nightly schedules of live music clubs, comedy clubs, and theatrical productions, as well as comprehensive listings of movie showtimes and other events, are printed in the *Chicago Sun-Times* Friday "Weekend Plus" section, the *Chicago Tribune* "Friday" section, and the free *New City* and *Chicago Reader* alternative newspapers.

Live Rock

Chicago has quietly replaced Seattle as the independent rock capitol of America. A slew of critically acclaimed record labels such as Bloodshot, Thrill Jockey, Minty Fresh, Pravda, Drag City, Wax Trax, and others have created a scene that filters through the city's live music clubs. Popular rock figures like Billy Corgan (formerly of the Smashing Pumpkins), Jeff Tweedy of Wilco, and Jon Langford (Mekons, Waco Brothers) also call Chicago home.

Metro (3730 North Clark Street; (773) 549-0203) is the motherlode for the independent rock movement. Owner Joe Shanahan has consistently championed up-and-coming bands in his lovingly sleazy theater-cabaret in the shadows of Wrigley Field. Metro is heavily into alternative and grunge with a sprinking of national acts such as Lucinda Williams, Tom Jones, and even Bob Dylan. Shanahan gave the Smashing Pumpkins their big break, allowing them to open for bands like Jane's Addiction at Metro. Demographics slide around as expected; young hipsters for alternative shows, old hippies for Dylanesque gigs. Shanahan also owns the smaller **Double Door** (1572 North Milwaukee Avenue; (773) 489-3160), which is a noisy dump. You are in luck if you find a night where the young neighborhood crowd is actually listening to the music.

A more connective experience can be had down the street at **Phyllis' Musical Inn** (1800 West Division Street; (773) 486-9862). Portions of the Michael J. Fox–Joan Jett film *Light of Day* were shot in this sweet, ramshackle, 100-seat family-run bar. After World War II and through the early 1960s, West Division Street was known as "Polish Broadway" because more than a dozen nightclubs on the strip featured live polka music. Open since 1954, Phyllis' is the last remnant of that era. The bar features alternative country and rock bookings before an easygoing audience that generally falls in the 20–30 age group.

One of the newer entries on the progressive rock music landscape is **The Abbey** (3420 West Grace at Elston; (773) 478-4408). The Abbey is an old-school Irish pub whose booking policy ranges from cutting edge national acts like Pere Ubu and Mark Eitzel to Chicago-based alternative country and rock bands. Sight lines can get a little fuzzy when the pub gets crowded, but a balcony affords a better view. The Abbey gets bonus points for live rugby matches broadcast via satellite on Sunday morning and a dinner and weekend breakfast menu. The event dictates the audience. Young slackers come for the alternative rock shows, toothless beer drinkers roll in for the Sunday-morning rugby sessions.

During the 1970s and 1980s, the Lincoln Park neighborhood was a focal point of live rock and blues and the **Wise Fools Pub** was a smart player in that scene. The Wise Fools has reopened in its original location (2270 North Lincoln; (773) 929-1300). You won't catch many big names playing the 250-seat listening room, but there's ample local pop and rock bands for a crowd made up of a lot of students from nearby De Paul University. You can also catch a sense of history: George Thorogood made his Chicago debut in this room in 1979, and blues queen Koko Taylor used to hold court here.

The Wrigleyville neighborhood (near Wrigley Field, of course) is the home of one of America's oldest live reggae clubs, **The Wild Hare: A Singing Armadillo Frog Sanctuary** (3530 North Clark Street; (773) 327-4273). Co-owned by former members of the Ethiopian band Dallol, who toured behing reggae superstar Ziggy Marley, this cozy nightclub has presented live reggae and lots of dancing seven nights a week since 1979. It has evolved into a cultural mecca for transplanted Jamaicans and Africans. And the joint never runs short of Red Stripe and rum.

Just a few blocks south of Wrigleyville is **Schubas Tavern** (3159 North Southport Avenue; (773) 525-2508), a very comfortable restaurant-bar-music-room heavy on acoustic music and small jazz outfits. American roots artists such as Steve Earle, Steve Forbert, and Alex Chilton have performed for folks of all ages in the pristine 100-seat room.

Other essential (and deeply intimate) rooms on the live alternative rock/pop circuit include **Martyrs'** (3855 North Lincoln Avenue; (773) 404-9494), the grungy **Empty Bottle** (1035 North Western Avenue; (773) 276-3600) and **The California Clipper** (1002 North California; (773) 384-2547), a delightfully restored 1940s cocktail lounge that also sails off into live jazz and alternative country.

The Chicago area (don't call it Chicagoland) has several mega- and middle-sized rock concert venues. Chicagoans love summer due to the tempermental nature of the other seasons. The big outdoor sheds are very popular. The 28,000-seat **Tweeter Center** (formerly the World Music Theatre, Ridgeland Avenue and Flossmoor Road in south suburban Tinley Park; (708) 614-1616) is one of the largest outdoor concert facilities in the country. Acts like Bruce Springsteen, John Mellencamp, and Jimmy Buffett play to full houses here. Bring binoculars; even pavilion seats can be far away.

The **Ravinia Festival** in the northern suburb of Highland Park (phone (847) 266-5000) is older, prettier, and more intimate. The focus is generally on classical music, although light rock and roots acts pop up. Ravinia has a capacity for 15,000 fans on lawn seating and 3,500 in a rustic pavilion. The city's newest outdoor venue is **Skyline Stage** at Navy Pier (phone (312) 595-7437), located east of downtown and just off of Lake Michigan, which means it isn't a bad idea to bring a windbreaker.

The city and suburbs are sprinkled with diverse indoor live music venues. The home of the Chicago Bulls and Chicago Blackhawks, the 22,000-seat **United Center** (1901 West Madison Street.; (312) 455-4500) books mega-acts like the Rolling Stones, Paul McCartney, Neil Diamond, and Bruce Springsteen. Built in 1980, the **Allstate Arena** (6920 North Mannheim Road, in Rosemont, next to O'Hare Airport; (847) 635-6601) also features superstar caliber acts with a spin on country music. The Allstate Arena holds up to 18,500 folks for music events, and don't let the suburban location scare you off. It is accessible by the Chicago El.

Middle-range rock venues include the **Park West** (322 West Armitage Avenue; (773) 929-1322) a former strip club turned into an elegant 800-seat music room; the 1,200-seat **Vic Theatre,** a vaudeville house built in 1912 (3145 North Sheffield Avenue; (773) 427-0449); the cavernous **Riviera Theatre** (4746 North Racine at Lawrence and Broadway avenues; (773) 275-1012) where Warren Zevon fell off the stage into the orchestra pit during his drinking days; and the crazy **Aragon Ballroom** (1106 West Lawrence Avenue; (773) 561-9500). A popular spot for big band dancing in the 1940s, the Aragon (capacity 5,500) now almost exclusively features head-banging metal music, in which the room's horrible acoustics really don't matter. Tickets for all these shows are usually available by phone from TicketMaster at (312) 559-1212, but be on guard for "service" charges and handling fees.

Jazz

Chicago's live jazz scene has made a lively migration from downtown clubs and hotels into the neighborhoods. The first stop on any jazz lover's tour should be the historic **Green Mill Jazz Club** (4802 North Broadway; (773) 878-5552). The Green Mill is the anchor of the funky Uptown neighborhood. Al Capone drank here; check out the hideaway trap door behind the bar. Chicago's best-known jazz musicians—like Patricia Barber and Kurt Elling—hold court in this colorful club.

For authentic ambience, head to the **Velvet Lounge** (2128½ South Indiana Street; (312) 791-9050), which since 1982 has been owned by powerful Chicago tenor saxophonist Fred Anderson. He conducts jam sessions between 6 and 10:30 p.m. every Sunday. Anderson is a founding member of the South Side's respected Association for the Advancement of Creative Musicians.

The most dependable downtown jazz spots are **Andy's** (11 East Hubbard Street; (312) 642-6805), a soulful bar and grill that's known for vibrant after-work sets featuring top local players, and the historic **Jazz Showcase** (59 West Grand; (312) 670-2473). Irrepressible owner Joe Segal books many prestigious national acts into his intimate room, which features a blessing from a blown-up, black-and-white photograph of Duke Ellington that hangs between velvety blue curtains behind the stage. In almost 50 years of operation, Segal and his Jazz Showcase have moved through several Chicago locations; the current spot is well served by a tie-in with the nearby Maggiano's restaurant for dinner-show packages.

A little farther north, **Green Dolphin Street** (named after the classic tune "On Green Dolphin Street," 2200 North Ashland; (773) 395-0066) is the newest jazz club on the block, featuring straight-ahead local jazz with occasional salsa and funk-inspired acid jazz bookings. A cool decor is defined by a lofty ceiling, wood paneling, blinds, and white cloth–covered tables. The club seats around 120 and serves appetizer-type snacks and drinks. There is also an adjacent restaurant.

Country and Western

Although Chicago music is most closely identified with blues and jazz, it once was a mecca for country music. During the 1940s and 1950s, country artists from the South were drawn to Chicago, since it was the home of the WLS National Barn Dance (1924–1960). For its last 30 years, the live music show was broadcast from the Eighth Street Theater (now the site of the Conrad Hilton International Ballroom). The hardscrabble aura of the big industrial city also attracted a blue collar population that liked to work hard and play hard. During the 1950s, just the 3000 block of West Madison Street alone (not far from the current United Center) featured five live country music joints with colorful names such as the Casanova Club and the Wagon Wheel.

You can still feel this gritty spirit in the working-class Uptown neighborhood by visiting **Carol's Pub** (4659 North Clark; (773) 334-2402, open to 4 a.m. Friday–Sunday) and the **Lakeview Lounge** (5110 North Broadway, just a boot scoot north from Carol's; (773) 769-0994, open to 4 a.m. daily, 5 a.m. on Saturday). Lakeview Lounge is a tad cleaner than Carol's and has a better jukebox (Webb Pierce, Marty Robbins, Steve Earle; all on 45s). One country singer looked at the potted plants by the Lakeview front window and remarked how the place had become "feng shuied." You can sit at the bar and watch the El rumble by across the street. Snacks include Tombstone pizza and porkies. The house band Nightwatch has played here forever. The trio plays country standards from a small stage wedged behind the bar every Thursday through Saturday night (no cover). Carol's also features live music on weekends from another band with another generic name—Diamondback. They take requests, but don't ask for any Dixie Chicks. Carol's has a more ambitious menu (hamburgers, shrimp, fish, veal), but the kitchen looks unusually suspect from the U-shaped bar. Carol's has also gone full-tilt patriotic after the 2001 terrorist attacks; make special note of the red, white, and blue U.S.A. boxing gloves that hang above the bar.

More genteel country fans should trek out to the **Sundance Saloon** (Routes 176 and 83 in far north suburban Mundelein; (847) 949-0858). The saloon opened in 1975, which makes it the oldest continously running country bar in the state of Illinois. The Sundance has two dance floors and presents live music on weekends. Dance lessons nightly; the club is open Tuesday–Saturday, 7 p.m.–3 a.m.

Live Blues

An essential live blues experience still reflects the city's segregated tradition. A great majority of whites and tourists go to North Side clubs, and most African Americans go to South Side clubs. It has been that way since the Hoochie Coochie Man was a kid.

Still, there is not as much difference between North and South Side shows today as there was in the 1960s and 1970s. All South Side (and West Side) shows are casual, and there is more sitting-in on sets. South Side artists hang out in the street with their friends. The North Side clubs are more structured, have better sound, and in general, feature higher quality musicianship because artists are paid better.

Here are the best of the Chicago blues clubs:

Checkerboard Lounge (423 East 43rd Street on the south side; (773) 624-3240). Chicago blues guitarist Buddy Guy owned this club between 1972 and 1986, when it became known for jam sessions whenever blues-influenced guitarists such as Eric Clapton and Jimmy Page came to town. Guy cut his chops along 43rd Street listening to legends such as slide guitarist Earl Hooker and Muddy Waters before much of the neighborhood was gutted during the late-1960s riots. The Checkerboard is the last bastion of that precious history, which you can still get a feel for through black-and-white promotional photos of blues stars, a humble stage decorated by blue and silver rayon curtains, and a loud blues jukebox. Live music is featured Thursday through Monday nights. Take a cab.

Today, Guy has moved to the South Loop where he owns **Buddy Guy's Legends** (754 South Wabash Avenue; (312) 427-0333). Guy periodically plays to sold-out crowds in the spacious but spirited room, which mixes local and national bookings. The late Stevie Ray Vaughan, Jeff Beck, and Eric Clapton have performed at Legends. This is the only Chicago blues bar with a full kitchen, wide-screen television sets, and ample pool tables.

Rosa's Lounge (3420 West Armitage Avenue; (773) 342-0452) celebrates traditional values in the middle of a transitional Hispanic neighborhood. The 150-person-capacity club is owned by Italian blues drummer Tony Manguilo and his mother, Rosa. Their passionate approach to American blues stretches from a tenderly refurbished mahogany bar to a spacious stage and impeccable sight lines. Live blues start at 9:30 p.m. on weekdays, and at 10 p.m. on weekends. Street parking all around.

B.L.U.E.S. (2519 North Halsted Street; (773) 528-1012) is the longest-running North Side club with the same location and ownership. You can arrive at any time of the night (or morning) and be assured a good shot at the stage, even though the room—which holds 100 people max—is usually crowded. B.L.U.E.S. features top-notch live local bands every night of the year, attracting a throng of international and domestic tourists. You can get the blues in trying to find a place to park in this neighborhood; valet parking is available on weekends. And don't fret. B.L.U.E.S. doesn't stand for anything in particular.

Finally, **Kingston Mines** (2548 North Halsted Street; (773) 477-4646) draws hard-core fans from B.L.U.E.S. across the street because of its late license (4 a.m. Saturday, 5 a.m. Sunday). Local blues acts alternate on two stages, so there's rarely any dead time. This club has been around for 25 years in various North Side locations.

Comedy/Interactive Theater

Chicago used to be known for its comedy clubs. But if you can't beat 'em with the shtick, join 'em. Interactive theater is the hot trend in Chicago humor circles. Now in its seventh year at the **Pipers Alley Theater** (230 West North, directly behind Second City; (312) 664-8844), *Tony 'n' Tina's Wedding* is a two-hour and-45 minute production with 32 cast members, a huge set, and buffet Italian dinner. Audience members ("guests") enter a beautiful chapel for a wedding ceremony, which is followed by a dinner and dance reception (complete with a live band) that goes haywire. The wedding ceremony is scripted, but the rest of the show is free-form improvisation.

Tony 'n' Tina's Wedding features lots of hometown nuance, right down to local celebrities. Many media and sports figures (they're the biggest celebrities Chicago has to offer) have appeared in *Tony 'n' Tina's Wedding,* and the occasional "big name" like Frankie Avalon drops in for a short residency. *Tony 'n' Tina's Wedding* does such a good job of meshing actors with the audience that you can't always tell who is who. No weddings on Monday and Tuesday; performances are Wednesdays through Sunday nights. Tickets are $49 per person Wednesday and Thursday, $58 per person Friday and Sunday, and $65 per person Saturday (half price for children on Sunday).

Flanagan's Wake takes place in the fictional borough of Grapplin, County Sligo, to the west of Ireland. Old boys tell tall stories, sing ballads, and mourn the passing of dearly departed Flanagan. "Mourners" can share stories of their own experiences, or merely observe the customs of the "locals." The show is 60% scripted; the rest depends on audience interaction. *Flanagan's Wake* is one of the longest-running shows in Chicago theater history. Performances are Thursday and Friday night, Saturday afternoon and night, and Sunday afternoon. Flanagan's Wake takes place on the 150-seat main stage of **The Noble Fool** comedy theater center (16 West Randolph in downtown Chicago; (312) 726-1156). Comedy is presented in three separate performance spaces at the theater center, including an intimate downstairs cabaret bar. Tickets for *Flanagan's Wake* are $29 per person.

And if you're really hard up for free-form improvisation, check out **ComedySportz,** a rat-a-tat-tat series of improv games performed by two teams in "heated" competition. Be forwarned: The pace can get as dizzy as a Cubs rebuilding plan. ComedySportz is at 2851 North Halsted, not far from Wrigley Field, the Cubs' house of horrors (phone (773) 549-8080). Performances are Friday and Saturday nights; tickets are $17.

Dance Clubs

Chicago has always had a step up on the rest of the country when it comes to dancing. Popular 1960s soul dances like "The Monkey Time" and "The Woodbine Twine" came out of Chicago; in the 1980s, spikey-hair punks were pogoing at rank, long-gone storefront clubs; and during the 1990s, the industrial "house music" movement went worldwide after originating on Chicago's near south and west sides.

Of the dance-oriented clubs that follow, some are new, others are standbys. But this club scene is volatile; more dance clubs go in and out of style than any other Chicago nightlife pursuit. Be sure to call ahead.

In the last couple of years, the Lake Street corridor has been a breeding ground for cutting-edge dance clubs. This warehouse neighborhood is set under the noisy El tracks and is a cheap cab ride from downtown. Do not walk. **Transit** (1431 West Lake Street; (312) 491-8600) features a minimalist decor in a maximum setting. The upscale dance club is part of a 10,000-square foot complex. DJs deliver heavy doses of funk and rhythm and blues with no surrender. The dense beats can boggle your mind after a few hours. One warning: Transit is not cheap, which of course keeps out the riff-raff. Weekend covers are as high as $20.

Several blocks north of Lake Street, **Red Dog** (1958 West North Avenue; (773) 278-1009) is the centerpiece of the nightlife experience in Wicker Park. A dark, mysterious mood is set by the clandestine entry from an alley behind the Border Line Tap. Dense house music is the theme in a gothic atmosphere, checkered with religious artifacts and stained-glass windows. Red Dog consists of three bars and two dance floors, which helps handle overflow weekend crowds. Every Monday night, the club morphs into the "Boom Boom Room," which is one of the most popular gay dance nights in the city. Be warned: It's tough to park in Wicker Park on weekends.

Berlin (954 West Belmont; (773) 348-4975) is a beloved icon for the gay community, although everyone is welcome. The futuristic-storefront dance club has been operating for 18 years in a convenient location just steps from the Belmont El stop (Red Line). Contemporary house, acid jazz, and neo-soul are accented by 1980s video projection.

The stepping scene is a staple of Chicago's African-American community. Stepping is a stylized ballroom dance form—with attitude. A smooth, clearly defined beat is what sets stepping apart from other dance forms. Classic stepper's songs include "Love's Gonna Last" by Jeffrey and "Windows" by the Whispers. Chicago steppers congregate at the **Fifty Yard Line** (69 East 75th Street; (773) 846-0005), an easy-to-find place (just east off the Dan Ryan Expressway) that mixes a sports theme with a dance theme.Just don't request any Moby.

For those who prefer to look in the future, there's **Voyeur** (151 West Ohio Street; (312) 832-1717), whose hook is five closed-circuit monitors located throughout four cavernous rooms. Clubgoers sit down on a sofa in front of a monitor connected to a joystick. They scope out a room by making panoramic 360° turns like a nightclubbing Oliver Stoned. Voyeur also has an ample dance floor, with DJs spinning erotic house, hip hop, synth-pop, and acid jazz.

Lookin' for Love

Chicago is a predominately Catholic/puritan city, which means the sex and singles situation can be unpredictable. It's easy to get to know some singles in a nice tavern; other times the scene is as uptight as Martha

Stewart in a mosh pit. Chicago's rapture freaked out Frank Sinatra so much, he sang about how he actually "saw a man dance with his wife."

For grins, locals of all ages sail the "Viagra Triangle," three bars which anchor the legendary Rush Street neighborhood. From the 1950s through the 1980s, Rush Street was Chicago's answer to Bourbon Street with its colorful assortment of jazz clubs, honky-tonks, and strip joints with names like the Candy Store. The city cleaned up the street, and in true Chicago iconoclasm, Rush Street went south. The street hit a major slump and only recently returned through a combination of sleek retail and upscale nightclubs that are popular with the 35–60 age group.

Gibson's (1028 North Rush; (312) 266-8999) is the big shooter in the triangle. The dimly lit bar and restaurant opened in 1989 in what used to be Mister Kelly's nightclub, a place that featured jazz and pop singers from across America. Gibson's is known for its killer steaks and killer martinis. Packing four to six ounces of vodka, the popular house martini is $7. Gibson's is a favorite of movie stars and athletes visiting Chicago. Jack Nicholson and Shaquille O'Neal do the hang here, and Dennis Rodman was a Gibson's regular when he played for the Bulls. That alone will tell you not to worry about a dress code.

The swingin' Sinatra-doused **Jilly's Piano Bar** (1007 North Rush; (312) 664-1001) is across the street from Gibson's. Jilly's is named in honor of Jilly Rizzo, one of Sinatra's best pallies. From 1981 to 1983, co-owner Nick Caruso, Sr. ran another Jilly's down the street at Rush and Delaware. There has been talk of erecting a life-size statue of Frank Sinatra in a park across the street from Jilly's and Gibson's.

The third major stop on the "Viagra Triangle" would be **Tavern on Rush** (1031 North Rush; (312) 664-9600), another steakhouse with another bunch of older men and women with year-round tans. Tavern on Rush is so far beneath Gibson's and Jilly's on the buzz circuit that ex-Bull Michael Jordan can eat here with minimal hassle.

A few blocks north of the triangle, a younger crowd descends on Division Street. Here, you will see two of the city's most legendary singles bars: **Butch McGuire's** (20 West Division Street; (312) 337-9080), and across the street, the more diminutive **The Lodge** (21 West Division Street; (312) 642-4406). Both places have been around since the early 1960s, and on a clear night you can almost see the path through the two establishments. And don't miss Butch's during the holiday season, when more than 200,000 Christmas lights twinkle in two rooms.

Not far off of Divison Street, or what veterans call "The Street of Dreams," is the **River Shannon,** a cozy neighborhood tap (425 West Armitage Avenue; (312) 944-5087) in the De Paul University neighborhood. The jam-packed Friday night crowds consist of fewer outsiders and more local folks. The demographics are heavy on attorneys and law students who seem to enjoy the Dave Matthews on the jukebox. After last call, the bravest and boldest customers head down the street to **Gamekeepers** (1971 North Lincoln Avenue; (773) 549-0400), a late night Animal House–type establishment with lots of television sets. And if you were born before 1971, you don't belong here.

The Wicker Park neighborhood is known for its live rock 'n' roll and slacker bars, but a singles oasis is **Nick's** (1516 North Milwaukee Avenue; (773) 252-1155). Formerly in the De Paul neighborhood, Nick's has found a niche in Wicker Park. It boasts one of the best jukeboxes in the city, with ample Memphis soul, Chicago blues, and Carolina beach music.

Nick's owner, Nick Novich—a former high school football coach—also runs **The Note** (1565 North Milwaukee Avenue; (773) 489-0011), a too-cool-for-school tavern and live music room (alternative rock, salsa, neo-soul) that's very popular with Wicker Park artists and musicians on the sex trail. The 100-CD jukebox here leans more toward jazz and moody soul, and the crowd is not as diverse as it is a few blocks south at Nick's. Translated: Wear black and slap on a ponytail.

Should you find yourself striking out around the University of Chicago on the south side, check out **The Woodlawn Tap** (1172 East 55th Street; (773) 643-5516). Since 1948, more than 500 free-thinking University of Chicago students have tended bar at the funky working-class tavern. Notable drinkers have included Paul Butterfield, anthropolgist Margaret Mead, and poet Dylan Thomas, who once stopped in three different times in one day.

The dean of the piano bar scene is the cagey Bob Freitag, going on his 25th year at **Orso's** (1401 North Wells Street; (312) 787-6604), an Italian restaurant in the heart of the Near North Old Town neighborhood. Freitag is different from most piano men because he rarely sings. Instead, he brings a graceful style to such classics as Irving Berlin's "I Love a Piano" and Duke Ellington's "I Got It Bad (And That Ain't Good)." Freitag plays between 6:30 and 10:30 p.m. Thursdays through Sunday, and he is a real Chicago treasure.

Other grand piano bars (without restaurants) include the dark and tiny **Zebra Lounge** (1220 North State Street; (312) 642-5140) done in zebra decor, of course, and the subterrannean **Redhead Piano Bar** (16 West Ontario Street; (312) 640-1000), generally full of losers who have struck out in the "Viagra Triangle."

And for guys who have really tossed in the towel, in the last few years the strip club has made a comeback in Chicago. This time around they're called "gentleman's clubs," following a nationwide trend towards nightclubs where scantily clad or nude women are the attractions.

The more mainstream gentleman's clubs are **Crazy Horse Too** (1531 North Kingsbury; (312) 664-7400), a.k.a. "the only topless full liquor club in downtown Chicago," and **Heavenly Bodies** (1300 South Elmhurst Road; (847) 806-1121 in Elk Grove Village, about ten miles from O'Hare International Airport. Collars, shirt and/or nice sweater are required at Heavenly Bodies after 7 p.m. Note that dancers at both clubs are topless only (i.e. no full nudity).

Legitimate Theater

In recent years, Chicago theater has been a fertile arena of actors and directors for agents, producers, and casting directors from the East and West coasts. While the Loop (downtown) theaters enjoy success with safe straight-from-Broadway touring companies—or in a few cases workshop productions heading to Broadway (i.e. Billy Joel and Twyla Tharp's *Movin' Out*)—a cutting-edge-off-Loop scene has flourished.

Chicago features more than 1,000 theatrical venues, which range from established institutions to mid-level professional companies to smaller and younger troupes.

The **Goodman Theater** is the oldest and largest resident theater in Chicago. Since its founding in 1925, it worked out of the rear portion of the Art Institute, but in the fall of 2000 the Goodman moved to a glorious two-theater complex in the heart of Chicago's vibrant North Loop Theater District. The Goodman pioneered regional theater in America. Under artistic director Robert Falls, shows have ranged from experimental Shakespeare to Bertolt Brecht to James Baldwin. The Goodman Theater is at 170 North Dearborn (phone (312) 443-3800).

On the Loop commercial front, a Broadway-in-Chicago texture colors the occasional bookings a the **Shubert Theatre** (40 West Monroe Street; (312) 902-1500), the **Ford Center for the Performing Arts/Oriental Theatre** (24 West Randolph Street; (312) 782-2004), and the **Cadillac Palace** (151 West Randolph Street; (312) 782-1600).

The **Shubert** opened in 1906 as the Majestic Theatre and the tallest building in Chicago. Its stature attracted vaudeville acts who performed from 1:30 to 10:30 p.m. six days a week, and notable figures gracing the stage included Harry Houdini and Eddie Foy. The **Palace** and the **Oriental** theatres opened in 1926; the Palace is worth a look-see even if the theater is dark. Designed by noted theater architects, the Rapp Brothers, the interior features a spellbinding vision inspired by the palaces of Fountainebleau and Versailles. The lobby is flavored with huge decorative mirrors and breche violet and white marble, which sweeps through a succession of foyers. Chicago fun fact: During the mid-to-late 1980s, the palace was used as a rock venue, and the dance band Frankie Goes To

Hollywood had the stage collapse under them during a performance. No one was seriously injured.

All three beautifully restored theaters are a joint venture between Clear Channel Entertainment and the Nederlander Organization, the two largest commercial theater producers and owner/operators in the United States. Call or check local listings for performance information.

The **Steppenwolf Theater** is one of the pioneers in the off-Loop movement. Steppenwolf is unique for the consistency of its ensemble; audiences have been able to watch a group of actors develop over the years. The original 1976 ensemble included actors John Malkovich and Laurie Metclaf. Steppenwolf received international acclaim for *The Grapes of Wrath;* it has also portrayed works by Sam Shepard, Tom Waits, and Tennessee Williams. The immaculate 500-seat main stage and 100-seat experimental theater are at 1650 North Halsted Street (phone (312) 335-1650), a modest cab ride from downtown.

Some people perceive **Second City** as a comedy club, but it is a legitimate local theatrical institution that started in 1959. Major talent like Ed Asner, John Belushi, Chris Farley, Bill Murray, and George Wendt cut their teeth here. The original founding format is still used. With minimal costuming and props, six or seven actors lampoon life in a torrid series of topical skits. Recent events have raised the bar for actors in critically acclaimed productions like "Thank Heaven It Wasn't 7/11."

Following every show, the troupe draws ideas from the audience from which they improvise new sketches. There is no charge for these late-night sets. And producer emeritus Joyce Sloane has always pledged to keep the theater admission charge ($17) in the same ballpark as a movie ticket. The original 300-seat location at 1616 North Wells Street (phone (312) 337-3992) also features a 180-seat back room for **Second City E.T.C.,** which is sometimes regarded as more rebellious than its big brother. Lastly, the **Second City National Touring Company** performs Thursdays through Saturdays at the Metropolis Performing Arts Center in suburban Arlington Heights (phone (847) 577-2121).

The last of the established groups is the **Northlight Theater,** whose office is at 9501 Skokie Boulevard, but which mounts shows in various north-suburban locations. For just over 20 years, Northlight has been one of the largest and most innovative theaters in the Chicago area and is an artistic anchor of the northern suburbs. Northlight has won critical acclaim for its production of a wide range of new and contemporary plays and original chamber-size musicals. Call (847) 673-6300 for more information.

The **Apollo Theatre** (2540 North Lincoln Avenue; (773) 935-6100) has been a hot spot for all things female with the now-notoriously well known *The Vagina Monlogues*. The 90-minute production has featured local actors as well as guest performers, like Dawn Wells of *Gilligan's Island* fame. The premise is pretty basic: three women talk about vaginas, euphemisims for vaginas, and metaphors for vaginas. Unlike some relationships, the show is still going strong after two years, with performances Tuesdays through Sundays.

Quality mid-level theater includes **The Famous Door Theatre** at the Theatre Building (1225 West Belmont Avenue; (773) 404-2625); **Victory Gardens** (2257 North Lincoln Avenue; (773) 871-3000); **The Black Ensemble Theatre** (4520 North Beacon Street; (773) 769-4451); the **Mercury Theater** (3735 North Southport; (773) 325-1700); and the **Chicago Shakespeare Theater** (at Navy Pier, 800 East Grand Avenue; (312) 595-5600).

The best of the younger and smaller theaters are **The About Face Theatre** (3212 North Broadway Avenue; (773) 784-8565), which presents eveything from musical theater influenced by poet Walt Whitman to dark lesbian fairy tales; **Live Bait** (3914 North Clark Street; (773) 871-1212), named because the founders felt that attempting to attract an audience was like being bait on a line; the empathetic **Latino Chicago Theater Company** (1625 North Damen Avenue; (773) 486-5120); and the **Griffih Theater Company,** which explores works by James Agee and others at the Calo Theater (5404 North Clark Street; (773) 769-2228).

The days of Chicago dinner theater are long gone, but to immerse yourself in a total theatrical tourist experience, check out *The Spirit of Chicago.* The floating dinner theater cruises Lake Michigan with a mainstream song-and-dance revue. This *Love Boat* revisited also includes narrated sightseeing of Chicago's magnificent skyline. *The Spirit of Chicago* docks at Navy Pier (600 East Grand; (312) 836-7899). Advance reservations are recommended,

Apart from the young and experimental theater spaces, most of these shows can be expensive—and many often sell out. The League of Chicago Theatres offers a **Hot Tix** program where tickets are half-price the day of the performance. Hot Tix booths are at 78 West Randolph in downtown Chicago, the Chicago Water Works Visitor Center, 163 East Pearson near the Water Tower, and at the downtown Tower Records (214 SouthWabash). For booth hours, call (312) 554-9800. Many theaters also offer discounts for students, children, senior citizens, the disabled, and armed forces personnel. Call ahead.

The general dress code for Chicago theater is casual. Men need not wear ties, and women don't have to overdress. Jeans, slacks, and nice shirts are perfectly acceptable.

The Classics

The world-renowned **Chicago Symphony Orchestra** is the touchstone of the Chicago classical music landscape. Since 1960, the CSO has won 51 Grammy awards, 23 of them between 1972 and 1991 when the great music director Georg Solti was conductor. Overall, Solti won 31 Grammies, more than any other artist, including Michael Jackson. Solti's tradition is consistently celebrated in the CSO's clarity and logic.

The 112-year-old Chicago Symphony Orchestra is based in **Symphony Center,** 220 South Michigan Avenue. Visiting domestic and international orchestras also appear at Orchestra Hall as part of a "Symphony Center Presents" season (phone (312) 294-3000). Be sure to call ahead. Subscriptions account for roughly 75% of tickets sold for CSO concerts, and 2001 attendance filled more than 90% of Orchestra Hall's capacity. Sometimes tickets are available at the last minute, so call the box office on the day of the concert.

The Symphony Center also includes a beautiful gift shop and **The Club at Symphony Center,** which features special events like cabaret and a wine tasting series (phone (312) 294-3333).

On a smaller scale, the 15-year-old **Newberry Consort** is the city's premiere early music ensemble. Their season begins in the fall in various locations in Chicago, Oak Park, and Evanston (phone (312) 255-3700).

CHICAGO NIGHTCLUBS BY ZONE		
Name	**Description**	**Cover**
Zone 1—The North Side		
Charlie's	Gay country-and-western dance club	None
Green Mill Jazz Club	Hepcat speakeasy with live jazz	$3–$8
The Hideout	Eclectic live music in the middle of nowhere	$3–$10
Marie's Riptide	Quintessential Chicago dive	None
Metro	Concert venue with attitude	$5–$20
Old Town School of Folk Music	Folk- and world-music mecca	Varies
Pops for Champagne	Elegant cocktail bar	None–$10
Weeds	Retreat for Bohemian riff-raff	None
Zone 2—North Central/O'Hare		
Hala Kahiki	Tiki bar to the max	None
Zone 3—Near North		
Excalibur	Mondo super-sized dance club	$4–$15
House of Blues	Juke-joint opera house	$10–$60

CHICAGO NIGHTCLUBS BY ZONE (continued)		
Name	**Description**	**Cover**
Zone 3—Near North (continued)		
Jillyland	Sinatra central	None
The Lodge	Neighborhood singles bar	None
The Matchbox	Tiny, intimate, friendly tavern	None
Old Town Ale House	Classic pub for scribes and thespians	None
SLOW DOWN— Life's Too Short!	Key West in the Windy City	$5–$10
Zone 4—The Loop		
Funky Buddha Lounge	Urban-hip dance club and lounge	None–$20
Zone 5—South Loop		
Buddy Guy's Legends	Home of the legendary bluesman	$8–$15
Zone 6—South Central/Midway		
Baby Doll Polka Club	Polka as lifestyle choice	None
Zone 8—Southern Suburbs		
Fitzgerald's	Roots-music roadhouse	$8–$20

Nightclub Profiles

BABY DOLL POLKA CLUB

ROLL OUT THE BARREL

Who Goes There Bouncy Southwest-side Polish clientele, beady-eyed airplane groupies checking out arrivals and departures from the exciting Midway Airport landing strip across the street. They're all having a barrel of fun.

6102 South Central Avenue; (773) 582-9706   Zone 6 South Central/Midway

Cover None **Minimum** None **Mixed drinks** $2.50–$5 **Wine** On Tap! ($2.75) **Beer** $2–$3.50 (including bottles of Zywiec, a Pilsner imported from Poland) **Dress** Casual, leiderhosen-friendly **Specials** Live polka bands play at 9:30 p.m. Saturdays; 5:30 p.m. senior citizen set on Sundays **Food available** Snacks, chips, microwaved stuff

Hours Sunday–Friday, 4 p.m.–2 a.m.; Sunday, 4 p.m.–3 a.m.

What goes on Chicago is America's polka capital, and the intimate Baby Doll is where locals go to polka. The Baby Doll has been swinging at its current location for 21 years. The club got its name from the 1951 hit "Baby Doll Polka" by late Chicago button box player Eddie Korosa. He wrote the song in honor of his three daughters. His ex-wife Irene now owns and operates the bar.

Setting & atmosphere Wisconsin Rec Room; airplanes made out of beer cans, airplane memorabalia and a CD jukebox with non-polka legends like Hank Williams, Dean Martin, and Neil Diamond. Regulars squeeze in and out of a 24-seat bar like a trusty accordion. The bar is finished in dark wood and leafy brown carpeting that boogies across the floor and crawls up the bar. The rear of the club features a small stage and red tables and chairs. A glow-in-the-dark chalkboard hangs over the tiny dance floor. Irene has scrawled her favorite saying on the board: "Polka happiness to you, wherever you go, whatever you do."

If you go Impress your friends by riffing on the differernces between Bavarian, North Woods, Slovenian, and Chicago styles of polka. All you need to know is that the legendary Chicago style carries a slower and more deliberate beat (known in polka circles as the bellow shake) through a smaller, five- or six-piece band that you will see here on weekends. Live music or not, this is a classic Chicago experience.

BUDDY GUY'S LEGENDS

LIVE BLUES IN A DOWNBEAT, REC ROOM—TYPE SETTING

Who Goes There International tourists, more of a racial mix than North Side blues clubs, and sometimes even Buddy Guy, the Chicago guitar great

754 South Wabash Avenue; (312) 427-0333   Zone 5 South Loop

Cover $8–$15 **Minimum** None **Mixed drinks** $4 **Wine** $4 **Beer** $3.50–$5 **Dress** Everything from tees and sweats to after-work attire **Specials** Local record-release parties, spur-of-the-moment bookings such as Eric Clapton and occasional live recordings, like owner Buddy Guy playing with G. E. Smith of the *Saturday Night Live* band **Food available** Southern Louisiana cuisine: ribs, red beans and rice, and "Peanut Buddy Pie," a Buddy Guy–endorsed peanut butter pie

Hours Monday–Thursday, 5 p.m.–2 a.m.; Friday, 4 p.m.–2 a.m.; Saturday, 5 p.m.–3 a.m.; Sunday, 6 p.m.–2 a.m.

What goes on A stately approach to booking live local, national, and international blues acts seven nights a week. From 1972–1986, local guitar hero Buddy Guy (who influenced Eric Clapton and Stevie Ray Vaughan) ran the Checkerboard Lounge, a South Side blues club that still stands today. In 1989, he reopened in a bigger and safer location as part of Chicago's developing South Loop. The sprawling storefront club is popular with tourists because of Guy's international reputation and its prime location.

Setting & atmosphere Urban roadhouse. Four pool tables are almost always occupied at stage left. Portraits of blues greats like Muddy Waters, Lightin' Hopkins, and Howlin' Wolf hang throughout the museum-like space. Near the club entrance there's a display case featuring Guy's awards; guitars from the likes of Eric Clapton and Muddy Waters hang above the bar.

If you go Don't request Britney Spears. This is a blues sanctuary. It's also best to arrive early, as all shows are general admission and often sell out. The Southern Louisiana kitchen serves better-than-average bar food. And periodically check out the far west end of the bar. That's Guy's favorite spot.

CHARLIE'S

CHAPS, YOUNG AND OLD—IT'S A GAY COUNTRY-WESTERN DANCE CLUB

Who Goes There Predominantly gay men, some gay women; about 10% of the crowd are straight country-western fans; lots of neighborhood boot scooters

3726 North Broadway; (773) 871-8887   Zone 1 North Side

Cover None **Minimum** None **Mixed drinks** $4–$7 **Wine** $4–$6 **Beer** $4–$5.50 **Dress** No dress code; leather chaps and cowboy hats are okay **Specials** None **Food available** Occasional Sunday afternoon barbecue

Hours Monday and Tuesday, 3 p.m.–2 a.m.; Wednesday–Friday and Sunday, 3 p.m.–4 a.m.; Saturday, 3 p.m.–5 a.m.

What goes on Charlie's is one of the friendliest clubs in the city, gay or straight. Lots of line dancing on a floor lit up by a big mirrored boot, a Charlie's trademark. The gay country-western club chain kicked off in the early 1980s in Denver, Colorado, and has expanded to Phoenix and Chicago. The Saddle Swingers, a nine-member gay men's country line dance troupe, appear one Saturday night a month at Charlie's, and the Chi-Town Squares, a gay square dance club, practice at Charlie's on Sunday evenings.

Setting & atmosphere Clean, dark, and with a great sound system for listening to Brooks & Dunn hits like "Boot Scootin' Boogie" and "My Maria," Alan Jackson's "Chattahoochee," and other house favorites. At late night/early morning, the DJ throws in some progressive dance tunes to mix things up. The club holds 300–350 people, and the ample dance floor gives people room to boogie.

If you go Be sensitive to the fact that Charlie's tackles two extreme American stereotypes: country-western music and the gay lifestyle. Charlie's makes the evening a memorable experience with a sincere staff and keen musical programming. And Charlie's gives back to the community: The club's monthly "Mr. Charlie's" program (an award bestowed to the man who brings in the most money that night in the bar) has raised more than $224,000 for AIDS-related charities since it was organized in 1982.

EXCALIBUR

ROYAL ORDER OF ENDLESS NIGHTS IN A REAL NORTH SIDE CASTLE

Who Goes There 25 and over, big hair from the 'burbs, the office party circuit, some tourists

632 North Dearborn Street; (312) 266-1944   Zone 3 Near North

Cover $4–$7 Friday and Saturday; free other nights; $10–$15 for upstairs Vision Nightclub, according to event **Minimum** None **Mixed drinks** $3.75–$5.50 **Wine** $4.50 **Beer** $3.75–$4.25 **Dress** Club casual; nothing tattered, torn, or soiled **Specials** None **Food available** Full menu from Cajun chicken to steak sandwiches; appetizers served until 3 a.m.

Hours Sunday–Friday, 5 p.m.–4 a.m.; Saturday, 5 p.m.–5 a.m.; open 365 nights a year

What goes on Everything for the MTV generation. A downstairs game room features nearly 100 state-of-the-art video and pseudo–virtual reality games. Pool tables are all over the place, with eight in one billiard room. An upstairs space called Vision Nightclub holds 2,000 people. Vision includes three large dance floors surrounded by multiple stories of balcony lounge levels. Each room has its own sound system, DJ booth, and specific music styles. The $100,000 sound systems are among the finest in the world.

Setting & atmosphere Party in a historic building. Resembling a castle, this rambling 40,000-square-foot building is one of the few 19th-century Gothic buildings to survive the Chicago Fire; it was designed by American architect Henry Ives Cobb. It's previously been the home of the Chicago Historical Society, the Chicago Institute of Design, and before Excalibur, the hoity-toity Limelight nightclub.

If you go Locals view Excalibur as a tourist trap (it is across the street from the Hard Rock Cafe), but the new Vision Nightclub has featured internationally known DJs such as Darude, Deep Dish, Juan Atkins, Sandra Collins, Hybrid, Derrick Carter, DJ Sneak, and Doc Martin. Dance music has progressed with the times; expect high-energy electronic music, including trance, house, and techno. Cover charges are reasonable for a New York City–type experience.

FITZGERALD'S

LIVE AMERICAN ROOTS MUSIC IN A ROADHOUSE CLUB

Who Goes There Music lovers of all ages, a hearty portion of Lake Woebegone characters, Near West suburban folks; slacker factor very low

6615 West Roosevelt Road, Berwyn; (708) 788-2118; www.fitzgeraldsnightclub.com
Zone 8 Southern Suburbs

Cover $8–$20 **Minimum** None **Mixed drinks** $3.50–$5 **Wine** $4.50 **Beer** $3–$4.50 **Dress** Casual **Specials** Eclectic comfort food, sandwiches, and appetizers **Food available** Occasional event- related fare

Hours Tuesday–Thursday, 7 p.m.–1 a.m.; Friday and Saturday, 7 p.m.–3 a.m.; Sunday, 5 p.m.–1 a.m.

What goes on A family-run operation since it opened in 1980, FitzGerald's is one of the most passionately booked rooms in the Chicago area. Blues legend Stevie Ray Vaughan played the intimate 300-seat club in 1981, long before he hit it big. Other landmark shows that remain indicative of the club's musical mission include appearances from the late zydeco king Clifton Chenier and the Neville Brothers. Ample attention is also given to Chicago blues and folk, and Sunday night sets are generally reserved for traditional and big band jazz.

Setting & atmosphere Totally roadhouse. The backwoods feel has even attracted Hollywood. The Madonna jitterbug scene from *A League of Their Own* was filmed here, as well as the pool hall shots in the Paul Newman flick *The Color of Money*. Sound and sight lines are top-notch, and space for a dance floor is cleared when appropriate. A major 2002 renovation gave birth to a diner called the Roosevelt Grill. The grill, which seats 60, is anchored by a vintage oak bar with beveled and arched mirrors. Regional cuisine is served, and sometimes performing artists cook up some grub from their hometown (i.e. gumbo from New Orleans, ribs from Memphis). New bathrooms were installed in the club, and a new side bar/function room features a star-spangled roadhouse jukebox and television sets to monitor action during the rare moments Chicago sports teams are in the playoff hunt.

If you go Respect the experience. Over the years, FitzGerald's has cultivated fans who love roots music as well as the roots texture of the room. Rarely do you hear an acoustic performance drowned out by audience chatter. And don't be intimidated by the suburban location. Berwyn is a ten-minute drive from the Loop, and the Congress El goes to Berwyn. Get off at Oak Park Avenue, walk three blocks south and then three blocks east. Or call co-owner Bill FitzGerald and ask him to pick you up. If he has time, he probably will. It's that type of touch that makes FitzGerald's a local treasure.

FUNKY BUDDHA LOUNGE

URBAN-HIP DANCE CLUB AND LOUNGE THAT STANDS THE TEST OF TIME

Who Goes There An extremely unique group of African-American, Asian, Indian, Latino, and white folks aged 21–30 that create a collective groove. David Schwimmer of *Friends* visits the Buddah when in town, and it's a popular post-game hang for NBA stars (it's a cross-court pass away from the United Center, the home of the Chicago Bulls).

728 West Grand Avenue; (312) 666-1695   Zone 4 The Loop

Covers None early in the week; $10–$20 Friday and Saturday **Minimum** None **Mixed drinks** $5–$8 **Wine** $5–$7 **Beer** $4–$8 **Dress** Casually hip; no shorts, no tank tops, no tennis shoes **Specials** Occasional live African/Brazilian music early in the week. The Funky Buddah prides itself on a smoke-free environment, with huge smoke-eaters positioned throughout the club's three rooms. The Buddah was the first bar in the State of Illinois to be awarded a clean-air certificate. The lounge also features a non-smoking room. **Food available** None, but La Scarola across the street is one of the city's best Italian restaurants

Hours Monday, Wednesday–Friday, 9 p.m.–2 a.m.; Saturday, 9 p.m.–3 a.m.

What goes on One-stop shopping. You can drink, dance to DJs spinning neo-soul, hip hop, and funk, and then make out on exquisite leopard-print sofas.

Setting & atmosphere Loungy Eurotrash. The Buddah consists of three rooms: an up-front bar and lounge, a rear dance club, and a nonsmoking room. Decor is connected with (expensive) antique-store ambience, and lighting is soft and dark. Murals are depictions of vintage Mambo record albums from the 1950s and 1960s. Bass-heavy hip-hop can make conversation difficult on weekend nights.

If you go Make sure you are relatively young. The Buddah has been around for six years, which is a long time on the Chicago club scene. But the Buddah consistently reinvents itself and stays on top of music trends. Anyone over 35 could feel out of place here, unless they are Charles Barkley or Keith Richards.

GREEN MILL JAZZ CLUB

HEPCAT SPEAKEASY WITH QUALITY LIVE JAZZ

Who Goes There Sincere jazz fans, local poets, romantic couples on the last stop before home, 25–ageless

4802 North Broadway; (773) 878-5552   Zone 1   North Side

Cover $3–$8 **Minimum** None **Mixed drinks** $3–$5 **Wine** $2.50–$3.75
Beer $1.75–$4 **Dress** Casual and hip **Specials** Uptown Poetry Slam, 5–8 p.m. Sundays
($5 cover) **Food available** Bar snacks

Hours Sunday–Friday, noon–4 a.m.; Saturday, noon–5 a.m.

What goes on Top-notch local jazz artists and a steady influx of New York musicians
who aren't heard anywhere else in town. The Mill also is the city's premiere joint for
late-late jam sessions.

Setting & atmosphere Can't be beat. The dark, seductive Mill opened in 1907 and
enjoyed its first run of popularity in the 1920s during the neighborhood's vaudeville hey-
day. Proprietor Dave Jemilo purchased the club in 1986, and instead of gutting it, he lovingly restored it to its earlier splendor. The only additions were a dance floor and a new
stage. The piano behind the bar has always been there, and it's still used on Sunday nights.

If you go Listen to the music. It's rare that quality jazz can be heard at affordable
prices in a neighborhood setting.

HALA KAHIKI

TINY BUBBLES—LOTS OF THEM

Who Goes There 21–60, Chicagoans suffering from intense cabin fever, Jimmy
Buffett fans, visitors on layovers from O'Hare International Airport—less than
ten minutes north of the Chicago area's biggest tiki bar

2834 North River Road, River Grove; (708) 456-3222   Zone 2   North Central/O'Hare

Cover None **Minimum** None **Mixed drinks** $3.50–$10.50 (for two) **Wine** $5.50
Beer $5–$5.50 **Dress** Casual; no hats or tank tops; a Hawaiian shirt and hula skirt are
fine **Food available** Pretzels, pineapple

Hours Monday and Wednesday, 7 p.m.–2 a.m.; Thursday, 4 p.m.–2 a.m.; Friday and Saturday, 4 p.m.–3 a.m.; Sunday, 6 p.m.–2 a.m.

What goes on Located in near west suburban River Grove since 1967, Hala Kahiki
(meaning "House of Pineapple") serves almost 75 different tropical drinks, including
bizarre concoctions like Dr. Funk of Tahiti (licorice-flavored Pernod and rum), Skip and
Run Naked (a gut-wrenching gin and beer mix), and the house favorite, the Zombie, a
potent mix of fruit juice and three rums—including 151.

Setting & atmosphere The tiki hut holds more than 200 people in three separate,
dimly lit rooms and the bamboo-dominated front bar. The back room features a romantic
light blue water fountain, while the front bar's innocent 1950s feel is accented by seashell-
covered lamp shades and a dash of incense. In the back of the nightclub, there is a Hawaiian Seas Gift Shop, replete with Don Ho cassette tapes, Hawaiian shirts, and Kukui nuts
(authentic beads worn by Hawaiian royalty). A must-sea on any visit to Chicago, the Hala
Kahiki is the only full-tilt tropical bar and South Sea shop in the Midwest.

If you go Don't order beer. Do consider a designated driver. The drinks pack a punch,
and getting pulled over wearing a green Hawaiian shirt, a yellow lei, and listening to Don
Ho will not help your case.

THE HIDEOUT

AN URBAN ROADHOUSE IN THE MIDDLE OF NOWHERE, SURROUNDED BY EVERYTHING

Who Goes There Local musicians and music industry folks ages 25–35, older blue-collar workers, people trying to maintain a low profile

1354 West Wabansia; (773) 227-4433; www.hideoutchicago.com   Zone 1   North Side

Cover $5–$10 for live music; $3 when DJs spin (no cover on Mondays) **Minimum** None **Mixed drinks** $2.50–$3 **Wine** $3.50 **Beer** $1.50 (Pabst Blue Ribbon)–$5 **Dress** Very casual **Specials** Free bag of pretzels or a shot of Hot Damn! if you mention *The Unofficial Guide to Chicago* **Food available** Chips and peanuts

Hours Monday, 8 p.m.–2 a.m.; Tuesday, 4 p.m.–2 a.m.; Friday and Saturday, 7 p.m.–3 a.m.

What goes on The uncanny ability of the Hideout to reinvent itself is what makes the eclectic live music room a must-see. Although the tiny building's first deed dates back to 1890 and the club has been called the Hideout since 1934, only since the mid-1990s was the joint discovered by a young alt-country crowd. Popular "Americana" country singers such as Neko Case and Kelly Hogan not only perform at the Hideout, they tend bar there as well. That vibe is what put the Hideout on the map and attracted the attention of national publications such as *Rolling Stone* magazine. National acts such as Wilco and the Mekons have been known to stop in the Hideout for impromptu sets. More recently, the Hideout has branched out to feature harder live rock music, country and soul DJs, and art films, moving ever so slightly away from the country music that put the Hideout in the high life.

Setting & atmosphere Friendly. Live music is presented in a comfortable back room that resembles a Northern Wisconsin lodge. Adorned with Christmas lights and an efficient stage, the concert space seats about 100 people. The Devil in a Woodpile acoustic blues quartet performs for free every Tuesday in the low-ceilinged front bar space. The Hoyle Brothers play traditional country music at 5:30 p.m. every Friday, attracting the factory and city workers in the blue-collar neighborhood. Black-and-white pictures of the Chicago Cubs (circa 1969) hang behind the bar. Owners Tim and Katie Tuten found the pictures when they were cleaning up the bar. Tim Tuten is a history teacher in the Chicago public school system, which accounts for the Hideout's social conscience. There's seating for about 18 people along the bar, and the staff is personal. No jukebox; house tapes.

If you go Follow directions. The Hideout is in a hard-to-find industrial neighborhood. Known only by its crooked old-style sign out front, The Hideout is directly west of the City of Chicago Fleet Management parking lot, two blocks north of North Avenue and a block east of Elston Avenue. There's ample free parking, and any decent cab driver can find the place.

HOUSE OF BLUES

THE BLUES AS A TAP ROOT FOR A COLORFUL MUSICAL TREE

Who Goes There 21 and way over; very few blues fans; the audience demographic depends on the booking; always a smattering of tourists and a hard-core group of Chicago roots music listeners

329 North Dearborn Street; (312) 923-2000   Zone 3 Near North

Cover $10–$60, none in restaurant **Minimum** None **Mixed drinks** $5–$8 **Wine** $5–$7 by the glass **Beer** $4–$6.50 **Dress** Anything from Bourbon Street to State Street **Specials** The extremely popular Gospel Brunch ($15–$40)—seatings at 9:30 a.m. and noon every Sunday; "After 5 Live" concerts, held once a month inside the restaurant **Food available** Back Porch restaurant serves Creole-Southern cuisine; dinner till 10 p.m. daily, late-night menu available till 2 a.m. weekdays, 3 a.m. weekends

Hours Sunday–Friday, 8 p.m.–4 a.m.; Saturday, 8 p.m.–5 a.m

What goes on Live music seven nights a week. No American concert venue is booked with the adventure and passion of the House of Blues. The Chicago club opened Thanksgiving weekend 1996, and in the first three months of operation, acts as diverse as Soul Brother #1 James Brown, Johnny Cash, jazz guitarist Les Paul, rocker-hunter Ted Nugent, and Cuban salsa singer Celia Cruz all graced the HOB (as locals call it) stage. The 400-room House of Blues hotel with 30 suites is adjacent.

Setting & atmosphere House of Blues owner-founder Isaac Tigrett calls his Chicago music hall a "juke-joint opera house," and it is actually designed from the Tyl Theatre opera house in Prague, Czechoslavakia, where Mozart debuted *Don Giovanni* in 1787. The 1,465-capacity music room is the largest of the House of Blues chain. The four-tiered music hall is adorned with hundreds of pieces of eclectic Southern folk art and closed-circuit television monitors where fans can watch the live music while waiting for a drink. The music room is framed by 12 gold-plated private opera boxes that are sold to support House of Blues–related charities. Sound is impeccable, and sight lines are clear. If you want to sit down, arrive very early. There are a limited number of bar stools near serving areas. Otherwise, it truly is standing room only.

If you go It took a long time for musically provincial Chicagoans to get over the fact this is not a "blues" bar. Hello? Check your attitude at the door and you'll discover this club oozes with warmth and spirit. HOB is Chicago's showcase live music venue.

JILLYLAND

COME FLY WITH ME

Who Goes There 30–55, Sinatraphiles, Chicago jocks, Steve Lawrence and Eydie Gorme; lots of singles—the second, third, or fourth time around

1007–1009 North Rush Street; (312) 664-1001; www.jillys.com   Zone 3 Near North

Cover None **Minimum** None **Mixed drinks** $5–$12 **Wine** $5–$10 **Beer** $4.50–$6 **Specials** Sing and swing with "Chicago's Voice of Choice," Tony Ocean, who covers a lot of Dean Martin and some Rod Stewart, too (Tuesday–Saturday, until 1:30 a.m.) **Food available** Only for thought

Hours Monday–Friday, 3 p.m.–2 a.m.; Saturday, 1 p.m.–3 a.m.; Sunday, 5 p.m.–2 a.m.

What goes on "Jillyland" is the umbrella moniker for Jilly's Bistro, Jilly's Piano Bar, and Jilly's Retro Club. Jilly Rizzo was Frank Sinatra's best friend and bodyguard. In 1992, Rizzo was killed on his 75th birthday by a drunk driver in Palm Desert, California. Sinatra was devastated. Jilly's Bistro lives on as a tribute to Rizzo. The cozy 100-seat nightclub is a splendid Near North spot for sophisticated conversation and, quite frankly, a stiff drink. The Bistro opened on May 6, 1995 (Rizzo's birthday), and became so popular the owners quickly expanded into a separate downstairs 1970s dance club called Jilly's

Retro. The 400-capacity disco is open Tuesday–Friday, 8 p.m.–2 a.m.; Saturday, until 3 a.m. The disco is closed on Sunday and Monday. Covers vary between $5–$15. But for intense intimacy, stick with the Bistro.

Setting & atmosphere Ring-a-ding-ding. A seductive setting is accented by ornate walls filled with Sinatra and Rat Pack photographs. A model train chugs around the top of the Bistro's long cherry-oak bar. Sinatra, of course, was a train fanatic. Even bar receipts say "My Favorite Bistro—Frank Sinatra." Hanging in the hallway into the bistro is the tender eulogy delivered by Las Vegas comic Joey Villa at Rizzo's funeral. Celebrities like Don Rickles, Kevin Costner, Harrison Ford, Jimmy Buffett, and metal-head Ozzy Osbourne have dropped in, and Steve Lawrence and Eydie Gorme stop in when they are in town.

If you go Pretend it's 1960 all over again. A Kennedy kind of Camelot has been reborn on Rush Street.

THE LODGE

IN-YO-FACE DRINKING AND SCHMOOZING IN A NEIGHBORHOOD TAVERN

Who Goes There Jocks, aging jocks, wannabe jocks, real jocks like Charles Barkley, and conventioneers; curious suburban invasion on weekends

21 West Division Street; (312) 642-4406   Zone 3 Near North

Cover Only for St. Patrick's Day and New Year's throngs **Minimum** None **Mixed drinks** $4–$5.50 **Wine** $6.50 **Beer** $3.750–$4.505 **Dress** Anything goes **Specials** Stoli Sunday, Cuervo Monday, Kettle One Wednesday **Food available** Shelled peanuts on the floor

Hours Sunday–Friday, noon–4 a.m.; Saturday, noon–5 a.m.

What goes on Open since 1957, this is the longest-running act on Division Street, or what locals call "The Street of Dreams." One of the area's premiere singles bars, the Lodge has held its own against evil influences such as disco, punk, and herpes. Its late-night license and 1:1 male-female ratio makes it a popular stop for pro athletes winding down after a game. NBA superstar Charles Barkley and ex–Kansas City Royals infielder George Brett have made the Lodge a regular stop when they're in town.

Setting & atmosphere Less is more. The charm comes in a shoebox-size room resplendent in refined cedar and pseudo-antique paintings, accented by three tottering chandeliers and one of the loudest oldies jukeboxes in Chicago. You can't help but meet someone in this setting.

If you go Stock up on breath mints, cologne, and perfume. On a busy night, it's like riding an El train at rush hour. And know all the words to Meat Loaf's "Paradise by the Dashboard Light." It's a traditional Lodge sing-a-long.

MARIE'S RIP TIDE

A NEIGHBORHOOD BAR LOOKING FOR A NEIGHBORHOOD

Who Goes There Artists, musicians, working-class neighborhood people, and folks who swing in memory of Bobby Darin

1745 West Armitage Avenue; (773) 278-7317   Zone 1 North Side

Cover None **Minimum** None **Mixed drinks** $5 **Wine** $3.50 **Beer** $3.50 **Dress** Hello sailor **Specials** None **Food** available Chips, peanuts, hard-boiled eggs

Hours Monday–Friday, 8 p.m.–4 a.m.; Saturday, 8 p.m.–5 a.m.; Sunday, 8 p.m.–4 a.m.

What goes on People get ripped. People slow dance to the Sinatra–Elvis–Patsy Cline jukebox. People contemplate other people in a driftwood world.

Setting & atmosphere Unpretentious in a psychedelic Wisconsin way. A long main bar is sourly accented by 1950s-style diner booths. Even the regulars slip off the slick vinyl barstools. The staff redecorates the room in elementary school motif according to most approaching holidays. Rip Tide was included on the set of the *Crime Story* television series. And the back bar features the smallest bidet on the North Side.

If you go Notify your next of kin. Marie's is directly west of the Kennedy Expressway at the Armitage Avenue exit, so it's safe and well lighted at night. Neighborhood parking is available. Parking spaces open up as the night goes on.

THE MATCHBOX

SPARKS FLY IN ONE OF THE CITY'S MOST INTIMATE TAVERNS

Who Goes There A compelling group of characters, including cops, musicians, raconteurs, and folks visiting the INTUIT (The Center for Intuitive and Outsider Art) gallery next door. Chicago can be a segragated city, but you would never know it by spending time at the Matchbox.

770 North Milwaukee Avenue; (312) 666-9292   Zone 3 Near North

Cover None **Minimum** None **Mixed drinks** $4.50–$6.50; higher for single-malt scotches, single-barrel bourbons, aged rums, and ports **Wine** $5–$10.50 **Beer** $2.75–$14; high end is "Mad Bitch" from Belgium in a 750-ml bottle, and "Fin du Monde" ("the end of the earth") from Quebec **Dress** Casual, but know that someone could spill something on you due to tight quarters **Specials** None **Food available** An avid train buff, Matchbox owner David Gevercer has opened the Silver Palm restaurant in a stainless-steel 1947 Atlantic Coast Line Railroad dining car behind the Matchbox. Pumped-up American cuisine (demi-glacé brushed on the hamburgers, duck wings, aged prime rib) is served Monday–Saturday, 7 p.m.–2 a.m.

Hours Sunday–Friday, 4 p.m.–2 a.m.; Saturday, 4 p.m.–3 a.m.

What goes on The mere size of the Matchbox dictates a sense of community—3 feet wide at its narrowest, 10 feet at its widest. The friendly bartenders will be the first to tell you that if you don't like being sociable, the Matchbox is not the place for you. The diversity of the crowd can also be attributed to the wide range of drinks, which go as low as a pint of Double Diamond for $2.50 to a $10 scotch. A high-end tequila selection includes Patron, Porfidio, and Del Maguey Mezcal.

Setting & atmoshere Really friendly. The Matchbox opened seven years ago in a former shot-n-beer bar and package liquor store of the same name. The back bar contains a collection of poster art, Matchbox toy cars, and a bouquet of flowers brought in every Thursday by a local florist. The cigar fad has passed through Chicago, but the Matchbox still sells Punch, Arturo Fuente, dunhill, and Montecristos, which means the place can get smoky.

If you go Arrive early so you can secure a barstool. During late spring and summer months, the Matchbox has sidewalk seating which offers a colorful view of a gentrified Near North neighborhood. No need to wear "Hello My Name Is ..." tags in this joint, and no need to ask anyone for a light.

METRO

ALTERNATIVE CITY CONCERT VENUE WITH AN ATTITUDE

Who Goes There 18–30, anybody who knows anything about music or happens to have a friend in the band

3730 North Clark Street; (773) 549-0203   Zone 1 North Side

Cover $5–$20 **Minimum** None **Mixed drinks** $4–$6 **Wine** $4 **Beer** $4–$6 **Dress** A potpourri of flannel, Doc Martens, leopard coats, Dr. Seuss hats (yuck!), and anything in black leather **Specials** Occasional record-release parties, last-minute guerilla bookings; for example, Bob Dylan played this intimate hall a couple of years ago **Food available** None

Hours Saturday, 7 p.m.–4 a.m.; also nights of concerts

What goes on Local and national alternative rock bands love playing this former cabaret theater because of the appreciative crowds. Metro presents all-ages shows and over-21 concerts. The downstairs Smart Bar is a dark and brooding dance club for concertgoers and people-watchers. It is open 9 p.m.–4 a.m. Sunday–Friday, and 10 p.m.–5 a.m. Saturday. There's a separate cover that ranges between $7 and $10 on Friday and Saturday, depending on the DJ. However, admission is waived for Metro concertgoers.

Setting & atmosphere With body surfing and moshing in the concert hall upstairs and blue-hazed zebra motif in the Smart Bar, there's something for every nonconformist. People come to Metro strictly to hear the music, therefore the aesthetics are underplayed.

If you go You can say you knew them when. Metro has been the launching pad for breakout alternative bands from Chicago like Smashing Pumpkins and Urge Overkill. Even superstars like Axl Rose of Guns n' Roses like to hang around Metro/Smart Bar.

OLD TOWN ALE HOUSE

FROM BACH TO BUKOWSKI

Who Goes There Whoever dares, 25–70, but a sanctuary for artists, journalists, Second City actors, and late-night waitresses and bartenders

219 West North Avenue; (312) 944-7020   Zone 3 Near North

Cover None **Minimum** None, nor is there a maximum **Mixed drinks** $5.25–$6 **Wine** $4–$5 **Beer** $3.75–$5 **Dress** Old raincoated; funky; cigars are welcome **Specials** None **Food available** Snacks, but it's okay to bring in fast food

Hours Sunday–Friday, noon–4 a.m.; Saturday, noon–5 a.m.; open 365 days a year

What goes on Serious talking and serious drinking. Classic Chicago writers like Studs Terkel and the late Mike Royko used to pound a few here. The original Ale House opened across the street in 1958. It burned down in 1970, maybe due to negative karma. The original Ale House was run by a German who owned a pack of German shepherds named after Nazi generals. Only the long bar was salvaged from across the street. The Ale House's late-night license makes it a popular stop for nightcrawlers getting off work late.

Setting & atmosphere Sleazy, which is a word even the proprietors use. The jukebox is heavy on jazz, soul, classical, and opera. A cornucopia of crazy artifacts include a gorilla bust that is decorated for appropriate seasons, a crooked "Jurassic Park" sign, and strange newspaper clippings bartenders cut and paste on the wall. Chicago folk singer–humorist Larry Rand best summed up the Ale House as "a fern bar where the customers are often more potted than the plants."

If you go You won't be sorry. This is as authentic as a Near North Side drinking experience can get. Just don't cross the stray punch lines from the Second City folks, still winding down from their late-night sets across the street.

OLD TOWN SCHOOL OF FOLK MUSIC

I'D LIKE TO TEACH THE WORLD TO SING; THE COUNTRY'S PREMIERE RESOURCE CENTER FOR FOLK AND WORLD MUSIC IDIOMS

Who Goes There Everyone between age 8 and 88; people who have either attended or taught here include John Prine, Roger McGuinn of the Byrds, Billy Corgan of Smashing Pumpkins, and Jeff Tweedy of Wilco

4544 North Lincoln Avenue; (773) 728-6000; www.oldtownschool.org
Zone 1 North Side

Cover Varies **Minimum** None **Mixed drinks** None **Wine** $3.50 **Beer** $2.50–$3.50 **Dress** No code; flannel welcomed **Specials** Two-day outdoor roots music festival during July; Latin festival in October; Do-It-Yourself Chanukah in December **Food available** Sandwiches and snacks, $1–$5

Hours Monday–Thursday, 9 a.m.–10 p.m.; Friday and Saturday, 9 a.m.–5 p.m. (for concerts, the school closes at 1 a.m.); Sunday, 10 a.m.–5 p.m.

What goes on The Old Town School of Folk Music services more than 6,000 adult and youth students weekly in classes as eclectic as Bulgarian singing, flamenco guitar playing, the songs of Bob Dylan, and Hawaiian hula dancing. Nearly 30,000 people attend Old Town School concerts annually. Singer-songwriter Joni Mitchell christened the Old Town School in the fall of 1998. Other concert regulars include Guy Clark, folk legend Odetta, bluegrass great Del McCoury, roots artist Taj Mahal, and Hungarian folk legends Muzsikah. The Old Town School's previous home (909 West Armitage) remains open as the Old Town School of Folk Music's Children's Center. Some adult classes are offered at the old homestead.

Setting & atmosphere The Old Town School of Folk Music was restored from the 43,000-square-foot Hild Library, an Art Deco treasure built in 1929. The acoustically perfect $2 million concert hall is the crown jewel of the center. With 275 seats on the main floor and 150 in the balcony, no audience member is more than 45 feet from the proscenium stage. The $150,000 sound system features 38 speakers that ring throughout the intimate hall. Vintage acoustic instruments are hung on the hall's 14 pillars to absorb sound. The center also includes 31 teaching spaces. The Different Strummer music store sells instruments and rare recordings—instruments are also rented and repaired.

If you go   This can be one of the most rewarding musical experiences in Chicago. During the day, the concert hall transforms into a cafe area where folk music fans can relax, talk, and hear impromptu concerts by students. The Old Town School of Folk Music began in 1957 as an offshoot of the humanist movement in folk music—a notion of bringing people together under the belief that music belongs to the masses.

POPS FOR CHAMPAGNE

COZY, CLASSY, AND CLEVERLY UNDERSTATED

Who Goes There   Upper echelon, 30–50, well-dressed connoisseurs of fine bubbly, young urban professionals, fancy neighborhood folks

2934 North Sheffield Avenue; (773) 472-1000   Zone 1 North Side

Cover $6–$10; no cover Sunday or Monday **Minimum** None **Mixed drinks** $6–$12 **Wine** $7–$13 (glass), $30–$400 (bottles, including champagne) **Beer** $5–$8 **Dress** Business casual **Specials** Champagne tasting parties **Food available** Nightly appetizers, including osetra caviar

Hours   Monday–Friday, 5 p.m.–2 a.m.; Saturday, 5 p.m.–3 a.m.

What goes on   Although the ambience can be intimidating, the easygoing staff and patrons could be found in any neighborhood pub. Conversation flows from the newest plays in town to the latest imports in champagne. The sophistcated jazz club opened in 1986 and entertains nightly to crowds that generally pour in around 11 p.m. Private parties can be arranged.

Setting & atmosphere   This once-Spanish grocery store envelops you in a highly elegant world. Vaulted ceilings, two-story windows, and marbleized walls accent the cozy lounge with 25 small tables and an elevated stage (complete with a black baby grand piano) behind the bar. Art Deco accents and burgundy curtains add a nice touch. Weather permitting, customers can adjourn to a small back patio lined with beautiful evergreen and relax under the evening sky.

If you go   Don't order a beer. Prepare yourself for the prices; this is no cheap route. Bring a date to make a good impression, bring a boss to ask for a raise. Patrons run next door to the attached, more casual Star Bar—also owned by Pops—but always return for a touch of real class.

SLOW DOWN—LIFE'S TOO SHORT!

WASTED AWAY AGAIN IN . . . CHICAGO? A BIG HUNK OF KEY WEST FLOATS NORTH

Who Goes There   Young professionals, singles, fans of Jimmy Buffett, Bob Marley, and (in season) boaters from the adjacent Chicago River

1177 North Elston Avenue (at Division Street); (773) 384-1040   Zone 3 Near North

Cover $5–$10 for live shows **Minimum** None **Mixed drinks** $3–$5.75 **Wine** $7 **Beer** $3.50–$5.75 **Dress** Casual; shorts and halter tops okay in summer **Specials** Drink specials daily **Food available** "Swamp" cuisine includes burgers, chicken, pork chop sandwiches, and spicy BBQ wings, which are regarded as some of the best in the city

Hours Sunday–Tuesday, 11 a.m.–2 p.m.; Wednesday–Friday. 11 a.m.–4 a.m.; Saturday, 11 a.m.–5 a.m.

What goes on No tropical depression here. Live reggae, pop, and contemporary blues on weekends, better-than-average bar food, and sports on a flotilla of TVs.

Setting & atmosphere One of the most colorful bars in Chicago, SLOW DOWN—Life's Too Short! is located on the shores of the Chicago River (there's a boat valet for up to 30 boats) and has a breathtaking view of the Chicago skyline. SLOW DOWN features three multilevel outdoor decks, lots of beach bric-a-brac, and an outdoor shower. The building's history dates back to the late 1940s when it was called "The Snake Pit," run by a bunch of renegades from the Chicago Yacht Club. Parts of the Drew Barrymore film *Never Been Kissed* were filmed at SLOW DOWN. And of course, Florida-based singer-songwriter Jimmy Buffett gave an impromptu concert here a while back.

If you go Be prepared to have fun. Management truly believes life is too short, which is why they serve a free dessert before every meal. Another bonus is the industrial neighborhood setting, which makes it easy to park and equally easy to get to by cab from downtown.

WEEDS

CULTURAL ANARCHY FOR A NEW BEAT GENERATION

Who Goes There Lovable riffraff between 21–65, artists and/or slackers, newspaper people, cab drivers, and strippers

1555 North Dayton; (312) 943-7815   Zone 1   North Side

Cover None **Minimum** None **Mixed drinks** $3–$6 **Wine** $4 **Beer** $2–$4 **Dress** Grateful Deadish **Specials** Free shot of tequila if it's late enough; a surreal beer garden in season **Food available** Bar snacks, chips, peanuts, etc.

Hours Monday–Friday, 4 p.m.–2 a.m.; Saturday, 4 p.m.–3 a.m.; Sunday, noon–9 p.m.

What goes on Just about anything. Monday is poetry night, hosted by Gregorio Gomez, artistic director of the Chicago Latino Theater. Tuesdays and Wednesdays are "Comfort Nights," which means there are no scheduled activities. Some of the city's top jazz players jam on Thursday nights, featured rock bands play on Friday nights, and Saturday nights are reserved for open stage. There are bizarre special events like Lawrence Welk Bubble Day and Birth Control Day (where customers wear IUDs as earrings). Never a cover.

Setting & atmosphere Twisted Bohemian. Old bras and unused condoms hang from the ceiling along with the year-round Christmas lights thing. Most of the bar's furnishings were gathered from neighborhood dumpsters. Sabbath candles and incense burn along the bar, and a funky beer garden is utilized in season. The bar gets its name from being at the corner of Dayton and Weed Streets.

If you go Owner-proprietor-poet Sergio Mayora—who once ran for mayor of Chicago—wrote of his bar: "A place with a difference; where what you are or who you are is only as important as where you are." Be prepared to rub shoulders with all walks of life, hell-raisers, hillbillies, chicks, and tricks. A once-in-a-lifetime experience.

Restaurant Index

Nightclub Index

Subject Index

Unofficial Guide to Chicago Reader Survey

If you would like to express your opinion about Chicago or this guide-book, complete the following survey and mail it to:

> *Unofficial Guide to Chicago* Reader Survey
> PO Box 43673
> Birmingham AL 35243

Inclusive dates of your visit: _____

*Members of
your party:*   Person 1   Person 2   Person 3   Person 4   Person 5
Gender: M F   M F   M F   M F   M F
Age: _____

How many times have you been to Chicago? _____
On your most recent trip, where did you stay? _____

Concerning your accommodations, on a scale of 100 as best and 0 as worst, how would you rate:

The quality of your room? _____   The value of your room? _____
The quietness of your room? _____   Check-in/check-out efficiency? _____
Shuttle service to the parks? _____   Swimming pool facilities? _____

Did you rent a car? _____   From whom? _____

Concerning your rental car, on a scale of 100 as best and 0 as worst, how would you rate:

Pick-up processing efficiency? _____   Return processing efficiency? _____
Condition of the car? _____   Cleanliness of the car? _____
Airport shuttle efficiency? _____

Concerning your dining experiences:

Including fast-food, estimate your meals in restaurants per day? _____
Approximately how much did your party spend on meals per day? _____
Favorite restaurants in Chicago: _____

_____

Did you buy this guide before leaving? ☐   while on your trip? ☐

How did you hear about this guide? (check all that apply)

Loaned or recommended by a friend ☐   Radio or TV ☐
Newspaper or magazine ☐   Bookstore salesperson ☐
Just picked it out on my own ☐   Library ☐
Internet ☐

Unofficial Guide to Chicago **Reader Survey**
(continued)

What other guidebooks did you use on this trip? _____

_____

_____

_____

On a scale of 100 as best and 0 as worst, how would you rate them?

_____

_____

_____

Using the same scale, how would you rate *The Unofficial Guide(s)?*

_____

Are *Unofficial Guides* readily available at bookstores in your area? _____

Have you used other *Unofficial Guides?* _____

Which one(s)? _____

_____

_____

_____

_____

Comments about your Chicago trip or *The Unofficial Guide(s):*

_____

_____

_____

_____

_____

_____

_____

_____

_____

_____

_____

_____

_____